Bioethics in a Cultural Context

Philosophy, Religion, History, Politics

VINCENT BARRY
Professor Emeritus of Philosophy, Bakersfield College

WADSWORTH
CENGAGE Learning

Australia • Brazil • Japan • Korea • Mexico • Singapore • Spain • United Kingdom • United States

WADSWORTH
CENGAGE Learning

Bioethics in a Cultural Context: Philosophy, Religion, History, Politics
Vincent Barry

Publisher/Executive Editor: Clark Baxter

Senior Sponsoring Editor: Joann Kozyrev

Editorial Assistant: Marri Straton

Assistant Editor: Joshua Duncan

Media Editor: Kimberly Apfelbaum

Marketing Manager: Mark T. Haynes

Marketing Communications Manager:
  Laura Localio

Content Project Management: PreMediaGlobal

Art Director: Jennifer Wahi

Print Buyer: Mary Beth Hennebury

Marketing Coordinator: Joshua Hendrick

Cover Designer: Kate Scheible

Cover Image: Shutterstock 3602589 Dandelion

Compositor: PreMediaGlobal

For product information and technology assistance, contact us at
Cengage Learning Customer & Sales Support, 1-800-354-9706
For permission to use material from this text or product,
submit all requests online at **www.cengage.com/permissions**
Further permissions questions can be emailed to
permissionrequest@cengage.com

Library of Congress Control Number: 2010935861

ISBN-13: 978-0-495-81408-5

ISBN-10: 0-495-81408-3

Wadsworth
20 Channel Center Street
Boston, MA 02210
USA

Cengage Learning is a leading provider of customized learning solutions with office locations around the globe, including Singapore, the United Kingdom, Australia, Mexico, Brazil, and Japan. Locate your local office at **www.cengage.com/global**

Cengage Learning products are represented in Canada by Nelson Education, Ltd.

To learn more about Wadsworth, visit **www.cengage.com/wadsworth**

Purchase any of our products at your local college store or at our preferred online store **www.cengagebrain.com**

Printed in the USA
2 3 4 5 6   28 27 26 25 24

To Jen-Li Rose at 12,
keep that breathless charm

Preface

The seeds of this book were sown in the spring of 2005 when Congress intervened in the matter of Terri Schiavo, a patient described by physicians as "vegetative." The widely publicized case pitted the wishes of Terri's husband, Michael, who wanted his wife's feeding tube removed, against the objections of her birth family, the Schindlers. The courts and prominent bioethicists framed the conflict as a dispute over what Terri wanted and who should say. Mainstream media used it to show how politicized bioethics had become. Largely left unexamined, it seemed to me, were deeper, philosophical questions stoking the controversy.

Schiavo passed but not its hold on me. The more I thought about it, the more the case struck me as paradigmatic for what frequently happens whenever we go beyond the procedural aspects of bioethical decision making and think deeply about the decisions themselves. We come to realize that controversial ethical issues often are not about ethics at all but about other more philosophical concerns, such as our understanding of human nature and destiny, truth and authority, meaning and value, or the proper relationship between individual and society. Indeed, many of the controversial moral problems of today's biological science and medicine are like this. It is not so much that they invite opposed moral viewpoints but that they evoke irreconcilable answers to profound, underlying questions:

- *What is a human being or a person?*
- *When does human life begin and death come?*
- *How do medicine and the broader culture situate death in human life?*
- *Are illness, pain, suffering, and death evils to be defeated, or can they have transcendent value?*
- *What kind of universe do we occupy—one with meaning and purpose or a universe utterly indifferent to human affairs, including our pain and suffering?*
- *What is the ideal society? What practices does it allow and prohibit?*

- *How are we to know all these things—on whose authority? Must we, in the end, rely totally on ourselves or is there some higher knowledge?*

Such questions suggest that much of the controversy in bioethics is traceable to perennial philosophical debates.

Is there any value in placing today's bioethical dilemmas in their ancient philosophical context? I think there is. It can depoliticize them and put them at a more human level. We see that these dilemmas play out in bioethics but they are not limited to this and addressing them in bioethics requires addressing them elsewhere as well.

Reflections such as these inspired *Bioethics in a Cultural Context—Philosophy, Religion, History, Politics. BCC* offers a fresh approach to introductory bioethics by examining the subject through a wider lens than the customary issue analysis. Yes, the text covers all of today's hot-button bioethical controversies related to life's beginning and end. But rather than merely scanning views with their supporting argumentation, the text places the issues in cultural and historical context and delves into the philosophical and religious subsoil that makes them so divisive and, daresay, so interesting. *BCC*, in brief, endeavors to enrich the material that is generally considered in introductory bioethics by going beyond today's most polarizing bioethical controversies to show how they have arisen and why the answers are important.

STRUCTURE

BCC is divided into four parts, with introduction and conclusion.

- The introduction sets the theme, provides a road map for the book as a whole, and helps students make sense of moral conflict.
- PART I SACRED AND SECULAR FOUNDATIONS provides a survey of the major historical influences on Western bioethics and its practice.
- PART II ORIGINS AND CONTEXT OF BIOETHICS surveys the figures, thought, and events that contributed to the founding of modern bioethics; it also discusses the field's basic principles, the contemporary critique of them, and several alternative perspectives.
- PART III ISSUES AT THE BEGINNING OF LIFE extends understanding of the foundations, origins, and context of bioethics to notable issues in reproductive medicine.
- PART IV ISSUES AT THE END OF LIFE joins the main controversies that surround personal decisions and public policy at life's end.
- The conclusion gives unity to the text as a whole by reviewing its key concepts and controlling idea in the context of the divide between secular and religious perspectives in modern bioethics.

ORGANIZATION

The central notion around which *BCC* is organized is that controversial bioethical issues and cases raise ultimately persistent questions whose origins are not really unique to bioethics and whose answers have implications ranging far beyond. A lively introductory chapter sets this theme by using *Schiavo* as a focal point for showing that, while many biomedical issues are new, the fundamental differences they raise between ways of knowing and understanding are as old as Western civilization itself.

Given its historical sensibilities, the text turns immediately in Chapter 1 to the West's two major traditions of knowing and understanding: medieval religion and Enlightenment science. Chapter 2 shows how these different ways of perceiving the world led to different and enduring ways of doing ethics, with particular regard to divine command theory, religious and secular natural law, Kant's ethics, and utilitarianism. Taken together, Chapters 1 and 2 provide rarely given but valuable background for understanding the historical tensions between the religious/theological and the secular/philosophical that came to shape the conception of bioethics and were ultimately resolved in favor of secularism, only to reassert themselves in the bioethical and political controversies that today surround issues of birth and death.

Discussion of the philosophical and religious roots of bioethics sets up in Chapters 3 through 7 a presentation of the field's origins and context. Chapter 3 shows how Enlightenment-bred values and ideals of secular modernity characterized the intellectual milieu that formed after World War II and peaked at the dawn of modern bioethics. It surveys the social climate, medical advances, and court rulings that contributed to the urgency for bioethics in the late 1960s and early1970s; it also profiles many of the philosophers and theologians who pioneered the field. Given that the groundwork of these trailblazers ultimately took the form of the so-called Belmont principles of 1979, Chapters 4 and 5 take a close examination of these comprehensive standards of bioethics and their applications. Although these foundational principles remain influential, Chapter 6 shows why a perceived overweening attachment to one of them, individual autonomy, has invited assorted criticism. Chapter 7 considers alternative perspectives, including feminist ethics of care and narrative ethics.

Having traced the development of bioethics from its origins to current state, the book then turns to the two predominant kinds of bioethical issues that tax us today. Chapters 8–16 cover the major controversies at the beginning of life—abortion, embryo screening, surrogate mothering, commercial egg donation, genetic testing, prenatal sex selection, and stem cell research. Chapters 17–22 take up the major controversies that surround the end of life, as they pertain to the definition and criteria of death, suicide, assisted suicide, euthanasia, and judgments of medical futility as a means of rationing health care. The coverage reprises the book's linchpin idea by showing how these issues owe their inherent controversy to fundamentally different ways of knowing and understanding, specifically to opposed views about the definition of human life and personhood, the purpose for existence, the reach of personal liberty, and the nature of the ideal society.

The text's concluding chapter invites further discourse by discussing the concept of individual autonomy and rights in the liberal democracy. It addresses the challenge to bioethics posed by trying to balance, on one hand, Western concepts of rights with, on the other, religious concepts of divine sovereignty or commitment to religious principles that may conflict with individual autonomy.

FEATURES

I wrote *BCC* mindful of a general audience unfamiliar with bioethics as a subject and activity. The text had to be accessible and substantive, with a good range of topics and issues that were contextualized, clearly explained, and sparked with copious examples and real-life cases. Here are some of the text's features that aim to give students with varying learning styles and experiences opportunities to understand the moral implications of the dramatic changes occurring today in American health care.

1. **Introductions to Parts** Helping give the work a sense of unity and coherence, each part has its own introduction that ties the forthcoming material thematically to the book as a whole.

2. **Conversation Starters** Chapters begin with an event, a situation, a case, or an illustration that draws attention to the chapter's main point of interest.

3. **Conclusions** Chapters close with some judgments and opinions suggested by their contents.

4. **Examples and Illustrations** Liberal use of popular and public materials are designed to make the content clear and the narrative compelling.

5. **Bioethics Across Cultures** Scattered throughout the text, these fifty-four inserts are intended to impart cross-cultural awareness and appreciation of how different religions and cultures work to resolve complex issues in bioethics. Some of these global excursions feature individuals who, though perhaps obscure in the United States, have headlined bioethical imbroglios abroad—Eluana Englaro in Italy, Angelique Flowers in Australia, and Richard Latimer in Canada, for instance. Following all of the cross-cultural presentations are questions as diverse as

   - "What's the morality of drugs not being available in the country where the drug trials are taking place?"
   - "Is the value of a person's life in an impoverished developing nation the same as the value of an affluent Westerner's life?"
   - "Is Major League Baseball morally justified in conducting genetic testing on promising young Latin American players?"
   - "Does feminist bioethics offer a unique perspective on global violence against women?"

- "Is it right for the United States to withhold aid from foreign reproductive care agencies that discuss or offer abortion services?"
- "What moral issues are involved in outsourcing surrogacy?"
- "What are the principal differences between Buddhist understanding of illness and suffering and that of Judaism, Christianity, and Islam?"

6. **Cases and Controversies** Several real-life cases and controversies with questions for analysis appear at the end of every chapter, seventy-four in all. Well-toned and neutrally presented, this mix of classic and contemporary material, of suitable length for classroom use, provides an opportunity to extend the ideas and principles laid out in the chapters, while encouraging self-examination and critical analysis. Sometimes showcased are famous events or court decisions, such as the Sherri Finkbine thalidomide tragedy, the Baby M surrogate motherhood ruling, and the *Griswold v. Connecticut* birth control decision. Just as often, however, it's a fresh case or controversy, including:

- medical workers' involvement in C.I.A. interrogations;
- the Steve Jobs liver transplant;
- conscientious objection to selling the morning-after contraceptive pill;
- the 2009 *Benitez* decision involving denial of artificial insemination based on marital status;
- selling blood across the U.S.-Mexico border;
- mandated vaccination with Gardasil;
- the first gene therapy death;
- mercy deaths during Hurricane Katrina; and
- the creation of "synthetic life."

7. **Multidisciplinary Coverage** Besides the philosophical and religious, this text strives to include diverse clinical, academic, historical, legal, and scientific perspectives. This accounts for the uncommon treatment of some familiar material and the inclusion of unique topics. For example, as a prelude to issues at the beginning of life, Chapter 8 treats conceptual issues in reproductive technology, including scientific views about when life begins and whether they're compatible with traditional religious teaching. In Chapters 9 and 10, the usual arguments for and against abortion are interwoven with a narrative about the philosophical/religious thought, medical advances, social/political activism, and legal landmarks in reproductive rights that led up to and have followed *Roe*. Chapter 19 overviews the intellectual history surrounding suicide in the West and shows how this mix of religious and secular opinion, modified by cultural conditions and demands, has come to shape contemporary law, morality, and feeling about physician-assisted death. Chapter 22 places medical judgments of futility in the economic context of health care prioritization. And the aforementioned conclusion takes up the challenge of navigating the chasm between secular and religious

bioethics in the liberal democracy. Typically ignored or downplayed in bioethics texts, these disciplines help illuminate today's bioethical debates, placing what may be unfamiliar content into more familiar contexts.

8. **Extensive Documentation** Numerous online resources provide opportunities for convenient reference and research.

WAYS OF USING THE TEXT

Recognizing the wide range of ways for teaching bioethics, I've tried to make *BCC* easy to customize without losing its individual voice. The book's tidy organization, myriad topics, and numerous cases should give instructors great flexibility in how they use the text and structure their courses.

BCC can be broken into parts for abbreviated courses and for additions or omissions. Easily digestible sections allow a similar adaptability within chapters. As the chapters themselves are relatively self-contained, they generally can be assigned in any order without loss of coherence. Common sense exceptions would be the introduction and conclusion and chapters dealing with conceptual matters (e.g., Chapters 8, 17, and probably 15).

Because many instructors prefer to dwell only on some parts of a lengthy book and assign others for outside reading, it's important that the text be clear and accessible to a wide variety of readers. This is especially true with controversial content of a philosophical and religious nature. I've tried to address this challenge by presenting the material in a frank and respectful tone, and in a style plain enough to serve both those who need background and those ready to engage the serious biomedical issues facing society. The brevity of each section and, I trust, the fair and balanced explanations should appeal to a wide breadth of readers.

Like many texts, this one can be taught cover to cover. Where time constraints or other factors prevent this, the text as a whole can be conveniently tailored to meet individual preferences. Instructors eager to get to the issues, for example, can skip immediately from the introduction to Parts III and IV, perhaps assigning select chapters from the earlier parts for outside reading. Alternatively, those wanting to introduce basic bioethical principles before proceeding to the issues could move immediately to Chapters 4, 5, 6, and 7, after the introduction. It's also possible to focus exclusively on the cases and, perhaps, cross-cultural inserts, with the text assigned as background. Ideally, most of the chapters are crafted such that a lecturer or seminar leader would have little additional work to do in preparation to teach the material.

Chapter 1 warrants a special word because it offers something singular for a bioethics text: a concise history of Christian religion and the intersection of secularism. How one uses this chapter, if at all, largely depends on how much attention one wishes to pay to the intellectual history of Western civilization from the rise of Christianity to the Enlightenment, with specific regard to such crucial matters as our views of human nature and personhood; our understanding of illness, suffering, and death; and our conception of science and medicine and their relationship to religion. In general, those inclined to make the inclusion of theology and cross-cultural religious perspectives more explicit in their teaching of bioethics probably would assign all of Chapter 1, whereas those disinclined would pick and choose or even skip it entirely, again without loss of textual coherence.

My personal feeling is that it's very difficult, if even possible, to engage bioethics in the United States today without seriously acknowledging the formidable influence of religion on social policy and clinical practice. It's a sure bet that many students who read this book, not to mention the instructors who teach from it, hold sincere, religiously inspired moral opinions on such matters as abortion, preconception sex selection, stem cell research, suicide, or assisted death. And those who don't are no less affected by the highly influential religious voices and opinions of those occupying seats of institutional or political power. Add to this (1) the contribution of religious thinkers some forty-odd years ago to the nascent field of applied medical ethics, and (2) the current tensions between religious and moral interests in the making of national science policy, as doctors and patients must weigh the issues and the options.

It seems to me, then, that the inclusion of the sacred alongside the secular in treating bioethics in the context of culture is not only felicitous today but also imperative. At the very least, it can show students how they've come by their beliefs and that religious approaches to difficult, ethical questions are not purely monolithic but are themselves diverse and even at odds with one another. It can also inform them of the historical relationship between religion and philosophy, and how religious ideas can influence ideas we later come to define as philosophical ones, nowhere more so than in bioethics. Finally, it can take students to the next level: a critical examination of the role of religious belief in shaping bioethical policy and practice. These observations notwithstanding, I realize that some instructors will more lament than welcome the inclusion of religious perspectives in a bioethics text. Again, they can freely adapt *BCC* to their tastes without sacrificing coherence.

ACKNOWLEDGMENTS

The abundant end-of-chapter citations suggest the profound debt I owe to the great many scholars and writers whose thought and work helped shape this book. For the humbling opportunity to tap into their knowledge and wisdom, my sincere thanks to sponsoring editor Joann Kozyrev. For her scrupulous attention to the details of production, my gratitude extends to Sushila Rajagopal. And for their generous commentary and encouragement, I gratefully acknowledge the following reviewers:

Joseph Aieta III, Lasell College

Kem Barfield, Three Rivers Community College

Barbara Bellar, DePaul University

Nancy Billias, Saint Joseph College

David Boersema, Pacific University

Paul Boling, Bryan College

Kae Chatman, Arkansas State University, Beebe

Mary Giegengack-Jureller, Le Moyne College

Brian Glenney, Gordon College

Paul Haught, Christian Brothers University

Mitra Huber, The College of St. Elizabeth

Phil Jenkins, Marywood University

Jeffery Johnson, Eastern Oregon University

Joel Martinez, Lewis & Clark College

Michael McKeon, St. Gregory's University

Mark McLeod-Harrison, George Fox University

Rolland Pack, Freed-Hardeman University

Hannah Love, Pacific Lutheran University

Roger Russell, University of St. Francis

J. Aaron Simmons, Hendrix College

Les Stanwood, Skagit Valley College

Cindy Wesley, Lambuth University

Introduction

Bioethics, *Schiavo*, and Cultural Politics

O n the evening of March 19, 2005, the US Congress did something it had never done before. With time running out on how much longer she could remain alive, Congressional leaders announced that they would allow the parents of a 41-year-old Florida woman to petition the federal courts to have a feeding tube replaced for their brain-damaged daughter. The next day President Bush flew back to Washington from his Texas ranch to sign the emergency legislation. Two days earlier the president had told the nation:

> The case of Terri Schiavo raises complex issues. Those who live at the mercy of others deserve our special care and concern. It should be our goal as a nation to build a culture of life, where all Americans are valued, welcomed, and protected—and that culture of life must extend to individuals with disabilities.[1]

It was in 1990 when Terri Schiavo (1963–2005) incurred severe neurological damage when a chemical imbalance stopped her heart, cutting the oxygen supply to her brain. The then 26-year-old was left in what physicians term persistent vegetative state (PVS), capable of breathing on her own but unable to eat or speak. No fewer than seven board-certified neurologists said her condition was permanent and irreversible, though not terminal. With proper care Terri could live many years, a fate her husband and legal guardian didn't think she would want. So Michael Schiavo requested that doctors stop the artificial feeding. When his wife's Catholic parents objected, the stage was set for a lengthy legal battle that culminated in a court order to remove Schiavo's feeding tube.

Once the feeding tube was removed, evangelical Christian conservatives, who had helped reelect President Bush in 2004 and swell Republican majorities in Congress, requested and obtained the unprecedented emergency legislation allowing the Schindlers to petition federal courts to resume tube feeding. But their legal tactic failed, and Terri Schiavo died on March 31, nearly two weeks after the removal of her life-sustaining feeding tube.

In a message to supporters and media shortly after her death, Terri Schiavo's brother said, "Throughout this ordeal we are reminded of the words of Jesus' message on the cross: 'Forgive them for they know not what they do.'"[2] Bobby Schindler's biblical allusion was to the bitter feud between the Schindlers and Michael Schiavo. But his words were suggestive of something larger, for *Schiavo* wasn't only about a divided family. It was also about a divided country. As widely depicted, *Schiavo* was a dramatic battle in the struggle to define America known popularly as the "culture war."

Over the past two decades, the term culture war (or culture wars) has become a catchphrase for a variety of polarizing political and social issues: teen pregnancy, sex education, pornography, drugs, gun control, same-sex marriage, funding for the arts and public broadcasting, feminism, immigration, multiculturalism, environmentalism, judicial nominations, religion in public life. Although the issues touch almost every aspect of social life, in no field are they more numerous or contentious than in medicine and health care. It is there that matters at life's beginning and end invite especially passionate debate and irreconcilable positions.

In the case of Terri Schiavo, public opinion was divided, albeit not evenly, on the question of proper treatment for PVS patients. Advances in medical science and technology have contributed to like disagreement in other areas: abortion, infertility treatment, prenatal testing, preconception sex selection, organ transplantation, and stem cell research, to name a few. All have forced upon us difficult choices in our personal and professional lives, as well as in public policy. This book deals with these matters and the spirited social debates they have triggered. It's about bioethics in the context of culture, including philosophy, religion, history, and politics.

BIOETHICS

Etymologically, bioethics consists of two Greek words: *bios* for "life" and *ethos* for "character or custom." From *ethos* comes "ethics," which suggests the view of bioethics as an application of ethics to the life sciences, especially medicine and health care. For this reason bioethics is sometimes called biomedical ethics. So conceived, bioethics derives its content largely from biology and medicine and its theory and guiding principles from the larger field of ethics.

ETHICS

Ethics may be defined, broadly, as the general term for the philosophical study of morality or, simply, moral philosophy. This label says something important about what ethics does and how it does it: It studies morality philosophically.

To say that ethics studies morality means that it is concerned with an individual's or culture's standards of character and conduct. Consider that in growing up we absorb from our families and societies all sorts of notions about good and bad, right and wrong, rights and responsibilities. Later we may think philosophically about what we've inherited: We may critically examine and test our acquired moral values and standards by closely inspecting the reasons for and against them. When we undertake this close inspection of our inherited moral customs, we're doing ethics, specifically normative ethics.

Normative Ethics

Normative ethics is the area of ethics or moral philosophy concerned with judgments and theories about obligation and value, good character, well-being, and right action. It is basically interested in answering two "ought questions." One is a question of conduct: "What ought I do?" The other is a question of character: "What ought I be?" In both instances, normative ethics seeks prescriptions, that is, authoritative rules or directions, for right action and good character. Its prescriptive interest distinguishes normative ethics from fields with merely a descriptive or scientific interest in ethics, such as cultural anthropology or sociology.

Cultural anthropologists sometimes give accounts of permissible cultural practices that our society finds objectionable, including polygamy, arranged marriages, suicide as requirement of widowhood, killing for honor, severe punishments for blasphemy or adultery, and female circumcision, or genital mutilation. The anthropologist generally is interested in reporting and culturally explaining these practices, not judging them. As a scientist she's simply saying what *is*, rather than what *ought to be*, the case. The normativist, on the other hand, wants to know whether such practices are preferable, whether they are ever moral, and on what grounds. The anthropologist's interest in morality, then, concerns how things *are*, whereas the ethicist's interest concerns how things *should* or *ought to be*. The sociologist, to take another example, is more interested in how people assign credit and blame than when it's right to do so. In describing, the anthropologist and sociologist engage in *descriptive* or *non-normative* ethics. In prescribing, the ethicist (or moralist) does *prescriptive* or *normative* ethics.

Frequently today prescriptive, or normative, ethics extends to specialized areas such as the environment; or to professions such as business, government, law, or medicine. What is thought of value and obligation, in general, is applied to specific areas, practices, or activities. Bioethics is like this. It often analyzes what moral standards and judgments ought to drive health care matters. Thus: *What ought we do in a case like Schiavo? What rules, guidelines, or principles are we to follow? What should we most honor in deciding—the patient's biological existence? The quality of her life? Her wishes? If she hasn't left "clear and convincing" evidence of what she would want, how are we to proceed?* Other circumstances elicit similarly normative questions. *What principles, standards, or norms are we to use in matters involving human cloning, stem cell research, or genetic screening*, as examples?

Trying to answer questions like these gives bioethics its normative edge. But *Schiavo* wasn't only about what Terri wanted and who was to say, and neither is bioethics. *Schiavo* was also about something that often happens whenever we go beyond procedural aspects of bioethical decision making and think deeply about the decisions themselves. It is then that we confront some of the most basic questions we can formulate about ourselves and our destiny. *What is a human being? What is a person? What is the meaning of life and suffering? What is death and when does it come? What do we owe those who, though not dead nor dying, are profoundly disabled and dependent?* And perhaps the most important question of all: *How are we to answer these questions? What guidelines do we follow?* Inquiries such as these bear directly on judgments of value and obligation, and they indicate another area of ethics relevant to bioethics. It's termed metaethics.

Metaethics

Of importance to many modern theorists, metaethics is the branch of ethics that goes beyond the interests of normative ethics into the origins of ethical concepts. For example, whereas normative ethics is interested in knowing what things are morally good and bad, metaethics ponders the meaning of *moral goodness*. Trying to understand the nature of ethical properties and evaluations requires an exacting study of the meanings of moral terms like *good* and *bad*, the sentences in which they appear, and the methods of reasoning involved in making moral evaluations.

Additionally, metaethics often is drawn into the orbit of highly speculative questions. For instance, whereas normative ethics asks what is right and wrong, metaethical theory seeks to determine whether we live in the kind of universe where there is anything that is right or wrong apart from what any of us thinks, feels, or believes. In other words, metaethics, in part, seeks an answer to the question: *Is there or is there not anything objectively right or wrong independent of human opinion?* A related metaethical question involves whether some things are always moral or always immoral. *Are there discoverable absolute standards for determining right and wrong? Or do right and*

BIOETHICS ACROSS CULTURES

Canada's Terri Schiavo

In October 2007, Grace Hospital in Winnipeg, Canada, admitted 84-year-old Samuel Golubchuk with multiple organ failure. Earlier, in 2003, Golubchuk had part of his brain removed after a fall. His condition deteriorated rapidly while in the hospital, and Grace doctors told the family they wanted to take him off life support. The family balked, citing their Orthodox Jewish faith. To do so, they said, would be contrary to their father's wishes and his religious beliefs as an Orthodox Jew who held life to be sacred. "Doctors don't know everything," Golubchuk's son told *Canadian Television News*, "God is the major doctor."

The family went to court and obtained an injunction forbidding the hospital and doctors "from removing the plaintiff ... from life support care, ventilation, tube feeding, and medication"—an order that if violated could lead to fines or imprisonment. Rather than obey the court order, Dr. Anand Kumar, a critical care specialist, resigned, as did two other Grace physicians. In explaining his decision, Dr. Kumar said: "If we honestly attempt to follow the court mandate to focus on keeping Mr. Golubchuk from his natural death, we will likely have to continue to surgically hack away at his infected flesh at the bedside in order to keep the infection at bay." Calling further treatment "tantamount to torture," Dr. Kumar protested: "This is grotesque. To inflict this kind of assault on him without a reasonable hope of benefit is an abomination. I can't do it."

Golubchuk, the man whom conservative groups in the United States took to calling "Canada's Terri Schiavo," died of "natural causes" at Grace Hospital on June 24, 2008.

Question

Do you think Dr. Kumar did the right thing in resigning, or should he have followed the court order? In the midst of the Golubchuk affair, an article appeared in the *Canadian Medical Association Journal*, co-authored by its editor-in-chief, responding to the charge that physicians were trying to "murder" Golubchuk. It stated in part:

> If this is murder, many of Canada's doctors belong in jail. Legally, doctors are practitioners of a duty of care. An obligation to provide extraordinary care to dying patients, including patients who are minimally responsive, forces one to breach the everyday duty of care, which is to provide the best balance between probable harms and foreseeable benefits. That is why an approach that excludes the option to withhold or withdraw life-sustaining care is unworkable.

Do you agree that in cases like these physicians should have the authority to make medical decisions to withhold or withdraw life-sustaining treatment from a patient without the consent of the patient or the patient's family? Or do you agree with the Golubchuks, that competent religious authority should be permitted to make crucial decisions in the event of incapacitation?

(SOURCES: Amir Attaran et al, "Ending Life with Grace and Agreement," CMAJ, April 22, 2008, pp. 1115–1116. Retrieved March 15, 2009, from http://www.pubmedcentral.nih.gov/articlerender.fcgi?artid=2292789); Sam Solomon, "End-Of-Life War Outlives Golubchuk," National Review of Medicine, July 2008. Retrieved March 20, 2009, from www.nationalreviewofmedicine.com/issue/2008/07/5_patients_practice_07.html; The College of Physicians and Surgeons of Manitoba, "Statement Withholding and Withdrawing Life-Sustaining Treatment." Retrieved March 17, 2000, from www.cpsm.mb.ca/cgi-bin/perlfect/search/search.pl?q=withholding; Hillary White, "Samuel Golubchuk Dies Naturally," *LifeSite News*, June 25, 2008. Retrieved March 20, 2009, from http://www.lifesitenews.com/ldn/2008/jun/08062504.html.)

wrong depend on context or consequence? These questions are of theoretical interest. But more than that, they suggest why cases such as *Schiavo,* and bioethics, itself, can be so controversial.

Consider, for example, that many people today believe that some things are always right or wrong, regardless of their context; others believe that right and wrong always depend on cultural or individual preference. Obviously, these basic beliefs clash; they can't both be true. They represent radically different ways of making sense of life. An action that is acceptable according to one belief may not be acceptable according to the other. Individuals or groups holding these opposed beliefs are said to be in moral conflict. Moral conflicts occur when disputants are acting within different beliefs about how the world operates. *Schiavo* was an example of a moral conflict. But *Schiavo* was hardly unique. Indeed, no field today is driven more by moral conflicts than biomedicine.

MAKING SENSE OF MORAL CONFLICT

Many scholars have attempted to make sense of the moral and cultural conflicts that continue to confront us. One of the more careful overviews comes from James Davison Hunter, a professor of sociology and religious studies at the University of Virginia.

Writing in the 1990s, Hunter suggested that the United States was locked in a competition to define social reality that involved a unique realignment in American politics based upon conflicting beliefs about what we are as human beings and who we are as a nation. Unlike past cultural clashes, typically fought along class, religious, or political party lines, the contemporary one, according to Hunter, was being waged along unfamiliar lines defined by conceptions of reality and transcendent values. He described it as a struggle to define America, or more precisely: a struggle to define what and who we are. Although Hunter was not talking about bioethics specifically, his conception of the cultural struggle's issues and adversaries is worth sketching because it provides a window into the nature of the moral conflicts that often make bioethics so divisive today.

Issues

Briefly, Hunter frames the competition to define *what we are* as a struggle to define such fundamental matters as human nature and destiny, good and evil, truth and authority, meaning and value. Despite their complexity, we might initially express the clashing cultural views about these subjects simply as oppositions. For example:

- On one hand, the belief that we are here on earth for a reason and with some ultimate destination such as heaven; on the other, the belief that we live in an indifferent universe, that life has no more or less defined meaning than what each of us makes of it

- On one hand, the belief in the sanctity of life, that every human life is inherently valuable regardless of its state or circumstance; on the other, the belief in the quality of life, that life has value so long as it is meaningful and enjoyed

- On one hand, the belief that we are persons from when we are unborn to when we die; on the other, the belief that only after birth do we become persons, which we may cease to be before death

For Hunter, opposed perspectives such as these speak to the struggle to define social reality.

Given the bulk of its content—ultimate reality, human nature and destiny, the meaning of life, the ultimate sources of knowledge—the question of what we are is largely speculative. Hunter's next question—the *who we are* question—is, by contrast, more practical. It has political overtones, because it's about social relationships involving power, authority, and social policies. It also has moral and religious import, because it's about the standards that will guide those relationships and policies. The *who we are* question is about how we as Americans will order our lives and govern ourselves. It's about the limits of public and collective life, about what we will permit and prohibit. *Who we are,* in a word, is about something that has vexed human beings through all of recorded history: the notion of the ideal society.

What *is* the ideal society? Is it the one that permits, limits, or prohibits: gay marriage and adoption; "obscene art"; prayer, sex education, and the teaching of intelligent design in public schools? In the realm of bioethics: *Is the ideal society the one that does or does not permit access to "morning after" birth control pills, mandatory vaccinations, medical marijuana, stem cell research, experimentation on early stage embryos, preconception trait selection, noncoital reproduction, assisted death, compensation for human tissue donation, and research cloning? Does the ideal society largely permit freedom of research and individual action in these biomedical areas, or does it restrict and even deny such freedom at home and actively discourage it abroad? Does the ideal society mandate health care services to everyone or doesn't it?*

BIOETHICS ACROSS CULTURES

Religion and HIV/AIDS in Africa

In January 2006, Ambassador Randall Tobias, who served as President George W. Bush's global AIDS czar, issued written guidelines that spelled out the Bush administration's conservative religious approach to preventing HIV/AIDS in Africa. Groups that received US funding, Tobias warned, should not target youth with messages that presented abstinence and condoms as "equally viable, alternative choices ..." in their sex education programs. Meanwhile, groups that supported the president's conservative religious agenda started to receive money that traditionally went to more experienced organizations. One such group, the Children's AIDS Fund, received roughly $10 million to promote abstinence-only programs overseas. FreshMinistries, a Florida organization with little experience in tackling AIDS, also received $10 million. A Bush administration directive further said that two-thirds of global AIDS-prevention money was to go to promoting abstinence and fidelity, and before overseas groups could receive US funding they were take a "loyalty oath" to condemn prostitution.

Supporters of the program said it was working, and two months before leaving office President Bush was recognized for his international efforts in the fight against the spread of AIDS. In presenting him with the International Medal of PEACE, California megachurch

pastor Rick Warren said, "No world leader has done more for world health than President George Bush.... Literally millions of lives have been saved in the last five years." But AIDS experts told a different story. They claimed that the preoccupation with abstinence was handicapping the fight against the deadly virus. Health workers saw the influence of America's Christian Right in the chastity message and believed the Bush administration was using its financial might to pressure them into accepting evangelical ideology at the expense of public health. They encouraged the new Obama administration to rethink Bush's policy.

Meanwhile, Pope Benedict XVI came in for criticism when, during a March 2009 trip to Africa, he reaffirmed his predecessors' long-standing opposition to condoms. "You can't resolve [the spread of AIDS] with the distribution of condoms," the pontiff told reporters. "On the contrary, it increases the problem." Health workers battling the epidemic on the front lines reacted much as they did to the president's program. They said the Pope valued religious dogma above the lives of African people. The British medical journal *Lancet* (3/28/2009) weighed in, calling on the Pope to retract is statements:

> When any influential person, be it a religious or political leader, makes a false scientific statement that could be devastating to the health of millions of people, they should

---

Adversaries

Hunter gives substantial coverage to the sides locked in cultural and moral conflict. He defines them in terms of where they stand on the issue of what and who we are. Today approximately 15 to 20 percent of the nation considers itself profoundly religious and staunchly conservative; another 15 to 20 percent considers itself profoundly secular and staunchly liberal.[3] These groups fall within the cultural adversaries that Hunter terms *orthodox* and *progressivists*. The labels don't matter, but what they signify does, for it throws light on some of the most influential voices in today's public debates about bioethical issues.

According to Hunter, orthodoxy is committed to a view of reality that is "independent of, prior to,

and more powerful than human experience."[4] It is inclined to believe in "an external, definable, and transcendent authority" from which we come to know what is true and good, how to live, why we are here, and where we are going. For the orthodox, this objective, higher authority defines, at least in the abstract, "a consistent, unchangeable measure of value, purpose, goodness, and identity, both personal and collective."[5] Orthodoxy, in short, deals with the issue aspect of cultural conflict by telling us once and for all what and who we are.

Not for all but for the great many orthodox, the superior authority is the God of the Bible. These religious orthodox believe in a higher knowledge that comes from faith, revelation, Scripture, or religious

BIOETHICS, *SCHIAVO*, AND CULTURAL POLITICS   **7**

retract or correct the public record. Anything less from Pope Benedict would be an immense disservice to the public and health advocates, including many thousands of Catholics, who work tirelessly to try and prevent the spread of HIV/AIDS worldwide.

The Catholic Church teaches that fidelity within marriage and abstinence are the best ways to stop AIDS.

On the other hand, *The New York Times'* Nicholas D. Kristof has written of "many Catholic nuns and priests heroically caring for AIDS patients— even quietly handing out condoms." Indeed, a growing number of conservative Christians have expressed concerns about evangelicals so preoccupied with sexual morality that they seem to forget or ignore the poor, needy, and ill. Richard Stearns, head of World Vision in the United States, a Christian organization with evangelical roots, asks, "Where were the followers of Jesus Christ in the midst of perhaps the greatest humanitarian crisis of our time?," the AIDS crisis in Uganda, which records the highest proportion of AIDS orphans in the world, many of whom head families or are parts of communities without any adult supervision. "Surely," writes Stearns, "the Church should have been caring for these 'orphans and widows in their distress.' (James 1:27)."

Question

"The evangelicals are absolutely right: abstinence is the best way of preventing the spread of HIV/AIDS." So says Sigurd Illing, who specializes in providing diplomatic advice for disadvantaged and marginalized African nations such as Somaliland. "But," the Bavarian diplomat is quick to add, "some people aren't receptive. We need an end to this bedevilling of condoms by people who take a high moralistic stance and don't care about the impact that this has on reality." Do you agree with Illing? Or do you think that sexual-based morality has a place in the formation of public health policy? Discuss the controversy in the context of moral and cultural conflict.

(SOURCES: Geraldin Sealey, "Epidemic Failure," *Rolling Stone*, June 2, 2005. Retrieved March 10, 2009, from http://www.rollingstone.com/politics/story/7371950/an_epidemic_failure/; NA, "Public Health and Religion: AIDS, America, Abstinence," *The Independent*, June 1, 2006. Retrieved March 15, 2009, from www.independent.co.uk/news/world/africa/public-health-and-religion-aids-america-abstinence-480593.html/; Brittney Bain, "President Bush Awarded For Fight Against AIDS," December 1, 2008, *The PEW Forum on Religion & Public Life*. Retrieved March 16, 2009, from http://pewforum.org/news/display.php?NewsID=17044/; NA, "Vatican Defends Pope Condoms Stand," *Reuters*, March 18, 2009. Retrieved March 18, 2009, from http://www.reuters.com/article/worldNews/idUSLI43220920090318; Carol Hilton, "*Lancet* Calls for Pope's Repentance on HIV Comments," March 30, 2009. Retrieved March 30, 2009, from http://www.medicalpost.com/news/article.jsp?content=20090224_171348_2428/; Nicholas D. Kristof, "Learning From the Sin of Sodom," *The New York Times*, February 28, 2010, p. 11; Richard Stearns, *The Hole in Our Gospel: What Does God Expect of Us?*, Nashville: Thomas Nelson, 2009.)

tradition. (In far fewer numbers are secular, or non-religious, orthodox, who find transcendent authority and objective values and truth in something other than God and the consolation of revealed truth, perhaps in nature, the social order, or human evolutionary development.) Hunter counts among the predominant religious orthodox: evangelical Protestants, orthodox and neo-conservative Jews, and conservative Roman Catholics. Also included would be *social conservatives*, a political label for those who generally believe that government has a role in enforcing traditional values, such as the importance of the biological family and respect for human life from conception to natural death.[6] Social conservatives are overwhelmingly Christian.

It wasn't surprising to find many of the orthodox—evangelical Christians, traditional Jews and Catholics, social conservatives—bitterly outspoken in their condemnation of withholding artificial nutrition from Terri Schiavo. Members of these groups variously likened the withholding of food and water to letting a helpless infant starve to death or to "cruel and unusual punishment."[7] The Vatican, through its newspaper *L'Osservatore Romano*, even compared Schiavo's situation to that of an innocent person sentenced to capital punishment, a view largely shared by US bishops and Muslim authorities.

For these religious and social conservatives, Terri Schiavo's life plainly had value regardless of her condition, because they believe that life's worth doesn't depend on "what a person can do, experience or achieve," to quote *The New York Times* politically conservative columnist David Brooks. Rather, Brooks explained at the time, they believe that "[t] he life of a vegetative person or a fetus has the same dignity and worth as the life of a fully functioning adult."[8] This makes life's value absolute. Life is a sacred or divine gift that the ideal society recognizes by treating Terri Schiavo's life as worthwhile as her husband's, yours, or mine. The ideal society protects the unconditional value of life by prohibiting death-hastening policies and decisions at the end of life as well as at life's beginning. Such a view inspires prohibitions on what otherwise would be freedom of action or self-determination, whether of individual or scientist.[9]

In opposition to cultural orthodoxy, Hunter sets cultural progressivism, which does not tell us once and for all who we are but subscribes to a reality, truth, and authority that are ever unfolding. For cultural progressivists, there is no higher or transcendent authority of good and bad, right and wrong. Such matters are for us humans to determine. So is defining ultimate truth. This doesn't mean that the progressivists lack or are indifferent to standards of conduct. But unlike most of the orthodox, who overwhelmingly source notions of goodness and badness to divine higher authority, the progressivists mainly attribute them to human beings. They believe that people set the ground rules of conduct, personal and social. This makes those guidelines and directives debatable, flexible, and changeable.

For the progressivists, the view that lives such as Terri Schiavo's must be preserved at all costs is wildly unrealistic, even cruel, given the advanced state of medical technology today, which can blur the distinction between living and merely existing. It isn't life that counts, the progressivists tend to say, it's life's dignity or quality. Like Terri Schiavo's, life can pass into mere existence, and it's up to the individual and family to say when that happens. For many progressivists, therefore, the ideal society recognizes the conditional value of life and honors it, perhaps by permitting death-hastening policies

and decisions at the end of life. It also allows the individual and scientist a large measure of freedom of action, or self-determination, at the beginning of life.

Predictably within the progressivist camp Hunter numbers various secularists, or those without religious beliefs. But, significantly, he also includes reform Jews and liberal Catholics and Protestants. Thus, some *religious* progressivists described the withdrawal of Schiavo's artificial feeding as appropriate. A prominent rabbi, for example, said that artificial nutrition was not food but medical treatment; and, therefore, he said it could be withdrawn, given the medical hopelessness of Schiavo's condition. He also urged people to accept their mortality, as he said the Bible makes clear. Even some evangelicals agreed, saying that feeding tubes are like breathing machines, which would make removing them no more starvation than removing ventilation is suffocation. A professor of Christian ethics at an evangelical university thought that withdrawing the feeding tube would be appropriate if that was what Schiavo wanted. And, taking aim at the Vatican and US bishops, a professor at a leading Catholic university, Daniel C. Maguire of Marquette, said that both were out of step with "mainstream Catholic theology against extraordinary measures to sustain life." Maguire called *Schiavo* a "15-year atrocity" that represented a tendency to idealize physical life and forget the natural process of death.[10] For his part, Catholic theologian and priest Richard McBrien of Notre Dame attacked the Vatican's capital punishment analogy as "theologically erroneous—and irresponsibly so, given the highly public nature of this controversy."[11]

Cultural historians can judge the merits of Hunter's culture war concept. For us it serves as an appropriate entrée to our study, because it brings out the philosophical differences and disputants that largely drive today's spirited cultural discourse in bioethics. This book takes the position that contemporary bioethics is less about specific issues and more about their subterranean moral conflicts. Certainly, *Schiavo* was controversial. But the view here is that, ultimately, *Schiavo* owed its controversy, as does bioethics itself, not to procedural matters but to fundamental disagreements about which of opposed conceptions of reality, truth, and goodness will mainly shape society.

ABOUT THIS BOOK

Over 2,000 years ago, in his dialogue *Euthyphro*, Plato (427–348 BCE) posed the question: *Is it the case that something is good because God approves it, or is it the case that God approves what is good?* If the former, then ethics is properly understood as an aspect of religion and theology. If the latter is the case—that God approves what is good—then ethics is properly understood as moral philosophy, or a rational study of moral values and rules independent of religion and theology.

Plato's question cannot be settled to everyone's satisfaction. This partly explains the irresolvable moral tensions and conflicts in a culture such as ours, that inherits both moral traditions, the sacred and the secular. These fundamentally different ways of doing ethics especially show up in bioethics, which engages content of the highest religious interest and value, such as what makes a human being, when life begins and ends, and how properly to determine human sexuality and make a baby.

To tap the ancestral lines of these interlacing perspectives, as we do in Part I, Sacred and Secular Foundations, is to begin to understand the historical influences that still resonate in today's moral conflicts and debates in bioethics. Also to be discovered in the past, and the more recent, are the signal political events, scientific advances, and social developments, along with the religious, political, and philosophical thought that profoundly shaped the founding of modern bioethics in the 1960s and early 1970s. These we'll sketch in Part II, Origins and Context of Bioethics. Parts III and IV will extend our understanding of the foundations, origins, and context of bioethics to Issues at the Beginning of Life and Issues at the End of Life, respectively.

The often-wrenching personal decisions at life's beginning and end, together with their related divisive social policies, are made today in a medical, social, and political environment that's quite different from the early days of modern bioethics. Of special note is the biblically inspired bioethical vision of the religious conservatives that currently is challenging the field's dominant secular construction. A prominent US religious figure has even suggested that civil law should support a "Christian bioethical vision."[12] Should it? Does religion have a role in public bioethics? Do arguments based on religious principles have a place in society's debates about bioethical policy? Such questions, which speak to the relationship of religion, medical science, and public policy are an increasingly important part of the cultural discourse in bioethics. The book's Conclusion, Bioethics, Religion, and Liberal Democracy, addresses these matters.

CASES AND CONTROVERSIES

Reproductive Flashpoints

The new reproductive technologies that allow people to begin life outside the womb or prevent it—or *end* it—the "morning after" have produced intense bioethical debates. Here is a handful of culturally divisive issues that we'll examine in detail elsewhere in this text.

- Many people are concerned that we are acting as if it is a right to have children. Religious people generally say that children are a gift from God, a

privilege, not something that is ours by right. *Is infertility a medical problem to be overcome, or are children a gift we can't demand?*

- In order to maximize the chances of a successful pregnancy, many ova are collected and many spare embryos are made. But what to do with the spares? They can be thrown away, frozen for future attempts, used for medical research, or even put up for "adoption." Religious and social conservatives are especially unhappy with the

(Continued)

CASES AND CONTROVERSIES (CONTINUED)

destruction of embryos, as they believe that life begins at conception and to experiment on or destroy life is morally wrong. *What do you think is the best use of the estimated 400,000 frozen embryos stored in the United States?*

- Many religions teach that sex has a dual purpose—to unite the couple and to procreate. Some of them, such as Roman Catholicism, are concerned that treatments for infertility separate the two purposes, and they would say that infertility treatments are therefore wrong. Many Christians, however, including Catholics and Protestant and Anglican denominations, as well as Jews and Muslims, say that as long as infertility treatment isn't used to replace sex within marriage it's permissible. *What do you think the purpose of sex is? Do infertility treatments interfere with its purpose?*

- In January 2009 Nadya Suleman, an unmarried mother on public assistance with six children, was dubbed "Octomom" when she gave birth to octuplets after taking fertility drugs. *What does your faith tradition say about the Suleman case? Is it an example of science being properly used in the cause of new life, as desired by a woman who sees bringing new children into the world as her highest good?*

- The pregnancy rate among 15- to 19-year-olds increased 3 percent between 2005 and 2006—the first jump since 1990–before dropping 2 percent between 2007 and 2008. Abortion also inched up for the first time in a decade, according to 2006 data. Teen pregnancy and abortion have long been among the most pressing social issues and have triggered intense political debate over sex education. According to a landmark study reported in 2010, sex education classes that focus on encouraging children to remain abstinent can convince a significant proportion to delay sexual activity.[13] *Should the federal government fund programs that encourage abstinence until marriage or focus on birth control?*

CASES AND CONTROVERSIES

Refusal Legislation

"Right of Conscience" bills, also known as health care refusal measures, were introduced in several states' legislatures in 2008. In a later chapter we'll take a closer look at such legislation. Suffice it here to point out that these measures generally immunize facilities and providers from any form of liability for choosing not to inform, refer, or provide health care services of which the provider or facility has a religious, moral, or ethical objection. The measures are promoted by the "Medical Right," a term coined to show the connection of religiously influenced medical organization to the "Religious Right," a political force primarily comprising fundamentalists in the Protestant and Roman Catholic traditions. The Christian Medical and Dental Society, the Catholic Medical Association, Americans United for Life, and Pharmacists for Life International are among the organizations active in advocating for health care refusal clauses. About half of the proposals would shield pharmacists who refuse to fill prescriptions for birth control and morning-after contraceptive pills because they believe the drugs cause abortions. Many of the proposals are far broader measures that would shelter a doctor, nurse, aide, technician, or other employee who objects to any therapy. Included might be in vitro fertilization, physician-assisted suicide, embryonic stem cells, and possibly even providing treatment to gays and lesbians.

Questions for Analysis

1. To their critics, refusal measures represent the triumph of religious ideology over the full range of legal medical services. Do you agree?

2. Julian Savulescu, former editor of the prestigious *Journal of Medical Ethics*, says that conscience has little place in the delivery of modern medical care. If individuals are not prepared to offer legally permitted, efficient, and beneficial care to a patient because it conflicts with their values, the Oxford University professor says they shouldn't be doctors. "Doctors should not offer partial medical services or partially discharge their obligations to care for their patients." Is Savulescu correct?[14,15]

CASES AND CONTROVERSIES

Religion and Termial Care

For many patients and their physicians, avoiding the pain and suffering of a terminal disease is top priority. This is not necessarily the case, however, with very religious patients. One study that followed 345 cancer patients to their deaths found that patients who wanted aggressive care and received it had lower ratings of physical distress.[16,17] According to Betty Ferguson, a registered nurse who studies end-of-life issues, "We've had patients who said, 'Well, God suffered.

Jesus suffered. So if I suffer, it's going to make me more like God.'" Ferguson's Orthodox Jewish patients often express the belief that life is worth living no matter how debilitated they are.[18] What does your faith tradition teach about the meaning and purpose of suffering, pain, and death? What in your view is a "good death"? Do you think doctors should talk to their patients about their patients' religious views to determine what is motivating their preferences for aggressive care?

REFERENCES

1. President's Statement on Terri Schiavo, March 17, 2005. Retrieved July 23, 2008, from http://www.whitehouse.gov/news/releases/2005/03/20050317-7.html.

2. "'May God give grace to our family,'" *CNN.com*, April 1, 2005. Retrieved July 23, 2008 from http://www.cnn.com/2005/US/03/31/schiavo/.

3. E. J. Dionne, Jr., "Why the Culture War Is the Wrong War," *The Atlantic Monthly*, January/February 2006. Retrieved August 4, 2008, from http://www.theatlantic.com/doc/200601/culture-war.

4. James Davison Hunter, *Culture Wars: The Struggle To Define America*, New York: Basic Books, 1991, p. 120.

5. Ibid., p. 44.

6. Tim Rutten, "War, After the Smoke Clears," *Los Angeles Times*, January 17, 2007, p. E8.

7. Teresa Watanabe and Larry B. Stammer, "Diverse Faiths Find No Easy Answers," *Los Angeles Times*, March 24, 2005, p. A21.

8. David Brooks, "Arguments of Morality and Reality," *The New York Times*, March 29, 2005, p. A1.

9. Mark Mellman, "Another Country," *The New York Times*, September 17, 2008, p. A27.

10. Tim Rutten, "Schiavo Case Bares Political Sea Change," *Los Angeles Times*, March 26, 2005, p. E18.

11. See note 7 above.

12. Francis Cardinal George, "The Need for Bioethical Vision," in *Cutting-Edge Bioethics: A Christian Exploration of Technologies and Trends*, John F. Kilner, C. Christopher Hook & Diann B. Uustal, eds., Grand Rapids, MI: William B. Eerdmans Publishing. 2002, p. 97.

13. John B. Jemmott III, Loretta Jemmott, and Geoffrey T. Fong, "Efficacy of a Theory-Based Abstinence-Only Intervention Over 24 Months: A Randomized Controlled Trial With Young Adults," *Annals of Pediatric and Adolescent Medicine*, February 2010, pp. 152–159.

14. Rob Stein, "Health Workers' Choice Debated," *Washington Post*, January 30, 2006, p. A1.

15. Julian Savulescu, "Conscientious Objection in Medicine," *BMJ*, February 4, 2006, pp.2294–2297.

16. Andrea C. Phelps et al. "Religious Coping and Use of Intensive Life-Prolonging Care Near Death in Patients With Advanced Cancer," *JAMA*, March 19, 2009, pp. 1140–1147.

17. Roni Caryn Rabin, "Study Links Religion and Terminal Care," *The New York Times*, March 18, 2009, p. A18.

18. Karen Kaplan, "For Many, Faith Leads to Aggressive Treatments," *Los Angeles Times*, March 18, 2009. Retrieved March 24, 2009, from www.spokesman.com/stories/2009/mar/18/for-many-faith-leads-to-aggressive-treatments.

PART I

Two Enduring Traditions

INTRODUCTION: SACRED AND SECULAR FOUNDATIONS

For centuries thoughtful people have pondered and disagreed on basic questions about human nature and destiny, suffering and death, truth and meaning, and right and wrong. Placed in an historical context, then, the deep cultural divisions evident in a case like *Schiavo* are not new. Rather, they can be viewed as part of an ongoing dialogue—sometimes civil and muted, sometimes uncivil and strident—that extends back into the distant past. Many of the issues, of course, are fresh, certainly those in biomedicine. But the fundamental differences between ways of knowing and understanding are as old as Western civilization itself.

This part of the book surveys the West's two great traditions of knowing and understanding. Chapter 1 deals with the legacies of medieval religion and Enlightenment science, while Chapter 2 examines their enduring moral and political endowments. The theme of Part I is that these two distinct and venerable ways of knowing and understanding—one sacred, the other secular—are active philosophies helping to shape today's bioethical controversies.

Chapter 1

Medieval Religion and Enlightenment Science

The Institute on Biotechnology & the Human Future in Chicago offers assessments of the scientific benefits and risks of new developments in biotechnology, while at the same time analyzing their cultural and ethical significance.[1] One of the Institute's fellows is C. Ben Mitchell, an associate professor of Bioethics and Contemporary Culture at Trinity International University in Deerfield, Illinois, just north of Chicago. Mitchell is also a consultant with the Center of Bioethics and Human Dignity at Johns Hopkins University and editor of *Ethics & Medicine: An International Journal of Bioethics*. The widely published Mitchell, who holds a doctorate in philosophy with a concentration in medical ethics, has a name for the present age. He calls it "Technopian" for its daunting list of technologies that worry as much as thrill him.

WELCOME TO TECHNOPIA

In the brave new world of "Technopia" Mitchell forecasts, we can expect to enjoy:

- the ability to clone humans and predetermine the sex of children and their genetic makeup;
- drugs tailor-made to the genetic makeup of individual patients;
- genetically derived therapies for the prevention and cure of most cancers, heart disease, AIDS, and other diseases, including new strains of vaccine-resistant ones such as malaria;
- the ability to "program" out of human genes the propensities to contract various diseases and illnesses;
- repair of damaged brain cells, spinal cord, and other diseased or damaged human tissues;
- animals that grow replacement organs for the 50 percent of humans who currently die before getting a transplant organ from a human donor; and

- a "smart mouse" that points the way to eliminating aging in humans.

"Clearly," Mitchell admits, "the future may reap great benefits from biotechnologies such as genetic engineering, cloning, cybernetics, nanotechnology, and a litany of other neologisms yet to be invented." But Mitchell, a Christian bioethicist who consults on matters of public policy, is quick to add: "The future may also portend tragedy, a loss of human dignity, and a world which is increasingly hostile to concerns which transcend the world of contemporary scientific research."

For Mitchell and many others,[2] one of those concerns is "to re-establish what, exactly, it means to be human." After all, as he explains, "[I]f being human is all about the brain, then supercomputers might be able to contain all the information in the brain and then be designated as 'human'." That possibility especially horrifies religious and social conservatives. They say that the Bible establishes profoundly different criteria for humanhood and offers a moral vision that, strictly speaking, does not include many of the wonders of modern biotechnology. (Biotechnology refers to the application of biological research techniques to the development of products and processes to improve human health.)

This scriptural outlook, which is associated with but not limited to religious fundamentalism and social conservatism, provides millions of Americans with a religious framework for understanding human nature, knowing human destiny, interpreting misfortune, finding meaning, relating to others, and evaluating government. It also helps shape their opinions about social policy, particularly in bioethics. The roots of this highly influential scriptural view trace back to Christian-dominated Europe in the millennium between approximately 500 and 1500 CE, known as the Middle Ages.

THE MEDIEVAL CHURCH

Established as the state religion in 391 CE, the Roman Catholic Church became the most powerful organization of the time following the collapse of the Western Roman Empire in the fourth and fifth centuries. Embracing most Western Europeans, the Church offered to the spiritual lives of people what the feudal and manorial system offered to their political and economic lives: unity, solidarity, and security.[3] In a time of tumult and uncertainty, the medieval Church gave assurance and hope of a better life to come. Its theological orientation, summarized as follows, left no doubt as to the meaning of life and death

> [T]he stretch on earth is only a short interlude, a temporary incarceration of the soul in the prison of the body, a brief trial and test, fated to end in death, the release from pain and suffering. What really matters is the life after the death of the body. One's existence acquires meaning not by gaining what this life can offer but by saving one's immortal soul from death and eternal torture, by gaining eternal life and everlasting bliss.[4]

Surrounding this view was a constellation of biblical stories considered to have profound explanatory or symbolic significance.

Descriptively, these scriptural narratives and their interpretations accounted for human origin, nature, and destiny, as well as for the presence of evil in the world, including illness, suffering, and death. They helped people understand what and who they were, where they were going, and why they faced so much adversity along the way. Prescriptively, they told people how they should live, including how to structure such social institutions as marriage, family, and government.

Crucial to the development and expression of this biblical perspective were the views of the Church's most brilliant and influential of writers and thinkers, Saint Augustine (354–430) and Saint Thomas Aquinas (1225–1274). Although separated by 800 years, and despite many sharp differences between them, Augustine and Aquinas both treated the Bible as the ultimate source of knowledge about humankind's origin, nature, destiny, and relationship with God. Millions of people still do.

THE AUTHORITY OF THE BIBLE

The Bible, which contains the sacred writings of all Christian religions, includes the Hebrew Scriptures, termed Old Testament (written between 1400 and 400 BCE), and Christian Scriptures, or New Testament, (completed and preserved between 50 and 100–150 CE). Significantly, the word testament comes from the Greek *diatheke* meaning "covenant." For believers, the Bible remains a sacred covenant, or agreement, between God and his people, in which God reveals himself, makes certain promises, and requires certain behavior in return. For both Augustine and Aquinas, as well as for people generally during the Middle Ages, the Bible was the chief, if not exclusive, source of knowledge and understanding about themselves, their world, and the fate of both.

But early Christians also recognized that the Scriptures could be obscure and difficult. The imperfect, fallible human mind could misunderstand and be led astray by them. To correct for this possibility, according to its founders, God established the Church as his representative on earth.

As the Bible's infallible interpreter, the Church existed to make revelation rational. It also functioned to spread biblical truth, which included suppressing heresy, or opinions at variance with official teaching. In this way, the early Church strove to avoid confusion and safeguard the sum of truths revealed in the Scriptures.

THE BIBLICAL ACCOUNT
OF CREATION

"In the beginning God created the heavens and the earth" (Gen. 1:1). With these primordial words, the first book of the Bible asserts the existence of a single, unchanging, divine sovereign who created the universe. This monotheistic belief is regarded as Judaism's unique contribution to the ancient religions of the Mediterranean, all of which—Egyptian, Babylonian, Assyrian, Greek—subscribed to polytheism, the belief in many gods, often quarrelsome and typically

indifferent to the world and its inhabitants. The God of Genesis, by contrast, is one and personal, righteous, and loving. By expressing himself in creation, this biblical God gives to the world unity and meaning, and to its inhabitants intrinsic value and significance.

Human Nature

Of the human aspect of creation, Genesis records that the first human, Adam, was made a "living being" or psycho-physical self by the "breath" or spirit of God: "The Lord god formed man of dust from the ground, and breathed into his nostrils the breath of life; and man became a living being" (Gen. 2.7; cf. Ps. 104. 29–30; Job 34.14–15). The first human, then, was both corporeal and spiritual; a unity of a material body and a spiritual, animating soul. Being *imago Dei*, made in the image of God, he shared something of the divine intellect and will. Through the intellect he could know that a single God exists, and through the will he could choose and act to love God. This uniquely human capacity to choose and act was fundamental to the covenant between God and Adam.

The Relationship and the Covenant

According to Genesis 3:2–3, God commanded Adam: "You may freely eat of every tree of the garden, but of the tree of knowledge of good and evil you shall not eat, for in the day that you eat of it you shall die." Clearly, then, the first human is depicted as naturally free to obey or disobey, to do good or evil, to choose life or death. Thus is established the relationship of God's lordship and the human's subservience.

The essence of this covenant or contract was that Adam would use his God-given faculties properly. In the classical Greek construction, proper use of uniquely human faculties basically meant rational development. Through reason, the Greek philosophers taught, one was to control destructive impulses, discover moral law in the universe, and find meaning in life. In the biblical view, by contrast, the unique human faculties of intellect and will characterized the first human as a beloved and compliant child of God. According to the biblical covenant, Adam could expect from a righteous God love, mercy, and justice; God, in turn, could expect of him fidelity and obeisance. Man, in brief, must act responsibly, that is, to choose to do right, not as he saw it, but as God willed it. In this way, order and harmony were established in the divine-human relationship and in creation, generally.

Signifying the station of this completely good creature, the Creator then crowns the first human with "glory and honor" (Ps. 8.5) by giving him "dominion over all the earth and everything in it" (Gen 1.26). God then completes man's happiness by placing him in a divine garden, Eden, and creating Eve to be Adam's wife. (Gen 2:21–22)

Given this idyllic account of creation, the earliest theologians, and later ones, faced what is called "the problem of the existence of evil."

THE PROBLEM OF EVIL

We generally think of evil as being either "natural" or "moral." Natural evil refers to an apparent malfunctioning of the physical world, whereas moral evil is human made. Natural evil includes not only so-called disastrous acts of nature such as storms and earthquakes, but also illness, disease, pain, suffering, and ultimately death. Moral evil includes destructive behavior by humans toward others, such as lying, cheating, and killing.

While perceptions of evil may vary, evil always threatens our ability to act in the world and to understand it. Church historian Walter Sundberg puts it this way: Evil "raises the fundamental human question of intelligibility. If we cannot order evil, then both practical and theoretical reason are threatened."[5] In her book on the subject, philosopher Susan Neiman even goes so far as to call this fundamental question of intelligibility raised by evil the guiding force of modern thought.[6] In any event, for theologians the "intelligibility" that the presence of evil threatens is the belief in an all-good, all-powerful God. Expressed as a question, then, the problem of evil is this: *If God is all good,*

why is there evil; and if God is all powerful, why does he permit it? Must it be concluded that God is not all good or not all powerful? An attempt to answer this question is sometimes called a theodicy (from the Greek *theo* meaning "god" + *dike* meaning "justice or order").

Theodicy is the traditional theological term for a reasoned attempt to vindicate God's goodness and power in the face of evil. Theologically, a theodicy tries to establish the compatibility of evil and divine justice so that the existence of evil cannot shatter our trust in the world, forcing us, unaided, to make sense of the seemingly senseless. Although Augustine didn't invent the term—the German philosopher Gottfried Leibniz (1646-1716) did in his book *Theodicy* (1710)—Augustine did attempt to reconcile the existence of evil with the existence of an omniscient, omnipotent God. His explanation is an important aspect of the medieval religious view that still has wide appeal, especially in many people's feelings and attitudes toward illness, suffering, and death.

The Augustinian Theodicy

Consistent with the Bible, Augustine's theodicy involved man's fall from grace, or state of divine influence and sanctification. The biblical basis of the fall is two passages from Genesis. The first—"God saw all that he had made and saw that it was very good" (Gen. 1:31)—establishes a divine creation free of evil. The second describes the human's first recorded act, an act of free choice proposed by the serpent, who, addressing Eve, contradicts God's admonition to man: "You shall not die. For God knows that when you eat of it your eyes will be opened and you will be like God, knowing good and evil" (Gen. 3.4–5). Succumbing to pride, Adam is persuaded by Eve to betray his creaturely position and, figuratively, make of himself God, thereby breaking the sacred relationship and covenant.

Because of this misuse of freedom, according to Augustine, the first human organism was cut off from the source if its life: God's breath or spirit. Where there was harmony, there was now discord. Where God ruled man through his human spirit, he now governed in a more external way: by subjecting man to the laws of nature. Evil followed, natural and moral, both the consequences of Adam's original sin of prideful disobedience. With this explanation, Augustine, in effect, rescued human inquiry from the futile task of attempting to make sense of the senselessness of evil. As Nieman puts it:

> Why do bad things happen? Because bad things were done. Better to have some causal explanation than to remain in the dark. To connect sin and suffering is to separate the world into moral and natural evils, and to create thereby a framework for understanding human misery.[7]

To connect sin and suffering is also to create a framework for ultimately blaming humans for evil, another important element in the medieval worldview.

THE DOCTRINES OF THE FALL AND DEPRAVITY

Corrupted by pride and ambition, the first man and woman suffered the wrath of God, physically and spiritually. Their bodies would not only die, their souls would be dead to all things good. Even worse, this condition of physical and spiritual death would pass on to all future generations, who, according to Augustine, were "seminally present in the loins of Adam" (cf. Heb. 7:9–10). The upshot would be a new kind of human, a new species, never made by God but sinned into existence. The original sin of Adam and Eve, in short, became in Augustine's theology the condition of sin that marked all humans. It effected what theologian C.S. Lewis (1896–1963) once called "a radical alteration of [the human's] constitution, a disturbance of the relation between his component parts, and an internal perversion of one of them."[8]

Elaborating further on the doctrine of the fall, Lewis, one of the last century's most influential Christian writers, described its catastrophic impact on the human mind as follows:

> … the organs, no longer governed by man's will, fell under the control of

ordinary biochemical laws and suffered whatever the inter-workings of those laws might bring about in the way of pain, senility and death. And desires began to come up into the mind of man, not as his reason chose, but just as the biochemical and environmental facts happened to cause them. And the mind itself under the psychological laws of association and the like which god has made to rule the psychology of the higher anthropoids. And the will, caught in the tidal wave of mere nature, had no resource but to force back some of the new thoughts and desires by main strength, and there uneasy rebels became the subconscious as now know it. The process was not, I conceive, comparable to mere deterioration as it may now occur in a human individual; it was a loss of status as a species.[9]

What the human lost by the fall from grace, then, was its "original specific nature." As a result, it was returned to dust, its position of origin. "Thus," Lewis concluded, "human spirit from being master of human nature became a mere lodger in its own house, or even a prisoner; rational consciousness became what it now is—a fitful spotlight resting on a small part of the cerebral motions."[10]

The fall, therefore, was not only the first humans'; it is all of humanity's. In the words of Psalm 51: "Behold, I was shapen in iniquity; and in sin did my mother conceive me" (see also Gen 25:22–23). By a single human trespass, human nature was essentially corrupted; and for both—our corrupt actions and our corrupt nature—each of us is to be considered blameworthy.

MORAL FAILURE AND ILLNESS

In his book *Blind Faith* (2006), about the relationship of religion and medicine, Richard Sloan reminds us that, besides monotheism, a key feature that distinguished Judaism from ancient Egypt and the Near Eastern cultures was the relationship between moral failure and illness. "In Judaism," writes the Columbia University behavioral scientist, "this was a central feature. In ancient Egypt, it was not," adding:

> In the Old Testament, Adam's sin allowed evil, including illness, into a previously perfect world. Faithfulness to God was associated with health and prosperity. Lack of faith led to illness. Thus, ancient Judaism heralded a concern that still confronts us today: the moral responsibility for illness.[11]

The medieval theologians largely adopted this Old Testament view of human affliction as a religious problem that sin brought on. Thus, as Christianity took on the practical mission of tending to the sick and suffering, it also became acutely mindful of its own theology. Especially relevant was its conception of sin, which was central to its creation theory; its theodicy; and its eschatology (from the Greek *eschatos* meaning "last"), or beliefs about death and human destiny.

Bi-level Conception of Sin

Embedded in the doctrine of the fall from grace is actually a bi-level conception of sin. First, there is the particular level of someone breaking God's commandments, as with Adam's prideful disobedience. But on a deeper, universal level that Lewis wrote about, there is the sin of humanity's fallen nature inherited from Adam's rebellion against God (Gen 3:14–19; 4:1–15; Rom 8:20–22). For his sin, Adam suffered—he lost Paradise. But humanity suffers also from this original sin. From Adam's choice not to love follow all the world's evils, notably in this context: illness, disease, pain, suffering, and death, the greatest penalty for the inherited sin of the willful Adam. A "debt contracted through sin" is what Augustine called death. As he wrote in the *Enchiridion,* his handbook on faith, hope, and love:

> … there is one form of punishment peculiar to man—the death of the body. God had threatened him with this punishment of death if he should sin,

leaving him indeed to the freedom of his own will, but yet commanding his obedience under pain of death; and He placed him amid the happiness of Eden….
> Thence, after his sin, he was driven into exile, and by his sin the whole race of which he was the root was corrupted in him, and thereby subjected to the penalty of death….[12]

For this Church Father, then, death and its prefiguration, decrepitude, were the wages of sin. This had the inevitable, though not unique, effect of linking medicine with the supernatural.

MEDICINE AND THE SUPERNATURAL

Sloan notes:

> Medicine and religion have been intimately connected throughout history, and in most eras they have been connected to magic, too. Throughout, they all have attempted to answer the same basic questions. One of these is "What causes illness?" A related question is "Why did I get sick?"[13]

To both questions the medievalist answered: "*Sin*—illness and disease, pain and suffering, inevitable death and certain knowledge of it, all are the consequences of *sin*."

Accordingly, the sick in the Middle Ages were largely offered the cure of prayerful contrition dispensed by the cleric, who was more philosopher than scientist. This physician/priest was expected to be steeped in Greek sources—Hippocrates (460–377 BCE), Plato (427–348 BCE), Aristotle (384–322 BCE)—adapted, always, to Christian teaching. "Particularly striking," writes one historian of medicine, was "the recourse to authority, that is, to the written sayings of the ancients, which were more important in establishing a diagnosis, prognosis and therapeutic advice than the actual experience of the practitioner."[14] Apparently as interested in supernatural meaning as with scientific description, the ancient Greek physician Galen (129–200 CE), who was the dominant medical authority of the day, epitomized this admixture of medicine, philosophy, and religion.[15]

Illness as Salvific

Theologically, the most important part of the supernaturalization of health and medicine in the Middle Ages was the potentially salvific value of illness. However well deserved the destiny of all, death and its familiar foreshadowings didn't mean ultimate annihilation or nothingness. For, judging it "better to bring good out of evil, than to permit any evil to exist," Augustine's words, "God ... determined that in the case of men [unlike] in the case of fallen angels, there should be ... restoration to happiness."[16] This meant not only individual survival of death as a personality, but also a blissful afterlife for those who kept the covenant by using this life for spiritual renewal.

The promise of personal immortality effectively completed the West's evolutionary creation narrative whereby life had a beginning and not an end, but a goal: death. Henceforth, death in the West would be the gateway to a new personal existence. Theologically, it would be the portal to eternity, the final test, and the ultimate dread and suffering before divine judgment of one's earthly life. Fundamental to the medieval mind, then, was the view of the present life as the determinant of eternal destiny. Life's travails, notably sickness and suffering, were thereby transformed from evils to be avoided to potential instruments of spiritual renewal for winning heaven and avoiding hell. Enduring hardship in devout faith was a biblically grounded form of spiritual renewal, a way to show the depth of one's belief and trust in God, and thereby to gain personal salvation (Ps 116:10). For medieval Christians, in short, pain and suffering offered opportunities of faith and reconciliation with God.

ROLE OF GOVERNMENT AND LAW

One final point about the medieval religious outlook. Although it did not dictate a particular form of government, the medieval religious theory of human nature and destiny provided a basis for government and law, as well as a template for evaluating political systems. Thus, the general thinking of Aquinas was that, as children of a God of law and order, human beings (1) needed and sought the discipline of governmental structures; and (2) they could bring the divine traits of intellect and will to the task of self-government. Earlier, Augustine gave emphasis to the human's fallen nature and the consequent need to have its potential for evil and sinfulness regulated through civil government and law. For both Augustine and Aquinas, then, government was a divinely ordained, necessary instrument of external control. Its basic function was to prevent chaos and anarchy, and establish order and harmony on earth.[17] So conceived, government was granted broad powers, including war making when in the righteous cause of defeating evil. Another important implication was that, as a divine and necessary instrument of regulation, government, in general, was owed obedience, and could punish and levy taxes (Rom 13:1-6). At the same time, reflective of the overarching covenant between God and humanity, government was expected to treat its charges as creatures of God. It was to do this by ensuring that the laws it enacted reflected God's plan for creation.

ENLIGHTENMENT SCIENCE

Although medieval religious thought would dominate Europe until about the sixteenth century, a shift in thinking and attitude began centuries earlier that ultimately would transform how people viewed themselves, their world, and even God. Far too many to mention here were the events and forces behind this drift away from medieval supernaturalism to a more human-oriented, secular view of life. Certainly among the factors were the Crusades,

BIOETHICS ACROSS CULTURES

Buddhism, Health, and Disease

Buddhism has a 2,500-year history of involvement in medicine theory and practice. Like other religious philosophies, what this tradition teaches about health and disease is inseparable from its worldview, which is based on the interdependence of all phenomena. According to the Buddhist doctrine of dependent origination, the existence of every being is mutually interdependent, forming a kind of web of cause-and-effect relationships. This implies, first, that whatever happens in the world affects everything else; and, second, that nothing is independent: Everything in the temporal world is subject to change, including human beings. Therefore, it's useless to think about some enduring reality such as "self" or "soul," or an underlying human nature such as the Judeo-Christian-Islamic belief that that humans are made in the image of God and destined for personal immortality. Consistent with this worldview, according to Pinit Ratanakul, professor of philosophy at Mahidol University of Bangkok, "health and disease involve the overall state of a human being and are interwoven with many factors such as economics, education, social and cultural milieu." All of these conditional factors, Ratanakul points out, need to be seriously taken into account in the understanding of health and disease, as well as diagnosis, prevention, and treatment. Health is therefore to be understood in terms of holism, an approach to health that addresses the body, mind, and spirit; or the physical, emotional, and spiritual aspects of an individual. When framed holistically, health becomes "the expression of harmony–within oneself, in one's social relationships, and in relation to the natural environment." Therefore, from the perspective of Buddhism, to be concerned about a person's health means "to be concerned with the whole person, his (her) physical and mental dimensions, social, familial, and work relationships, as well as the environment in which he (she) lives and which acts on him (her)." Healing, then, is not merely treating measurable symptoms. Rather, "It is more an expression of the combined effort of the mind and the body to overcome disease than a fight between medicine and disease." The overcoming of physical disease, in turn, is part of the larger project of overcoming the "dis-ease" of living. This involves stepping permanently out of the cycle of rebirth—ending the continuous process of birth and death, loss and suffering. How to do this? Siddhartha Gautama (563–483 BCE), the founder of Buddhism, taught that if one wishes to be released from suffering, one must sever ties with worldly

which introduced new ways of thinking and living. So, too, the rise of cities increased freedom and mobility and introduced a new class of profit-minded "entrepreneurs." Also stimulating worldly interests were the medieval universities, which openly debated ideas that threatened mysticism and revelation as main sources of knowledge. Outside the universities, Gutenberg's invention of the printing press in 1456 put a Bible into the hands of ordinary people, which the Protestant Reformation of the next century encouraged them to use to have a personal, non–clerical-mediated relationship with God. The ferocious religious wars that followed the birth of Protestantism further undercut religious faith.

Emblematic of the age was a new breed of natural scientist, one trying to construct an accurate representation of the world based on reason and evidence, as opposed to the Bible, religious authority, or received wisdom. For a long time, however, the stunning discoveries of the new science simply proved the greatness and glory of God, even to those who made them. The English mathematician and physicist Isaac Newton (1642–1727), for example, saw divine majesty operating behind the mechanical universe he depicted in his monumental *Principia* (1687). Carl Linnaeus (1707–1778), the Swedish natural scientist and progenitor of Charles Darwin (1809–1882), proclaimed in his small but highly influential book, *Systema Naturae* (*The System of Nature*, 1735), that the study of nature revealed the mind of God. Both Newton and Linnaeus drew their inspiration from the Christian doctrine of a divinely created and ordered world.

passion, which is the cause of suffering. The way of life free from all worldly passion, and thus suffering, can only be known through Enlightenment, and Enlightenment can only be attained through the discipline of the Noble Path, which is the fourth of Buddhism's Fourfold Noble Truths:

1. The Truth of Suffering—The world is full of suffering. Birth is suffering, old age is suffering, sickness and death are suffering. A man full of hatred is suffering, to be separated from a beloved one is suffering, to be vainly struggling to satisfy one's needs is suffering. In fact, life that is not free from desire and passion is always involved with distress.
2. The Truth of the Cause of Suffering—The cause of human suffering is undoubtedly found in the thirsts of the physical body and in the illusions of worldly passion. If these thirsts and illusions are traced to their source, they are found to be rooted in the intense desires of physical instincts. Thus, desire, having a strong will-to-live at its basis, seeks that which it feels desirable, even if it is sometimes death.
3. The Truth of the Termination of Suffering—If desire, which lies at the root of all human passion, can be removed, then passion will die out and all human suffering will be ended.

4. The Truth of the Noble Path to the Termination of Desire—In order to enter into a state where there is no desire and no suffering, one must follow a certain Path. The states of this Noble Path are: Right View, Right Thought, Right Speech, Right Behavior, Right Livelihood, Right Effort, Right Mindfulness, and Right Concentration.

(SOURCES: Pinit Ratanakul, "Buddhism, Health and Disease," *Eubios Journal of Asian and International Bioethics* 15 (2004), pp. 162–164. Retrieved March 26, 2009, from http://www.eubios.info/EJ145/ej145b.htm; *The Teaching of Buddha*, Bukkyo Dendo Kyokai, 1976, pp. 38–39; James J. Hughes and Damien Keown, "Buddhism and Medical Ethics: A Bibliographic Introduction," *Journal of Buddhist Ethics*, Volume Two, 1995. Retrieved March 29, 2009, from http://www.changesurfer.com/Bud/BudBioEth.html.)

Question

What do you think are the principal differences between the Buddhist understanding of illness and suffering and that of Judaism, Christianity, and Islam? Contrast the function of moral excellence in Buddhism, on the one hand, and the three Abrahamic religions on the other. Would "the problem of evil" pose a problem for Buddhism? Why, perhaps, does Buddhism, of all religions, best complement medicine?

But an orderly, logical, machine-like world governed by universal laws of motion suggested something else: an absent God. Eventually, the thousand-year-old construct of a meaningful, purposeful universe defined by reference to a personal deity actively involved in human affairs, faced the challenge of a rival conception: a deity akin to a grand engineer detached from the workings of the universe and the lives of people and, like both, subject to the laws of physics.

This new way of viewing the human mind and the world was termed by the age itself Enlightenment, to signify movement from what it perceived as medieval darkness of ignorance and superstition to modern light of knowledge and truth. The familiar label *Age of Enlightenment* ordinarily refers to the eighteenth century in European philosophy. However, because its foundations for a new conception of the human mind and human relationship to nature were set in the seventeenth century, here the Enlightenment will be taken in its longer form to include that earlier period termed the *Age of Reason*. The Enlightenment's ideas represented a revolution in both science and social science that still influences our views of health, illness, and medicine, as well as our conception and practice of bioethics.

For now, we'll focus on two conceptual upheavals in science and their implications. The first was a new way of thinking termed *scientific method*. The other, inseparable from the first, was a new way of envisioning the world: as a machine. Together, scientific method and mechanism eventually would transform how human beings thought about themselves and their world; their relationship to God; the nature of medicine; and the problem of evil including illness, disease, suffering, and death.

SCIENTIFIC METHOD

"[S]cience," writes Harvard psychologist Steven Pinker, "is just the attempt to understand the world with a special effort to ensuring that the things you say about it are true."[18] Central to that endeavor is scientific method, a process of collecting data, making interpretations, and doing experiments in order to construct a reliable, consistent, and nonarbitrary picture of the world. Often associated with the English philosopher Francis Bacon (1561–1626), scientific method rests firmly upon the tripod of observations, hypotheses, and experimental testing.[19]

Commonplace throughout the physical and social sciences, and archly defended today by thinkers like evolutionary biologist Richard Dawkins (*The God Delusion*, 2006), four centuries ago scientific method represented nothing less than a new faith, professing that empirical human inquiry could yield an understanding of the universe. For scientists, this new method of thought meant freedom to find answers by using evidence and reason, rather than relying solely on tradition. In severing thought from religious faith, scientific method enthroned the autonomy of the mind as the chief means of acquiring knowledge about the world. And it did something else: Scientific method separated secular matters from any ultimate, transcendent goal and purpose. In short, it provided a way for sorting out the sacred and the secular.

Rene Descartes

The new "faith" of science found its preeminent theoretician in "as devout a Catholic as anyone of his time"[20]: Rene Descartes (1596–1650), considered the founder of modern philosophy. Descartes, a modern commentator writes:

> experimented and observed and made real progress in optics, physiology and mathematics, all the time hoping to synthesize

what he found into a unified system, a crystalline structure of "clear and distinct ideas." He wanted to know not just how events do fall out, but why they have to fall out as they do, why it stands to reason that the laws of nature have to be as they are. And he thought that by finding that out we would, quite literally, be reading the mind of God.[21]

Descartes' bold ambition took root in an original, mathematically inspired, analytic method of thought based on a handful of logical precepts, commencing with the historic principle of universal doubt. As he wrote in his *Discourse on Method* (1637),

> The first of these [precepts] was to accept nothing as true which I did not clearly recognize to be so: that is to say, carefully to avoid haste and prejudice in judgments, and to accept in them nothing more than what was presented to my mind so clearly and distinctly that I could have no occasion to doubt it.[22]

This foundational precept of universal doubt led Descartes to the one truth he could not doubt: the truth of his own existence as a thinking being.

While he could doubt everything else, even to supposing life a demon-controlled dream, he could not doubt the truth of *Cogito, ergo sum*, Latin for "I think, therefore I am." And so, with the *cogito* as his foundational clear and distinct idea, Descartes came to conclude that a human being is essentially a "thing which thinks." What the ancients and medievalists had called "soul" meant for Descartes a "thinking being," that is, "[a] thing that doubts, understands, affirms, denies, is willing, is unwilling, and also imagines and has sensory perceptions."[23] This most clearly and distinctly apprehended truth—thought itself—was the evidence that proved to Descartes the hypothesis of his own existence.

From this one indubitable truth, Descartes then moved into complex systems of belief by which he realized the existence of God as the source of truth and knowledge about the world. Not to be read as a mere recapitulation of the biblical narrative, the Jesuit-trained philosopher-scientist was saying: We can have reliable, accurate knowledge of the world because the existence of a perfect God—that is, one not given over to trickery or deceit—guarantees it. In this manner, Descartes attempted to accommodate the central concept of the old medieval theology—the existence of an all-good, all-loving, all-powerful God—within the new development of scientific method. He was, in effect, asserting: Observation, description, prediction, and experimentation—the new faith's antidote to relying on ecclesiastical authority and ancient tradition—are trustworthy, because God is.

At the same time, by giving rational justification to the empirical discoveries of the day's science, the "Cartesian Revolution" made reason and sense experience, not authority and tradition, primary sources of knowledge. It announced, in brief, that humans, unaided by received wisdom, could attain reliable knowledge. This is what makes *Discourse on Method* one of the most influential works in the history of science, medicine included.

The Emergent Scientific Medicine

Seeking what he termed "a clear and assured knowledge useful for life," Descartes was confident that his method of thought would eventually yield "an infinity of devices that would enable us to enjoy without pain the fruits of the earth and all the goods one finds in it, but also principally the maintenance of health" (*Discourse*, part 6, par. 2). This made Descartes, in the words of another commentator, one of those Enlightenment thinkers who was confident that "reason would function alongside faith to increase human happiness and life span, end disease, reduce suffering of all kinds and give people greater power over nature and greater freedom in their lives."[24] In this Descartes agreed with Bacon, who famously advocated a science devoted to "the glory of the Creator and the relief of man's estate" (*The Advancement of Learning*, 1605).

For Enlightenment medicine, "the relief of man's estate" required forsaking traditional teaching and theories of supernatural intervention, and retrieving the rational spirit of early Greek medicine. By associating medicine with science, the ancient Greek physician Hippocrates had disconnected it from magic and superstition, training medicine on

rational, and away from supernatural, explanations for illness and disease. Medieval Christianity had preserved the moral, humane spirit of Hippocratic thought but not its scientific thrust. Now, Enlightenment medicine proposed to recapture the Hippocratic separation of medicine from religion in several important ways, such as by discrediting supernatural explanations, testing religious belief, and challenging tradition.[25] Always the goal was to gain an understanding of how things worked as they did, not why. This was exactly what Descartes had in mind in seeking clear and assured knowledge useful for health and life, free of supernatural embellishment. In the years ahead, this commitment to natural explanation would lead to a full-fledged medical, as opposed to theological, understanding of illness and death, culminating in 1892 with the publication of *The Principles and Practice of Medicine*, authored by the Canadian physician William Osler (1849–1919), considered the founder of modern medicine.

MECHANISM

Descartes' contribution to the scientific revolution did not stop with his elaboration of scientific method. He was also committed to providing a thoroughly mechanical account of nature.

The Christian tradition, as had the Greek before it, embraced *vitalism*, the belief that there is in living organisms a life principle that provides purpose or direction. In *L'homme* (*Treatise on Man*), published posthumously in 1664, Descartes strived to discredit this medieval, spiritual teleology, inherited from Aristotle, that posited a goal or purpose working in biology. ("Teleology" is from the Greek *telos* meaning "end or purpose.") In opposition, Descartes posed *mechanism*, the view that everything can be explained in terms of laws that govern matter and motion. Like a machine, natural objects could be taken apart, analyzed, and ultimately understood in terms of physical causes. In this fashion, Descartes demystified nature, leaving it no longer the object of contemplation and significant of mystery and moral purpose it had been for the ancients and was for the medievalists.

BIOETHICS ACROSS CULTURES

Islamic Science

The term *Islamic science* refers to science that developed in the medieval Islamic world between the 7th seventh and 10th tenth centuries, also known as the Islamic Golden Age. Although most of the period's texts were written in Arabic, the scientists were of diverse ethnicities and religions. Medieval Muslim physicians and doctors pioneered scientific method in medicine, including experimentation, clinical trials, dissection, and postmortem autopsy. In the tenth century, the Persian physician/philosopher Razi (865–925) introduced controlled experiments and clinical observation into medicine, while rejecting, in *Doubts about Galen,* several of Galen's theories that couldn't be verified. Razi also carried out one of the earliest, and most ingenious, medical experiments in order to find out the most hygienic place to build a hospital. He simply hung pieces of meat throughout tenth century Baghdad and observed where the meat decomposed least quickly—that was where he built his hospital. His *Comprehensive Book of Medicine* was one of the first explorations of evidence-based medicine. Another Persian, known in English by his Latinized name Avicenna (980—1037), wrote hundreds of treatises on a wide range of subjects. Considered the "father of modern medicine," this physician/philosopher is best remembered for two monumental works. The first, *The Book of Healing,* published in 1027, was a scientific and philosophical encyclopedia; the second, *The Canon of Medicine,* completed in 1025, served as the standard medical text

not only in the Islamic world but throughout Europe as late as 1650. Much of that book was also translated into Chinese as the *Hui Hui Yao Fang* (*Prescriptions of the Hui Nationality*) by the Hui people in Yuan China. *The Canon* also formed the basis of Unani medicine, a form of traditional medicine practiced in India. The principles of medicine described by Avicenna ten centuries ago in *The Canon* are still taught at UCLA and Yale University, among other medical schools, as part of the history of medicine. A scanned copy of *The Canon of Medicine* is available at http://ddc.aub.edu.lb/projects/saab/avicenna/contents-eng.html.

(SOURCES: "Avicenna," *Wikipedia.* Retrieved March 30, 2009, from http://en.wikipedia.org/wiki/Avicenna; "The Canon of Medicine," *Wikipedia.* Retrieved March 30, 2009, from http://en.wikipedia.org/wiki/The_Canon_of_Medicine.)

Question

Well before the Europeans, Muslim scientists reached "the research-based conclusion that illnesses were caused by tiny creatures invisible to the naked eye and that patients needed to be isolated from healthy people during their treatment." Can the relative progress of Muslim physicians and scientists, on the one hand, and Christian Europeans, on the other, in part have a theological explanation?

(SOURCE: Irfan Kumar, "Muslim Contributions to Science," *The Daily Rising Kashmir,* Retrieved March 27, 2009, from http://www.risingkashmir.com/index.php?option=com_content&task+view&id=7956.)

By the Cartesian account, nature was deterministic, meaning it operated in fixed and predictable ways. If laws of matter and motion governed nature's operations, then they were accessible to the human mind. This implied a separation and fundamental difference between human beings and the natural world. The human mind, Descartes taught, was simple and immaterial, in contrast to all natural objects, including the human body, which were composites with extension. That made the human being essentially mind: an immaterial, thinking "I," or autonomous self, who transcended environment and biology and was, thus, capable of knowing and understanding the world.

Descartes' thought is sometimes termed a "radical dualism" because of its separation between the knower and the known; between the observing/knowing subject and the observed/known object. Practically, this separation between the human being and the natural world meant that, as thinking beings, humans could control and direct the world that they were at once a part of (as body) and apart from (as mind). By mastering nature, humans could transform their environment for the better, as *they* defined the better. As for the "soul," since it defied mathematical understanding, it didn't exist as the principle of animation in all living things, as conceived of by Aristotle and adopted by Aquinas. For Descartes the human "soul" was simply mind, whose purpose it was to manipulate the mechanism of nature, using self-directed willpower.

Later philosophers generally rejected Descartes' radical dualism, just as they and scientists discredited "the world as machine" model. But both Cartesian-inspired views have had lasting influence on Western thought and institutions. The autonomous, rational self, for example, became the foundation for Enlightenment humanism, a philosophy that stressed human values, including: individual liberty and responsibility, freedom of thought, tolerance of ideas, personal achievement, the liberal political state, and free market economy. Above all, Enlightenment humanism emphasized the sensible and reasonable as bases for belief and action. For its part, the "modern world machine" has served as a metaphorical model for subsequent generations of reductive models.[26] A reductive model is any hypothetical description of the world that reduces it to its fundamental or material basis, such as the nineteenth century's view of the universe as a network of invisible electromagnetic force fields or the twentieth century's conception of the universe as a digital computer.[27] It was during the Enlightenment that reductionism became the predominant model of Western medicine.

Reductionism is the view that a system can be fully understood in terms of its isolated parts. For example, seeing their role as searching out disease, diagnosing, and treating, physicians quickly began to focus on a "single problem with a single part of the body without looking at the whole person."[28] As a result, their lens for viewing patients and their medical problems became decidedly positivistic, meaning narrowed to scientific investigation and methods, and to an understanding of health largely in terms of the proper mechanical functioning of the body.[29,30]

IMPLICATIONS FOR RELIGION

Although scientific method and mechanism by no means displaced the medieval religious tradition, it did represent a new way of thinking about things that was destined to put and keep religion on the defensive. The scientific revolution introduced modern understandings of reality; of human nature and destiny; and of knowledge, truth, and meaning that directly challenged fundamental religious beliefs and teachings. Henceforth, religious truth would have to be interpreted within evidence and reason or risk being increasingly marginalized. Specifically, religion had to adapt to the following implications of the scientific revolution.

Deism

Descartes' mechanistic view didn't extend only to the world and its inhabitants. It could also be taken to imply that behind everything was something akin to a grand engineer or divine clock maker with no personal, ongoing relationship with his creation. In other words, a deistic god.

Deism is associated with two core beliefs. First, reason or logic, rather than tradition and revelation, should be the basis of belief in God. In this, deism opposes fideism, which relies on faith, not reason, to realize religious truth. Second, deism is also associated with the classical view that, having created it, "nature's god"—an impersonal, all-powerful force or energy—variously termed "providence," "creator," or "mind"—abandoned the world to humankind.

During the Enlightenment neither of these core beliefs was taken as suggesting that the world wasn't intelligently disposed or that it operated according to blind chance or pure luck. But they did imply that, although the universe might operate according to intelligent design, humans could say nothing intelligent about the designer, who was impervious to what happened in the universe. Questions about the essence of God, including his relationship to humans and role in their affairs, were simply beyond experience and, therefore, rationally unaddressable. The best humans could do was glimpse the mind of God reflected in the known laws of physics. This was possible by closely and methodically examining nature in the manner suggested by scientific method, and not through religion and revelation. Even some theologians of the day adopted this position, notably Anthony Collins

(1676–1729) (*Philosophical Inquiry Concerning Human Liberty*, 1715).[31]

The deistic way of understanding the deity also supported the emergent new biology based upon the principle of natural selection proposed in Darwin's *The Origins of the Species* (1859). Briefly, Darwin taught that in nature slight variations in an organism occur randomly. Some of these variations, if useful for survival, are preserved and passed on to subsequent generations, while some aren't. This means that only organisms best adapted to their environments survive; the less adapted tend to perish. Natural selection, as the process of genetic transmission is termed, struck Darwin as more compatible with an impersonal than a personal deity.[32,33]

Anthropic Mechanism

Another implication of the scientific revolution further threatened traditional understanding of human nature and the human's relation to God and nature.

Consider that Cartesianism taught that, as a natural system, the human body could be expected to function mechanically, or in predictable and rational ways. This meant that all human functions or faculties—muscular action, reflexes, sensations—could be explained, say, by reference to nerves and brain, and their governance by a uniform chemistry. Indeed, while working on *L'homme* in 1632, Descartes, a student of chemistry and anatomy, dissected the heads of animals in order to understand cognitive processes such as memory and imagination.[34] A contemporary went even further. Anticipating modern neurobiology, the English physician Thomas Willis (1621–1675) anatomized the human brain, confident of discovering clues to human intellect, passion, and memory. For religion, the suggestion of such experiments and underlying theory was decidedly unsettling: Like the universe itself, everything about humans could be explained mechanically. This view is sometimes termed *anthropic mechanism*.

Personhood as Consciousness

If the scientific revolution suggested an alternative view of human beings, it also implied a view of personhood at odds with the established religious view. *Personhood* refers to what makes a person a person, that is, the quality(ies) thought necessary for an individual to be recognized as a person. The traditional biblical view made no distinction between being human and being a person. Indeed, conservative Judeo-Christian teaching still holds that "a human being is a person from conception and at every subsequent moment." According to bioethicist Dennis M. Sullivan, "This means a human being/person has fundamental value, regardless of condition, state, or circumstance."[35]

Descartes, by contrast, put mind and thought on a different plane from the physical world. For Descartes it was the soul as immaterial mind that constituted a person. This is generally taken as suggesting that personhood is tied up with its capacity for consciousness, a view most of today's philosophers hold. In other words, recognition of status as a person derives from cognitive considerations. Therefore, whatever the cognitive attribute(s) may be—such as autonomy, rationality, self-awareness—the value of personhood is assigned and not inherent as in the biblical view.

Whether personhood is intrinsic or acquired currently divides religious and secular bioethicists. The controversy arises from the fact that if some cognitive character defines personhood, then presumably individuals who lack it are to be considered non-persons. In that event, they would not automatically enjoy all the rights ordinarily ascribed to persons, most notably the right to life. Imagine the potential enormity of the category of such individuals, including, as it might, the unborn; the recently born; the mentally ill and retarded; the frail elderly; and the permanently and irreversibly "awake but unaware," such as a Terri Schiavo.

As we'll see in subsequent chapters, the critical importance of one's understanding of personhood cannot be overstated in the study of modern bioethics. As noted by Sullivan, who is a physician as well as the Director of the Center for Bioethics at (Baptist) Cedarville University:

> The personhood question is central to biomedical ethics, where the nature of

humanity touches every issue at hand: abortion, reproductive technologies, human stem cell research, cloning, assisted suicide, euthanasia, genomics [i.e., the study of genes and their functions], and resource allocation.[36]

The Problem of Evil

The Enlightenment's scientific revolution also unsettled the medieval understanding of evil in the world. Illustrative are the reactions to an enormous earthquake that rocked the city of Lisbon on the morning of All Saints' Day, November 1, 1755. Firestorms and floods followed the ten-minute earthquake, destroying most of the city, including all of its important churches and perhaps as many as one-third of its population, upwards of 90,000 souls.[37]

True to its theodicy, the religious response interpreted the earthquake as a divine message.[38] Catholics, for example, saw it as God's punishment for a wicked and decadent city akin to the biblical Sodom and Gomorrah. Protestants, on the other hand, viewed the Lisbon earthquake in strictly sectarian terms: as God punishing Catholic Lisbon for Portugal's part in the Inquisition, the Roman Catholic tribunal for investigating and punishing heresy that had been established in Portugal in the sixteenth century. So, while they differed about specifics, Christians generally agreed that the earthquake was a reflection of God's design; and, therefore, it served a religious purpose, such as getting people to abandon sin, pray, and repent.

In contrast, the deistic response consisted of trying to account for the disaster rationally, not morally or supernaturally. Although the explanations were scientifically crude—such as "overexcited electrical currents" or, in the case of Immanuel Kant (1724–1804), subterranean explosions of gases—they shared the deistic view that the presence of a natural evil, such as a killing earthquake, was immaterial to the natural order of things because that was established before God abandoned the world and its inhabitants. In short, the rules governing nature were rigid and discernible, and the best way to explain any event was through reason and evidence, not faith, authority, and tradition. Typical of the new, enlightened thinking was the view of French philosopher Jean-Jacques Rousseau (1712-1778), who attributed the Lisbon deaths to reckless urban planning.[39-41]

From the general view that we own our misfortune, it was a short leap to demystifying illness and disease. To the emerging scientific mind, illness and disease were no more divinely ordained punishment for sin than was the Great Lisbon Earthquake. Rather, they were natural phenomena amenable to medical explanation. Thus, by the end of the nineteenth century, according to Bonnie Miller-McLemore, the medieval culpability before illness and death would be largely managed within the modern medical model. The Vanderbilt professor of religion sums up the change this way:

> The medical establishment at that time exhaustively explained illness and death in rational, scientific, "morally neutral" terms. Doctors certified that the causes of disease resided in micro-organisms, not in personal, moral or religious factors. This assertion eliminated religious questions of meaning, mystery or moral imperative. People no longer used the concept of divine providence to explain death; they considered religious, spiritual and moral meanings superfluous. They felt blameless and by attributing illness to natural causes, the physician supported that view.[42]

CONCLUSIONS

If scientific medicine challenged the supernatural basis of illness, it also called into question the biblical account of a world created by God in its present state. More sensible and reasonable to the nascent modern mind was a conception of the universe as an unfolding, historical process governed by natural laws, albeit perhaps divinely ordained ones. This made history more a product of human action than divine will, more a disclosure of humanity itself than of God's purpose for it. Rather than focused on a defined Augustinian end point such as final divine judgment, historical progress began to mean a steady and unlimited improvement by humans following predictable and rational laws. Inexorably, the natural orientation of the present life became less death and the world to come, more prolongation of life and happiness now. The word "meliorism" captures this incipient view of historical change, progress, and human happiness. Meliorism—from the Latin *melior* meaning better—is "the view that the world is neither all good nor all bad, but can be improved through human effort."[43]

The scientific revolution implied that as active participants in the world, rather than its passive victims, humans could influence the natural processes and thereby animate history for the betterment of themselves, their society, and future generations.

Human beings might be machinelike, but, according to Descartes and contrary to medieval theology, they were not, by nature, sinful and destitute. After all, they possessed an "autonomous self," or immaterial thinking "I," that stood above and apart from nature and was ultimately the master of its own fate. By reason and will, humans could define their humanity and shape their future, especially as it pertained to health.

It was Benjamin Franklin (1706–1790), a vivid embodiment of Enlightenment thought in colonial America, who captured this unbridled optimism in a letter (1780) to the esteemed English scientist Joseph Priestley (1733–1804), where he wrote: "It is impossible to imagine the height to which may be carried, in a thousand years, the power of man over matter.... All disease may be prevented or cured." Behind Franklin's utopian fervor stood the overwhelming appeal of modernization introduced with the Enlightenment's scientific revolution: the promise of infinite progress through science and technology, embracing the conquest of disease and the indefinite extension of life.

CASES AND CONTROVERSIES

What Doctors Think about Religion and Health

According to a survey reported in 2007 in the *Archives of Internal Medicine*, most physicians in the United States believe that religion and spirituality have a positive effect on patients' health and that God sometimes intervenes on patients' behalf. Overall, only 1 percent of the 1,144 questioned believed that religion has a negative effect on health, and 2 percent said it has no influence one way or the other. But 54 percent said God sometimes affects a patient's health, and 33 percent said religion and spirituality help prevent medical events such as heart attacks, infections, and death.[44] The survey's most striking finding—at least in the opinion of Harvard professor of medicine Jerome E. Groopman—was "the perception that God is micromanaging clinical outcomes at the bedside." That view—"that the natural course of the world is altered on a regular basis by God intervening"—reflects "a fundamentalist reading of the Bible where God does

intervene in those ways," according to Groopman, author of *How Doctors Think* (2007).[45]

Questions for Analysis

1. What would you say is the significance of this study? For example, does it say anything about how physicians might interpret scientific data and clinical evidence or how they might interact with patients?

2. Do you think that religion can give some patients false hope or cause guilt or other negative emotions that could lead to increased patient suffering?

3. Do you believe "that the natural course of the world is altered on a regular basis by God intervening"?

4. How do the study's findings jibe with the medieval view of the world?

CASES AND CONTROVERSIES

Faith Flags

Physician Walter L. Larimore and medical journalist William Carr Peel believe that the workplace is the most strategic place of spiritual influence for Christians. According to Carr,

> Your workplace, the place where you spend the bulk of your time during the week is the most strategic place of spiritual influence in the world. Whether you work at a restaurant, bank, school, manufacturing plant, airport, ad agency, hospital—wherever, God wants to use you .... right where you are for His Kingdom purpose.[46]

In their book *The Saline Solution*, Larimore and Carr advise physicians to issue probes, called "faith flags," designed to determine how receptive their patients are to escalating efforts at evangelizing. To a patient facing surgery, for example, the doctor asks: "Do you know anyone who prays? You may want to consider asking them to pray for you because the research clearly shows that prayer improves surgical outcome." Alternatively: "It may not be important to you, but it would mean a lot to me if you would let me pray for you. Is that OK?"[47]

Questions for Analysis

1. Richard P. Sloan thinks that doctors who evangelize patients have a professional obligation to advertise themselves as Christian physicians; otherwise, he says, they're acting unethically. Do you agree?

2. Even with disclosure, do you find anything objectionable about physicians making their faith public to patients; or do you think it is a legitimate way to take evangelism out of the religious box and weave it into the work world?

3. How would you feel and respond as a patient to a "faith flag"?

4. Investigate the claim that "research clearly shows that prayer improves surgical outcome."

CASES AND CONTROVERSIES

Criticism of Science and Its Method

By utilizing scientific method, science uses a reductionistic approach to knowledge. The reductionistic approach of scientific method purports to gain knowledge of the whole by breaking it up into small pieces. The underlying idea is that we can understand the whole by isolating and dissecting its parts. This implies that nature can be disassembled and reassembled under human control.

The reductionistic approach has led to spectacular discoveries and advances in scientific knowledge, but it has also been criticized as myopic. Critics say, for example, that it overlooks and even denies the innate relatedness of systems; it avoids the truth that the whole possesses more than the sum of its parts. Existential philosophers such as Soren Kierkegaard (1813–1855) and Martin Heidegger (1889–1976)—one a Christian, the other an atheist—while acknowledging the importance of rational clarity, denied that reason or science and its method could answer life's most pressing questions about the meanings of illness and suffering, of life in general, or of one's own life in particular. Their intellectual heirs are no less skeptical of the capacity of reason and science to solve unknowns that, nonetheless, humans must confront, such as change, risk, uncertainty, and vulnerability.

Questions for Analysis

1. How do you view this criticism of science and its method?

2. Can you think of problems that seem unresponsive to the reductionistic approach? Curing cancer or predicting earthquakes, for example?[48]

3. What events in the last and present centuries would you point to as humbling examples of the limitations of science and technology to control nature and minimize uncertainty?

4. Does illness, especially a serious one, introduce the kinds of unknowns that existentialists say science is incapable of solving? If so, what are the implications for patient care?

CASES AND CONTROVERSIES

The Life and Death of Jane Tomlinson

In 1991, at the age of 26, Jane Tomlinson (1964–2007) was treated for breast cancer, with a poor prognosis. In 2000, doctors found that the disease had spread throughout her body. Thereafter, Tomlinson became famous throughout the United Kingdom for raising millions of dollars for charity by completing athletic challenges including marathons, triathlons, and long distance cycling across Europe, the United States, and Africa. Following her death in 2007 at the age of 43, Jane's husband, Mike, paid tribute to her courageous seven years of sporting achievements and charity fundraising by saying that his wife's example could "redefine what it means to be a cancer patient."

But not everyone agrees that Jane Tomlinson provides an appropriate role model for cancer patients. Dr. Mike Fitzpatrick, for one, says that Tomlinson's model revives the nineteenth-century concept that disease can be challenged by will. "This notion is always closely linked to the idea that disease is itself an expression of character," he says. As a result of this interpretation, cancer, or any disease for that matter, is given a punitive meaning. "Jane Tomlinson is offered as the model of the active patient who refuses to take a passive role in their treatment" Fitzpatrick says. "But where does this leave somebody with cancer who does not want—or is not able—to fight or struggle, does not want to spend their remaining months or years running or cycling or becoming a high profile campaigner?"[49]

Questions for Analysis

1. Do you think that Jane Tomlinson offers an enlightened approach toward cancer; or do you think that that any attempt to confer meaning on cancer inevitably is moralistic and punitive?

2. Does Dr. Fitzpatrick's criticism get to the point that McLemoore made in this chapter?

3. The writer Susan Sontag (1933–2004), who died of cancer, was one of the first to point out "the accusatory side of the metaphors of empowerment that seek to enlist the patient's will to resist disease."[50] Discuss Sontag's insight in the context of Enlightenment thought and the acclaim for Jane Tomlinson.

4. Do you know people who felt guilty about their illness or attributed it to their own moral failure?

REFERENCES

1. C. Ben Mitchell, "Bioethics in the New Millennium: Ethical Challenges Ahead," *Dignity*, Bannockburn, IL: The Center for Bioethics and Human Dignity, Spring, 2001. Retrieved April 30, 2007, from http://www.cbhd.org/resources/bioethics/mitchell_2001-spring_print.htm.

2. Francis Fukuyama, *Our Posthuman Future: Consequences of the Biotechnology Revolution*, New York: Farrar Straus & Giroux, 2002.

3. Neal Cross, Leslie Dae Lindou, and Robert C. Lamm. *The Search for Personal Freedom*, 3rd ed., vol. 1, Dubuque: Wm. C. Brown Company Publishers, 1968, Ch. 14.

4. Karl Baier, "The Meaning of Life," in E. D. Klemke. *The Meaning of Life*, New York: Oxford University Press, 2000, p. 102.

5. Walter Sundberg, "The Conundrum of Evil," *First Things*, January 2003, pp. 53–58. Retrieved April 30, 2007, from http://www.leaderu.com/philosophy/evil_modernthought.html.

6. Susan Neiman, *Evil In Modern Thought*, Princeton, N.J.: Princeton University Press, 2002.

7. Ibid., p. 23.

8. C.S. Lewis, *The Problem of Evil*, San Francisco: Harper San Francisco, 2001, p. 79.

9. Ibid., p. 77.

10. Ibid., p. 78.

11. Richard Sloan, *Blind Faith: The Unholy Alliance of Religion and Medicine*, New York: St. Martin's Press, 2006, p. 17.

12. Saint Augustine, *Enchiridion on Faith, Hope, and Love*, J.B. Shaw, trans., Washington: Regnery Publishing, Inc., Gateway Edition, 1996, pp. 31–34.

13. Sloan, p. 15.

14. Fernando Salmon, "Pain and Medieval Medicine, The Welcome Trust. Retrieved April 30, 2007, from http://www.wellcome.ac.uk/en/pain/microsite/history2.html.

15. Sherwin B. Nuland, *Doctors: The Biography of Medicine*, New York: Vintage Books, 1988, p. 33.

16. Saint Augustine, *Enchiridion*, p. 33.

17. Kerby Anderson, *Christian View of Government and Law*, Richardson, TX: Probe Ministries International, 1999.

18. Steven Pinker, "The Known World," *The New York Times Book Review*, May 27, 2007, p. 12.

19. Frank Wolf, "APPENDIX E: Introduction to Scientific Method." Retrieved April 30, 2007, from http://teacher.nsrl.rochester.edu/phy_labs/AppendixE/AppendixE.html).

20. Russell Shorto, *Descartes' Bones: A Skeletal History of the Conflict Between Faith and Reason*, New York: Doubleday, 2008, quoted in Gary Rosen, "Body of Knowledge, Judging," *The New York Times Book Review*, November 2, 2008, p. 10.

21. Simon Blackburn, "Benefits of Doubt," *The New York Times Book Review*, Feb 4, 2007, p. 21.

22. Rene Descartes, *Discourse on Method* (1637), in *The Philosophical Works of Descartes*, vol. 1, Elizabeth S. Haldane and G. R. T. Ross, trans., Cambridge: Cambridge University Press, 1911, p. 92.

23. Rene Descartes, *Meditations on First Philosophy* (1642), *The Philosophical Writings of Descartes*, vol. 2, J. Cottingham, R. Stoothoff, and D. Murdoch, trans., Cambridge University Press: Cambridge, 1984, pp. 16–23.

24. Shorto, p. 10.

25. Ronald Bruce Meyer, Andreas Vesalius (1514). Retrieved April 30, 2007, from www.unm.edu/~humanism/dissection-moratorium-vesalius.htm.

26. Margaret Wertheim, "Cosmic Data," *Los Angeles Times Book Review*, April 2, 2006, p. R12.

27. Seth Lloyd, *Programming the Universe: A Quantum Computer Scientist Takes on the Cosmos*, New York: Alfred A. Knopf, 2006.

28. Daryl Kulak, "Alternative Medicine Is Holistic, Western Medicine Is Reductionistic," *Ezine Articles*. Retrieved December 8, 2008, from http://ezinearticles.com/?expert=Daryl_Kulak

29. See note 19 above.

30. See note 20 above.

31. See note 22 above.

32. Judith Shulevitz, "When Cosmologies Collide," *The New York Times Book Review*, p. 10.

33. Richard Dawkins, "Inferior Design," *The New York Times Book Review*, July 1, 2007, p. 14.

34. John Sutton, "Rene Descartes," *Encyclopedia of Life Sciences*, New York: Macmillan Publishers, 2000. Retrieved April 30, 2007, from http://www.phil.mq.edu.au/staff/jsutton/DescartesELSbiography.htm

35. Dennis M. Sullivan, "The Conception View of Personhood: A Review," *Ethics & Medicine*, Spring 2003. Retrieved April 30, 2007, from http://findarticles.com/p/articles/mi_qa4004/is_200304/ai_n9232530.

36. See note 35 above

37. "1755 Lisbon Earthquake," Answers.com. Retrieved April 30, 2007, from http://www.answers.com/topic/1755-lisbon-earthquake.

38. Robert K. Reeves, "The Lisbon earthquake of 1755: confrontation between the church and the enlightenment in eighteenth-century Portugal." Retrieved April 30, 2007, from www.dickinson.edu/~quallsk/thesis_reeves.doc.

39. Rousseau, Jean Jacques. "Letter to Voltaire 18 August 1756." Retrieved April 30, 2007, from http://www.missouri.edu/~histzut/voltaire/html.

40. Susan Neiman, *Evil In Modern Thought*, Princeton: Princeton University Press, 2002, p. 47.

41. Ibid., p. 55.

42. Miller-McLemore. Retrieved April 30, 2007, from http://www.religiononline.org/showarticle.asp?title=928.

43. Manuel Velasquez, *Philosophy: A Text with Readings*, eighth edition, Belmont, CA: Wadsworth/Thomson Learning, 2002, p. 720.

44. Church Communication Network, "The Going Public with Your Faith," March 13, 2008. Retrieved March 24, 2009, from http://www.ccn.tv/programming/event/evt_13mar08.php.

45. Nicholas Bakalar, "Most Doctors See Religion as Beneficial, Study Says," *The New York Times*, April 17, 2007, p. D7.

46. See note 44 above.

47. Quoted in Richard P. Sloan, *Blind Faith*, New York: St. Martin's Press, 2006, pp. 198–199.

48. Patricia Ryaby Backer, "What is the Scientific Method?" October 29, 2004. Retrieved March 30, 2009, from www.engr.sjsu.edu/pabacker/scientific_method.htm.

49. Mike Fitzpatrick, "The Meaning of Cancer," *British Journal of General Practice*, October 1, 2007, p. 847.

Retrieved April 1, 2009, from http://www.pubmedcentral.nih.gov/articlerender.fcgi?artid=2151832.

50. NA, "Illness as Metaphor and AIDS and Its Metaphors," *Susan Sontag Foundation*. Retrieved May 10 2009, from www.susansontag.com/SusanSontag/books/illnessAsMetaphor.shtml.

Chapter 2

Religious and Secular Ethics

Immanuel Kant is regarded as one of the most influential thinkers of the modern world and the last major philosopher of the Enlightenment. In 1784 he wrote an essay entitled *What Is Enlightenment?*, in which he described it as:

> ... man's emergence from his self-incurred immaturity. Immaturity is the inability to use one's own understanding without the guidance of another. This immaturity is self-incurred if its cause is not lack of understanding, but lack of resolution and courage to use it without the guidance of another.[1]

Kant believed that it was "laziness and cowardice" that kept people from thinking for themselves and allowed others to control them: "... a book to have understanding in place of me, a spiritual adviser to have a conscience for me, a doctor to judge my diet for me, and so on." "It is so convenient to be immature!" Kant bluntly wrote, urging as a motto for enlightenment, "*Sapere aude!*" Latin for "Dare to know."

As counterpart to the new breed of Enlightenment natural scientist, Kant represented a new generation of moral theorist, one confident in the power of reason, unaided by traditional understanding, to discover moral law. This conviction inspired a forum of secular ethical theories in the seventeenth and eighteenth centuries with lasting influence on moral analysis and bioethics, as well as on the modern understanding of political systems and social institutions. These fresh moral and political philosophies, while not opposed to religious teaching, didn't require it. Although frequently clashing, they shared a focus on the well-being of humankind in the present life, not in some possible hereafter. They agreed that morality was important to human well-being and that rationality, not faith or dogma, should be the principal guide to human conduct. They thus posed a direct challenge to the old way of doing ethics with which we begin: following the will of God.

DIVINE COMMAND THEORY

Beyond the proper posture to take toward life's limitations and struggles, the medieval Church also addressed the proper relationship with others. As children of God human beings were to treat one another properly, by following the will, or command, of God. In the study of ethics, this view that all of morality is dependent on the will of God is often called divine command theory.

According to divine command theory, what God expects of us derives from his immutable moral nature. Given that God's moral nature never changes, neither do his expectations of us. The moral obligations that flow from God's unchanging moral nature are fixed, unchanging, and absolute. In this manner, the divine command—"Always follow the will of God"—applies to everyone, at all times, everywhere.

Scriptural Basis

Medieval theology allowed for two interpretations of divine command. According to one interpretation, the specifics of God's will were revealed in the Sacred Scriptures, as interpreted by the Church. Traditional examples were the Ten Commandments of the Old Testament (Ex 20:2–17) or the New Testament's Golden Rule, by which we are enjoined to treat others as we ourselves would want to be treated (Luke 6:27–31). Augustine's writings and teachings show that he considered the Bible the chief source of Christian ethics.[2] For his part, Aquinas proposed an alternative divine command theory called natural law as providing a rational basis for scriptural moral revelation.

Natural Law

Aquinas reasoned that, because God created the world and everything in it with an order and purpose reflective of his will, by examining the nature of things we should be able to discover what God expected of us. Our God-given intellect, though flawed and imperfect, could discover the creator's behavioral imperatives or moral law. This general revelation, complementary to the Bible's special revelation, meant that knowledge of God's will was open to all, non-believer as well as believer, through nature and the human mind and heart, independently of divine revelation (Ps 19:1–6; Rom 1:18–20; 2:14–15; Acts 14:14–18; 17:24–31). In other words, the mental powers given by God for discerning his existence also enabled us to discern moral law. Although neither Aquinas nor the Catholic Church viewed this analysis as undermining the special revelation of the Bible, Protestant reformers did. To Martin Luther (1483–1546) and John Calvin (1509–1564), for example, both of whom held Augustine in high regard, the derivation of God's existence and moral law from human nature effectively diminished the relevancy of God and the supernatural, as well as the centrality of sin upon human life.[3]

Aquinas, in fact, did not originate natural law theory but adapted it from the ancient Greek view that moral principles were objective truths that could be discovered in the nature of things, much like laws of nature could be discovered in the physical universe. Laws of nature are statements about the physical world based on observation. The law of gravitation, for example, describes the natural phenomenon of attraction between massive bodies. Its moral counterpart, natural law, discerns something else in nature: rules for how humans are to conduct their lives and relate to one another. So, as distinguished from laws of nature, natural law is based on interpretation and not merely observation of nature; it is prescriptive and normative, not merely descriptive and non-normative.

What is morally appropriate behavior, according to any natural law view, is determined by the kind of creature the human is—that is, by reference to a theory of human nature, which, presumably, reason can discover. Aquinas' view of human nature reflected, of course, the biblical narrative of the human created in the image of God. But the pre-Christian Aristotle also influenced Aquinas.

Borrowing from Aristotle, Aquinas taught that the basis of moral obligation resided in our very nature in the form of various natural inclinations or dispositions, such as the preservation of life, the propagation of the species, and the search for truth and a peaceful society. The moral law, presumably, was founded on these natural dispositions and the ability of reason to discern right course of action. Nothing less than our fulfillment as human beings lay in the balance. For Aristotle that fulfillment resided in the present world, achievable in a reasonable balance between behavioristic extremes. For Aquinas our fulfillment resided in the world to come, achievable through obedience to a divine lawgiver. For both, living by nature's law, as understood by reason, was the road to self-fulfillment. By following this moral law, Aristotle said that we could live a good and happy life that ended at death. For Aquinas, following nature's divinely ordained precepts, which were also revealed in the Sacred Scriptures (e.g., Jer 31:33; Rom 2:15–16) and taught by the Church, meant we could win eternal salvation in the postmortem life.

Thomistic natural law didn't upset basic moral precepts of medieval Christianity but proposed another avenue to them. For example, Augustine used the biblical commandment "Thou shalt not kill" to condemn suicide. Aquinas also condemned self-killing, but not merely because of scriptural prohibition. Suicide was wrong, according to Aquinas, because it violated the command of God not to destroy what our reason knows is a fundamental good, our life.[4]

The Doctrine of Double Effect

Thomas Aquinas is credited with introducing the principle of double effect, in his discussion of the permissibility of self-defense, in his monumental work, *Summa Theologica* (II-II, Qu. 64, Art. 7) The doctrine (or principle) of double effect is often invoked to explain the permissibility of an action that causes a serious harm, such as the death of a human being, as a side effect ("double effect") of promoting some good end, such as self-preservation. Thus, the death of an assailant is justified so long as it wasn't intended, but resulted as an unavoidable side effect (or "double effect") of defending oneself. Again, a doctor who injected a large dose of morphine into a patient with the intention to kill the patient would act impermissibly, whereas one who did the same thing with the intention of pain relief would act permissibly, even though she knew that death would be hastened. The principle of double effect, then,

recognizes that sometimes it is permissible to bring about as a merely foreseen side effect a harmful event that it would be impermissible to bring about intentionally.[5] Specifically, under the doctrine of double effect, a harmful effect is indirect and morally permissible if and only if: (1) the act itself is morally good or neutral, (2) only the good effect of the act is intended directly, (3) the bad effect of the act is not the means for achieving the good effect, and (4) the good effect outweighs the bad effect.

Over the years Roman Catholicism has given special attention to morality in medicine. Literally for centuries it has engaged questions that we today term bioethical, carefully crafting the theoretical scaffolding for moral analysis and resolution. Its positions, grounded in Thomistic natural law and double-effect analysis, continue to influence laws, institutions, and professional codes of conduct. As we'll repeatedly see in issues Parts III and IV, the reach of its moral theology extends from decisions and policies at the beginning of life to those at life's end.

Following the tradition of Aquinas, several moralists of the Dominican order of priests, writing in the sixteenth century, articulated a distinction between ordinary and extraordinary means of preserving life. Basically, the distinction is this: "Ordinary" refers to all reasonable and beneficial medicines and treatments that can be obtained and used without excessive burden to the patient; whereas "extraordinary" refers to all medicines and treatments that can be obtained or used only with excessive burden to the patient, or ones that wouldn't offer the patient reasonable hope of benefit. According to the ordinary/extraordinary distinction, a patient is not morally obligated to use any means, natural or artificial, that does not offer a reasonable hope of ameliorating the patient's condition.

Beyond this, contemporary revisions have breathed new intellectual life into Aquinas' natural law theory. The Catholic Australian philosopher John Finnis, for one, has argued, controversially, that the truth of natural law doesn't depend on any prior acceptance of God's existence or upon revelation. Rather, it is self-evident, that is, we can know the principles of natural law through our subjective experience, which is always directed toward fundamental goods. In contrast to the four fundamental goods or objectives that Aquinas said God commands us to pursue—human life, family, knowledge, and an orderly society[6]—Finnis identifies seven basic forms of good: "life, knowledge, play, aesthetic experience, friendship, practical reasonableness, and religion."[7]

In any event, the Thomistic version of natural law consisted of rationally discoverable rules of conduct corresponding to dispositions supposedly inscribed by God in human nature. Enlightenment thinkers favoring natural law accepted its classical non-revelatory basis for human conduct. However, they replaced its divine prescriptions with the physical, biological, and behavioral laws discoverable without appeal to religious authority. In other words, as an alternative to religious natural law, some Enlightenment philosophers proposed secular natural law.

SECULAR NATURAL LAW

It is typical of secular natural law theorists to pose an early, pre-societal stage of human development and speculate about the rules people in this hypothetical primitive state of nature would naturally agree to live by. For example, the English philosopher John Locke (1632–1704), a preeminent natural law theorist and intimate of Newton, envisioned an original, free state of nature, characterized by happiness, reason, and tolerance. In this pre-social state hypothetical, all were equally free to pursue life, liberty, health, and possessions. From this model Locke then derived certain inalienable rights that supposedly flowed from nature's law, independent of and prior to the establishment of any state or its primary instrument, government (*Two Treatises of Government,* 1688). Specifically, Locke viewed life, liberty, and property as natural rights. He said that it was precisely and only to protect these natural rights and ensure equal treatment against the threats to them posed by conflicting and unrestrained self-interests that people formed societies.

In order to appreciate the significance of Locke's thought and what he understood by "natural rights," it's useful, initially, to distinguish between legal and moral rights.

Legal and Moral Rights

Broadly defined, a right is an entitlement to act or have another act in a certain way. If you claim a "right" to vote, for example, presumably you mean that you're entitled to vote and others should—that is, have a duty—to permit you to vote. Your right to vote under certain conditions is derived from our legal system and is, thus, considered a legal right.[8]

In addition to legal rights, we also speak of moral or, perhaps more often today, human rights. Unlike a legal right, which is supported by a legal system, a claim to a moral, or human, right is supported merely by one's humanity, regardless of law. So, whereas a legal right is derived from law or a legal system, a moral right is derived merely from being a human being.

For example, if you claim a right to free speech, you're probably asserting that, as *human beings,* you and anyone else are entitled to express or listen to an opinion expressed in public without censorship or government interference. Your moral right to free speech, or anyone else's, does not depend on a human institution for its legitimacy, as legal rights do. You would likely say that, even if a law didn't protect it, you would still have the moral right to free speech. You'd also likely say that your right to free speech should be supported by law, and that the ideal state is the one that does that. More broadly, the just state protects all moral or human rights.

Conceptually, moral or human rights are descended from *natural rights,* Locke's locution. Sometimes they're even taken to mean the same thing. The renowned American historian Lynn Hunt, for example, says that moral, or human, rights require three interlocking qualities: They must be "*natural* (inherent in human beings), *equal* (the same for everyone) and *universal* (applicable everywhere)."[9] Hunt's depiction of moral rights fairly captures what Locke meant in asserting that human beings, as human beings, have natural rights to life, liberty, and property. It also reflects the sentiment of Thomas Jefferson, (1743–1826) as expressed in the *Declaration of Independence* (1776):

> We hold these truths to be self-evident,
> that all men are created equal, that they are

endowed by their creator with certain unalienable rights, that among these are life, liberty and the pursuit of happiness.

In 1789, the French *Declaration of Rights of Man and Citizen* similarly declared that "all men are born free and equal in rights," among which it listed liberty, private property, inviolability of the person, as well as equality before the law and freedoms of speech and religion.

Clearly implied in a natural rights political construction is a healthy tolerance for diverse, often-opposed private interests and values, especially in the spheres of religion and conscience. This fundamental premise fell under the so-called Enlightenment Project, which can be understood by reference to a collection of beliefs, such as:

- a belief in the power of human rationality to establish reliable, universally recognized scientific and moral knowledge;

- a rejection of beliefs that claim truth based solely on authority and tradition;

- a belief in the equality of humans in terms of their ability to be rational and an impulse to remove all barriers to the exercise of that rationality via the promotion of individual liberty, autonomy, and choice; and

- a belief in the capacity of humankind to use rationality to promote individual and communal progress.

One profound implication of a commitment to these beliefs was that religion could no longer define "political community," as it had in the Middle Ages. In its place, as the American philosopher and political economist Francis Fukuyama notes, would be "a neutral framework of laws and institutions that would guarantee rational individuals the right to pursue whatever ends they chose under a social contract."[10]

Social Contract Theory

Social contract refers to a theory on how states and governments come into being. The key concept of contract theory, or contractarianism, is the claim that it is the people who bring the state or government into being to secure and promote their basic rights and well-being. Empowering civil authority to spell out legal rights based on natural or moral rights, presumably, ensures the requisite mutual trust for the social cooperation needed to protect those rights.

Thomas Hobbes (1588–1679) and Locke were two of the period's three great contractarians, the third being Rousseau (*Le Contrat,* 1762). Mindful of the time's divisive religious wars and the desperate need for peace, Hobbes suggested, in *Leviathan* (1651), the possibility of establishing legitimate political institutions without grounding them on divine revelation. To this end he proposed consolidating power in the hands of a sovereign ruler in order to suppress human evil. Locke, on the other hand, envisioned what in the West came to be viewed as the only legitimate political order, namely one:

> … in which power would be limited, divided and widely shared; in which those in power at one moment would relinquish it peacefully at another, without fear of retribution; in which public law would open relations among citizens and institutions; in which many different religions would be allowed to flourish, free from state interference; and in which individuals would have inalienable rights to protect them from government and their fellows.[11]

Their differences aside, Hobbes, Locke, and Rousseau, seeking to escape "the destructive passions of messianic faith," replaced a "political theology centered on God [with a] political philosophy centered on man." Professor of Humanities Mark Lilla, for one, has termed this the Great Separation.[12]

Contract theory, then, was basically a declaration of war on medieval notions of kingship by which royalty ruled by divine right and, therefore, was accountable only to Church and God. Social contract, by contrast, proposed two revolutionary political ideas: (1) Governments are formed by the consent of the people as the rational means, not to acquire rights, but to secure them more efficiently than in the primitive state of nature. (2) When governments fail, the people have a right to dissolve them and form new governments.

The US Constitution   In America the social contract was spelled out in the US Constitution (adopted in 1787), which is notable here in several respects.

As theory, the Constitution is the preeminent example of natural law influencing social law. The Constitution is also a good example of the political reach of scientific method. As physicist Heinz Pagels points out:

> ... the political principles drafted into the Constitution... are indebted in large measure to the emergent ideas of seventeenth- and eighteenth-century science.... The necessity for experimentation and modification through amendment are scientific principles embedded in the Constitution [for example]."[13]

In the same vein, popular science writer Timothy Ferris finds in the Constitution the underlying principle that citizens should "be free to experiment, assess the results and conduct new experiments." In *The Science of Liberty* (1010), Ferris compares the American Republic to "a scientific laboratory [designed] not to guide society toward a specified goal, but to sustain the experimental process itself."[14]

Most importantly, the Constitution formally altered the medieval relationship between law and religion. Thus, Article VI, sometimes referred to as the "Supremacy Clause," establishes the Constitution as the supreme law of the land, while the "Establishment Clause" of the First Amendment prohibits the government from (1) installing a religion, (2) preferring religion to irreligion (e.g., atheism or agnosticism), or (3) preventing the practice of religion. Evangelist Robert Price makes clear the further political implications of the Supremacy and Establishment Clauses, as well as the Constitution generally:

> Our Constitution does not really posit a system of values and virtues to be inculcated among the people. Instead it presupposes simply that we will not get in each other's way. We maximize individual freedom, we live and let live. Our laws are based not on morality but rather simply on non-interference. Thus for the

government not to outlaw abortion means not that it considers abortion to be morally right and good, but that it feels it has no business interfering in the matter. Religiously, you can do whatever you want to do—except draft me as a human sacrifice! Your freedom ends where mine begins. Such an argument is purely pragmatic, and it is a great way of dealing with pluralism. Live and let live.[15]

But what happens when "live and let live" comes up against majoritarian values? In other words: How are we to resolve what constitutional scholar John A. Robertson terms "the recurring dilemma of rights in a society of limited governmental powers"? As he explains:

> Recognition of fundamental rights is essential in the constitution scheme, yet it permits activities that may run counter to the values that a majority holds and may even lead to changes in those values. Yet the community through law may not stop the exercise of those rights, even though an impact on its value structure may occur. Thus, abortion, in vitro fertilization, non-coital reproduction, conscientious refusal of needed medical care, and sometimes even assisted death are left to the "moral discretion of patients, physicians, and other actors in the private sector."[16]

So, as a moral theory, secular natural law of the Enlightenment posited rationally discoverable rules of conduct in human nature. However, as it came to be mediated—socially and politically through rights theory, contractarianism and, in America, the US Constitution—it left the individual largely the rule maker and assigned government a minimal, protective role. The result was a robust individual autonomy or personal freedom that contrasted sharply with religious natural law, which cast the individual as discoverer and follower of rules legislated by a theistic God, who embedded them into human nature, established a Church to interpret them, and expected a civil government strong enough to administer them.

Today's secular natural law theorists still adhere to the core belief in rationally discoverable, non-revelatory rules of conduct in human nature. For example, a number of conservative thinkers—termed "Darwinian conservatives" by political scientist Carson Holloway (*The Right Darwin,* 2006)—claim that evolutionary biology provides a scientific basis for natural moral law, effectively making religion superfluous. Political analysts Larry Arnhart (*Darwinian Conservatism,* 2005) and James Q. Wilson (*The Marriage Problem,* 2002), as well as political economist Fukuyama (*Our Posthuman Future,* 2002) and *National Review's* John Derbyshire, argue that the Darwinian account of human nature—that human behavior, thought, and feeling are innately or biologically based—supports, rather than undermines, morality. They say controversially, for example, that Darwinism supports the natural status of the traditional family and traditional sex differences and roles.

Other conservatives, however, notably George Gilder and John West, find the coupling of natural law and Darwinian evolution a troubling stretch. Both men are associated with the Discovery Institute, a think tank best known for challenging evolutionary thought and advocating intelligent design, a theory that attributes the origin of life and the universe to intelligent causes. To conservative thinkers like Gilder and West, Darwinian evolution doesn't support natural law. They say that accepting it, in fact, destroys any basis for natural law by undercutting religious faith and producing "an amoral, materialistic worldview that easily embraces abortion, embryonic stem cell research and other practices they abhor."[17]

KANT'S THOUGHT AND ETHICS

Kant was another proponent of moral rights, but as truths of reason, rather than of human nature.

In 1785, the year following *What Is Enlightenment?,* Kant published *Foundations of the Metaphysics of Morals* (1785). In this work he proposed a moral system based on rationality and duty, applying the technique of using reason to analyze itself that he had developed earlier in his groundbreaking *Critique of Pure Reason* (1781).

Philosophy's "Copernican Revolution"

In the *Critique* Kant had set out to understand how the mind received and processed information. His conclusion, briefly, was that we could never know things as they really were, but only as we perceived them to be. Knowledge was perception, and the world as it really was—"things in themselves" or, in Greek, *noumena*—were inaccessible to the human mind. All we could ever know were "phenomena," or things as they appeared to us and were interpreted by us. In Kant's words: "The mind ... brings something to the object it experiences.... The mind imposes its way of knowing upon its objects."

This startling notion—that objects conform to mind, rather than mind to objects—has been termed philosophy's "Copernican Revolution." The phrase suggests that Kant's idea—that our understanding of the world and its objects has as much to do with our own minds as with the world and its objects—represented a change in perspective that was as important to philosophy and the social sciences as Copernicus' idea that the earth was not the center of the universe was to astronomy.

Besides challenging traditional assumptions about logic, history, and science, philosophy's Copernican Revolution also disputed the reliability of experience, tradition, and religious authority for developing moral principles. In Kant's view, "God" and many other speculative topics, including the problem of evil, simply exceeded the limits of human knowledge. However, that he couldn't say anything intelligible about God or how an all-good and all-powerful Being could create a world full of innocent suffering didn't stop Kant from linking both to his theory of morality.

God, Morality, and the Problem of Evil

The Bible's book of Job does not attempt to explain the mystery of suffering but to probe the depths of faith in spite of suffering. As such, the ancient parable of a long-suffering man provides one of the most poignant of imponderables: "Why do bad things happen to good people?" For Kant, it was precisely life's unrelieved suffering and unrighted injustice that persuaded him that reason demanded that happiness and virtue be connected. In other words, by no other dictate than that of rationality: The righteous should be blessed, and the unrighteous punished. That's how it ought to be. When it isn't, which is often, we can, like Job, feel confounded.

But the palpable disconnect between virtue and happiness didn't upend Kant. For one thing, he treated it as one of those unfathomable supernatural matters. For another, and more positively, he thought that trying to comprehend the connection between virtue and happiness was morally disastrous because it precluded the very possibility of morality. It was precisely *not* understanding the connection between virtue and happiness (or vice and unhappiness) that led to both faith in God and the possibility of morality, he argued. For if we lived in a morally transparent world, we'd lack the freedom that morality required, because "[t]o act freely is to act without enough knowledge or power—that is, without [divine] omniscience or omnipotence."[18] Therefore, according to Kant, "[S]olving the problem of evil is not only impossible but immoral." "Theodicy," he wrote, "is not merely impossible and immoral it also tends toward blasphemy."[19] In the face of life's unrelenting, undeserved suffering and injustice, then, ours was not to ask, "Why?" Rather, we were to affirm, "There must be a God to right such things," then act like that God by becoming, as it were, moral legislators.

Moral Choice

As in the *Critique of Pure Reason*, so too in his *Critique of Practical Reason* (1788), a more-developed version of *Foundations,* Kant turned reason on itself to elucidate moral choice. Basically, he claimed that reason without recourse to experience, religious authority, or tradition could discover moral laws, which, like the laws of physics, implied absolute necessity. In Kant's celebrated words: "Two things fill the mind with awe and wonder the more often and more steadily we reflect upon them: the starry heavens above me and the moral law within me" (*Critique of Practical Reason*).

According to Kant, by telling us what to do—what principles of action were objectively required—reason enabled us to go beyond natural instinct and narrow self-interest. Reason told us what principles of action had the force of an unconditional moral duty, that is, one that was both universal and absolute; one that always applied, unexceptionally, to all rational creatures. Moral choice, in turn, was the freedom to act in accordance with unconditional duty or discoverable laws of reason. This made reason the means to personal freedom or individual autonomy. Because we were subject only to the laws of our reason, we were autonomous, self-governing beings. And by Kant's account, it was autonomy that gave rational beings dignity and worth beyond all measure and, thus, made them deserving of respect.

Kant believed that there was only one formally unconditional duty found in pure reason. He termed this universal basis of moral obligation the categorical imperative (CI) and made it the centerpiece of his ethics.

The Categorical Imperative

Kant expressed his CI as follows: "Act as though the principle of your action were to become by your will a universal law of nature" (*Groundwork of the Metaphysics of Morals*). In other words, in deciding something morally significant, we were to imagine the maxim that all rational beings would adopt as a law governing that decision and derivative action. In this way Kant offered an answer—a *secular* answer—to the question of moral obligation: "What ought I do?": "I ought always to follow the CI." The CI was Kant's attempt to secure ethics by reason alone.

Kant believed that properly applying the CI necessarily led to universal prohibitions of actions such as lying, stealing, murdering, and suicide. In other words, it was against the moral law of reason to lie, steal, murder, or take one's own life. Anyone who did such things was governed not by reason but by something else—passion, desire, convenience, happiness. Their actions, therefore, flouted rational self-rule by violating the inherent worth and dignity of other persons and themselves.

Of course, as a Lutheran, Kant certainly realized that religious law also prohibited these practices. However, his test of morality was not compliance with the law of God, any more than liberal Protestant Locke's was. For Locke moral law was found in human nature, for Kant in reason. Both were theists who viewed their ethics as supportive of religious morality but justified independently of it.

Social Interests

Although rooted in individual autonomy, Kant's ethics were saved from narrow self-interest by a social component required of rationality. His two alternative formulations of the CI show this: the principles of humanity and reciprocity.

The Principle of Humanity   One version of the CI, sometimes termed the principle of humanity, said: "Always act to treat humanity, whether in yourself or in others, as an end in itself, never merely as a means." This meant that rational beings ought never intentionally use other rational beings merely as a means of satisfying selfish needs and desires. Why? Because so doing disrespected others by effectively removing their autonomy and, therefore, not treating them as an ultimate end. Of course, being autonomous, we were always free to treat others that way; but in so doing, we would be acting irrationally. Therefore, as rational beings, we should never so exploit other rational beings by breaking promises, lying, cheating, or stealing.

Principle of Reciprocity   Another formulation of the CI, sometimes termed the principle of reciprocity and akin to the Golden Rule, stated: "Always treat others as you would have them treat you." Here Kant explicitly recognized that through our own acts of will we legislated moral law. The moral rules we obeyed were not imposed on us from the outside by custom, tradition, and authority; or by Church, Bible, and God. They were self-imposed and self-recognized, fully internalized principles. Although as moral beings we gave ourselves the moral law and accepted its demand on ourselves, we could not morally prescribe anything we wanted.

We were bound by reason and its demands. And given that reason was the same for all rational beings, we all gave ourselves the same moral law.[20]

To determine whether a maxim of our action was a moral law, we could ask whether what it commanded would be acceptable to all rational beings thinking impartially and rationally. Would such beings accept it regardless of whether they were the doers or the receivers of the actions? If yes, then to exempt ourselves would offend the dictates of reason. Once again, as autonomous beings we were always free to exempt ourselves, but that would contradict our role as moral legislators and, therefore, would be an irrational act. Exempting ourselves from general prohibitions of promise breaking, lying, cheating, and stealing was simply unfair, according to the CI.

By applying the categorical imperative as either a principle of humanity or reciprocity, Kant, in effect, showed how rationality saved us from the natural tendency to favor ourselves and consider only our own interests. He showed that truly rational individuals considered the interests of others, and, in fact, were duty-bound to do so. Hence, it was precisely as rational beings, according to Kant, that we were able to connect with the rest of humanity. It was by thinking as social beings that we helped create a human community by establishing a basis for cooperation, consensus, and conflict resolution based on a rich conception of moral rights.

Moral Rights

Implicit in Kant's ethics were moral rights as truths of reason, specifically equality and freedom. Without equality, the categorical imperative would lack universal application. There simply would be no basis for saying that *all* rational human beings should be treated with respect and dignity (or as ends in themselves) unless we assumed that all were fundamentally equal. By the same token, without assuming that all were fundamentally free, reason could not act to do what duty demanded.

Kant discovered in reason itself, then, the rights contractarians discovered in the hypothetical, original state of nature. Consequently, Kant's assumption of moral rights provided another secular basis of social contract, or popular sovereignty, besides secular natural law.

Negative and Positive Rights   Kant offered further grounds for social cohesion in distinguishing two kinds of rights: negative and positive. The distinction between them sometimes is conveniently expressed as the difference between "freedoms from" and "freedoms to." Thus, negative rights are rights that protect *freedoms from* interference of various kinds, whereas positive rights are *freedoms to* various things.

Illustrative of negative rights, according to philosopher Manuel Velasquez: "The right to privacy, the right not to be killed, the right to travel, and the right to do what one wants with one's property are all negative rights because they all protect some form of human freedom liberty."[21] Negative rights impose negative duties or obligations on others not to interfere with a person's choice and activities in certain areas such as privacy, life, travel, or property. The first ten amendments to the US Constitution, or the Bill of Rights (ratified in 1791), address negative rights. Their intent is to limit governmental power and protect basic liberties of individuals.

Positive rights are "rights that guarantee people certain goods: the right to an education, to adequate medical care, food, housing; the right to fair trial; the right to a job; and the right to a clean environment."[22] Positive rights impose positive duties on others to help a person have or do something. In Kant, positive duties delineated a sphere of conduct (i.e., helping, supporting, or assisting) that *could be* wrong when unmet, whereas negative duties delineated a sphere of conduct (i.e., lying, stealing, murdering) that violated the categorical imperative and, therefore, were *always* wrong when unmet.

A great many of today's social controversies, at base, involve disputes about the relative role of the state in relation to freedom. *How active a role ought the state, as the highest authority in society, and the government, as its primary instrument, play in the lives of its citizens? In other words, is the ideal state the one that guarantees only negative rights, that is, freedoms from interference, such as the rights spelled out in the original Bill of Rights? Or is the ideal state the one that supports positive rights, or freedoms to have certain things?* In his State of the Union Address of January 11, 1944, Franklin Delano Roosevelt (1882–1945) asked Congress to adopt a "second Bill of Rights," one that would guarantee, among other things: work, adequate housing and income, education, and medical care.[23] The three-term president (1933–1945) clearly had in mind a free and democratic society with ambitious social goals, as opposed to a minimalist conception of it, as providing a framework for democracy to operate without imposing constraints on its goals. President Obama acted in this tradition of activist government when he signed health care reform into law (the Patient Protection and Affordable Care Act, 2010), saying: "We have now just enshrined … the core principle that everybody should have some basic security when it comes to their health care." Many Republicans, by contrast, saw the landmark legislation as an example of big government run amok and an abandonment of our founding principles. These competing views of democracy don't resound only in the public debate about the role of government, as opposed to market forces, in providing health services. They also inform the social discourse about today's most hotly contested bioethical issues—abortion, in vitro fertilization, human cloning, egg donation for research, and assisted death, for example.

UTILITARIANISM

Four years after the publication of Kant's *Metaphysics of Morals*, the English philosopher Jeremy Bentham (1748–1832) proposed a different Enlightenment theme as a secular basis of morality, rights, and social cohesion. In the opening words of his *Introduction to the Principles of Morals and Legislation* (1789), Bentham powerfully expressed one of the most enduring of human impulses:

> Nature has placed mankind under the governance of two sovereign masters, *pain* and *pleasure*. It is for them alone to point out what we ought to do, as well as to

determine what we shall do. On the one hand the standard of right and wrong, on the other the chain of causes and effects, are fastened to their throne. They govern us in all we do, in all we say, in all we think: every effort we can make to throw off our subjection, will serve but to demonstrate and confirm it. In words a man may pretend to abjure their empire: but in reality he will remain subject to it all the while.[24]

So thinking, Bentham said that the purpose of morality was to maximize human happiness, as measured by pleasure and pain. And that, he added, a rational calculation could determine.

For Bentham pleasure and pain were merely types of sensations measurable by their quantitative differences, especially by their intensity and duration. This empirical, "hedonic calculus," he believed, made possible an objective, scientific determination of the morality of anyone's conduct, individual or collective, on any occasion.[25]

Bentham's moral objectivism didn't mean that right and wrong were unchanging or that there were absolute standards against which moral questions could be judged. On the contrary, lying, cheating, stealing, promise breaking, and other actions universally prohibited by Kant's categorical imperative and by religious and secular natural law were, in theory, permissible under a utility calculation. It all depended on outcome or consequence. For Benthamism, the moral action, ultimately, was the one likely to yield the greatest net happiness of all the alternatives.

Utility Principle

Philosophers like Bentham, who believed that the value of something depended on its utility, called themselves utilitarians, a term that his godson, the English philosopher John Stuart Mill (1806–1873), popularized.

In doing ethics, utilitarians like Mill followed the greatest happiness or utility principle, which they considered a scientific approach to morality.

Thus, in answer to the question of conduct, "What ought I do?," utilitarians replied: "Do what likely will yield the greatest net happiness." This utility principle—the greatest happiness for the greatest number—effectively substituted majoritarian rule for divine will, natural law, or abstract imperatives, as a test of morality. But their commitment to *hedonism*, the belief that pleasure is the highest good, didn't make the early utilitarians any less respectful of individual freedom. On the contrary, freedom was central to their utility principle; without it, presumably, individuals lacked the essential ingredient of happiness.

Moral Rights and the Harm Principle

Utilitarians did not appeal to reason alone or to natural law as a basis for moral rights, Indeed, Bentham famously referred to the idea of natural rights as "nonsense upon stilts," because it effectively precluded any utilitarian calculation of social consequences. Still, utilitarians considered the best or ideal society the one that recognized a sphere of inviolable personal liberties. They also invoked utility, rather than contract or reason alone, to define the relationship between the individual and the state or government. Thus, for utilitarians the best government was the one that advanced the ideal society, which, in turn, was the one that respected the sanctity of the individual by honoring moral rights, particularly individual freedom.

The utilitarian case for moral rights received its most eloquent and influential expression in the middle of the nineteenth century with the publication of *On Liberty* (1859).[26] In that essay, Mill wrote: "Over himself, over his own body and mind, the individual is sovereign." Hardly just a rhetorical flourish, by *sovereign* Mill meant a mature individual liberty that included freedoms of thought, speech, taste, action, and political assembly, no matter how unpopular or offensive. The sole limit to individual freedom Mill expressed as the celebrated *harm principle*: "… the only purpose for which power can be rightfully exercised over any member of a civilized community, against his will, is to prevent harm to others."

BIOETHICS ACROSS CULTURES

Bentham in Bhutan

In the 1970s King Jigme Singye Wangchuck of Bhutan in the Himalayan mountains proposed the notion of "gross national happiness" (GNH) as an alternative to "gross domestic product" (GDP) as a way to measure his tiny kingdom's wealth. Now the Bhutanese are refining the country's guiding philosophy into what they see as a new political science. "You see what a complete dedication to economic development ends up in," says Kinley Dorji, Secretary of Information and Communications, referring to the global economic crisis. "Industrialized societies have decided now that GNH is a broken promise."

As an alternative and a way to counter the encroachments of the outside world, the Bhutanese, who are Buddhists, have produced an intricate model of well-being that features the four pillars, the nine domains, and the seventy-two indicators of happiness. Specifically, the government has determined that the four pillars of a happy society involve "the economy, culture, the environment and good governance." It breaks these into nine domains: "psychological well-being, ecology, health, education, culture, living standards, time use, community vitality and good governance, each with its own weighted and unweighted GNH index." All of this is to be analyzed using seventy-two indicators. Under the domain of psychological well-being, for example, indicators include "the frequencies of prayer and meditation and of feelings of selfishness, jealousy, calm, compassion, generosity and frustration as well as suicidal thoughts." Even time is broken down, such as how much time is spent with the family. Mathematical formulas have been devised to reduce happiness to its tiniest component parts. The GNH index for psychological well-being, for example, includes the following:

One sum of squared distances from cutoffs for four psychological well-being indicators.

Here, instead of average the sum of squared distances from cutoffs is calculated because the weights add up to 1 in each dimension.

This is followed by a set of equations. Every two years, these indicators are to be reassessed through a nationwide questionnaire overseen by the Gross National Happiness Commission. To the pristine culture of Bhutan, snuggled between the world's two most populous nations, India and China, the GNH represents cultural survival, "by being distinct, by being different."

(SOURCE: Seth Mydans, "Recalculating Happiness in a Himalayan Kingdom, *The New York Times*, May 6, 2009. Retrieved May 6, 2009, from http://www.nytimes.com/2009/05/07/world/asia/07bhutan.html.)

Question

Apparently tiny Bhutan isn't alone in proposing an alternative to economic benefits as a way to judge government programs. France recently summoned a committee headed by economist and Nobel laureate Joseph Stiglitz to suggest new ways of measuring the wealth and well-being of a nation other than its GDP. The factors that could potentially be used to gauge prosperity include:

the amount of charitable or volunteer work a country produces, or how much political activity and domestic work are worth. Negative factors could include environmental damage. Social values such as health, education and leisure could also come into the mix.

Do you think this proposal has merit? Identify some of the health costs and benefits of using the GDP as a measure of a nation's progress.

(SOURCE: Sebastian Seibt, "How Representative is GDP of a Nation's Wealth?" *France International News*, March 12, 2009. Retrieved May 9, 2009, from http://www.france24.com/en/20090312-quality-life-more-important-gdp-stiglitz-french-commission.)

Clearly Mill had in mind a negative freedom that permitted people the opportunity to live their lives as they saw fit, according to their own values and beliefs without outside interference. Although this conception didn't preclude a role for government in providing resources for individual self-development, it did mean minimal state intrusion into demonstrably private affairs, among which, incidentally, Mill, who was an atheist or agnostic, included suicide and euthanasia.

Social Interests

Although early utilitarianism readily acknowledged a sphere of inviolable private affairs and decisions, it was social or community interest that gave the moral theory its urgency. For Bentham and Mill, morality was about maximizing *collective* pleasure and minimizing *collective* pain. That meant looking beyond self-interest—beyond the pleasure/pain calculation for self—and considering the impact of one's acts on others, now and in the future.

Subsequently, some utilitarians, termed *rule* as opposed to *act,* urged going beyond the isolated act to inquire: "What if *everyone* in a similar circumstance did this? What would the social impact be?" If from this universal or bird's-eye perspective more happiness and less pain likely would result than from everyone's doing the alternative, then we should adopt that rule. Otherwise, we shouldn't, regardless of the particular outcome.

Preference Satisfaction

Today some utilitarians have broadened the scope of utility to include *preference satisfaction.* A preference is anything we seek to obtain or avoid. Anything that benefits or harms us, then, corresponds with the satisfaction or frustration of one or more of our preferences as they might relate, for example, to our reputation, desires, plans, projects, and other interests and goals.[27] So-called preference utilitarians define happiness broadly in terms of satisfying and maintaining "integrated satisfaction" of preferences. The conceptual difficulties of defining "integrated satisfaction" aside, this expanded

understanding of happiness bears on an understanding of illness, death, and the value of life, among other health matters.

By a preference account, for example, the tragedy of a premature death, such as a young traffic fatality, is not that the young person is deprived of any opportunities for future pleasure, as hedonistic utilitarians might say. The harm is, rather, that the premature death leaves the young person's preferences largely unmet, and that's tragic. Similarly, the tragedy of a Terri Schiavo is not that the person can no longer experience pleasure. After all, she can't experience pain either. The real tragedy is that Terri Schiavo, though existing, can no longer satisfy a single preference, including to live or die. Indeed, because a Terri Schiavo has no capacity to suffer or feel satisfaction, there is really nothing to weigh in deciding to end life support.

Some philosophers think that a preference analysis of such events better accounts for why we consider it so unfortunate for the individuals themselves even though those individuals may be "experiential blanks." Perhaps it also better accounts for why we generally can accept the death of the elderly more easily than the death of the young. In any event, one thing is certain: For preference utilitarianism, not all lives are of equal value. And it's precisely that belief that has made preference utilitarians like the Australian philosopher Peter Singer a favorite target of social conservatives who have branded the Princeton professor "the most dangerous man in the world" for asserting, among other things, that fetuses and some of the seriously impaired have less moral status than, say, adult gorillas and chimpanzees.[28]

CONCLUSIONS

The utilitarians and Kant usually are treated as moral antipodes. Thus, utilitarianism is taken as representing *teleological* ethics, which says an action's consequences are the only criteria for determining the morality of an action. Simply put: We should do something because it maximizes happiness. By contrast, Kant, as well as Locke and medieval

moralists, are considered representative of *deontological* ethics, which denies the teleological view and insists that some things are right or wrong, not because they produce a certain ration of good to evil but because of the nature of the action itself. By the deontological account, only the action done from regard for the moral law itself, not its consequences,

BIOETHICS ACROSS CULTURES

Spain Extends Rights to Apes

On June 25, 2008, Spain became the first nation to officially recognize the rights of non-humans when its parliament voiced support for the rights of great apes to life and freedom. Under Spain's penal code, it will be illegal to use great apes in experiments or for circuses, TV commercials, or movie making. Keeping an estimated 315 apes in Spanish zoos will not be illegal, but supporters of the bill say conditions will need to improve drastically in 70 percent of establishments to comply with the new law. The parliament's order complies with the Great Apes Project (GAP), devised by scientists and philosophers who say our closest genetic relatives deserve rights hitherto limited to humans. Philosophers Peter Singer and Paola Cavalieri of Italy founded GAP in 1993, arguing that "non-human hominids" such as chimpanzees, gorillas, orangutans, and bonobos should enjoy the right to life, freedom, and not to be tortured. Supporters say that this "community of equals" with humans should not be killed except in carefully defined circumstances such as self-defense; that they shouldn't be deprived of their liberty without due cause and a right to appeal; and that they shouldn't undergo deliberate infliction of severe pain, even because of a perceived benefit to others.

(SOURCE: Martin Roberts, "Spanish Parliament to Extend Rights to Apes," *Reuters*, June 25, 2008. Retrieved April 15, 2009, from www. reuters.com/article/scienceNews/idUSL256586320080625?feedType=RSS& feedName=scienceNews&rpc=22.)

Question

Do you think we have ethical obligations that transcend our species? Was Mill right when he responded to Kant's lack of interest in animals by saying: "The question is not, Can they *reason*? nor, Can they *talk*? But, Can they *suffer*?"

---

is truly moral. This makes deontology a moral absolutism, the view that certain actions are right or wrong, regardless of context. By contrast, teleology, which emphasizes consequences, is moral contextualism, the view that the same action can be right in one situation but wrong in another. Aphoristically, deontologists say "Do the right thing even though the heavens fall," whereas teleologists exhort: "Do the right thing lest the heavens fall."

Despite their fundamentally different approaches to ethics, when placed in the larger context of the Enlightenment revolution in moral and social thought, the differences between deontology and teleology give way to striking commonalities. Both deontologists and teleologists represented, in the moral sphere, the Enlightenment's affection for rational/empirical methodology in the scientific sphere. As much as in the natural sciences, these emergent social sciences of secular morality were to be grounded in reason and facts, not religion.

Locke, Kant, Bentham, and Mill (as well as their intellectual heirs) all shared the age's effort to justify moral truth intellectually, not theologically. Each offered a lodestar for determining moral value and obligation without relying on revelation or church teaching. Conceptually, each provided a nonreligious basis for objective morality—for saying that certain actions were morally right or wrong, independent and regardless of human opinion. Thus, opposed to the law of God, which based moral actions on divine approval:

- secular natural law based right actions on some facts about human nature, as described by the fledgling sciences;

- Kant based right actions on a self-evident moral principle, the categorical imperative; and

- utilitarianism based moral actions on empirical calculation of the greatest net happiness, or the utility principle.

Additionally, deontologists and teleologists alike opposed medieval paternalistic government, albeit for different reasons.

- For Locke, intrusive government represented a coercion disrespectful of the distinctiveness of individuals, each with a unique life to lead.

- For Kant, intrusive government posed a potential threat to one's choosing to obey the law of reason as revealed by reason, itself.

- For utilitarians, intrusive government threatened one's freedom to pursue happiness that didn't interfere with another's like pursuit.

Beyond this, despite their different rationales for doing so, all three opposed medieval paternalism specifically with freedom protecting self-governance. In their respect for individual autonomy and popular sovereignty, they formed a united front that, taken with the complementary revolution in science, signaled nothing less than a tectonic shift in the locus of political power and moral authority away from Church and State to individual and body politic.

Practically, this shift can be depicted in a sampling of conceptual oppositions between pre-Enlightenment and post- Enlightenment thought.

- Before the Enlightenment, Church-sponsored government had a moral function; after the Enlightenment, it is limited to protecting of individual rights.

- Before the Enlightenment, morality was defined by reference to the law or will of God, knowable by revelation or reason; after the Enlightenment, morality is defined by reference to the autonomous individual. Moral codes derive largely from rationality alone (as with Kant) or from calculative rationality (as with utilitarians).

- Before the Enlightenment, obligations were more important than rights; after the Enlightenment, rights take priority.

- Before the Enlightenment, the just society was the achievement of the Church; after the Enlightenment, it's the achievement of politics, which involves the autonomous use of reason.

- Before the Enlightenment, human nature was viewed as fundamentally corrupt and in need of divine guidance and deliverance from itself; after the Enlightenment, human beings are viewed as fundamentally rational, educable, and capable of self-government.

- Before the Enlightenment, there was a single path to full knowledge about the meaning and purpose of life, the Church; after the Enlightenment, a variety of conceptions of the good life are thought to cohere with right and justice.

- Before the Enlightenment, goodness and morality resided in God; after the Enlightenment, they have a non-transcendent source, such as practical reason or the capacity for rational choice, as with Kant; or simply pleasure and human happiness, as with the utilitarians; or preference as with many contemporary utilitarians.

For a fledgling America, the Enlightenment's overarching values of reason and freedom inexorably coalesced to form the basis of its so-called religious liberty principle: that laws "will be fashioned through democratic processes in which every perspective is subject to critical analysis."[29] This principle stood in stark opposition to the pre-Enlightenment faith in Church or Bible as supreme authority. In practice, the nascent republic's religious liberty principle required two things: (1) Any proposed public policy had to be open to critical scrutiny, including revision and rejection; and (2) it must not unnecessarily restrict choice. The first was a test of reasonableness, the second of individual liberty. Both were secular criteria that were to play a central role in the conception and practice of bioethics two centuries later.

The Jodie and Mary Twins' Tragedy

When Michaelangelo and Rina Attara learned that Rina was carrying twins, they traveled from their home in Malta to Great Britain, one of only a few locations for dealing with highly unusual births. Their twin daughters, born in October 2000 and known to the public as "Jodie" and "Mary," were joined at the pelvis with a fused spine. Although surgeons had separated other infants successfully, they knew that in this case both babies could not survive the surgery.

Jodie, the larger and stronger of the two, was active and breathing voluntarily with a good heart and lungs, and moving all four limbs. Mary, who was smaller and weaker, showed minimal response and had so poorly developed heart and lungs that she was totally dependent on Jodie for oxygen and blood circulation. In other words, Mary could not exist without Jodie. Doctors recommended separation surgery, which they believed Jodie could survive because her long-term problems were "functional" rather than life threatening. The only threat posed to Jodie, they said, was that Mary was sapping her strength. Without the operation both babies would die. With the operation, Mary certainly would.

The twins' Catholic parents, however, would not okay the operation. In their eyes, both twins were God's creatures, each having a right to life. They could not sanction the shortening of Mary's life to extend that of Jodie. If it was God's will that they both die, then so be it. "We could not possibly agree to any surgery being undertaken that will kill one of our daughters," they said. "We have faith in God, and we are quite happy for God's will to decide what happens." Their priest and friends supported them in their decision.

Under English law, however, parents' wishes do not take precedence. Therefore, the medical team sought court permission to separate the twins and assurance that the procedure, which they knew would result in the death of Mary, would not be unlawful, that is, murder.

Although one of the justices suggested that the hospital was asking the court to "save Jodie but murder Mary," the court supported doctors at the hospital and ruled that Jodie should be saved by detaching Mary. The ruling in part was based not on Jodie's interests but Mary's, reasoning that her harsh life would only worsen as low levels of oxygen in her blood further destroyed her brain. Furthermore, in the court's opinion, stopping delivery of Jodie's blood wouldn't be a positive act of killing but a passive by-product of saving Jodie, like withdrawing food and water from a terminally ill patient.

The separation took place on November 7, 2000, and, as expected, Mary died. In the days following separation, Jody rapidly improved, although she still faced the prospect of substantial reconstructive surgery.[30]

Questions for Analysis

1. Was saving one of the children morally better than losing both?

2. Let's say the court punted the decision back to the parents. Would the parents of Mary and Jodie have been morally justified in refusing treatment and allowing both babies to die?

3. In arguing against the surgery, Archbishop Cormac Murphy-O'Connor, Head of the Catholic Church in England and Wales, said, "There is a fundamental moral principle at stake. No one can commit a wrong action that good may come of it." Was the surgery that ended Mary's life a "wrong action"?[31]

4. Archbishop Murphy-O'Connor also said that Mary possessed the same "basic worth and dignity" of every human being, adding: "She has done nothing which could justify killing her."[32] Place this comment in the context of medieval theology.

5. It was the court's opinion that the case involved self-defense—the right of the stronger twin to be released from a sister who would eventually kill them both. As such it could be justified by the doctrine of double effect. However, it was argued elsewhere, by the Christian Institute, that the separation surgery would fail the test of double effect. Did the operation meet the four conditions of the doctrine of double effect, or didn't it? What do the different interpretations suggest about the doctrine and ecclesiastical moral authority?

6. The complexities of this case split the religious ranks. For example, a Muslim spokesperson pointed out that "[t]he general view of Islam is that life and death are in the hands of the Almighty alone, and human beings should not play God." An Anglican bishop, on the other hand, offered this opinion: "I would say that God's activity is at work in the care that the hospital has given, and the skills of the surgeons to possibly give life out of a situation that could bring death for both children."[33] How do you account for these seemingly opposed views of two church leaders whose moral systems are based on divine command and natural law theory?

7. How would secular natural law, Kant's ethics, and utilitarianism approach and resolve this case?

CASES AND CONTROVERSIES

Life vs. Law

Jay Weaver, a paramedic for more than twenty years and specialist in health case law, recalls the following facts about an incident he witnessed while working as a paramedic for the city of Boston.[34]

The patient was an 11-year-old girl paramedics found at home late at night gasping for air. She could understand English, but her stepfather, the only other person in the house, could not. A "stack of medical records nearly three inches thick" revealed a tangle of heart-wrenching medical and social issues:

- the girl had never known her father;
- her mother had been murdered just two weeks earlier;
- she was related to her stepfather by marriage, but he had no authority to make medical decisions on her behalf since she was a ward of the state; and, worst of all,
- the girl had lung cancer.

Paramedics also learned that when the cancer was found to have spread to her brain, a physician had declared the girl's condition terminal and the hospital had suspended treatment. After meeting with her privately, during which he had posed questions about "life, sickness, medical procedures and death," a judge had determined that the girl was mature enough to understand the consequences of her decision as to her resuscitation status. The girl indicated that she didn't want to be resuscitated in the event of respirator or cardiac arrest.

On the night they were called to the girl's house, paramedics found the judge's order attached to her medical documents. The language left no doubt that it applied to them. The note was addressed to "all health care providers, including EMS professionals."

The girl was in severe respiratory distress, capable of uttering just a few words at a time. Just as they were about to lift her inside the ambulance, she looked up and, with a terrified expression, whispered, "Please don't let me die." Then she stopped breathing. Although Weaver knew what the court order meant and that only the issuing judge could rescind it, he says that he couldn't resist the patient's plea. Knowing he was breaking the law, he ventilated the 11-year-old all the way to the hospital. She didn't regain consciousness, but her heart kept beating and she remained alive. In the emergency department,

a nurse continued the ventilation while an administrator called the hospital's lawyer at home. Stop the resuscitation, the lawyer advised. You're breaking the law. A doctor ordered the nurse to stop. The girl's heart slowed. After a few minutes, it stopped entirely. The doctor pronounced her dead.

Questions for Analysis

1. What moral issues does this case raise?
2. What rights are involved?
3. What moral principle or principles do you think should mainly have guided the respective decisions of the judge, Weaver, and emergency personnel?
4. Some people would say that what Weaver did was legally wrong but morally right? Do you agree? How would you describe the relationship of law and morality?
5. Evaluate the judge's order, Weaver's decision, and staff's action from the perspectives of natural law (both secular and religious), Kant's ethics, and utilitarianism.

CASES AND CONTROVERSIES

Crossing the Border to Sell Blood

BioLife is one of several companies that have established themselves in the main Texas border cities. These companies capture the blood of hundreds of

low-income Mexicans with visas who can cross legally into the United States, like Olga Garcia.

Buses carry the message in Spanish to Mexicans like Garcia: "¡Gane dinero hoy!" (Earn money today!), to get the attention of visitors crossing the border.

(Continued)

CASES AND CONTROVERSIES (CONTINUED)

To earn the maximum amount, donors go twice a week and sell between 690 and 880 milliliters of blood each time, depending on their weight. BioLife Plasma Services currently pays $25 for the first donation of the week and $55 for the second. The firm gives an additional $20 for eight consecutive donations. At 150 pounds, Garcia donates 880 milliliters during each visit. As a plasma donor, she gets $70 weekly, compared to the $56 she earns per week working eight-hour days in textile factories. For a year, Garcia went twice each week to the BioLife Plasma Services laboratories and sold 1.76 liters of her blood. With that money, she paid the mortgage on her house, as well as electricity and phone bills.

"At times, I did not have enough money to buy shoes for my son," Garcia says. "So I went to BioLife, and with that money I bought them."[35]

Questions for Analysis

1. What moral issues do commercial transactions in blood raise?

2. What rights are involved in these kinds of transactions?

3. Evaluate commercial transactions in blood from the perspectives of religious and secular natural law, Kant's ethics, and utilitarianism.

4. Do you think that companies like BioLife are really no different from any other kind of legal business, or are they open to moral criticism? Explain by appeal to moral principle.

CASES AND CONTROVERSIES

Is Vaccinating Part of the Social Contract?

When children first began to receive vaccinations in the 1930s, they typically received just a single one. By 2009 the Centers for Disease Control and Prevention (CDC) was recommending vaccination against fourteen vaccine-preventable diseases, including measles, mumps, rubella (German measles), varicella (chickenpox), hepatitis B, diphtheria, tetanus, pertussis (whooping cough), Haemophilus influenza type B (Hib), polio, influenza (flu), and pneumococcal disease. Because some of these vaccines have to be administered more than once, today a child may receive up to twenty-three shots by the time he or she is two years of age. Depending on the timing, a child might receive up to six shots during one visit to the doctor.

According to the CDC, "vaccines are our best defense against many diseases, which often result in serious complications such as pneumonia, meningitis (swelling of the lining of the brain), liver cancer, bloodstream infections, and even death." The CDC also claims that immunization has wiped out smallpox and polio in the United States and greatly reduced the cases of measles, mumps, tetanus, whooping cough, and other life-threatening illnesses. At the same time, neither the CDC nor any other medical body claims that vaccines are 100 percent effective or that children can't have reactions, ranging from the trivial to the severe.

Nationally, there's a growing movement of parents who are getting exemptions from laws requiring children to get vaccinated before attending school. Ashland, Oregon, site of the world famous Shakespeare Festival, has one of the highest rates at 28 percent, compared with about 4 percent statewide. One of Portland's alternative schools has a 67 percent exemption. Mistrust of government and of pharmaceutical companies motivate some parents to opt out of vaccinations, whereas others fear the possible side effects. The CDC and other health experts, on the other hand, say that not getting immunized puts children at greater health risks than immunization does and that one of the ironic side effects of immunization success is that too many young parents have grown complacent. Because they see very little incidence of a disease, they neither respect it nor immunize for it.

In the growing debate over whether to vaccinate, those getting exemptions often point to cases of unvaccinated children who, nonetheless, didn't get a disease. However, public health officials say this supports immunization. When the majority of children are vaccinated, what is called a "herd community" is formed, making the spread of a disease within a group unlikely because there are so few susceptible members. Those getting vaccinated are helping to prevent the non-vaccinated from contracting a disease. In other words, parents who don't vaccinate their children can only do so safely because most parents accept the risk of vaccination for their own children, thereby raising the overall protective community.

Sometimes parents can't even count on herd protection for their unvaccinated children. With whooping cough, or pertussis, the theory of herd immunity doesn't appear to work well. Researchers who studied children enrolled in a Colorado health plan between 1996 to 2007 found that the unvaccinated children were about 23 times as likely as the vaccinated children to get whooping cough. In other words, about 1 in 20 unvaccinated children were infected, compared with 1 in 500 who were vaccinated.[36]

Questions for Analysis

1. Is social contract theory applicable to the vaccination issue?

2. What rights does vaccination involve?

3. Do you think that parents who don't vaccinate their children are socially irresponsible?

4. Are elementary schools justified in requiring vaccinations for admission?

5. Discuss the morality of parents' refusing to vaccinate their children for pertussis.

6. Which of the moral theories do you think makes the strongest case for a duty to vaccinate?

REFERENCES

1. Immanuel Kant, "An Answer to the Question: *What Is Enlightenment?*," Konigsberg in Prussia, 30th September, 1784. Retrieved May 1, 2007, from http://ethics.sandiego.edu/Books/Kant/Enlightenment/what-is-enlightenmentKant.htm.

2. Tracy Wilkinson, "A Holy Week Marked by an Absence," *Los Angeles Times*, March 25, 2005, p. A1.

3. Carl F. Henry, "Natural Law and a Nihilistic Culture," *First Things*, January 1995, pp. 55–60.

4. Manuel Velasquez, *Philosophy: A Text with Readings*, 8th ed., Belmont, CA: Wadsworth/Thomson Publishing, 2002, p. 535.

5. NA, "Doctrine of Double Effect," *Stanford Encyclopedia of Philosophy*, July 28, 2004. Retrieved March 25, 2009, from http://plato.stanford.edu/entries/double-effect.

6. Velasquez, p. 535.

7. John Finnis, *Natural Law and Natural Rights*, Oxford: Oxford University Press, 1980, p. 90.

8. William H. Shaw and Vincent Barry, *Moral Issues in Business*, 9th ed., Belmont, Ca.: Wadsworth/Thomson, 2004, p. 73.

9. Gordon S. Wood, "Natural, Equal, Universal," *The New York Times Book Review*, April 8, 2007, p. 30.

10. Francis Fukuyama, "Adam Smith and the Virtues of Enlightenment," *Public Interest*, Summer 1999. Retrieved May 1, 2007, from http://findarticles.com/p/articles/mi_m0377/is_136/ai_55174708.

11. Mark Lilla, "The Politics of God," *The New York Times Magazine*, August 19, 2007, p. 33.

12. Mark Lilla, *The Stillborn God: Religion, Politics and the Modern West*, 2007.

13. Gene Garfield, *The Bicentennial of the US Constitution: The American Philosophical Society and the Role of Scholarship in the Creation of the US Republic*, Institute for Scientific Information, Philadelphia, May 25, 1987, p. 131. Retrieved May 1, 2007, from http://www.garfield.library.upenn.edu/essays/v10p131y1987.

14. Quoted in Gary Rosen, "Freedom's Laboratory," *The New York Times Book Review*, February 14, 2010, p. 21.

15. R M. Price, "The Future Fate of Religions," 2004. Retrieved May 1, 2007, from www.robertmprice.mindvendor.com/art_future.htm.

16. John A. Robertson, "Noncoital Reproduction and Procreative Liberty," in *The Ethics of Reproductive Technology*, Kenneth D. Alpern, ed., New York: Oxford University Press, 1992, p. 255.

17. Patricia Cohen, "Darwin's Theory Sets Off a Debate By Conservatives," *The New York Times*, Maya 5, 2007, p. A22.

18. Susan Neiman *Evil, in Modern Thought*, Princeton: Princeton University Press, 2002, p. 68.

19. Ibid. p. 69.

20. Shaw and Barry, p. 63.

21. Velasquez, p. 655.

22. Ibid., p. 607.

23. Cass R. Sunstein, *The Second Bill of Rights: FDR'S Unfinished Revolution and Why We Need It More Than Ever*, New York: Basic Books, 2004.

24. Jeremy Bentham, *Introduction to the Principles of Morals and Legislation*, Oxford: Oxford University Press, 1823, p. 1.

25. Shaw and   Barry, p. 60.

26. John Stuart Mill, *On Liberty* (1859), New York: Penguin Classics, 1982.

27. Peter Singer, *Practical Ethics*, Cambridge: Cambridge University Press, 1993.

28. Ronald Bailey, "The Pursuit of Happiness, Peter Singer Interviewed by Ronald Bailey," *Reason Magazine*, December, 2000. Retrieved May 11, 2007, from www.reason.com/news/show/27886.html.

29. Paul D. Simmons, "Religious Liberty and Abortion Policy: *Casey* as Catch-22," in *The Ethics of Abortion*, 3rd ed., Robert M. Baird and Stuart E. Rosenbaum (eds.), Amherst, NY: Prometheus Books, p. 148.

30. J. F. O. McAllister, "Kill Mary to Save Jody?," TIME, September 10, 2000. Retrieved May 26, 2009, from http://www.time.com/time/printout/0,8816,54436,00.html.

31. "Jodie and Mary: The Medical Facts," BBC News, December 7, 2000. Retrieved May 28, 2009, from http://news.bbc.co.uk/2/hi/health/920487.stm.

32. NA, "Siamese or Conjoined Twins," *Religions Now*, August 9, 2000. Retrieved May 28, 2009, from http://members.lycos.co.uk/ReligionsNow/evidence/siamesetwins.htm.

33. Colin Hart, "Judges and Doctors Must Not Play God," *The Chritian Institute*, September 21, 2000. Retrieved May 26, 2009, from http://www.christian.org.uk/pressreleases/2000/PressRelease210900.html.

34. Jay Weaver, "Life vs. Law: When the Mandates Are At Odds," Arehttp://www.emsresponder.com/print/EMS-Magazine/Why-EMS-Needs-Its-Own-Ethics/1$6382 at Odds," in Craig M. Klugman, "Why EMS Needs Its Own Ethics," *EMS.com Responder*, October 2007, pp. 114–122. Retrieved April 4, 2009, from http://www.emsresponder.com/print/EMS-Magazine/Why-EMS-Needs-Its-Own-Ethics/.

35. Jorge Luis Sierra and Peter Micek, trans., "Crossing the Border To Sell Blood," *Rumbo News Report*, August 9, 2007. Retrieved April 5, 2009, from: http://news.newamericamedia.org/news/view_article.html?article_id=3e985017e737ef2604c7d2352e6f61c9.

36. Jason M. Glanz, et al., "Parental Refusal of Pertussis Vaccination Is Associated With an Increased Risk of Pertussis Infection in Children, *Pediatrics*, June 2009, pp. 1446–1451.

PART II

Origins and Context
of Bioethics

INTRODUCTION: TRIUMPH OF SECULARISM

Cultural historians generally agree that the Enlightenment revolutions in science and the social sciences laid the foundation for modern Western civilization. Enlightenment values—reason, freedom, tolerance, scientific method, individuality, confidence in human progress—all profoundly shaped the character and Constitution of the United States and remain indomitable forces in modern society. At the core of these values is secularism.

Secularism—from the Latin *saeculum*, meaning "from or of this world"—is often understood as the separation between church and state in making government and public policy. More broadly, secularism refers to a doctrine that develops its worldview—its perspectives on reality, knowledge, ethics, and governance—without reliance on religious authority, although not necessarily excluding its influence. So understood, secularism substitutes a human-centered for a god-centered view of the world. It focuses on human needs, desires, and material progress, and enlists the power of science and its method to attain them.

The shift that we sketched in Part I—from medieval faith and obeisance to divine authority to Enlightenment science, rationality, and liberty—ushered in new ways of seeing the world, of constructing society and political systems, and of defining success and improvement that have come to mark the modern world, its significant institutions and organizations, as thoroughly secular. It is these Enlightenment-bred values and ideals of secular modernity that form the backdrop of Part II. All were part of the intellectual milieu that formed after World War II and crested in the 1960s, at the dawn of modern bioethics.

In that quarter century or so, modern medicine's adherence to science and its method brought stunning achievements but also new moral challenges. Chapters 3, 4, and 5 will review the factors that helped create the need for bioethics, its basic principles, and subsequent applications. Today, as we'll see in

Chapters 6 and 7, the defining tenets of bioethics are under attack, while alternative viewpoints test its original, Enlightenment-bred assumptions and biases.

The theme of Part II is that bioethics came into being during a decidedly secular era and today owes its controversy largely to its ingrained secular outlook.

Chapter 3

The Birth of Bioethics

"**M**ost of the participants were young, white, middle-class, college-educated women who had been active in the Civil Rights Movement or had helped draft resisters during the Vietnam War."[1] That's how Kathy Davis, a professor of women's studies at Utrecht University in Holland, describes the group of Boston women who met on May 4, 1969, in a workshop on "Women and Their Bodies." Although the activists were merely planning "to make sense of the medical muddle then surrounding women's health," says another commentator, what they ended up making was history.[2]

THE EMERGENT PATIENT CONSCIOUSNESS

A year after the momentous meeting, the Boston seminar, known as the Doctor's Group (now the Boston Women's Health Book Collective), published one of the most influential books of its era, *Our Bodies, Ourselves* (*OBOS*). The original *OBOS* booklet, a stapled newsprint edition selling for 75 cents, was a concise, readable manual on women's bodies and health, written by women, based on their own experiences. As such, it was filled with practical information on a wide range of topics of interest to women. It also combined "a scathing critique of patriarchal medicine and the medicalization of women's bodies as well as an analysis of the political economics of the health and pharmaceutical industries," according to Davis. Above all, she writes: "*OBOS* validated women's embodied experiences as a resource for challenging medical dogmas about women's bodies and, consequently, as a strategy for personal and collective empowerment."[3] Since its 1970 publication, *OBOS* has sold over 4 million copies and has been translated into seventeen languages and Braille. Davis credits its simple, direct message with galvanizing the woman's health movement and reaching twenty million readers worldwide.

It's fitting that we begin this chapter about the people and events important to the birth of modern bioethics with reference to *OBOS*, for that groundbreaking work owed its inspiration and urgency to the same social, political, and medical forces that fashioned the new bioethics of the 1960s and early 1970s. From John F. Kennedy's election in 1960 to Richard Nixon's resignation in 1974, America was a troubled land, with the civil rights movement and the Vietnam War catalyzing unprecedented social protest against the established order and authority. During the turbulent sixties, individuals and groups with power were increasingly pressured

---

BIOETHICS ACROSS CULTURES

Africa Still Waiting for "The Sanitary Revolution"

The dazzling medical advances of the last half-century can easily blind us to what many regard as the most important medical milestone ever: the introduction of clean water and sewage disposal, collectively known as "the sanitary revolution." The newest medical tools, procedures, and breakthroughs can also insulate Americans from an unpleasant reality: for millions of people the sanitary revolution of the nineteenth century has not yet occurred.

Three of the original champions of clean water and sewage disposal were a lawyer, a doctor, and an engineer. The lawyer, Edwin Chadwick (1800–1890), pioneered the introduction of piped water to people's homes and sewers rinsed by water. The physician, John Snow (1813–1858), a legendary figure in the history of public health, epidemiology, and anesthesiology, discovered that cholera was spread by water. Cholera is an acute diarrheal disease caused by a bacterium that is transmitted to humans through contaminated food or water. Without treatment, death can result in a matter of hours. The engineer, the visionary Joseph Bazalgetteto (1819–1891), was inspired by Snow's discovery to establish an effective means of preventing the ancient scourge: the provision of municipal sanitation.

Through the collective genius of these three Englishmen, cholera was one of the first infections whose mode of transmission was understood and for which effective prevention measures were developed and implemented. As a result of their work, cholera has been rare in the United States and other developed countries for at least 100 years. But not so in many parts of the developing world, where inadequate sanitation is still a major problem. In 2001 alone, unsafe water, sanitation, and hygiene accounted for over 1.5 million deaths from diarrheal disease in low- and middle-income countries. (That's still less than the number of children who die of pneumonia in these countries annually.)

Drs. Eric D. Mintz and Richard L. Guerrant, both leaders in global health, recently reported that, while case fatality rates for cholera in the rest of the world are now well below 1 percent, rates in excess of 5 percent are still commonly reported in many African countries. In 2005, the reported incidence of cholera in Africa was 95 times that in Asia and 16,600 times that in Latin America. In 2007, the reported rate of death from cholera in Africa was seven times that in Asia; no cholera-related deaths have been reported in Latin America since 2001. According to United Nations agencies, the cumulative case fatality rate in the ongoing cholera epidemic in Zimbabwe remained stubbornly above 4.7 percent through February 2009, by which point five months had elapsed since the epidemic began, and more than 73,000 cases and 3,500 deaths had been reported. The epidemic in Zimbabwe shows no signs of waning and has spread to neighboring South Africa and Zambia, causing thousands of additional cases.

(SOURCE: Eric D. Mintz, and Richard L. Guerrant, "A Lion in Our Village," *The New England Journal of Medicine*, March 12, 2009, pp. 1060–1063.)

Question

Are there good religious and secular reasons for saying that the international community has a moral responsibility to protect vulnerable African populations by extending the sanitary revolution, along with basic health care services and supplies?

---

to negotiate with those with less power. Within these unequal relationships, war protesters, students, black Americans, women, consumers, and many types of workers struggled to win a measure of independence, the very thing the Doctor's Group attempted to carve out in the sphere of women's health. Indeed, the demands for equality and individual rights were especially intense in medicine and health care, as a whole. It was there, as public health historian Amy L. Fairchild observes, that "[t]he forces that gave birth to ... changes provided the context

for and were in turn energized by the new bioethics, which had as its lodestar a commitment to patient autonomy and a rejection of medical paternalism."[4]

THE NEW FRONTIER OF MEDICINE

If, like *OBOS*, the new bioethics drew its inspiration from the politics of social protest and demand for individual rights, both book and discipline found their urgency in the stunning post-war advances in medical science. The years after World War II were ones of unprecedented possibility in health care, and by the 1960s medicine found itself on an exciting new frontier of dazzling breakthroughs that were making the aspirations of enlightened thinkers like Bacon, Kant, and Franklin come true in the fight against disease, illness, and human deprivation. But along with the impressive successes came unparalleled uncertainty about professional conduct and social policy. The new technologies and treatments, even medical research itself, straightaway posed complex questions and difficult choices.

New Technology and Treatments

Along with new technology and treatments for disease came fresh moral controversies. The invention of the kidney dialysis machine (1945) and shunt (1962), for example, made it possible for patients suffering from chronic kidney disease to receive ongoing hemodialysis treatments. For some of the desperately ill, dialysis, the procedure for cleaning wastes from blood after kidneys have failed, was a medical miracle. Others, however, were left wondering: *Is death, perhaps, preferable to the extreme burden of being supported by a machine?*[5]

A similar question soon shrouded the invention of the heart-lung machine. First used on a human in 1953, this device "breathed" for people who couldn't breathe on their own. A godsend if temporary, the "breathing machine" became an invention of dubious value when used to sustain respiration and heartbeat indefinitely in patients with permanent, irreversible neurological impairment. *Were such patients being helped or hurt? Were they better off dead than alive? Indeed, were patients who had lost all brain function really alive?*

One of the truly spectacular achievements made possible by the new, post-war medical technology was the organ transplantation, or transference of an organ from human-to-human or animal-to-human (called xenotransplant). In 1964 six baboon kidneys were transplanted into humans, all of whom died of infections within weeks. Then, in 1967, a South African surgeon, Dr. Christiaan Barnard (1922–2001), together with a team of thirty associates, performed

the first human heart transplant. The recipient, Louis Washkansky, was a 55-year-old wholesale grocer who had suffered progressive heart failure. The donor, Denise Ann Darvall, was a 25-year-old automobile accident victim. The surgery took five hours. Barnard, a minister's son, said of his achievement: "My moment of truth—the moment when the enormity of it all really hit me—was just after I had taken out Washkansky's heart. I looked down and saw this empty space...."[6] Washkansky died eighteen days after the astonishing feat, his new heart still strong, but his body the victim of pneumonia.

Like Washkansky, the earliest heart transplant patients didn't face the Hobson's choice of kidney patients, since they soon died of either rejection or infection. But their plight, nevertheless, raised misgivings. By 1971, when 146 of the original 170 heart recipients were dead, many professionals and laypeople were left asking: *Is modern medicine selling desperate patients false hope? When exactly does life end? What matters more—quantity or quality of life?*

Transplant surgery also created a need for fresh organs from newly dead bodies. High on the list of potential organ donors were those artificially supported patients with dead brains but sustained circulation. By religious and medical tradition, only when blood stopped circulating was a person considered dead. That meant patients with heart-lung function were to be considered alive and, thus, might not have life-sustaining organs removed without killing them. This placed surgeons, researchers, and institutions in legal limbo. *How could they utilize the new technology and do transplantations while, at the same time, being protected from civil and criminal liability?*

Advances in Reproductive Technologies

Of the formidable post-war breakthroughs in reproductive technology, four stand out: amniocentesis, in vitro fertilization, surrogacy, and cloning.

Amniocentesis Amniocentesis is the process of removing from a pregnant woman's uterus a sample of the amniotic fluid, which surrounds the fetus. This fluid contains fetal cells that are analyzed to identify genetic defects of the fetus.[7] Although tapping of amniotic fluid had been practiced for over a hundred years, it wasn't until the 1950s that it was first used to diagnose genetic disease. Prior to that, diagnostic techniques were severely limited. But while amniocentesis enabled detection of a wide range of fetal defects, it also forced prospective parents of a seriously abnormal fetus and their physicians to consider the troubling question: *Should such pregnancies be ended or carried to term?*

In Vitro Fertilization   In vitro fertilization, or IVF involves fertilizing an egg outside the womb, then transferring it into the uterus to begin a pregnancy or preserving it for future use. In 1978, as Chapter 11 will recount, the first baby produced by an IVF procedure was born. An inestimable gift to many, IVF immediately raised questions about its "unnaturalness"; the normality and well-being of IVF babies; and especially about the disposition of unused fertilized eggs, because doctors often create more eggs than are used in a course of trying to become pregnant. The unused eggs are usually frozen, and many are eventually discarded as medical waste. At its inception, then, IVF raised the still contentious question: *If a human being exists from or at conception—the teaching of many religions—is it proper to destroy fertilized eggs? Is their destruction tantamount to murder?* Concern with the fate of human fertilized eggs during prenatal life was (and still is) part of the broader issue of the appropriate use of laboratory collected genetic material.

Surrogacy   In human reproduction, the term surrogacy is used when a woman carries a pregnancy and gives birth to a baby for another woman. Although surrogacy is as old as the Bible, the first recognized surrogate mother arrangement in the United States was made in 1976. The story of this extraordinary medical achievement is told in a case presentation following this chapter. Suffice it here to say that surrogacy raised a knot of difficult moral questions about rights, marriage, and transfer of genetic material.

Cloning   Cloning is the process of making a genetically identical copy of a cell or an individual. The first vertebrate, a frog, was cloned in 1962 by British biologist John B. Gurdon. By the late 1960s,

many scientists believed that human cloning was on the near horizon. For the optimists, that prospect promised superior individuals and rejection-proof organ transplants. Some, like molecular biologist Joshua Lederberg, a Nobel Laureate in Medicine (1958), even proposed human cloning as a way to ensure a healthy and superior gene pool. To skeptics, however, human cloning was morally troubling. *Would a human clone—a subhuman or parahuman—be a human being? Could such a creature be bred for its parts and then discarded? What impact would human cloning have on the traditional Judeo-Christian understanding of "the covenant link between personal union and procreation in marriage"?*

Scientific Research

The vigorous scientific medicine of the nineteenth century continued apace in the twentieth, establishing a broad knowledge base for a brave new world of medicine. But too often the means involved nonconsensual, nontherapeutic experimentation on vulnerable populations,[8] as in the following egregious instances:

- From 1960 to 1971, researchers at the University of Cincinnati exposed at least 90 cancer patients to large radiation doses and recorded their physical and mental responses. Most of the patients were poor or working-class people; about 60 percent were black. Twenty-one died within a month or so.[9]

- In the so-called Jewish Chronic Disease Hospital case of 1963, prominent researchers injected live cancer cells into uninformed nursing home residents, some Holocaust survivors, to test their immune systems.[10]

- In 1966, the esteemed Harvard physician Henry Beecher (1904–1976) detailed twenty-two examples of experiments conducted in the United States between1948 and 1965 on human subjects without their understanding of consequences or their consent.[11] The most shocking involved purposely infecting institutionalized mentally defective children with hepatitis virus and injecting live cancer

---

BIOETHICS ACROSS CULTURES

Globalization of Clinical Research

The complex history of medical experimentation contains many grim chapters. Some are quite familiar, including Nazi concentration camp inmate "studies." Less known, however, is how the poor, under-informed, or simply powerless continue to bear the weight of medical advances as pharmaceutical companies embrace globalization as a core component of their business models, especially in the realm of clinical trials. In *Body Hunters: How the Drug Industry Tests Its Products on the World's Poorest Patients*, journalist Sonia Shah tells their story.

An expose of the pharmaceutical industry, Shah's book focuses mainly on the issue of clinical trials, as they're conducted in India, Latin America, and Africa, where oversight is minimal. The great advantage of conducting clinical trials in these countries is that potential subjects abound. In the United States where the Food and Drug Administration (FDA) prefers, if not requires, drugs be tested against placebos to prove effectiveness, Americans (and Western Europeans, for that matter) are reluctant to take placebos. The same cannot be said of much of the underdeveloped world, where desperate test subjects abound. These "warm bodies," Shah calls them, satisfy the industry's main interest, which is collecting data. Shah gives the examples of placebo groups, who receive little or no medical

care, and countries that can provide them with a high death rate, so crucial to their data.

According to the International Guidelines for Biomedical Research Involving Human Subjects (published in 1993), clinical research should be responsive to the health needs and priorities of the communities in which the research is conducted. And yet, a recent examination of clinical trials sponsored by US-based companies in developing countries shows no trials for tuberculosis, which disproportionately affects these populations. There was, however, a variety of trials for conditions such as allergic rhinitis and overactive bladder. Clearly, developing countries do not realize the benefits of trials if the drugs being evaluated do not become readily available there once they have been approved.

(SOURCE: Seth Glickman et al., "Ethical and Scientific Implications of the Globalization of Clinical Research," *The New England Journal of Medicine*, February 19, 2009, pp. 816–823.)

Question

Does it matter morally if the growth in clinical trials worldwide is not accompanied by greater availability of drugs in the countries where the trials are conducted? Do you think that the social ecology and genetic makeup of the study population in developing countries allow trial results to be generalized to populations in which the treatment will most likely be used?

---

cells into senile and demented hospitalized patients.

- In 1972, researcher Peter Buxtun disclosed the details of experiments conducted by the US Public Health Service (PHS) under the title *Tuskegee Study of Untreated Syphilis in the Negro Male*. Because the study is detailed in an end-of-chapter case presentation, it's enough to say for now that syphilis patients in the study went untreated for forty years.

Emerging with the new post-war medicine, then, were thorny ethical matters that defied the expertise of scientists and technicians and strained the established medical codes of conduct. The significance of human life and death; the definition of parenting; the meaning of suffering; the responsibilities

of researchers, including their goals and methods, all were fresh issues that hewed more toward moral philosophy than science and medicine. As a result, the rights and interests of patients and human research subjects drew attention as never before. Indeed, as *OBOS* famously announced in 1970, the days of deferring to doctors and researchers, drug companies and federal officials, were numbered.

COURT DECISIONS

It wasn't only transformative events in medicine that awakened patient consciousness in the years after World War II. So did case law about matters at life's beginning and end.

Law at the Beginning of Life

In 1965 the US Supreme Court expanded individual rights to privacy in matters of sexuality and family planning. *Griswold v. Connecticut*, for example, specifically recognized the possession of birth control as "right of privacy" covered within the due process clause of the Fourteenth Amendment. The right to possession of birth control was subsequently extended to non-married couples in *Eisenstadt v. Baird* (1972). Building on these privacy in procreative-choice rulings, advocates of liberalizing state abortion laws, such as attorney Lawrence Lader (1919–2006), successfully pressed their cause. Primarily as a result of their public information campaigns, popular support for abortion shot up to 64 percent in 1972 from 49 percent just four years earlier.[12] The stage was thus set for *Roe v. Wade*, the controversial 1973 Supreme Court ruling that established the right to abortion (see Chapters 9 and 10). While *Roe* brought together feminists, most Jews, liberal Catholics and atheists, it also created a backlash of religious fundamentalism; triggered conservative Christian activism; and, arguably, ignited the so-called culture war.[13-15] Two other rulings in the seventies further deferred to physician judgment and patient choice, *Planned Parenthood of Central Missouri v. Danforth* (1976) and *Colautti v. Franklin* (1979).[16]

Law at the End of Life

During these turbulent times patient rights activism was not confined to reproductive choice but extended to end-of-life decisions as well. In 1968, for example, Florida proposed the first living-will bill; five years later such a law was enacted in California. For the first time people were permitted to put in writing their wishes for end-of-life medical treatment if they became unable to communicate. Ever mindful of its members' professional prerogatives, five years later, in the year of *Roe*, the American Medical Association (AMA) branded these living wills an intrusion into the doctor-patient relationship, and the American Hospital Association (AHA) did not acknowledge a patient right to a living will in its historic 12-point *Patient's Bill of Rights* (1973).

Then, in 1976, the New Jersey Supreme Court dramatically heightened end-of-life consciousness. At the behest of her parents, the court ordered doctors to remove a respirator from a young woman in a chronic vegetative state, the result of ingesting a mix of alcohol and barbiturates the year before. Breathing on her own and fed through a tube, a procedure which only then was becoming widespread, Karen Ann Quinlan (1954–1985) survived for ten more years.

Quinlan, also featured at the end of this chapter, came to symbolize the dawn of a new era in medicine. Ahead lay complex, technology-driven moral, social, and legal issues, with patients and health teams determining appropriate end-of-life treatment. Little wonder, then, that at the advent of this new era the phrase "right to die," complementary to "right to choose" (as with abortion), came into use, referring broadly to the right to make the tough end-of-life decisions that the new technology required. Recognition of other patient rights soon followed.

In 1980 the Florida District Court of Appeals affirmed (in *Satz v. Perlmutter*) a competent patient's constitutionally protected privacy, liberty, and autonomy interests in removing life-sustaining treatment and in choosing to "die with dignity," another coined phrase with lasting impact on cultural discourse. In 1990, five years after Quinlan's death and the year Terri Schiavo was slipping into her own fateful coma, the US Supreme Court permitted the removal of a feeding tube from 32-year-old Nancy Cruzan, who had been in persistent vegetative state (PVS) since being injured in an automobile accident in 1983 (*Cruzan v. Director, Missouri Department of Health*). *Cruzan* was the high court's first "right-to-die" case, though more accurately: the right to refuse nutrition and hydration. The ruling meant that the constitutionally protected liberty interest of formerly competent persons in refusing unwanted medical treatments such as ventilators, as with Quinlan, also extended to artificial food and water, as with Cruzan.

Worth noting is that all these decisions about what was permissible at the beginning and end of life were indebted to a view of freedom borrowed from Mill and the utilitarians and popularized by philosopher Isaiah Berlin (1909–1997) in his 1958 lecture titled *Two Concepts of Liberty*. In that highly influential address, Berlin cast freedom as a negative liberty that defined the Enlightenment political ideal of the liberal democracy. By this account, the main purpose of a liberal democracy such as the United States was to create the social environment in which individuals were free from interference, "to do what they wanted, provided that their actions didn't interfere with the liberty of others." It was in this liberal democratic spirit that cases including *Griswold, Einstadt, Roe, Quinlan,* and *Cruzan,* all were decided.

Scientific advances and new technology, the mistreatment of human subjects in research, the clamor for patient rights, the judicial expansion of individual liberty—such were the chief medical and legal developments that marked the founding and early years of modern bioethics. They represented the confluence of two powerful currents of the secular Enlightenment: progress through science and technology and individual rights.

But the development of medical technology from an ever-expanding base of scientific knowledge, together with a robust conception of court-backed individual rights, weren't only raising unprecedented questions of professional values, practice, and relationships. They were also testing established social limits. *What new ground rules would govern the new biology, the new liberties, and the new research? How and where would the permissible limits be drawn?* And, most important of all: *Who would make the new rules and how would they do it?* It was to meeting such challenges that a group of bold minds, rightly considered the pioneers of bioethics, turned their attention.

THE PIONEERS AND THEIR MIND-SET

From its beginnings, many disciplines contributed to the content of bioethics, including law, medicine, and sociology. But it was mainly from theology and philosophy that the trailblazers came who fashioned the field's theory and methods.

The Theologians

As students of the nature of God and religious truth, theologians naturally took an early interest in the new technologies' implications for understanding such fundamental matters as human nature and destiny, the value of life, and the meaning of illness and suffering. Among them were the following figures, ranked chronologically by key publications or accomplishments:

- the Episcopal priest Joseph Fletcher (1905–1991), whose *Morals and Medicine* (1954) endorsed patient rights and individual choice and set the stage for his better known and more controversial *Situational Ethics: The New Morality* (1966), which provided a utilitarian framework for abortion and euthanasia;

- the Methodist theologian Paul Ramsey, whose prescient *The Patient as Person: Explorations in Medical Ethics* (1969) called attention to the crucial and fragile bonds of the physician-patient partnership;

- the ecumenical theologian James Gustafson, whose 1970 essay "Basic Issues in the Bio-Medical Fields" was one of the first to identify prickly issues in genetics and neurosciences;[17] and the Catholic theologian Warren Reich, whose *Encyclopedia of Bioethics* (1978, rev. 1995) grounded the field; and who in 1971 helped found The Kennedy Center for the Study of Human Reproduction from a Catholic viewpoint (now called the Kennedy Institute of Ethics).

Although of similar backgrounds and traditions, theologians were hardly of one mind on all the issues. As do their counterparts today, they, too, differed on fundamental questions about the beginning and end of life, the nature of values, and the ultimate authority of right and wrong. The response to Lederberg's cloning suggestion is a striking example, with liberal Fletcher curious about the new technology's uses (*Ethics of Genetic Control,* 1974) and the more conservative Ramsey troubled by its potential abuses (*Fabricated Man,* 1970). Both theologians could claim biblical bases, depending on their preferred version of the creation story: Gen 1, in the case of Fletcher; or Gen. 2 in the case of Ramsey. Fletcher's and Ramsey's perception of progress also clashed. As characterized by bioethics historian Albert Jonsen, himself one of the field's groundbreakers:

> Fletcher... affirmed the new things would advance human good and saw ethics as the willingness to accept the new medical technology with a reasonable awareness of possible misuse. Ramsey glimpsed ... the power of evil hidden even in the good. He played the prophet, pointing to the moral problems that plague all progress and urging rules that would contain those problems. Joseph Fletcher endorsed the vision of advance toward human betterment with cautions about possible tyrannies; Paul Ramsey preached the supremacy of the moral imperative that must guide and sometimes curtail those advances.[18]

There was, then, no more a single monolithic "religious" voice at the birth of bioethics than there is today. What's more, the earliest debates, such as about cloning and progress, foreshadowed major lines of argumentation in contemporary bioethics,[19] as well as the current disagreements between the religious orthodox and the religious progressivists.

Adding to the mix were the differences in theological traditions. Catholic theologians such as Richard McCormick (1922–2000), Charles E. Curran, and Bernard Haring (1912–1998), could consult centuries of thought and explicit teaching about reproduction, end-of-life treatment and decisions, and the physician-patient relationship based on Thomistic natural law.[20] They could also draw on a deep reservoir of theory and action in the arena of politics and civil society, or social justice.

For their part, Protestant thinkers, generally favoring Enlightenment liberty of individual conscience in the interpretation of moral doctrine and conduct, could tap into the more recent thought of theologians like H. Richard Niebuhr (1919–1962). Niebuhr along with his better-known brother Reinhold Niebuhr (1892–1971), Helmut Thielicke (1908–1986), Karl Barth (1886–1968), Dietrich Bonhoeffer (1906–1945), and Paul Tillich (1886–1965), were associated with a highly influential movement at the time termed Protestant neo-orthodoxy.[21] The neo-orthodox theological renaissance depicted a transcendent God "working through humanity to establish justice on earth." It saw its mission as "giving shape and meaning to modern culture," and believed that society must confront social injustice. In a real sense, then, these theologians were "public Protestants," a term that religion historian Martin Marty coined to describe those late nineteenth-century Protestants who believed that good works were the road to salvation. Opposed to public Protestants, Marty set "private Protestants," who believed that salvation lay in a personal relationship with God. The thrust of Protestant thinking, then, was toward inclusion, not exclusion, of secular opinion, specifically dialogue and engagement with the other major group of bioethical pathfinders represented by the philosophers.[22] In the spirit of Vatican II (1962–1965), Catholic theologians also were amenable to abandoning "a centuries-old embattled stance toward modernity for one emphasizing dialogue and shared struggle for human dignity."[23,24]

Less heard in the early days were theological voices from the Judaic tradition, according to Jonsen.[25] Still, the distinctive perspective of traditional Judaism did have its representatives including: Immanuel Jakobovits (*Jewish Medical Ethics*, 1959), Fred Rosner (*Modern Medicine and Jewish Law*, 1972), David Feldman (*Marital Relations, Birth Control, and Abortion in Jewish Law*, 1974), and J. David Bleich (*Contemporary Halakhic Problems*, 1977).[26]

The Philosophers

Because the new biology raised fundamental, yet practical, questions of character and conduct, it caught the eye of another group of thinkers and scholars whose interests traced back to the ancient pursuit of wisdom and enlightenment about how best to live. Prominent among these moral philosophers or ethicists were the following, again listed chronologically by key work:

- Samuel Gorovitz, whose 1966 essay "Ethics and the Allocation of Medical Resources" posed the problem of allocating crucial but scarce medical resources such as dialysis;

- Han Jonas (1903–1993), whose 1967 essay "Philosophic Reflections on Experimenting with Human Subjects" anticipated the moral implications of biomedical research;

- Daniel Callahan, whose essay "Bioethics as a Discipline" (1973) helped establish bioethics as a legitimate academic discipline; and who in 1969 founded (with psychoanalyst Willard Gaylin) The Hastings Center, an internationally acclaimed institute for bioethics with a secular moral bent;

- Robert Veatch, "the original bioethicist,"[27] who served as ethics representative to the parents of Karen Ann Quinlan in 1975–1976; and

- H. Tristram Engelhardt, Jr., philosopher/physician, who co-founded (with physician Edmund Pellegrino) the *Journal of Medicine and Philosophy* in 1976.

These and other moral philosophers—Arthur Caplan, Stuart Spicker, Howard Brody, Baruch Brody, Ruth Macklin—joined the theologians and staffed the institutions that helped establish bioethics as an acceptable interdisciplinary field dealing with the ethical, social, and legal aspects of advances in medical science. Together with scientists and scholars from other fields, they set the stage for the social policy of the 1970s and beyond. But that policy and the events it set in motion would not have been possible had theologians and philosophers been unable to bridge their differences.

Points of Difference

It has been said that philosophy is like standing in a dark room looking for a black cat. Theology, on the other hand, is like standing in a dark room looking for a black cat and shouting: "Found it!" This old saw can be explained by reference to why each believes as it does.

Although both share an interest in first principles and reality, theologians trust in faith and generally assent to a revealed, fixed, and universal truth. Philosophers trust in reason and assent only to what can be rationally demonstrated. Theologians, typically, have found their final truth, whereas philosophers are still searching for theirs. These fundamentally different sources of authority for beliefs—the one divine, the other secular—account for both the theologian's claim to have objective certainty and the philosopher's skepticism toward the theologian's faith-based certitudes. Metaphorically, the theologian can claim to have found the black cat that the philosopher continues to search for in the dark room.

The crucial difference in sources of authority for belief between the two midwives of bioethics posed a potential sticking point when Congress passed the National Research Act (NRA) on July 12, 1974. The NRA charged the Secretary of Health Education and Welfare (now Health and Human Services, or HHS) to appoint a commission to "identify the basic ethical principles" that the federal government should use to protect human subjects of medical experiments. But how was the new National Commission for the Protection of Human Subjects of Biomedical and Behavioral Research, as the body was named, to articulate a coherent position when its primary authors—theologians and philosophers—didn't share the same belief system?

COMMON GROUND

Over the ensuing years the commission met on a monthly basis and convened at the Smithsonian's

Belmont Conference Center in February 1976 for an intensive four days of deliberations. Although the theologians and philosophers didn't have common belief systems, they did share a number of views, interests, and purposes as heirs to both the Judeo-Christian and Enlightenment traditions.

For one thing, both could agree that the ultimate goal of medicine was health and that medical science was to be used for the benefit and use of life. They could also agree on the inherent dignity and worth of human beings, thereby making treatment of human subjects in research and elsewhere of vital mutual concern. Additionally, the religious and secular founders of bioethics realized the critical importance of gaining the support of the medical professionals. After all, the end-product, a summary of basic bioethical principles, was intended for clinical practice, with the audience primarily physicians, nurses, and research scientists, whose training, though not faith based, nonetheless dealt with universal (scientific) truths.

Beyond this, theologians and philosophers shared a state of mind profoundly influenced by the values and goals of the Enlightenment, specifically in (1) their desire to balance utility and autonomy, (2) their faith in rationality, and (3) their inheritance of a national religious identity.

Utility and Autonomy

Agreeing on the overriding goal of medicine and the inherent value of human beings, both groups were especially determined to find the moral overlap in answering the hard questions that the new biotechnology posed. Toward that end, both tended to frame moral dilemmas largely in pragmatic terms of calculating risk-benefit.[28] But as they strove in utilitarian fashion to balance risks and benefit, they also harbored a deep respect for individual autonomy and rights.[29] Clinically, this meant giving patients a voice in health decisions within a medical environment increasingly shaped by powerful technologies and medical specializations.

Faith in Rationality

Perhaps the theologians didn't share the philosophers' supreme faith in rationality, but their own traditions recognized its importance and value.

The Bible, for example, recorded the words of the prophet Isaiah: "Come, let us reason together" (Isaiah 1:18); and natural law theory stood as a monument to the power of the intellect to discover moral law. What's more, theologians were as much "children of the Enlightenment" as were the philosophers. Both shared the Enlightenment's optimism that, reasoning together, they could find a common morality within which to frame bioethics for a pluralistic society with members of seemingly incompatible moral traditions, including medical professionals. At the beginning, then, the founders of bioethics were unified in their acceptance of the history and context of the Enlightenment tradition, with its value-laden presuppositions and understanding of rationality.

A National Religious Identity

Finally, as Americans, both groups shared two important commitments. The first was to the Constitution's presupposition of negative freedom, or freedom as non-interference. Both theologian and philosopher could generally endorse Berlin's view of freedom as non-interference as being "the only concept of liberty that could be actualized in the 'real world' of inevitably conflicting interests, diverse concepts of the good, and competing human projects."[30]

The second commitment that both groups shared as Americans was to a national religious identity. Sociologist Robert N. Bellah ("Civil Religion in America," 1967) famously called this national identity "American civil religion," and Robert M. Price, Professor of Biblical Criticism, lucidly describes it as follows:

> Our common scripture is the Declaration, Constitution, and Bill of Rights.
> Our Exodus was the Revolutionary War.
> Father Abraham was George Washington,

Moses was James Madison, Solomon was Ben Franklin, and Jesus was Abe Lincoln. The Founding Fathers equal the Church Fathers.... Our holidays are holy days.[31]

Whatever their personal religions, then, both theologians and philosophers had, as it were, a second religion: Americanism. They could generally agree that this national religious identity could be given full play in shaping concepts, decisions, and public policy, whereas the personal religion was to be kept private. The trick, of course, was to propose a moral framework for all persons regardless of any particular faith commitment,[32] one with appeal to "rational individuals without the special illumination of some divine grace," in the words of philosopher Engelhardt, writing in the first edition of his text *The Foundations of Bioethics* (1986). The Belmont Commissioners met this ideal and challenge by agreeing, in effect, to a compromise that mimicked the one that the Enlightenment had made with religion two centuries earlier.

THE "JEFFERSONIAN COMPROMISE"

In a 1994 essay titled "Religion as Conversation-Stopper," philosopher Richard Rorty (1931–2007) invented the term "Jeffersonian compromise" for the arrangement that the Enlightenment reached with the religious in order to negotiate the tension between religion and democracy.[33] Rorty's analysis was indebted to the tradition of church-state separation put forth by contractarians Hobbes and Locke.

Mindful of the devastating religious wars of early modern Europe, Hobbes argued that religious premises were inherently divisive and offered futile grounds for establishing government and arguing public policy. For his part, Locke conceived of religion as essentially private and

argued (in *Letter Concerning Toleration*) that it be practiced in the church or temple, not in the arena of political action. Both believed that introducing irreconcilable personal, religious preferences into the so-called public square was a recipe for stalemate, or worse. Following this analysis, the Enlightenment proposed a pragmatic solution: Religious opinions were to be kept out of the public square. This view, subsequently adopted by the writers of the US Constitution, meant that, while religious liberty was to be protected, "assertions of religious authorities" had to be submitted to "the critical scrutiny of common sense and reason."[34] Rorty called this arrangement the "Jeffersonian compromise."

The founders of bioethics reached their own "Jeffersonian compromise" in order to appeal to as wide an audience as possible. Their goal, after all, was to propose methodology friendly to the theologian and the moral philosopher, the conservative and the liberal, the scientist and the non-scientist, the physician and the patient. And so, like the Enlightenment thinkers, they too adopted the view that the idiom of any particular religion or philosophy was not only inappropriate for shaping policy in a secular, pluralistic society, but potentially divisive—a "conversation stopper," to use Rorty's picturesque phrase. Only "publicly acceptable reasons" would provide the desired conceptual framework of universal appeal.

The requisite language of publicly acceptable reasons meant that, while theologians such as Ramsey could make contributions in their own terms, ultimately their language and arguments would get translated into secular terms in ways acceptable to them. What couldn't be so secularized was to be considered private and personal and, therefore, inappropriate for social and public policy. By so channeling public awareness of bioethics through the language of ethics or culture, the federal Belmont Commission did maintain religious and philosophical neutrality. But the commission's methodology also had the effect of marginalizing religious questions, analysis, and insight about many bioethical issues. "The result," says biochemist/philosopher Dianne N. Irving, "was the secularization of both theology and philosophy for public policy purposes."[35]

A few years before his death in 2007, Rorty, perhaps the preeminent cultural philosopher of his time, allowed that the "'compromise' between the Enlightenment and religion is now considered to be itself a public issue which is 'open to continual renegotiation.'"[36] What this "renegotiation" means for bioethics is something we'll leave for this book's

Conclusion. Suffice it here to observe that today, some thirty years after the commission issued its Belmont Report of 1979, the "Jeffersonian compromise" that produced the trade-off of religious neutrality for religious integrity has, itself, become, a political flashpoint, with conservative and liberal factions, both within and without religion, openly disagreeing about the role of religion in public life and the precise meaning of "separation of church and state."[37]

CONCLUSIONS

At the birth of bioethics, the private/public separation that today is being rethought seemed eminently reasonable, prudent, and even necessary. Not only did it enable the founders to converse, it helped them to define common values and ideals that, though discernible in religion, were not based exclusively on the principles of any one religion. Privatizing religion, then, not only seemed tasteful, it helped the founders speak the same language, which was, essentially, the language of the Enlightenment.[38]

Recall that during the Enlightenment, tolerance, rationality, self-determination, and change replaced tyranny, authority, community and tradition as core European values. Fueled by a belief in progress and democracy—in the capacity of individual self-determination to solve problems and make progress—these new values formed the mentality of the modern world, especially the "New World," where Enlightenment ideals largely shaped America's self-image and sense of destiny or purpose, at no time more so than at the peaking of secularism in the 1960s.[39]

As heirs to this Enlightenment thought, the pioneers of modern bioethics, theologian and philosopher alike, generally shared its optimistic belief in the capacity of reason to illuminate universal understanding and resolution of the stubborn moral problems posed by modern medical science and

technology. As citizens and supporters of the exemplar liberal democracy, they accepted this nation's basic principles and values, notably individual freedom and tolerance of diverse viewpoints, as being compatible with religious faith and consistent with Judeo-Christian tradition. And as members of a federal commission, the trailblazers viewed their mission as drafting public policy, which in our society continues to mean "a *minimal*, lowest common denominator ethics capable, it is thought, of securing public consensus."[40]

The Belmont Commission implicitly endorsed, then, political pluralism, that is, "the conviction that legitimate authority is multiple rather than singular." Commission members agreed "no one locus of authority, secular or religious, individual or collaborative, enjoys a comprehensive priority over the rest."[41] Unsurprisingly, the founders set aside as private and personal the potentially divisive issue of transcendent moral authority or truth, as to its existence, nature, and role in the fledgling field of bioethics. They discounted "the need to put ethics within the larger framework of an interpretation of life and human destiny," the very essence of religious belief.[42]

The upshot was the publication in the *Federal Register* of April 18, 1979, of a brief document whose secular principles, to be considered in the next chapter, came to define bioethics.

CASES AND CONTROVERSIES

The Tuskegee Study

Lured by the offer of free medical care, about 600 black sharecroppers in Macon County, Alabama, became part of an experiment conducted from 1932 to 1972 by the US Public Health Service (PHS) working with the Tuskegee Institute to examine the impact of syphilis involving black men. It was called the "Tuskegee Study of Untreated Syphilis in the Negro Male."

Syphilis is a potentially deadly, sexually transmitted disease that can result in damage to the liver, heart, lungs, and brain; produce ulcerated skin; and lead to dementia. The Tuskegee subjects, most of whom were illiterate, were not told that they had syphilis, but that they were being treated for "bad blood," a local term used to describe several ailments, including syphilis, anemia, and fatigue. In exchange for taking part in the study, the men received free medical exams, free meals, and burial insurance. Although originally projected to last six months, the study actually went on for forty years.

Even though treatment for syphilis was available in the form of arsenic and bismuth before 1945 and penicillin afterward, the men were not given either treatment during the course of the study. Indeed, their local physicians were instructed not to treat them with penicillin, even to feign treatment, such as by giving them aspirin. The researchers also worked with the local draft board to prevent the subjects of the study from being drafted for World War II, because as soldiers they would have been tested for syphilis and properly treated if they had the disease.

In 1966, Peter Buxtun, a young college graduate who was working in San Francisco as a venereal disease investigator for PHS, learned of the study and began to ask uncomfortable questions. Although Buxtun's concerns led to an investigation by the Centers for Disease Control, the CDC concluded that the study should go on. Subsequently, Buxtun told a reporter about the Tuskegee study, and in July 1972 the Associated Press story was headline news, triggering a public outcry that forced the Assistant Secretary for Health and Scientific Affairs to appoint an Ad Hoc Advisory Panel to review the study.

The panel had nine members from the fields of medicine, law, religion, labor, education, health administration, and public affairs. It found that the men had agreed freely to be examined and treated. However, there was no evidence that researchers had informed them of the study or its real purpose. In fact,

the men had been misled and had not been given all the facts required to provide informed consent. They were never given adequate treatment for their disease, even after 1947 when penicillin became the standard treatment for syphilis. The advisory panel also found nothing to show that subjects were ever given the choice of quitting the study, even when this new, highly effective treatment became widely used. The panel concluded the study was "ethically unjustified."

In the summer of 1973, a class-action lawsuit was filed on behalf of the study participants and their families. In 1974, a $10 million out-of-court settlement was reached. As part of the settlement, the US government promised to give lifetime medical benefits and burial services to all living participants. The Tuskegee Health Benefit Program (THBP) was established to provide these services. In 1975, wives, widows, and offspring were added to the program. In 1995, the program was expanded to include health as well as medical benefits. The CDC was given responsibility for the program, where it remains today in the National Center for HIV/AIDS, Viral Hepatitis, STD, and TB Prevention. The last study participant died in January 2004. The last widow receiving THBP benefits died in January 2009. There are sixteen offspring currently receiving medical and health benefits.

On May 16, 1997, at a special White House ceremony, President Clinton apologized to the Tuskegee participants and their families on behalf of the federal government. In attendance were eight surviving subjects, ranging in ages from 87 to 110. "What the United States did was shameful, and I am sorry," President Clinton said.[43,44]

Questions for Analysis

1. The PHS defended the study as necessary because, with the availability of antibiotics, researchers would never again be able to study the long-term effects of syphilis. Do you think the end justified the means?

2. Evaluate the morality of the study from the perspectives of natural law (religious and secular), utilitarianism, and Kant's ethics.

3. Although many articles were published about the Tuskegee study between 1932 and 1966, not a single one mentioned anything about the ethics of the investigations. Today we probably find it shocking that a 1936 article even referred to the men as "the material included" in the study. Can

(Continued)

CASES AND CONTROVERSIES (CONTINUED)

you think of things occurring today at home or abroad that years from now might shock generations about our moral insensibilities?

4. As the federal government didn't require that subjects in experiments give written informed consent to participate in studies until the mid-1960s, is it fair to judge the Tuskegee Study by today's standards?

5. Today African Americans are under-represented as organ donors and under-represented as individuals who donate blood. In the wake of the terrorist attacks of 9/11, it was reported that many African-American postal workers were reluctant to follow recommendations of the US Centers for Disease Control after being exposed to anthrax. Do you think that apparent African-American

mistrust of the medical community could be part of the Tuskegee legacy? What about the conspiratorial theories about the origins of AIDS in the black community; or, more recently in Georgia, about abortion being a decades-old tool to kill off African Americans?[45–50]

6. Henrietta Lacks (1920–1951) was a poor, illiterate African-American tobacco farmer who died of cervical cancer at 31, leaving behind five children and an extraordinary scientific legacy. What did this rather obscure figure contribute to medical research and why is it controversial? *The Immortal Life of Henrietta Lacks* (2010) by Rebecca Skloot is an excellent source for learning about Lacks' gift to medicine that wasn't a gift.

CASES AND CONTROVERSIES

The Death of Karen Ann Quinlan

On the evening of April 15, 1975, Karen Ann Quinlan (1954–1985) collapsed after ingesting a mix of alcohol and barbiturates. For at least two fifteen-minute periods, the 22-year-old woman ceased breathing. When she failed to respond to mouth-to-mouth resuscitation, paramedics took her by ambulance to Newton Memorial Hospital in New Jersey. She had a temperature of 100 degrees, her pupils were unreactive, and she didn't respond even to deep pain. Examining physicians characterized Karen as being in a "chronic, persistent, vegetative state," and later it was determined that no form of treatment could restore her to cognitive life. After she was kept alive on a ventilator for several months without improvement, her parents, convinced that their daughter would not want to be so maintained, requested the hospital discontinue active care and allow her to die. When the hospital refused, Joseph Quinlan, a Catholic, asked to be appointed his daughter's legal guardian with the expressed purpose of discontinuing the use of the respirator. The hospital refused, and a series of widely publicized legal battles ensued. Eventually the Supreme Court of New Jersey granted Joseph Quinlan's request, and the respirator was turned off. However, artificial feeding was continued until June 11, 1985, when Karen Quinlan died of pneumonia at the age of thirty-one.

The New Jersey Supreme Court made several important points in *Quinlan* about formerly competent persons. One was that patients like Karen Ann Quinlan have a constitutionally protected privacy interest, based on liberty, in refusing unwanted medical care, even if that refusal leads to their deaths. Another was that others, called surrogates or proxies, might represent their interests. The Quinlan case also led directly to the development of living wills and advance directives, and to hospital ethics committees.

Questions for Analysis

1. What moral issues did *Quinlan* raise?

2. Discuss *Quinlan* in the context of Enlightenment values.

3. In *Quinlan* the court rejected the family's argument that the manner in which a dying person chooses to die is a religious act entitled to First Amendment protection. Philosopher Ronald Dworkin in his book *Life's Dominion* characterizes such a life-altering decision as "quintessentially religious" and entitled to First Amendment protection.[51] Which is it, in your opinion?

4. Discuss the impact of a strong belief in God on an ethics committee member's ability to consult, educate, advise, and recommend choices in difficult clinical situations.[52]

CASES AND CONTROVERSIES

Surrogate Mother Elizabeth Kane

In 1976 attorney Noel Keane, who is generally recognized as the creator of the legal idea of surrogate motherhood, arranged the first formal agreement between a couple and a surrogate mother in the United States. Three years later, Elizabeth Kane, a housewife from Pekin, Illinois, became the first public case of a surrogate-for-hire. Responding to a classified ad placed by a Kentucky couple advertising that they wanted a woman to give birth to a child for them after becoming artificially inseminated with the husband's sperm, Kane, a mother of three, answered the ad. In an unprecedented legal arrangement, she agreed to relinquish all rights to the baby at birth. For her services, she was to receive $10,000. It was thus that on November 9, 1980, Elizabeth Kane, a pseudonym, gave birth to an 8-pound, 10 ounce baby boy in the maternity ward of Audubon Hospital in Louisville, Kentucky.

Only a month after the birth, Kane, 37, admitted in an exclusive interview with *People* magazine, itself only six years old at the time, that her experience had not been simple or easy. Her friends and family questioned her judgment in carrying a stranger's child, while theologians, ethicists, and lawyers debated the implications of surrogate birth. She admitted to empathizing with relatives and friends who were childless and often wondered why she couldn't bear a child for one of them. When she read the ad placed by the Louisville couple, she said she felt "an overwhelming desire to help."

Kane's husband, David, was at first less enthusiastic, but he was kind and thoughtful throughout the pregnancy. Kane reported that they said nothing to anyone for almost two months, and when they eventually told their immediate families, his was supportive, hers less so. "My mother has been in touch since," Kane said, "writing long, chatty letters that never mention the baby. It's as if I had a disease, not a pregnancy." Kane expressed concern that the strains with her family might be beyond repair.

Then there were Kane's own three children, the eldest an eleven-year-old daughter. When the news came out that Kane was accepting the $10,000 fee, she said the children were taunted at school with remarks like, "What's the going price of a baby today?" Their friends stopped coming around and playing with them. "So there were problems," she told *People*, "but I

always knew I was doing the right thing, as a woman and a Christian."

After sixteen hours of labor, the baby was born. David, who had studied Lamaze and had learned the breathing, soothed Kane during the delivery. Kane said she hardly noticed the presence of the baby's parents.

> All I could concentrate on was the baby's head as he emerged. "He's beautiful," was my first thought, "and large." He was also a stranger. He didn't look like any of my other children. The parents, who had been watching in sterile gowns and masks, came over to the table and we all babbled excitedly as new parents would. His mother said to her husband, "He looks just like you." Then she came over to the table and hugged me. There were tears in her eyes and she said, "Thank you for my baby. He's so beautiful." I asked the new mother if it was all right if I held him, and she looked sort of surprised and said, "Of course." That was the last time I held him, and I never nursed him.

Kane concluded the interview affirming that all of them—she, husband, and children—would do it again. "My hope is that this child will be loved as I love my children, that his parents will encourage him and guide him. I don't ever want his mother to feel that she has to share him with someone else. She is his mother. My part is over."

In 1988, eight years after giving this interview, Elizabeth Kane published *Birth Mother*, an account in diary form about her experiences. In the book she wrote that, in retrospect, she felt manipulated by her doctor, her lawyer, and even her minister, and acknowledged a despondency that eventually affected her. Kane is currently an active member of the National Coalition Against Surrogacy.[53]

Questions for Analysis

1. Because Kane's arrangement involved payment, many of the social concerns at the time veered toward the commercial aspects of the arrangement. What do you think some of those concerns were?

2. Even where no payments were involved, analysts of the day said that surrogacy raised many

(Continued)

CASES AND CONTROVERSIES (CONTINUED)

difficult moral and legal problems. What would some of them be?

3. What were some of the basic ideas about motherhood that Kane called into question?

4. What does your faith tradition teach about surrogate mothering?

5. Surrogacy is far less the spectacle today that it was thirty years ago. Nevertheless, do you think that the culture still tends to stereotype surrogates?

6. Evaluate surrogacy from the perspectives of natural law, utilitarianism, and Kant's ethics.

REFERENCES

1. Kathy Davis, "Translating *Our Bodies, Ourselves*," *The European Journal of Women's Studies,* London: SAGE Publications, p. 223. Retrieved April 15, 2008, from www.ourbodiesourselves.org/about/davis.asp.

2. Molly M. Ginty, "Our Bodies, Ourselves Turns 35 Today," *We News,* May 4, 2004. Retrieved April 25, 2008, from http://www.womensenews.org/article.cfm/dyn/aid/1820.

3. Davis, p. 224.

4. Amy L. Fairchild,, "Leprosy, Domesticity, and Patient Protest: The Social Context of A Patients' Rights Movement in Mid-Century America," *Journal of Social History,* Summer, 2006, pp. 1011–1043.

5. Albert R. Jonsen, *The Birth of Bioethics,* New York: Oxford University Press, 1998, pp. ix–x.

6. David Walleschinsky and Irving Wallace, *The People's Almanac,* New York: Doubleday, 1975. Retrieved May 10, 2009, from www.trivia-library.com/a/first-human-heart-transplant.htm.

7. Jonsen p. 306.

8. James V. Lavery, Christine Grady, Elizabeth R. Wahl, and Ezekiel J. Emanuel, eds., *Ethical Issues in International Biomedical Research,* New York: Oxford University Press, 2007.

9. William Dicke, "Eugene Saenger Is Dead; Controversial Doctor, 90," *The New York Times,* October 11, 2007, p. C16.

10. Ezekiel Emanuel, "Unequal Treatment," *The New York Times Book Review,* February 18, 2007, p. 18.

11. "Ethics and Clinical Research." *The New England Journal of Medicine,* June 16, 1966.

12. Susan Jacoby, *Freethinkers,* New York: Metropolitan Books, p. 343.

13. Ibid., pp. 342, 344.

14. Alan Wolf, "Political Science 358: American Culture War," Spring 2008. Retrieved May 2, 2008, from www.bc.edu/centers/boisi/meta-elements/pdf/PO_358_Spring_2008.pdf.

15. Paul D. Simmons, "Religious Liberty and Abortion Policy: *Casey* as Catch-22," in *The Ethics of Abortion*, Robert M. Baird and Stuart E. Rosenbaum, eds., Amherst, NY: Prometheus Books, 2001. p. 152.

16. Simmons, p. 348.

17. Jonsen, p. ix.

18. Ibid., p. 397.

19. Courtney Campbell, "Religion and the Controversy of Human Cloning," *Second Opinion*, Chicago: Park Ridge Center, September 1999, p. 5.

20. Jonsen, p. 36.

21. Allen Verhey, ed., *Religion & Medical Ethics: Looking Back, Looking Forward,* Grand Rapids, MI: William B. Eerdmans Publishing Company, 1996, p. 11.

22. David Mackey, "Protestant Neo-Orthodoxy and Spirituality," *Philosophical Studies in Education,* 2005, pp. 45–52. Retrieved April 15, 2008, from www.ovpes.org/2004/Mackey.pdf.

23. Peter Steinfels, "New Book Reaffirms Depth of Changes Wrought by Vatican II," *The New York Times,* December 20, 2008, p. A19.

24. John W. O'Malley, *What Happened at Vatican II,* Cambridge, MA: Belknap/Harvard University, 2008.

25. Jonsen, p. 35.

26. David Smith, "Religion and the Roots of the Bioethics Revival," in *Religion & Medical Ethics,* Allen Verhey, ed., Grand Rapids, MI: William B. Eerdmans Publishing Company, 1996, p. 13.

27. Jonsen, p. 57.

28. Jonsen, p. 184.

29. Ibid., pp. 396–397.

30. George Weigel, "A Better Concept of Freedom," *First Things: A Monthly Journal of Religion and Public Life*, March 1, 2002. Retrieved April 10, 2008, from http://goliath.ecnext.com/coms2/summary0199-1586478ITM.

31. Robert Price, "The Future Fate of Religions," 2004. Retrieved April 20, 2008, from http://www.robertmprice.mindvendor.com/art_future.htm

32. Stephen E. Lammers, "The Marginalization of Religious Voices in Bioethics," in *Religion & Medical Ethics*, Allen Verhey, ed., Grand Rapids, MI: William B. Eerdmans Publishing Company, 1996, pp. 19–43.

33. Richard Rorty, "Religion as Conversation-stopper," *Philosophy and Social Hope*, London: Penguin, 1999, pp. 168–174.

34. Simmons, p. 150.

35. Dianne N. Irving, "The Bioethics Mess," *Crisis Magazine*, May, 2001. Retrieved April 10, 2008, from http://www.lifeissues.net/writers/irv/irv_37bioethicsmess.html.

36. Richard Rorty, "Religion in the Public Square: A Reconsideration," *Journal of Religious Ethics*, Spring, 2003, pp. 141–149.

37. Peter S. Wenz, *Abortion Rights as Religious Freedom*, Philadelphia: Temple University Press, 1992, p. 112.

38. Lammers, p. 23.

39. Paul Brians, "The Enlightenment," May 18, 2000. Retrieved March 12, 2008, from http://www.wsu.edu/~brians/hum_303/enlightenment.html.

40. Gilbert Meilander, *Bioethics: A Primer for Christians*, Grand Rapids, MI: William B. Eerdmans Publishing Company, 2005, p. xi.

41. Ed Kromer, "Two Views on Religion in Liberal Democracy," *McGill Reporter*, October 24, 2002. Retrieved April 10, 2008, from http://www.mcgill.ca/reporter/35/04/beatty/.

42. Daniel Callahan, "Dialogue: Religion and Bioethics," *Lahey Clinic Medical Ethical Newsletter*, Winter, 2000. Retrieved April 11, 2008, from http://lahey.org/NewsPubs/Publications/Ethics/JournalWinter2000/Journal_Winter2000_Dialogue.asp.

43. Jean Heller, "Syphilis Victims in the U.S. Study Went Untreated for 40 Years," *The New York Times*, July 26, 1972, p. 1.

44. Shamin M. Baker, Otis W. Brawley, and Leonard S. Marks, "Effects of Untreated Syphilis in the Negro Male, 1932 to 1972: A Closure Comes to the Tuskegee Study, 2004," *Urology*, June 2005, pp. 1259–1262. Retrieved September 1, 2008, from www.usrf.org/uro-video/Tuskegee_2004/Tuskegee_study.pdf. http://www.archives.gov/southeast/exhibit/6.php)

45. Cheryl J. Sanders, "Religion and Ethical Decision Making in the African Community: Bioterrorism and the Black Postal Workers," in Lawrence Prograis, Jr., and Edmund D. Pellegrino, *African American Bioethics: Culture, Race, and Identity*, Washington, DC: Georgetown University Press, 2007, pp. 93–104.

46. A.V.N. Gamble, "Under the Shadow of Tuskegee: African Americans and Healthcare," *American Journal of Public Health* 87 (11), pp. 1173–1178.

47. Peter A. Clark, SJ, "Prejudice and the Medical Profession," *Health Progress*, September–October 2003, pp. 12–23.

48. Centers for Disease Control and Prevention, "U.S. Public Health Service Syphilis Study at Tuskegee." Retrieved April 25, 2009, from www.cdc.gov/tuskegee/timeline.htm.

49. Kennedy School of Ethics, "High School Bioethics Curriculum Project," Georgetown University. Retrieved April 23, 3009, from http://highschoolbioethics.georgetown.edu.

50. Shaila Dewan, "To Court Blacks, Foes of Abortion Make Racial Case," *The New York Times*, February 26, 2010. Retrieved March 1, 2010, from http://www.nytimes.com/2010/02/27/us/27race.html.

51. Winthrop Thies, "The Ethical Equivalence of Refusal of Treatment, PAD and Euthanasia," *Compassion & Choices*. Retrieved May 10, 2009, from http://compassionandchoicesnj.org/papers/equivalent.php.

52. Richard E. Thompson, "Is God Happy with the Ethics Committee?" *BNET*, July–August 2007. Retrieved May 10, 2009, from http://findarticles.com/p/articles/mi_m0843/is_4_33/ai_n19394970/.

53. Elizabeth Kane, "Surrogate Mother Elizabeth Kane Delivers Her 'Gift of Love'—Then Kisses Her Baby Goodbye," *People*, December 8, 1980. Retrieved April 17, 2009, from www.people.com/people/archive/article/0,20078051,00.html.

Chapter 4

The Basic Principles of Bioethics

The brief document that appeared in the *Federal Register* on April 18, 1979, was titled the *Belmont Report*.[1] Historically, the document represented still another of a long line of medical prayers, oaths, and codes of conduct that had been shaped by Greco-Roman and Judeo-Christian traditions. Still, the Belmont principles and guidelines for biomedical research signaled a dramatic shift away from traditional Hippocratic paternalism to patient autonomy.

HIPPOCRATIC PATERNALISM

According to the ethic of medical paternalism, it is the physician's prerogative to act in what she or he sees as the patient's best interest. Clinically, this means more attention ordinarily is given to the patient's care and outcomes, less to her needs, preferences, and rights.[2] Codifying this view, the *Oath of Hippocrates,* composed between 460–389 BCE, committed physicians to practice "for the benefit of the sick" according to their "ability and judgment." Toward this end, the oath pledged fidelity to Apollo, the Greek god of medicine, suggestive of the solemnity of the physician's commitment, as well as the historic and universal interconnection of medicine, spirituality, and religion.

Until the 1960s, Hippocratic paternalism ruled Western medical ethics. It was only then that the notion of the "ideal physician" began to change, as physician power, rather than character, became the issue. As proper procedure began to rival correct conclusions in ethical importance, so too the question "Who is to decide?" became as important as "What is to be done?"[3] Increasingly, the ideal physician was the one who saw the doctor-patient relationship less patriarchal and more democratic, less about power exercising and more about power sharing. Although traditional dedication to the welfare of the patient and to a certain set of professional virtues remained important, the new model had the effect of blunting Hippocratic paternalism by impressing on physicians that, in the end, the choice of medical treatment was the patient's not theirs—even if that choice was medically imprudent.

The *Belmont Report* was a powerful impetus to this rethinking of the physician's role. Devoid of religious terminology and concepts, drafted largely by a philosopher (Tom Beauchamp), the report set forth an "objective, non-partisan, philosophical ethic"[4] and defined a range of patient rights, inspired by neglected needs, that came to be known as the Belmont principles. Originally intended as guidelines for human experimentation, these principles, as Jonsen says, soon "found their way into the general literature of the field and, in the process, grew from the principles underlying the conduct of research into the basic principles of bioethics."[5] With that, the age of medical paternalism—when doctors alone decided what was best for patients—was over. Here to stay was the age of patient autonomy—when patients would choose medical treatment.

THE BELMONT PRINCIPLES

The core of the *Belmont Report* were three principles—respect for persons, beneficence, and justice. These principles were, in effect, construed as extensions of two responsibilities: (1) the time-honored primary and overriding duty of physicians to patients, and (2) the state's responsibility to protect its members.

In both contexts, *patients* was (and remains) understood broadly as anyone who had or could have a medical condition for which he or she sought professional treatment or advice. Included were not only those receiving immediate treatment or care, but also anyone for whom treatments were being prepared or researched, that is, potentially everyone in society. By the same token, those treating patients was (and is) understood as including not merely physicians, but any personnel involved in the patient's treatment, including researchers and those charged with organizing and managing the health system.[6]

While acknowledging the relevancy of other principles, the Belmont commissioners felt that respect for persons, beneficence, and justice warranted the status of fundamental principles, given their high regard in Western culture. Comprising a veritable moral constitution of bioethics, these core principles received their definitive formulation and development by Beauchamp and religious scholar James Childress in their 1979 publication, *Principles of Biomedical Ethics*, where the original triad was cast as a quartet: autonomy, nonmaleficence (non-injury), beneficence, and justice. To the authors and other leaders in the emerging field of

bioethics, these four principles constituted an appealing philosophical framework for efficiently analyzing bioethical cases and provided a rational structure for justifying moral judgments. Their eminently rational or "self-evident value" is still touted, as shown in this description appearing on the ethics page of a medical school Website:

> ... the notion that the physician "ought not to harm" [nonmaleficence] any patient appears to be convincing to rational persons. Or, the idea that the physician should develop a care plan designed to provide the most "benefit" to the patient in terms of other competing alternatives [beneficence], seems self-evident. Further, before implementing the medical care plan, it is now commonly accepted that the patient must indicate a willingness to accept the proposed treatment, if the patient is cognitively capable of doing so [autonomy]. Finally, medical benefits should be dispensed fairly, so that people with similar needs and in similar circumstances will be treated with fairness [justice].[7]

From their inception, all of the Belmont principles were to be taken into account when applicable in a case, and no one of them was supposed to overrule the other. Each was *prima facie*, meaning always binding unless in conflict with other duties, when a rational calculation had to be made to determine which of the conflicting duties was the weightier and was, therefore, the actual duty. Illustrative is this simple example of a conflict between nonmaleficence and beneficence, again cited by the same medical school:

> ... [C]onsider a patient diagnosed with an acutely infected appendix. Our medical goal should be to provide the greatest benefit to the patient, an indication for immediate surgery [beneficence]. On the other hand, surgery and general anesthesia carry some small degree of risk to an otherwise healthy patient, and we are under an obligation "not to harm" the patient

[nonmaleficence]. Our rational calculus holds that the patient is in far greater danger from harm from a ruptured appendix if we do not act, than from the surgical procedure and anesthesia if we proceed quickly with surgery. In other words, we have a "prima facie" duty to both benefit the patient and to "avoid harming" the patient. We must balance the demands of these principles by determining which carries more weight in the particular case to determine what our actual duty is.[8]

In large part, the eminent reasonableness of the principles was attributable to their leading secular sources of the eighteenth and nineteenth centuries, particularly Kant and Mill; and, in the twentieth century, the American philosopher John Rawls (1921–2002), who, borrowing from Kant, had revitalized social contract theory just a few years earlier, in his influential work, *A Theory of Justice* (1971).[9] At the same time, religious tradition supported the Belmont principles, thereby offering the overlapping consensus between religious and secular values discussed in Chapter 3.

Although initially intended to guide medical research involving human subjects, the *Belmont Report* quickly won general acceptance as proposing applicable nonsectarian standards for a pluralistic society doing bioethical analysis. Its debt to earlier codes of medical conduct notwithstanding, "principlism," as the new method came to be known, effectively supplanted its predecessors and soon became the dominant method for doing bioethics, the "shared

---

BIOETHICS ACROSS CULTURES

Transcultural Human Rights

According to the Preamble to the World Health Organization Constitution, "The enjoyment of the highest attainable standard of health is one of the fundamental rights of every human being." Since 1975 the Transcultural Nursing Society (TNS) has endeavored to implement this statement by bringing culturally competent nurses and health care providers to people of diverse and similar cultures. Its global health care outreach is based on the following Statement of Human Rights:

Regardless of race, ethnicity, national origin, religious and philosophical beliefs, gender, sexual orientation, cultural values, age, and other diversities, people have the following universal human rights:

- Access to quality care including qualified healthcare professionals, organizations and resources
- Access to culturally and linguistically competent healthcare providers
- Respectful care with recognition for personal dignity, privacy and confidentiality
- Informed participation in one's own healthcare
- Involvement of family members and significant others in healthcare delivery and decision making if desired by the care recipient

- Accept or refuse care and negotiate with healthcare providers to achieve culturally congruent care
- Freedom from healthcare treatments that involve coercion, bribery and illicit activities that place one's well-being at risk
- Receive care in an environment in which physical, psychological, spiritual and cultural safety is assured for the person and his/her family, and significant others
- Receive care without putting one's self or loved ones in jeopardy or harm's way

(SOURCE: Dr. Margaret Andrews, et al, "Position Statement on Human Rights." *Transcultural Nursing* Society, 2008 Retrieved June 8, 2009, from http://www.tcns.org/tcnshumanrights.shtml)

Question

Do you agree with the Preamble of the WHO Constitution and the TNS Statement of Human Rights? TNS doesn't see its work as extending charity but meeting an obligation. Do you think that meeting the worldwide crisis in health and health care is best viewed as charity or obligation? Explain by reference to religious and secular moral principles.

language" of all parties to bioethical discourse, in both the professional and public realms. Even today the principles of autonomy, nonmaleficence, beneficence, and justice are virtually synonymous with "bioethics."

AUTONOMY

Defined as a freedom from interference enjoyed by the mentally competent, autonomy figured prominently in what Jonsen calls "the first defining moment for bioethics,"[10] the debate over human experimentation. At issue was the proper balance of social interests and those of autonomous persons as research subjects. The debate forced bioethics to answer the following question: "Should the social good to which the results of biomedical experimentation contributed overrule the freedom, wishes, and choices of individuals?"[11] The *Belmont Report* came down decisively on the side of "respect for autonomy," which it defined as giving "weight to autonomous persons'" considered opinions and choices while refraining from obstructing their actions unless they are clearly detrimental to others.

For its understanding of "respect for autonomy," the report borrowed from Kant, the "philosopher of autonomy," particularly his notion of respect for humans as "ends in themselves" capable of determining their own destinies. Recall that, according to Kant, as autonomous beings we make choices based upon what we consider the best reasons, including our own values, goals, and priorities. Showing respect for persons acknowledges this. It means treating others as capable of choosing, and not interfering with their choices. In terms of Kant's Categorical Imperative, respecting autonomy follows the principle of humanity: that we always treat others as ends in themselves, never merely as means to our own ends. Respecting autonomy also honors the principle of reciprocity: that we treat others as we would want to be treated, that is, showing the same respect for their reasons for acting as we feel our own deserve.

Autonomy became firmly fixed among the principles of bioethics with the publication of *Principles of Biomedical Ethics*, in which authors

Beauchamp and Childress cast it as "a form of personal liberty of action where the individual determines his or her own course of action in accordance with a plan chosen by himself or herself."[12] A later edition defined autonomy in terms of "freedom from external constraint" and associated it with the presence of critical mental capacities such as understanding, intending, and voluntary decision capacity. Significantly, respecting autonomy, the authors explained, means recognizing "with due appreciation" individuals' own considered value judgment and outlooks, even when they appear mistaken. In this way, as Jonsen notes, Beauchamp and Childress fused the Kantian notion of respect for persons with Mill's and Berlin's notion of liberty as freedom from interference in matters strictly personal and private, or actions that don't infringe on the liberty of others. So conceived, the principle of autonomy soon came to mean simply that "persons should be free to perform whatever action he wishes—even if it involves serious risk for the agent and even if others consider it to be foolish."[13]

Although the principle of patient autonomy was intended to safeguard free treatment choice, it also recognized that not every patient was capable of exercising that choice, because some lacked the requisite mental capacities. So, the principle was intended not only to respect mentally able individuals as autonomous agents but also to protect those not mentally able—such as children or those declared legally or medically mentally incompetent—by treating them paternalistically. As depicted in the report, then, autonomy implied two separate moral requirements that subsequently have come to govern medical matters: freedom and protection. Thus, the first requirement of autonomy is to acknowledge the freedom of treatment choice of the mentally able patient; the second is to protect those with diminished mental ability by acting in what's thought to be their best medical interests.

It is notable that, consistent with the "Jeffersonian compromise," (see Chapter 3), the *Belmont Report* separated autonomy from any notion of goodness or obligation motivated by either philosophy or religion. It identified autonomy strictly with human will, while remaining silent about how the self-directed will was to be used. For Aristotle,

Aquinas, and Kant, on the other hand, autonomy always was to be directed toward some ultimate good, such as happiness, union with God, or rationality. In each of these traditions, when we don't use our autonomy as prescribed, we sin, that is, break either religious or moral law. This makes immorality the product of misdirected autonomy, a distinct theme of today's religious and social conservatives. By contrast, the new secular bioethics submitted no comparable notion of ultimate good and how to pursue it, derived from a view of humanity. In that sense, the *Belmont Report* left autonomy philosophically ungrounded. What it offered instead of a moral theory embracing a conception of goodness and conduct were guidelines. This didn't mean, however, that the Belmont commissioners viewed the autonomy principle as a guideline without moral limits.

Moral Limits

It is, perhaps, commonplace today to view personal autonomy as self-authenticatingly the highest good, the ultimate source of all value, and the chief goal of all human action. Although early on and increasingly, bioethics tacked in this direction, the commissioners never conceived of autonomy as an absolute right, any more than did Kant, for whom a robust respect for the interests of others was integral to being rational. Recall (from Ch. 2) that Kant's truly rational being was the social being. This tight connection between the rational and social being cuts to the conception of autonomy that the commissioners seemed to have in mind: moral autonomy as having a moral limit and itself being limited.[14]

As a moral limit, autonomy was to function as a constraint on certain actions, such as medically treating people against their express wishes. By the same token, being limited in weight and scope, autonomy was sometimes to be constrained by social considerations. A person with a contagious disease, for example, could not refuse therapy and by so doing endanger the public well-being. From the outset, then, the commissioners viewed the health, welfare, or rights of others as the natural limits of autonomy.[15]

Also worth remembering is what *OBOS* was calling attention to: paternalistic medicine. According to Veatch, at the birth of bioethics "the dominant moral problem in medicine was a paternalistic physician who forced life-prolonging technologies on a patient or withheld bad news or treated without real consent."[16] For the commissioners, then, the function of autonomy was to liberate the patient from the oppression of such a physician. This gave autonomy a limited role designed to fulfill the transient, narrow purpose of challenging a smug, arrogant paternalism.

Still, drawing the line between individual freedom and community interest is not always as easy as in the matter of a contagious disease or an overweening medical paternalism. *Should a competent, pregnant woman be allowed abortion on demand? Should a couple be permitted to design the baby they want? Is a competent patient entitled to medical treatment that physicians deem futile? Should a terminally ill patient be granted a mercy death? Should patients with life-threatening or untreatable diseases have access to experimental drugs that haven't been established as safe and effective? Should couples be allowed to screen embryos for genes that raise the risk of developing cancer or to select the sex of their child?*

Like these, virtually all of today's bioethical controversies pit freedom of choice, of individual or scientist, against the nature of the choice, regarding its social or religious implications. *Just what limitations ought be placed on individual autonomy?* With the emergence of autonomy as the preeminent bioethical principle, this question has come to dominate bioethical debates. Indeed, it has been suggested that the first salvo of the culture war was a spirited defense of individual autonomy against traditional religious morality that occurred when bioethics was just starting to take shape. As political scientist Alan Wolfe opines:

> There is no precise date at which the American culture war began, but the best guess would be in 1973, when the U.S. Supreme Court decided *Roe v. Wade*. Women, the Court essentially ruled, had the right to control their own bodies, especially after the first trimester of a

pregnancy, and no state could refuse to allow them access to abortion. In thereby choosing the importance of individual autonomy over moral prohibitions rooted in many religious beliefs, the Court's decision contributed to the mobilization of groups determined to overrule the decision or at least to limit its applicability.[17]

In the spirit of the "Jeffersonian compromise," the Belmont Commission, like the high court in *Roe*, chose "the importance of individual autonomy over moral prohibitions rooted in many religious [or philosophical] beliefs." Indeed, to its members, both theologians and philosophers, the principle of autonomy not only addressed the problem of human experimentation, its broad application recommended it as a core principle of bioethics.

Secular and Religious Appeal

As a requisite of human liberty, presupposition of non-sectarian ethics, basis for contractarian theory, and hallmark of a pluralistic society, the principle of autonomy clearly played a vital role in the development of secular ethical and political theory. This made it inherently appealing to the Belmont Commission's philosophers.

For the theologians, autonomy underscored the theological doctrine about the sacredness of the individual. By way of illustration, consider the opening pages of Ramsey's powerful 1970 publication, *Patient as Person,* in which the conservative Protestant theologian and ethicist wrote:

> Just as man is a sacredness in the social and political order, so he is a sacredness in the natural, biological order.... The sanctity of human life prevents ultimate trespass upon him even for the sake of treating his bodily life, or for the sake of others who are also only a sacredness in their bodily lives.[18]

Ramsey's theological belief in the sanctity of human life was hardly Kantian autonomy. As Jonsen notes, "[I]t would take Renaissance and Enlightenment thought to reach Kant's autonomy,

in which rational beings are 'self legislators' and, further, even creators of their own moral values." Still, as a secular remnant of their own belief in the sanctity of the individual person, the principle of autonomy struck a cord with the commission's theologian members.[19] It also appealed to them in another respect.

Because autonomy is about self-governance or self-rule, it's at the heart of the liberal, democratic state. It is, more specifically, about what a liberal democracy seeks to safeguard: matters of conscience, most notably in this context: *religious* belief. Thus if, as a practical matter of religious belief, a mentally able adult refuses life-saving surgery or blood, the principle of autonomy supports his right to choose. Jehovah's Witnesses, for example, base their belief that "true Christians will not accept a blood transfusion" mainly on two biblical passages, Leviticus 17:13, 14 and Acts 21:25. Regardless of how recklessly imprudent this may appear to most, to reprise Beauchamp and Childress, this religious conviction is safeguarded by law and medicine, even if death will result. (Consistent with autonomy's second requirement, protection of the mentally unable, health authorities and courts may intervene on behalf of children whose parents, for religious reasons, are denying them life-saving medical treatment.) From a secular perspective, then, autonomy or self-determination is fundamental to democracy, while from a religious perspective it's fundamental to freedom of conscience and its expression. Both aspects appealed to the Belmont commissioners.

NONMALEFICENCE

The principle of nonmaleficence, or non-injury, basically requires of physicians that they not intentionally create a needless harm or injury to the patient by acts of commission or omission. In other words, physicians must not harm patients either by what they do or don't do.

Curiously, the familiar dictum "First do no harm" never appears in the famous Hippocratic Oath, although it is often associated with Hippocrates.

Even if Hippocrates never said it, it's generally acknowledged that the "Father of Medicine" in the West considered the injunction "Strive to help, but above all, do no harm" the ruling maxim of medical ethics. So did all other medical ethicists and medical oaths, codes, and prayers up to the founding of modern bioethics, when personal autonomy gained prominence.

Nonmaleficence is closely related to two legal concepts: medical negligence and due care. *Medical negligence* involves a violation of nonmaleficence that results in serious harm to the patient, a determination that hinges on the concept of due care. Broadly speaking, *due care* refers to the care or quality of care that a reasonable person would exercise under the circumstances. Thus, a physician may be morally and legally negligent for failing to meet the standards of due care should she breach a duty to a patient and, as a result, the patient experiences harm.

As with autonomy, the notorious human experiments cited in Chapter 3 gave the Belmont commissioners ample reason to be concerned with nonmaleficence, aside from its deep-rooted secular and religious traditions. Also still fresh in their minds was the Nuremberg trial of physicians, which revealed evidence of the sadistic human experimentation of Josef Mengele (1911–1979) upon Jews, homosexuals, and others deemed "diseased," according to the warped eugenics of Adolf Hitler (1889–1945).

Also not lost on the commissioners was the strong utilitarian bias of medical research in the decades after World War II, with the US government and pharmaceutical industry teaming up to enlist vulnerable people in socially beneficial experiments involving "new vaccines, antibiotics and other drugs, and to test radiation and other toxicities."[20] The anticipated benefits for society were considered reason enough for subordinating the interests of the human subjects, prompting the following observation from the medical historian and influential public health official Walsh McDermott (1900–1981) at a 1967 colloquium:

"We have seen large social payoffs from certain payoffs from certain experiments in humans…. We could no longer maintain, in strict honesty, that in the study of disease the interest of the individuals are invariably paramount."[21]

Certainly, ethical medical research remains an ongoing issue.[22,23] But, nowadays, substantial harm results from the improper treatment of disease and patients. In fact, medical errors are one of the nation's leading causes of death and injury today, estimated to result in close to 100,000 annual deaths, according to the landmark 1999 *Institute of Medicine Report: To Err Is Human: Building a Safer Health System*. Fatalities from medication errors alone—more than 7,000 annually and often caused by illegible physician handwriting—exceed those from workplace injuries. Significantly, the *IMR* found that the majority of medical errors are not the result of "individual recklessness" but from failed systems and procedures, that is, basic flaws in the way the system is organized. "These stunningly high rates of medical errors—resulting in deaths, permanent disability, and unnecessary suffering—are simply unacceptable in a medical system that promises first to 'do no harm,'" said the report's author, William Richardson.[24–26] Sometimes it's a lifesaving tool that turns deadly. A 2010 *New York Times* investigative piece reported that while accurate in attacking tumors, powerful new technology such as linear accelerators have also created avenues for error—"through software flaws, faulty programming, poor safety procedures or inadequate staffing and training." These errors can be life crippling or even fatal.[27]

The quality of care, or lack of it, in the nation's nursing homes offers another grim example of contemporary, systemic medical maleficence. Despite legislation passed in 1987 to improve care of the elderly (*Nursing Home Reform Act*), the United States has too many bad nursing homes and too few good ones. According to "Nursing Home Quality Monitor," a report published in the September 2006 issue of *Consumer Reports*, of 16,000 nursing homes analyzed for deficiencies in reports, staffing, and patient care indicators, such as decreased mobility of residents, only 9 percent could accurately be described as providing good care.

Cross-Cultural Care

In 2003, a national survey of resident physicians in their last year of training was conducted to determine whether the nation's future physician workforce felt sufficiently prepared to deliver quality care to diverse populations. The objectives of the survey were to assess the resident physicians' self-perceived levels of preparedness, assess the educational climate for cross-cultural training, and determine whether respondents received formal training and evaluation in cross-cultural care during their residency. Results of this study were published in *JAMA* (*Journal of the American Medical Association*) in 2005 and again reviewed in 2007.

The survey of over 2,000 residents found that nearly all of the respondents thought it was important to consider the patient's culture when providing care. Many residents felt that cross-cultural issues "often" resulted in negative consequences for clinical care, including longer office visits, patient noncompliance, delays obtaining consent, unnecessary tests, and lower quality of care. But many residents felt unprepared to deliver care to patients with specific characteristics likely to arise in cross-cultural situations. For example, more than one out of five residents felt unprepared to treat patients with "mistrust, cultural issues at odds with Western medicine (25%), or religious beliefs that affect care." Similarly, some residents felt unprepared to treat users of complementary medicine, new immigrants, or patients with limited English proficiency.

Most resident physicians—particularly those in emergency medicine, general surgery, and obstetrics/gynecology—reported receiving little or no instruction in cross-cultural skills beyond what is learned in medical school. Approximately half reported receiving minimal training in understanding how to address patients from different cultures or in identifying patient mistrust, relevant religious beliefs and cultural customs, and decision-making structure. Whereas family-medicine residents received more instruction than did those in any of the other six specialties, residents in general surgery and emergency medicine reported having very little instruction in cross-cultural skills. A total of 66 percent of residents had received little or no evaluation on cross-cultural aspects of doctor-patient communication. About 30 percent cited the lack of good role models as a problem, and 31 percent stated that they had no role models or mentors during their residencies who were good at providing cross-cultural care.

(SOURCE: J. R. Betancourt, J. S. Weissman, M. K. Kim et al., "Resident Physicians' Preparedness to Provide Cross-Cultural Care: Implications for Clinical Care and Medical Education Policy," *The Commonwealth Fund*, May 9, 2007. Retrieved April 17, 2009, from http://www.commonwealth fund.org/Content/Publications/Fund-Reports/2007/May/Resident-Physicians-Preparedness-to-Provide-Cross-Cultural-Care–Implications-for-Clinical-Care-and.aspx)

Question

The majority of residents expressed confidence that, when it came to managing common clinical problems and delivering services that would be expected of them in their medical careers, they were well prepared. Does it matter, then, that they lack cross-cultural preparedness? What are some of the implications of this study for clinical care and medical education?

BENEFICENCE

Besides directing them not to do harm, the Hippocratic tradition also said to physicians: "Strive to help," or act beneficently. The principle of beneficence enjoins physicians to maximize possible benefits, while minimizing possible harms to patients and the larger society.

Although Beauchamp and Childress individuated them, by tradition beneficence was taken to encompass nonmaleficence, which was how the *Belmont Report* handled it. So construed, beneficence can be placed on a continuum, with the negative obligation to avoid harm on one end and the positive duty to do good on the other. In between fall the duties of preventing and eliminating harm. In this Kantian configuration, the more pressing obligations are the ones that involve harm. Thus, first avoid harm, then prevent it, then eliminate it. After these come the positive duties to maximize possible benefits and minimize possible harms. This is why many of today's bioethicists understand beneficence as "doing or producing good by promoting happiness" and thus, "not much different from utilitarian happiness or the principle of utility."[28] (See Ch. 2 for the principle of utility.)

As with the other principles, the *Belmont Report* related beneficence to the realm of research involving human subjects. Thus, in the case of particular projects, it addressed (with harm in mind) potential injury to subjects, including children. More broadly, in the case of scientific research it stressed that members of the larger society are obliged to recognize the longer term benefits and risks that may result from the improvement of knowledge and from the development of novel medical, psychotherapeutic, and social procedures.

More than any of the other principles, the inclusion of beneficence reflected the historical importance of upright character and technical competence as the determinants of the ideal physician. Appropriately, then, beneficence continues to embrace acts of kindness or charity that go beyond strict obligation to avoid, prevent, or eliminate harm. The model doctor not only fulfills the letter of the law but its spirit as well. Like the Good Samaritan in the well-known New Testament parable, recounted by the physician/apostle Luke (Luke 10:29–37), a model doctor unhesitatingly renders aid to those in distress and works to promote the good of society. This traditional *ideal physician* shows compassion, mercy, kindness, and generosity. In acting virtuously she becomes a professional embodiment of neighborly love, thus expanding her circle of relationships to include more than merely her own patients.

At the same time, the principle of beneficence continues to focus attention on the moral importance of physicians' doing what they believe serves the best interests of patients, which involves more than a calculation of medical risks and benefits or the details of intervention options in a feverish climate of malpractice litigation. Against the rigors of a pressured practice, beneficence still reminds the physician of the original "call" to medicine—"the desire to make a difference in people's lives and the alleviation of pain and suffering."[29] This includes taking stock of the emotional, social, cultural, and spiritual aspects of the patient, almost in the ancient sense of physician as the doctor of the body and of the soul. As Leon Kass (see Ch. 3) wrote a year after the publication of the *Belmont Report*:

The physician, who is the knower of health and the numerous forms of its absence, who seeks to assist the healing power in the human body, also must tend particular, necessitous human beings who, in addition to their symptoms suffer from self concern and often fear and shame-about weakness, esteem, and the fragility of all that matters to them.[30]

It's worth noting that, in sharp distinction from the emphasis on autonomy of the new bioethics, the traditional, paternalistic Hippocratic model of medical ethics gave priority to beneficence. Given the parent/child configuration of their relationship, unanimity between physician and patient was presupposed. Thus, the patient was to assume that the physician would act in the patient's best interest, and the physician was to assume patient agreement with his professional assessment of the risks, benefits, and burdens of treatment. In short, trusting to beneficence or professional integrity, both parties tacitly agreed that doctor knew best. Unsurprisingly, then, autonomy was not even listed among the Hippocratic tradition's three defining principles: beneficence, nonmaleficence, and confidentiality. Neither was autonomy expressly mentioned in the AMA's first *Code of Ethics*, published in 1847.

Today's followers of this venerable tradition, such as Edmund Pellegrino and David Thomasma (1939–2002), the renowned team of physician and philosopher, explicate Hippocratic beneficence as "beneficence-in-trust." In so doing, they place patient autonomy within beneficence by centering autonomy in the patient's desire to accept appropriate clinical management.[31] In other words, some of those who would revive paternalism today (sometimes called "neo-paternalists") argue that the Hippocratic tradition, in fact, honors patient conscience and choice, but, properly in their view, always within a physician-patient relationship characterized by "mutual trust, respect for each other's integrity, and reasonableness in expectations and demands."[32] Thus, both becoming informed and giving consent for appropriate treatment are required.

BIOETHICS ACROSS CULTURES

Traditional Medicine for the Hmong

The United States recently has experienced a great surge in immigration, with one in five residents now a recent immigrant or a close relative of one, according to *The New York Times*. In Minneapolis alone, where Swedes and Norwegians once had separate hospitals, Hennepin County Medical Center (HCMC) spends $3 million a year on interpreters fluent in fifty languages to communicate effectively with foreign-born patients. Some of these patients resist conventional medical wisdom or practices, forcing changes in the hospital. For example, the objections of Somali women to having babies delivered by male doctors has led HCMC, gradually, to develop an obstetrical staff made up almost entirely of women.

One of the recurring issues in providing health care to immigrants is the clash between health care systems—the conflict between the rational, scientific biomedical model and the immigrants' emphasis on spiritual and non-physiological etiologies, or causes of disease. Actually, this tension between opposed health systems is not new in the United States.

America's secret war in Laos during the Vietnam era displaced hundreds of thousands of Hmong refugees, over 150,000 of whom eventually resettled in the United States. One of the most difficult aspects of displacement and resettlement for the Hmong has concerned health practices and beliefs stemming from its traditional animistic worldview. It's generally accepted among Hmong that the natural world consists of good, bad, and ancestral spirits, and that the physical and spiritual welfare of the living hangs delicately on their relationships and interactions with these spirits. Those who run afoul of the spirits fall ill and can only be made whole by a special healing practice, such as shamanism or supplicating powerful spirits.

Many of the Hmong's traditional healing practices have set up confrontations with US doctors, citizens, and government. At the same time, however, as the research of anthropologist Jacob Hickman has documented, "The Hmong ideology has adapted to include biomedical concepts of etiology and pathology, while retaining the core aspects of the traditional Hmong health system." The upshot, says the University of Chicago anthropologist, is an "integration of spiritual and biological causes" of illness that represents a "holistic medical perspective in the Hmong community." Hickman writes:

This has lead to a diagnostic system which must account for social, spiritual, and physical context, as well as changes and constancies in the course of the sickness or condition. Consequently, it is often difficult to assign an appropriate treatment to an illness, and the efficacy of the healing technique reveals additional information about the source of the problem. The integration of spiritual and biological causes constitutes a diverse, holistic medical perspective in the Hmong community, leading the Hmong to seek both traditional and modern medical practitioners as primary health care providers.

In 2009 Mercy Medical Center in Merced, California, became the first hospital in the country to recognize the cultural role of traditional healers like shamans. At Mercy, which serves a large Hmong population, shamans may perform nine ceremonies, including "soul calling" and "chanting in a voice not to exceed three decibels."

(SOURCE: Denise Grady, "Foreign Ways and War Scars Test U.S. Clinic," *The New York Times*, March 29, 2009, p. 1; Jacob R. Hickman, "Is It the Spirit or the Body? Syncretism of Health Beliefs Among Hmong Immigrants to Alaska," *National Association for the Practice of Anthropology, Bulletin* 27, 2005, pp. 176–195. Retrieved March 30, 2009, from orca.byu.edu/Reports/Journals/2004%20Final%20reports/FHSS/Hickman,%20Jacob%20Randall.doc.; Patricia Leigh Brown, "A Doctor for Disease, A Shaman for the Soul," *The New York Times*, September 20, 2009, p. 21.)

Question

Like many legal refugees coming to the United States from war zones around the world, the Hmong have a preference for healers who can address the spiritual in parallel with the physical health. This has led to a kind of "mix-and-match" approach to health-seeking behavior—choosing between either traditional medicine or modern medicine, depending on the nature of illness or health problem. Do you think that our health care system should accommodate both traditional and modern biomedical practice? Or should refugees and immigrants be expected and acculturated to alter their attitudes and behaviors to more closely resemble those of Americans? Which of the two approaches is more equitable?

It's also worth calling attention to the parallel view in religious traditions. Of the Jewish tradition, for example, physician Daniel Eisenberg writes:

> Judaism takes a paternalistic view of many human endeavors, including the practice of medicine. Since man was created in the image of G-d and his body is the property of the Creator, man is given only custodial rights to his body.... The secular emphasis on autonomy inescapably leads to the conclusion that the patient has the right to refuse any and all medical information. In Judaism, both becoming informed and giving consent for appropriate treatment are required....

And further:

> The situation is akin to a money manager entrusted with the funds of a client. He is obligated to research all reasonable investment options. After accumulating the necessary information, he MUST decide where to invest his client's money. He MUST invest the money because that is his mandate. Only if he feels that all investment options are unacceptable for his client, based on sound reasoning, may he leave the money as cash. Similarly, as the prudent steward of one's own body, one MUST acquaint oneself with all reasonable medical options, including inaction, before making a decision. But after evaluating all reasonable options, the Torah requires one to choose the sensible option, the one that the prudent steward would choose.[33]

To the founders of modern bioethics, however, the historic physician-patient relationship, characterized by competence and probity, and supported for centuries by medical tradition and religious texts, was a vestigial ideal of a mystified past. In their collective opinion, a smug and arrogant paternalism too willing to act on judgments of a patient's best interests without the patient's knowledge or consent needed to be countered with a healthy patient autonomy. Accordingly, in the spirit of the times, they placed choice of treatment with the patient, however unwise and ill-considered, and

not the physician, however upright and competent. As ethicist Janet Smith notes:

> The PRA [principle of respect for autonomy] clearly challenges paternalism by making patients responsible for choosing what care they receive. Whereas paternalism has been advocated as a means to ensure the best medical care for a patient, the widespread acceptance of the PRA stems from quite different concerns. It is advocated not so much as a means of restoring health, but rather as a means of ensuring good medical ethics.[34]

As an upshot, more than occasionally today, professional judgment or beneficence, clashes with patient autonomy, something we'll consider elsewhere.

JUSTICE

In addressing justice as a core ethical principle, the Belmont commissioners clearly had in mind what is called distributive justice. Distributive justice concerns the proper allocation or distribution of benefits and burdens in a society. "Who is to get what when there isn't enough for all?" is a classic question of distributive justice.

With regard to benefits and burdens, the *Belmont Report* (and Beauchamp and Childress) conceived of justice as "what is deserved," or "fairness in distribution." Thus, when people get what they deserve, that's considered just or fair; when they do not, that's considered unjust or unfair. Alternatively, justice requires that equals be treated equally. In other words, according to Belmont, in the absence of some allowable distinction—such as one based on "experience, age, deprivation, competence, merit, or position"—like parties were to be treated alike. As for the respects in which people were to be treated alike or equally, the report named several widely accepted formulations of just ways to distribute burdens and benefits according to some relevant property. Thus:

- to each person an equal share;
- to each person according to individual need;
- to each person according to individual effort;

- to each person according to societal contribution; and

- to each person according to merit.

It's notable that the report's understanding of justice as equal treatment shared with the civil rights movement opposition to justice understood as procedural equality. Recall that, according to procedural equality, individuals are treated justly so long they are treated alike *under law*. Especially between the years 1954 and 1968, civil rights activists challenged this view, insisting that a law, policy, or regulation could be unfair to begin with, such as ones that supported racial discrimination. In that instance, procedural equality, no matter its social utility, masked and perpetuated deep social injustice.

For the civil rights movements and the emergent bioethics, justice as fairness had to do with rights, not procedure; with fairness, not law, although the law was expected to support what was fair. For racial minorities or women, fairness meant the right to equal treatment, regardless of color or sex. For the new bioethics it meant the right to have basic health needs met and the right to make health decisions consistent with one's values. To the authors of the *Belmont Report*, rights to health care, choice, or privacy didn't need to be proved any more than did minority or female rights to equal treatment with white males. In the tradition of secular deontological theory, the right to fair or equal treatment could be considered, from a Lockean perspective, a derivative of nature's law, an extension of "life, liberty, and the pursuit of happiness" guaranteed individuals under the social contract; or, from a Kantian or Rawlsian view, a self-evident truth. At the same time, justice as a moral right could be argued strictly from social utility, as being crucial to a wholesome society. For their part, the commission's religious traditions could wholeheartedly agree that fair or equal treatment was appropriate for all God's creatures.

In the three decades since Belmont, medicine has made its services available to more and more people. The result has been scarcities in many important facets of heath care, from equipment and drugs to organ donors, nurses and physicians in minority communities. With scarcity, temporary or chronic, have come problems of allocation and,

along with them, serious and stubborn questions of distributive justice that go well beyond research involving human subjects, which, again, was the purview of the *Belmont Report*.

Consider that allocation has both economic and ethical dimensions. Economically, allocation concerns the most efficient distribution of resources; ethically, it concerns the *fairest* distribution. Neither aspect of allocation—economic or ethical—can be neatly separated from the other. Complicating things further today is that the allocation problem exists at two interconnected levels.[35]

The first level is macroallocation, which refers to the amount that a society should expend for medical resources and how it will be distributed. Where, for example, should we spend more: on primary care (the broad spectrum of preventive and curative care offered by physicians) or crisis intervention (e.g., surgery, kidney dialysis, intensive care units, organ transplants)? That's a question of *macro*allocation.

No matter which side one takes on the issue of preventive versus crisis medicine, one can then ask: *Who will have access to the available resources and how will that be determined? Will the resources be distributed to each patient equally, as Medicare is to all those over 65 years of age? Or should they be distributed in some other way: according to need, merit, social contribution, or possibly a mix?* Such questions of resource accessibility, which are taken up in Chapter 22 in the context of end-of-life care, involve *micro*allocation.

Another point worth remembering: Policies at the macro level inevitably affect what happens at the micro level. The ill poor, for example, more than any other group, stand to benefit from a preventive emphasis and to lose from a crisis intervention approach. For example, about 30 percent of Medicare dollars are spent during the last year of life, and half of that is spent during the last sixty days. In 2009 dollars, that amounted to about $70 billion a year, much of it spent on medically futile care. This expensive end-of-life care detracts from the health care system's ability to finance preventive care.[36]

Again, a program of universal health care, like the one instituted in Massachusetts, can mean low-cost insurance options for low-income families but also less consumer freedom, because it imposes heavy taxes on those who choose not to purchase a health insurance plan that covers treatments that they don't use or desire. Critics of the historic Affordable Health Care Act (2010) find similar inequities in the nation's new health reform law.

In sum, as bioethics pioneer Ruth Macklin has pointed out: "Our society has not yet agreed on who has what kinds of rights and—the other side of the coin—who has the obligation to fulfill them."[37] At the dawn of modern bioethics, this issue could be sidestepped; today soaring health care costs make that option an unaffordable luxury.[38]

CONCLUSIONS

Although autonomy, nonmaleficence, beneficence, and justice largely accounted for the success of the newly emergent discipline of bioethics, their respective weight and influence was not equal. In short order, patient autonomy gained primacy. The presumption in favor of autonomy, says Professor of Religion Stephen E. Lammers, jibed with the Enlightenment ideal of "a universal understanding that permits all persons to make arguments for their conception of a good life" and, toward that end, the institution of "political and social arrangements that do not permit anyone to impose their conception of a good life upon others." Practically, as Lammers further notes, this has meant: "[P]atients should be permitted their visions of a good life, and what physicians and nurses should learn to do is to respect the patients without making any assessments of the patients' plans for a good life."[39]

What came to be termed *principlism*, then, was essentially about self-governance, liberty, rights, individual choice, and following one's own will. As such, principlism quickly set the stage for making powerful ethical arguments based on individual "visions of a good life" in favor of a variety of hot button issues, including abortion, in vitro fertilization (IVF), preconception sex selection, cloning, assisted death, and medically futile care at the end of life. This partly explains the fusillade of criticism directed at principlism as well as secular bioethics with which it's virtually synonymous. Before examining this criticism (in Chapter 6) and proposed alternatives to principlism (in Chapter 7), we will first consider how the emphasis on autonomy shows up in some familiar applications of the Belmont principles.

CASES AND CONTROVERSIES

Drugs, Devices, and Disclosure

In the fall of 2008, congressional investigators found that one of the nation's most prominent psychiatrists had taken large, undisclosed payments from a drug company whose products he evaluated. According to the report, Dr. Charles Nemeroff of Emory University, the lead investigator on a government-financed study of antidepressant drugs made by GlaxoSmithKline, took some half-million dollars in fees and expenses while he led the study, although he promised to keep his fees below the $10,000 a year in compliance with federal and university conflict-of-interest rules. Between 2000 and 2007, Dr. Nemeroff earned more than $2.8 million in consulting arrangements with drugmakers.[40]

Dr. Nemeroff was only the most prominent figure in a series of disclosures that shook the world of academic medicine in 2007 and 2008. In the spring of 2007, Dr. Melissa P. DelBello of the University of Cincinnati reported her connections to drugmakers, including $200,000 she earned from 2005 to 2007 from eight drugmakers and $28,000 alone from AstraZeneca. In June of 2007, it was reported that Dr. Joseph Biederman, the world-renowned Harvard child psychiatrist who helped fuel an explosion in the use of powerful antipsychotic medicine in children, earned at least $1.6 million in consulting fees from drugmakers from 2000 to 2007, but didn't report much of this income to university officials. Biederman's colleague, Dr. Timothy E. Wilens, also reported earning at least $1.6 million from 2000 to

2007, and another Harvard colleague, Dr. Thomas Spencer, reported earning at least $1 million after being pressed by Congressional investigators. The Harvard group's consulting arrangements with drugmakers were already controversial because of its advocacy of unapproved use of psychiatric medicines in children.[41]

Also attracting professional and political attention during this period was the drug and medical device companies' sponsorship of "continuing medical education." In 2007 the Senate Finance Committee launched an inquiry into the practice and estimated that drug- and device-makers had spent more than $1 billion in 2004 alone to sponsor continuing medical education—most of it passing through professional medical organizations. Gifts, travel expenses, or payments made for consulting, researching, or speaking can amount to millions of dollars yearly for "key opinion leaders"—many of them medical association officials—and extra income for many doctors in regular practice. Investigators, and increasingly well-known physicians, have charged that industry's support of medical education courses compromises the objectivity of the instruction, often in ways that are not evident to the physicians taking them.

In 2009 a group of prominent doctors, led by David J. Rothman, president of Columbia University's Center on Medicine as a Profession, drafted a "road map" for doctors' groups to establish their financial independence from the makers and marketers of prescription medications and medical devices. Rothman said it would be "tough" for many physicians' groups to operate without drug- and device makers' financial sponsorships. But, he added, "[Y]ou do not want the piper calling the tune."[42] Authored by eleven physicians, the proposal, which appeared in the April 1, 2009, issue of *JAMA*, urged medical associations to "work toward a goal of accepting $0 contributions from industry." Some of the nation's leading academic institutions— Johns Hopkins, Stanford, and Yale—already had tightened rules that limit interactions between pharmaceutical sales representatives and their physicians. Park Nicollet Health Services, one of Minnesota's largest health systems, banned all industry gifts and nearly all free drug samples and made public all doctor consulting payments.[43] In 2010 Boston-based Partners HealthCare, which includes some of the nation's leading teaching hospitals, began sharply limiting the amount of compensation institutional officials may receive for serving on boards of directors of biomedical companies or companies that are likely to do business with Partners.[44]

Vermont has the most stringent state effort to regulate the marketing of medical products to doctors. Also in 2010, Harvard Medical School announced that its

faculty no longer would be permitted to give promotional talks for drug and device makers or receive gifts, travel, and meals. Any financial relationships for consulting would be closely monitored. Effective July 1, 2009, the law requires drug-and device makers to publicly disclose all money given to physicians and other health care providers, naming names, and listing dollar amounts. It also bans nearly all industry gifts, including meals to doctors, nurses, medical staff, pharmacists, health plan administrator, and health care facilities. In practice, each year Vermonters would learn "which doctors have been paid and how much, by the makers of brand-name drugs for which they wrote prescriptions— or how much money certain surgeons have received from the makers of the stents, pacemakers, artificial knees, and such that the doctors implanted."[45]

Questions for Analysis

1. What is wrong, if anything, with researchers demanding profitable consulting agreements or getting lucrative consulting fees?

2. To whom do you think physicians and medical researchers owe their primary allegiance—the drug companies, the universities who may employ them, the medical profession, or patients?

3. Are the Belmont principles at all relevant to cases like these?

4. Few physicians believe their clinical judgments are influenced by the payments, and they may be right. But a growing number of physicians clearly are worried that increasingly publicized financial conflicts either cloud physicians' judgments or erode their patients' trust or both. Do you share this concern?

5. For many analysts the troubling aspect of these cases is that the physicians-researchers ran afoul of the established fee and disclosure "rules of the game," set by Congress or their university employers. But to Dr. Rothman, his group, and many physicians who want a zero-contributions policy, these infractions are not the most worrisome part. What is objectionable to them is the relationship itself between the drug companies and the physicians, which they regard as injurious. Who are the stakeholders in the physician-drug company relationship?

6. Doctors who have seen details of their consulting deals made public say they have been tarred. One, Dr. Richard Grimm, a Minnesota researcher, twice served on government-sponsored hypertension panels that create guidelines about when to

(Continued)

CASES AND CONTROVERSIES (CONTINUED)

prescribe blood pressure pills. But when state records revealed that he had earned more than $798,000 from drug companies from 1997 to 2005, he claimed that invitations to serve on such panels dried up. "There's this automatic assumption that

if you make money from a drug company, you must be corrupt," Dr. Grimm said.[46] Are physician/researchers like Dr. Grimm being treated unfairly?

7. Do you support the Vermont law?

CASES AND CONTROVERSIES

Medical Workers Involved in CIA Interrogations

In his book *Oath Betrayed*, physician and Professor of Bioethics at the University of Minnesota Steven Miles wrote about modern medical complicity in torture.[47] Unfortunately, the link between torture and medical personnel is not a new one. In the Renaissance, for example, special "torture doctors" helped inquisitors choose their interrogation methods. Still, Miles' disclosure of US medical complicity in abuse of prisoners at Abu Ghraib, Guantanamo Bay, and elsewhere shocked the medical profession and the country. Not only were doctors, nurses, and medics silent while prisoners were abused, according to Miles, physicians and psychologists provided information that helped determine how much and what kind of mistreatment detainees could endure without dying. Additionally, Miles said that health professionals operating under the purview of the US military monitored these harsh examinations. And he provided compelling evidence for his charges, as have *New York Times* journalist Mark Daner, and *The New Yorker*'s Jane Meyer, in her 2008 book, *The Dark Side*.[48] So, when a long-secret Red Cross report surfaced in the spring of 2009 about the involvement of medical workers in abusive CIA interrogations, it wasn't exactly news. Nevertheless, the report's conclusion that such involvement was a "gross breach of medical ethics" was shocking.[49]

According to the International Committee of the Red Cross (ICRC), the chief independent monitor of detention conditions around the world, US medical professionals working for the CIA were present when prisoners were undergoing waterboarding. In waterboarding, a prisoner is immobilized, has rags put over his face, and has water pour over him to create a sensation of drowning. Waterboarding can actually result in drowning, and presumably the medical personnel were present to prevent that from occurring. They also were present when guards confined prisoners in small

boxes, shackled their arms to the ceiling, kept them in frigid cells, and slammed them repeatedly into walls, according to the Red Cross report.

None of this, of course, came as a surprise to Miles. Since World War II, he counts about seventy cases worldwide of physician punishment for participation in torture or related crimes. Most, he says, were in Brazil, Argentina, Uruguay, and Chile. None have been in the United States.

Questions for Analysis

1. What moral issues does the Red Cross report raise?

2. Would it make a moral difference if the medical workers' intentions were to prevent death or injury, rather than support the interrogators?

3. Evaluate the conduct of the medical personnel in terms of the Belmont Principles.

4. Evaluate the conduct of the medical personnel from the perspectives of religious and secular natural law, Kant's ethics, and utilitarianism.

5. By policy the Red Cross keeps its reports to government confidential to encourage officials to grant access to prisoners. When Mark Danner obtained and posted the ICRC report on the Website of *New York Review of Books*, a Red Cross spokesperson declined to comment on it, saying: "We deplore that confidential material attributed to the ICRC was made public." Do you agree or disagree with this policy? Support your answer with moral principle(s) such as utility or the categorical imperative.

6. Do you think that medical personnel who participated in torture should be held accountable? If so, what moral principle(s) would you enlist to support your recommendation?

CASES AND CONTROVERSIES

The Steven Jobs Liver Transplant

Whenever someone rich and famous gets an organ transplant, questions usually surface about whether the person leapfrogged others on a waiting list and received the first available organ. Recall baseball great Mickey Mantle, who waited all of one day for a liver in 1995, then died of liver cancer anyway, just two months later. So, when Apple's chief executive, Steven P. Jobs, 54, got his liver in April 2009, it wasn't surprising that questions popped up about the fairness of the system for allocating scarce organs to sick people.

Doctors insist there's no way that Jobs or anyone else can cheat the system. Under current procedures, transplant centers keep waiting lists with patients ranked in descending order based on how sick they are and how long they've been sick. A patient with the highest MELD (model for end-stage liver disease) rating is first in line for an available liver. But there's a catch: geography. Waiting times for a liver vary in different parts of the United States. For example, patients wait longer on the East and West Coasts than in the Midwest or elsewhere because of greater demand and lesser availability on the coasts. Thus, if you need a liver and you can afford to travel, you might go to a state with the shortest waiting list and sit tight until your name reaches the top. Some patients even rent rooms or apartments and wait patiently, or anxiously, by the phone.[50] Jobs, a resident of Silicon Valley, California, had his transplant thousands of miles away, at Methodist University Hospital in Memphis, where the median waiting time is 3.8 months, compared with a national waiting time of 12.3 months.[51]

Another way to improve your chances is to register at more than one transplant center. When an organ such as a liver becomes available, the United Network for Organ Sharing, or UNOS, which is the agency that distributes donated organs to those on waiting lists, searches for patients who need it most and have registered at the transplant center where the organ is available. So, the more transplant centers you're registered at, the more likely you are to get one of these scarce commodities. Conversely, the fewer the centers that have you in their databases, the less likely you'll get a liver. Of course, such a strategy isn't cheap. You'll need generous insurance coverage or personal means enough to pay for the medical workups, not to mention the cost of the transplant, which could run upwards of $200,000. But if you can afford it, there's nothing preventing you from registering at multiple centers. And to make things easier, there's plenty of easily accessible data about waiting times and other information about the nation's transplant centers.

Beyond these perfectly legal ways of improving the odds of securing an organ, there is a flourishing international black market for kidneys, where a network of greedy organ brokers prey on the desperate and destitute. A 2009 *New York Daily News* probe found that the wretchedly poor in India, for example, are paid $2,000 to $10,000 for kidneys that ultimately sell for as much as $180,000 to transplant recipients in the world's richer nations, some in the United States. "In India, China, Africa and Latin America the poor are selling their kidneys to wealthy buyers through an underground set of networks," says Dr. Stephen Post, professor of Bioethics at Stony Brook University.[52] But it's not just overseas where black markets for organs flourish. In the summer of 2009, forty-four people in New Jersey, rabbis and politicians among them, were charged with organized crimes, including selling livers for $160,000 apiece.

Currently, according to UNOS, more than 80,000 Americans are waiting for kidney transplants and about 16,000 are on the national liver waiting list. In the first quarter of 2009, roughly 1,500 got livers in the United States, none of them with any form of cancer. Jobs had surgery for pancreatic cancer in 2004, and, though unconfirmed, the suspicion was that the cancer had spread to his liver, which would explain the need for the transplant. Some transplant surgeons wouldn't even recommend a transplant under such circumstances because there's no evidence that a transplant will stop or even slow the spread of cancer.[53] According to the hospital where Jobs received his liver transplant, Jobs was "the sickest patient on the waiting list at the time a donor organ became available," and he was the patient "with the highest MELD score of his blood type."[54]

Questions for Analysis

1. Assuming that Jobs' cancer has likely spread to his liver, do you think that this was the best use of a liver?

2. Is the current system the fairest means possible of organ allocation?

3. In 2008 the parents of 17-year-old Nataline Sarkisyan sued insurance giant Cigna Healthcare for declining to guarantee payment for a liver

(Continued)

CASES AND CONTROVERSIES (CONTINUED)

transplant at UCLA Medical Center. Since the family couldn't pay, Nataline wasn't admitted to the transplant program, and died. Should an organ be treated like any other commodity in the marketplace, available only to those who can afford it?

4. Suppose that your life depended on a liver transplant. How would you want that allocation to be determined?

5. Discuss the ethics of trading in kidneys and other organs. If it meant your survival and you could afford it, would you get a black market kidney?

REFERENCES

1. National Commission for the Protection of Human Subjects of Biomedical and Behavioral Research, "The Belmont Report: Ethical Principles and Guidelines for the Protection of Human Subjects of Research," *Federal Register*, April 18, 1979, p. 23, pp. 192–197. Retrieved May 1, 2008, from http://ohsr.od.nih.gov/guidelines/belmont.html.

2. See note 1 above.

3. William Ruddick, "Medical Ethics," *Encyclopedia of Ethics*, 2nd ed., Lawrence and Charlotte Becker, eds., New York: Garland Publishing, 1998. Retrieved April 20, 2008, from http://www.nyu.edu/gsas/dept/philo/faculty/ruddick/papers/medethics.html.

4. Albert R. Jonsen, *The Birth of Bioethics*, New York: Oxford University Press, 1998, p. 104.

5. See note 4 above.

6. Austin Cline, "Introduction to Bioethics." *About Religion and Spirituality*, New York: New York Times Company, 2008. Retrieved May 1, 2008, from http://atheism.about.com/library/FAQs/phil/blphil_ethbio_principles.htm.

7. Thomas R. McCormick, "Principles of Bioethics," *Ethics in Medicine*, April 11, 2008. Retrieved May 1, 2008, from http://depts.washington.edu/bioethx/tools/princpl.html.

8. See note 7 above.

9. Dianne N. Irving, "The Bioethics Mess," *Crisis Magazine*, May, 2001. Retrieved May 15, 2008, from www.hospicepatients.org/prof-dianne-irving-bioethics-mess.html.

10. Jonsen, p. 334.

11. See note 10 above.

12. Ibid., p. 335.

13. See note 12 above.

14. James Childress, "The Place of Autonomy in Bioethics," *Hastings Center Report*, January–February, 1990, pp. 12–17.

15. Dan E. Beauchamp, *The Health of the Republic: Epidemics, Medicine, and Moralism* as *Challenges to Democracy*, Philadelphia: Temple University Press, 1988.

16. Robert Veatch, "Which Grounds For Overriding Autonomy Are Legitimate?" in "Can the Moral Commons Survive Autonomy?" *The Hastings Center Report*, Garrison, NY: Hastings Center, November 1, 1996. p. 41.

17. Alan Wolfe, "Seminar: American Culture War," Spring, 2006. Retrieved May 2, 2008, from http://www.bc.edu/bc_org/research/rapl/courses/political_science_358.html.

18. Paul Ramsey, *The Patient as Person: Exploration in Medical Ethics*, New Haven: Yale University Press, 1970, p. xiii.

19. Jonsen, p. 345.

20. Ezekiel Emanuel, "Unequal Treatment," *The New York Times*, February 18, 2007. Retrieved May 2, 2008, from http://www.nytimes.com/2007/02/18/books/review/Emanuel.t.html?_r=1&pagewanted=print&oref=slogin.

21. See note 20 above.

22. Steven H. Miles, *Oath Betrayed: Torture, Medical Complicity, and the War on Terror*, New York: Random House, 2006.

23. David J. Rothman and Sheila M. Rothman, *Trust Is Not Enough: Bringing Human Rights to Medicine*, New York: *New York Review of Books*, 2006.

24. L. T. Kohn, J. M. Corrigan, and J. M. Donaldson, *To Err Is Human: Building a Safer Health Care System*, Washington: National Academies Press, 2000.

25. Philip Aspden, Julie A. Wolcott, J. Lyle Bootman, and Linda R. Cronenwett, eds., *Preventing Medication Errors*, Washington, DC: National Academies Press, 2007.

26. Michael R. Cohen, ed., *Medication Errors*, 2nd ed., Washington: American Pharmacists Association, 2007.

27. Walt Bogdanich, "A Lifesaving Tool Turned Deadly," *The New York Times*, January 24, 2010, p. 14.

28. Pamela Sue Anderson, "Unselfish Love: A Contradiction in Terms," in Lieven Boeve, Joeri Schrijvers, and Wessel Stoker, eds., *Faith in the Enlightenment: The Critique of the Enlightenment Revisited*, Amsterdam: Rodopi, 2006, p. 255.

29. Deborah I. Fahnestock, "Partnership for Good Dying. (A Piece of My Mind)," *Dying, Death, and Bereavement*, 6th ed., George E. Dickinson and Michael R. Leming, eds., Guilford, Conn.: McGraw-Hill/Dushkin, 2002-03, p. 81).

30. Leon Kass, *Toward a More Natural Science: Biology and Human Affairs*, New York: The Free Press, 1980.

31. E. D. Pellegrino and D. C. Thomasma, *For the Patient's Good: The Restoration of Beneficence in Health Care*, New York: Oxford University Press, 1988.

32. Patrick Guinan, "Why Not Give Hippocrates a Place at the Table?" *Ethics & Medicine*, Chicago: Bioethics Press, Fall, 2002. Retrieved June 1, 2008, from http://findarticles.com/p/articles/mi_qa4004/is_200210/ai_n9126859.

33. Daniel Eisenberg, M.D., "Medical Informed Consent—from the Patient's Side," *Jewish Law, Examining Halacha, Jewish Law and Secular Law*, 1999. Retrieved June 3, 2008, from http://www.jlaw.com/Articles/MedConsent.html.

34. Janet Smith, "The Preeminence of Autonomy in Bioethics," in *Human Lives; Critical Essays on Consequentialist Bioethics*, David Oderberg and Jacqueline A. Laing, eds., London: McMillan Press, Ltd., 1997. Retrieved June 5, 2008, from http://www.aodonline.org/SHMS/Faculty+5819/Janet+Smith+9260/Dr.+Janet+Smith+-+Published+Articles.htm.

35. T. L. Beauchamp and L. R. Walters, *Contemporary Issues in Bioethics*, 6th ed., Belmont, CA: Wadsworth Publishing, 2002.

36. Jane E. Brody, "One Piece of Health Reform: Avoiding 'Bad' Deaths," *The New York Times*, August 18, 2009, p. D7.

37. Carol Levine, ed., *Taking Sides: Clashing View on Controversial Bioethical Issues*, 6th ed., Guilford, CT: The Dushkin Publishing Group, Inc., 1995. p. xxii.

38. Lisa Potetz, "Financing Medicare: an Issue Brief," *The Kaiser Family Foundation*, January 2008.

39. Stephen E. Lammers, "The Marginalization of Religious Voices in Bioethics," in Religion & Medical Ethics, Allen Verhey, ed., Grand Rapids, Michigan: William B. Eerdmans Publishing Company, 1996, p. 24.

40. Gardiner Harris, "Top Psychiatrist Didn't Report Drug Maker's Pay," *The New York Times*, October 3, 2008. Retrieved April 15, 2009, from http://www.nytimes.com/2008/10/04/health/policy/04drug.html.

41. Gardiner Harris and Benedict Carey, "Researchers Fail to Reveal Full Drug Pay, *The New York Times*, June 8, 2008. Retrieved April 15, 2009, from http://www.nytimes.com/2008/06/08/us/08conflict.html.

42. Melissa Healy, "Medical groups should pare financial ties to drug companies, doctors say," *Los Angeles Times*, April 1, 2009. Retrieved April 15, 2009, from http://latimesblogs.latimes.com/booster_shots/2009/04/doctors-groups-should-pare-financial-ties-to-drug-companies-jama.html.

43. Editorial, "Drugs and Disclosure," *The New York Times*, October 10, 2008. Retrieved April 15, 2009, from http://www.nytimes.com/2008/10/11/opinion/11sat2.html.

44. Bernard Lo, "Serving Two Masters—Conflicts of Interest in Academic Medicine," *The New England Journal of Medicine*, February 25, 2010, pp. 669–671.

45. Natasha Singer, "Doctor Gifts To Be Public in Vermont," *The New York Times*, May 20, 2009, p. B1.

46. Gardiner Harris, "Crackdown on Doctors Who Take Kickbacks," *The New York Times*, March 5, 2009. Retrieved May 10, 2009, from www.pharmfree.org/news?id=0039.

47. Steven Miles, *Oath Betrayed: Torture, Medical Complicity, and the War on Terror*. New York: Random House, 2007.

48. Scott Shane, "Report Outlines Involvement of Medical Workers in Abusive C.I.A. Interrogations," *The New York Times*, April 7, 2009, p. A6.

49. Peter D. Kramer, "Medical Complicity and The War on Terror," *The Washington Post*, July 23, 2006, p. BW 04. Retrieved April 5, 2009, from http://www.washingtonpost.com/wp-dyn/content/article/2006/07/20/AR2006072001021.html.

50. Denise Grady and Barry Meier, "A Transplant That Is Raising Many Questions," *The New York Times*, June 23, 2009, p. B1.

51. Ibid., p. B5.

52. Brian Kates and William Sherman, "Rogue Kidney Brokers Resell Organs from Poorest Nations on Black Market," *New York Daily News*, July 26, 2009. Retrieved July 26, 2009, from http://www.nydailynews.com/news/ny_crime/2009/07/26/. 2009-07-26_rogue_kidney_brokers_resell_organs_ fetched_from_poorest_nations_on_black_market. html?page=0.

53. Arthur Caplan, "Did Steven Jobs' Wallet Help Cut Transplant Wait?" *MSNBC*, June 23, 2009. Retrieved June 23, 2009, from http://www.msnbc. msn.com/id/31509368/ns/health-health_care/.

54. Rick Whiting, "Hospital Confirms Liver Transplant for Apple's Steve Jobs," *Channel Web*, June 24, 2009. Retrieved June 24, 2009, from www.crn.com/it-channel/218101102.

Chapter 5

Applications

Consistent with its charge, the *Belmont Report* included some applications of the general guidelines for medical research, including informed consent, risk/benefit assessment, and the selection of human subjects. But as the core principles underlying the conduct of research grew into the basic principles of bioethics, so, too, their applications reached beyond the laboratory into the clinic. As they did, they provided a principled basis for various patient rights that, in fact, already were circulating in medicine and health care, thanks in part to a statement of patient rights adopted a few years earlier by the American Hospital Association (AHA).

A PATIENT'S BILL OF RIGHTS

In 1970 a study was undertaken by the AHA's board of trustees and four consumer representatives for the purpose of formulating a statement of patients' rights. Three years later, and seven years before the *Belmont Report*, the group released *A Patient's Bill of Rights (APBR).*[1] Although the AHA acknowledged that hospitals would not lose accreditation if they failed to adopt the statement, they expressed the hope that all member institutions would adopt it.

Although it never used the word, from its inception the *APBR* clearly was an elaboration on the theme of patient autonomy, including its nature and function. According to the bill, respecting patient autonomy encompassed: giving patients information about treatment options, including at the end of life; safeguarding their privacy and confidentiality; permitting them to consent or refuse to participate in research and treatment; and disclosing potential conflicts of interest to them. And because patient autonomy isn't only about entitlement but also personal responsibility, the statement concluded with a brief list of patient responsibilities, such as disclosing information about past illnesses and recognizing the impact of lifestyle on health.

Given its empowerment of all patients, the *APBR* effectively challenged the status quo and paternalistic authority even more so than had *OBOS* (See Chapter 3) two years earlier, on behalf of women. The statement of patient rights also provided a context for the new bioethics and was in turn strengthened by it. Thus, on one hand, the Belmont principles provided a principled basis for the rights expressed in *APBR*. On the other, the principles made explicit what was implied in the *APBR* and has been the lodestar of bioethics ever since: a strong commitment to patient autonomy and a rejection of medical paternalism.

In this chapter we'll see how autonomy continues to drive some familiar applications of the Belmont principles: truthtelling, informed consent, participation in medical research, advance directives, and privacy and confidentiality. We'll also review the status of these derivative principles in the contemporary clinical setting.

TRUTHTELLING

Although the physician obligation of truthtelling can be derived from any of the principles, it's tightly linked to autonomy. For patients to choose for themselves, they need to have the truth about their diagnoses, treatments, and prognoses. Therefore, the physician is obligated to be trustworthy and truthful with patients, families, and colleagues regarding these medical matters. When it isn't medically advisable to give such information to patients, it must always be made available to an appropriate person on his behalf.

Whereas the *Belmont Report* was most concerned with truthtelling in the context of human subjects research, nowadays most violations of truthtelling relate to poor communication between physician and patient. Inadequate disclosure, including professional or institutional relationships that might affect patient care; deception by what is omitted as well as expressed; evasion and denial; and unrealistic medical hope, any of these examples of poor physician communication can affect adequate health care and physician accountability.

Consider, for example, end-of-life care. Despite the 1995 multi-million dollar effort to improve communication between patients and doctors on end-of-life care—called the *Support Study*—many physicians remain unwilling to talk seriously with their ill patients and families about death.[2] According

to research, doctors typically avoid making prognoses or are falsely optimistic, even when death is likely in a matter of months or less. In one study of 5,000 hospitalized adults who, by the best medical estimate, had about six months to live, only 15 percent were given clear prognoses. In another study, of end-stage cancer patients with about a month to live, only about one-third of physicians interviewed said they would share an accurate prognosis with their patients and then only if pushed to by family. "By not making or communicating prognoses," writes physician and Harvard sociologist Nicholas A. Christakis,

> [D]octors can make the end of life more unpleasant. Patients are given no chance to draft wills, see distant loved ones, make peace with estranged relatives or even discuss with their family their wishes about how to live the end of their lives. And they are denied the chance to make decisions about what kind of medical care they want to receive.[3]

In end-of-life cases the problem is that the requisite information may not be accurately communicated to the patient or family. Indeed, as at least one study has shown, false optimism about recovery can lead to collusion between physician and patient to conceal the hard truth about an illness.[4] In other instances, the information is communicated but not intelligibly. As a result, the patients don't follow the physicians' orders.[5] The number of Americans unable to adequately understand basic health information is estimated upwards of 90 million. And "health illiteracy" plays no favorites; it "affects people of all ages, races, income and education levels."[6]

Compounding the problem is the estimated 14 percent of adults in the United States with a "below basic" level of "prose literacy"—defined in a large survey as the ability to use "printed and written information to function in society, to achieve one's goals, and to develop one's knowledge and potential."[7] Some studies have put the figure of the functionally illiterate as high as 55 percent of the adult population. In any event, despite the

BIOETHICS ACROSS CULTURES

East Asian Autonomy

In the West, the principle of autonomy is individual-oriented. In other words, the patient is the final authority on clinical decisions for herself, and the physician must respect that, by disclosing diagnosis, prognosis, and treatment options directly to the patient, no matter how bitter the information is. The two exceptions permitted are when the truth will severely harm the patient or when the patient doesn't want to know the truth.

In contrast, East Asians understand autonomy as a family-oriented principle. Highly influenced by the long-standing Confucian tradition, the countries of East Asia—including China, Japan, and the Koreas—view each family as an autonomous unit in which all its members flourish or suffer as a whole. Medical challenges are no exception. The medical problems of one family member are taken as the problems of the entire family. One member's illness is borne by the rest of the family, including the burden of receiving information and consenting to treatment. Indeed, a family representative is expected to arrange all matters with the physician. This means that the entire family, not just the individual patient, has final authority over clinical affairs.

While the family's decision should be made for the best interests of the patient, it is also expected to uphold the interdependence of family members rather than individual differentiation. Accordingly, East Asian physicians ordinarily do not offer medical information to the patient directly but to a family representative. The family is left to decide whether to tell the patient the truth. The custom especially holds with severe diagnoses or fatal prognoses.

(SOURCE: Ruiping Fan, "Truth Telling to the Patient: Cultural Diversity and the East Asian Perspective," in *Bioethics in Asia*, Norio Fujiki and Darryl R. J. Macer, eds., Bangaok Eubios Ethics Institute, pp. 107–109. Retrieved May 15, 2009, from www.eubios.info/ASIAE/BIAE107.htm)

Question

Do East Asians have a sense of truthfulness? How is their practice of truthtelling different from ours? Bioethicist Edmund Pellegrino has written that truthtelling to the patient is not a cultural artifact and that "autonomy is a valid and universal principle because it is based on what it is to be human." (Edmund Pellegrino, "Is Truth Telling to the Patient a Cultural Artifact?" *JAMA*, October 1992, pp. 1734–1735) Evaluate this view in the light of the East Asian experience.

National Literacy Act of 1991, which was created to help 30 million illiterate Americans over sixteen to become literate, the problem has increased. According to a multi-year study of Medicare patients begun in 2003 and reported in 2007 in the *Archives of Internal Medicine*: After taking into account other potential factors, such as participants' health when they entered the study, those with inadequate health literacy were 52 percent more likely to have died than those with adequate health literacy.[8]

Making matters worse are barriers of language and culture that can easily lead to misconstrual of physician orders. Often cited as a poignant example of the need for cultural competency in medicine is the book *The Spirit Catches You and You Fall* (1998), which tells the story of an immigrant Hmong family whose epileptic daughter is poorly treated and eventually dies when the family belief system isn't considered.

As an upshot, according to the *New England Journal of Medicine*, some experts today advocate an approach to physician-patient communication similar to universal precautions for preventing HIV infection. "Health care workers, they say, should assume that all patients have a limited understanding of medical words and concepts, whether or not they have passable general-reading skills." One expert advises physicians to "organize their discussions with patients around three key points per visit and use a teach-back approach, asking patients to explain what they have been told" in order to ensure good communication and meet the obligation of truthtelling in the modern clinical setting.[9,10]

INFORMED CONSENT

In the years leading up to the *Belmont Report*, characterized as they were by individualism and anti-authoritarianism, protecting patient autonomy was already emerging as a key concern of medical ethics. As previously noted, Belmont further advanced autonomy, casting it as a guard against subject abuse in medical research and the imposition of unwanted and burdensome medical treatment. Respecting autonomy, then, came to be viewed as a way to balance power in the physician-patient relationship, primarily by establishing a solid foundation for informed consent.

Informed consent basically means that a patient (or research subject) freely agrees to a procedure or treatment on the basis of a correct understanding of what it involves, especially risks. The legal foundation for the doctrine of informed consent was laid by the US Supreme Court in 1891 when it recognized the right of every individual to "possession and control of his own person, free from all restraint or interference of others, unless by clear and unquestionable authority of law" (*Union Pacific Railway Company v. Botsford*). In 1914 the doctrine was firmly established when the New York Court of Appeals found that a surgery done without a patient's consent constituted medical battery. In that case the eloquent jurist Benjamin Cardozo (1870–1938), who would later served on the US Supreme Court, famously wrote:

> Every human being of adult years and sound mind has a right to determine what shall be done with his own body; and a surgeon who performs an operation without his patient's consent commits an assault for which he is liable in damages. This is true except in cases of emergency where the patient is unconscious and where it is necessary to operate before consent can be obtained. (*Schloendorff v. New York Hospital*, 1914).

Later in the century, the Connecticut Supreme Court invoked Cardozo when upholding an appeals court decision against a physician who had failed to provide enough information for a patient to give informed consent to surgery (*Logan v. Greenwich Hospital Association*, 1983). The decision meant that

> the physician is ... charged with the duty to disclose to the patient that information that "a reasonable patient would have found material for making a decision whether to embark upon a contemplated course of therapy."

It is out of the court-established doctrine of informed consent that legal remedies have come against doctors who fail to obtain consent. Performing surgery without consent, for example, is legally an assault and a basis of a malpractice claim against the physician.

Legally and morally, there are two relevant aspects of informed consent that define it, unmistakably, as an aspect of autonomy. The "informed" part requires deliberation; the "consent" part requires voluntariness.

Deliberation

Consider the actual cases, of (1) a 29-year-old patient left paraplegic after exploratory surgery; (2) a woman who developed a serious vaginal disorder (vesicovaginal fistula) after an elective hysterectomy; and (3) a middle-aged school teacher, wife and mother of five, left facially disfigured and without speech following surgery. All of these patients sued their physicians for the same reason: They claimed they didn't give informed consent to the procedures that left them impaired.

Whether these patients agreed to certain medical procedures was not at issue; they had. The cases turned on the answer to the following question: Was their agreement the result of a *deliberative process* that included the means and opportunity for making an informed decision to participate in the medical procedure or treatment?

For patients to deliberate, they basically need significant and understandable information. Except in emergencies the information for deliberation includes but isn't always limited to: (1) the specific procedure and/or treatment, including the medically significant risks involved and probable duration of incapacitation; (2) alternatives for care or treatment; and (3) the name of the person responsible for the procedures and/or treatment. For these facts to be useful in the deliberative process, they need to be understandable to the patient. The patient also needs time and opportunity for weighing options, doing research, asking questions, considering alternatives, and so on. In short, if consent is to be informed, that is, valid and legitimate, patients must be allowed to deliberate on the basis of enough of the right kind of information expressed in terms that a layperson can understand, not in medical jargon.

It's notable that informed consent includes informed *refusal*. Thus, like informed consent, informed refusal requires that patients be made aware of the risks they run in not undergoing treatment, including diagnostic procedures. The precedent-setting case here occurred around the advent of bioethics. It involved a 30-year-old California woman who died in 1970 of cervical cancer that was detected by an ob-gyn to whom the woman had been referred by a general practitioner (GP) who had treated her from 1963 to 1969. The woman's children sued the GP for never having done a Pap smear, which might have detected the cancer early enough to treat successfully. In agreeing, the California Supreme Court (*Truman v. Thomas*, 1980) did not say that the physician had to do the test but that he was obligated to provide enough information about it, especially the potentially lethal risks of refusing it, to allow the patient to give informed refusal. The ruling effectively set a precedent for physicians to educate patients about diagnostic as well as therapeutic procedures.

Refusal of treatment raises a host of questions about the reach of patient autonomy, the obligations of physicians to treat, and the role of the courts. When patients are suffering from terminal or incurable illnesses, refusal of treatment also raises considerations about the sanctity of life compared with the quality of life, as well as about the proper utilization of limited medical resources. These matters figure prominently in end-of-life decisions, as we'll see in Part IV of this book.

Voluntariness

For consent to be legitimate, it must be voluntary as well as informed. Patients must willingly agree to the procedure or treatment, or willingly refuse it.

Whether voluntarily agreeing to or refusing treatment, a person obviously must be in a position to act voluntarily—he or she must have the capacity and legal competence to make a self-determined decision about her health. Competence, in other words, is always necessary for informed consent. Unless proved otherwise, anyone who has reached the age of majority (ordinarily 18 years of age) is assumed competent to make decisions about his health, including decisions contrary to the opinions of others. Such individuals are presumed rational enough to understand and process information, and assess the consequences of their choices and actions.

But determining a patient's capacity for rational thought in a medical matter isn't always easy. Is the person who refuses a needed operation or blood transfusion on religious grounds rational? How about the humanitarian who is willing to submit to an experiment that will help others but hurt herself? Or the elderly patient who has recently squandered away a fortune on individuals he hardly knows and on frivolous activities? From a strict medical viewpoint, all of these decisions could be interpreted as irrational, since they go against narrow, medical self-interest. From a subjective perspective, however—from the viewpoints of the individuals' values, goals, and life plans—the choices might make sense.

Today a body of law addresses matters of competence. That aside, the following facts about competence are worth remembering. (1) There are degrees of competence. (2) Incompetence in one area—for example, managing one's financial affairs—doesn't always mean incompetence to decide medical treatment. (3) Although incompetence is not always easy to determine, it is always easier to determine than competence.

Then there are problems of determining the competence of certain classes of patients, such as children, the aged, or the mentally retarded and

BIOETHICS ACROSS CULTURES

A Japanese Woman with Aggressive Leukemia

A 66-year-old Japanese woman, who had come to the United States with her family twenty years earlier, had hypertension and hypothyroidism, but was otherwise healthy. When spontaneous bruises appeared on her legs, accompanied by fever, she went to the emergency room, with family members. Fearing a serious diagnosis, her family asked the doctors to reveal test results to them, not directly to her. The family would then huddle to determine whether it was best to tell the woman. When the blood tests showed very aggressive leukemia, the health care team was conflicted. Most, including the doctors, felt they had to tell the patient of the diagnosis. They felt it was her right to know, particularly if she was to undergo difficult chemotherapy. Some staff, however, sided with the family. One member, a nurse who was Korean, felt that the family was within its rights to decide whether to give or

withhold the information since they best knew how she might react to this life-threatening condition.

(SOURCE: Joseph R. Betancourt, Alexander R. Green, and J. Emilio Carrillo, "The Challenges of Cross-Cultural Healthcare—Diversity, Ethics, and the Medical Encounter, Bioethics Forum, *Bioethics Forum*, Fall 2000, pp. 27–32. Retrieved April 20, 2009, from www.practicalbioethics.org/FileUploads/The%20Challenges%20of%20Cross%20Cultural%20Healthcare.16.3-2.pdf)

Question

Should this patient be told the truth? Who should decide? If the family won't tell the woman the truth about her diagnosis, should the doctor? Do you think any family can be justified in refusing treatment on behalf of a competent patient without consulting the patient? Would problems like these be avoided by determining at the outset whether patients prefer to let their families make decisions about their diagnoses, thereby waiving their own right to know?

disturbed. Consistent with the paternalistic aspect of autonomy, those who can't give informed consent are entitled to protection and assent. In general, this means having their interests adequately represented and including them in the decision making as much as possible. Today, under the doctrine of *substituted judgment*, someone, such as the next of kin, may be designated to exercise judgment for a patient who cannot give or refuse consent to treatment, as with Karen Ann Quinlan (see case presentation, Chapter 3) or Terri Schiavo (see Introduction).

Kinds of Informed Consent

According to medical law experts, Jaime Staples King and Benjamin Moulton,[11] currently state jurisdictions are almost evenly split between two types of standards for informed consent: the physician-based standard and the patient-based standard. Physician-based standards, in effect, require physicians to assume the role of a "reasonably prudent practitioner" in informing a patient of the risks, benefits, and alternatives to a treatment; whereas the patient-based standards require that

physicians assume the role of a "reasonable patient" and provide their patients with all information on the risks, benefits, and alternatives to a treatment that this hypothetical "reasonable patient" would attach significance to in making a treatment decision. The underlying assumptions of both standards are open to conceptual and empirical challenges.

For example, conceptually, except in the most egregious of cases, doctors likely will differ in their understanding of what constitutes a "reasonably prudent practitioner" and "reasonable patient." Empirically, research shows that "around one-third of all medical decisions should depend largely on the values and preferences of the patient, rather than the norms of physician practice, as is the law under the physician-based standard." Other research demonstrates that patients vary widely in their disclosure preferences and needs. This would indicate that, contrary to the principle of individual autonomy, reliance on the "reasonable patient" standard might, in fact, deny many patients the amount of information they require to give an informed consent to treatment.

Such problems have led some medical and legal scholars, King and Moulton among them, to call for a revision of the current methods of informed consent in favor of shared medical decision making. "Shared medical decision-making," they explain, "is a process in which the physician shares with the patient all relevant risk and benefit information on all treatment alternatives and the patient shares with the physician all relevant personal information that might make one treatment or side effect more or less tolerable than others." Both parties then use this information to come to a mutual medical decision.

To its advocates shared medical decision making improves patient autonomy and comprehension, reduces unwanted medical procedures and services, and improves communication and trust between physicians and patients. To its critics, many physicians among them, it's impractical. They say it's not only time consuming but places an unbearable financial strain on an already overburdened system, including doctors who don't have the support and resources to implement it. What's more, say critics, patients don't really understand or want the information. (See end-of-chapter Cases and Controversies: The Merenstein Case of Informed Consent.)

ADVANCE DIRECTIVES

The statutes that permit the state to select a "health care representative" also allow individuals to pick a person who can exercise substituted judgment on their behalf should they become unable. Various documents, generally termed advance directives (or advanced directives), have been developed as a way of prolonging the autonomy of patients by allowing them to declare formally how much of what kind of treatment they wish to receive should they no longer have decision-making capacity. Although available in 1972, advance directives were never mentioned in the original *APBR*, but were included in the 1992 revision under patient responsibilities.

For the purpose of refusing unwanted life-sustaining treatment, attorney Louis Kutner devised the first of these directives, termed living wills, in 1969.[12] The American lawyer-activist was

responding to the growing fear brought on by the new life-sustaining technology that could keep patients alive longer than they might wish. Kutner's idea was to create a document that gave patients control over how they were to be treated should illness and disability render them incapable of representing themselves. Legally, it was based on the precept of refusal of treatment. Since then, the documents have been refined to minimize ambiguity and permit greater detail.

It was the New Jersey Supreme Court that first legally validated advance directives, in the groundbreaking *Quinlan* case of 1976. The next year California, as part of its *Natural Death Act*, created a version of a living will, called the *Directive to Physician*, that had the same legal power as an estate will. Its successor today, the *Durable Power of Attorney for Health Care* (*DPAHC*), allows competent adults to designate in writing a party (termed "agent," "proxy," or "surrogate") to make health care decisions, or substituted judgments, for them should they lose decision capacity. As required by the federal *Patient Self-Determination Act* of 1991, patients must be informed about the DPAHC and directives, in general, upon admission to a health care institution. For many people of religious faith as well as others who feel that living wills and directives have an objectionable, even fearsome, death presumption, there is an alternative today that has a strong pro-life emphasis and allows for expressed desires for ventilators, feeding tubes, medications, and the like. It's called *The Will To Live* and is available from The Will To Live Project in Washington, DC.

It's important to remember that health care institutions are not obligated always to comply with patient end-of-life requests. Nor must physicians follow patient requests that violate their consciences, although they are expected to remove themselves from the case in a way that doesn't abandon patient or family. This broad legal right of institutional or professional refusal can be troublesome for both those who give and receive end-of-life care.

Take, for example, the practice of terminal sedation that came into usage in the 1980s. Terminal sedation, which may be requested in an advance directive, is pain management in terminally ill patients that uses sedation to control pain, even if it hastens death. A practice such as terminal sedation or the withholding of food and water "creates unique problems for religious institutions involved in the provision of health care." As physician/ethicist Eran Klein also points out:

> Catholic institutions have been able to avoid, often by carefully created structural divisions and partnerships with other health care centers, participation in practices like abortion, contraception and assisted reproduction. End-of-life treatment, like terminal sedation or withdrawal of artificial nutrition and hydration, is in some ways more complicated for Catholic institutions, given that care of the dying is more intimately woven into the daily practice of acute medical care. While it may be acceptable to transfer patients pursuing elective abortions to other hospitals, transferring acutely ill patients to other facilities to receive their desired end-of-life care is less obviously so. Spelling out roles for those working in this field... is an ongoing challenge for Catholic hospitals.[13]

Chapter 6 lays out the issue of conscientious objection more fully.

A couple of aspects about advance directives—one practical, the other philosophical—are also worth noting. Practically speaking, it's very difficult to anticipate or to imagine the medical condition one will ultimately be in that would warrant an advance directive. As a result, directives tend to be general in nature. Also, appointing someone to speak for us when we no longer can speak for ourselves is benign enough so long as the person understands what we want and is willing to say so. But can we be sure of that? Perhaps not. A 1998 study showed that patients and their proxies are in agreement only two-thirds of the time.[14] The deeper, philosophical aspect of advance directives is the underlying assumption that what we want when incompetent is what we said we wanted when competent. But can we accurately anticipate our own state of mind when dying or even when receiving significant medical treatment?

PARTICIPATION IN MEDICAL RESEARCH

The *Belmont Report* recognized that respecting personal autonomy included a right to participate as a subject in medical research. At the same time, it also made clear that medical research involving human subjects called for keen vigilance with respect to informed consent. Its general conclusion, therefore, was that the consent of human subjects to participate in medical research must be based on their clear understanding of the nature of the trial, test, or experiment; its risks, as well as its benefits to themselves and others; and the implications of randomization. Randomization is a method used to assign participants to treatment groups. In ethical research involving human beings, according to Belmont, the subjects have a right to know that being assigned to a control group ordinarily means not receiving any benefit from a possibly promising therapy and, therefore, losing precious time for alternative treatment.

Despite its laudable goals, three decades after Belmont, research subjects still aren't always protected as envisioned.[15] According to Dr. Adil Shamoo of the University of Maryland Medical School, throughout the United States today the politically powerless—children, people of color, the poor, the incarcerated, the decisionally incapacitated—are used as subjects of medical research.[16]

Recognizing, as did the *Belmont Report,* the potential for abuse but also the need for medical research, states have grappled with drafting protective legislation that does not stifle research science. In 1999, for example, Maryland proposed a statute to enhance the rights of human subjects in medical experimentation, specifically the decisionally incapacitated. While the bill was widely viewed as an improvement, it was also severely criticized for allowing institutional review boards that monitor and review medical research projects to substitute their judgments for those who can't judge for themselves.[17]

Other states, South Carolina among them, have flirted with offering prison inmates early release in exchange for an organ. But even without the incentive of reduced prison times, ethicists generally agree that such an incentive would be unethical because prisoners have little autonomy and live in highly coercive environments. Indeed, federal law prohibits inmates from entering clinical trials of drugs under development, even if they have cancer or AIDS.

In 1996 the Secretary of HHS announced a waiver requiring informed consent for a limited number of patients. Under the new Emergency Consent Exception, the requirement of informed consent from each human subject prior to initiation of an experimental intervention would be waived in a limited class of research activities. Excepted would be patients in need of emergency medical intervention who cannot give informed consent because of their life-threatening medical condition and who do not have a legally authorized person to represent them. According to the FDA:

> The intent of the emergency consent exception is to allow research on life-threatening conditions for which available treatments are unproven or unsatisfactory and where it is not possible to obtain informed consent, while

establishing additional protections to provide for safe and ethical studies....[18]

Although supposedly limited in scope, "[w]hat's been happening," according to bioethicist Nancy M.P. Kind at Wake Forest School of Medicine, "is that narrow window seems to be expanding."[19] Indeed, under the consent exception, the government is currently undertaking studies that involve thousands of patients in numerous sites in the United States and Canada, designed to improve treatment after car accidents, cardiac arrest, and other emergencies. Supporters of the research say that this is the only way scientists can do this kind of potentially life-saving research, which is necessary because current treatments are unsatisfactory. But George J. Annas of Boston University is among those who think investigators are just not trying hard enough to obtain informed consent in difficult situations. "I don't think we should use people like this," the renowned bioethicist says, "especially given that children as young as 15 might be included in the research."[20] Others have expressed concern that patients may be getting experimental therapies that could turn out to be inferior to standard treatments.

BIOETHICS ACROSS CULTURES

A Slow Dying in Nigeria

"By the time word of the little girl's death reached the United States, her name had been replaced by numerals: No. 6587-0069. She was 10 years old and a scant 41 pounds. She lived in Nigeria, and in April 1996 she ached from meningitis."

That was the lead of a story that *The Washington Post* broke on December 16, 2000, about a 1996 medical experiment conducted by Pfizer researchers in Kano, Nigeria, during a major meningitis epidemic in that West African nation. Somehow the girl had found the medical camp where two groups of foreign doctors were dispensing expensive medicines for free. One group, a humanitarian charity, Doctors Without Borders, had erected a treatment center solely in an effort to save lives. The other group, Researchers for Pfizer Inc., had set up a second center and was using Nigeria's

meningitis epidemic to conduct experiments on children with what the huge American drug company believed was a promising new antibiotic—Trovan, a drug not yet approved in the United States. The company wanted to test the drug for use against meningitis, including an epidemic strain. Because it couldn't find enough patients in the United States, its researchers had come to Kano, "among the dying." According to the *Post* exposé:

> Doctors working with Pfizer drew spinal fluid from the girl, gauged her symptoms and logged her as patient No. 0069 at testing site No. 6587 in experiment No. 154-149. They gave her 56 milligrams of Trovan. A day later, the girl's strength was evaporating, Pfizer records show, and one of her eyes froze in place. On the third day, she died. Pfizer

records are explicit. Action taken: "Dose continued unchanged." Outcome: "Death."

The story of the girl's slow death created a sensation, especially the part about how Pfizer researchers, following the protocol design to test Trovan in children, monitored her dying apparently without modifying treatment.

The families of the Kano subjects subsequently sued Pfizer in Nigeria and, later, in the United States, charging the company with conducting medical experiments without informed consent. Pfizer argued that there was no international norm requiring its physicians to obtain informed consent for the use of experimental drugs. In 2006, an internal report by the Nigerian Ministry of Health concluded that the Pfizer study violated Nigerian law, the Declaration of Helsinki (promulgated in 1964 and revised eight times since), and the United Nations' Convention on the Rights of the Child. The Nigerian government then filed both a criminal and a civil suit against Pfizer, and a settlement in this case was reportedly reached. Meanwhile, the case continues to wend its way through the US courts. According to George Annas of Boston University School of Public Health, the central allegation that the Nigerian families need to prove is that "Pfizer, working in partnership with the Nigerian government, failed to secure the informed consent of either the children or their guardians and specifically failed to disclose or explain the experimental nature of the study or the serious risks involved" or to inform them that alternative treatment proven to be effective was immediately available from Doctors Without Borders at the medical camp.

(SOURCES: Joe Stephens, "Where Profits and Lives Hang in the Balance," *The Washington Post*, December 17, 2000, p. A1. Retrieved May 18, 2009, from http://www.washingtonpost.com/wp-dyn/content/article/2007/07/02/AR2007070201255_pf.html; George Annas, "Globalized Clinical Trials and Informed Consent," *The New England Journal of Medicine*, May 14, 2009, pp. 2050–2053)

Question

Pharmaceutical companies say that the human subjects are better off participating in research like this, because they at least have a chance of getting a medicine that might benefit them. Do you agree? Do you think that the doctrine of informed consent should be given the status of an international human right that the world's courts can enforce? What likely impact would that have on international corporations and researchers?

PRIVACY AND CONFIDENTIALITY

Since its inception, the *Belmont Report*'s commitment to respect for persons and personal autonomy has provided a sturdy conceptual basis for two of the most familiar patient rights: privacy and confidentiality, both of which are threatened today.

"The most comprehensive of rights and the right most valued by civilized men"—that's how the famous Supreme Court Justice Louis Brandeis (1856–1941) once described the right to privacy (*Olmstead v. United States*, 1928). Although definitions of privacy vary—Brandeis simply called it "the right to be let alone"—a consensus of expert opinion has formed around the notion of control, specifically over information about ourselves and who can experience or observe us, physically or psychologically. An extension of this concept of privacy, confidentiality refers to identifiable data and relates to agreements between participant and investigator, in medical research; or between physician/institution and patient, in clinical practice. Confidentiality specifically addresses how the participant or patient's data will be handled and to whom it will be disclosed.[21]

At a time when vast computer networks can collect and store reams of personal data, it's understandable that privacy and its extension, confidentiality, are more tightly connected to the control of information than ever before. But because of that, it's easy to miss what's ultimately at issue, which has less to do with who knows what about us than with the value of privacy itself, sometimes termed "the cornerstone of a liberal democracy."

Medical ethicist Joseph Kupfer, for one, finds the value of privacy in its connection to autonomy. Privacy, says Kupfer, is essential to having an "autonomous self-concept," that is, "a concept of oneself as in control of your life." Elaborating, Kupfer explains as follows:

> An autonomous self-concept requires identifying with a particular body whose thought, purposes, and actions are subject to one's control.... autonomy requires

awareness of control over one's relation to others, including their access to us... privacy contributes to the formation and persistence of autonomous individuals by providing them with control over whether or not their physical and psychological existence becomes part of another's experience.[22]

Kupfer's argument here is that autonomy is impossible without a concept of oneself as autonomous, and privacy (and its extension, confidentiality) is essential to such a self-concept. Without privacy, without being let alone, we can't be the most autonomous person possible, that is, the one who evaluates her deepest convictions or the most fundamental aspects of his life plan. Put another way: When the most intimate aspects of our lives are up for scrutiny, we are vulnerable to ridicule, censure, coercion, and manipulation by others—no more so than in the area of personal health.

It's little wonder, then, that privacy, and by implication confidentiality, are medical values and obligations as old as the profession itself. Nowhere in the *Oath of Hippocrates*, as noted earlier, does it say, "First, do no harm," but it is written: "What I may see or hear in the course of the treatment or even outside the treatment in regard to the life of men I will keep to myself." The ancients clearly recognized that absent openness and honesty—impossible without privacy and confidentiality—there's no chance for a productive and wholesome physician-patient relationship.[23] As physician and bioethicist Pellegrino writes:

> In a state of vulnerability and inequality, we are forced to trust our physicians.... We are ill equipped to evaluate their competence. We are forced to reveal our intimate selves—baring our bodies, our personal lives, our souls and our failing to another person who is a stranger. Without these invasions of our privacy, we cannot be healed or helped. Moreover, the professional invites our trust. Professionals begin their relationship with us with the question: How can I help you? Implicitly they are saying, "I have knowledge you need; trust me to have it and to use it in

your best interests." In the case of medicine, that promise is made in a public oath at the time of graduation when the graduate announces to all present that, henceforth, he can be trusted to serve interests other than his own. It is repeated in the codes of medicine....[24]

By long-standing legal and professional tradition, Americans could generally count on their health records being protected from prying eyes, but that has changed over the years since *Belmont*. Today we're treated not only to sensational breaches of the personal and confidential medical records of celebrities and public figures, but everyday people as well.[25] In Georgia, for example, a company hired by the state to administer health benefits for low-income patients had to send letters to notify tens of thousands of residents that their private records had been exposed on the Internet for nearly seven weeks before being removed.[26] More ominous than these worrisome breaches, however, are the judicially sanctioned moves at the highest level of government to permit access to health data by private companies and public organizations without one's consent or even notification.[27]

DNA: The Genetic Fingerprint

Potentially the gravest threat to autonomy-guarding privacy today is the expansion of opportunities to learn about our DNA, or genetic fingerprint, and subsequently construct our personal identities. Despite the fact that as many as 95 percent of "breakthrough" linkages between genes and disease or behavior are "false positives," we're often encouraged to have our DNA tested for genetic predispositions to disease, morbid conditions such as obesity, and certain potentially destructive behaviors such as overeating or aggression. As a result, in the future more and more genetic samples likely will be collected and stored. For well-known figures of the past, this means extending modern scientific technology right into the grave; or, in the case of pharaohs, into the pyramids. In 2010, DNA testing showed that Egypt's most famous pharaoh—Tutankhamun (1341–1323 BCE), or King Tut—likely died of a combination of bone

BIOETHICS ACROSS CULTURES

Baseball's Genetic Testing in Latin America

When he signed out of the Dominican Republic in 1993 with the Oakland Athletics, baseball player Miguel Tejada said he was sixteen. Today the star shortstop of the Baltimore Orioles admits he was nineteen. Except to adolescents rushing to grow up, the difference between sixteen and nineteen seems trivial. But in the eyes of professional baseball, there's a huge difference between a 16- and 19-year-old. "It's night and day," as one international scout for a major league team puts it.

By carefully studying visa documents, the federal government has determined that more than three hundred players in professional baseball have falsified their birth dates. In an effort to stop identity and age falsification by Latin American prospects, Major League Baseball (MLB) now conducts genetic testing on promising young Latin players, such as Miguel Sano. Sano, a top Dominican prospect, was given DNA tests and a bone marrow scan to help confirm that he was sixteen. His parents also had DNA testing to prove Miguel was their son; and Sano's sister underwent a bone scan to help confirm that she was his older sibling, and not a younger one whose birth certificate was used to falsify Sano's age. Sano was asked to submit to the tests when questions about his declared identity and age remained after investigation.

As MLB sees it, prospects like Sano are being given a chance to clear up concerns by submitting to the genetic tests, which, according to baseball officials, are used only "in very rare instance and only on a consensual basis to deal with the identity fraud problems that the league faces in that country." The results of the tests are not used for any other purpose, according to MLB.

But many experts in genetics and bioethics don't view these tests so benignly. They see them as an invasion of personal privacy and an instance of the type of employer-employee arrangements that the Genetic Information Nondiscrimination Act (GINA) was intended to prohibit. "DNA contains a host of information about risks for future diseases that prospective employers might be interested in discovering and considering,"

says Kathy Hudson, the director of the Genetics and Public Policy Center and an associate professor at Johns Hopkins University. "The point of GINA was to remove the temptation and prohibit employers from asking or receiving information," according to Hudson.

Even some baseball people concede the potential for "fishing expeditions," that is, using the tests for other purposes beyond age and identity verification. As one scouting director puts it:

> It's a tough area to figure morally and in all kinds of directions. Can they test susceptibility to cancer? I don't know if they're doing any of that. But I know they're looking into trying to figure out susceptibility to injuries, things like that. If they come up with a test that shows someone's connective tissue is at a high risk of not holding up, can that be used? I don't know. I do think that's where this is headed.

A professor of bioethics notes the irony of baseball's excursion into genetic testing. "The funny thing about this," says Mark Rothstein of the University of Louisville School of Medicine, "is that the most famous baseball player with a genetic disorder was Lou Gehrig. Would they have signed him if they knew he was predisposed to A.L.S. [amyotrophic lateral sclerosis]?" On July 22, 2010, MLB announced that it would immediately begin drawing blood from minor league players to test for human growth hormone, thereby becoming the first U.S. professional sports organization to conduct testing for HGH.

(SOURCE: Michael S. Schmidt and Alan Schwarz, "Baseball's Use of DNA Tests on Prospects Find Controversy, Too," *The New York Times*, July 22, 2009, p. A1.)

Question

Is MLB's genetic testing warranted? Should GINA cover cases of American companies conducting DNA tests abroad on citizens of other countries? Do you think the Sanos gave informed consent?

---

disease and malaria. Interesting, to be sure. But this medical find left some ethicists asking whether major historical figures have a right to privacy after death just as private citizens do in life.[28]

Perhaps the most important thing surrendered with one's DNA is the "autonomy to discover and

use one's own genetic information for one's own purposes...," according to Annas and Patricia M. Roche. The lawyers/medical ethicists write:

> A fundamental concern is that the possession and storage of a personally identifiable

DNA sample give the possessor access to a wealth of information about the person and his or her genetic relatives. This includes information derivable from new DNA tests that were not available, or even anticipated, when the sample was relinquished. Consequently, as long as personally identifiable DNA samples are stored, there is the possibility of unauthorized access to and use of genetic information—an invasion of genetic privacy. To the extent that we see our future and ourselves as influenced by our genes, such invasions can disrupt our very sense of self.[29]

Although the majority of states have begun to regulate testing and the fair use of genetic information, the regulations are generally anti-discrimination statutes that do no address the ultimate disposition of collected and analyzed DNA. More encouraging is federal legislation that bans genetic discrimination.

In May 2008, a full thirteen years after such legislation was first introduced, the US Congress finally approved the *Genetic Information Nondiscrimination Act*, which protects consumers from discrimination by health insurers and employees on the basis of genetic information.

Despite their traditional value and importance in fostering the physician-patient relationship, there are times when privacy and confidentiality must be breached, notably when, in the words of The World Health Organization (WHO), the expected harm of maintaining them is believed to be "imminent, serious and unavoidable except by unauthorized disclosure." Documenting a drug allergy in the medical record or complying with a court order or a law (as in cases of child abuse) are obvious examples. Doctors must also betray confidentiality when it is in the "public interest," as with reporting infectious diseases or warning potential victims of violence.

CONCLUSIONS

The core principles underlying the *Belmont Report* and their applications have served for three decades as a leading source of guidance regarding the ethical standards that should govern research with human participants and, more broadly, policies and decisions on a range of issues that arise in clinical settings. Indeed, in the United States today the principlism that was first formulated by philosophers and theologians remains the dominant method of doing bioethics, and it has come to be defined largely by reference to patient autonomy. This helps account for why analyses of truthtelling, informed consent, advance directives, and privacy and confidentiality inevitably orbit around the right of the patient to make decisions about their medical care without physician influence. In short, driving most discussions about the core principles and their extensions is the overriding assumption that the physician may educate, but not decide for, the patient.

As we enter deeper into the post-Belmont era, where patient autonomy outweighs traditional Hippocratic paternalism, philosophical analyses of autonomy anchor coherent, reasonable arguments for individual and scientific freedom across the spectrum of bioethical issues. From prenatal testing and preconception sex selection to stem cell research and cloning, assisted death, and euthanasia, bioethics seems to have as its goal patient (or physician/scientist) autonomy. And yet, in the words of one observer, each of these issues continues to elicit "anger, fear, and revulsion,"[30] especially, though not exclusively, among religious and social conservatives. The upshot has been a backlash against what critics view as an overemphasis on patient autonomy and, more generally, against the secular bioethics with which it is so closely identified. In the following chapter, we'll see why many analysts today, including secularists, argue that the texture of human values is richer and more complex than an ethic of autonomy confers.

CASES AND CONTROVERSIES

The Merenstein Case of Informed Consent

Early in his resident program in Virginia, Dr. Daniel Merenstein gave a physical exam to a highly educated patient in his mid-fifties. As part of the exam, Dr. Merenstein said he discussed with the patient "the importance of colon cancer screening, seat belts, dental care, exercise, improved diet, and sunscreen use." He also discussed with the patient all of the relevant risks and benefits regarding screening for prostate cancer via the prostate specific antigen, or PSA, test. While PSA screening, which consists of a benign blood test, can detect early-stage prostate cancer, there's no conclusive evidence that it improves health outcomes. It can, however, produce false positives, which can lead to unnecessary surgery or radiation treatments with significant side effects, such as impotence and incontinence. In short, while the harms of PSA screening can be established, its benefit currently cannot be. As a result, a number of national medical associations advise that each asymptomatic patient should determine whether to have the test upon reaching a certain age or wait until symptomatic. After Dr. Merenstein shared all of this information with his patient, who declined the test, he never saw the man as patient again.

Some time after Merenstein completed his residency program, the patient was examined at a different clinic, and his PSA level was found to be very high. Further tests led to a diagnosis of incurable, advanced-stage prostate cancer. Dr. Merenstein was sued for malpractice; the trial began on June 23, 2003.

Although Merenstein was convinced that he followed all disclosure guidelines, he listened to the plaintiff's attorney argue that his behavior constituted malpractice in Virginia. In all states, to win a malpractice suit it must be established that the physician violated the standard of care, which in turn resulted in the patient's injury. Due to the minimal risks associated with the simple blood test, the plaintiff argued that Merenstein should have ordered the PSA screen without discussing it with his patient. When four Virginia physicians supported that assessment, the plaintiff won his case against Merenstein's residency program.

Questions for Analysis

1. Explain how this case illustrates the tension between the two types of standards for informed consent.

2. Which of the standards did the court go with, and do you agree with its decision?

3. As a patient, would you want a physician to order a controversial but benign test for you without first discussing its risks, benefits, and alternatives with you?

4. Who should bear responsibility when the risks accepted in a difficult situation come to fruition?

CASES AND CONTROVERSIES

Jaffee v. Redmond (1996): Safeguarding Patient Communication

Mary Lu Redmond was a police officer for the Village of Hoffman Estates, Illinois, when, on June 21, 1991, she was the first to respond to a call from the relatives of a man named Ricky Allen about an altercation between two men at a suburban apartment complex. The relatives met Redmond as she arrived, and the officer saw two men run out of a building. The man trailing had a knife in his hand, which he raised to stab the man in front of him, an arm's length away. Redmond shouted, "Stop, police!" When no one responded, she shot the man with the knife to prevent a homicide. Ricky Allen fell, mortally wounded and bleeding from an artery in his neck. Redmond called an ambulance while Allen's relatives stared in horror and anger. They had called the police to stop the fight, and now their cousin and brother lay dying. Redmond was white, and Allen was black.

So troubled was Redmond by these events that she sought counseling from her employer's internal employee assistance program. As director of the department, psychotherapist Karen Beyer decided it would be best if she took on the therapy in what was shaping up as a high-profile case.

Redmond and Beyer worked together for almost two years and then a subpoena arrived for the records of their work. Redmond balked. She wanted the records of her sessions with Beyer kept private, and Beyer acceded. The psychotherapist did, however, assure the judge and attorneys that Redmond's account of the facts never varied from her original report. Moreover, both the police department and the State of Illinois found Redmond's actions appropriate according to department guidelines. Nevertheless, pressure on both to release the records continued to mount. Eventually, Ricky Allen's mother, Carrie Jaffee, brought a civil right suit against Redmond and the police department for wrongful death due to excessive use of force. Because it was a civil rights case, it was heard in a federal court, in Chicago.

The federal judge soon joined the chorus of attorneys who advised Beyer to turn over her client's records. Beyer refused because of "the devastating effect I believed this would have had on Redmond." Beyer told the court that Redmond was "a proud and very private person who had been traumatized by the shooting and the events that followed. Her records contained nothing more than her private struggle to heal." The federal judge instructed the jury in the case that they could assume that Redmond and Beyer were concealing damaging information. With those instructions, the jury found for the Jaffees.

At the appeals level the decision was overturned. The judges in the Circuit Court of Appeals applied "balancing theory," which takes into consideration the public's right to know what is in the records versus an individual's right to privacy. The circuit court judges ruled in this case that the privacy of records of a police officer who sought therapeutic help after a traumatic incident outweigh the need for the public to know the contents of the record to determine her state of mind at the time of the shooting.

But the matter didn't end there. Jaffee succeeded in getting the case accepted by the US Supreme Court, and on June 13, 1996, five years after the shooting, the high court issued its decision. The 7-2 majority stated that psychotherapists could not be forced to provide evidence about their patients in federal court cases. The majority asserted:

> Significant private interests support recognition of a psychotherapist privilege. Effective psychotherapy depends upon an atmosphere of confidence and trust and therefore the mere possibility of disclosure may impede development of the relationship necessary for successful treatment. The privilege also serves the public interest, since the mental health of the Nation's citizenry, no less than its physical health, is a public good of transcendent importance.

In dissenting, Justice Antonin Scalia expressed skepticism about the special standing the majority was giving to psychotherapy:

> Effective psychotherapy undoubtedly is beneficial to individuals with mental problems, and surely serves some larger social interest in maintaining a mentally stable society. But merely mentioning these values does not answer the critical question: Are they of such importance, and is the contribution of psychotherapy to them so distinctive, and is the application of normal evidentiary rules so destructive to psychotherapy, as to justify making our federal courts occasional instruments of injustice [by excluding evidence from court]?

Additionally, Scalia said he didn't see why therapists like Beyer should be granted special privilege to keep secrets. "For most of history," Scalia wrote, "men and women have worked out their difficulties by talking to… parents, siblings, best friends, and bartenders— none of whom was awarded a privilege against testifying in court."[31]

Questions for Analysis

1. *Jaffee* established the psychotherapist-patient privilege in the federal courts. Should communications between therapists and patients enjoy absolute protection from disclosure?

2. Is Scalia's analogy correct, or are psychotherapists significantly different from "parents, siblings, best friends, and bartenders"?

3. In a related case, a man named John Auster informed his therapist, Dr. Fred Davis, that unless the managers of his workers' compensation claim continued to pay the benefits that he believed he was owed, he would "carry out his plan of violent retribution" against them and others. Dr. Davis informed authorities; Auster was arrested and indicted for extortion. Though denying Auster's motion to dismiss the indictment, a district court ruled that communications between Auster and his therapist were inadmissible at trial under the psychotherapist-patient privilege. On appeal, however, the lower court's decision was reversed. In *U.S. v. Auster* (2008) the US Court of Appeals for the Fifth Circuit said that Auster had no reasonable expectation of confidentiality when he made his threat. Do you agree with this decision, or do you think the therapist-patient protection should extend even to cases like Auster's?

CASES AND CONTROVERSIES

Jesse Gelsinger: The First Gene Therapy Death

In 1999 the field of gene therapy held great promise for treating and even curing dozens of diseases, including ornithine transcarbamylase (OTC) deficiency, a metabolic liver disease that causes a dangerous buildup of ammonia in the body and usually is fatal at birth. Jesse Gelsinger (1981–1999) was one of the fortunate OTC victims. Jesse's version of OTC was not inherited but the result of a genetic mutation. As such it wasn't as severe, and with a restricted diet and special medications the 18-year-old from Tucson was doing pretty well when, in the fall of 1999, he joined a clinical trial run by the University of Pennsylvania that aimed to correct the mutation that resulted in OTC. Researchers planned to create a needed enzyme by infusing a corrective gene into the body of a human subject like Jesse.

Three months before his actual participation in the clinical trial, Jesse and his father, Paul, who had a science background, met with one of the principal investigators, who spelled out the risks. There was the possibility of an immune response, including serious liver damage; and a subsequent liver biopsy after the infusion also could produce serious side effects. But, in general, son and father were told that the most likely downside would be "flu-like symptoms." About a month later they received further reassurance from another principal investigator, this one an expert on OTC, who reported that the most recent patient had significantly benefited from the treatment. With their concerns allayed, says Paul Gelsinger, "We totally dropped our guard and Jesse made arrangements to participate."

On September 13, 1999, Jesse was injected with adenoviruses carrying a corrected gene and suffered a massive immune response. Straightaway, multiple organs failed, and four days later, on September 17, Jesse Gelsinger was dead.

Within six weeks of his son's death, Paul Gelsinger settled a suit against the University of Pennsylvania; James Wilson, the Penn investigator who headed the trials; and Arthur Caplan, the Penn bioethicist who provided ethical oversight on the study. The FDA conducted its own investigation, and in 2005 announced a $517,000 settlement with Penn and said research restrictions would be placed on three doctors involved in the case, including Wilson. According to the FDA investigation, the scientists involved in the trial broke several rules of conduct:

- making false statement and claims about the gene therapy trial, including the misrepresenting of information that would have halted the

experiment ("the study had produced toxicities in humans that should have resulted in termination");

- failing to disclose all possible dangers in patient consent forms;

- including Gelsinger, despite having high ammonia levels that should have led to his exclusion from the trial;

- failing to report that two patients had experienced serious side effects from the gene therapy;

- failing to disclose that animals had died in the research;

- underreporting side effects;

- failing to notify the FDA and university monitors of critical changes in the study; and

- having a potential conflict of interest. (Wilson, for example, was the founder of a biotechnology firm set up to take gene therapy from the laboratory to the marketplace. His company, Genova Inc., provided about a quarter of the budget for Penn's gene therapy institute. When Genova was sold in 2000 to Seattle-based Targeted Genetics Corp., Wilson was to receive one million shares, then worth about $13.5 million.)

In the years since the death of Jess Gelsinger, the nation's top medical schools have instituted a number of reforms, including conflict-of-interest guidelines requiring researchers to disclose any financial interest they have in patient studies. The results have been, at best, uneven, as shown in a previous case presentation (Drugs, Devices, and Disclosure, Chapter 4).[32-35]

Questions for Analysis

1. Identify the factors that undermined informed consent in this case.

2. Do you agree with Paul Gelsinger's assessment that "[t]he system failed my son at every level"?[36]

3. Under the settlement, Penn and the three researchers did not admit to the government's allegations and contended "that their conduct was at all times lawful and appropriate." Do you agree?

4. One of the complaints against bioethicist Caplan was that he advised the researchers that parents of terminally ill children, who were initially viewed as the subject pool, were incapable of giving informed consent, and suggested it

would be better, ethically, to use otherwise healthy adults with the mild form of OTC.[37] Apparently, then, Caplan was exercising care in his dealing with the researchers. Do you think that his moral obligation extended to Gelsinger and his family?

5. "Anyone considering joining a clinical trial needs to be aware that they are dealing with a system that is seriously flawed" is Paul Gelsinger's warning to prospective participants in clinical trials. What corrective measures would you make to ensure participant safety?[38]

REFERENCES

1. *A Patient's Bill of Rights*, Chicago: The American Hospital Association, 1992.

2. Pauline W. Chen, "The Most-Avoided Conversation in Medicine," *The New York Times*, December 26, 2007, p. A27.

3. Nicholas A. Christakis, "The Bad News First," *The New York Times*, August 24, 2008, p. A19.

4. Anne-Mei, The, "Collusion in doctor-patient communication about imminent death: an ethnographic study," *BMJ*, December 2, 2000, p. 7273. Retrieved February 24, 2008, from http://www.pubmedcentral.nih.gov/articlerender.fcgi?artid=27539.

5. Jane E. Brody, "Just What the Doctor Ordered? Not Exactly," *The New York Times*, May 9, 2006, p. D8.

6. Jane Brody, "The Importance of Knowing What the Doctor Is Talking About," *The New York Times*, January 30, 2007, p. D7.

7. M. Kutner, E. Greenberg, and J. Baer, *A First Look at the Literacy of America's Adults in the 21st century*. Washington, D.C.: National Center for Education Statistics, Department of Education, December, 2005. Retrieved June 5, 2008, from http://nces.ed.gov/naal/.

8. David W. Baker, et al, "Health Literacy and Mortality Among Elderly Persons," *Archives of Internal Medicine*, July 23, 2007, pp. 1503–1509. Retrieved June 1, 2008, from http://archinte.ama-assn.org/

9. Erin Marcus, "The Silent Epidemic—The Health Effects of Illiteracy," *The New England Journal of Medicine*, July 27, 2006, pp. 339–341.

10. "Special Issue on Health Literacy," *Journal of General Internal Medicine*, August, 2006.

11. Jaime Staples King and Benjamin Moulton, "Rethinking Informed Consent: The Case for Shared Medical Decision-Making," *American Journal of Law & Medicine*, vol. 32, 2006, pp. 429–501. Retrieved May 11, 2009, from www.informedmedicaldecisions.org/pdfs/shared_med_decisions.pdf.

12. Louis Kutner, "Due Process of Euthanasia: The Living Will, A Proposal," *Indiana Law Journal*, vol. 44, 1969, p. 549.

13. Eran Klein, "The Hard Case of Palliative Sedation," *Virtual Mentor*, May 2007, pp. 345–349. Retrieved June 10, 2008, from virtualmentor.ama-assn.org/2007/05/ccas3-0705.html.

14. D. Sulmasy, et al, "The Accuracy of Substituted Judgments in Patients with Terminal Diagnoses," *Annals of Internal Medicine*, April 15, 1998, pp. 621–629.

15. National Bioethics Advisory Commission, *Ethical and Policy Issues in Research Involving Human Subjects*, Bethesda, MD, August 2001. Retrieved June 20, 2008, from http://bioethics.georgetown.edu/nbac/human/oversumm.html.

16. Mike Ervin, "Guinea Pigs Don't Get To Say 'No'," *The Ragged Edge*, Nov./Dec. 1998, The Disability News Service, Inc. Retrieved June 2, 2008, from http://www.ragged-edge-mag.com/1198/b1198ff2.htm.

17. See note 16 above.

18. "Exception from Informed Consent For Studies Conducted in Emergency Settings: Regulatory Language and Excerpts from Preamble," *Information Sheets: National Review Boards and Clinical Investigators 1998 Update*, Washington: U.S. Food and Drug Administration, 1998. Retrieved June 9, 2008, from www.fda.gov/oc/ohrt/irbs/except.html

19. Rob Stein, "Critical Care Without Consent," *The Washington Post*, May 27, 2007, p. A1.

20. See note 19 above.

21. "Chapter 5: Ensuring Voluntary Informed Consent and Protecting Privacy and Confidentiality (Research Involving Human Participants V1)," *Online Ethics Center for Engineering*, June 14, 2006. Retrieved May 30, 2008, from www.onlineethics.org/CMS/research/resref/nbacindex/nbachindex/hchapter5.aspx.

22. Joseph Kupfer, "Privacy, Autonomy, and Self-Concept," *American Philosophical Quarterly*, vol. 24, 1987, p. 82.

23. Sandeep Jauhar, "Break a Confidence? Never. Well, Hardly Ever," *The New York Times*, May 29, 2007, p. D5.

24. Edmund D. Pellegrino, "Character, Virtue, and Self-Interest in the Ethics of the Professions," *Loma Linda University, Provonsha Lecture*, February 15, 1989. Retrieved June 3, 2008, from http://www.llu.edu/llu/bioethics/prov89.htm.

25. Charles Ornstein, "Just 'Nosy,' Says Figure in Medical Data Scandal," *Los Angeles Times*, April 9, 2008, p. A1.

26. Brenda Goodman, "Georgia Patients' Records Exposed on Web for Weeks," *The New York Times*, April 11, 2008, p. A19.

27. Eve Bender, "Advocates Ask Federal Court To Overturn Privacy Rule." *Psychiatric News*, May 16, 2003, p. 5.

28. *JAMA*, February 17, 2010.

29. Patricia A. Roche and George J. Annas, "DNA Testing, Banking, and Genetic Privacy," *The New England Journal of Medicine*, August 10, 2006, p. 345.

30. Courtney S. Campbell, "Religion And Moral Meaning In Bioethics," *Hastings Center Report*, July–August 1990, pp. 4–10. Retrieved May 10, 2008, from http://ccbs.ntu.edu.tw/FULLTEXT/JR-MDL/camp.htm.

31. King and Moulton, Retrieved May 1, 2009, from www.informedmedicaldecisions.org/pdfs/shared_med_decisions.

32. Karen Beyer, "*Jaffee v. Redmond* Therapist Speak," *American Psychoanalyst*, September 2000. Retrieved April 14, 2009, from http://jaffee-redmond.org/articles/beyer.htm.

33. Alla Katsnelson, "Fixing Gene Therapy Trials," *The Scientist: NewsBlog*, January 23, 2008. Retrieved May 17, 2009, from http://www.the-scientist.com/blog/print/54207/.

34. Paul Gelsinger, "A Comment from Paul Gelsinger on Gene Therapy and Informed Consent," *blog.bioethics.net*, January 31, 2008. Retrieved May 19, 2009, from http://blog.bioethics.net/2008/01/a-comment-from-paul-gelsinger-on-gene-therapy-and/.

35. Susan Fitzgerald and Virginia A. Smith, "Penn to pay $517,000 in gene therapy death," *Philadelphia Inquirer*, February 10, 2005. Retrieved May 20, 2009, from http://www.irbforum.org/forum/read/2/95/95.

36. Sheryl Gay Stolberg, "The Biotech Death of Jesse Gelsinger," *The New York Times*, November 28, 1999. Retrieved May 20, 2009, from http://www.nytimes.com/1999/11/28/magazine/the-biotech-death-of-jesse-gelsinger.html.

37. Mary R. Anderlik, "Legal Liability for Bioethicists Involved in Research," *Health Law & Policy Institute*, October 2, 2000. Retrieved May 20, 2009, from http://www.law.uh.edu/healthlaw/perspectives/Research/001002Best.html.

38. Kristen Philipkoski, "Perils of Gene Experimentation," *Wired*, February 21, 2003. Retrieved May 20, 2009, from www.wired.com/techbiz/media/news/2003/02/57752.

Chapter 6

Beyond Principlism I: Autonomy Under Attack

Since the Enlightenment, we've grown comfortable with two notions about morality that help explain why principlism and contemporary bioethics are under attack. The first is the view of morality as a matter of "human agency and decisive action." In other words, individuals choose their moral commitments and are held accountable for their choices.[1] This is the practical meaning of personal autonomy. We're also at ease with a second Enlightenment affection: the social contract model. Indeed, contractarianism provided a conceptual framework for the Belmont principles and has had the effect of encouraging physicians to frame their relationship with patients largely in terms of a contracted agreement, with special attention to patient autonomy.

For many physicians, then, honoring patient autonomy within a model of contractarianism has come to mean adherence to patient choice based on informed consent, something that the law stringently requires. From this procedural or legalistic standpoint, it's a short step to viewing the governing principles of bioethics—that is, doing the "right" thing—as merely sound risk management strategies, or ways of avoiding civil wrongs such as tort, malpractice, and assault and battery. Consider, for example, the following actual case and its impact on the physician.

FEELING BETRAYED BY PRINCIPLISM

The patient was a seventeen-year-old girl from an Orthodox Jewish community on the East Coast. Three weeks prior to her hospitalization the young woman had consulted with her rabbi about Jewish laws covering her upcoming arranged wedding to a young man she'd met only once. In the medical phase of marital counseling, the woman was found to have dysfunctional uterine bleeding, which subsequently was tracked to uterine cancer. Dr. John Lantos and his colleagues recommended radiation followed by a hysterectomy, which would leave the woman infertile. But the young woman's father feared that the news would devastate his daughter and jeopardize the wedding; so he requested that she not be told that the treatment would leave her infertile.

Of the decision he faced, Dr. Lantos writes:

> In one sense it was easy. Informed consent, respect for persons, truth telling. From a risk-management point of view, it was a no-brainer. You tell her; if she refused treatment, that's her choice. It may be tragic, but it isn't tort. Treat without consent and she sues later; it is at least malpractice and maybe assault and battery.[2]

From a principlism perspective, then, the right course of action seemed clear-cut: Tell the patient the whole truth.

But, on second thought, the matter was a bit more complex. Whose interests were paramount, the patient's or the hospital's? And what about the principles used to decide? The Belmont principles were neither timeless nor universal. Had the young woman not been in the United States, for example, or had it been a few decades earlier than the 1990s, perhaps nobody would have told her. She was, after all, a minor, and her concerned and sincere parents had the legal right to decide for her. Then there was the matter of her religion, which didn't acknowledge the primacy of autonomy. As her father said, "She must have treatment. Law requires it. Why add to her suffering now, when she needs hope and strength?"

When the young woman was told the whole, hard truth, she said she didn't want the treatment and stormed out of the room, leaving Dr. Lantos questioning his decision:

> Did we do the right thing? We followed all the rules. Our actions were based on adherence to the most idealistic moral principles. In a certain sense, what we did was unassailable. In the most difficult and trying circumstances, we had confronted ugly truths instead of hiding from them. We had helped a patient who clearly had the capacity to make her own decisions, to understand the choices before her, and

to make a choice based on her own deeply felt moral values. This was a triumph for patient autonomy, for feminism, for children's rights, a culmination of twenty-five years of work in health law, civil liberties, and bioethics. But it felt as if we had betrayed everything that medicine stands for and had become zealots in a cause that looked less like moral excellence and more like political dogma.

Although Dr. Lantos did what he ought to have done, according to principlism, in retrospect he is not persuaded that he best served this young woman. In fact, he feels that he placed physician and institutional values and interests above his patient's. To him this suggests that playing by the rules perhaps is not the same as "moral excellence," which means more than not doing what is wrong. Moral excellence also means doing what is right, and that's where, in this instance, Lantos feels betrayed by principlism. Although he studiously acted on principle to avoid wrongdoing, both moral and legal, he somehow feels that, in this instance, he and the philosophy of principlism failed the test of moral excellence.

Dr. Lantos is hardly alone in his feelings. As strict autonomy, defined largely by the criteria of informed consent, has come to dominate the social contract between physician and patient, some say the other principles—nonmaleficence, beneficence, justice—have been neglected. They also say that the primacy of autonomy has been to the detriment of significant existential and spiritual aspects of the physician/patient relationship. Most troubling is the charge that, uncoupled from a larger vision of societal good or human ends, principlism turns the complexity of moral decision making and argument in medicine into very thin gruel.[3] Of course the Belmont principles matter, critics concede, but they also believe that bioethics needs to go beyond the philosophy of principlism, beyond the belief that any medical ethical dilemma can be reduced to the core principles and their applications.

This chapter and the next examine these serious criticisms. We begin where contemporary attacks on principlism often do: with a critique of the primacy of patient autonomy.

THE CRITIQUE OF AUTONOMY

To critics, a strict emphasis on patient autonomy variously (1) impoverishes bioethics, (2) disallows conscientious objection, and (3) overrides professional judgment.

Patient Autonomy as Impoverishing Bioethics

One line of criticism attacks the preeminence of autonomy as emptying ethics of its contents. Janet Smith, for example, feels that the principle of autonomy has crowded out of bioethics both deontological and utilitarian arguments, leaving patient treatment choice as the quasi-absolute moral value and normative standard. Smith, a Catholic moralist, says:

> Neither bioethicists, doctors, or patients need to justify their choices in terms of moral principles: the overriding concern is whether or not a patient's autonomy is being respected. This turn from considering the moral acceptability of issues to ensuring the autonomy of choices renders the discipline of bioethics rather vacuous.[4]

Fr. Richard McCormick, one of the Belmont theologians, shares Smith's concern. "If the primary and exclusive emphasis is on autonomy," McCormick warns, "we will have excluded from consideration those goods and values that make choices right or wrong." But those "goods and values" are precisely some of the key factors that make bioethics a moral enterprise; for, according to McCormick, "they are the factors that support or undermine, promote or harm the person." McCormick is convinced, then, that "[w]hen the rightness or wrongness of choice is reduced to the single factor that it is this individual's choice, morality has been impoverished."[5]

Smith and McCormick are among a number of philosophers and theologians who, since the mid-1990s, have expressed concern that autonomy has gone well beyond being merely a means to good. Daniel Callahan, for another, argues that, given its cultural power, "every benefit of every doubt is given to autonomy" as a matter of "working public policy." As a result, Callahan believes we are losing the "moral commons in medicine."[6] *Moral commons* refers, roughly, to the specific good shared by and beneficial for the community at large. Callahan's point is that the more considerations of autonomy drive public policy the less consideration is given to the common good. Illustrative, he says, is artificial reproduction where anonymous sperm donations degrade the traditional understanding of fatherhood. In other cases, as with resistance to mandatory testing for AIDS, claims of autonomy and liberty thwart the promotion of public health, according to Callahan.

Physician Albert Tauber, on the other hand, is more concerned with what an emphasis on autonomy does to the traditional nature of medicine. He sees the idea of patient autonomy as an extension of an Enlightenment political and social philosophy that fails to ground the moral character of medicine. Rather than focusing on patient self-determination, he believes that his medical colleagues need to reconstitute their commitment to beneficence, which, together with the traditional professional responsibility of restoring health and reducing suffering, he argues is compatible with and supportive of patient autonomy. Striking a balance between autonomy and beneficence, Tauber says, is an aspect of the inevitable larger search for balance between "individualism and communal concerns [that] is no less than the search for the social glue that ties us together in a highly pluralistic culture."[7]

Patient Autonomy Disallows Conscientious Objection

As noted earlier, the primacy of autonomy has come to mean that physicians must faithfully honor patient informed consent, by disclosing all options, including risk assessments, and allowing patients to choose among them. But where does that leave physician autonomy and that of other health care professionals? Is their sole or overriding professional responsibility to ensure patient autonomy? Models that emphasize strict patient autonomy have been criticized for diminishing *professional* autonomy, including responsibility, by making physicians and others mere technicians or vendors of health care goods and services. More specifically, critics say that the primacy of patient autonomy disallows professional, conscientious objection.[8]

Cases of conscientious objection usually involve either reproductive or end-of-life scenarios. The former include providing emergency contraception or "morning after" pills, performing abortion for failed contraception, prescribing birth control to adolescents without parental approval, artificially inseminating unmarried women, inseminating gay women, or assisting in abortions. End-of-life scenarios might involve deliberately hastening death, administering terminal sedation to dying patients, or treating patients deemed "medically futile." The debates that these practices spark pit professional conscience against patient choice. On one hand, it's widely acknowledged that physicians should not have to engage in medical practices that violate their morals or religious beliefs. On the other hand, it's also acknowledged that patients should have access even to legal treatments that morally trouble health care providers.[9] At issue are serious questions about the balance of rights and obligations within the doctor-patient relationship. *Is it ethical for physicians or other health professionals to describe their objections to patients? May they keep their objections to themselves, or are they obligated to disclose them? May they refuse to discuss, provide, or refer patients for medical interventions to which they have moral objections?* A related issue involves depriving patients a treatment that others may receive, such as denying young, unmarried women birth control. (See case "When Plan B Doesn't Work," end of chapter.)

R. Alta Charo, a University of Wisconsin lawyer and bioethicist, suggests that the conflict about conscience clauses "represents the latest struggle with regard to religion in America," and she criticizes those medical professionals who would claim

"an unfettered right to personal autonomy while holding monopolistic control over a public good."[10] Regarding "pro-life pharmacies," Charo worries about what will happen if they proliferate, especially in rural areas.

> We may find ourselves with whole regions of the country where virtually every pharmacy follows these limiting, discriminatory policies and women are unable to access legal, physician-prescribed medications. We're talking about creating a separate universe of pharmacies that puts women at a disadvantage.[11]

Some doctors agree, invoking the physician's remit according to the *Oath of Hippocrates* to "prescribe regimens for the good of my patients according to my ability and my judgment and never do harm to anyone." Like Charo and philosopher Julian Savulescu, they remind their colleagues that there is no mention of sentiment or conscience here, that a doctor gives the advice or acts in a manner that is medically sound.[12] The Hastings Center's Nancy Berlinger concurs. "If you are a health-care professional," she says, "you are bound by professional obligations. You can't say you won't do part of that profession."[13]

Others doctors, however, point to the primary goal of health service—to protect the health of its recipients—which they feel obligates physicians to protect life at all stages, regardless of patient preference.[14] Just because abortion, emergency contraception, and terminal sedation are legal, they say, doesn't make them moral. In this spirit, the American Pharmacists Association (APA) permits its 50,000-strong membership to refuse to fill prescriptions if they object on moral grounds, and Pharmacists for Life International actively promotes a pharmacist's right to refuse to fill prescriptions he or she feels "stops a human life in any way."[15] Bioethicist Loren E. Lomasky of the University of Virginia welcomes the so-called pro-life pharmacy as consistent with national values that accommodate a spectrum of beliefs. "In general," she says, "I think product differentiation expressive of differing values is a very good thing for a free, pluralistic society. If we can have 20 different brands of toothpaste, why not a few different conceptions of how pharmacies ought to operate?"[16]

Some health care providers go even further in defense of conscientious objection. They say the right of conscience includes not only refusal to treat but also to refer. "To knowingly send a patient to someone I knew was going to cause them harm [e.g., terminate a pregnancy]," says Al Weir, a former oncologist and director of the Tennessee-based Christian Medical Association, "to me that would be the wrong thing to do."[17] Sharing this sentiment is a pharmacist who says: "If I don't believe something is right, the last thing I want to do is refer to someone else. It's up to that person to be able to find it."[18]

But Charo insists that informing the patient is not only acceptable but also obligatory. Otherwise, she says, the patient doesn't have the option to access other physicians, and that is "a raw imposition of our personal beliefs on all those who come to you for professional services."[19] The APA urges conscientious objectors to arrange for patients to get the pills. Yet some pharmacists have refused to hand the prescription to another druggist to fill. In some cases they've refused to give the prescription back to a woman so that she can fill it in another pharmacy.

The apparent division of opinion within the medical profession regarding conscientious objection has serious clinical implications. A recent study conducted by ethics researchers at the University of Chicago reported a substantial proportion of physicians who object to certain treatments. For example, 52 percent of the physicians in this study reported objections to abortion for failed contraception, and 42 percent reported objections to contraception for adolescents without parental consent. Nearly 30 percent of physicians surveyed would have a problem referring a patient to another physician for procedures that are legal but controversial; and about half that number didn't feel obligated to inform their patients of options that they, the physicians, thought to be immoral. Female physicians were substantially more likely to say doctors must give all the information and make referrals than

were male physicians. The authors of the study concluded:

> If physicians' ideas translate into their practices, then 14% of patients—more than 40 million Americans—may be cared for by physicians who do not believe they are obligated to disclose information about medically available treatments they consider objectionable. In addition, 29% of patients—or nearly 100 million Americans—may be cared for by physicians who do not believe they have an obligation to refer the patient to another provider for such treatments.[20]

As tensions escalate between the patient's right to choose and the physician's right to refuse, Dr. Farr A. Curlin, lead author of the study, has some advice for patients concerning informed consent:

> They should know that many physicians do not believe they are obligated to disclose information about or provide referrals for legal yet controversial treatments. Patients who want full disclosure from their own physicians might inform themselves of possible medical interventions—a task that is not always easy—and might proactively question their physicians about these matters. Patients may not have ready access to information about physicians' religious characteristics and moral convictions. Thus, if patients are concerned about certain interventions for sexual and reproductive health and end-of-life care, they should ask their doctors ahead of time whether they will discuss such options. If a patient wants a treatment that the physician will not provide, the patient may choose to consult a different physician.[21]

Many doctors, however, think that this advice places too much responsibility on the patients and ignores the fact they often have no choice of physician. Such concerns drew this comment from an Oregon physician:

> In the dark ages of medical paternalism, doctors alone decided what was best for patients. Full disclosure about the PAR

[procedure, alternatives, and risks] of treatment is a secular ethical concept based on human rights. Sadly, as Curlin's data show, paternalism remains—particularly among Christian male doctors fighting culture wars instead of serving patients. This means patients must work to get professionals to conduct a full PAR conference—particularly true if seeking reproductive or end of life care.[22]

California, New Jersey, Illinois, and Washington State recently began requiring pharmacies to fill all prescriptions or help patient/customers fill them elsewhere. Other states are considering such requirements.

In 2008 HHS proposed a regulation to protect health care workers who object to abortion and to birth control methods they consider tantamount to abortion. Under the proposal, federal funding would be denied to any hospital, clinic, health plan, or other entity that did not accommodate employees who wanted to opt out of participating in care that ran counter to their personal convictions, including providing birth control pills, IUDs, and the Plan B emergency contraceptive. The most controversial section of the proposal defined abortion as

> any of the various procedures—including the prescription, dispensing and administration of any drug or the performance of any procedure or any other action—that results in the termination of life of a human being in utero between conception and natural birth, whether before or after implantation.[23]

The proposal had the support of conservative groups and abortion opponents, including the US Conference of Catholic Bishops and the Catholic Medical Association, which said the regulation would protect workers' religious freedom. Opposed were the National Association of Chain Drug Stores, the American Hospital Association, and the American Medical Association, as well as family planning advocates and women's health activists, who claimed that the regulation would create overwhelming obstacles for women seeking abortions and birth control.[24] As of August 2009, the HHS was still reviewing hundreds of thousands of public comments it had received on the matter and weighing options.

BIOETHICS ACROSS CULTURES

Unmarried and Pregnant in Saudi Arabia

An adolescent, unmarried girl in Saudi Arabia was brought to a hospital for an unrelated spinal problem, when her American doctors discovered that she was pregnant. Two of the doctors, familiar with the gender expectations of young women, knew that the pregnancy would bring great dishonor to the family and that punishment could bring death to the girl. They arranged for her to have an abortion in a neighboring country. They told her parents that treatment for the spinal problem was only available in this other country. A third doctor, who had only been in Saudi Arabia a short time, felt that he could not be a part of this deception. The other two doctors urgently convinced the third doctor that the girl would be in serious danger if her pregnancy was revealed to her family. The third doctor reluctantly agreed to say nothing. At the last minute, however, as the girl started to board the plane, the doctor uncontrollably felt he could not go through with what he felt was an ethical violation of truthtelling and told the father that the girl was pregnant. The father immediately grabbed the girl and left with her. Several weeks later, the third doctor ran into the girl's brother and asked about her condition. The boy shook his head and explained that the girl was dead. The family's honor had been restored, and the distraught doctor left Saudi Arabia.

(SOURCE: G. A. Galanti, *Caring for Patients from Different Cultures: Case Studies from American Hospitals*, 2nd ed. Philadelphia: University of Philadelphia Press, PA, 1997. Quoted in "Cultural Competency in Medicine," *American Medical Student Association*, 2008. Retrieved April 29, 2009, from http://www.amsa.org/programs/gpit/cultural.cfm)

Question

What bioethical principles are in conflict? Characterize the physicians' competing values in terms of deontological (duty) and teleological (consequences) ethics. Who, in your opinion, was morally right and why? Do you think that this case shows that bioethical principles can or cannot be used to make justified cross-cultural judgments?

Autonomy As Overriding Professional Judgment

The "placebo effect" is a long-known phenomenon in which patients given a fake or ineffective treatment often improve anyway, simply because they expect to get better. In a recent survey, about half of American doctors said they regularly give patients placebo treatments—usually drugs or vitamins that won't really help their conditions. Nearly 60 percent of the surveyed physicians said they would recommend a sugar pill for patients with chronic pain if it had been shown to be more effective than no treatment. Since it isn't known whether the placebo effect would be undermined if patients were told they were getting a fake pill, many doctors admit not being honest with their patients about what they're doing, the survey found.[25] To Franklin G. Miller, director of the research ethics program at the National Institutes of Health and one of the study authors, the finding was disturbing. "There is an element of deception here which is contrary to the principle of informed consent," he said. In their defense, doctors who use placebos say they are merely helping their patients get better.[26]

Is it ever ethical for physicians to deceive patients for the patients' own good? The dilemma that was raised by the placebo survey—between honoring informed consent and prescribing without the patient's knowledge—is representative of a third category of objections to the primacy of patient autonomy. It pits (patient) autonomy against (physician) beneficence. Thus, in the surveyed instances, what is generally owed the patient, informed consent, clashes with what the physician believed to be in the medical interest of the patient, namely, prescribing a placebo without patient knowledge. Unlike matters of conscience, in these disputes the physician objection to honoring autonomy lies in professional judgment rather than moral integrity.

With placebos, it could be argued that most patients would gladly be duped if that was the only way to get relief. Since what the physician wants is exactly what the patient wants, where's the harm?

But that rationalization isn't available in cases in which patient wishes conflict with professional judgment. What then? Take, for example, mammograms, which use low-dose x-rays to examine the human breast for tumors. In 2009, the US Preventive Services Task Force recommended that women start routine scans at age fifty rather than forty and reduce the frequency to every two years rather than once a year. In response, doctors generally said they would follow the recommendations, while most women said they would not, even if doctor recommended, according to a study reported in *Annals of Internal Medicine* (February 16, 2010). So, who should decide—physician or patient? Sometimes these conflicts grow torturous, as we'll see elsewhere, in Chapter 22, where we place them in the context of end of life decisions.

SUGGESTED OFFSETTING PRINCIPLES

Criticisms like the foregoing have led some bioethicists to suggest procedural offsets to the primacy of autonomy in bioethics. Callahan, for one, has offered two: the ecological and vital institution principles. For their part, various religions advocate a biblical alternative to autonomy termed theonomy.

The Ecological Principle

Callahan's ecological principle addresses what are termed incremental and symbolic harms. *Incremental harms* are acts that individually cause little or no harm but have a dramatic effect when taken together. Philosopher Bonnie Steinbock gives the example of the PAS permit, which is often resisted because its dangers are believed to outweigh its need, even though some individual cases of PAS would be morally correct.

Other times an activity is considered wrong "not because of the tangible danger to individuals, but because it violates an important value or principle." Steinbock terms these *intangible* or *symbolic harms*. She gives the example of using embryos to make cosmetic products and asks why this is any worse than using embryos in medical research.

"If, as many commentators (myself included) insist, embryos cannot be harmed, then why not use them for purely commercial purposes? If it doesn't matter to the embryos, why not use them to make money as well as cure cancer? The answer is that making money is not as morally important as saving lives. Using embryos for purely commercial purposes demonstrates insufficient respect for human life, an intangible or symbolic consideration."[27]

Callahan's ecological principle essentially disallows a claim of autonomy until after a thorough canvassing to determine both its incremental and symbolic harms. In theory, then, autonomy could be overridden by consideration of the "common good" or "social interest."

The Vital Institution Principle

The second of Callahan's autonomy limiting principles, the vital institution principle calls for an assessment of our autonomous choices on vital social interests and institutions. For example:

> If our free reproductive choices will have an effect on the family, on the relationship between men and women, and on childbearing and childrearing, then we should bend over backwards to protect those institutions. . . . Similarly, if population health is a basic goal of a health care system, then claims of liberty should not be allowed to drive up costs with high-technology options or enable the elderly in the future to claim expensive rescue medicine to make up for a lifetime of poor health behavior.[28]

Like the ecological principle, the vital institution principle is utilitarian in nature and would not allow claims of liberty to prevail as easily as they

now do against what it perceived as the "common good" or "community values."

In response, defenders of autonomy don't deny that it must sometimes yield to social benefit. But for them the crucial question is: When must autonomy give way? Indeed, Robert Veatch has called this "the central moral project for the future of biomedical ethics."

Veatch is especially concerned about the implication of Callahan's ecological principle that permits some unspecified "aggregate impact" to suppress individual autonomy. As Veatch says:

> This would justify conscripting people into dangerous research against the will of subjects if the social benefits were great enough. It would justify refusing to save a life if that life is of such minimal social value that spending the resources on others would do more good.[29]

Steinbock expresses similar reservations:

> Although incremental and symbolic harms are relevant considerations, the assessment of such harms poses epistemic difficulties. How do we know when the feared harm actually threatens and thus justifies the restriction of liberty and autonomy? Virtually every medical and technological innovation has been greeted with predictions of doom and claims that it will change society for the worse. Dan Callahan's "vital institution" principle, which restricts individual liberty when this threatens our vital social interests and institutions, could become simply stick-in-the-mud conservatism. A related problem is the temptation to engage in post hoc ergo propter hoc (after this therefore on account of this) reasoning. There is more reproductive freedom today than fifty years ago and the family is in crisis. But is the plight of the family due to increased reproductive freedom or other social forces? Those of us concerned with both incremental and symbolic harms have to do more thinking about the kind and amount

of evidence sufficient to restrict individual liberty and prevent change.[30]

For both Steinbock and Veatch, talk about "moral commons," "common good," or "common interest" is vague, sometimes negligently so. There may be legitimate counterclaims to autonomy, they admit, but these need to be distinguished from the nebulous "aggregate social impact." In the end, says Veatch,

> Just as Hippocratic paternalistic consequences for the individual patient can never be allowed to outweigh autonomy for the single patient, so at the social level mere aggregate social consequences should never be permitted to outweigh autonomy.[31]

Today's champions of individual freedom, in effect, echo Kant, that human dignity consists in the autonomy of self-legislation. Like him, they seem to be contrasting autonomy with heteronomy (from the Greek *hetero* for "another" and *nomos* for "law"), which subjects one's rational freedom to the power or rule of another. For those favoring limitations on patient autonomy, that higher, limiting authority may be strictly secular, as with Callahan's concerns about the collective effect of individual choice on society and its institutions. For many others today, the higher authority is God, and the offsetting principle is divine will.

The Theonomy Principle

Theonomy, literally "God's law," is sometimes used in Christian ethics instead of the term *biblionomy*, or biblical law. Theonomy is the view that the Bible contains God's plan for personal and social ethics. This puts theonomy (or biblionomy) in opposition to autonomy, whereby the self provides the basis of ethics.

Some contemporary theonomists, notably Christian Reconstructionists, believe that biblical or divine law should rule all spheres of public and private life. In our times, perhaps the chief apologist of this extreme view was Greg L. Bahnsen (1948–1995), an ordained minister in the Orthodox

Presbyterian Church with a doctorate in philosophy. Nearly forty years after its publication, his *Theonomy in Christian Ethics* is still considered a foundational text of Christian Reconstuctionism.[32] In that work, Bahnsen claimed:

> everyone is held responsible to God to obey all of his laws in every area of their lives; both Church and state, as well as the home, are subject to God's law; civil government must enforce God's law; and civil rulers are duty-bound to enact and enforce the law of God as taught in the Old and New Testament.

Theonomists like Bahnsen and the Rev. William O. Einwechter reject the claim that the influential natural law should be the ethical standard, regarding it as imperfect as human reason, compared to what they consider to be the infallible revelation of Scripture. Einwechter is the vice president of the National Reform Association, whose stated mission is to maintain and promote Christian principles in public life and governance. As Einwechter asks in his own introduction to theonomy: "Why choose natural law which reveals no specifics on the nature of civil government, or the use and limits of state power, over the Word of God which does give these specifics?" Then, anticipating objections, Einwechter continues:

> Some may respond by saying that we live in a secular society that does not accept the authority or the ethical standards of biblical law. However, if natural law and biblical law are the revelation of the same moral law, how will the ethical standards of natural law be any easier for the unbeliever to accept than the ethical standards of the Bible? If there is no hope that a pluralistic society will ever accept the standard of biblical law, what basis is there to hope that such a humanistic culture will ever come to a true and common understanding on what constitutes natural law?[33]

The theonomy of Christian Reconstructionism has been criticized as being, variously, non-Scriptural,

BIOETHICS ACROSS CULTURES

Egyptian Doctor's Honesty Backfires

In January 2009, two women who had recently moved to the area and were looking for a physician approached Dr. Kamelia Elias, who practiced medicine in Egypt before relocating to Winnipeg, Canada. After discovering that the two were lesbians, Dr. Elias told them that, though homosexuality was incompatible with her religious beliefs, she had never had occasion to treat lesbians during her twenty years as a physician, and suggested they seek someone with more experience. The two lesbian women, who were legally married in Canada, filed a complaint against Dr. Elias with Physicians and Surgeons of Manitoba, alleging she discriminated against them for suggesting they find a physician who had experience with homosexuals.

"They get a lot of diseases and infections," Dr. Elias told the *Winnipeg Free Press*. "I didn't refuse to treat them. I said it's better to find someone who has experience and will take this type of patient. There [are] some doctors who can treat them."

Bill Pope of the College of Physicians and Surgeons of Manitoba said many physicians who come to Canada from diverse cultural backgrounds may not understand "Canadian norms." "It was becoming clear that we're getting people from cultures that are very different from (ours), and you can't blame someone when your culture teaches you one thing, you can't understand what the expectations are in Canada," Pope told the press. The medical director of the center that employed Dr. Elias released an equally sympathetic statement that read in part:

> Dr. Elias at no time refused to accept these women into her practice. It was only when one of the two women became defensive

when asked about their relationship, and Dr. Elias was pointedly asked if she had a problem with their relationship, that Dr. Elias felt it necessary to be up-front with regards to her own religious beliefs and inexperience in treating homosexual patients. Please understand that her inexperience stems not from unwillingness to treat these patients, but solely due to lack of exposure to them in her practices in Cairo, Egypt and Steinbach, Manitoba. Her disclosure of her religious background was in the interest of being as honest and transparent as possible so that the patients themselves could decide if they wanted her as their physician.

Andrea Markowski, one of the two lesbian women, disagreed with that characterization. She said that she and her partner interpreted Dr. Elias's statement of her religious beliefs that she would not treat them. "We took that to mean that she wouldn't care for us because it conflicted with her religion," Markowski said. "She clearly was shocked by our relationship, unable to recover."

(SOURCE: Thaddeus M. Baklinski, "Lesbians File Human Rights Complaint Against Canadian Physician," *LifeSiteNews.com*, January 29, 2009. Retrieved April 17, 2009, from www.lifesitenews.com/ldn/2009/jan/09012908.html)

Question

Does a physician have the right to refuse to treat a patient because she has a religious objection to the patient's sexual orientation? Do you think that principlism adequately addresses a case like this?

---

antidemocratic, authoritative, legalistic, and, in general, likely to be more harmful than helpful in a pluralistic nation like the United States. Noteworthy is that such criticism has come from leaders within the reformed Christian movement, such as Michael Horton, who is the President and Chairman of the Council of the Association of Confessing Evangelicals (ACE) and editor of *Modern Reformation*.[34] Beyond this, theonomy raises the problems of internal logic of any plan to impose "God's law" on society and its institutions. If, after all,

the imperfect human mind can't be trusted to properly interpret natural law, why can it be trusted to interpret biblical law? And if it can't, why take one authority's interpretation of it over another's?

Problems of interpretation can make application of broad biblical principles especially tricky, such as the Ten Commandments, Golden Rule, Sermon on the Mount, and other sources of divine will. Sincere people can and do differ, especially in bioethics, where, as the Schiavo case (see Introduction) demonstrated, people of the same faith traditions can have more in common with secularists than with each other. The obvious reason is that the Bible is inchoate, if not silent, on cloning, IVF, assisted death, and other modern issues, thereby inviting diverse, often opposed, interpretations. As for the claim of universal validity of many bible-based religions, including almost all branches of Christianity, they can't all be right, since they invariably contradict each other in important ways. Therefore, to return to Horton's criticism, either all of them are wrong or all less one are. If only one of the multitude is correct, how will that be determined? If not by force of logic, then, perhaps, by force of arms?[38]

Participated Theonomy

Catholicism's answer to the theonomy of Christian Reconstructionism is *participated theonomy*, which makes use of the Thomistic natural law that Einwechter dismisses as unspecific compared with biblical standards.

As we saw in Chapter 2, Thomistic natural law takes root in God's divine and eternal law. By this account, the normative requirements of natural law are *"truths* meant to help us choose rightly." It is through natural law, then, that human beings can share or participate in divine wisdom, which is expressed in divine law. Thus, in one of his encyclicals, Pope John Paul II spoke of our moral life as a:

> ...*theonomy, or participated theonomy,* since man's free obedience to God's law effectively implies that human reason and human will participate in God's wisdom and providence. By forbidding man to "eat of the tree of the knowledge of good and evil," God makes it clear that man does not originally possess such "knowledge" as something properly his own, but only participates in it by the light of the natural reason and of Divine Revelation, which manifests to him the requirements and promptings of eternal wisdom. Law must therefore be considered an expression of divine wisdom: by submitting to the law,

freedom submits to the truth of creation. Consequently one must acknowledge in the freedom of the human person the image and the nearness of God, who is present in all (cf. Eph 4:6). But one must likewise acknowledge the majesty of the God of the universe and revere the holiness of the law of God, who is infinitely transcendent: *Deus semper maior* [God is always greater].[36]

The pope seemed to be saying that human beings are, by nature, free and self-determining, but also have a relational character. Therefore, a right understanding of meaning and value must consider both the autonomous individual and the relational individual—the individual who is self-determining and at the same time stands in relation to others, with whom he and she share a divine kinship. This leaves us free only to the extent that we turn toward and give ourselves to others. As cast by the Catholic theologian and Cardinal Avery Dulles (1918–2008):

> This "law of the gift," as the Pope calls it, is inscribed deep in the dynamic structure of the person as fashioned in the image of the divine. He confirms this insight by quoting from Vatican II: "The human being, who is the only creature on earth that God willed for itself, cannot attain its full identity except through a disinterested gift of self." The citizen serves the common good out of a free commitment or devotion. Those who love God serve him freely, and if they refuse that service they undermine the freedom that love has given them. Those who obey the commandments out of fear are not fully free, but they fall into even deeper slavery if they disobey God in order to gratify their own impulses. The truly free person is one who does what is good out of love for goodness itself.[37]

Consistent with centuries-old teachings, then, human freedom consists in the freedom to love

God and do as he wills, as mediated through religious teaching.

To its critics, participated theonomy is really a form of heteronomy or self-alienation. In the light of the dire consequences of willful disobedience, they ask: What kind of freedom does participated theonomy leave humans with—the freedom to do as the church says God wills or suffer eternal damnation? Then there's the whole supposition of the existence of a God with a plan for his creation. Thus, even if one doesn't view participated theonomy as coercion in disguise, it still invites the query of atheistic existentialism: Is the assumption of God's existence and divine law still another excuse for living inauthentically, that is, another way to avoid freedom and responsibility?

For some moralists today, secular as well as religious, the reassessment of the primacy of autonomy is merely preamble to ways of doing bioethics that differ markedly from the entrenched principlism. What these alternatives are and how they challenge principlism are the interests of the next chapter.

CASES AND CONTROVERSIES

When Plan B Doesn't Work

The Pulzes long ago decided that they could not afford a fifth child. So when the condom they were using broke, they panicked. Their fear really spiked when the Walgreens pharmacy down the street from their home in Milwaukee refused to fill an emergency prescription for the morning-after pill. Sometimes referred to as "Plan B," the morning-after pill consists of higher doses of the hormones found in standard birth control pills. Taken within seventy-two hours of unprotected sex, Plan B has been shown to be highly effective at preventing pregnancies.

"I couldn't believe it," said Kathleen Pulz, 44. "How can they make that decision for us? I was outraged. At the same time, I was sad that we had to do this. But I was scared. I didn't know what we were going to do."

Kathleen Pulz is among today's women and men caught in the crossfire over the nation's battle over reproductive rights, as some pharmacists across the country refuse to fill prescriptions for birth control and morning-after pills. They say that dispensing the medications violates their personal moral or religious beliefs.

"This is a very big issue that's just beginning to surface," says Steven H. Aden of the Christian Legal Society's Center for Law and Religious Freedom in Annandale, Virginia, which defends pharmacists. "More and more pharmacists are becoming aware of their right to conscientiously refuse to pass objectionable medications across the counter. We are on the very front edge of a wave that's going to break not too far down the line."[38]

The trend has opened a new front in the national debate over reproductive rights. At issue are competing rights: the right of pharmacists to refuse to cooperate in something they consider immoral and the right of women to get physician-prescribed, legal medications. The clash has spilled over to statehouses nationwide, with politicians siding with one side or the other.

"There are pharmacists who will only give birth control pills to a woman if she's married. There are pharmacists who mistakenly believe contraception is a form of abortion and refuse to prescribe it to anyone," says Adam Sonfield of the Alan Guttmacher Institute in New York, which tracks reproductive issues. "There are even cases of pharmacists holding prescriptions hostage, where they won't even transfer it to another pharmacy when time is of the essence."

Rachel Laser, of the National Women's Law Center in Washington, sees the battle as another indication of the current political atmosphere and climate. "It's outrageous," Laser fumes. "It's sex discrimination. It prevents access to a basic form of health care for women. We're going back in time."

Karen L. Brauer, president of Pharmacists for Life, vehemently disagrees. Brauer, who was fired from a Kmart pharmacy in Delhi, Ohio, for refusing to fill birth control prescriptions, defends the right of pharmacists not only to decline to fill prescriptions themselves but also to refuse to refer customers elsewhere or transfer prescriptions. She thinks that referring while refusing is like saying: "'I don't kill people myself but let me tell you about the guy down the street who does.' What's that saying? 'I will not off your husband, but I know a buddy who will?' It's the same thing." Brauer now works at a hospital pharmacy.

By the time Suzanne Richards, 21, finally found another pharmacy to fill her morning-after pill prescription—after being rejected by a drive-through Brooks Pharmacy in Laconia, N.H., one late Saturday night in September— the seventy-two hours had long passed. "When he told me he wouldn't fill it, I just pulled over in the parking lot and started crying," says the single mother of a 3-year-old. "I just couldn't believe it. I was just trying to be responsible."

In the end, Richards turned out not to be pregnant, and Kathleen Pulz was able to obtain her prescription last June directly from her doctor, though she does not think she was pregnant, either. "I was lucky," Pulz said. "I can sympathize with someone who feels strongly and doesn't want to be involved. But they should just step out of the way and not interfere with someone else's decision. It's just not right."[39]

Questions for Analysis

1. Discuss conscientious refusal in the context of principlism, including objections to principlism.

2. "The United States was founded on the idea that people act on their conscience—that they have a sense of right and wrong and do what they think is right and moral," says Tom Brejcha, president and chief counsel at the Thomas More Society, a Chicago public-interest law firm that is defending a pharmacist who was fined and reprimanded for refusing to fill prescriptions for birth control pills. "Every pharmacist has the right to do the same thing," Brejcha says. Do you agree with Brejcha?[40]

3. Does refusing to fill a prescription for birth control prevent access to a basic form of health care for women?

4. Brauer explains that her group was founded "with the idea of returning pharmacy to a healing-only profession." She says that "what's been going on is the use of medication to stop human life. That violates the ideal of the Hippocratic oath that medical practitioners should do no harm." Does filling, or presumably writing, contraception prescriptions violate the most basic of biomedical principles, "Do no harm"?

5. Pharmacists are governed by state laws and disciplined by licensing boards. Wisconsin law prohibits pharmacists from refusing treatment on moral grounds. In 2002 Neil T. Noesen refused to fill a University of Wisconsin student's birth control pill prescription at a Kmart in Menomonie, Wis., or transfer the prescription elsewhere. An administrative judge recommended Noesen be required to take ethics classes, alert future employers to his beliefs, and pay what could be as much as $20,000 to cover the costs of the legal proceedings. The state pharmacy board basically agreed, whereupon Noesen appealed the decision and lost. On April 23, 2008, the Thomas More Society filed an appeal with the Wisconsin Supreme Court on behalf of Noesen to hear his appeal of court-ordered punishments. The court has discretion over the cases it hears. Explain why you think this case, which pits religious belief against professional duties, should or should not make it to the floor of the Wisconsin Supreme Court and, perhaps ultimately, to the US Supreme Court.[41]

6. Assess conscientious refusal policy from the viewpoints of Callahan's ecological and vital institution principles.

CASES AND CONTROVERSIES

Guarded about Gardasil

Gardasil, which was approved by the Food & Drug Administration (FDA) in 2006, is meant to protect against four forms of the human papilloma virus (HPV) that cause cervical cancer. The vaccine requires a series of three injections given over six months at a cost of about $360. Clinical trials have found few side effects, though these include pain, swelling, itching, redness,

fever, nausea, and dizziness. Gardasil's manufacturer, the pharmaceutical giant Merck, suggests that all females between ages 9 and 26 receive the vaccine, even if they have already been infected with HPV. Indeed, Merck has waged an aggressive campaign to convince state legislatures to make it mandatory for girls before they are likely to become sexually active. In 2007, the governor of Texas, Rick Perry, ordered that all girls be

(Continued)

CASES AND CONTROVERSIES (CONTINUED)

vaccinated with Gardasil before entering the sixth grade. By 2008, twenty states were considering similar mandates.[42]

In the United States alone, it is estimated by WHO that 75 percent of adults aged 15 to 40 will be infected with HPV over their lifetime. Although males can be infected with HPV, they rarely seem to suffer its diseases. Twenty million people are currently infected, and there are 6.2 million new infections yearly. About 11,000 cases of cervical cancer are diagnosed in the United States annually, leading to about 3,500 deaths. US women diagnosed with cervical cancer have a 5-year survival rate of 72 percent, according to the American Cancer Society. The Centers for Disease Control & Prevention (CDC) also recommends that all females from 9 to 26 should be vaccinated with Gardasil, and says that only if enough people get the vaccination can the spread of HPV be prevented.

But many people are opposed to making the vaccine mandatory, and in some states, such as Massachusetts, mandatory efforts have stalled. In 2007 Michigan lawmakers defeated a bill, saying it would interfere with family privacy. Some parents are opposed to mandatory vaccination on moral grounds, believing that vaccinating their daughters against a sexually transmitted disease sends the message that sexual activity at such a young age, or even prior to marriage, is acceptable. Some Christian advocacy groups believe that the vaccine is not necessary because a decent young woman will not have pre-marital sex. Others simply believe that the government has no right to usurp parental authority by mandating a vaccine for a disease that is not spread through casual contact. Still others worry that Gardasil is too new and hasn't been subjected to enough scrutiny. They fear harmful side effects may not become apparent for several years, and would like to wait before subjecting their daughters to the vaccine.

The Gardasil controversy is not likely to go away anytime soon, despite criticism of cost, potential side effects, and removing parental consent. It's widely acknowledged that Gardasil is a good thing. But far from settled is the question of whether as a public health measure states ought to require its use.[43]

Questions for Analysis

1. If Gardasil is mandated, it will mark a shift in public health policy. Until now, mandatory inoculations have been reserved for communicable diseases representing a public health risk. Gardasil is designed to protect against a virus whose transmission can be prevented through individual behavior. In other words, HPV does not pose an imminent and significant risk to the health of others. Does this make a parental decision about a Gardasil vaccination of their 11-year-old significantly different from a decision about vaccinating the child for, say, mumps, measles, or chickenpox?

2. Does the fact that a vaccine like Gardasil likely will prevent much morbidity and mortality with few side effects justify government intrusion into family privacy and autonomy?

3. Would mandatory vaccination cause "symbolic" or "intangible" harm?

4. Would mandated Gardasil keep or violate Callahan's "vital institution principle"?

5. Should there be a religious/philosophical exemption if Gardasil vaccine is adopted as public policy by a state?

6. Rather than allowing an "opt out" on religious or medical grounds, would autonomy be better served by letting those who want the vaccine to "opt in" voluntarily? What might the drawbacks be?

7. Since Gardasil is meant to be given to girls over 10 years of age, should they have any say in receiving the vaccine?

CASES AND CONTROVERSIES

Benitez v. North Coast Women's Care Medical Group

In 1999 Guadalupe Benitez, a lesbian woman from Oceanside, California, was treated for infertility at North Coast Women's Care Medical Group. Two of the clinic's physicians, Christine Brody and Douglas Fenton, refused to perform artificial insemination treatment on Benitez because they said that such treatments to unmarried women violated their Christian religious beliefs. In 2000 Benitez sued the fertility clinic and the two doctors, arguing that the physicians' decision was based on objections to her sexual orientation.

"For me this is a case about doing the right thing and being fair," Benitez was quoted as saying. "Not discriminating against people and doctors not playing the role of God, saying because you are gay, you are not worthy of having a child or a family. I did it not only for me, my partner and my children but for other people coming after me, so they don't have to go through the humiliation and frustration and abandonment as a patient."[44]

The case drew more than forty friends of the court briefs from a wide variety of religious organizations, medical groups, and gay civil rights organizations. The physicians and clinic drew support from the American Civil Rights Union, the Islamic Medical Association of North America, the Christian Medical & Dental Associations, and anti-abortion groups. Filing papers on Benitez's behalf were the American Civil Liberties Union, the California Attorney General, the National Health Law Program, and the Gay and Lesbian Medical Association. For its part, the California Medical Association reversed initial support of the Christian doctors after receiving criticism from the gay rights community. Health care provider Kaiser Foundation Health Plan also opposed the Christian doctors.[45]

Legal pre-trial wrangling delayed the hearing of the case for three years. Finally, in 2004, a trial court ruled in Benitez's favor based on sexual-orientation discrimination, only to be reversed in 2005 when an appellate court upheld North Coast's claim of religious freedom. The California Supreme Court ultimately ruled, in 2009, that guarantees of religious freedom in the state and federal constitutions do not permit doctors to refuse to artificially inseminate a patient because she is a lesbian. Justice Joyce Kennard wrote in the unanimous ruling that Brody and Fenton had neither a free speech right nor a religious exemption from the state's law, which "imposes on business establishments certain antidiscrimination obligations."

Questions for Analysis

1. What moral relevancy would you give to the fact that the physicians refused to provide treatment to Benitez that they would provide to another patient, as opposed to refusing to provide a treatment to anyone on religious grounds?

2. Benitez's lawyer compared the clinic's response to the civil rights era: "I don't treat black patients, but I will refer you to someone who will." Do you agree with this characterization?

3. Do you think that physicians should or should not be permitted to pick and choose on the medically irrelevant characteristics of a patient?

4. How do you view this decision—as a victory for equal access to treatment from health care providers or an infringement on the right of health care providers to free exercise of religion?

5. Compare this case with the earlier one, "Egyptian Doctor's Honesty Backfires," in one of this chapter's Bioethics Across Cultures.

REFERENCES

1. Sidney Callahan, "Abortion and the Sexual Agenda," *Commonwealth*, April 25, 1986, p. 232.

2. John Lantos, "To Tell or Not to Tell," *The Park Ridge Center Bulletin*, March 1999. Retrieved February 20, 2008, from http://www.parkridgecener.org/Page61.html.

3. Courtney S. Campbell, "In Whose Image? Religion and the Controversy of Human Cloning," *Second Opinion*, September 1999.

4. Janet Smith, "The Preeminence of Autonomy in Bioethics," in *Human Lives: Critical Essays on Consequentialist Bioethics*, David Oderberg and Jacqueline A. Laing, eds., New York: St. Martin's Press, 1997. Retrieved June 5, 2008, from http://www.aodonline.org/SHMS/Faculty+5819/Janet+Smith+9260/Dr.+Janet+Smith+-+Published+Articles.htm.

5. Quoted in David B. Fletcher, "The Ethics of Bioethics," *The Center for Bioethics and Human Dignity*, Summer 2001. Retrieved July 2, 2008, from www.cbhd.org/resources/bioethics/fletcher_summer-2001.htm.

6. Robert M. Veatch, Willard Gaylin, Bonnie Steinbock, "Can the Moral Commons Survive Autonomy?" (includes commentaries) ("In Search of the Good Society: The Work of Daniel Callahan,"), *The Hastings Center Report*, November-December 1996. pp. 41–47.

7. Alfred Tauber, *Patient Autonomy and the Ethics of Responsibility*, Cambridge: MIT Press, 2005, p. 15.

8. Farr A. Curlin, et al, "Religion, Conscience, and Controversial Clinical Practices," *The New England Journal of Medicine*, February 8, 2007, pp. 593–600.

Retrieved July 2, 2008, from http://content.nejm. org/cgi/content/full/356/6/593.

9. Katherine A. White, "Crisis of Conscience: Reconciling Religious Health Care Providers' Beliefs and Patients' Rights," *Stanford Law Review*, May 1999, pp. 1703–1749.

10. Alta Charo, "The Celestial Fire of Conscience— Refusing To Deliver Medical Care," *The New England Journal of Medicine*, June 16, 2005, pp. 2471–2473. Retrieved July 1, 2008, from http://content.nejm.org/ cgi/content/full/352/24/2471.

11. Rob Stein, "'Pro-Life' Drugstores Market Beliefs: No Contraceptive for Chantilly Shop," *The Washington Post*, June 16, 2008, p. A1.

12. Michael Gillan Peckitt, "Savulescu on Conscience," *BMJ*, February 5, 2006. Retrieved July 8, 2008, from www.bmj.com/cgi/eletters/332/7536/294.

13. See note 11 above.

14. Trevor G. Stammers, "Six Objections to Savulescu's Salvo," *BMJ*, February 5, 2006. Retrieved July 8, 2008, from www.bmj.com/cgi/eletters/332/7536/294.

15. See note 11 above.

16. See note 11 above.

17. Jeremy Manier, "Medical Options Withheld, Stud Finds," *Los Angeles Times*, Feb 8, 2007, A15.

18. See note 11 above.

19. See note 17 above.

20. Farr A. Curlin, Ryan E. Lawrence, Marshall H. Chin, and John D. Lantos, "Religion, Conscience, and Controversial Clinical Practices," *The New England Journal of Medicine*, Feb. 8, 2007, pp. 593–600.

21. See note 20 above.

22. Dr. Rick Bayer, "Physicians' Perspective: Conscience and Ethics Paternalism versus Patient Autonomy," *Alternatives*, Fall, 2007. Retrieved July 2, 2008, from http://www.alternativesmagazine.com/43/fall07.html

23. Rob Stein, "Workers' Religious Freedom vs. Patients' Rights," *Washington Post*, July 31, 2009, p. A1. Retrieved July 31, 2008, from http://www.washingtonpost.com/wp-dyn/content/article/2008/07/30/AR2008073003238.html?.

24. David Stout, "Medical 'Conscience Rule' Is Issues, *the New York Times*, December 18, 2008. Retrieved December 18, 2008, from http://www.nytimes.com/2008/12/19/washington/19rule.html?em.

25. Jon C. Tilburt et al, "Prescribing 'placebo treatments': results of national survey of US internists and rheumatologists," *BMJ*, October 23, 2009, p. 1938. Retrieved October 25, 2008, from http://www.bmj.com/cgi/content/short/337/oct23_2/a1938.

26. Maria Cheng, "Placebos Don't Make Ethicists Feel Better," *Los Angeles Times*, October 24, 2008, p. A17.

27. Bonnie Steinbock, "Liberty, Responsibility and the Common Good," in Veatch, Gaylin, and Steinbock, p. 45.

28. Ibid., p. 42.

29. Ibid., p. 45.

30. Ibid., p. 43.

31. See note 29 above.

32. Greg Bahnsen, *Theonomy in Christian Ethics*, Phillipsburg, NJ: Presbyterian and Reformed Publishing Company, 1984.

33. William O. Einwechter, *Ethics and God's Law: An Introduction to Theonomy*, Mill Hall, PA: Preston/ Speed Publications, 1995.

34. Michael Horton, *A Better Way: Rediscovering the Drama of God-Centered Worship*, Grand Rapids, MI: Baker Books, 2003.

35. Michael Horton, "In God's Name: Guidelines for Proper Political Involvement," *Modern Reformation Magazine*, September/October 1994. Retrieved May 2, 2008 from http://www.modernreformation.org/default.php?page=issuedisplay&var1=IssRead&var2=78.

36. Pope John Paul II, *Veritatis Splendor* (*The Splendor of Truth*), August 6, 1993. Retrieved April 15, 2008, from http://www.vatican.va/holy_father/john_paul_ii/encyclicals/documents/hf_jpii_enc_06081993_veritatis-splendor_en.html.

37. Avery Dulles, "John Paul II and the Truth about Freedom," *First Things*, August/September, 1995, pp. 36–41. Retrieved May 1, 2008, from www.firstthings.com/article.php3?id_article=4077.

38. Rob Stein, "Pharmacists Rights at Front of New Debate," *The Washington Post*, March 28, 2005, p. A01.

39. See note 38 above.

40. Rob Stein, Pro-Life' Drugstores Market Beliefs, *The Washington Post*, June 16, 2008, p. A01.

41. Editorial, "No Merit To Noesen Appeal," *The Daily Cardinal*, Madison: University of Wisconsin, April 29, 2008.

42. National Health Federation, "Efforts to Make Gardasil Mandatory Stall in Some States," *NewsInferno.com*, April 24, 2008. Retrieved April 24, 2009, from http://www.thenhf.com/vaccinations/vaccinations_183.htm.

43. Craig M. Klugman, "Public Health Principlism," *Online Journal of Health Ethics*, vol. 1, no.1, 2007. Retrieved April 20, 2009, from http://ethicsjournal.umc.edu/ojs2/index.php/ojhe/article/view/61/76.

44. Susan Donaldson James, "Doctors Deny Lesbian Artificial Insemination," *ABC News*, May 28, 2008. Retrieved October 1, 2009, from http://abcnews.go.com/TheLaw/Story?id=4941377&page=1.

45. See note 44 above.

Chapter 7

Beyond Principlism II: Alternative Perspectives

B esides procedural offsets to principlism—such as the ecological, vital institution, and theonomy principles—four alternative perspectives have received wide attention. They are virtue theory, an ethic of care, existential and spiritual dimensions of illness, and narratives.

VIRTUE THEORY

Principle-based theorists—natural law, categorical imperative, utilitarianism—assume that there is a decision procedure or mechanical rule for doing ethics and generating morally correct action. Virtue theorists deny this. They say that the complexity of life precludes the formulation of simple moral rules such as the utility principle or the categorical imperative. As a fruitful alternative to focusing on the principle-generating question "What ought I do?," virtue theorists turn their attention to the question of character interest: "What ought I be?" They argue that we can only determine what we ought to do in reference to what it means to be a morally good person, that is, a virtuous person, or one of good character. In the West the tradition that associates individual morality with character strengths or virtues has its roots in ancient Greek philosophy, particularly in the thought of Aristotle.

For Aristotle the virtuous act, or moral virtue, was the one that steered clear of the two undesirable extremes of deficiency and excess and, thereby, achieved the Golden Mean. This made every moral act or virtue an appropriate middle between the two defects of too little or too much of something. The virtue of courage, for example, was the mean between cowardice (a deficiency) and recklessness (an excess); generosity was the mean between stinginess (a deficiency) and prodigality (an excess); truthfulness was the mean between understatement (a deficiency) and boastfulness (an excess). The virtuous person, then, was able to navigate, felicitously and habitually, between these and other character defects and thereby attained the proper excellence of a human being.

Aristotle taught that by practicing the doctrine of the Golden Mean human beings could achieve their natural purpose: *eudaimonia*, a Greek word for happiness but probably better understood as total well-being.[1] Taken as the latter, eudaimonia sometimes is translated as "flourishing," or developing one's potential, including living well within the community.

Achieving eudaimonia by aiming at the mean wasn't easy, like determining an arithmetic mean. As Aristotle took pains to point out in Books II–IV of his monumental *Nicomachean Ethics*, acting in the mean was acting in the right manner, with the right motive, at the right time, to the right degree, in the right relationship, and for the right duration. Given its non-formulaic nature, keeping to the moderate course called for a clear vision, including an ability to discern and examine all sides of a matter and place them in due perspective. Acting in the mean also required a passion tempering, keen and calm intellect; a proper use of reason in the context of a well ordered life not given to immoderation; and a display of emotion only when appropriate, and then only to the appropriate degree. Aristotle had a term for this habit of mind that he believed enabled us to choose well both in a particular situation and the whole of our lives. He called it *phronesis*, or "practical wisdom."

The publication of two books in 1980 renewed interest in the role of virtues in the moral life and medicine. In *After Virtue* Alasdair MacIntyre urged a return to the Aristotelian notions of Golden Mean, eudaimonia, and phronesis. In *Ethical Options in Medicine*, Gregory Pence applied virtue ethics specifically to medicine as a practice and institution. Pence, a philosopher and medical ethicist, identified a number of virtues of the ideal physician, including compassion, competence, justice, and courage. Building on this tradition, Pellegrino and Thomasma have written extensively on the need to balance the modern emphasis on technical expertise with moral excellence in medicine. They point out—in *A Philosophical Basis of Medical Practice* (1981) and *Virtues in Medical Practice* (1993), for example—that, while technical competency is expected of physicians, competency alone doesn't lead to successful clinical interactions. The truly excellent physician also exhibits character qualities, or moral virtues, including benevolence, compassion, honesty, humanity, courage, respect, fortitude, justice, and prudence. Such qualities are

necessary to elevate medical care and its practitioners from being merely competent to being excellent. They also save bioethics from being merely a robotic exercise in following rules or attempting to apply them to given situations. Yes, the principles are important, these virtue theorists concede; but the principles and rules need to be directed and guided by the virtues. Principlism, in brief, needs to be informed by character qualities that define excellence in clinical encounters and in medicine as a profession.

FEMINIST ETHICS OF CARE

In 1985, in the midst of the virtue theory revival, moral psychologist Carol Gilligan published a book that basically focused on a single virtue: care. The work, *In a Different Voice*, challenged the conceptual foundations of moral philosophy by contrasting an *ethic of care* with the well-established *ethic of justice*.

Justice

At heart, an ethic of justice involves the formulation and impartial application of universal moral principles, such as the categorical imperative or utility. It associates moral development with an understanding of the rights and rules associated with these principles, and prescribes principled conduct, regardless of relationships to others, even close ones such as family. Sometimes termed a rationalist model of moral judgment, an ethic of justice tends to objectify the parties to a moral decision by casting them in a formal relationship characterized by duties and obligations. It views them as parties to a contract based on autonomy and pre-established guidelines. By this account, morality consists exclusively of weighing matters of harm, rights, and justice. As one commentator puts it: "If no condemning evidence is found, no condemnation is issued."[2]

In her book, Gilligan maintained that since the Enlightenment moral philosophy had been dominated by an ethic of justice. By extension, the new bioethics practiced the justice, or rational, method of ethical decision making. Thus, principlism

BIOETHICS ACROSS CULTURES

Buddhist Virtue

Professor of Philosophy Pinit Ratanakul notes that, traditionally, the ethical imperative for Buddhist physicians is based on love. Specifically, it is loving kindness (*metta*) or compassion (*karuna*) as manifested in the practice of loving care, according to Ratanakul, who is the director of religious studies at Mahidol University in Bangkok, Thailand. Physicians from the earliest times have been called upon to practice this Buddhist moral ideal by serving all patients. This means, for example, "accepting the patients as full persons with feelings, beliefs and cultural values and act with due regard to their need in accordance with moral imperative." Thus, when faced with a difficult decision, physicians are to ask themselves: What is the most loving action I can take, given all relevant considerations?

Ratanakul thinks that the Buddhist concept of loving care is comprehensive enough to embrace all other moral principles in Western bioethics, such as respect for persons and their autonomy, beneficence, nonmaleficence, and justice. However, in emphasizing the principle of loving care—as opposed to individual autonomy and rights—"Buddhist bioethics recognizes the complexity of life situations where legalistic observation of moral rules can unintentionally lead to greater evils and abdication of compassion." As he puts it:

> In real life there are many cases, which are in the twilight zone. In such cases the nature of intention behind deed is of primary significance and thus should be taken into account before we rush in negative judgment on the party concerned. When life situations force people to make unpleasant decisions, hard choices between greater and lesser harms, greater and lesser good, we should not overburden them with a sense of guilt but evaluate the reality with compassion to lessen their suffering caused by wrong decisions. Only by avoiding the rigidity and laxity can the practice of compassion be achieved. Where would society be, where would medicine be were it not for the example of those who practice the Buddhist ideal of loving kindness or compassion consecrated themselves to the welfare of others even at the cost of their own comfort and benefit.

Ratanakul believes that it is now time for a "paradigm shift" from overemphasis on individual rights to loving care as a moral imperative in the practice of medicine.

(SOURCE: Pinit Ratanakul, "Love in Buddhist Ethics," *Eubios Journal of Asian and International Bioethics*, March 1999, pp. 45–46. Retrieved April 20, 2009, from http://www.eubios.info/EJAIB92.htm)

Question

Do you agree with Ratanakul that there is an overemphasis on individual rights in the practice of medicine? What does Buddhist ethics share with other critiques of principlism? Apply the principle of loving care to the cross-cultural case presented in "Egyptian Doctor's Honesty Backfires," Chapter 6.

---

framed bioethical decisions in terms of balancing the competing interests of individuals and sorting out relevant principles, with patient autonomy ordinarily being the main consideration. Gilligan's groundbreaking book proposed an alternative version of ethical decision making that she called an ethic of care, or care ethics.

Care

An ethic of care challenges the dominant justice approach by having us view ourselves as part of a web of relationships, a notion akin to Aristotle's conception of the human being as by nature a social (and political) animal. Aristotle used the word *philia*, usually translated "friendship," to refer to the emotional bonds between human beings that make social relationships possible. He even considered human friendship a necessary virtue for living well. Care theorists similarly note that some of our relationships have powerful emotional charges, and the involved parties must empathically relate to each other's needs for the relationships to survive. This, in turn, calls for partiality and committed involvement rather than the impartiality and abstract reasoning of the justice perspective, which views individuals as self-interested, autonomous agents, as opposed to interdependent beings.

Philosopher Virginia Held has suggested some characteristics of an ethics of care, notably:

- a focus on "the compelling moral salience of attending to and meeting the needs of the particular others for whom we take responsibility"[3];

- an appreciation for the relevancy of emotional attachment between individuals in moral decision making; and

- a preference for "the particular claims of others with whom we share actual relationships" over the impartiality and abstract reasoning of a principle-based ethic.[4]

Other scholars have pinpointed three closely related virtues that seem to lie at the heart of all ethic of care constructs: sympathy, or the power of sharing the feelings of another; empathy, or identification with and understanding another's situation, feelings, and motives; and compassion, or a deep awareness of the suffering of another, coupled with the wish to relieve it.[5]

Relating this perspective to medicine leads nurse Diann Uustal to believe that the nature of the healing relationship is the key feature of an ethic of care. She views the relationship of caregiver-care receiver as distinguished by certain virtues, values, and concepts, including:

> ... compassion, concern for others, the strengthening of relationships, enhancing a sense of connectedness, improving communication, being attentive to the uniqueness of the individual and the context of the situation, taking into account the importance of feelings and how they influence decisions, and being responsive and responsible for one's actions.[6]

By this measure, the patient is always to be considered as a *whole person*. "This means," according to Uustal, and reminiscent of Aristotle, "... considering and including the physical, emotional,

spiritual social (relational), and intellectual needs of the individual."[7]

The Emergence of Feminist Bioethics

Gilligan was one of the first scholars to observe that the emphasis of care ethics, on the responsibilities imposed by relationships, was a way of looking at morality generally more characteristic of women than men. In this sense, *In a Different Voice* was a clarion call for revising and rethinking traditional ethics so as to understand and value women's moral experience. This is why today Gilligan's approach sometimes is termed "feminist care ethics."

In a Different Voice included research suggesting that for women morality is largely a matter of caring and being responsible for others with whom they are involved in personal relationships; whereas for men it lists toward the impartial application of rules and principles, and an emphasis on autonomy and rights, all characteristic of an ethic of justice and patriarchy, generally.[8] In this sense, Gilligan was suggesting that traditional ethics, both secular and religious, tends to be more masculine- than feminine-oriented. By contrast, she called attention to the experience of women, to their issues and interests. Specifically, her ethic of feminist care balanced the prominent moral heritage of Kant and utilitarianism in three particular ways:

> First, ... that actual relationships can be central to morality, thus challenging the impartial and universalistic view of others characteristic of the dominant moral tradition. Second, in contrast to the rationalism of the dominant tradition, the emotions are allowed to be of value to morality in the ethics of care. Finally, the ethics of care offers an alternative conception of persons: we are connected to others, rather than isolated individuals.[9]

Later, feminists such as Alison Jaggar (*Feminist Ethics*, 1992) showed how traditional ethics overrates "masculine traits" such as independence, intellect, and domination; and underrates "feminine traits" such as interdependence, feeling, and cooperation.

Other feminists have argued that traditional ethics favors "male" ways of moral reasoning that emphasize rules, rights, universality, and impartiality over "female" ways of moral reasoning that emphasize relationships, responsibilities, particularity, and partiality.[10]

The feminist emphasis on specific individuals in actual encounters with other specific individuals, with care and concern as the major determinants of the relationship, stands in opposition to the impartial, universalistic principles that still dominate modern bioethics. The mainstream rationalist model, in which moral emotions such as empathy do not directly cause a moral judgment, might be appropriate in impersonal relationships; but to care theorists, such detachment is unacceptably facile in many personal relationships. In therapeutic encounters, says medical ethicist Nancy Jecker, "Keeping an abstract and distant gaze … becomes a way of retreating and pulling back. It renders moral reasoning instrumental to the purpose of denying the moral claims personal relationships make," which have more to do with "caring" than justice.[11]

To be sure, Gilligan's gender-differentiated, caregiving morality came in for its share of criticism from feminists who objected to an ethic focusing on gender differences and, perhaps, reinforcing women's subordination as caregivers.[12-15] Still, her view bore significant implications for the freshly minted Belmont principles. After all, if, as Gilligan argued, traditional ethics carried a male bias, so did its descendant, bioethics. And if traditional (masculine) ethics of justice needed to be balanced by a (feminine) ethics of care, so, too, the bioethics of principlism needed the corrective of a feminist bioethics. It is perhaps revealing that Ruth Macklin was one of the rare early bioethicists in what Jonsen wryly describes as "a field dominated by white (but not yet dead) males."[16]

In the early 1990s a feminist bioethics did, in fact, emerge as a distinctive area of academic interest. From the outset, feminist bioethics offered a full-throated critique of mainstream bioethics aimed at its well-established rights- or consequences-based mode of analysis, abstract rules and principles,

liberal individualism, and socially elite clientele (e.g., teaching hospitals, biotech companies, medical societies). Although the pursuit of a more satisfactory bioethical theory led feminist scholars in a variety of directions, care remained a common concern. Indeed, today a robust conception of care is probably the best-known feature of feminist theory.

Feminist bioethicists generally see resources within the ethic of care for highlighting what they view as shortcomings in mainstream bioethics. Susan Dodds, for example, laments the tendency to restrict patient autonomy strictly to informed consent and choice. Overlooked, she points out, are the myriad social and economic factors that impinge on choice, not to mention the unequal-power relationship between patients and physicians/institutions. Sensitivity to the contextual details of personal experience has inspired other feminists to extend the ethic of care to issues of justice and social policy. Alisa Carse, Hilde Lindemann, and Nel Noddings, for example, have offered sustained analyses of the differences among social groups, particularly of the social forces that require some groups to oppress others. Of concern to these feminist scholars are how power in the guise of race, class, gender, sexual orientation, and ethnicity plays itself out in the health care practice and its theory.[17] It's worth remembering that feminist bioethicists undertake this examination not only from the viewpoint of women but also from the perspectives of all social groups that have been forced to serve the interests of other, more powerful groups or have been marginalized in our society. Feminist bioethics thus gives voice to all of the oppressed, neglected, and unempowered.[18]

In later chapters we'll see how the feminist perspective applies to specific issues, such as abortion and assisted death. Suffice it here to emphasize that today the tendency in feminist bioethics is to extend the ethics of care beyond interpersonal problems to social and political issues that require a more generalized treatment of justice. In this sense Gilligan's initial interests have come full circle: Care and justice—*both* play a leading role in the ongoing feminist bioethical debate.

BIOETHICS ACROSS CULTURES

Global Violence Against Women

In April 2009 a group of young women stepped off a bus in Kabul, Afghanistan, and moved toward a protest march that was forming on the other side of the street. "Get out of here, you whores!" a mob of men shouted at them. "Get out!"

Scattering as the men moved in, the women shouted, "Want our rights. We want equality." The women melted into a group of about three-hundred angry Afghan women who then marched on the streets of the capital to demand that Parliament repeal a new law that introduced a range of restrictions on women and permitted, among other things, marital rape.

Marital rape is just one of the numerous acts of violence directed at women around the world. The United Nation defines violence against women as any act of gender-based violence that results in, or is likely to result in, physical, sexual or mental harm or suffering to women, including threats of such acts and coercion or arbitrary deprivation of liberty, whether occurring in public or private life.

By this measure, millions of girls and women worldwide suffer from violence and its consequences. While men also are victims of violence, females of all ages are victims of violence, in part because of their limited social and economic power compared with men. Globally, at least one in three women has experienced some form of gender-based violence during her lifetime. Cross-cultural research shows that violence against girls and women can begin before birth and continue throughout their lives into old age. It also suggests that women are reluctant to discuss abuse, and may even accept it as part of their role in a culture.

As in Afghanistan, the most common forms of violence against women are physical, sexual, and emotional abuse by a woman's spouse or intimate partner. In some parts of the world, as many as one-half of women have experienced domestic violence, according to a World Health Organization (WHO) Multi-Country Study on Women's Health and Domestic Violence. A list of the various forms of violence against women include:

■ 12 to 25 percent of women being forced by an intimate partner or ex-partner to have sex at some time in their lives;

■ rape as a part of warfare used to disrupt communities and perpetuate ethnic cleansing;

■ sexual violence in refugee camps;

■ forced sexual initiation and sexual abuse;

■ early marriage of girls, in Saharan Africa and South Asia, as early as seven or eight in parts of East and West Africa;

■ sex-selective abortion, female infanticide;

■ systematic neglect of the welfare of girls, contributing to the estimated 60 to 100 million "missing" girls and women worldwide; and

■ trafficking in women and girls for forced labor and sexual exploitation.

Beyond this, health care professionals participate in culturally supported forms of abuse, such as virginity examinations, forced cesarean-section deliveries, and female genital mutilation.

Women who are abused have poorer mental and physical health, more injuries, and a greater need for medical resources than non-abused women. The WHO study found that abused women in Brazil, Japan, and Peru are almost twice as likely as non-abused women to report their current health status as poor or very poor. And the effects of abuse are long lasting, often contributing to alcohol and drug abuse. Reproductively, abused women have been found to have three times the number of gynecological problems as non-abused women.

(SOURCES: Dexter Fiolkins, "Afghan Women Defy Convention, and Crowds, to Protest New Law on Home Life," *The New York Times*, April 16, 2009, p. A1; Barbara Shane and Mary Ellsberg, *Outlook*, September 2002. Retrieved April 16, 2009, from www.path.org/files/EOL20_1.pdf; Nicholas D. Kristof and Sheryl WuDunn, "Why Women's Rights Are the Cause of Our Time," *The New York Times*, August 23, 2009, p. 28.)

Question

Were you aware of the prevalence of global violence against women? If not, what do you think accounts for your unawareness of what is, arguably, the number one health issue confronting women around the world? Does feminist care ethics offer a unique perspective on global violence against women?

EXISTENTIAL AND SPIRITUAL DIMENSIONS OF ILLNESS

In *Leaky Bodies and Boundaries* (1997), an examination of women and contemporary biomedicine, feminist Margrit Shildrick made the point that the broken body of sickness has important consequences for our self-perception. "The loss of a leg or a breast, for example, affects not simply corporeal integrity, but also the sense of who we are," she wrote.[19] Even more extreme is a potentially life-threatening diagnosis such as cancer. Indeed, the word itself, *cancer*, is enough to terrify most of us, especially at the outset of a diagnosis, when we're dealing with all kinds of uncertainties and tend to feel overwhelmed by what's happening to us. It is then that the primacy of individual existence blows away all theoretical abstractions. It is also when we most often protest, "It can't be me," or ask of life's unfathomable unfairness, "Why me?" That state of panic that may result from feeling isolated in a diseased or broken body—of thinking life has no meaning, of losing one's autonomy or self-identity, of fearing the unknown, of searching for purpose in our illness, or of dreading death—is sometimes termed an *existential crisis*. That's what Shildrick was getting at when she said that a serious medical problem attacks not only our body but also our very "sense of who we are."

To some of its critics, it is the failure to address the existential aspect of illness that partly explains the widespread dissatisfaction with mainstream medicine. For example, in *The Cure Within* (2008), a history of mind-body medicine in the West, Harvard historian Anne Harrington observes that,

> like all cultures, ours has traditionally provided people a stockpile of religious, moral and social stories to help them answer the great 'why' questions of their suffering, and to connect their experiences to some larger understanding of their identities and destinies. Today, however, the story offered by mainstream medicine "is as impersonal as they come."[20]

What Harrington means is that contemporary medical science can offer knowledge, but not meaning; and it's meaning that we seek when we're ill.

The Death of Ivan Ilyich (1886), a major exploration of the consciousness of death, is, perhaps, the best literary example of what Harrington is driving at. The classic story by Leo Tolstoy (1828–1910) is also a powerful example of Aristotle's conception of the human being as "thoroughly rooted in social context," as well as the dangers of living an unexamined life given over to the pursuit of self-interest at the expense of compassion, sympathy, and community.

In *Ilyich*, Tolstoy created an existential and spiritual crisis for the materially successful title character. Ilyich's personal crisis was brought on by a fatal illness that forced him to confront questions like: *What has my life meant? Did I make the right choices? What is death, now that it is I who must die? What will become of me? What, if anything, will I leave behind?* For Ilyich, it was his looming mortality that raised these existential concerns, but any serious illness can have the same effect, as Shildrick showed. Whatever the trigger, an existential crisis is spiritual in nature and calls for a compassionate response. Unfortunately for Ivan Ilyich, his family and friends responded with practiced indifference or denial, while his physicians could only meet his crisis as a biological or physical problem to be met with medical nostrums. The palpable gap between what Ilyich desperately needed as a whole person and what he was given as a patient is suggestive of an inherent conflict in the physician's scientific orientation that Tolstoy, a precursor of existentialism, homed in on when scientific medicine was still in its infancy.[21]

Consider another example, this one a contemporary woman's actual account of being informed by her specialist that she had breast cancer and her subsequent reluctance to have the offered mastectomy:

> "His management of my crisis consisted of a pat on the hand and the assurance that he was very sorry. I was pretty sorry myself.

This was the ultimate existential crisis and it packed a terrific punch. My medical team were dealing with a diagnosis as a physical problem in terms of their personal and technological resources, while I was trying to handle it on a mental and emotional level as a spiritual challenge. It seemed incredible that whatever attention had been afforded to me generally was now withdrawn, and instead focused exclusively on my left breast. Doctors, studiously avoiding eye contact, came, examined me and left. Risking the agony of deep exposure, I asked to see the doctor who seemed to have played the role of chief negotiator. He arrived, briskly pleased, imagining no doubt that I had finally come to see things his way [i.e., to consent for mastectomy]. 'I think I know why I'm ill,' I announced. I was absolutely shattered by his exasperated reply. 'Well, that doesn't make any difference to the way we treat you,' he said."[22]

The patient's subsequent refusal to accept the prescribed mastectomy so infuriated the doctor that he ended the discussion with a blunt, "The decision will obviously have to be taken out of your hands." Later, when she asked him what she could do to improve her chances of survival, he replied tersely, "Nothing." (In fact, some evidence suggests that health professionals, by increasing their awareness of the patient's emotional and spiritual needs, as opposed to only the physical and intellectual, can help a patient's will to live.)[23,24]

As with Ivan Ilyich, the communication gulf between this patient and her physicians was further widened by other aspects of their opposed outlooks.

- For her, a personal understanding of why she was ill was important to the treatment she would choose; for them, it was irrelevant.

- For her, how she chose to respond to her situation mattered; for them, it only mattered insofar as she consented to appropriate treatment.

- For her, introspective knowledge, knowledge of herself, was crucial; for them, it was trivial against the objective, factual, and scientific.

- For her, the maintenance of personal identity was the key concern; for them, defeat of the disease was.

- For her, technology and specialization threatened her individuality; for them, medical know-how was her only hope of survival.

- For her, she was more than her left breast; for them, her diseased body could be viewed independently of her as a person, including her beliefs, values, and social context.

- For her, she could influence the course of her disease; for them, her cancer would run its well-defined course independent of her or, for that matter, their relationship with her.

- For her, the enshrined medical notion of the "detached observer" was callously shocking; for them, it was the ideal way to relate to a patient.

- For her, patient autonomy meant acting for her own reasons, based on her own goals and aspirations; for them it meant giving informed consent to the mastectomy.

- For her, the disease was something to give meaning to; for them, it was an evil to be eradicated.

Perhaps most important, this woman saw herself as *ill*, whereas her physicians saw her as having a *disease*. Of the difference, physician Tauber writes:

> Disease is a synthesis and condensation of signs and symptoms, test finding, and a web of sorting categories. Indeed, in the United States, every disease has an international bar code, and if a patient does not have such a code, the doctor does not get paid! Illness, on the other hand, is the experience of disease and thus is a composite of all those elements that conspire to incapacitate a person.[25]

This patient's reaction against her physicians' "mechanistic model of disease" is reminiscent of early existentialism's reaction against the rationalism of the Enlightenment and positivism. Existentialists such as Soren Kierkegaard (1813–1855) and Martin Heidegger (1889–1976)—one a Christian, the other an atheist, and both familiar with the Tolstoy story—while acknowledging the importance of rational clarity, denied that reason or science could answer life's most pressing questions about the meanings of illness and suffering, of life in general, or of one's own life in particular. The intellectual heirs of these seminal existentialists are no less skeptical of the capacity of reason and science to solve unknowns that, nonetheless, must be faced, such as change, risk, uncertainty, and vulnerability. Philosopher Thomas Attig has expressed these mysteries as questions:

> Is it OK that we are small and insignificant when compared with the vast expanses of space, time, and history that surround us? Is it OK that change and impermanence pervade our lives, and that we have little to no control over many of the things that happen in them? Is it OK that we are imperfect; that we fall far short of our highest aspirations? Is it OK that our knowledge is limited, our judgment is fallible, and certainty eludes us? Is it OK that we are vulnerable to suffering and death?[26]

Sociologist and medical ethicist Renee C. Fox, one of bioethics' pathfinders, calls questions like these the "transcendent aspects of the human condition."[27] For Fox, as well as for theologians Courtney S. Campbell and Stanley Hauerwas, these "enduring questions of meaning that are integral to health, illness and medicine have been relegated to the borderlands of bioethical concerns," largely due to an overweening attachment to principlism. What sometimes remains, they feel, is an anemic response to the patient, wherein *respect for persons* means little more than patient choice, preferably shaped by medical interests. Thus, "Will you or won't you undergo mastectomy or (as in the Dr. Lantos example in Chapter 6) the hysterectomy?" A century earlier, with the rise of scientific medicine, the prescient Tolstoy wrote that physician response to Ilyich consisted of "impressive talk... about the kidney and the caecum, and questions and answers exchanged with such an air of importance... instead of the real question of life and death, the only one confronting Ivan Ilyich...."[27]

Because existentialists are interested in the perceived experience of the individual, they often use narratives or stories, such as *Ilyich*, to convey their messages. Not surprisingly, then, the perceived inattention paid the existential dimensions of illness has led to an interest in reviving, as an antidote to a potentially excessive scientific objectivity, the ancient tradition of storytelling or narratives in the teaching and practice of medicine, a mode of reasoning also favored by the care perspective.

NARRATIVES

In an article about narrative-based medicine, physicians Trisha Greenhalgh and Brian Hurwitz write:

> The processes of getting ill, being ill, getting better (or getting worse), and coping (or failing to cope) with illness, can all be thought of as enacted narratives within the wider narratives (stories) of people's lives.[29]

Again, recall Ilyich. His death, or dying, *cannot* be properly understood outside the context of his lived life. That's why Tolstoy revealed it. Ilych's backstory, his life's narrative, helps us understand his existential crisis. It provides meaning, context, and perspective for his predicament; and, ironically, it is also *totally absent* in his medical record. In a real sense, then, it is Ivan Ilyich, not his physician, who defines how, why, and in what way he is ill, and in what existential state he will die.

The same can be said of the woman with breast cancer. Her personal story provides what Greenhalgh and Hurwitz term a potential "framework for approaching her problems holistically, as well as revealing diagnostic and therapeutic options." It also implicatively locates her medical-existential crisis within the larger narrative of her life. By providing a window into such "existential qualities as hurt, despair, hope, grief and moral pain," the method of narrative, then, offers a possibility of developing a necessary understanding of a patient that cannot be arrived at by the problem-solving bias of principlism. This is one reason that feminist scholars such as Nel Noddings prefer narrative interpretation to the application of principles in bioethical analysis.[30]

As an upshot, today some take a narrative perspective on the moral life as a needed complement to principlism. Whereas the latter approaches a moral problem as a kind puzzle to be solved, a narrative approach treats it as a chapter within the context of an individual's ongoing life story, characterized with its own personalities, relationships, themes, significant events, values, commitments, and symbolic meaning. As MacIntye writes: "In our moral lives, we are engaged in enacting our own narrative,"[31] and "… my life has the unity of a story with a beginning, a middle, and an end."[32] By this account, the task of living is to determine how best to live out that unity and bring it to completion. Again, consider Ivan Ilyich, isolated in his angst largely because, narrativists would suggest, no one had narrative skills enough to recognize and respond to his suffering for what it was: a struggle to find meaning, to make sense of what was happening to him within the framework of his life's story. As Campbell notes:

> … within the vision of life as a journey, the hard cases, quandaries, and dramatic scenarios of bioethics are disclosed as but a time-slice in the narrative of a person's moral quest. A devotion to problem-solving both reflects and reinforces a cultural tendency to excise an individual from the social and temporal ties, from community and history, that present sources of meaning in the moral life.[33]

These words, coming as they do from a Christian professor of theology, suggest that the value of narrative has not been lost on Christian ethicists whose departure point is to treat theology primarily as the story of God working in human history and lives.

Narrative Theology and Ethics

Narrative theology, as it is sometimes called, emphasizes a pre-Enlightenment reading of the Bible as a realistic narrative of the world from creation to last judgment, rather than merely as a moral primer or a history of the ancient Jews and early Christians. Accordingly, says professor of philosophy and religion William Placher, "Much of the most interesting recent work in Christian ethics discusses the way narratives shape our understanding of Christian life." Besides the groundbreaking work of theologian Hans Frei (1922–1988), Placher reminds us that "ethicists as different as Hauerwas, Gilbert Meilaender, and James McClendon, as well as philosophers like MacIntyre, propose that ethics is not primarily a matter of making particular decisions in isolation [i.e., principlism]—moral-problem solving or what Hauerwas calls 'quandary ethics.'" Rather, in their view,

> we make decisions on the basis of beliefs about what sorts of virtues seem important, what sort of human life we believe to be good. To answer that kind of question, a principle or a rule is often less helpful than a story. I may get more help in deciding how to make ethical decisions as a Christian by reading [John Bunyan's classic 17th century allegory] *Pilgrim's Progress* or a biography of [the American journalist and Catholic social activist] Dorothy Day [1897–1980] or [civil rights champion] Martin Luther King, Jr. [1929–1968]—or by reading the Gospels—than by reading an academic discussion of medical ethics.[34]

By the narrative theology measure, then, the stories of the Bible can shape readers morally by, first, showing them how to act. This is accomplished mainly through the Bible's depiction of characters who model moral behavior. Beyond this, and more importantly, Bible study can develop moral capacities to meet real-life challenges by immersing readers in complex tales, with nuanced characters of complex motives, attempting to navigate circumstances that present problems and challenges that defy easy resolution. Biblical narratives, moreover, can provide readers the broader context of life's ultimate meaning and purpose for situating such troubling matters as illness, disease, suffering, and death. By giving moral insights that "can be expressed in language that speaks across the boundaries of cultural and moral differences, evoking engagement and response,"[35] these enduring narratives respond to our existential needs for order, sense, and coherence in our lives.

Consider as illustrative an actual case, provided by Campbell, of a couple whose first child was born with serious congenital abnormalities, evidenced visibly by facial disfigurement and substantial respiratory difficulties. After little Angela had spent a short while in a neonatal intensive care unit, neonatologists indicated that, though they could not be sure when death would occur, they were certain that the child's prognosis was terminal and asked the parents for their preferences regarding continuing or stopping treatment. "How might we think about such a problem in contemporary bioethics?" Campbell asks, before suggesting:

> We might invoke a benefits versus burdens calculation or a best interests standard, or take procedural recourse to an ethics committee, perhaps recommending withdrawal of life support. Or, we might consider the cogency of arguments supporting active killing as a compassionate act to spare the child what would inevitably be a painful life, whatever its duration.[36]

Importantly, Campbell's surmise is as true of most religious bioethicists as secular ones, for as Leon Kass has observed:

> Perhaps for the sake of getting a broader hearing, perhaps not to profane sacred teachings or to preserve a separation between the things of God and the things of Caesar, most religious ethicists entering the public practice of ethics leave their special insights at the door and talk about "deontological vs. consequentialist," "autonomy vs. paternalism," "justice vs. utility," just like everybody else.[37]

But, in this instance, the parents did not ask the questions or mull the principles cited by Campbell and Kass. "Instead," Campbell says,

> they ... brought to that very difficult situation an understanding that our lives are subject to ultimate powers which are creative, nurturing, and redeeming, and a way of construing the world shaped decisively by a set of religious convictions about the purpose of life, the meaning of death, and ultimate human destiny. Within that moral vision, Angela was not seen by her parents as a tragedy to be prevented (by prenatal diagnosis and abortion) or an unwanted burden whose life could easily be shortened, but instead as a girl in need of care. With minimal medical support, my friends took Angela home to begin their family life bound together, and over the next few months gave devoted and unceasing care until she died.[38]

Campbell is not arguing that the parents made the ethically right decision to take the child home rather than let her die in the hospital. (Indeed, in a later chapter we'll see narrative theology used in support of mercy death.) Campbell's point is, rather, "that a world view provided meaning in a situation that seemed pervaded by arbitrariness and cruelty, a meaning that could not be supplied or sustained by our conventional bioethics maxims about 'best interests' or 'substituted judgment.'" This leads Campbell to conclude, biblically: "The tragedy seen by others, including myself, was transformed into a girl. 'Suffer the little children ... for of such is the kingdom of God.'"

Dr. Lantos reports a similar ending in the case of the young woman with the malignant uterus (Ch. 6). A few days after bolting out of his office, the woman agreed to the procedure. In the interim she'd consulted with her rabbi, who told her: "If God wants you to have children, you'll have children. Not to believe that would be worse than death. It would be idolatry." The young woman's fiancé, we're told, didn't desert her, but joined her in daily prayer, reciting the entire Book of Psalms every morning. Six months after surgery, her cancer in remission, the couple married with the intention of adopting children. In retrospect, Dr. Lantos feels that everyone was trying to do the right thing, as they saw the right:

> The rabbi interpreted Torah and Talmud to come to a truth that differed somewhat from the truth of the doctors. Could the doctors have offered hope in the same way the rabbi did? Perhaps. But they felt morally bound to convey the truths science,

not religion. The parents stood with a foot in each truth community clearly trusting the doctors with their daughter's life but not trusting the doctor's moral vision. The young woman chose life over death and obedience to her parents and teachers over an individualistic tragedy that her doctors and lawyers would have allowed.[39]

BIOETHICS ACROSS CULTURES

Bioethics in the Twenty-first Century

Masahiro Morioka is a philosopher and writer whom many consider one of today's most important thinkers in the field of philosophy and sociology. As a professor of contemporary thought and ethics at Japan's Osaka Prefecture University, Morioka is accustomed to pondering big questions, such as "What should bioethics become in the 21st century?" He believes that in this century "bioethics should leave behind today's principle-based, male-centered, medicine-oriented, American bioethics, and become an international, cross-cultural, more feminist, more environmentally oriented study of life, science and society."

Although biomedical ethics will remain an essential part of this effort, Morioka's vision is closer to that of the American biochemist Van Rensselaer Potter (1911–2001), who coined the word "bioethics" in 1970. By "bioethics" Potter had in mind "interdisciplinary ethics" which cuts across natural sciences and the humanities. As such Potter's "bioethics" included both "medical bioethics" and "ecological bioethics." So does Morioka's. Also, Potter's bioethics was closer to today's environmental ethics than to medical ethics, as is Morioka's. Thus, in the twenty-first century Morioka anticipates bioethics as an integrated study of life, science, and society. Issues of medical ethics will be researched and studied in relation to other social problems such as poverty, sexism and ageism, environmental pollution, racial and ethnic conflicts, and so on.

Besides broadening its outlook by restoring its original cross-disciplinary character, Morioka envisions bioethics for making sound policy. He anticipates a "process of making health care policy for domestic and worldwide health problems such as AIDS, transplantation, and care for the aged." Bioethics for making sound policy would also include everyday clinical ethics in the hospital, and our activities in creating mutual

support networks for the weak and the disabled. Morioka believes that this process must be cross-cultural and international, and respect different value systems and worldviews. He gives the example of shoehorning "informed consent" into a community whose value systems and customs won't easily accommodate it. "We are going to be confronted with the difficult problem of deciding what ideas in bioethics we should view as universal and what values and customs in a given tradition we should leave as they are," he says.

Beyond this, Morioka believes that bioethics for making sound policy must also acknowledge the psychological factors influencing both patient and physician when making medical decisions in a clinical setting. Heretofore, bioethics has concentrated largely on logical analysis of moral rules "and made light of the psychological aspects of human nature." Morioka thinks this is unwise. "People's conduct," he maintains, " is often deeply influenced by personal psychological relationships, not by moral rules and sermons."

(SOURCE: Masahiro Morioka, "Toward International and Cross-cultural Bioethics," *Proceedings of the Third International Bioethics Seminar,* Eubios Ethics Institute, 1994, pp. 293–295. Retrieved June 5, 2009, from http://www.lifestudies.org/international01.html)

Question

What would be the value in bringing bioethics more in line with Potter's conception of an integration of biology, ecology, medicine, and human values? What are the implications of Morioka's proposal for ethical analysis and evaluation? What are some medical examples of how people's conduct is "deeply influenced by personal psychological relationships"? Apply Morioka's conception to the following cross-cultural inserts: "East Asian Autonomy" (Ch. 5), "A Japanese Woman with Aggressive Leukemia" (Ch. 5), and "Unmarried and Pregnant in Saudi Arabia" (Ch. 6).

CONCLUSIONS

Largely because of the *Belmont Report*'s mandate and its pragmatic character, principlism, perhaps, was bound to give an incomplete picture of the moral life. For example, although principlism was embraced as a neutral and universal moral language for saying "what is good to do or not to do in and through medicine," it was actually speaking to a particular time and place.[40] More broadly, it was a Western Anglo-American bioethics that did not take into account how race, culture, and religion can and do shape views of medicine and, thus, bioethics.[41] Additionally:

- Although principlism offered a structure for analyzing and solving moral problems, it also separated individual patients from their social and temporal ties, from their community and history, and thus severed them from their sources of moral meaning.

- Although principlism respected the autonomy of selves, it didn't ground the self in anything enduring, such as community or God.

- Although principlism was motivated by concern about the concrete circumstances of clinical life, it offered up abstract principles open to multiple, even opposed interpretations.

- Although principlism addressed the doctor-patient relationship from the viewpoint of patient rights and physician responsibilities, it said little about patient responsibilities and physician and societal rights.

- Although principlism was adopted as an ethic for health care, it offered nothing about the meaning of health care.

- Although principlism came to enshrine individual choice in medical matters, it was silent on the choice itself and its limits.

Most important, in bringing a language of individual rights into a clinical setting, the 1979 *Belmont Report* gave patients a much-needed voice in decision making and established a basis for moral consensus within a pluralistic society with both secular and sacred traditions. But, as we've seen in the last two chapters, it also left bioethics unmoored from the larger questions of human nature and reality, of truth and meaning, of transcendent values and destiny. Perhaps unavoidably ignored at its birth, such matters can't be dodged three decades later; for even when they don't bubble up, they're always present just beneath the surface of today's cultural discourse in bioethics—no more so than in matters at the beginning and end of life.

CASES AND CONTROVERSIES

Forever Small: The Ashley Treatment

Caring for children with profound developmental disabilities is difficult and demanding. For nonambulatory children with severe, combined neurological and cognitive impairment, caregivers, usually parents, must provide all of life's necessities. As the child grows, and these tasks become more difficult, many parents would like to continue caring for their child with special needs at home but find it difficult to do so as the child increases in size. If growth could be permanently arrested while the child was still small, both child and parent could benefit from continued care in the home.

In 2006 doctors in Seattle General Hospital deliberately stunted the growth of a severely disabled young girl to keep her from growing too large for her family members to carry. Drs. Daniel F. Gunther and Douglas S. Diekema described the surgical/pharmaceutical treatment as "growth attenuation," in the October 2006 issue of *Archives of Pediatrics and Adolescent Medicine*. In the article, the physicians gave the case of a girl named Ashley as a powerful illustration of the merits of growth attenuation.

Ashley, then nine, was born with static encephalopathy, severe brain impairment. She couldn't walk or talk, keep her head up, or roll over or sit up by herself.

(Continued)

CASES AND CONTROVERSIES (CONTINUED)

She was fed with a tube. Her parents called her "Pillow Angel," because she stayed right where they placed her, usually on a pillow. They said they feared that their angel would become too big one day to care for.

Under treatment by Gunther and Diekema, who worked in the pediatrics department at Children's Hospital and Regional Medical Center in Seattle, Ashley was given high doses of estrogen over several years to inhibit her growth and underwent a hysterectomy and the removal of her breast buds to avoid menstrual cramps and the possibility of pregnancy, and to decrease the likelihood of sexual abuse. The treatment is expected to keep Ashley's height at about 4 feet 5 and her weight at about 75 pounds for the rest of her life. She is expected to have a normal lifespan. Had she not been given the treatment, doctors estimate, she would have grown into a woman of average height and weight—about 5 feet 6 inches and 125 pounds.

The parents' decision drew criticism and even outrage from some doctors and caregivers who said such treatment was a violation of personal dignity. Some said it was also a violation of the medical oath: First do no harm. The governance board of directors of the National Catholic Partnership on Disability condemned the treatment as immoral and unethical. Ethicist Arthur Caplan called it "indefensible under any circumstances."

But Ashley's parents and physicians said the move was a humane one, allowing the child to receive more care, more interaction with her younger brother and sister, and more of the loving touch of parents and others who can carry her. In a written account posted on their website, the parents wrote:

We will continue to delight in holding her in our arms and Ashley will be moved and taken on trips more frequently and will have more exposure to activities and social gatherings (e.g., in the family room, backyard, swing, walks, bathtub, etc.) instead of lying down in her bed staring at TV (or the ceiling) all day long.[42]

A year after the surgery, Ashley's parents told CNN in a lengthy e-mail interview that they were delighted with the outcome. "The 'Ashley treatment' has been successful in every expected way," they said. "It has potential to help many others like it helped our precious daughter."

Questions for Analysis

1. Can you think of good historical reasons to proceed cautiously when considering *any* medical intervention directed at persons with developmental disabilities?

2. Should parents be permitted to choose the "Ashley treatment"?

3. Explain why you agree or disagree with those who say that growth attenuation is playing God.

4. Evaluate growth attenuation from the perspective of religious natural law.

5. Discuss the "Ashley treatment" from the perspectives of virtue, care, existential and spiritual dimensions of illness, and narrative ethics.

6. Explain how both Kant's ethics and preference utilitarianism could justify the "Ashley treatment."

CASES AND CONTROVERSIES

Dax Cowart: Burn Victim Wants to Die

In the Texas summer of 1973, Dax Cowart, 25, was severely burned over 65 percent of his body in a freak accident, propane gas explosion that killed his father. Dax's face and hands suffered third-degree burns, and both eyes and ears were irreparably damaged. His very survival was in doubt.

When finally stabilized, Dax underwent amputation of several fingers and removal of his right eye. During much of his 232-day hospitalization, he

repeatedly insisted that treatment be discontinued and that he be allowed to die. The physicians at Parkland Hospital in Texas conferred with his mother to obtain consent for all his treatments, even though she had not been appointed his legal guardian and psychiatric evaluation had determined that Dax had full decision-making capacity. But, ultimately, his mother was given the power of attorney, while her son was declared mentally incompetent. Despite Dax's demands and the constant struggle between son and mother, doctors continued wound care, performed skin grafts, and provided nutritional fluid support.

Dax finally recovered from his burns and left the hospital, totally blind, with minimal use of his hands, badly scarred, and dependent on others to assist in personal functions. He successfully sued the oil company responsible for his burns, which left him financially secure. Later, he attended law school at Baylor University. He attempted suicide twice after his rehabilitation period. He eventually finished law school, started his own practice advocating the "right to die" movement, and married. Dax Cowart is now apparently happy but still believes the doctors were wrong to follow his mother's wishes over his.[43,44]

Questions for Analysis

1. What moral issues are involved in this case?

2. Identify the values, interests, and responsibilities of each of the involved parties: Dax, his mother, and physicians.

3. Do you think that medical paternalism was justified to save Dax's life, or was Dax's autonomy violated?

4. Evaluate Dax's desire to die to avoid suffering, from the perspectives of virtue, care, existential and spiritual dimensions of illness, and narrative.

5. Should people like Dax be allowed to die if they are judged mentally competent and that is what they want? Justify your answer by appeal to moral principle(s).

CASES AND CONTROVERSIES

Gatekeepers Without Empathy

In 2004 the US government cited Harvard University for ethical lapses in research experiments involving human subjects, including some in China and Tanzania. About one-third of the university's research projects turned out to have problems, generally involving a failure to provide complete information to the people involved, according to government investigators.

While no one was hurt as a result, the omissions came despite intense scrutiny of human-subject research by US universities following several deaths, including ones at the University of Pennsylvania, Johns Hopkins University, Indiana University, and the University of California. Other universities were accused of ignoring rules requiring that human-subject research be peer reviewed. Among them were Duke University and the Universities of Alabama, Colorado, Illinois, Texas, and Chicago.[45] Meanwhile, across the pond the prominent British medical journal *The Lancet* retracted a 1998 article linking childhood vaccinations and autism, a condition whose roots are not understood. In its February 2010 statement, the editors cited as a reason for the full retraction the dishonest and unethical behavior of the article's author, who they said showed a "callous disregard" for the suffering of children he studied.[46]

How to account for these lapses, some thirty years after the Belmont principles were formulated

specifically to protect human subjects of medical research? If we asked Daniel Vasgird, he'd urge us to reflect on "the empathetic divide that often exists between researchers, including those who support them, and the research participants, who are the foundation of the enterprise."[47] A social psychologist, Vasgird maintains that this gulf exists despite the best of intentions. "As a result," he says, "there can be considerable ambiguity about the motives of those gatekeepers who behave without due regard for the welfare of research participants."

As an example Vasgird cites his own experience as chair of a behavioral and biomedical science Institutional Review Board (IRB) for a New York institution in line for many collaborative national research investigations. About midway through his time there, "a particularly sensitive and apparently risky joint protocol came before the IRB from a principal investigator (PI) who was associated with a major research institution in our area." Although the proposal promised great benefit if conducted properly, the IRB decided that several changes needed to be made to protect the human subjects of the research. Since the changes were substantially higher than the minimum protections required by federal regulations, the research institution balked. It called the IRB's requests "arbitrary and capricious," unprecedented, and impossible to meet. Vasgird pointed out that the federal and state regulations were minimal standards and that the IRB had the "flexibility, discretion and empowerment to

(Continued)

CASES AND CONTROVERSIES (CONTINUED)

raise that bar as it feels necessary for each individual case." For this protocol, the IRB, acting as the participants' advocate, had decided a higher bar was necessary to protect their well-being.

In the middle of his explanation, Vasgird reports being cut off by the institution's own president, who furiously ordered him to make the adjustments to fit the client's criteria. Vasgird refused, even when the president, a usually "charming, witty and gracious person," threatened to have his "head on a plate." Over the next few months the PI submitted a series of revisions that ultimately complied with all of the IRB's original requests.

From his experience, Vasgird draws many lessons. One is that those who endeavor to maintain both research integrity and human subject protection need to feel "an obligation to those we represent to do all that we can to expand our imaginative range to what might be missing relative to the issues and cases we deliberate about and ultimately decide on." True ethical behavior, he says, is impossible without "a feeling of identification and solidarity with those we represent and advocate for."

Questions for Analysis

1. Vasgird titles his anecdote "A Case Study in Virtue Ethics." Explain what he means.

2. Why was the president not open to the IRB's explanation?

3. Vasgird believes that if the IRB had allowed the study to run as originally presented, the president would not have been accused of intentional harm had something gone amiss and the participants took the brunt of the consequences. Why does he believe this?

4. In terms of the four basic bioethical principles, the original proposal failed the test of nonmaleficence, in Vasgird's view. However, Vasgird doesn't talk about principles. Instead he relates the mission of the review board to reaching "outside our usual sources of information to those we might not at first be able to relate to" and expanding "our imaginative and empathetic parameters." What do you think he's driving at?

5. Vasgird and the president clearly are intelligent men who certainly must have been aware of the basic bioethical principles. And yet, they arrive at opposed judgments about the research proposal. How do you account for the difference?

6. Do you think that this case shows how "legalistic observation of moral rules can unintentionally lead to greater evils and abdication of compassion," in the words of Pinit Ratanakul (see Bioethics Across Cultures, "Buddhist Virtue")?

REFERENCES

1. Jeffrey Olen, Julie C. Van Camp, and Vincent Barry, *Applying Ethics,* 8th ed., Belmont, CA: Thomson/ Wadsworth, 2005, p. 12.

2. Jonathan Haidt, "The Emotional Dog and It Rational Tail: A Social Intuitionist Approach to Moral Judgment," *Psychological Review,* vol. 108, 2001, pp. 814–834.

3. Virginia Held, *The Ethics of Care: Personal, Political and Global,* New York: Oxford University Press, 2006. p. 10.

4. Ibid., p. 11.

5. Thomas Bivins, "Caring and Harm," 2000. Retrieved April 19, 2008, from http://jcomm.uoregon.edu/~tbivins/J397/LINKS/LECTURE_NOTES/Caring.html.

6. Diane B. Uustal, "The Ethic and Spirit of Care," in *Cutting-Edge Bioethics: A Christian Exploration of Technologies and Trends,* John F. Kilner, C. Christopher Hook, Dianne B. Uustal, eds., Grand Rapids, MI: 2002, pp. 147–148.

7. Ibid., p. 149.

8. Carol Gilligan, *In a Different Voice,* Cambridge: Harvard University Press, 1993.

9. Catherine Villanueva Gardner, "Varieties of Ethical Theories," *APA Newsletters,* Spring, 1999. Retrieved April 1, 2008, from www.apaonline.org/apa/archive/newsletters/v98n2/feminism/gardner.asp.

10. NA, "Feminist Ethics," *Stanford Encyclopedia of Philosophy,* May 4, 2009. Retrieved May 17, 2009, from http://plato.stanford.edu/entries/feminism-ethics/.

11. Nancy Jecker, "Giving Death a Hand: When the Dying and the Doctor Stand in a Special Relationship," in Ralph Baergen, *Ethics at the End of Life,*

Belmont, CA: Wadsworth/Thomson Learning, 2001, p. 171.

12. Sandra Lee Bartky, "Feeding Egos and Tending Wounds: Deference and Disaffection in Women's Emotional Labor," in *Femininity and Domination: Studies in the Phenomenology of Oppression*, New York: Routledge, 1990, pp. 99–119.

13. Hilde Lindemann Nelson, "Against Caring," *Journal of Clinical Ethics*, vol. 3, 1992, pp. 8–15.

14. Helga Kuhse, "Clinical Ethics and Nursing: 'Yes' to Caring, but 'No' to a Female Ethics of Care," *Bioethics*, vol. 9, 1995, pp. 207–219.

15. E. F. Kittay and D. T. Myers, eds., *Women and Moral Theory*, Totowa, NJ: Rowman and Littlefield, 1987.

16. Albert Jonsen, *The Birth of Bioethics*, New York: Oxford University Press, 1998, p. 79.

17. See note 16 above.

18. Hilde Lindemann, *An Invitation to Feminist Ethics*, New York: McGraw Hill, 2006.

19. Margrit Shildrick, *Leaky Bodies and Boundaries: Feminism, Postmodernism and Bioethics*, New York: Routledge, 1997, p. 15.

20. Quoted in Jerome Goopman, "Faith and Healing," *The New York Times Book Review*, January 27, 2008, p. 15.

21. Albert Tauber, *Patient Autonomy and the Ethics of Responsibility*, Cambridge, MA: The MIT Press, 2005, p. 47.

22. T. Brohm, *Gentle Giants*. London: Century, 1986, pp. 8–10. Quoted in Hamish Wilson, "The Myth of Objectivity: Is Medicine Moving Towards a Social Constructivist Medical Paradigm?" *Family Practice*, April 2000, p. 203. Retrieved May 1, 2008, from http://fampra.oxfordjournals.org/cgi/content/full/17/2/203.

23. Dean Whitehead, "Beyond the Metaphysical: Health-Promoting Existential Mechanisms and Their Impact on the Health Status of Clients," *Journal of Clinical Nursing*, September 2003, p. 678.

24. Bjorg T. Landmark, "Living with Newly Diagnosed Breast Cancer—The Meaning of Existential Issues. A Qualitative Study of 10 Women with Newly Diagnosed Breast Cancer," *Cancer Nursing*, June 2001, p. 220–226.

25. Tauber, p. 49.

26. Thomas Attig, "Relearning the World: Making and Finding Meanings," in *Meaning Reconstruction & the Experience of Loss*, R. A. Neimeyer, ed., Washington, D.C.: American Psychological Association, 2001, p. 45.

27. Rene Fox, "Back from the Borderlands," *The Park Ridge Center Bulletin*, March 1999, p. 10. Retrieved May 12, 2008, from http://www.parkridgecenter.org/Page62.html.

28. Leo Tolstoy, *The Death of Ivan Ilyich*, New York: Bantam Books, 1981, pp. 112–113.

29. Trisha Greenhalgh and Brian Hurwitz, "Narrative Based Medicine: Why Study Narrative?" *BMJ*, January 2, 1999, pp. 48–50. Retrieved May 1, 2008, from www.bmj.com/cgi/content/#3D7047.

30. Nel Noddings, *Caring*, Berkeley: University of California Press, 1984.

31. Alasdair MacIntyre, *Three Rival Versions of Moral Enquiry*, Notre Dame, Indiana: University of Notre Dame Press, 1990, p. 80.

32. Ibid., p. 197.

33. Courtney S. Campbell, "Religion And Moral Meaning In Bioethics," *Hastings Center Report*, July-August 1990, pp. 4–10. Retrieved May 10, 2008, from http://ccbs.ntu.edu.tw/FULLTEXT/JR-MDL/camp.htm.

34. William Placher, "Hans Frei and the Meaning of Biblical Narrative," *Religion-online*. Retrieved May 9, 2008, from www.religion-online.org/showarticle.asp?title=15

35. Lisa Sowie Cahill, "Finding Common Ground: Religion's Role in the Ethics Committee," *The Park Ridge Center Bulletin: Religion in Bioethics*, March/April 1999, p. 3. Retrieved June 12, 2008, from www.parkridgecenter.org/Page547.html.

36. See note 33 above.

37. Leon R. Kass, "Practicing Ethics Where's the Action?," *Hastings Center Report,* January/February 1990, pp. 6–7. Quoted in Campbell.

38. *Campbell*, p. 6.

39. John Lantos, "To Tell or Not to Tell," *The Park Ridge Center Bulletin*, March 1999. Retrieved February 20, 2008, from http://www.parkridgecener.org/Page61.html.

40. Stephen Lammers, "The Marginalization of Religious Voices in Bioethics," in *Religion & Medical Ethics*, Allen Verhey, ed., Grand Rapids, MI: William B. Eerdmans Publishing Company, 1996, pp. 29–30.

41. Lawrence Prograis, Jr., and Edmund D. Pellegrino, *African American Bioethics: Culture, Race, and Identity*, Washington: Georgetown University Press, 2007.

42. Sam Howe Verhovek, "Parents Defend Decision to Keep Disabled Girl Small," *Los Angeles Times*,

January 3, 2007. Retrieved April 15, 2009, from http://articles.latimes.com/2007/jan/03/nation/na-stunt3.

43. NA, "Dax," *Health Care News*, St. Louis, MO, 2007. Retrieved April 20, 2009, from http://www.ascensionhealth.org/ethics/public/cases/case12.asp.

44. Albert R. Jonsen, Mark Siegler, and William J. Winslade. "Introduction: Case Analysis in Clinical Ethics," *A Practical Approach to Ethical Decision in Clinical Medicine*, 4th ed. New York: McGraw-Hill, 1998. Retrieved April 20, 2009, from http://depts.washington.edu/bioethx/tools/ceintro.html.

45. Jon Marcus, "Harvard Quizzed on Research Ethics," *Times Higher Education*, May 28, 2004. Retrieved April 16, 2009, from http://www.timeshighereducation.co.uk/story.asp?storyCode=188971&sectioncode=26.0.

46. NA, "Taking It Back," *The New York Times*, February 7, 2010, p. 2.

47. Daniel R. Vasgird, "Resisting Power and Influence: A Case Study in Virtue Ethics," *Journal of Empirical Research on Human Research Ethics,* June 2006, pp. 19–22. Retrieved April 20, 2009, from http://caliber.ucpress.net/loi/jer.

Issues at the Beginning of Life

INTRODUCTION: HEADLINES FOR REPRODUCTIVE ETHICS

The first half of 2007 featured three headline events with significant implications for reproductive ethics and policy, which are the interests of Part III. Then, two days before Thanksgiving, came a blockbuster.

1. January 2: *Testing for Down Syndrome Recommended for All Pregnant Women* The new year had hardly begun when a new *Practice Bulletin* was issued by the American College of Obstetricians and Gynecologists (ACOG), recommending that all pregnant women, regardless of age, should be offered a new, safe screening for Down Syndrome (DS).[1] Doctors had long recommended amniocentesis testing before the twentieth week of pregnancy for women thirty-five and over, since their age put them at risk for chromosomal abnormality. Because the test carried a small risk of miscarriage, it was not recommended for younger women. Now, the ACOG recommendation made the new simpler and safer test, consisting of a sonogram and two blood tests, the preferred screen for DS.

   DS is a common disorder caused by an extra chromosome that can result in congenital heart defects and mental retardation. The DS population in the United States is more than 350,000, with about 5,500 DS babies born annually. With an average life expectancy of forty-nine, some DS adults hold jobs, but many have difficulty living independently. Upwards of 90 percent of all DS pregnancies are aborted, despite the waiting list of families eager to adopt such children.[2]

   "There are many couples who do not want to have a baby with Down syndrome," said Deborah A. Driscoll, chief of the obstetrics department at the University of Pennsylvania and a lead author of the new ACOG recommendation. "They don't have the resources, don't have the emotional stamina, don't have the family support. We are recommending this testing be offered so that parents have a choice."[3]

But parents of DS children saw it differently. Some of them viewed the ACOG's recommendation as "painting a bull's eye on Down Children."[4] George F. Will, conservative journalist and father of a DS adult, labeled the new recommendation a "search and destroy mission."[5] Another DS parent said: "For me, it's just faces disappearing…. It isn't about abortion politics or religion, it's a pure ethical question."[6] For her part, Republican vice-presidential candidate Sarah Palin said she felt "blessed" to give birth to a DS baby.

Beyond DS, today's sophisticated prenatal testing technologies permit detection of a wide variety of abnormalities. An influential federal advisory group has recommended that all neonates be screened for twenty-nine rare medical disorders, ranging from the well known, such as sickle cell anemia, to the extremely uncommon. Indeed, the day is quickly coming when we'll be able to screen for literally everything known to have a genetic component. Of course, for most of the tested disorders it won't be known whether a treatment will help, or even if a baby who tests positive will develop the disease. So, prospective parents and their physicians will have to decide whether having such tests will do more good than harm, emotionally and physically. They also may be deciding which embryos will be deemed fit for life and forcing society to decide the limits of reproductive choice.[7]

2. April 18: *Partial-Birth Abortion Ban Upheld* In the spring of 2007, the Supreme Court ruled, in *Gonzales v. Carhart*, that Congress can prohibit doctors from performing the late-term abortion procedure opponents call "partial-birth abortion," even when the pregnant woman's health is at risk. The ruling prevents physicians from intentionally delivering

vaginally a living fetus and then deliberately killing it when it is leaving the womb. *Carhart* does not prohibit the most common method for late-term abortion, called dilation and evacuation (D&E), which consists of removing fetal tissues from the womb piecemeal. Nor does it prohibit delivering a fetus that isn't viable or using the method to save the woman's life. Still, by prohibiting a particular abortion procedure, the *Carhart* decision broke new ground and promised to reframe the abortion debate. (See case presentation *Gonzales v. Carhart*, Ch. 10).

3. May 30: *Fate of Frozen Embryos In Dispute* Shortly after the *Carhart* decision, a case with further implications for abortion made the front page of a national newspaper.[8] Publicized as the "Texas Frozen Embryo Custody" case, *Roman v. Roman* concerned the fate of three frozen embryos created by a Texas couple who divorced before the woman was artificially fertilized.

Just hours before Augusta Roman was scheduled to undergo the fertilization procedure, her husband at the time, Randy Roman, insisted that the procedure be canceled and that the embryos be frozen. The couple later began divorce proceedings and disputed ownership of the embryos. Augusta Roman sought to have the three embryos that survived the freezing process implanted in her and brought to term, but husband Randy wanted to have them destroyed or to remain frozen indefinitely. A trial court subsequently ruled in favor of Augusta, only to have its decision reversed, leading to Augusta Roman's petition to the US Supreme Court.

At stake in *Roman* was more than who owned the frozen embryos. It also had implications for *Roe v. Wade* (1973), the land-mark case that disallowed many state and federal restrictions on abortion. In that politically controversial decision, the US Supreme Court ruled that, by the standard of the Fourteenth Amendment, the unborn were not "persons." Unburdened of having to balance the rights of the unborn against those of the pregnant woman, the high court recognized a woman's right to privacy allowed her to terminate a pregnancy. But now, buoyed by *Carhart,* social conservative legal theorists were hopeful that a case involving frozen embryos could give an increasingly conservative court one vehicle for reconsidering the rights of the unborn and to do so apart from the woman's right to control her own body. If that happened, then Augusta Roman, 48 and childless, would gain control of the embryos, and *Roe* would be undermined.

On March 17, 2008, the Supreme Court denied Augusta Roman's petition and, thereby, sealed the fate of the frozen embryos. They would be destroyed by the fertility clinic unless the parties agreed to have them disposed of differently.

4. November 21: *Stem Cell Milestone Achieved* It was a week after the Romans made national headlines when a Democratic Congress gave final approval to legislation aimed at easing restrictions on federal financing of human embryonic stem cell (ESC) research. Given that stem cells have the unique ability to generate all kinds of cells in the body, the great hope is that, when placed in the proper environment, they can make cells to fight conditions such as diabetes, Parkinson's disease, epilepsy, and spinal cord injury. Proponents of ESC research say that only the stem cells found in human embryos can yield cells to produce the desired

effects. They want to make use of the routinely discarded embryos grown by fertility clinics such as the Romans'. But to capture the stem cells in the cause of alleviating human suffering, the embryos must be destroyed.

Arguing for the bill's passage, House Speaker Nancy Pelosi (D-CA) said, "Science is a gift of God to all of us and science has taken us to a place that is biblical in its power to cure. And that is the embryonic stem cell research."[7] In a strongly worded disagreement, President Bush characterized the legislation as needlessly encouraging a conflict between science and ethics. The next day he vetoed the proposal, saying that if it were to become law, "American taxpayers would for the first time in our history be compelled to support the deliberate destruction of human embryos...."[10]

With both sides gearing up to make ESC research a political issue in the 2008 presidential campaign, the fall of 2007 brought a stunning breakthrough in stem cell research. Just before Thanksgiving, researchers from Japan and Wisconsin reported that they had reprogrammed mature human skin cells to behave almost exactly like embryonic stem cells. Presto!—the thorny controversy over the morality of destroying embryos to obtain stem cells seemingly had vanished. But had it? In fact, experts warned, while the new technology might avoid the ethical problem of killing embryos, it brought a whole new set of issues.[11] Meanwhile, skin cell scientists at the University of Wisconsin insisted that work with ESCs had to continue. Research was in its early stages, they said, and comparison studies had to be done to ensure that genetically engineered skin cells did not behave in unexpected ways.

Genetic research and fetal testing, abortion, assisted reproduction, stem cell research—Chapters 9 through 16 review the science, social context, and ethics of these culturally divisive core issues in human embryology. The theme of Part III is that nowhere more so than in the ethics of reproductive technology is what drives today's bioethical controversies, namely, clashing views about what and who we are. We begin, in Chapter 8, with some important conceptual matters.

REFERENCES

1. Bulletin #77, "Screening for Fetal Chromosomal Abnormalities," *Obstetrics & Gynecology,* January 2007.

2. George Will, "Golly, *Did* Jon Do?" *Newsweek,* January 29, 2007. Retrieved July 5, 2007, from http://www.msnbc.msn.com/id/16720750/site/newsweek/

3. Amy Harmon, "Prenatal Testing Puts Down Syndrome in Hard Focus," *The New York Times,* May 9, 2007. Retrieved August 1, 2007, from http://www.nytimes.com/2007/05/09/us/09down.html

4. Tom Strode, "Life Digest: Stem Cells from Amniotic Fluid May Help Avoid Ethical Dilemma," *BP News,* January 8, 2007. Retrieved August 15, 2007, from www.bpnews.net/BPnews.asp?ID=24727-67k

5. See note 2 above.

6. See note 3 above.

7. Peter Braude, "Preimplantation Diagnosis for Genetic Susceptibility," *The New England Journal of Medicine,* August 10, 2006, pp. 541–543.

8. Kevin Sack, "Her Embryos or His?" *Los Angeles Times,* May 30, 2007, p. A18.

9. Jeff Zeleny, "House Votes to Expand Stem Cell Research," *The New York Times,* June 8, 2007, p. A23.

10. Joel Havemann, "Stem Cell Bill Passes House, but Faces Certain Veto," *Los Angeles Times,* June 8, 2007, p. A16.

11. Karen Kaplan, "Stem Cell Milestone Achieved," *Los Angeles Times,* November 21, 2007, p. A1.

Chapter 8

Conceptual Matters in Abortion and Reproductive Technology

O n March 6, 2006, Governor Mike Rounds of South Dakota signed into law the nation's most far-reaching ban on induced abortion: the Women's Health and Human Life Protection Act.

BANNING ABORTION IN SOUTH DAKOTA

The law, approved by the South Dakota Legislature by a wide margin, made it a felony to intentionally terminate a pregnancy except to save the life of the mother. Even then, physicians were required to do their utmost to save the fetus, otherwise face five years in prison.

Incensed abortion rights advocates nationwide branded the law blatantly unconstitutional. That charge didn't in the least faze its supporters, however. Indeed, they welcomed the law as a direct challenge to *Roe*. But instead of suing, abortion rights activists took to the streets, collecting enough petition signatures to put the law to a popular vote. After a bruising emotional campaign, involving thousands of volunteers and costing millions of dollars, South Dakota voters soundly rejected the abortion ban.

Undaunted, supporters of the total ban, many of whom had participated in months-long round-the-clock prayer vigils to ask God for the law's success, vowed to fight on. "We have an army now that we didn't have before," said the campaign manager. One of the army's leaders, newly consecrated Bishop Paul Swain issued a strong statement in favor of the legislation, following in the path set by his predecessor, Bishop Robert J. Carlson, who had actively encouraged Catholic voters to be guided by the issue of abortion in election votes. For its part, the opposition expressed equal confidence in its ability to prevail again, if necessary. "We have galvanized people from every part of the state," boasted a lobbyist for Planned Parenthood. "We are so much stronger today."[1]

When the votes were counted, a clear majority (55%–45%) again had rejected the broad ban on abortion whose stated purpose included, in language

149

that foreshadowed the following year's *Carhart* ruling, the protection of "the mother's fundamental natural intrinsic right to a relationship with her child."

Two years later, with all eyes on Barack Obama's historic 2008 win in the November presidential election, 55 percent of South Dakota's voters again rejected a slightly revised version of the high-profile proposed abortion ban. Undeterred, proponents vowed to try again to outlaw abortion in the 2010 election, in hopes of forcing a challenge to *Roe*. Still resonating with them was the sentiment expressed by Gov. Rounds in 2006 when he signed the abortion bill into law:

> In the history of the world, the true test of a civilization is how well people treat the most vulnerable and helpless in their society. The sponsors and supporters of this bill believe that abortion is wrong because unborn children are the must vulnerable and most helpless persons in our society agree with them.[2]

The governor's rhetoric and the reach of the short-lived South Dakota law left no doubt that, to its proponents, abortion was not only the termination of a pregnancy, it was murder. "We're coming back," said Leslee Unruh, an anti-abortion activist and prime proponent of the South Dakota ban. "We're not going away…. Third time's the charm."[3]

Whether abortion is the taking of human life, indeed murder, depends, initially, on what is meant by *human life*. According to the South Dakota law, the unborn is a member of the human species and as such is a human being and, thus, has rights, the most basic being the right to its life. But critics of the law and supporters of choice offered an alternative view. They said that it isn't the unborn's membership in the species *homo sapiens* that makes it a human being but its mental development. If human beings have rights, it's because they are sufficiently developed mentally to show distinctly human mental or psychological properties associated with the ability to think. Prior to such development, the unborn is not, properly speaking, a human being

at all; and, therefore, its abortion is morally non-problematic.

Still other parties to the South Dakota debate expressed the view that the unborn's human status is morally insignificant. What matters is whether the unborn is properly considered a *person*, because it is to persons that we ordinarily ascribe rights. According to the South Dakota law, the unborn is a person merely by virtue of its being biological human life. But it could be argued that *personhood* is defined by those mental properties that make the unborn human; and, therefore, lacking those capacities, the unborn aren't persons.

Although never using the term, then, the South Dakota law implicitly took a stand on what's termed the *ontological status of the unborn*, which is the focus of this chapter. "Ontology" literally means the study of being or existence. When we speak of the ontological status of the unborn, we mean basically to things: (1) the kind of entity the unborn is, that is, whether it is a human or a person; and (2) when it becomes that kind of entity. As by the South Dakota dispute showed, the ontological status of the unborn is an unsettled matter that bears directly on the issue of fetal rights and, subsequently, on permissible treatment of the unborn.[4] Indeed, the ontological status of the unborn—the kind of being it is—is at the heart of all issues of reproductive ethics, from abortion and fetal testing to artificial reproduction, cloning, and stem cell research.

We begin our discussion of the ontological status of the unborn with some basic embryology.

DEVELOPMENTAL SEQUENCE OF HUMAN LIFE

Although a knowledge of developmental biology will not answer the question "When does human life begin?," it does provide a scientific basis for various viewpoints, including religious ones.

In general, pregnancy is dated from the first day of the woman's last normal menstrual period, and the birth date is approximately 40 weeks from the beginning of the last period. During this time the unborn will grow from an egg to a fetus to a fully grown baby, with different parts of the body developing at different stages of the pregnancy. The average pregnancy lasts for 280 days, 40 weeks or nine months, from conception to birth. This is called the gestation period. If a pregnancy ends prior to the twentieth week due to natural causes, it is referred to as a *miscarriage* or a *spontaneous abortion*, and thereafter as a *preterm delivery*.[5] An abortion, or the termination of a pregnancy, may also be induced. An *induced abortion* is the purposeful termination of a pregnancy that physicians refer to as either *therapeutic* or *elective*. Therapeutic abortions are those recommended to protect the mother's physical or mental health. Elective abortions are those initiated by personal choice and account for the vast majority of abortions, upwards of 95 to 98 percent.[6] In everyday parlance, *abortion* denotes any artificial means to induce the loss of a pregnancy.

The nine months of pregnancy are traditionally divided into three trimesters: distinct periods of roughly three months in which different phases of fetal development take place. During the pregnancy the unborn has various technical names depending on its stage of development: *zygote*, first through third day; *blastocyst*, second day through second week; *embryo*, third week through eighth week; and *fetus*: ninth week until birth. However, the term fetus is also used non-technically to refer, in a general way, to the developing young in the uterus at any stage.

First Trimester

The first trimester of pregnancy, a time of basic cell differentiation begins when a fertilized egg implants into a woman's uterus. The following are the significant developmental events during the first trimester. (*Bear in mind the approximate nature of this sequential process, given that pregnancies differ and that development varies from fetus to fetus.*)

- sperm meets eggs; cells differentiate and divide into a zygote: week 1
- zygote implants in uterine wall, commencing pregnancy: weeks 2–3

- embryonic heartbeat, sometimes seen on ultrasound as flickering in the chest: week 5
- faint electrical activity from fetal nervous system: week 6
- fetal heartbeat, heard with a Doppler instrument, which bounces harmless sound waves off the fetal heart: weeks 9–12

Second Trimester

The second trimester is a period of rapid growth and maturation of body systems. A second-trimester fetus born prematurely may be *viable*, or capable of surviving outside the womb, but only if given the best hospital care possible and, generally speaking, having reached 24 weeks gestation. Amillia Taylor, born in 2006 in Florida, is the first baby known to have survived after a gestation of fewer than 23 weeks—21 weeks, 6 days in her case.[7] The following are the significant developmental events during the second trimester:

- quickening, or mother's perception of fetal movement: week 16 (within a range of 13-25)
- early connections between thalamus and cortex: weeks 22–24
- air sacs forming in lungs: week 23

Third Trimester

The third trimester marks the final stage of fetal growth. Systems are completed, fat accumulates under the skin, and the fetus moves into position for birth. During this time the fetus can "experience the self/other perceptions that form the basis of human consciousnesses."[8] The third trimester ends with the birth itself. The following are the significant developmental events during the third trimester:

- cerebral cortex "wired"; higher brain activity started; viable fetus: week 24
- cell structure of fetal brain begins to resemble a newborn's: week 26
- well-organized cerebral activity, partly overlapping with adult brain activity, as shown by fetal EEG (electroencephalograph): week 27

- fetal brain pattern almost identical to that of a full-term baby: week 32

Nearly 90 percent of all abortions occur in the first trimester, well before viability. Many providers won't do abortions thereafter because the procedure becomes more difficult. According to the AMA, third trimester abortions to save the mother's life are required only under extraordinary circumstances. It is estimated that of the approximately 1.3 million abortions that occur annually in the United States, about 1,000 are third trimester abortions.[9]

THE ONTOLOGICAL STATUS
OF THE UNBORN

The kind of entity the unborn is, that is, its ontological status, depends on one's understanding of two terms: *human life* and *person*.

The Meaning of *Human Life*

Popular opinion notwithstanding, the term *human life*, as used in "Abortion is the taking of human life," is not exactly clear. As philosopher Harry J. Gensler observes:

> Suppose we found a Martian who could discuss philosophy; would he be "human"? We need to make distinctions: the Martian would be "human" in the sense of "animal capable of reasoning" ("rational animal") but not in the sense of "member of the species *Homo sapiens*"—so the Martian is "human" in one sense but not in another. Which of these senses should be used in the abortion argument? The fetus is not yet an "animal capable of reasoning." Is it a "member of the species *Homo sapiens*"? That depends on whether the unborn are to be counted as "members" of a species— ordinary language can use the term either way. In the biology lab we all (regardless of our views on abortion) distinguish between "human" fetuses and "mouse" fetuses—so

in this sense (the "genetic sense") the fetus is human. But in counting the number of mice in the city of Chicago we all (regardless of our views on abortion) count only the born—so in this sense ("the population-study sense") the fetus is not a human. So is the fetus a "human"? In two senses of this term that we have distinguished the answer would be NO while in the third sense the answer would be YES ....[10]

As we saw earlier, the two great belief traditions in the West, the one sacred and other secular, offer contrasting conceptions of *human life*. According to the traditional Western religious view, it is divine likeness that makes life *human*. By contrast, the Western secular tradition understands *human life* in some biological or functional sense, as in *all* uses of the term in Gensler's illustration.

Understood biologically, *human life* means being a member of the human species or having the human genetic code. A related view holds that *human life* is defined by the ability to function as an integrated whole. As neurobiologist Maureen Condic notes, "While organisms are made of living cells, living cells themselves do not necessarily constitute an organism."[11] In other words, it's not just the presence of human cells that defines human life, but their working together for the continued life and health of the body as a whole.

For others, it's not biology, or at least not biology alone, that defines *human life*. Following the leads of Descartes and Locke, they connect being human with a capacity for consciousness or with the possession of certain *psychological* properties uniquely human. The abilities to use symbols, to think, and to imagine have been identified as some of these distinctive human properties.[12] This has led some, like the census taker in Gensler's example, to the view that not until birth does a human being come into existence, a belief, incidentally, of many Jews and Muslims.

Although the sacred may exclude the secular and vice versa, the two views needn't be mutually exclusive. Believing that divine likeness defines human life, for example, does not, of itself, rule out understanding human life either biologically or psychologically. In fact, historically, as we'll soon see, most theologians have implicitly endorsed biological *and* psychological conceptions of human life. This is why they generally have not viewed abortion as always homicide. By the same token, it's not unusual today to incorporate current embryological knowledge to support a traditional religious view of humanhood. Gilbert Meilander, for example, who is a professor of Christian Ethics at Valparaiso University and a member of the President's Council on Bioethics, writes:

> … the newly fertilized ovum has a top-bottom axis that sets up an equivalent axis in the embryo. Thus, for example, where the head and feet will sprout is established in the first hours after egg and sperm unite. Even the earliest embryo, it seems, is more than just a featureless collection of cells; it is an integrated, self-developing organism, capable (if all goes well) of the continued development that characterizes human life—and we are right to react with awe and wonder at the mystery of its individual existence.[13]

Whether one views human life biologically or psychologically greatly matters in the abortion debate. The South Dakota law, for example, clearly was referring to the broader category "biological human life" than the more restrictive "psychological human life," because it made no distinction among abortions. This explains why religious conservatives and fundamentalists championed the law, while many religious liberals opposed it, even though both camps agreed that abortion involves the destruction of biological life. For religious and social conservatives, the willful destruction of even the earliest stage of human development is always wrong. For religious liberals and secularists, it is generally the intentional termination of *psychological* life, a later stage, that is morally problematic.

The Meaning of *Personhood*

Intertwined with the question of the meaning of *human life* is the conception of personhood, which may or may not differ from the meaning of human

life. For example, conservative religious views, such as the official position of Roman Catholicism, make no distinction between a human being and a person, since both are defined by a God-given immortal soul. To biochemist and Catholic educator Dianne N. Irving, the biological counterpart of the soul is the unique strand of DNA that defines the human nature of both a human being and person. Because fertilization creates a unique strand of DNA in the human egg, a human being and a person come into being at fertilization. This makes terms like pre-*embryo*, *pre-person*, or *pre-human being* largely irrelevant, or worse, "illusions and distortions." "All these [terms]," according to Irving, who has published extensively on bioethics, "consider a person only in terms of exercising 'functions,' rather than in terms of his/her nature." By that standard, she adds, there is

> [s]cientifically … no point from fertilization … to death when the human nature of [a] human being changes at all; it keeps on continuously creating specifically human enzymes, proteins, tissues and organs—which only a human being can do…. Scientifically, the immediate products of … fertilization are the same—an already existing, living, unique, individual, embryonic human being and person.[14]

Gregory Koukl, who is a professor of Christian Apologetics at evangelical Biola University, agrees:

> The unborn offspring of human parents is fully human [i.e., a human person]—not potentially human—at every stage of her development. She will go through many physical changes from conception to old age, but will never change from one kind of being into another.[15]

In the same vein, philosopher Stephen Schwartz of the University of Rhode Island writes:

> My capabilities have changed, they have increased as my basic inherent capacity to function as a person has developed; but I remain always *the same person*, the same essential being, the being who has these

growing capabilities. If I am essentially a person now, I was essentially a person then, when I was a [fetus].[16]

In contrast, following Locke, the vast majority of bioethicists, as well as some Christian theologians,[17] focus mainly or exclusively on activities or attributes that they believe indicate personhood. A person, said Locke, is "a thinking intelligent being, that has reason and reflection, and can consider itself, as itself, the same thinking thing, in different times and places" (*Of Identity and Diversity*, 1689). Although people ordinarily equate *person* with *human being*, by a consciousness-related abilities standard, *person* could refer to anyone possessing those abilities, regardless of whether they are humans. Thus, Gensler's Martian. Philosopher David DeGrazia makes the point this way:

> The concept of personhood seems to extend beyond humanity. For we often categorize as persons certain imaginary nonhuman beings and certain nonhuman beings whose existence is debatable. Thus E.T., the extraterrestrial, Spock from *Star Trek*, and the speaking, encultured apes of *The Planet of the Apes* impress us as being persons. Furthermore, if God and angels exist, they too are persons. (Interestingly, many people who are inclined to equate personhood with humanity also assert, contradictorily, that God is a person.) This suggests that *person* does not mean *human being*. The term refers to a kind of being defined by certain psychological traits or capacities: beings with particular complex forms of consciousness. So, in principle, there could be nonhuman persons, for it is conceivable—and perhaps true—that certain nonhumans have the relevant traits.[18]

Most philosophers today and some liberal theologians tend to associate personhood with not just a single trait but also a cluster of them, such as "autonomy, rationality, self-awareness, linguistic competence, sociability, the capacity for intentional action, and moral agency." DeGrazia, for example, suggests that the "present meaning of *person* is

roughly *someone (of whatever species or kind) with the capacity for sufficiently complex forms of consciousness.*" He also endorses the consensual view of philosophers that "capacity" be understood "in the sense of current capabilities; mere potential to develop them is not enough."[19]

For their part, contemporary conservative theologians generally do not deny that personhood is "constituted by a set of ultimate capacities of thought, belief, sensation, emotion, volition, desire, intentionality and so forth."[20] But they contend that these are the constituents of an essentially immaterial, rational nature that human beings share with God. "God is the paradigm case ... of a person," write J. P. Moreland and Scott B. Rae, and "... it is clear that God is an immaterial reality (John 4:24)." Therefore, these two theologians conclude, human persons are essentially immaterial entities or souls.[21] Similarly, the Calvinist Christian theologian Alvin Plantinga writes:

> The first point to note is that on the Christian scheme of things, God is the premier person, the first and chief exemplar of personhood ... and the properties most important for an understanding of our personhood are properties we share with him.[22]

By this account, humanness or personhood is a nature that an individual exemplifies from conception, rather than a set of functional states that it attains.

WHEN ONTOLOGICAL STATUS IS ATTAINED

Whatever the view of the unborn's ontological status, the question then arises: *When is it attained in fetal development?* According to the South Dakota ban, the unborn has full ontological status at conception. In other words, the human being begun at conception is a human person. The opposed view is that the unborn attains full ontological status at some point after its conception. Thus, even if a human being begins at conception, it becomes a human person later. These opposed positions about when ontological status is attained reflect an old theological debate about hominization and ensoulment.

Hominization and Ensoulment

In Roman Catholic theology, *hominization*, from the Latin word *hominem* meaning "man," is the point in gestation at which the unborn attains full human status. The current official teaching of the Roman Catholic Church dates back only to 1869 when Pope Pius IX (1792–1878) implicitly endorsed the doctrine of immediate hominization in ruling that abortion at any stage is homicide (*Apostolicae Sedis, Apostolic See*). *Immediate hominization* means that the unborn is a human being from conception and, therefore, has full ontological status at conception. Prior to the pope's proclamation, Catholic theologians, including Augustine and Aquinas, generally favored *delayed hominization*, which holds that the unborn does not attain full human status until after a certain point in the process of development.

Although historically a minority view, immediate hominization did have its proponents in the ancient world, notably Hippocrates, who taught that a human soul was created at conception. It was this belief that evidently led to the Hippocratic Oath's explicit prohibition of giving a woman "an instrument to produce abortion." Still, even in the early and medieval Church immediate hominization was not the prevailing view, which can be inferred from the allowance for early abortions. In prohibiting abortion at any state of pregnancy, then, Pius IX was, in fact, ending a debate over the doctrine of ensoulment that had raged within the Western Church since about 100 CE.

Ensoulment refers to the creation of a soul within a human being or other creature. Aristotle had taught that the soul or spirit was what made living things different from non-living things. This led him to propose a hierarchy of souls (*On the Soul*, Book II). On the lowest level of vegetable life Aristotle placed the vegetative or nutritive soul, which

he associated with growth and reproduction. Next was the sensitive soul, which was present in non-human animals. Besides the processes of nutrition, growth, and reproduction, the sensitive soul was capable of sensation and desire. Finally, superior to the sensitive soul was the rational soul. It was this rational spirit, or capacity to reason, that Aristotle believed distinguished humans from other life forms. Aristotle guessed that the earliest the unborn attained a rational soul, that is, personhood, was forty days after conception, before which he permitted abortion.

Although directly at odds with current conservative thought and orthodox religious teaching,[23] Aristotle's doctrine of delayed ensoulment, or hominization, was for centuries the model for the Western Church's understanding of the moral status of the unborn. Aquinas, for example, taught that the unborn progressed in development from a vegetative soul, to an animal soul, and ultimately, "when the body is developed," to a rational soul. Prior to Pius IX's, then, as Catholic theologian Jean Porter points out, most Catholic theologians

> were well aware that the early-stage embryo was an organism distinct from the body of its mother, but they denied precisely what [the Catholic Church] is now claiming to be not only true, but obviously true—namely, that this human organism is a human person in the full sense.[24]

Although talk about "soul" and its relation to the body may seem quaint today, in fact it is ensoulment as a moral doctrine, and specifically immediate ensoulment, that underlies conservative Christianity's moral objection to an array of reproductive procedures.

Take, for example, therapeutic stem cell research, which the Bush administration rejected in 2001 and again in 2007. In the view of the president, a born-again Christian, the unborn from conception is a "human life" that cannot be destroyed for scientific research. Probably Bush, and certainly religious conservatives, consider a pre-embryo or blastocyst "human life" within the religious notion of ensoulment. Specifically, they believe that it is a

---

BIOETHICS ACROSS CULTURES

Jewish Beliefs about Personhood

Although it accords the fetus great value because it is potentially a human life, Halacha (Jewish law) does not define when a fetus becomes a *nefesh* (person). According to rabbinical law: "... a baby... becomes a full-fledged human being when the head emerges from the womb. Before then, the fetus is considered a 'partial life.'" There has been no consensus among historical Jewish sources about when ensoulment happens, but several abortion-related passages in the Hebrew Scriptures and Talmud give insight into the traditional status given the fetus. For example, the Babylonian Talmud Yevamot 69b states that "the embryo is considered to be mere water until the fortieth day." Afterwards, it is considered subhuman until it is born. The Talmud also refers to the fetus as "the thigh of its mother," based partly upon a passage in Exodus

21:22, which outlines the Mosaic law regarding a man who causes a miscarriage. If the woman survives, then the perpetrator is fined. But if the woman dies, the man is also killed. This passage is generally taken to indicate that the fetus has value, but does not have the status of a person. Accordingly, to Rashi, the great twelfth century commentator on the Bible and Talmud, the fetus was not a person.

(SOURCE: B. A. Robinson, "When Does Human Personhood Begin? Belief 4: Jewish Beliefs," *Tolerance*, Ontario Consultants on Religious Tolerance, August 6, 2000. Retrieved April 25, 2009, from: www.religioustolerance.org/jud_abor.htm.)

Question

Do historic Jewish beliefs about personhood suggest a single, unambiguous position on abortion?

---

divinely infused soul at conception that makes the unborn a human being and, therefore, entitled to the same life-protection as any other innocent human being. It is their view, then, that those frozen embryos disputed in *Roman* and the other 400,000 stored in fertility clinics are entitled to the same protection as an infant. For example, these embryos have a right to informed consent to be subjects in life-ending research, and their donors can no more substitute their own consent to their "offspring's" participation than any parent may for a child.[25] So, substantially underlying the Bush administration's moral objection to stem cell research was a particular and controversial theological view.[26]

MORAL STATUS OF THE UNBORN

The moral status of the unborn generally is discussed in terms of its rights and, thus, bears on virtually all issues of reproductive ethics. What rights, if any, the unborn have stem from a view of its ontological status. Therefore, if the ontological status of the unborn remains uncertain, so does its moral status. Indeed, until recognized as persons, for all intents and

purposes the unborn have no rights; or, if they do, those rights don't have the same status as the rights of those recognized as persons.[27]

Religious Views

Adopting Aristotle's doctrine of delayed ensoulment, neither Augustine nor Aquinas regarded abortion as homicide when performed in the early stages, since merely a vegetative or sensitive soul was believed to be terminated. Only abortion of a more fully developed "*fetus animatus*" (animated fetus), taken as after forty days, was punished as murder. Even then, abortion to save the mother's life was permissible. Moreover, the thinking at the time was that the sin of abortion, at least insofar as to require penance, was the intent to conceal fornication and adultery, that is, interference with the procreative purpose of sexual activity.[28]

Adopted by the early Church, this view was confirmed as Catholic dogma by the Council of Vienne in 1312. Curiously, the Vatican has never officially repudiated it, although it has abortion.[29,30] When Pius IX set aside previous Church teachings and questions on hominization, and endorsed the doctrine of immediate ensoulment, he was asserting

---

BIOETHICS ACROSS CULTURES

Islamic Understanding of Fetal Development

Both revelation and prophetic inspiration remain crucial ways of understanding fetal development from an Islamic perspective. The following Qur'anic verses, for example, are central to understanding some of the ways in which Muslim thinkers approach these issues.

> He creates you in the wombs of your mothers
> In stages, one after another
> In three veils of darkness
> Such is Allah, your Lord and Cherisher (Q 39:6).

> We created the human being from a quintessence of clay
> Then we placed him as semen in a firm receptacle
> Then we formed the semen into a blood-like clot
> Then we formed the clot into a lump of flesh
> Then we made out of that lump, bones
> And clothed the bones with flesh
> Then we developed out of it another creation
> So Blessed is Allah the Best Creator
> (Q 23:12–13).

These verses provide Muslim scholars a scriptural basis for asserting a process of fetal development from an organism to a human being. To these words are then added a prophetic understanding of the time and pace of this development. Thus:

Each of you is constituted in your mother's womb for 40 days as a *nutfa* (semen), then it becomes an *alaqa* (clot) for an equal period, then a *mudgha* (lump of flesh) for another equal period, then the angel is sent and he breathes the *ruh*, (spirit) into it.

Together the Qur'anic verses and the prophetic tradition are taken to describe a sequential process whereby the fetus undergoes a series of changes and finally culminates in becoming a full human being when it is "ensouled." According to the Qur'an, this culmination point denotes a significant shift, because the fetal organism is transformed into something substantively different from its previous state as is reflected in the verse "then we developed out of it another creation" (i.e., a human being). The prophetic tradition describes this same point of transition into a human being as the point at which the angel breathes the spirit into the fetus at 120 days.

(SOURCE: Sa'diyya Shaikh, "Family Planning, Contraception and Abortion in Islam," in *Sacred Choices: The Case for Contraception and Abortion in World Religions,* Daniel C. Maguire, ed., Oxford: Oxford University Press, 2003. Retrieved April 21, 2009, from: www.religious consultation.org/family_planning_in_Islam_by_Shaikh_p1.htm.)

Question

Compare the Islamic, Jewish and early Christian analyses of personhood. Would you expect Islamic scholars to express a single position on the morality of abortion?

---

full moral status of the unborn and, thus, rejecting permissible abortion based on the traditional non-person/person distinction. Henceforth, abortion at any stage for any reason was to be considered homicide. Currently this is the official position not only of the Catholic Church but also the "Christian Right," a variety of Christian political and social movements and organizations characterized by their strong support of conservative social and political values. As a politically active social movement, the Christian Right includes individuals from a spectrum of theological beliefs, ranging from moderately traditional movements within Lutheranism and Catholicism to theologically more conservative movements such as Evangelicalism, Pentecostalism, and Fundamentalist Christianity.[31] Strong opposition to abortion is one of the positions that give the disparate members of the Christian Right solidarity and distinguish it from Jewish, Muslim, and Buddhist traditions.

Secular Views

Unencumbered by questions of ensoulment, many secular views of the unborn's moral status are nonetheless shaped by its understanding of the unborn's ontological status. If, for example, the unborn is granted biological but not fully human status until birth, then presumably it would have no significant rights that would prohibit abortion. In the mid-1980s, for example, philosopher Tristam Engelhardt expressed the view that *moral agency*, or the ability to make responsible decisions, is the most distinctive mark of personhood. In other words, we're recognized as persons when we can act autonomously, or make choices based on our personal, internal values, goals, and principles. This would make the unborn "pre-persons," and once-competent adults "former persons."[32] Writing in that same decade, Stephen Tooley, who identified seventeen capacities for personhood, didn't even grant the neonate's absolute right-to-life status. Tooley saw no moral objection, in theory, to ending a life within three months of birth of, say, a seriously deformed infant, because the infant, measured by the capacities for personhood, was not yet a person.[33]

If, on the other hand, the unborn attains full ontological status prior to birth, then at that point it would be assigned rights. In theory, this means that abortions conducted prior to that time would not raise serious moral questions, whereas those conducted thereafter would. *But what should that point be?*

Today *viability* is a widely endorsed point for assigning ontological status. Thus, many theorists, following the lead of *Roe* and descendant decisions (e.g., *Danforth, Colautti, Casey* 1992), argue that abortion raises significant moral questions only after the fetus has attained viability and with it rights. The problem is that even if *viability* can be defined—as, for example, "that stage of development at which the fetus has sufficient neurological and physiological maturation to survive outside the womb"—there's no sure way of determining exactly when that gestational time or point is.[34] Indeed, it was precisely because judgments of viability are inexact and vary with pregnancy that the Supreme Court ruled, in *Danforth*, that fixed gestational limits for determining viability were unconstitutional. Determining viability, it said, was a matter of subjective physician judgment—a medical opinion, in other words. This is why the aforementioned rulings, while seeming to outlaw

late-term abortions, actually did not, since ultimately the physician makes the call on viability. Beyond that, viability is actually just one view of several scientific views about when life begins that bear on the ontological and moral status of the unborn for both religious and secular views.

SCIENTIFIC VIEWS ABOUT WHEN LIFE BEGINS

After surveying the relevant scientific literature, Scott F. Gilbert, Professor of Biology at Swarthmore College, provides the following classification scheme regarding the beginning of human life.[35] Although these views don't settle the matter, they are for many scholars, religious as well as secular, the entry point for an informed opinion about the beginning of human life. Such scientific data increasingly are shaping the standards of moral acceptability and, thereby, conceptually framing the discourse in abortion and other reproductive matters.

The Genetic View

According to the genetic view, a new individual is created at fertilization, when the genes from the two parents combine to form an individual with unique properties. As Princeton Professor of Jurisprudence Robert George and philosopher Christopher Tollefsen write in their book, *Embryo* (2008): "To be a complete human organism an entity must possess a developmental program (including both its DNA and epigenetic factors) oriented toward developing a brain and central nervous system." Because such a program begins at conception, so does personhood, according to these authors.[36]

Conservative religions—the Roman Catholic Church, the Lutheran Church-Missouri Synod, the Southern Baptist Convention—favor the genetic view. So do many physicians, biologists, and other scientists. Among them are neurobiologist Condic and geneticist Markus Grompe; Jerome

Lejeune of Paris, often referred to as the "father of modern genetics," and the scientist who discovered the chromosome pattern of Down Syndrome; and Professor Hymie Gordon, the distinguished chairman of the department of medical genetics at the renowned Mayo Clinic.[37]

The Embryological View

A common objection to the genetic view is that in humans identical twinning can occur as late as day twelve, producing two individuals with different personalities and lives and, theologically, different souls. Therefore, according to the embryological view, a single individual cannot be fixed earlier than day 12, when a series of cell movements, termed gastrulation, precludes the embryo from giving rise to twins or other multiple births.[38]

In 1979, the year of the *Belmont Report,* Clifford Grobstein (1916–1998) coined the word *pre-embryonic* to refer to earlier stages. By *pre-embryonic,* the renowned embryologist meant an indispensable precondition to human existence but not an individual human being as such.[39] Catholic theologians Richard A. McCormick,[40] Norman Ford,[41] Thomas Shannon, and Allan Wolter[42] have endorsed Grobstein's view.

Significantly, the embryological view would allow contraception, including "morning-after" pills and contragestational agents, but not abortion after two weeks. Still, this view has been criticized for an "ill-defined and inaccurate" use of terms like *pre-embryo* and *individuation.*[43] Even so, this hasn't stopped some governments from endorsing the embryological view to set abortion policy. The official British position, for example, is that human life begins at fourteen days, when the rudimentary nervous system starts to form.[44] At present in England and Wales there is a 24-week limit on abortions.

The Neurological View

Given that US law accepts as a definition of death the loss of cerebral function as measured by cerebral EEG (electroencephalogram) pattern, some scientists think that the acquisition of the human EEG (at about 27 weeks) should be defined as when a human

life begins. Others have set the date around week 24, when connections for brain function are made.[45] Still others who favor the neurological view date it earlier, around the sixth to eighth weeks, with faint electrical activity and, thus, the foundation of neural pathways essential for brain activity. In theory, the neurological view and any of the following additional views could allow abortions into the third trimester.

Additional Views

Beyond the genetic, embryological, and neurological views, Gilbert identifies several others: the ecological or technological, the immunological, the integrated physiological, and the metabolic views.

- The ecological/technological view: Human life begins when it can exist separately from its maternal biological environment. The natural limit of viability occurs when the lungs mature (usually by week 36), but technological advances can now enable a premature infant to survive at about 24 weeks gestation with a lot of intervention and sometimes even 23 weeks, with experienced specialists and a state of the art neonatal intensive care unit. (Amillia Taylor's birth was descibed as a "miracle.") This is the view currently operating in many states.

- The immunological view: Human life begins when the organism recognizes the distinction between self and non-self. In humans, this occurs around the time of birth.

- The integrated physiological view: Human life begins when an individual has become independent of the mother and has its own functioning circulatory system, alimentary system, and respiratory system. This is the traditional birthday, or when the baby is born into the world and the umbilical cord is cut.

- The metabolic view: There is no one point when life begins. The sperm cell and egg cell are as alive as any other organism. All "marker events" after metabolic processes start—such as the fourteenth day dividing line between zygote and embryo—are entirely artificial constructions of biologists and doctors in order to

BIOETHICS ACROSS CULTURES

Buddhism, Personhood, and Abortion

There are two fundamental teachings that shape Buddhist beliefs and practices around birth and death: the denial of the self and reincarnation, or postmortem embodiment. According to Buddhism, it is an illusion that there is a unique individual self that persists in time as a personal identity. This basic teaching of the nonexistence of the self is termed *anatta*, and it raises a question with regard to personhood. If there is no soul or unique, discrete self, what, then, is an individual "person"?

Buddhism proposes a composite of five "skandhas" or components: a body and, working with the body, four mental states: sensation, perception, will, and consciousness. It's these skandhas, according to most Buddhists, that reincarnate or pass from one body to another after death. An interruption of transmigration of the reincarnating, as through abortion, could be akin to murder. It all depends on timing, which comes back to the Buddhist understanding of "person."

It is one thing, for example, to associate embodiment or reincarnation with the creation of a sentient being, but another to say exactly when sentience occurs. Is it just the first of the five skandhas, the embryonic body, that constitutes a sentient being? Or does sentience emerge later in fetal development, perhaps even not until all five of the elements, including consciousness, are present? How those questions are answered, in part, affects the morality of abortion for Buddhists. To complicate things further, as bioethicist James Hughes points out:

> [I]nsofar as Buddhism is similar to a utilitarian ethics towards general happiness, or an ethics of care, or an ethics of virtuous intent, then the immorality of the abortive act of violence can be outweighed by the intentions of the mother and the greater suffering that it may prevent to mother, potential child and society.

(SOURCE: James Hughes, "Buddhist Bioethics," in *Principles of Health Care Ethics*, 2nd ed., Richard Edmund Ashcroft, Angus Dawson, Heather Draper, and John McMillan, eds., West Sussex: John Wiley & Sons, Ltd., 2007, p. 128.

Question

With which ontological issue would you associate the matter of reincarnation and abortion? Would it be fair to say that, according to Buddhism's basic teachings about birth and death, abortion is a personal and private decision whose morality circumstances determine?

better categorize development for academic purposes. This view is supported by recent research that shows fertilization to be a process that takes twenty to twenty-two hours rather than a single event.

In an article published just a month before her death, the esteemed developmental biologist Anne McLaren (1927–2007) offered an opinion about what she considered to be the consensual viewpoint of her colleagues. Notwithstanding the many competing views of when human life begins, McLaren said that biologists are in general agreement that a new, unique genetic constitution is formed at fertilization. Addressing the debate about exactly when life begins, she wrote:

> Whether there is a precise moment in the protracted process of fertilization when this occurs seems to be of greater interest to

politicians and philosophers than to those biologists who actually study the process.

Indeed, according to McLaren, the question "When does life begin?" is not a meaningful question to most biologists, since life is a continuum. Nonetheless, she said,

> [S]cientists that I have talked to who actually use donated human embryos in their research do view them in a rather special light because they are human, and would not want to use them for trivial or scientifically worthless research.

McLaren's observations tend to suggest that most biologists view the moral status of the human embryo developmentally. If so, they would view its moral value as increasing as it develops into a fetus, then into a baby.[46]

CONCLUSIONS

Professor of Law Paul Campos of the University of Colorado writes:

> Whether or not abortion should be legal turns on the answer to the question of whether and at what point a fetus is a person. This is a question that cannot be answered logically or empirically. The concept of personhood is neither logical nor empirical: It is essentially a religious, or quasi-religious idea, based on one's fundamental (and therefore unverifiable) assumptions about the nature of the world.[47]

Even if unverifiable, any assumption about the ontological status of the unborn nevertheless has profound medical, moral, and social implications. What we believe about human life and personhood inevitably determine our view of the moral status of the unborn.

If, for example, as religious and social conservatives generally claim, the unborn has full ontological status at conception, it also enjoys the same rights that we attribute to an adult human. This means that all core issues of human embryology—abortion, partial birth abortion, in vitro fertilization, human fetal research, human embryo research, cloning, and stem cell research—must address the unborn's claim to life. Presumably only conditions that would justify the killing of an adult human, such as self-defense, would morally justify deliberately taking the life of the unborn. This would prohibit all the aforementioned embryological procedures except therapeutic abortions, that is, abortions performed to save the mother's life or to correct some life-threatening condition. Indeed, even therapeutic abortions aren't permitted according to the most conservative of religious views.

If, on the other hand, as secularists and religious liberals generally claim, the unborn attains full ontological status at some developmental point after conception, then, presumably, it is only at that point that it enjoys the same rights we attribute to an adult human. Before then, no significant moral questions pertaining to the unborn's claim to life would arise concerning the aforementioned embryological practices. (Afterward, of course, it could still be argued—and often is—that it is morally permissible to have an abortion, even in cases where birth control was not used, the woman's life was not in danger, and the pregnancy was not the product of rape but of consensual sex.)

The ontological status of the unborn not only influences its moral status, but its legal status as well. To the extent that the unborn is considered a "person" under the law, it presumably has legal rights that may be used to restrict the mother's rights. As a result, there are currently underway well-organized efforts to elevate the legal status of the fetus, even to granting citizenship. The creation of the so-called fetal citizen is the most recent development in the politics of abortion, a most controversial topic, to which the next two chapters are devoted.

CASES AND CONTROVERSIES

The Language of Embryology

The authors of a textbook about bioethics caution their readers about the language describing embryos. "One must remember that science is always done in the context of society," they write, "and this is especially true when studying something as socially sensitive as embryology and birth." The authors go on to point out that "even the wording of human development differs from that of other animals." For example, "embryo," as applied to humans, refers specifically to the developing organism's first 8 weeks. After that, the organism is designated as a "fetus." Recently there have been attempts to further subdivide the terminology of human development. Thus, "pre-embryo" is used to

(Continued)

CASES AND CONTROVERSIES (CONTINUED)

refer to the early ends of gestation, roughly the first two weeks. At the other end of gestation, roughly from weeks 28–38, one hears of the "unborn fetus." None of these terms, the authors point out, are needed or used when discussing or studying the development of any other animal.[48]

Questions for Analysis

1. What moral and political distinctions placed on the biological processes of human development do terms like "pre-embryo," "embryo," "fetus," and "unborn fetus" reflect?

2. How do religious and social conservatives, on the one hand, and religious and social liberals, on the other, make use of such terms to advance their positions on abortion?

3. Research and report on the use of images of human embryos to influence public perception of their status.

4. What does the term pro-life mean in the context of the ontological status of the unborn? Could "pro-life" as easily be called "zygote rights"?

CASES AND CONTROVERSIES

Is Commander Data a Person?

In an episode of *Star Trek: The Next Generation* ("The Measure of a Man"), one of the main characters, a highly sophisticated android called Commander Data, objects to being removed from the *Starship Enterprise* to be dismantled and experimented upon. At Data's insistence that he's a "person" with "rights," a hearing is convened to settle the matter. Self-awareness is one of three criteria—the other two being intelligence and consciousness—that the panel agrees to use in defining "person." In the following dialogue from the movie, Captain Picard attempts to show that Data has self-awareness, while Commander Maddox challenges his assertion:

PICARD: What about self-awareness? What does that mean? Why am I self-aware?

MADDOX: Because you are conscious of your existence and actions. You are aware of your self and your own ego.

PICARD: Commander Data. What are you doing now?

DATA: I am taking part in a legal hearing to determine my rights and status. Am I a person or am I property?

PICARD: And what is at stake?

DATA: My right to choose. Perhaps my very life.

PICARD: "My rights" ... "my status" ... "my right to choose" ... "my life". Seems reasonably

self-aware to me.... Commander... I'm waiting.

MADDOX: This is exceedingly difficult.[49]

Questions for Analysis

1. Presumably, Maddox is thinking about subjective experiences when he speaks of being "conscious" of one's own existence and actions. Is Picard's response satisfactory?

2. Is it only necessary that Data have information about his own beliefs to be self-aware or must an inner feeling or experience of some kind accompany that information?

3. Commander Data gave every evidence of having an inner or mental life. Of course, just because he spoke and acted *as if* he had subjective experiences—as if he was really conscious and self aware—he might not actually be so. In other words, the judge had no reason to conclude either way: that Data was or was not conscious and self-aware. Still, a decision had to be made whether or not to accord Commander Data the status of conscious, self-aware being, or not. What would you decide and why?

4. Here's the decision of the Starfleet judge Lavoir:

   It sits there looking at me but I don't know what it is. This case has dealt with questions best left to saints and philosophers. I am neither competent nor qualified to answer that. I've got to make a ruling, to try to speak to the future. Is Data a machine? Is he the property of Starfleet? No. We've all been dancing around the main question: Does Data have a soul? I don't know that he has.

I don't know that I have. But I have to give him the freedom to explore that question himself. It is the ruling of this court that Lieutenant Commander Data has the freedom to choose.

Is Commander Data a person?

CASES AND CONTROVERSIES

Fetal Life and Personhood

Professor Jean Schroedel of Claremont Graduate University writes that "the question of when it can be said that a fetus is endowed with 'personhood' is fundamentally religious and theological." The political scientist and author of *Is the Fetus a Person?* (2000) adds:

> This question raises a complex and multifaceted issue that itself encompasses a host of deeper questions. Fundamentally, what is the meaning of "personhood"? Personhood implies self-awareness, the knowledge of oneself as a being separate and apart from the rest of the world. What is it that makes someone a person, what is it that makes each of us a distinct, unique being? Does it come from the mind or the heart or that elusive, ill-defined unseen quantity known as the soul? At what point in human development does the soul enter the body, and is that the same thing as saying that the fetus has become a unique and self-aware human being?[50]

Schroedel concludes that "[t]hese are questions of religious belief, not of science, law or public policy."

Questions for Analysis

1. Do you agree with Schroedel that "the question of when it can be said that a fetus is endowed with 'personhood' is fundamentally religious and theological"?

2. Assuming Schroedel is correct, what are the implications for law and public policy?

3. When would you say that "self-awareness" as "the knowledge of oneself as a being separate and apart from the rest of the world" occurs in human development?

4. Is awareness of things external to the self sufficient for defining "person," or must "self awareness" include such other capabilities as being aware of one's own mental states and being capable of critically reflecting upon and making judgments about those mental states?

REFERENCES

1. Stephanie Simon, "South Dakota Scraps Abortion Ban," *Los Angeles Times*, November 8, 2006, A16.

2. "South Dakota Bans Most Abortions," *CNN.com*, March 6, 2006. Retrieved April 18, 2008, from http://www.cnn.com/2006/POLITICS/03/06/sd.abortion/index.html.

3. Nicholas Riccardi, "Initiatives To Curb Abortions Defeated," *Los Angeles Times*, November 5, 2008, p. A18.

4. Jeffrey Olen, Julie C. Van Camp, and Vincent Barry, *Applying Ethics: A Text with Readings*, 9th ed., Thomson/Wadsworth, 2008, pp. 131–132.

5. "Duration of Pregnancy," *Ninemsn*, 2006. Retrieved April 22, 2008, from http://health.ninemsn.com.au/article.aspx?id=2397.

6. William Robert Johnston. "Reasons given for having abortions in the United States," *Abortion Statistics*, October 1, 2005. Retrieved April 20, 2008 from http://www.johnstonsarchive.net/policy/abortion/abreasons.html.

7. Lloyd de Vries, "Earliest Preemie's Release De-layed," CBS NEWS, February 20, 2007. Retrieved May 18, 2010, from http://www.cbsnews.com/stories/2007/02/20/health/main2493294.shtml.

8. Ibid., p. 347.

9. Guttmacher Institute, *The Limitations of U.S. Statistics on Abortion*, January 1997. Retrieved August 1, 2008, from http://www.guttmacher.org/pubs/ib14.html.

10. Harry J. Gensler, "An Appeal for Consistency," in *The Ethics of Abortion*, in Robert M. Baird and Stuart E. Rosenbaum, eds., Amherst, NY: Prometheus Books, 2001, p. 281.

11. Maureen L. Condic, "Life: Defining the Beginning by the End," *First Things*, May 2003, pp. 50.

12. Olen, Van Kamp, and Barry, p. 122.

13. Gilbert Meilander, *Bioethics: A Primer for Christians*, William B. Eerdmans Publishing Company, Grand Rapids, MI: 2005, p. 30.

14. Dianne N. Irving, "Cloning: When Word Games Kill," *American Bioethics Advisory Committee*, 1999. Retrieved April 22, 2008, from www.all.org/abac/dni001.htm.

15. Gregory Koukl, *Precious Unborn Human Persons*, San Pedro, CA: Stand to Reason Press, 1999, p. 43.

16. Stephen Schwartz, *The Moral Question of Abortion*, Chicago: Loyola University Press, 1990, p. 93.

17. Robert N. Wennberg, *Terminal Choices: Euthanasia, Suicide and the Right To Die*, Grand Rapids, MI: Eerdmans Publishing, 1989.

18. David DeGrazia, Human Identity and Bioethics, New York: Cambridge University Press, 2005, p. 4.

19. Ibid., p. 9.

20. J. P. Moreland & Scott B. Rae, *Body & Soul: Human Nature & the Crisis in Ethics*, Downers Grove, IL: InterVarsity Press, 2000, p. 25.

21. Ibid., p. 24.

22. Alvin Plantinga, "Advice to Christian Philosophers," *Faith and Philosophy*, July 1984, p. 265.

23. P. E. Devine, "'Conservative'" Views on Abortion," *Advances in Bioethics*, St. Louis, MO: Elsevier, 1997, pp. 183–202.

24. Jean Porter, "Is the Embryo a Person? Arguing with the Catholic Traditions," *Commonweal*, February 8, 2002. Retrieved August 25, 2008, from http://www.pfaith.org/catholic.htm.

25. Moreland and Rae, p. 2032.

26. Richard Owen, "Pope Chastises Bush over Death Penalty, Stem Cell Research, Globalization, and …," *The Times of London*, July 24, 2001. Retrieved August

15, 2008, from http://www.mindfully.org/Reform/Pope-Chastises-Bush.htm.

27. Carol Tauer, "The Tradition of Probabilism and the Moral Status of the Early Embryo," in *Abortion and Catholicism: The American Debate*, Patricia B. Jung and Thomas A Shannon, eds., New York: Crossroad Press, 1988, pp. 54–84.

28. Tribe, Lawrence H., *Abortion The Clash of the Absolutes*, New York W. W. Norton and Company, 1990.

29. Jane Hurst, *The History of Abortion in the Catholic Church: The Untold Story*, Washington: Catholics for a Free Choice, 1983.

30. David L. Perry, "Abortion and Personhood: Historical and Comparative Notes." Retrieved May 2, 2008, from http://home.earthlink.net/~davidlperry/abortion.htm.

31. "Christian right," *Wikipedia*, April 16, 2008. Retrieved April 20, 2008, from http://en.wikipedia.org/wiki/Christian_right.

32. Tristram Engelhardt, *The Foundations of Bioethics*, New York: Oxford University Press, 1986, p. 108.

33. Stephen Tooley, *Abortion and Infanticide*, Oxford: Clarendon Press, 1983.

34. Gregg Easterbrook, "Abortion Brain Waves," in *The Ethics of Abortion*, Robert M. Baird and Stuart E. Rosenbaum, eds., Amherst, NY: Prometheus Books, 2001, p. 348.

35. Scott Gilbert, "Summary: When Does Human Life Begin?" *Developmental Biology*, 8th ed., Sunderland, MA: Sinauer Associates Inc., 2006. Retrieved May 3, 2008, from http://8e.devbio.com/article.php?ch=21&id=7.

36. Robert P. George and Christopher Tolelfsen, *Embryo: A Defense of Human Life*, New York: Doubleday Books, 2008. Quoted in William Saletan, "Little Children," *The New York Times Book Review*, February 10, 2008, p. 24. Retrieved April 22, 2008, from www.nytimes.com/.webloc.

37. Brad Harrub, "The Inherent Value of Human Life," *Reason & Revelation*, July 2002, pp. 49–55. Retrieved April 25, 2008, from www.apologeticspress.org/articles/print/132.

38. Scott, Gilbert, Anna Tyler, and Emily J. Zackin, *Bioethics and the New Embryology*, Sunderland, MA: Sinnauer Associates, Inc., 2005, p. 19.

39. Clifford Grobstein, "External Human Fertilization," *Scientific American*, June 1979, pp. 57–67.

40. Richard A. McCormick, "Who or What Is the Pre-Embryo?" *Kennedy Institute of Ethics Journal*, March 1991, pp. 10–15.

41. Norman Ford and Mary Warnock, *When Did I Begin?: Conception of the Human Individual in History, Philosophy and Science,* New York: Cambridge University Press, 1989.

42. Thomas A. Shannon and Allan B. Wolter, "Reflections on the moral status of the pre-embryo," *Theological Studies*, December 1990, pp. 603–626.

43. C. WardKischer, "The Corruption of the Science of Human Embryology," *American Bioethics Advisory Committee (ABAC) Quarterly*, Fall 2002. Retrieved May 2, 2008, from http://www.all.org/abac/aq0203.htm#aa.

44. Brenda Maddox, "You Gotta Have Soul," *The Guardian*, April 4, 2005. Retrieved May 15, 2010, from http://www.guardian.co.uk/science/2005/apr/04/pope.religionwww.guardian.co.uk/g2/story/0,3604,1451653,00.html.

45. Harold Morowitz and James Trefil *The Facts of Life: Science and the Abortion Controversy,* New York: Oxford University Press, 1994.

46. Anne McLaren. "A Scientist's View of the Ethics of Human Embryonic Stem Cell Research," *Cell Stem Cell*, June 7, 2007, p. 39.

47. Paul Campos, "Opinions: Abortion and the Rule of Law," *Scripps Howard News Service*, January 2002. Retrieved February 24, 2009, from http://www.religioustolerance.org/abo_when.htm.com.

48. Scott F. Gilbert, Anna L. Tyler, Emily J. Zackin, *Bioethics and the New Embryology*, Sunderland, MA: Sinmauer Associates, Inc., 2005, pp. 42–43.

49. David L Anderson, "What Is a Person?" *Consortium on Cognitive Science Instruction*, Normal, IL: Illinois State University, 2000. Retrieved April 22, 2009, from http://www.mind.ilstu.edu/curriculum/listByAuthor.php.

50. Jean Schroedel, "Extending Legal Personhood to Fetal Life," Religious Coalition for Reproductive Choice, Education Series No. 16. Retrieved April 2, 2009, from www.rcrc.org/pdf/RCRC_EdSeries_-FetalLife.pdf.

Chapter 9

The Abortion
Debate I: Pre-*Roe*

Almost half of the six million pregnancies that occur annually in the United States are unplanned. Of these, about one in five, or 1.2 million, end in elective abortions.[1] At some time in their reproductive lives, more than 40 percent of all women will end a pregnancy in abortion. These women will tend to be young, unmarried, and poor. Black women get almost 40 percent of the nation's abortions, even though African Americans make up only 13 percent of the population. Nearly 40 percent of black pregnancies end in induced abortion, a rate far higher than for white or Hispanic women.[2] At present, more than 6 in 10 abortions occur within the first 8 weeks of pregnancy, and almost 3 in 10 take place at 6 weeks or earlier. Medication, as opposed to surgical, abortion provides women with an additional option early in pregnancy.[3] Since its legalization in 1973, there have been over 30 million abortions in the United States.[4] To many of its opponents, abortion is nothing less than murder. A few have even killed to stop it.

THE MURDER OF DR. GEORGE TILLER

The last day of May 2009 was the last day in the life of Dr. George Tiller. On that Sunday morning, the late-term abortion provider was fatally shot as he stood in the foyer of Reformation Lutheran Church in Wichita, Kansas. Three hours later 51-year-old Scott Roeder, a fierce abortion opponent who was once arrested with bomb components in his car, was arrested about 170 miles away. Tiller was the fifth American doctor killed for providing abortions. The killing occurred not long after President Obama lifted a ban on US funding for international health groups that support abortion.

In his more than three decades of providing abortion services, the 67-year-old Tiller had become a lightning rod in the struggle over legalized abortion. The father of four and grandfather of ten had once seen his clinic bombed and had been shot in both arms. He was also the defendant in a series of unsuccessful legal challenges intended to shut down his operations.[5] Warren Hern, a Colorado physician and close friend of Tiller, said Tiller's death was predictable.

"I think it's the inevitable consequence of more than 35 years of constant anti-abortion terrorism, harassment and violence."[6] Hern had predicted that anti-abortion violence would increase after the president's election of because Obama supports legalized abortion and, said Hern, its foes "have lost ground.... They want the doctors dead, and they invite people to assassinate us. No wonder that this happens.... I am next on the list."[7]

Less than two weeks after Tiller's murder, the Kansas abortion clinic he ran was permanently shut down. Supporters like Dr. Hern described the outcome as horrifying, while detractors saw it as an answer to their prayers. A militant wing of the anti-abortion crusade, Army of God, proclaimed on its web page of June 10:

> The lives of innocent babies scheduled to be murdered by George Tiller are spared by the action of American hero Scott Roeder. George Tiller the Baby killer reaped what he sowed and is now in eternal hell. Psalm 55:15 Let death seize upon them, and let them go down quick into hell: for wickedness.

About four months after the Tiller killing, longtime anti-abortion protester Jim Pouillon suffered the same fate at the hands of a local truck driver in Owosso, Michigan. The killer said he'd been bothered by Pouillon's graphic opposition to abortion, displayed as children came to school.

These killings challenged the notion of finding common ground between proponents and opponents of legalized abortion that just a month before Tiller's death President Obama had broached while at the University of Notre Dame, one of the country's preeminent Catholic institutions. The university had come under fire from conservative Catholics for inviting Obama to give its commencement speech and receive an honorary degree. Nearly 65,000 people signed an online petition protesting Obama's scheduled May 17 commencement address at the university, saying the president's views on abortion and stem cell research "directly contradict" Roman Catholic teachings.[8] Obama spoke, all the same. He devoted much of his speech to a plea

for respectful discourse, but admitted at one point, "The fact is that at some level, the views of the two camps are irreconcilable."

Less than a fortnight later, the president was describing the Tiller killing as a heinous act of violence, a sentiment that even some anti-abortion activists shared, such as the political activist Rev. Pat Mahoney and Troy Newman, head of Operation Rescue, who had moved to Kansas from California to try to put Tiller out of business. On the other hand, Operation Rescue founder Randall Terry said, "George Tiller was a mass-murderer. We grieve for him that he did not have time to properly prepare his soul to face God."[9]

Testimony in the Roeder case began on January 22, the same day the Supreme Court made abortion legal in 1973. A week later, on January 29, 2010, it took a Kansas jury just 40 minutes to convict Roeder of first-degree murder. Roeder expressed no remorse or regrets for the shooting. He said he had to kill the doctor to save the lives of unborn babies.

Are women who have abortions and those who assist them murderers, as abortion foes such as Roeder, Mahoney, and Newman claim?[10] Is abortion a "moral abomination"? Should the practice of intentionally terminating the unborn be stopped? Or is abortion sometimes justifiable? Should a woman continue to have the right to make an abortion decision and have access to a safe one? Such are the questions that have roiled the nation, at times violently, for the four decades since the passage of *Roe*.

Groups favoring and opposing access both desire that abortions be rare and safe and that having attained personhood the unborn's life be respected. The sticking point concerns when personhood is attained and whether, thereafter, the woman has a right to make an abortion decision. Some say that from conception the status of the unborn matters most, and therefore all elective, and possibly even therapeutic, abortions are immoral because they deny the unborn its right to life. Others assert that the woman's moral status matters most, specifically her right of choice and, therefore, not only is therapeutic abortion moral but elective abortion can be, as well.

In the abortion wars, these deep-seated convictions inspire forces on both sides of the moral divide to political and social activism in what has become a struggle over *Roe*. For cultural conservatives, the movement to overturn *Roe* is a crusade to turn back a monumental decision against human life and dignity. For cultural liberals, keeping *Roe* is saving the means by which modern women take control of their fertility and their lives. This makes *Roe* the pivotal decision around which leaders of the respective movements gather their forces. The one, "pro-life," seeks to outlaw most if not all abortions; the other, "pro-choice," seeks to eliminate most restrictions on abortions. Meanwhile, as these opposing sides dominate the cultural discourse, a consensus of Americans, likely more than 60 percent, favor legal abortion with restrictions, although they lean lightly toward the view that abortion is wrong.[11]

This chapter and the next deal with this intense debate that likely will continue to inflame society for years to come. We begin with a brief history of abortion before examining the conservative religious view and the pro-choice consciousness that it helped mobilize in the lead-up to *Roe*. Chapter 10 will review the abortion debate in the years after *Roe* to the present.

A BRIEF HISTORY

In the abortion debate, the most spirited opposition is to elective, or non-therapeutic, abortion. This translates to opposition to virtually every abortion performed annually in the United States. At the same time, most of these anti-abortion groups, denominations, and individuals are open to therapeutic abortions. For them, therefore, the moral status of the unborn matters, but not absolutely. They grant that the right of the unborn to its life may be overridden, for example, by the competing right of the mother to her life or, less so, her health. The most conservative views, however, oppose even therapeutic abortion, arguing that it is the status of the unborn, not the welfare of the woman, that most matters morally.

Historically, concern for the life of the unborn is a relatively modern objection to the practice of abortion, which was widely permitted up until the nineteenth century. When restrictions were first passed, they invariably expressed concern for the mother's health and safety, not the life of the unborn.

For example, the first restrictive abortion statute—Lord Ellenborough's Act, passed in 1803 by the British Parliament—prohibited abortion after quickening (taken then as the 16th week), not because a human being was destroyed but because "[abortion] rarely or never can be effected by drugs without sacrifice of the mother's life." In the 1820s American states began to follow Britain's lead and restrict abortion, again not to safeguard fetal life but the woman's. New York, for example, permitted the execution of female felons condemned to death while pregnant with a non-quickened fetus and postponed the execution of any with a quickened fetus until after the delivery of the baby. In 1858 the New Jersey Supreme Court, reviewing that state's 1849 law, declared: "The design of the statute was not to prevent the procuring of abortions, so much as to guard the health of the mother against the consequences of such attempts."[12]

By 1900, due mainly to concern for the woman expressed by physicians, the AMA, and state legislators, most abortions had been outlawed.[13] During the next two decades, as surgical procedures improved, abortion mortality began to decline, until eventually abortion, competently performed, became less dangerous to the woman than childbirth. Nevertheless, restrictions remained in place.

By mid-twentieth century, elective abortions, though illegal in all fifty states, were frequent, and the bans were unevenly enforced. According to Mark Graber of Columbia Law School, a million illegal abortions were performed annually in the United States in the 1950s and 1960s. For generally white, middle- and upper-class pregnant females, there was access, with impunity, to safe abortions performed by competent physicians. For many poor and minority women, however, there was access only to dangerous illegal abortions. During this period, according to Graber, between 5,000 and 10,000 women died and as many as 350,000—largely poor and black women—were injured annually by illegal abortions.[14] In the 1970s abortion care dramatically improved, with advances in local anesthesia and suction equipment, and the development of the Karman cannula, a device for performing simple, early abortions, named after its creator, psychologist Harvey Karman (1924–2008).[15]

By mid-twentieth century, then, the prevailing, nationwide abortion ban was having the effect of driving many women to unsafe abortions, when improved surgical procedures offered a safe alternative for women with personal and social proximity to competent physicians. In short, properly supervised, or legal abortions, were safer for women than illegal abortions (and still are).[16] As an upshot, notes journalist Roberta Brandes Gratz:

> … the argument that restrictive laws protected the woman's health and life no longer applied. Thus, restrictive abortion laws that had been constitutional when adopted became unconstitutional by, in effect, forcing women to accept the more dangerous of two procedures.[17]

With the collapse of the traditional argument that abortion bans protected women from an unsafe medical procedure, abortion foes staked out a different ground for retaining restrictive laws in the years leading up to *Roe*. They forsook the protection of the woman's life for the protection of fetal life. Prominent among the forces for retention were the Roman Catholic Church and like theologically conservative Christian groups, who assiduously and publicly began to defend the view that fetal life was sacred and had to be protected and nurtured.

In the lead-up to *Roe* in 1973, it was the religious beliefs of these groups that mainly drove the opposition to the legalization of abortion. Since *Roe*, they have continued to influence state abortion policy, with conservative Protestants shaping it indirectly through public opinion, while a strong, unified Catholic Church directly influences the passage of more restrictive abortion legislation. At the same time, ironically, their activism has also contributed to strengthening pro-choice mobilization and indirectly promoting liberal state abortion policies.[18]

Given their traditional and ongoing influence on abortion opinion and policy, it is important to grasp exactly why religious conservatives and many social conservatives consider abortion morally repellent.

LIFE MATTERS MOST: THE CONSERVATIVE RELIGIOUS VIEW

For the most conservative side in the abortion debate, the moral status of the unborn continues to matter absolutely. The Roman Catholic Church, for instance, views all direct abortions murder, because it considers the unborn an innocent person from conception to birth and, therefore, deserving of protection under its interpretation of natural law theory. Referencing the teachings of some of his predecessors, Pope Paul VI (1897–1978) detailed church teaching "on the dignity of human life as it originates and on procreation" in the encyclical *Donum Vitae (Gift of Life,* 1987). "[I]n the light of the previous teaching of the Magisterium," the pope said,

> *The human being must be respected as a person—from the very first instant of his existence….*
> From the moment of conception, the life of every human being is to be respected in an absolute way because man is the only creature on earth that God has "wished for himself" and the spiritual soul of each man is "immediately created" by God; his whole being bears the image of the Creator. Human life is sacred because from its beginning it involves "the creative action of God" and it remains forever in a special relationship with the Creator, who is its sole end. God alone is the Lord of life from its beginning until its end: no one can, in any circumstance, claim for himself the right to destroy directly an innocent human being.[19]

In the following decade, Pope John Paul II (1920–2005) strengthened the church's position by declaring that even "if we cannot say for sure when the embryo attains fully personal status, we are sure enough to act as if it does." Then further, in the 1995 encyclical *Evangelium Vitae (The Gospel of Life)*, the pope employed extensive references to the Bible and Vatican texts, including the decrees of the Second Vatican Council, when he emphasized:

> What is at stake is so important that, from the standpoint of moral obligation, the mere probability that a human person is involved would suffice to justify an absolutely clear prohibition of any intervention aimed at killing a human embryo.[20]

Although the encyclical spoke of a "probability," theologian Jean Porter points out that some of her colleagues and Catholic activists go even further, "arguing that the possibility that the embryo is a person is enough to justify treating it as if it were." In other words, by the most conservative reading, "we are faced here with a situation in which a fully personal human life may be present, and therefore we are morally obliged to resolve our doubts on the side of protecting life."[21] In fact, in insisting that the Church's teaching on abortion was unchanged and unchangeable, John Paul II drew the same conclusion based upon Scripture and natural law:

> Therefore, by the authority which Christ conferred upon Peter and his successors ... I declare that direct abortion, that is, abortion willed as an end or as a means, always constitutes a grave moral disorder, since it is the deliberate killing of an innocent human being. This doctrine is based upon the natural law and upon the written word of God, is transmitted by the Church's tradition and taught by the ordinary and universal magisterium. No circumstance, no purpose, no law whatsoever can ever make licit an act which is intrinsically illicit, since it is contrary to the law of God which is written in every human heart, knowable by reason itself, and proclaimed by the Church.[22]

According to Catholic moral teaching, then, even when a pregnancy is due to rape or incest or involves fetal deformity, the unborn may not be held accountable and made to suffer through its death. In a word, no intervention that constitutes a direct abortion is ever morally permissible, according to Catholic interpretation of Thomistic natural law and sacred scriptures.

Religious Natural Law and the Principle of Double Effect

Although the Catholic version of natural law doesn't permit direct abortion, it does permit the indirect abortion.[23] Consider the classic example of a pregnant woman with a cancerous uterus. The only way to save her life is by chemotherapy or hysterectomy. But if this done, the fetus will die. What to do? Like this one, medical cases of two effects—one good, the other bad—usually are resolved according the principle of double effect.

Recall from Chapter 2 that, according to the principle of double effect, an action should be performed only if the intention is to bring about the good effect and only if the bad effect will be an unintended or indirect consequence. Specifically, four conditions must be satisfied to justify the action:

1. The action itself must be morally indifferent or good.

2. The bad effect must not be the means by which the good effect is achieved.

3. The intention must be to achieve the good effect only.

4. The good effect must be at least equivalent in importance to the bad effect.

The principle of double effect, then, permits the *indirect* termination of a pregnancy, or one that occurs as a consequence of an unavoidable action taken to save the life of the mother. Such a measure is viewed as a permissible act of self-defense on the part of the woman. But even so, the means taken to save the mother must never be intended to kill the fetus directly. In 2009 Arizona bishop Thomas Olmsted condemned and excommunicated Sister Margaret McBride, a longterm and highly regarded administrator at St. Joseph's Hospital and Medical Center in Phoenix, for approving an abortion that

BIOETHICS ACROSS CULTURES

Early Induction in Ontario

Late in 2008, a pro-life website, *LifeSiteNews.com*, launched a blistering attack on Father Michael Prieur, along with his colleagues at the Diocese of London and St. Joseph's Catholic Hospital in Ontario, Canada, charging them of secretly performing abortions for the past twenty-five years. The accusation was based on a procedure called early induction, which St. Joseph's performs when the fetus has a lethal anomaly, a situation that poses grave risks for the mother and child. Anomalies such as anencephaly or grossly compromised vital organs make life impossible for more than a few minutes or hours after delivery. And the closer such a fetus moves to term, the greater the danger it poses to the mother. Indeed, lethal fetal anomalies cause one-third of the deaths of pregnant women. About 8 to 10 such cases a year occur at St. Joseph's, all of which go through a hospital committee—which includes Fr. Prieur—before they are approved for early induced labor.

In all instances, labor is not induced at St. Joseph's until at least 23 weeks, when the fetus has reached viability. That way, if the baby is born alive everything possible could be done to save it; and if the diagnosis is wrong, the child would still have a chance. Secular hospitals needn't fine tune such cases because they have more options, notably direct abortion, which has been legal in Canada for any reason at any time up to delivery since the Supreme Court struck down an anti-abortion law in 1988. Further complicating matters is a fluke of geography: St. Joseph's just happens to be the major hub for high-risk maternal fetal medicine in southwestern Ontario. So, a quarter century ago,

Fr. Prieur and colleagues at St. Joseph's devised early induction "as both good medicine and good morals."

To its harshest critics, however, early induction is tantamount to abortion, because it uses a medical procedure to end a pregnancy rather than letting nature take its course. But twenty-five years ago, Fr. Prieur came to the conclusion, during his very first moral struggle with a deadly fetal anomaly, that early induction was not abortion, because the child would not be killed in the womb, but rather delivered early. He reasoned that in the end, the mother's life would be spared, but not because of an act of "evil" on the baby. Father William McGrattan, another member of St. Joseph's ethics committee, agrees. "… [T]he action being done is not an action that is direct killing of the child," he says. "It is an action that is trying to recognize that the life of this child is dying and we're trying to support that process in a natural way and balance that with the complications to the health of the mother."

(SOURCE: Charles Lewis, "Operating on Faith," *National Post*, February 21, 2009. Retrieved April 25, 2009, from http://www.nationalpost.com/news/canada/story.html?id=1313233&p=3)

Question

In 2008 Fr. Prieur won the Performance Citation Award by Ottawa-based Catholic Health Association for his "strengthening of the Catholic health ministry in an extraordinary way." Do you think he deserved it, or is he guilty of performing "eugenic abortions," as his critics claim? Is the principle of double effect applicable to early induction?

---

the hospital's ethics committee thought necessary to save a pregnant woman's life. Two of the three largest Lutheran denominations, the Missouri Synod, and the Wisconsin Evangelical Synod, are among other conservative Christian churches that take essentially the same position on abortion as Roman Catholicism.

Scriptural Teachings

For conservative evangelicals, the rational calculation of natural law theorists, as well as the hyperanalysis of abstract notions of "personhood," though useful and perhaps even necessary in the public form, are ultimately beside the point. For them,

the authority of the Bible establishes the sanctity of the unborn's life and forbids abortion, even though the subject of abortion is not specifically addressed in the Bible.

As backup, those given to scriptural argument often cite two biblical teachings. The first, "You shall not murder" (Exod. 20:13), is thought to establish that it's never right to kill an innocent person. The second, Psalm 139, is taken as establishing the person status of the unborn:

> For thou didst form my inward parts;
> Thou didst weave me in my mother's
> womb. I will give thanks to thee, for I am

fearfully and wonderfully made; Wonderful are Thy works, and my soul knows it very well. My frame was not hidden from Thee, when I was made in secret, and skillfully wrought in the depths of the earth. Thine eyes have seen my unformed substance; and in Thy book they were all written the days that were ordained for me, when as yet there was not one of them. (Ps. 139:13–16)

Commenting on this passage, in which the psalmist King David "reflects on the way in which God has intricately created him," Moreland and Rae write:

David sees the person who gives thanks and praise to God (vv. 13–16) as the same person who was skillfully woven together in the womb (v. 13) and as the same person who is known by God inside and out (vv. 1–6). In other words, there is continuity of personal identity from the earliest point of development to a mature adult. That is the significance of Psalm 139 to the discussion of the nature of the embryo. It is not solely that God painstakingly and intricately created David in the womb; it is also that the person who was being created in the womb is the same person who is writing the psalm.[24]

Like Moreland and Rae, professors of philosophy and biblical studies, respectively, many people of faith find in these two passages the most compelling argument against abortion, based upon the unborn's full ontological status "from the earliest point of development":

It's never right to kill an innocent person. The unborn is an innocent person. Abortion is the killing of an innocent person. Therefore, abortion is wrong.

Others scholars read scriptural opposition to abortion in the command to love all persons, which, like the prohibition of murder, derives from the creation narrative that we are all made

in the image of an all-loving God. As such, we are not only of inestimable worth and value but also are related to love one another as children of God (see Mark 12:28–31; John 13:34–35). Viewed as a human being and person, the unborn is a neighbor whose life has parity with the woman's. In this way, according to John T. Noonan, with the Notre Dame Center for Ethics and Culture, the commandment to love one's neighbor gives life to an otherwise "rational calculation." This leads Noonan to express the commandment in humanistic Enlightenment, as well as theological, terms. As the jurist writes in his widely anthologized essay "An Almost Absolute Value in History" (1970):

… Do not injure your fellow man without reason. In these terms, once the humanity of the fetus is perceived, abortion is never right except in self-defense. When life must be taken to save life, reason alone cannot say that a mother must prefer a child's life to her own. With this exception, now of great rarity, abortion violates the rational humanist tenet of the equality of human lives.

For Christians the commandment to love had received a special imprint in that the exemplar proposed of love was the love of the Lord for his disciples. In the light given by this example, self-sacrifice carried to the point of death seemed in the extreme situations not without meaning. In the less extreme cases preference for one's own interests to the life of another seemed to express cruelty or selfishness irreconcilable with the demands of love.[25]

Scripturally, then, abortion is thought objectionable because (1) it wantonly takes the life of a creature made in the image of God. Also, (2) it isn't the loving sort of activity that a creature *imago dei* should be engaging in, certainly not the mother, whose unique relationship to the life she bears makes special, divinely prescribed demands of trust, responsibility, and care.

Historically, when the theologically inspired view that fetal life was sacred and had to be protected emerged as the main argument against abortion, the moral locus of opposition shifted from concern for the mother to concern for the unborn. That, in turn, created a rift among the vast majority of traditional opponents of abortion, which included even early feminists such as Susan B. Anthony (1820–1906). Many in the opposition held fast, but now because the moral status of the unborn most mattered to them. At the same time, a large number continued to identify with the woman, no longer because of her safety but rather her moral status, which they viewed as at least equal to that of the life she was carrying. For them abortion was now a matter of whose putative rights took precedence: the unborn's "right to life" or the woman's "right to choose." Again, so long as abortion was banned, this issue largely lay dormant, given the sizable coalition of individuals and groups that condemned and opposed abortion as dangerous to women. But with the advent of the safe abortion and, with it, the protection of fetal life as the main argument against abortion, the question of competing rights quickly moved to center stage and continues to dominate the abortion debate.

THE MOBILIZATION OF PRO-CHOICE CONSCIOUSNESS

The new emphasis on the protection of fetal life had the unintended effect of helping mobilize pro-choice consciousness in the years leading up to *Roe*. But so did some of the same events that surrounded the birth of bioethics, such as the fresh attention to women's health and sexuality and the shift from medical paternalism to patient autonomy. Then, too, the nationwide civil rights revolution was defining rights that no state could abridge, including, to many, the right to abortion.[26] Indeed, the National Association for Repeal of Abortion Laws (now the National Abortion Rights Action League, or NARAL), organized in 1967, framed the woman's choice to end life within her as a civil right based upon ownership of her own body.

The year before NARAL was established, one of its co-founders, Lawrence Lader, wrote what is regarded as the first carefully documented book on abortion. In *Abortion* (1966), Lader, a widely published magazine writer and political activist, argued that the Supreme Court's recent ruling in *Griswold* could apply to abortion. That landmark 1965 decision, (which is presented as a case at the end of this chapter), had invalidated a Connecticut prohibition on the use of contraceptives because it violated "the right to marital privacy." Lader contended that the right of marital privacy against state restrictions on a couple's access to family planning counseling could be applied to abortion. Pro-abortion activists took up Lader's argument, as would the high court itself. In deciding *Roe*, not only did the justices lean heavily on *Griswold*, they cited Lader's book no less than seven times.[27]

Another dynamic mobilizing pro-choice consciousness in the lead-up to *Roe* was the new openness about human sexuality of the 1960s that had the effect of easing discussions of birth control, abortion, and other delicate matters of human reproduction. Representative was the best seller *Peyton Place* (1956). Made into a movie in 1957, the Grace Metalious (1924–1964) novel that sold sixty thousand copies in the first ten days of its release dealt with the then-taboo themes of illegitimacy, incest, rape, and abortion, all in the context of three women coming to terms with their identity as women and sexual beings in a small New England town.[28] Most significantly, the movie cast an abortionist in a positive light when he terminates the pregnancy of a central character who has been impregnated by her alcoholic stepfather. The following year another play/movie, *Blue Denim* (1958, 1959), depicted the unwanted pregnancy of two typical teens driven by fear of discovery to a backroom abortionist. The dangers and ugliness of the back-alley abortion were even depicted in the 1963 "comedy," *Love with the Proper Stranger*, starring two movie stars of the day, Natalie Wood (1938–1981) and Steve McQueen (1930–1980). For its part, *Revolutionary Road*, a finalist for the National Book award in 1962, brought readers right inside a middle-class American household to witness the death of a young, suburban mother of two, following a self-induced abortion.

Meanwhile, outside the theaters and bookstores a couple of real-life medical stories were further sensitizing the public to the restrictive nature of abortion laws. One involved a woman named Sherri Finkbine, who had taken the sedative thalidomide as an aid for pain. Only later in her pregnancy did Finkbine and the world learn of the inadequate testing that had preceded

the release of the drug in 1957 and of its catastrophic effects on an unborn's limb development when taken between the 26th and 60th days after conception. Because the details of Finkbine's pregnancy are covered in another end-of-chapter case presentation, it's enough here to say that Finkbine attracted wide media coverage when she arranged for an abortion, and faced strong opposition from Catholic and fundamentalist clergy.

BIOETHICS ACROSS CULTURES

Abortions in Kenya

Where abortions are illegal, the health and safety of the mother are conspicuously at risk, compared with places with legal abortion. In the East African country of Kenya, for example, abortion is illegal except to save the mother's life. An estimated 250,000 to 320,000 abortions are carried out in the country each year, with unsafe procedures causing a shocking toll. Whereas globally 13 percent of maternal deaths result from abortion-related complications, in Kenya it's as high as 40 percent.

In public hospitals such as Kenyatta National in Nairobi, the nation's capital and largest city, about 20,000 Kenyan women are treated each year for abortion-related complications, everything from excessive bleeding to injured organs to sepsis. As reported in a 2008 *Ms.* article, those sufferers include women such as "Wangui," who drank "a boiled concoction made from trees and took several doses of an anti-malaria drug in order to abort because her impoverished household couldn't support a fifth child." She ended up in Kenyatta when she needed a life-saving blood transfusion.

Women's rights groups in Kenya have been pushing for a new national law on reproductive rights, as well as supporting a continental protocol on the rights of African women and a patients' bill of rights. But they were not helped in their efforts to improve reproductive health care by the global gag rule, the policy by which the United States withheld aid to foreign reproductive care agencies that discussed or offered abortion services. The controversial policy, also known as the Mexico City policy for the city in which it was first announced, was introduced by President Reagan in 1984, repealed by President Clinton in 1993, re-implemented by President George W. Bush in 2001, and rescinded by President Obama in 2009. Rather

than abide by the controversial rule, many clinics, including a number in Kenya, have simply turned down US funds. As a result, several in Kenya have closed for loss of funds, according to a 2004 report from the Center for Reproductive Health Research and Policy in San Francisco.

The gag rule notwithstanding, maternity care in general is problematic in Kenya's public hospitals. The 2007 report "Failure to Deliver," produced by the Federation of Women Lawyers-Kenya (FIDA Kenya) and the Center for Reproductive Rights in New York, pointed out that public health facilities often suffer from lack of supplies and congestion. Claris Ogangah-Onyango, legal counsel for FIDA Kenya, notes that when women with post-abortion complications occupy the majority of beds in maternity hospitals, there is not enough space and care for other women. "The government is mostly concerned with post-abortion care," she says, "and most of the funding goes to that. But they're not doing anything to stop [unsafe] abortions."

(SOURCE: Michele Kort with Mary Kathomi Riungu, "Are US Policies Killing Women Abroad?" *Ms.*, Winter 2008. Retrieved April 25, 2009, from http://www.rhrealitycheck.org/blog/2008/02/16/are-u-s-policies-killing-women-abroad)

Question

Of its 222 members, Kenya's parliament had just 18 women in 2008. Do you think putting more women in government would help address the problems of maternal care? Is it ethical for the United States to impose its moral values through restrictions placed by the global gag rule? Evaluate the gag rule from the perspective of the Belmont principles. Are other moral perspectives relevant?

The other big medical story of the day with implications for abortion involved a rubella, or German measles, epidemic that broke out in the United States in 1964. Unlike the thalidomide tragedies, which had left thousands of children worldwide with severe deformities, the range of birth defects posed by rubella to a fetus from maternal infection in the first 20 weeks of the pregnancy was well known, and many pregnant women who could, got abortions. But tens of thousands of others were blocked by strict abortion laws.

As these social, cultural, and medical developments were unfolding, secular philosophers and liberal theologians were providing a fresh theoretical framework for the further heightening of pro-choice consciousness.

PHILOSOPHICAL ANALYSES OF ABORTION

If, in the lead-up to *Roe*, pro-choice activists were drawing inspiration from events and developments such as the aforementioned, they were getting conceptual clarity and strength from the contemporary thought of certain philosophers with an interest in the morality of abortion. Indeed, so fecund were philosophical reflections on the topic that even today it's a rare abortion anthology that does not feature the work of moral philosophers such as Judith Jarvis Thomson, Mary Anne Warren, and Michael Tooley.

In 1971, just two years before *Roe*, Thomson published the first bioethical essay to appear in *Philosophy and Public Affairs (PAPA)*, then a fledgling journal with an interest in the philosophical dimensions of social and cultural issues.[29] In "A Defense of Abortion," a classic essay in abortion literature, Thomson conceded, for debate's sake, the largely religious view of the unborn as a person from conception. Even so, she claimed, the unborn's right to life was not always stronger or more stringent than the mother's right to decide what happens to her body.[30]

Thomson's argument involved a thought experiment in which she asked the reader to imagine waking up one morning tethered to a famous unconscious violinist with a fatal kidney ailment. The violinist's survival for the next nine months depended upon the reader's kidneys extracting poisons from the violinist's blood. Then Thomson pointedly asked whether, under the circumstances, one would be absolutely duty-bound to stay tied to the violinist; or whether it would be moral to disconnect from the violinist, even if that meant the violinist's certain death.

Thomson saw no moral obligation owed the violinist by the unwilling donor. By the same token, she saw no obligation owed the unborn by the pregnant woman, save in cases of minimum inconvenience, in which, she admitted, abortion would be "positively indecent." Illustratively, she gave the case of a late-term abortion "to avoid the nuisance of postponing a trip abroad."

Thomson's provocative analogy came in for swift criticism as missing crucial distinctions or having narrow application. In 1972, for instance, philosopher Baruch Brody, also writing in *PAPA*, distinguished between disconnecting, on one hand, and "cutting to pieces" on the other.[31] The first, Brody likened to letting die, a foreseen harm; the second to killing, an intended harm. The distinction resembled the familiar one between the morally permissible letting a terminally ill patient die (under double effect), as opposed to the morally impermissible deliberately killing him, as in euthanasia. According to Brody, Thomson had missed this significant moral distinction in her abortion essay.[32]

Others found Thomson's comparison limited to the rare pregnancy from rape. By contrast, Mary Anne Warren was quick to point out, the woman contemplating abortion ordinarily had been involved in the decision-making process that led to the pregnancy, namely, sexual relations. Therefore, Warren said, such a woman couldn't plead the innocent victim, as could the person unwillingly connected to the violinist or raped. Still, Warren was hardly attacking abortion. Indeed, in one of her own essays, published in 1973, she vigorously defended the woman's right to choose at any stage of gestation, since the unborn couldn't satisfy five traits

Warren felt central to the concept of personhood: consciousness, reasoning, self-motivated activity, communication, and self-concept. As she wrote in the year of *Roe*:

> ... neither a fetus's resemblance to a person, nor its potential for becoming a person provides any basis whatever for the claim that it has any significant right to life. Consequently, a woman's right to protect her health, happiness, freedom, and even her life, by terminating an unwanted pregnancy, will always override whatever right to life it may be appropriate to ascribe to a fetus, even a fully developed one.[33]

Earlier, in a 1972 *PAPA* article (and again in a 1983 book), Tooley shared Warren's emphasis on the self-determination of the woman, in his essay "Abortion and Infanticide."[34] Also adopting a rationality view of personhood as old as Locke and Kant, and favored by philosophers generally, Tooley argued that the unborn had no moral status because it possessed neither "a concept of self as a continuing subject of experiences and other mental states" nor was capable of thinking of itself as such a "continuing entity." Tooley concluded that, because the unborn couldn't desire its continued existence, it was meaningless to talk of its "right to life." Then, most controversially, he extended his argument to newborns, who, Tooley said, had no more moral status, strictly speaking, than do the unborn. Tooley didn't mean that the neonate's existence was to be met with moral indifference. But he did, at least in theory, establish a case for strictly regulated infanticide shortly after birth.

Somewhat later, the Australian philosopher Peter Singer (*Practical Ethics*, 1979) and the British philosopher Jonathan Glover (*Causing Death and Saving Lives*, 1977) concurred with Tooley. It was (and remains) the position of Tooley, Singer, and Glover to permit strictly controlled infanticide in cases of serious birth abnormalities, such as anencephaly (the total or near total absence of the cerebral hemisphere) and spina bifida (malformation of the spinal cord).[35] They base their view on two key premises. First, suffering should be relieved without regard to species. Second, infants, like other animals, are neither rational nor self-conscious. Therefore, in Singer's words: "Since their species is not relevant to their moral status, the principles that govern the wrongness of killing nonhuman animals who are sentient but not rational or self-conscious must apply here, too." This has led Singer and like minds to say that parents and doctors should be allowed to kill newborns with drastic disabilities, such as the absence of higher brain function or an incompletely formed spine, instead of letting "nature take its course."[36] In 2006 Britain's Royal College of Obstetricians and Gynecology adopted this view, publicly urging health professionals to consider infanticide for disabled newborns. The proposal, which was generally backed by geneticists and bioethicists, followed an increase in the number of seriously deformed neonates surviving because of medical advances.[37]

It is worth noting that in today's super-charged abortion debate the specter of infanticide has given the pro-life side substantial ammunition for attacking the pro-choice side. Singer, who may be today's most influential living philosopher, has especially come in for a torrent of invective. Still, to his harshest critics, Singer's tolerance of regulated infanticide is merely pushing the abortion permit to its logical conclusion: "baby killing," which, again, was the characterization that supporters of restrictive laws favored once safe medical procedures made concern for the life and health of the mother a moot point. Thus, when political journalist Radesh Ponnuru, senior editor of the conservative *National Review*, conflates infanticide and abortion, as he recently did, he is reprising what a half-century ago became the predominant argument against the safe abortion:

> [P]erhaps most terrible about these apologias for child-murder is that they have a point. They are not correct about the justifiability of infanticide; but they are correct that if abortion is justified, so is infanticide. People who first hear of Singer's views are apt to respond that he is simply crazy. But ... the philosophers of infanticide ... are not people who have lost their reason, but people who have lost everything but their reason.

They are reasoning from deeply flawed premises that they share with people who avoid endorsing child-killing only by reasoning poorly from them....

It is easy, in advance, to imagine that our sensibilities will set limits on moral innovation. We will liberalize abortion laws, but only for the hard cases.... We will create human embryos for the purpose of experiments, but only up to the fourteenth day of life.... But crossing those limits is not so difficult once we have breached the principles that forbade all such actions. All it takes is a simple question: What's the difference...? What changes at the fifteenth day? A Supreme Court justice may tell us one day that killing should be permitted until birth, and on another day forget why he once thought birth mattered. And there will always be Peter Singers to form the advance guard of a movement to erase the remaining limits.[38]

Whatever their differences, the philosophers who were writing about abortion in the *Roe* era were of a mind that clearly set them apart from the opponents of abortion. Despite their nuanced positions, and unlike their abortion foes, they considered it morally significant that the unborn lacked consciousness or, more specifically, *self*-consciousness. The unborn lacked an awareness of its self as an identical self that endured over time. Lacking this kind of self-awareness, which has a hallowed tradition in philosophy,[39] the unborn lacked autonomy. A fetus couldn't think, evaluate, choose, or act. Therefore, the rights owed autonomous beings simply did not apply to the non-autonomous unborn. This overarching belief was what united Thomson and her critics, for all their differences, four decades ago. To them, the fetus was basically a theological artifact, in contradistinction to the woman, who, in the autonomous or self-governing sense, was a "real person."

It is noteworthy that this depiction of the fetus as a kind of alien invader of the woman's body, while serving the emergent pro-choice movement, did so without confronting the unique perspective of the pregnant woman. Even those bioethicists who thought that abortion should be permitted inevitably treated her as so much maternal background and the fetus as if it grew under "a cabbage leaf."[40] Virtually absent, then, in the lead-up to *Roe* was any serious consideration of the most obvious fact of all: Fetuses grow inside women's bodies.

Today by contrast, according to philosopher Hilde Lindemann, "[f]eminst bioethicists ... insist, like real estate agents, on the importance of location, location, location."[41] Making the location of the pregnancy—inside a woman's body—the locus of the debate implicitly takes a woman's experiences seriously. Granted, her experience of pregnancy doesn't of itself provide an adequate justification for the permissibility of abortion. To get that, as Lindemann contends, "we have to add to it another feature of women's experience: the experience of gender as power over women."[42] By this she means that gender has set up socially and institutionally entrenched "norms of subservience for women."[43] If, then, we (1) take women's experience of pregnancy seriously, and (2) acknowledge that women traditionally have been oppressed by being required to serve the interests of others, then we make the abortion argument not about the moral status of the unborn but about whether women should control their own bodies or a society that oppresses them should. The question thus becomes: "Should pregnant women be forced to do the creative work of pregnancy, birth giving and child rearing, or should they have the power to control their bodies by putting a halt to the process of bringing a child into being?" Largely unformulated in the lead-up to *Roe*, today this question occupies the center of the feminist bioethicists' critique of abortion.

A Young Muslim Woman with a Complicated Pregnancy

In the area of procreation, it is not always easy to reconcile religious belief with medicine's modern capabilities. But Antoine Bèclére Hospital en Clamart does its best. The first, and so far only, ethical-religious clinic is also one of France's state-of-the-art obstetric hospitals.

Once a week Dr. Paul Atlan attends couples or single women faced with complex decisions. Sometimes the urgency of the situations complicates matters even further, as in the case of a young Muslim woman Dr. Atlan treated.

The young woman in question suffered from a genetic illness that put her own health at great risk during pregnancy. After the birth of her second child, doctors recommended that she not have any more children. When she became pregnant again, their concerns were borne out. By the fourth month of her pregnancy, her blood pressure was dangerously high. Only an abortion could save her life. When the young woman rejected the idea, the helpless doctor sent her in an ambulance to Dr. Atlan.

After a 45-minute discussion, Atlan persuaded her to let him ask the Paris Mosque for permission to interrupt the pregnancy immediately. An hour later, Dr. Dalil Boubakeur faxed back a report from the commission of theologians that he had called together. According to the report, the texts of the *Sharia* authorized the woman not to place her life in danger. After a further hour and a half of discussion, the sobbing patient finally agreed to a therapeutic abortion. Two days later, her blood pressure returned to normal.

(SOURCE: NA, "The Challenges of Bioethics: What the Different Religions Have To Say," *Revista Envío*, August 2003. Retrieved April 16, 2009, from www.envio.org.ni/articulo/2114)

Question

Should religion play a part in secular hospitals like Antoine Beclere? Can you think of examples in which it already does? Since its creation, mainly people of the Jewish and Muslim faiths have attended the clinic. There have been few Catholics and even fewer Protestants and no Orthodox Christians. Why do you think this is so? Do you think it's unethical for a person who opposes abortion to use the non-obstetric services of a hospital that performs abortions?

RELIGIOUS SOCIAL TEACHING AND ACTIVISM

While the philosophers were providing conceptual clarification in helping to mobilize pro-choice consciousness in the years leading up to *Roe*, mainline Jewish and Christian groups were also lending support to greater reproductive freedom. Members of both denominations, in fact, were active as early as the 1930s in support of birth control, culminating in 1961 when the National Council of Churches declared a liberal policy on contraceptive use by consenting couples. Later, in 1962, a Maryland clergy coalition successfully pressed that state to permit the disbursal of contraception. The same decade witnessed several thousand ministers and rabbis nationwide banding together to give women information about birth control and to lobby for repeal of anti-abortion laws.[44,45] Once *Roe* was won, many of these individuals helped found the Religious Coalition for Reproductive Choice, a group of clergy and lay leaders from mainstream religions still established to preserve reproductive choice as a basic part of religious liberty.

Largely driving the religious activism in the pre-*Roe* years was an alternative, liberal interpretation of religious natural law and sacred scriptures that made allowance for the abortion of *tragic necessity*, or one that imposes a great burden on mother or child. For their part, liberal Catholic philosophers and theologians—Richard McCormick, Thomas Shannon, Lisa Sowle Cahill, Joan Timmerman, and Carol Tauer—also were suggesting that, given its own tradition of moral logic, the Catholic Church was wrong not to grant the benefit of doubt in the case of early abortions.[46] After all, they argued, such abortions occurred spontaneously in nature all the time. Indeed, modern embryology estimates that over 50 percent of eggs successfully fertilized during unprotected sexual intercourse fail to implant or do not remain implanted in the uterine wall.[47] "What were we to make of such spontaneous abortions?" these theologians were asking. Were they to be considered deaths of persons that must be stopped in order to show respect for God-created life?[48]

Surgical improvements in treating ectopic pregnancies soon raised another difficulty for conservative opposition to all abortions. An ectopic pregnancy occurs when the fertilized egg attaches itself outside the cavity of the uterus (womb), usually in a fallopian tube. First described in the eleventh century, an ectopic pregnancy was a potentially fatal condition until the advent of surgery and blood transfusions in the early twentieth century. Thereafter, it still remained risky and usually impaired future fertility, a grim outlook that changed dramatically in the 1970s when sophisticated diagnostic tools and surgical procedures meant not only that the woman's life could be saved but also her fertility could be preserved. However, the new treatments ran afoul of official Catholic teaching because they involved a direct attack on the fetus and, thus, couldn't be justified under double-effect theory. With, then, the availability of this safe, fertility-preserving surgical procedure, liberal theologians began to ask: "If the unborn will perish no matter the procedure, why not do the one with the least likely harmful effects to the mother and that maximizes the chances for a successful future pregnancy?" As with lost eggs, this question continues to trouble Catholic theologians.[49-53]

With these developments, then, the stage was set for a constitutional confrontation between those, influenced mainly by conservative religious beliefs, who opposed abortion; and those, influenced by secular or liberal religious beliefs, who supported choice, at least under certain circumstances. The opportunity arrived in 1970 when 21-year-old "Jane Doe," a pseudonym for Norma McCorvey, became the lead plaintiff in a class-action lawsuit filed to challenge anti-abortion laws in Texas, represented by Dallas County District Attorney Henry Wade. Although the district court had ruled in McCorvey's favor, based mainly on the Ninth Amendment and *Griswold*, it nevertheless refused to enjoin the state from enforcing its prohibitive laws. Ultimately, in 1973, *Roe v. Wade* reached the US Supreme Court, which had to decide the constitutionality of state laws prohibiting abortion.

CASES AND CONTROVERSIES

Sherri Finkbine and the Thalidomide Tragedy

In 1962, Mrs. Sherri Finkbine, the mother of four normal children, found herself pregnant. The pregnancy was going well, except that Mrs. Finkbine was experiencing trouble sleeping. Instead of consulting her physician, she simply took some of the tranquilizers her husband had brought back from a trip to Europe, where the sedative was a widely used over-the-counter drug.

Mrs. Finkbine subsequently read an article about the increase in the number of children with deformities being born in Europe, including babies born with missing or deformed limbs, blind, or deaf. She especially noted the suspected connection between the birth defects and the use in pregnancy of a supposedly harmless tranquilizer containing the active ingredient

thalidomide, a sedative-hypnotic drug widely sold in Europe during the late 1950s and 1960s. Indeed, by 1962, some 10,000 children, mostly in Europe, had been born with thalidomide-induced birth defects.[54]

Alarmed by what she'd read, Mrs. Finkbine visited her physician, who confirmed her worst fears. The tranquilizer she had taken did indeed contain thalidomide. Convinced that his patient stood little chance of delivering a baby without deformities, the physician recommended termination of the pregnancy. He explained to Mrs. Finkbine that getting approval for an abortion under such conditions should prove simple. All she had to do was present her case to the three-member medical board of Phoenix. Mrs. Finkbine followed her physician's recommendation and, as anticipated, the board granted approval for the abortion. Concerned for the welfare of similar

(Continued)

CASES AND CONTROVERSIES (CONTINUED)

pregnant women and their babies, Mrs. Finkbine then told her story to the editor of a local newspaper. While agreeing not to identify her, the editor ran the story bordered in black on the front page under the headline "Baby-Deforming Drug May Cost Woman Her Child Here."

Straightaway, the wire services picked up the story, and it wasn't long before Mrs. Finkbine's identity was known and published, turning her into the object of intense anti-abortion sentiment. *L'Osservatore Romano*, the official Vatican newspaper, condemned Mrs. Finkbine and her husband as murderers. Although she received some letters of support, many were abusive. "I hope someone takes the other four children and strangles them," one person wrote, "because it's all the same thing." Another wrote from the perspective of the fetus: "Mommy, please dear Mommy, let me live. Please, please, I want to live. Let me love you, let me see the light of day, let me smell a rose, let me sing a song, let me look into your face, let me say Mommy."

Feeling the heat of the controversy, the medical board began to waver. They decided that, if challenged, their approval couldn't survive a court test, because Arizona statute allowed abortion only to save the mother's life. Rather than try to defend its approval, the board withdrew it.

Thwarted in her attempt to get a legal abortion in some other state, Mrs. Finkbine went to Sweden. After a rigorous investigation by a medical board there, she was given an abortion in a Swedish hospital. Her surgeon told Mrs. Finkbine that her 3-month-old fetus had no legs, one arm, and likely would not have survived.[55]

Questions for Analysis

1. Why do you think the Finkbine case riveted the public's interest in abortion as it never before had been?

2. Discuss the Finkbine case in the context of the philosophical analyses of abortion that led up to *Roe*.

3. Evaluate Mrs. Finkbine's decision from the perspectives of religious natural law, utilitarianism, and Kant's categorical imperative. How would principlism likely frame the issue?

4. What bearing, if any, do you think probable or certain deformities have on the person status of the unborn?

CASES AND CONTROVERSIES

Griswold v. Connecticut (1965)

Griswold v. Connecticut involved a statute adopted by the state of Connecticut in 1879 which made it illegal for any person to use, or assist in using, any "drug, medicinal article, or instrument for the purpose of preventing conception," even among married couples. The prohibition followed a nationwide Victorian purity campaign led by Anthony Comstock (1844–1915), a politician and US Postal Inspector who persuaded Congress in 1873 to pass the Comstock Law. "Comstock laws," as the nation knew them, made it illegal to deliver or transport both "obscene, lewd, or lascivious" material as well as any methods of, or information pertaining to, birth control. In 1965 the state of Connecticut was sued by two members of the Planned Parenthood League of Connecticut, whose Executive

Director, Estelle Griswold, had been convicted of providing contraceptive information, instruction, and medical advice to a married couple. Griswold's conviction was affirmed by the state's high court, but on appeal the US Supreme Court reversed by a 7-to-2 margin. The majority determined that the statute and its Comstock basis were invalid mainly because they infringed on the constitutionally protected right to "privacy" of married persons.

What made *Griswold* a landmark case was the Court's willingness to explicitly invest unenumerated rights with full constitutional status. Thus, writing for five members, Justice William O. Douglas (1898–1980) referred to rights that are implicit in, or peripheral to, other express guarantees in the Bill of Rights. In his famous words, "specific guarantees ... have penumbras, formed by emanations from those guarantees that help give them life and substance." Just as the Court earlier had found that First Amendment rights to freedom of speech implied a peripheral "right to freedom of association," Douglas reasoned, so too the First, Third, Fourth, Fifth, and Ninth Amendments imply "zones of privacy" that form the basis for the general privacy right affirmed in *Griswold*. Expanding on the status of the right of privacy, Justice Arthur Goldberg (1908–1990) said that it emanated "from the totality of the constitutional scheme under which we live." Agreeing with the Majority, Goldberg wrote:

> The makers of our Constitution undertook to secure conditions favorable to the pursuit of happiness. They recognized the significance of man's spiritual nature of his feelings and of his intellect. They knew that only a part of the pain, pleasure and satisfactions of life are to be found in material things. They sought to protect Americans in their beliefs, their thoughts, their emotions and their sensations. They conferred, as against the Government, the right to be let alone—the most comprehensive of rights and the right most valued by civilized men.... Adultery, homosexuality and the like are sexual intimacies which the State forbids ..., but the intimacy of husband and wife is necessarily an essential and accepted feature of the institution of marriage, an institution which the State not only must allow, but which, always and in every age, it has fostered and protected. It is one thing when the State exerts its power either to forbid extramarital sexuality ... or to say who may marry, but it is quite another when, having acknowledged a marriage and the intimacies inherent in it, it undertakes to regulate by means of the criminal law the details of that intimacy.[56]

While expressing disdain for the Connecticut law, the dissents by Justices Hugo Black (1886–1971) and Potter Stewart (1915–1985) denied that it infringed on any implied constitutional right. Indeed, they expressed concern that "[u]se of any such broad, unbounded judicial authority would make of this Court's members a day-to-day constitutional convention." Black warned of a "great unconstitutional shift of

power to the courts which ... will be bad for the courts and worse for the country."

Although still relatively unknown, *Griswold v. Connecticut* has had a profound impact on American laws and society, especially by establishing the conceptual and legal ground for *Roe* eight years hence, and for the intense discourse about legal abortion that continues to roil the country.

Questions for Analysis

1. What does your faith tradition teach about allowing people access to drugs or devices designed to stop contraception, and thus be able to engage in sex without having to worry as much about pregnancy?

2. Since *Griswold*, the logic of privacy has been extended to protect many social relations, including women's choices regarding abortion (*Roe v. Wade*, 1973), the sale of contraceptives to unmarried individuals (*Carey v. Population Services International*, 1977), and relations among homosexuals (*Lawrence v. Texas*, 2003). Do you agree with these extensions of privacy? Would you extend privacy to all social relations or would you limit its application?

3. Should the government have to demonstrate why it is justified in interfering with your life rather than requiring you to demonstrate that the text of the Constitution specifically and narrowly prohibits the government's actions?

4. What moral principles support the *Griswold* decision?

5. How would *Griswold* violate the Catholic interpretation of natural law?

6. While the privacy logic has been useful to limit at least some unwanted state intervention in intimate sexual matters, it has also been employed to preclude a positive state role in educating citizens and providing funding essential for the exercise of rights to use birth control and receive an abortion. Some critics thus argue for the need to replace the privacy logic with a more affirmative conception of autonomy rights that is more consistent with the goals of equality and empowerment. Do you agree that the logic of privacy implies a positive as well as negative right?

CASES AND CONTROVERSIES

The Pre-*Roe* "Bad Old Days"

Waldo Fielding was an obstetrician and gynecologist in Boston for thirty-eight years. He spent his early formal training in New York City, from 1948 to 1953, in two of the city's large municipal hospitals. There he saw and treated "every complication of illegal abortion that one could conjure, done either by the patient herself or by an abortionist—often unknowing, unskilled and probably uncaring." In seeking medical help to complete the process or correct damage, patients revealed nothing, and physicians didn't press them. Yet, this much was clear, Dr. Fielding says: "The woman had put herself at total risk, and literally did not know whether she would live or die." It was also clear, Fielding adds, that her desperate need to end the pregnancy drove women to any method available, including "coat hangers, darning needles, crochet hooks, cut-glass salt shakers, soda bottles, sometimes intact, sometimes with the top broken off." When a hanger was found trapped in the cervix, as sometimes happened, the woman was placed under anesthesia, "and as we removed the metal piece we held our breath, because we could not tell whether the hanger had gone through the uterus into the abdominal cavity." (Ultrasound, CT scans, or any of the now accepted radiology techniques weren't available then.) Another abortive method Fielding recalls hearing about from colleagues was forcing a soap solution through the cervical canal with a syringe. Were a bubble in the solution to enter a blood vessel and get transported to the heart, death was almost immediate. The worst case Fielding saw involved a nurse who was admitted with what looked like a partly delivered umbilical cord. The cord was, in fact, part of her intestine, which had been hooked and torn by whatever implement had been used in the abortion. It took six hours of surgery to repair uterus, ovaries, and part of the bowel that was still functional.[57]

Questions for Analysis

1. Experiences like these certainly gave political impetus to pre-Roe abortion activism. How did abortion activists make them *morally* relevant?

2. Do you think anecdotes like Dr. Fielding's make a compelling case that women should not have to carry children they don't want?

3. Rev. Randy Alcorn, founder and director of Eternal Perspective Ministries (EPM), a nonprofit organization dedicated to teaching biblical truth and helping the needy, dismisses the fear of the return of the "back alley" abortion with these words:

> The coat hanger argument is valid only if the unborn are not human beings, with commensurate human rights. Typically those appealing to the emotions through use of this argument completely avoid the real issue, since it is easier to talk about coat hangers than dead children. From the child's point of view there is no such thing as a safe, legal abortion. It is always deadly. For every two people who enter an abortion clinic, only one comes out alive. Rape is a horrible attack on an innocent human being, so we do not attempt to make rape safe and legal. We do not try to make kidnapping or child abuse safe and legal. If abortion kills children, our goal should not be to make it as safe and legal as possible, but to provide alternatives and legal restrictions that help avoid it in the first place.[58]

Do you think that Rev. Alcorn successfully refutes Dr. Fielding?

REFERENCES

1. Emily Bazelon, "Is There a Post-Abortion Syndrome?" *The New York Times Magazine*, January 27, 2007, p. 43.
2. Shaila Dewan, "To Court Blacks, Foes of Abortion Make Racial Case," *The New York Times*, February 26, 2010. Retrieved March 1, 2010, from http://www.nytimes.com/2010/02/27/us/27race.html.
3. Rachel K. Jones, et al., "Abortion in the United States: Incidence and Access to Services, 2005," *Perspectives on Sexual Reproductivity*, March 2008, pp. 6–16.
4. "Elective Abortion," *eMedicine*, December 29, 2007. Retrieved May 11, 2008, from www.emedicine.com/med/topic5.htm.

5. Joe Stumpe and Monica Davey, "Abortion Doctor Slain by Gunman in Kansas Church," *The New York Times*, June 1, 1009, p. A1.

6. Nicholas Riccardi, "Abortion Doctor George Tiller Is Killed; Suspect in Custody," *Los Angeles Times,* May 31, 2009. Retrieved from August 26, 2010, from http://articles.latimes.com/2009/jun01/nation/na-tiller1

7. Mark Murray, "First Thoughts: Culture Wars Return?" *First Read*, June 1, 2009. Retrieved June 1, 2009, from http://firstread.msnbc.msn.com/archive/2009/06/01/1948701.aspx.2009jun01,0,7068875.story.

8. Joshua Rhett Miller, "Critics Blast Obama's Scheduled Notre Dame Commencement Address," *FoxNews.com*, March 2, 2009. Retrieved June 6, 2009, from www.foxnews.com/politics/first100days/2009/03/24/critics-blast-obamas-notre-dame-commencement-address.

9. See note 7 above.

10. *The Nuremberg Files*, Pathway Communications: Carrollton, GA: 2008. Retrieved May 1, 2008, from http://www.christiangallery.com/atrocity.

11. Sandra S. Stanton, "Since *Roe v. Wade*: American Public Opinion and Law on Abortion," *ProQuest*, January 2005. Retrieved August 7, 2009, from http://www.csa.com/discoveryguides/roe/overview.php.

12. Roberta Brandes Gratz, "Never Again: Death, Politics and Abortion (1973)," *Ms. Magazine*, Spring 2002. Retrieved May 18, 2008, from www.msmagazine.com/spring2002/brandesgratz.asp.

13. Jone Johnson Lewis, "A brief history of the abortion controversy in the United States," *About.com Women's History*. Retrieved April 25, 2008, from http://womenshistory.about.com/od/abortionuslegal/a/abortion.htm.

14. Mark Graber, *Rethinking Abortion: Equal, Choice, The Constitution, and Reproductive Politics*, Princeton: Princeton University Press, 1996.

15. Elaine Woo, "Creator of Device for Safer Abortions," *Los Angeles Times*, May 18, 2008, p. B11.

16. Kenneth Hill, et al, "Estimates of Maternal Mortality Worldwide Between 1990 and 2005: An Assessment of Available Data," *The Lancet*, October 13, 2007, pp. 1311–1319.

17. See note 12 above.

18. Mathieu Deflem, "The Boundaries of Abortion Law: Systems Theory from Parsons to Luhmann and Habermas," *Social Forces*, March 1998, pp. 775–818.

19. Congregation for the Doctrine of the Faith, *Donum Vitae*, February 22, 1987, Staten Island, NY: Priests for Life. Retrieved May 1, 2008, from www.priestsforlife.org/magisterium/donumvitae.htm.

20. Pope John Paul II, "Evangelium Vitae (The Gospel of Life)," *L'Osservatore Romano*, Weekly Edition in English, April 5, 1995. Retrieved April 17, 2008, from http://www.ewtn.com/library/ENCYC/JP2EVANG.HTM.

21. Jean Porter, "Is the Embryo a Person? Arguing with the Catholic Traditions," *Commonweal*, Feb 8, 2002. Retrieved June 2, 2008, from http://www.pfaith.org/catholic.htm

22. See note 20 above.

23. Edwin F. Healy, "Indirect Abortion," *Medical Ethics*, 1994. Retrieved May 16, 2010, from http://www.ewtn.com/library/PROLIFE/INDIRECT.TXT

24. J. P. Moreland & Scott B. Rae, *Body & Soul: Human Nature & the Crisis in Ethics*, Downers Grove, ILL: InterVarsity Press, 2000, pp. 232–233.

25. John T. Noonan, "An Almost Absolute Value in History," in Jeffrey Olen, Julie C. Van Camp, Vincent Barry, eds., *Applying Ethics*, 8th ed., Thomson/Wadsworth, 2005, p. 132.

26. See note 12 above.

27. Douglas Martin, "Lawrence Lader, Champion of Abortion Rights, Is Dead at 86," *The New York Times*, May 10, 2006, p. A20.

28. "Peyton Place," Wikipedia, March 21, 2008. Retrieved May 2, 2008, from http://en.wikipedia.org/wiki/Peyton_Place_%28novel%29.

29. Albert R. Jonsen, *The Birth of Bioethics*, New York: Oxford University Press, 1998, p. 295.

30. Judith Jarvis Thomson, "A Defense of Abortion," in Jeffrey Olen, Julie C. Van Camp, and Vincent Barry, eds., *Applying Ethics*, 8th ed., Belmont, CA: Wadsworth/Thomson, 2005, pp. 133–143.

31. Jonsen, p. 295.

32. Baruch Brody, "Thomson on Abortion," *Philosophy and Public Affairs*, Spring 1972, pp. 335–340.

33. Mary Anne Warren, "On the Moral and Legal Status of Abortion," *The Monist*, January 1973, pp. 43–61.

34. Michael Tooley, "Abortion and Infanticide," *Philosophy and Public Affairs*," Fall 1972, pp. 37–65; *Abortion and Infanticide*, Oxford: Clarendon Press, 1983.

35. See note 31 above.

36. Dennis Hevesi, "Harriet Johnson, 50, Activist for Disabled, Is Dead," *The New York Times*, June 7, 2008, p. A15.

37. Sarah-Kate Templeton, "Doctors: let us kill disabled babies." *The Sunday Times*, November 5, 2006. Retrieved April 15, 2008, from http://www.timesonline.co.uk/tol/news/uk/article625477.ece.

38. Ramesh Ponnuru, *Party of Death*, Washington: Regnery Publishing, Inc., 2006, quoted in *Between Two Worlds*, May 2006. Retrieved May 2, 2008, from theologica.blogspot.com/2006_05_01_archive.html.

39. Jeffrey H. Reiman, "Asymmetric Value and Abortion, with a Reply to Don Marquis," in *The Ethics of Abortion*, 3rd ed., Robert M. Baird and Stuart E. Rosenbaum, eds., Amherst, NY: Prometheus Books, 2001, p. 335.

40. Hilde Lindemann, *An Invitation to Feminist Ethics,* New York: McGraw-Hill, 2006, p. 121.

41. See note 40 above.

42. Ibid., p. 123.

43. See note 42 above.

44. M. Thiery, "Pioneers of Intrauterine Device," *The European Journal of Contraception and Reproductive Health Care*, March 1997, pp. 15–23. Retrieved August 26, 2009, from http://www.informaworld.com/smpp/content~db=all~content=a908533441.

45. Scott, Gilbert, Anna Tyler, and Emily J. Zackin, *Bioethics and the New Embryology*, Sunderland, MA: Sinnauer Associates, Inc., 2005. p. 58.

46. Neela Banerjee, "The Abortion-Rights Side Invokes God, Too," *The New York Times*, April 3, 2006, A12.

47. Tom Davis, *Sacred Work, Planned Parenthood and Its Clergy Alliances*, Piscataway, NJ: Rutgers University Press, 2005.

48. Madonna Kolbenschlag, "Abortion and Moral Consensus: Beyond Solomon's Choice," *The Christian Century*, February 20, 1985, pp. 179–193.

49. Audra Robertson, MD, "Miscarriage," *Medline Plus, Medical Encyclopedia*, September 19, 2006. Retrieved July 3, 2008, from http://www.nlm.nih.gov/medlineplus/ency/article/001488.htm.

50. Leon Kass, "The Meaning of Life—In the Laboratory," in The *Ethics of Reproductive Technology*, Kenneth D. Alpern, ed., New York: Oxford University Press, 1992, p. 103.

51. "Ectopic for Discussions: A Catholic Approach to Tubal Pregnancies," *Faith Facts: The Answers You Need*, December 2, 2003. Retrieved June 2, 2008, from http://www.cuf.org/faithfacts/details_view.asp?ffID=57.

52. Kevin O'Rourke, "Is the Human Embryo a Person?" *Newsletter of the Neiswanger Institute for Bioethics and Public Policy*, January 2006. Retrieved May 31, 2008, from www.domcentral.org/study/kor/Embryo%20as%20Person.pdf.

53. Kelly Bowring, "The Moral Dilemma of Management Procedures for Ectopic Pregnancy," *National Catholic Register*, August 29, 1999. Retrieved May 31, 2008, from www.uffl.org/vol12/bowring12.pdf.

54. Carl Zimmer, "Answers Begin to Emerge on How Thalidomide Caused Defects," *The New York Times*, March 16, 2010, p. D3.

55. Jeffrey Olen, Julie C. Van Camp, and Vincent Barry, eds., *Applying Ethics*, 8th edition, Belmont, CA: Thomson/Wadsworth, 2005, p. 161.

56. *Griswold v. Connecticut, FindLaw/Cases and Codes.* Retrieved April 18, 2009, from laws.findlaw.com/us/381/479.html.

57. Waldo L. Fielding, "Repairing the Damage, Before Roe," *The New York Times*, June 3, 2008. Retrieved April 25, 2009, from http://www.nytimes.com/2008/06/03/health/views/03essa.html.

58. Randy Alcorn, *ProLife Answers to ProChoice Arguments*, Sisters, OR: Multnomah Publishers, 2000, pp. 173–178. Retrieved April 25, 2009, from www.epm.org/artman2/publish/prolife_arguments/If_abortion_is_made_illegal.shtml.

Chapter 10

The Abortion Debate II:
Roe and Beyond

The two topics at the center of the public discourse in the lead-up to *Roe*—the life of the unborn and the free choice of the woman—ultimately would shape the legal analysis in *Roe* and *Doe,* the companion case decided on the same day. Thus, in the matter of abortion, the Supreme Court had to decide, first, which of competing views of personhood best suited a pluralistic society like ours; and then, second, what weight to give to the woman's choice.

CHOICE MATTERS MOST: THE *ROE* DECISION

In answering the first question, the court turned to the Constitution's religious liberty principle and what it guarantees: freedom of conscience. In deciding the second matter, the court discovered a guarantee of privacy throughout the constitution. Both rights-based arguments still stand as moral bulwarks against limitations of reproductive autonomous choice.

The Religious Liberty Principle

The religious liberty principle is expressed in the First Amendment where it is written: "Congress shall make no law respecting an establishment of religion, or prohibiting the free exercise thereof...." Regarding religion in the traditional sense, the amendment generally is viewed as consisting of two parts. The first part, known as the establishment clause, ensures that the government remains neutral toward religion; the second part, termed the free exercise clause, guarantees against governmental compulsion in religious matters. The establishment clause, then, prohibits the government from showing preference to any one religion, while the free exercise clause guarantees freedom of belief and, generally, freedom to act on that belief. As bioethicist Paul D. Simmons writes:

> The first [the establishment clause]—that public policy should not be based upon narrowly constructed sectarian perspectives—reflects the concern that First Amendment protections be safeguarded by

policymakers. The second [the free exercise clause]—that no group should seek to impose its own moral/theological beliefs upon others who hold differing beliefs regarded as equally personal and sacred—requests that religious communities and/or leaders be faithful to the social contract of tolerance.[1]

In this way, both religion and citizen enjoy freedom of expression and protection from government coercion.

What did this mean for the first issue facing the court, the moral status of the unborn? It basically meant that any ultimate understanding of personhood could reflect a religious teaching but, constitutionally, it could not be based solely upon it. Were a definition to be grounded on a sectarian perspective—as, for example, on unquestioning faith in transcendent authority of Church or Bible—it would violate the establishment clause.

It was still possible, in theory, to adopt a conservative immediate hominization view of the unborn that reflected, but was not based solely upon, a religious teaching. Doing so was ruled out, however, within a deeper understanding of the First Amendment's intent. Taken more expansively—in terms of fidelity to the ideal of tolerance for religious and moral belief—the free exercise clause, in particular, deals not only with religion in the traditional sense but with conscience. And it was freedom of conscience that implicitly came to shape *Roe* and descendant decisions, and has served, ever since, as the moral bedrock of all defenses of a woman's right to make an autonomous abortion choice.

Freedom of Conscience   In *Religion on Trial* (2005), their book about religious freedom and the First Amendment, authors Phillip E. Hammond, David W. Machacek, and Eric Michael Mazur write: "What the First Amendment protects is freedom of conscience—broadly understood as the 'moral powers of rationality and reasonableness in terms of which persons define personal and ethical meaning in living.'"[2] Freedom of conscience, these constitutional

scholars add, is "the very nature of what it means to be human."[3] The less freedom of conscience allowed, the less we can live our lives as we see fit, according to our own values and beliefs without outside interference. By contrast, expanded liberty of conscience means greater moral autonomy for individuals and further restrictions on government's ability to regulate personal behaviors.[4,5]

Constitutionally protected freedom of conscience, furthermore, has two specific requirements with respect to public policy. First, any proposal must be open to critical scrutiny, including revision and rejection. In other words, it must be fashioned "through democratic processes in which every perspective is subject to critical analysis."[6] Second, it must not interfere with individual choice without a "compelling interest." The first is a test of reasonableness, the second of liberty. Earlier, in Chapter 3, we saw how these Enlightenment values, together with tolerance of opposed viewpoints, influenced the thinking of not only this nation's constitutional framers but also the founders of bioethics. Now we see the same mind-set shaping the abortion debate, by holding any definition of personhood to those enduring secular Enlightenment ideals of reasonableness in public discourse and freedom of individual conscience characteristic of all liberal democracies.

By the measure of reasonableness and individual liberty, any attempt to define the unborn as a person from conception, whether or not religiously based, was doomed from the outset. First, not only was there reasonable disagreement about the personhood status of the unborn, the weight of informed opinion, even in the 1970s, favored a time and stage *after* conception. Second, reasonable people could, did, and do disagree about both natural law theory, in general, and religious natural law in particular, not to mention the meaning and value of Scripture. Third, any definition grounded in an abstract religious or philosophical principle would inevitably violate the teachings of some religious groups and, consequently, restrict freedom of conscience by prohibiting abortion. As philosopher and feminist Joan Callahan notes:

In a pluralistic society, the fact that a religious institution, or a religious contingency (no matter how large), holds something to be wrong is simply not a good reason for setting a public policy prohibiting or requiring action on the part of all citizens.[7]

Such considerations led the majority in the 7–2 *Roe* decision to declare: "whether or not life begins at conception is necessarily a conscience issue." In other words, a single definition of personhood could not serve all in a democratic society. Twenty years later, philosopher and constitutional scholar Ronald Dworkin would write that in *Roe* the court determined that "freedom of choice about abortion is a necessary implication of the religious freedom guaranteed by the First Amendment."[8,9] Thus, for the first time women's reproductive choice stood alongside other fundamental rights, such as freedom of religion. Beyond this, in explicitly recognizing that a woman's right to decide whether to continue her pregnancy was protected under the constitutional provisions of personal freedom, *Roe*, in effect, lent substantial lift to the ascendancy of patient autonomy in medical ethics.

Having so disposed of the personhood of the fetus—the first issue it faced—the court, in addressing the second issue, inevitably gave primacy to the woman's choice. It did so, largely, by expanding upon the nature and scope of privacy that was judicially constructed in *Griswold*.

Privacy

Besides freedom of conscience, the court gave another autonomy-related reason for favoring choice that, over the years, has drawn more cultural attention and discussion: privacy.

The Ninth Amendment reserves to the people rights not enumerated in the Constitution, while the Fourteenth prohibits states from abridging "privileges and immunities" of US citizens, defined as "all persons born or naturalized in the United States." Note that the Constitution makes no mention of the "unborn." (As a historical note, the British colonies considered abortions performed before "quickening," taken back then as about month 4, to be legal; also, though socially unacceptable, abortion was legal in most states until the mid-1800s.) Together, the court said, the two amendments establish a right to make fundamentally important personal decisions, including in the reproductive sphere the right to choose to forgo the following possible harms associated with pregnancy, as enumerated by Justice Harry Blackmun (1908–1999), author of the majority (7–2) opinion:

> Specific and direct harm medically diagnosable even in early pregnancy may be involved. Maternity, or additional offspring, may force upon the woman a distressful life and future. Psychological harm may be imminent. Mental and physical health may be taxed by childcare. There is also the distress, for all concerned, associated with the unwanted child, and there is the problem of bringing a child into a family already unable, psychologically and otherwise, to care for it. In other cases, as in this one [i.e., "Jane Roe"], the additional difficulties and continuing stigma of unwed motherhood may be involved. All these are factors the woman and her responsible physician necessarily will consider in consultation.

While the Court was framing abortion as a private matter left to the conscience of physician and woman, it also recognized the state's "important and legitimate interest in protecting the potentiality of human life." Despite their apparent incompatibility, these twin concerns—freedom of conscience and protection of fetal life—yielded the court's trimester framework to govern abortion, which, as reaffirmed in later cases (e.g., *Casey*), adopted third-trimester viability as the constitutionally significant demarcation in weighing in life and choice. The idea of viability—28 weeks into the pregnancy at the time of *Roe*, perhaps 22–24 weeks today, given advances in technology—had clear advantages over the largely religious standard of fertilized egg. As Simmons explains:

The notion of viability correlates biological maturation with personal identity in a way that can be recognized and accepted by reasonable people. It violates no group's religious teachings or any premise of logic to provide protections for a viable fetus. The same can hardly be said for those efforts to establish moral and legal parity between a zygote (fertilized ovum) and a woman, which create substantive First Amendment issues.[10]

According to the hierarchy established by *Roe*, then, the woman's claim to make her own choice was to be considered strong in the first trimester, moderate in the second, and weak in the third, "at which point the state acquires a 'compelling' interest in the protection of new life." Practically this meant: (1) no regulation of the physician/woman's relationship at all in the first trimester; (2) regulations to protect the woman's health in the second; and (3) permissible prohibitions in the third trimester unless abortion was "necessary, in appropriate medical judgment to preserve the life or health of the mother."

Significantly, in the companion decision, *Doe*, the court further defined "health" as a medical judgment that "may be exercised in the light of all factors—physical, emotional, psychological, familial, and the woman's age—relevant to the well-being of the patient." It was this allowance that abortion opponents viewed as, effectively, permitting unrestricted access to abortion, or abortion on demand.[11] Indeed, some doctors subsequently acknowledged interrupting post-viability pregnancies for reasons of rape, incest, psychiatric or pediatric indications, or social reasons such as "fear that relatives will disown, beat or even kill them [i.e., the pregnant women] for conceiving out of wedlock."[12]

As of January 22, 1973, then, the day of these decisions, the woman's choice for abortion was placed off limits to state interference, no matter how advanced her pregnancy, when her life or health was at stake. With that, concern for the welfare interests of the woman had turned from being the main argument for prohibiting abortions when they were unsafe to the main argument for permitting even the late-term abortion.

ROE AND CULTURAL CONFLICT

Roe and *Doe* gave physicians and regulators much to applaud. Clinically, the decisions meant what women's rights advocates had long been arguing: that an abortion decision was essentially a matter of individual choice and privacy to be decided between a woman and her physician. With *Roe*, any pregnant woman—not just one of privilege—and her doctor could define the personal and ethical meaning of the harms and risks associated with a pregnancy, according to their own values and beliefs. In so doing, they could consult an abortion hierarchy, which, however imperfect, gave some guidance for balancing maternal and fetal rights, for permitting and restricting abortions.

At the same time, the 1973 abortion decisions ignited a firestorm of protest, prompting a nationwide debate and polarizing much of society into pro-choice and pro-life camps. Journalist Susan Gorney reports, on the thirty-fifth anniversary of the decision, that within a few weeks "scattered opposition groups … coalesced into a passionate, implacable national opposition movement devoted to either a constitutional human-life amendment or a complete reversal of Roe."[13] In June one such group, the National Right To Life Committee (NRLC), was incorporated and held its first convention, gathering pro-life activists from around the nation to form what would become the nation's largest pro-life organization, representing over 3,000 chapters in all fifty states and the District of Columbia. By the mid-1970s, "the pro-life movement had become the dominant focus of Catholic action and even identity in the [emerging] culture war."[14] Anti-abortion activists won a major legislative victory in 1976 when Congress passed the Hyde Amendment, which bars the use of federal funds for abortions under Medicaid, the federal health insurance program for the poor. For its part, the National Association of Repeal of Abortion Laws changed its name to the National Abortion Rights Action League (NARAL), today called NARAL Pro-Choice America (NARAL PCA). Besides NARAL PCA and Planned Parenthood, the pro-choice movement currently embraces many groups, including Choice USA, the National Organization for Women, and the Center for Reproductive Rights.

In retrospect, it might be said that the incorporation of NRLC and NARAL institutionalized cultural conflict. As noted by Alan Wolfe, professor of Political Science and director of the Boisi Center for Religion and American Public Life at Boston College:

> There is no precise date at which the American culture war began, but the best guess would be in 1973, when the U. S. Supreme Court decided *Roe v. Wade*. Women, the Court essentially ruled, had the right to control their own bodies, especially after the first trimester of a pregnancy, and no state could refuse to allow them access to abortion. In thereby choosing the importance of individual autonomy over moral prohibitions rooted in many religious beliefs, the Court's decision contributed to the mobilization of groups determined to overrule the decision or at least to limit its applicability.[15]

Reflecting the conservative religious sentiments of the gathering anti-abortion groups, the magazine *Christianity Today (CT)* greeted *Roe* with a warning to its mainly evangelical readers: "Christians should accustom themselves to the thought that the American state no longer supports, in any meaningful sense, the laws of God." With palpable disappointment, the editorial quoted the *Roe*-sympathetic view of a prominent Southern Baptist pastor, W. A. Criswell (1909–2002):

> "I have always felt that it was only after a child was born and had life separate from its mother that it became an individual person, and it has always, therefore,

seemed to me that what is best for the mother and for the future should be allowed."[16]

Generally sharing Criswell's view were many Protestant churches that historically had opposed abortion, including: the Presbyterian Church (USA), the United Methodists, the Lutheran Church in America, the United Church of Christ, the Disciples of Christ, and the Southern Baptist Convention. Some, like the last, would later repudiate their position, as Criswell himself did. Others would hold fast in favor of choice. It was in this way that *Roe* created a wedge within the religious community that in the years following would widen to capture increasingly more reproductive issues.

Of note, *CT* was not attacking the abortion decisions on constitutional grounds. It wasn't echoing, for example, what is still the view of many abortion foes that, since there's no right to privacy specifically enumerated in the Constitution, the *Roe* decision is flawed and, therefore, should be repealed. Rather, *CT* was asserting what has become a mainstay position of the Christian Right, that all people answer to God and, therefore, have no right to be left alone, certainly not in reproductive matters. In a word, sexual liberty, including the choice of abortion, is simply contrary to God's will and, therefore, potentially a source of social disorder. To conservative Christians, then, Roe was, and remains, nothing less than an act of court-approved rebellion against God's law. In that sense, more than an attack on *Roe*, the *CT* editorial amounted to an attack on modernity itself and its signature expansion of individual liberties.[17,18]

Current Religious Sentiment

Today a number of denominations consider an abortion decision sometimes moral. One, the liberal Evangelical Lutheran Church in America, declared in 1991 its teaching statement about terminating fetal life:

> The position of this church is that, in cases where the life of the mother is threatened,

BIOETHICS ACROSS CULTURES

Outrage in Brazil

Abortion is illegal in Brazil except in cases of rape or when the mother's life is imperiled. At least one of those circumstances applied in early 2009 to a 9-year-old found to be pregnant with twins by her stepfather, who confessed to sexually abusing her for several years. Although the girl's life was not immediately endangered, her mother authorized an abortion. As a consequence, Catholic Archbishop Jose Cardoso Sobrinho excommunicated the physician who performed the abortion and the family members who authorized it. In Catholicism excommunication renders a church member an exile from Christian society and is the severest penalty that the church can inflict.

The archbishop's actions shocked even many Catholic Brazilians. "In this case, most people supported the doctors and the family. Everything they did was legal and correct," said Beatriz Galli of *Ipas Brasil*, a non-government organization that fights to give women more say over their health and reproductive rights. "But the Church takes these positions that are so rigid that it ends up weakened. It is very intolerant, and that intolerance is going to scare off more and more followers."

Although Brazil's pro-abortion President Luiz Lula denounced the excommunication, Archbishop Sobrinho refused to recant, telling one newspaper:

> I'm not sorry. What I did was to declare the excommunication. It is my obligation to alert the people, so that they may fear the laws of God.... The law of God is above all human law.... Therefore, when a human law, meaning a law promulgated by human legislators, is contrary to the law of God, this human law has no value.... [Abortion is] homicide against innocent life. We are talking about a silent holocaust, that kills one million innocents in Brazil and fifty million in the world every year, a holocaust worse than the six million Jews, which we lament every year.

The archbishop received public support from the Vatican and National Conference of Brazilian Bishops, who wrote: "The Church, in fidelity to the Gospel, positions itself always in favor of life, in an unequivocal condemnation of all violence done against the dignity of the human person.... We do not agree with the final outcome of eliminating the life of defenseless human beings."

Evangelical sects, whose numbers have been growing in once almost entirely Catholic Brazil, does not project a united pro-life platform in Brazil as monolithic as the Catholic Church's. One major sect, the Universal Church of the Kingdom of God, has taken a stance that showcases its differences with its Catholic rival. The Universal Church's television channel TV Record recently aired spots featuring a woman declaring,

> I decided who to marry. I decided to use the pill. With my vote I decided who'd be elected President. I decided to work so that I won't be discriminated against. Why can't I decide what to do with my own body? Women should be able to decide for themselves what's important.

The promotion didn't impress Archbishop Sobrinho, who told *TIME* that the Vatican rejects believers who pick and choose their issues. Rome "is not going to open the door to anyone just to get more members," the Archbishop said after comparing abortion to the Holocaust. "We know that people have other ideas, but if they do, then they are not Catholics. We want people who adhere to God's laws."

(SOURCES: Matthew Cullinan Hoffman, "Archbishop Announces Excommunication of Doctor and Family Members for Abortion on Nine-Year-Old Girl," *LifeSiteNews.com*, March 5, 2009. Retrieved April 22, 2009, from http://www.lifesitenews.com/ldn/2009/mar/09030601.html; Matthew Cullinan Hoffman, "Vatican Backs Bishop Who Excommunicated Doctor and Family Involved in Abortion," *LifeSiteNews.com*, March 8, 2009. Retrieved April 22, 2009, from www.lifesitenews.com/ldn/2009/mar/09030903.html; Andrew Downie, "Nine-Year-Old's Abortion Outrages Brazil's Catholic Church," *TIME*, March 6, 2009. Retrieved April 22, 2009, from www.time.com/time/world/article/0,8599,1883598,00.html)

Question

Was this abortion morally justified? Do you agree with Archbishop Sobrinho that a law that permits abortion is contrary to God's law? Are Brazil's one million abortions a year the moral equivalent of the Holocaust, the systematic extermination of approximately six million Jews by the Nazi regime and its collaborators during World War II?

where pregnancy results from rape or incest, or where the embryo or fetus has lethal abnormalities incompatible with life, abortion prior to viability should not be prohibited by law or by lack of public funding of abortions for low income women. On the other hand, this church supports legislation that prohibits abortions that are performed after the fetus is determined to be viable, except when the mother's life is threatened or when lethal abnormalities indicate the prospective newborn will die very soon. Beyond these situations, this church neither supports nor opposes laws prohibiting abortion.[19]

The General Assembly of the Presbyterian Church (USA) similarly declared in 1992 "the considered decision of a woman to terminate a pregnancy can be a morally acceptable, though certainly not the only or required, decision." Elsewhere the Presbyterian church teaches that "… it can be an act of faithfulness before God to intervene in the natural process of pregnancy and terminate it."[20]

Still another strong affirmation of abortion rights comes from the Episcopal Church, which in 1973 numbered among its members Justice Byron White (1917–2002)—the other dissenter in *Roe*, along with Rehnquist, a Lutheran (ELCA). In its 1994 "Statement on Childbirth and Abortion," the General Convention of the Episcopal Church declared:

We believe that legislation concerning abortions will not address the root of the problem. We therefore express our deep conviction that any proposed legislation on the part of national or state governments regarding abortions must take special care to see that the individual conscience is respected, and that the responsibility of individuals to reach informed decisions in this matter is acknowledged and honored as the position of this Church; and be it further

Resolved, That this 71st General Convention of the Episcopal Church express its

unequivocal opposition to any legislative, executive or judicial action on the part of local, state or national governments that abridges the right of a woman to reach an informed decision about the termination of pregnancy or that would limit the access of a woman to safe means of acting on her decision.[21]

Official church positions notwithstanding, abortion generally remains contentious throughout the religious communities. Conservative Christians, for example, vehemently oppose abortion, whereas liberal Christians are more permissive of it. Representative of the latter is the National Council of Churches, which counts 50 million Christians within its membership. In the words of General Secretary Bob Edgar: "Jesus never said one word about homosexuality, never said one word about civil marriage or abortion."[22] Similarly, Catholics for Free Choice, as well as Evangelicals for Free Choice, both agitate to relax their churches' opposition to abortion; and Concerned Clergy for Choice represents a network of more than 800 pro-choice interdenominational clergy. On the other hand, Presbyterians Pro-Life strive to reverse their church's liberal policies; while Culture for Life, a Catholic-oriented advocacy group in Washington, actively supports its church's absolute prohibitions of abortion and contraception.

In Judaism, similarly, competing views of personhood have led to different takes on abortion. According to one school of Jewish theology, the unborn is a person and, therefore, abortion is to be restricted to direct threats on the woman's life, in which case abortion is mandatory. However, another school of Jewish thought confers personhood at birth, and, consequently, permits abortion for psychiatric conditions, such as prepartum depression, and for fetal abnormality such as Tay-Sachs, an untreatable genetic disease with a high incidence among Eastern European Jews. Although no Jewish denomination permits indiscriminate abortion, two-thirds of Jewish abortions are done as a means of birth control.[23]

In general, the view of Protestant churches and normative Jewish and Muslim traditions hasn't changed since *Roe*. It is basically a progressive one, that circumstances, as defined by some objective criterion, can make an abortion decision morally responsible. Included is approximately 10 percent of Evangelicals who allow for abortion in the case of rape or incest.[24] Their relatively permissive position sets these denominations at odds with the conservative religious prohibition of all abortion, as powerfully advanced by Roman Catholicism and the Southern Baptist Convention.

CHOICE UNDER ATTACK

In recent years the pro-life movement has opened two fronts in its battle to reverse *Roe*: one moral, the other legal. On the moral front, pro-life proponents have made effective use of the phrase *culture of life* to refocus the abortion debate on the unborn's life as opposed to the woman's right to choose. On the legal front, it has successfully created the existence of the *fetal citizen*.

Culture of Life

The term *culture of life* is generally attributed to Pope John Paul II, who coined the phrase in the mid-1990s. At World Youth Day in 1994, the Pope stated: "The culture of life means respect for nature and protection of God's work of creation. In a special way it means respect for human life from the first moment of conception until its natural end."

For the Pope and social conservatives, *culture of life* stands in opposition to a *culture of death*. The latter term includes a number of bioethical practices viewed by the pro-life movement as destructive of human life, such as abortion, embryonic stem cell research, and physician-assisted suicide. For social and religious conservatives, "our present social context," to quote John Paul II again, is "marked by a dramatic struggle between the culture of life and the culture of death." As a result, in the Pope's words, "there is need to develop a deep critical sense capable of discerning true values and authentic needs."[25] Social conservatives, generally, are persuaded that it is

they, perhaps alone, who are "capable of discerning true values and authentic needs."[26]

More than a rhetorical flourish, *culture of life* calls attention to the nature of abortion decision and away from who should make the decision. With that, the debate shifts to "'what' instead of 'who'—[to] morality instead of autonomy...."[27] But the refocusing effect of the *culture of life* on the morality of abortion, as opposed to the autonomy of the woman, only works if the unborn has moral status. This has led anti-abortion activists in several states to promote constitutional amendments that would define life as beginning at conception, thereby effectively outlawing all abortions as well as birth control methods that prevent a fertilized egg from implanting in the uterus, such as the birth control pill or contraceptive sponge.

Typical of these constitutional tactics was the 2008 initiative sponsored by a group called Colorado for Equal Rights. Defeated by a margin of 73 percent to 27 percent the measure proposed to consider "any human being from the moment of fertilization as a *person* ... in those provisions of the Colorado Constitution relating to inalienable rights, equality of justice, and the process of law."[28] Similarly, in 2009 lawmakers in the North Dakota lower house voted 51 to 41 to pass the Personhood of Children Act, which confers the same basic rights on "all human beings from the beginning of their biological development, including the pre-born, partially born." In Montana, where legislators introduced more anti-abortion bills in 2009 than during any other session in the past twenty years, the focus in 2010 turned to a proposed constitutional amendment that would establish "personhood" from the moment of conception. At the federal level, anti-abortion groups continue to push for a federal Human Life Amendment that would define life as beginning at conception. In the latest of attempts that date back to the passage of *Roe*, the Sanctity of Human Life Act, from physician and Gideon ministry activist Paul Broun (R-GA), would define life as beginning with fertilization. If passed, the embryo would have "all the legal and constitutional attributes and privileges of personhood."

BIOETHICS ACROSS CULTURES

Mexico Legislates Personhood

Abortion is illegal for most purposes in every state in Mexico except for Mexico City, which legalized abortion in 2007 up to week 12 for any reason. Although abortion carries criminal penalties in the state of Guanajuato, the state's criminal code contains an exception in rape cases. In 2008 legislators from that state's National Action Party sought to change that by amending the state's constitution to declare that personhood extends from conception to natural birth. The amendment read: "With regard to this Constitution and the laws that emanate from it, a person is any human being from conception until natural death, and the State will guarantee to him the complete enjoyment and exercise of all of his rights." In an accompanying text, the legislators wrote:

> The right to life is an inviolable natural right inherent in all human beings, since it is the foundation of all other rights, and therefore should be respected, guaranteed, and protected by the state.... Medical science has demonstrated that in a fertilized ovum there is a new human life, because nothing happens during the period of gestation that modifies or complements its essence, ... from the point of view of ethics and law, societies should always protect the weakest members.

The legislators cited international treaties to which Mexico is a party, such as the Universal Declaration of Human Rights and the International Treaty on Civil and Political Rights, in support of the right to life. They also charged that pro-abortion opponents from the socialist Party of the Democratic Revolution (PRD) were half-hearted supporters of life, since they opposed capital punishment but favored abortion. Although the amendment does not yet have sufficient votes for passage, its supporters are seeking to convince members of other political parties to sign on.

(SOURCE: Matthew Cullinan Hoffman, "Mexican State Legislators Seek To Define Personhood as Being from Conception," *LifeSiteNews.com*, July 23, 2008. Retrieved April 25, 2009, from http://www.lifesitenews.com/ldn/2008/jul/08072311.html)

Question

Do you agree with the accompanying text of the proposed legislation? In your view, is the proposal good social policy? In the United States, many social conservatives who oppose abortion support capital punishment; and many social liberals who support abortion oppose capital punishment. Are both these factions being inconsistent in their own way, or aren't they?

Such efforts notwithstanding, the ontological status of the unborn continues to be contested, with no resolution in sight. So, while battling at the state level for constitutional amendments, pro-life activists have also waged a campaign to humanize the unborn without having to confront directly the contentious philosophical issue of its nature. If successful, that strategy would make the central question, again, not who should make the decision but what the decision should be.[29] In short, the more the unborn is humanized, the more the morality of abortion dominates the debate, and, with that, the more likely restrictions on abortion. Indeed, the anti-abortion movement already has had some success in humanizing the unborn by making them "citizens."

The Creation of the Fetal Citizen

Whereas in the 1980s and '90s pro-life activists typically defended *fetal persons*, today the more moderate elements tend to cast the issue in terms of *fetal citizens*. Thus, while some extremists continue to harass and threaten, sometimes even harm medical personnel and their patients, anti-abortion moderates work to establish the personhood of the unborn indirectly through administrative rules, laws, and judicial rulings. Ultimately, they hope "to elevate the status of the unborn by erecting a legislative and juridical framework that extends the state's already significant dominion over pregnant women." As sociologist/bioethicist Monica Casper and anthropologist Lynn Morgan further point out:

The campaign call[s] for persistent pressure on simultaneous fronts—a motion to appoint a fetal guardian here, a proposition to outlaw a medical procedure there, a move to rally sympathy for 'fetal victims of homicide' elsewhere.[30]

The pro-life movement has implemented these tactics in diverse ways.

Use of Orders, Rules, and Laws One of the significant victories won by pro-life activism is the Born-Alive Infant Protections Act (BAIPA) of 2002, which for the first time codified in federal law the personhood of any born-alive member of the human species. BAIPA prohibits a live-birth abortion on a fatally flawed fetus or one born so prematurely— say, prior to 22 weeks—that it has no chance of surviving long term. Killing a born-alive infant, in short, is considered murder.

Besides BAIPA, pro-life activism also won on the federal level during the Bush administration:

- a limitation on stem cell research funding to existing stem cell lines, in order to save embryos from destruction (2001);

- a regulation that permits states to define fetuses as "unborn children," under State Child Health Insurance Programs (2002);

- the addition of embryos to the list of "human subjects" whose welfare should be considered by the Health and Human Services Secretary's Advisory Committee on Human Research Protection (2002); and

- a 2008 HHS proposal to redefine abortion to include some forms of contraception and allow doctors and pharmacists to deny them to women as they see fit.

Beyond federal action, there has been a number of attempts at the state level to define, in effect, the unborn as a citizen and, thus, someone with rights. The most sensational, perhaps, occurred in 2003 when President Bush's brother, Governor Jeb Bush of Florida, tried to appoint a "fetal guardian" in the case of a mentally retarded woman who had

been rape-impregnated during her stay at a state-run group home, despite a state supreme court ruling that the governor's move was improper (*In Re: Guardianship of J.D.S.*).[31] Perhaps the most resourceful tactic of anti-abortionists is the grand jury by petition. Ordinarily, a prosecutor calls a grand jury to investigate official corruption. But in Kansas, pro-life tacticians have turned to an unusual state statute, adopted in 1887, that allows ordinary citizens who gather enough signatures on a petition to demand that a grand jury investigate an alleged crime, in this case second- and third-trimester abortions.[32] Not long before his 2009 assassination, abortion-provider Dr. George Tiller was a target of the tactic. Like this one, all of the other states' feticide laws are directed to third-party attackers, with the exception of Utah. In 2010 the Utah House and Senate passed a first-of-its-kind bill to make it a criminal homicide for a woman to induce a miscarriage or obtain an illegal abortion.

Collectively, federal and hundreds of state actions have nudged the abortion debate from ontology to citizenship, while chipping away at the sphere of freedom defined by *Roe*. As the issue shifts from the nature of the unborn to its treatment, it also moves from the biomedical to the juridical domain, where, as Casper and Morgan note: "Fetal citizens… can … be made by the state through executive committee appointments, regulatory changes, executive decrees, presidential vetoes and obscure budgetary line items."[33] Once decreed, fetal citizens, now *de facto* persons, would be entitled to the legal protections of any other citizen.

Consider, for example, the Unborn Victims of Violence Act (UVVA), popularly known as Laci and Conner's Law for a California woman and her presumptively viable fetus, whose remains washed up along the shore of San Francisco Bay in April 2003. (Husband and father Scott Peterson was convicted in the deaths.) Signed into law by President Bush in 2004, UVVA makes the death of a pregnant woman and her zygote, embryo, or fetus in the execution of a federal crime punishable as two separate criminal violations. Like the earlier UCPAA, UVVA states:

"... the term 'unborn child' means a child in utero, and the term 'child in utero' or 'child, who is in utero' means a member of the species homo sapiens, at any stage of development, who is carried in the womb."[34]

On the day President Bush signed UVVA into law, Cathy Cleaver Ruse, spokesperson for the US [Catholic] Bishops' Secretariat for Pro-Life Activities, praised him with the words:

"We applaud the President for bringing justice to women and their children who are victims of violent crime. Thanks to him, and to a bipartisan majority of Congress, a woman who loses her child to a brutal attacker in a federal jurisdiction will no longer be told that she has lost nothing."

While acknowledging that the new law exempts abortions, Ruse pointedly observed that "the abortion lobby fought it anyway because it commits the unpardonable pro-choice sin:... it recognizes that a child in utero is a human being."[35]

Use of Informed Consent   Another effective pro-life tactic involves personalizing the unborn to the prospective mother during the informed-consent process. For example, in the year following the enactment of UVVA, the South Dakota legislature passed one of the strictest informed-consent provisions for abortion in the United States. They include that the woman undergoing abortion be informed that "the abortion will terminate the life of a whole, separate, unique living human being." The 2005 law defines *human being* as an "individual living member of the species *homo sapiens*." Planned Parenthood successfully sued to block the law from taking effect, and the Eighth Circuit Court is currently reviewing the ruling. In 2009 the Missouri Senate passed a bill that would require a patient take two trips to the doctor to get "more information" before receiving an abortion. Mississippi, one of the most restrictive states in the country, also requires two trips to the clinic, spaced at least 24 hours apart.

Again, under the Unborn Child Pain Awareness Act (UCPAA), proposed in the Senate by Republican Sam Brownback of Kansas, any abortion provider would be required to inform a woman seeking an abortion at 20 weeks or later about possible fetal pain and obtain a signed form accepting or rejecting administration of pain-relieving drugs to the "unborn child," defined as: "a member of the species homo sapiens, at any stage of development, who is carried in the womb." In the 2006 bill in the House, Rep. Christopher H. Smith (R-NJ) said: "Is it our hope that this [bill] may dissuade a woman from allowing her child to be killed? Absolutely." Although the bill received a solid majority (60%) in the House, it fell short of the two-thirds vote required to limit debate. After the bill died, Wendy Wright of Concerned Women for America, an advocacy group for socially conservative causes, said:

Abortion not only kills a baby, it tortures them. Regrettably congressmen—many who denounced the use of torture against suspected terrorists—have voted to not let women know that abortion will torture their innocent unborn babies.[36]

The bill never became law.

Despite setbacks on the federal level, discussions with patients about fetal pain have been mandated in several states, including Minnesota in 2007.[37] Also in the same year, the South Carolina legislature debated a bill requiring women to review an ultrasound image of the fetus before terminating a pregnancy. Dr. Sandra M. Christiansen, medical director of a church-supported pregnancy center that has its own ultrasound machine, says, "The motivation is that man and woman are made in God's image, that life is precious."[38] According to the Heidi Group, a Christian evangelical nonprofit organization that advises such centers on fund-raising and administration, 90 percent of women considering abortion abandon the idea when counseling includes the use of the sonogram.[39] Nebraska overwhelmingly passed its own "Ultrasound Bill" in 2009, and then, in March of 2010, banned most abortions twenty weeks after

BIOETHICS ACROSS CULTURES

Abortion Around the World

Abortion is legal in many countries around the world, and it is estimated that more than 40 million abortions are performed worldwide annually, according to an October 2008 World Health Organization report. WHO also estimated that about 20 million unsafe abortions are performed every year. That's one unsafe abortion for every ten pregnancies and one unsafe abortion for every seven births. Although it's difficult to obtain reliable data on illegal and unsafe abortions, several well-known organizations and researchers, including WHO, Guttmacher Institute, and Family Health International, make the additional estimates:

- Ninety percent of unsafe abortions are in developing countries.
- One-third of all abortions worldwide are illegal.
- More than two-thirds of countries in the Southern Hemisphere have no access to safe, legal abortion.
- Anywhere from 70,000 to 200,000 women die worldwide from unsafe abortions each year. This means that between 13 and 20 percent of all maternal deaths are due to unsafe abortions—in some areas of the world, half of all maternal deaths. Of these deaths, 99 percent are in the developing world, and most are preventable.
- Half of all abortions take place outside the health care system.
- One-third of women seeking care for abortion complications are under the age of 20.

- About 40 percent of the world's population has access to legal abortion (almost all in Europe, the former Soviet Union, and North America), although laws often require the consent of parents, state committees, or physicians.
- Worldwide, 21 percent of women may obtain legal abortions for social or economic reasons.
- Sixteen percent of women have access to abortion only when a woman's health is at risk or in cases of rape, incest, or fetal defects.
- Five percent have access only in cases of rape, incest, or life endangerment.
- Eighteen percent have access only for life endangerment.

(SOURCE: Women's Health Book Collective, *Our Bodies Ourselves For the New Century*, Touchstone, 1998. Retrieved June 8, 2009, from www.feminist.com/resources/ourbodies/abortion.html; Kate Kelland, "Unsafe Abortions Kill 70,000 a Year, Harm Millions," *Reuters*, October 13, 2009. Retrieved October 13, 2009, from http://www.reuters.com/article/latest-Crisis/idUSLC332921)

Question

Were you aware of any of these statistics? If not, what factors do you think account for your unawareness? What conditions do you think make unsafe abortion a major cause of death and health complications for women of childbearing age? Would the state of abortion around the world support a feminist ethics perspective? What possible policies would you suggest as responses to abortion worldwide?

gestation on the theory that, by that stage in the pregnancy, the fetus can feel pain. The following month Okalahoma became, arguably, the most hostile state to women seeking to end a pregnancy, when its legislature voted overwhelmingly to override vetoes of two highly restrictive abortion measures. One makes it a law for women to undergo an ultrasound and listen to a detailed description of the fetus before having an abortion, with no exceptions for rape or incest victims. The second measure protects doctors from malpractice suits for deciding not to inform parents that a fetus has birth defects.

To abortion rights supporters, the aggregate effect of all the political activism, impassioned rhetoric, and carefully crafted legislation is, again, to redefine the legal status of a fertilized egg as a person and, thereby, increasingly limit, if not eliminate, a woman's right to abortion under *Roe* and descendant decisions. As Cynthia Gorney writes, defenders of *Roe* recognize that:

> In right-to-life ethical reasoning, a seven-weeks-pregnant abortion is as unacceptable as a thirty-weeks-pregnant abortion. Distinguishing between them, for someone who has fully absorbed the right-to-life view, is like distinguishing between the killing of two-year-olds and the killing of

eight-year-olds. "Live human being" is a yes-or-no proposition, according to this way of seeing things; the premise that there exists some in-between form of life (a not-quite human being, a being still under construction) is regarded as misguided, self-serving rationalization.[40]

To the most rabid anti-abortionists, the "misguided, self-serving rationalization" of abortion rights supporters apparently even functions to sponsor black genocide. The 2009 documentary *Maafa:21,* by white abortion foe Mark Crutcher, detects what it says are "connections among slavery, Nazi-style eugenics, birth control and abortion." The film is reportedly being screened by black organizations across the country.[41]

CONCLUSIONS

In 2003, the year of the first federal law restricting abortions since *Roe,* research published by Greg M. Shaw, a political scientist at Illinois Wesleyan University, showed that Americans' support for abortion rights in a general sense had remained at a slim 55 percent majority for the preceding decade. To Shaw this suggested that, despite considerable uproar on the issue, "people are pretty settled on their basic opinion on the question."

Shaw's study, which examined public opinion on abortion from the late 1980s to 2003, also found that opinion shifted dramatically in favor of or against abortion, depending on individual circumstances. When in the pregnancy an abortion was performed—in the first or second trimester, for example—or the woman's reasons for seeking an abortion could alter the public's opinion significantly. Asked about an amendment to the Constitution to prohibit abortion, an even stronger percentage of people expressed opposition. To Shaw, all of this indicated "that people are willing to tolerate other people doing things that are, in their view, morally wrong and are, therefore, willing to allow the practice to be legal." Such a "hands-off" idea, he added, gave abortion rights advocates hope for long-term success, despite the ban on so-called partial-birth abortions, subsequently upheld in *Carhart.*[42]

Tamping down that hope, however, is the palpable success of abortion opponents in building a new generation of activists. Having never known a time when abortion was not accessible and acceptable, a striking number of today's students and young adults seem determined to end that era, according to several polls. For example, Pew Research Center polls dating back to the late-1990s show 18- to 29-year consistently favoring strict limits on abortion, more than the general adult population. A 2007 Pew survey found that 22 percent of young adults supported a total ban on abortion, compared with 15 percent of their parents' generation. A 2003 Gallup survey found that 72 percent of teenagers called abortion morally wrong, while 32 percent believed it should be illegal in all circumstances. Among adults surveyed that year, only 17 percent backed a total ban.[43] Also heartening to pro-life supporters was a poll conducted in May 2009, which showed that, for the first time, more Americans consider themselves "pro-life" than "pro-choice," 49 percent to 43 percent. On the other hand, another poll conducted during the same period, showed Americans overwhelmingly oppose the overturn of *Roe,* 68 percent to 30 percent.[44] Add in the policy implications of an additional Pew survey. This one, reported in February 2010, found that the millennials are "slightly more supportive than their elders of government efforts to protect morality, as well as somewhat more comfortable with involvement in politics by churches and other houses of worship."[45]

This trend among young people may be suggesting that irresolvable disputes about the proper boundaries marking fetal personhood are, in the end, a superficial aspect of the abortion debate. Also, perhaps of little consequence today is the post-Enlightenment right-based ethic that drove the debate leading up to and immediately following *Roe*. Taking hold instead seems to be a perception of abortion as more morally complex than the simple and polarized arguments presented in the 1970s and 1980s that framed abortion as either murder or a woman's right to control her body.

Over twenty years ago, theologian Madonna Kolbenschlag (1936–2000) may have anticipated this direction when she suggested, as an alternative to the pro-life/pro-choice dichotomy, "an ethic that shows more respect for the symbiotic nature of very early uterine life by regarding a woman and her fetus as a single organism, with one informing consciousness—that of the woman." "The problem, as the American nun and feminist well knew, is that with our culture's tendency to objectify everything, we have little tolerance for such ambiguity." Nevertheless, according to Kolbenschlag:

> Neither a narrowly conceived pro-choice nor a pro-life agenda can provide an adequate standard for the future. Neither the imperial self nor the imperialism of dogma and sanction (law) can solve the abortion dilemma. A responsible new ethic must certainly take into account the primacy of personal conscience and of women's experience, as well as the effects and consequences of reproductive choices on the common good.

Kolbenschlag suggested an "ethic of cocreation" as a term for the new ethic she was suggesting.

> Such an ethic would assume that we exist as individuals only within larger life systems. These constitute concentric envelopes of responsibility. Our relationships to the earth, to our culture and to our families of origin are not intentional—we did not choose our planet, our civilization or our ancestry. But this absence of choice does not excuse us from taking responsibility for

all that these areas encompass. An ethic of cocreation would counterbalance our tendency to a rationalistic and individualistic bias. It would make us more open to exigency and to the unpredictable—to creation as surprise. It would also help us to regard death, imperfection and dissolution as normal phenomena in the continuum of life. At the same time, it must be based on the moral agency and autonomy of women, the primary guardians of life for the species. For too long we have had to make either-or choices about whether to regard the fetus as a person or a nonperson. Could we not assign, instead, a unique value to this nascent human life, without criminalizing and traumatizing those who, caught in overwhelming predicaments, choose not to carry it to term?[46]

An ethic of cocreation aside, even some cultural liberals admit that ignoring the increasing visibility of the fetus makes them appear insensitive, "a bit too pragmatic in a world where the desire to live more communitarian and 'life affirming' lives is palpable," in the words of Frances Kissling and Kate Michelman. Both women have strong pro-choice credentials, Kissling with Catholics for a Free Choice and Michelman with NARAL PCA. And yet, they recognize that if pro-choice values are to regain the moral high ground they must address the challenges of a society that's moving ever-deeper into the post *Roe* era. Commemorating the thirty-fifth anniversary of the monumental decision, the pro-choice activists wrote in 2008:

> Our vigorous defense of the right to choose needs to be accompanied by greater openness regarding the real conflict between life and choice, between rights and responsibility. It is time for a serious reassessment of how to think about abortion in a world that is radically changed from 1973.[47]

CASES AND CONTROVERSIES

Gonzales v. Carhart (2007)

On November 5, 2003, President Bush signed into law the Partial-Birth Abortion Ban Act. The law prohibits a form of late-term abortion it calls "partial-birth abortion" and that the medical community terms "intact dilation and extraction," or D&E. Under the law, "partial-birth abortion" is defined as:

> An abortion in which the person performing the abortion, deliberately and intentionally vaginally delivers a living fetus until, in the case of a head-first presentation, the entire fetal head is outside the body of the mother, or, in the case of breech presentation, any part of the fetal trunk past the navel is outside the body of the mother, for the purpose of performing an overt act that the person knows will kill the partially delivered living fetus; and performs the overt act, other than completion of delivery, that kills the partially delivered living fetus. (18 US Code 1531)

Since it was first coined in the mid-1990s, the term partial-birth abortion had been used in many states and federal bills and laws, including one in Nebraska. In 1998, Dr. Leroy Carhart, a Nebraska physician who performed abortions in a clinical setting brought a lawsuit in Federal District Court seeking a declaration that the Nebraska statute violated the Federal Constitution, and asking for an injunction forbidding its enforcement. A district court agreed with Carhart, as did an appeals court in 2000. (*Stenberg v. Carhart*) In part, the decisions that the prohibition was unconstitutional were based on the vagueness of the law's language defining "partial-birth abortion."

Not long after it became law in 2003, doctors like Carhart challenged the Partial-Birth Abortion Ban Act. Again, three different US district courts found the new law unconstitutional, citing in each case the law's omission of an exception for the health of the mother, as opposed to the exception for the mother's life. The decisions were upheld on appeal, and the US Supreme Court agreed to hear *Gonzales v. Carhart*. On April 18, 2007, the high court upheld federal Partial-Birth Abortion Ban Act in a 5-to-4 decision.

Carhart wasn't the first time the Supreme Court permitted states to restrict abortion. Fifteen years earlier (in *Planned Parenthood v. Casey*, 1992), the court said states could restrict abortions done for nonmedical reasons, even in the first trimester. As a result, many states have rules in place, such as requiring young, pregnant women to involve their parents or a judge in their abortion decisions. Some states also have introduced waiting periods between a first visit to an abortion clinic and the actual procedure.

Still, *Carhart* represents the first significant limitation on *Roe v. Wade*. Not until *Carhart* has a particular abortion procedure been banned, or abortion restricted by the nation's high court without an exception for the health of the mother. In effect, then, *Carhart* marks a departure from the core principle that has stood since *Roe*, namely, that abortion restrictions could not endanger the woman's health. In *Carhart*, the court ruled that the "State's interest in promoting respect for human life at all stages of pregnancy" could outweigh a woman's interest in protecting her own health.

Carhart also inserts the court between physician and patient, since the court held that in the face of "medical uncertainty" lawmakers could overrule a doctor's medical judgment. In other words, the court sanctioned placing medical decisions in the hands of politicians, not doctors. This largely explains why the American Congress of Obstetricians and Gynecologists called the ruling "shameful and incomprehensible," a view that some bioethicists publicly echoed.[48,49]

To other critics the *Carhart* ruling suggests the emergence of a "new paternalism" toward women, especially in the light of sentiments expressed in the majority opinion by Justice Anthony Kennedy, considered the swing vote in the split decision. Kennedy said that the ban was, in fact, good for women because it protected them against terminating their pregnancies by a method they might not fully understand in advance and would come to regret later. While conceding that "we find no reliable data" on whether late-term or any other abortion causes women emotional harm, Kennedy nevertheless said it was "self-evident" that some women might suffer "severe depression" or "loss of self esteem." Had these women been better informed, Kennedy suggested, they might have chosen not to abort and thus been spared the "grief more anguished and sorrow more profound" caused by discovering how their pregnancy had been terminated.

In a bitter dissent read from the bench, Justice Ruth Bader Ginsburg, at the time the court's sole female member, said the majority's opinion demeaned women and "cannot be understood as anything other than an effort to chip away a right declared again and

(Continued)

CASES AND CONTROVERSIES (CONTINUED)

again by this court, and with increasing comprehension of its centrality to women's lives." Even anti-abortionists gave the decision mixed reviews. Incrementalists—those who seek to reduce the total number of abortions—saluted the ruling, whereas absolutists read in it an implicit endorsement of other forms of abortion, which they want totally banned.

Questions for Analysis

1. Do you agree with the court's decisions in *Carhart*?

2. Is the "ability [of women] to realize their full potential … intimately connected to their ability to control their reproductive lives," as Justice Ginsburg argued?

3. Does *Carhart* deny women the right to make an autonomous choice, even at the expense of their safety?

4. In response to the statute, some abortion providers now give the fetus a lethal injection before all late-term abortions, since *Carhart* doesn't make it clear what exactly might subject a doctor to criminal and civil liability under the ban. The American Civil Liberties Union claims that this shows that *Carhart* is forcing doctors to treat patients based on politics and not on their best medical judgment.[50] Do you agree? What are the implications for bioethics?

5. Some of its critics say *Carhart* reflects a bias toward Catholic doctrine, given that the five justices who decided for the majority are Catholic. Do you think this is a fair characterization? (When Sonia Sotomayor joined the high court in 2009, she became its sixth nominally Catholic member, along with Anthony M. Kennedy, John G. Roberts, Antonin Scalia, Clarence Thomas, and Samuel A. Alito, Jr. When Elena Kagan joined the court in 2010, she became its third Jewish member, together with Stephen B. Breyer and Ginsburg.)

CASES AND CONTROVERSIES

The South Dakota Script

Planned Parenthood v. Casey (1992) established that states can require physicians to give pregnant women information that "a reasonable patient could consider material to the decision of whether or not to undergo the abortion." But in formulating those requirements, states are supposed to adhere to biologic or scientific language, as opposed to language that is essentially religious or philosophical and carrying an ideological message.

Under a proposed 2006 informed-consent law, referred to as "the script" by the media, physicians in South Dakota would have been required to tell any woman seeking an abortion that she is terminating the life of "a whole, separate, unique, living human being" with whom she has an "existing relationship," that her relationship "enjoys protection under the United States Constitution and under the laws of South Dakota," and that abortion terminates that relationship along with "her existing constitutional rights with regards to that relationship."(S.D. Codified Laws, § 34-23A-10.1, 2006). The law also required that doctors inform pregnant women of the following:

A description of all known medical risks of the procedure and statistically significant risk factors to which the pregnant woman would be subjected, including: depression and related distress; increased risk of suicide ideation and suicide. A statement setting forth an accurate rate of deaths due to abortions, including all deaths in which the abortion procedure was a substantial contributing factor; all other known medical risks to the physical health of the woman, including the risk of infection, hemorrhage, danger to subsequent pregnancies, and infertility; the probable gestational age of the unborn child at the time the abortion is to be performed, and a scientifically accurate statement describing the development of the unborn child at that age; and the statistically significant medical risks associated with carrying her child to term compared to undergoing an induced abortion.[51]

When Planned Parenthood Minnesota, North Dakota, South Dakota sued to prevent the law from taking effect, Judge Karen Schreier decided in their favor, only to be overruled on appeal in 2008. On rehearing the case, Judge Schreier made a seemingly Solomonic determination by upholding part of the law. Women, the judge ruled, must be told that abortion ends a human life, but not that they have an existing relationship with the fetus or that the procedure increases the likelihood of suicide. Also, in making the human being disclosure, the judge ruled that doctors must use the term in a biological sense, not a religious or ideological one.

Both sides claimed victory. Lawyers for Planned Parenthood applauded the part of the ruling that emphasized the physician obligation to provide biological and factual information, rather than religious or ideological. For their part, the intervening parties in the lawsuit said that the human being ruling was significant. "This is the unraveling of *Roe*," said Leslee Unruh, founder of a pregnancy-counseling center in Sioux Falls. "[The ruling] is a huge, fatal blow."[52]

Questions for Analysis

1. Zita Lazzarini of the University of Connecticut Health Center and Johns Hopkins Bloomberg School of Hygiene and Public Health wrote in the *New England Journal of Medicine* that SD script is merely using "the iteration of definitions to cloak religious, philosophical or metaphysical language in statutory garments and call[ing] it 'scientific' or 'biologic.'"[53] Do you agree with Lazzarini that the SD script, as it was proposed, in effect violated *Casey*?

2. Lazzarini also wrote: "By assuming that women are incapable of making decisions about abortion as competent adults in consultation with their physicians," laws such as the South Dakota statute "tend to reduce women to their reproductive capacity and suggest that they need the paternalistic protection of legislatures and society." Do you agree with Lazzarini?

3. Do you think that Judge Schreier did or did not meet Lazzarini's objections?

4. Explain why, in your opinion, the new consent requirements will help or hurt communication between physicians and patients.

5. Some commentators interpreted Kennedy's words in *Carhart* as an open invitation to state legislatures to amend abortion statutes to add informed-consent requirements. Do you think that the addition of such requirements, as in the SD script, generally helps, hurts, or has no effect on informed consent?

CASES AND CONTROVERSIES

Redefining Pregnancy

According to a 2001 Zogby Poll, 49 percent of Americans believe that human life begins at conception. Undoubtedly, many who hold this belief think that any action that destroys human life after conception is the termination of a pregnancy, and so would be included in their definition of the term "abortion." In 2008, the Department of Health and Human Services, at the urging of the Religious Right, proposed a public policy that reflected this polling data. Specifically, the "Definitions" section of the HHS proposal stated:

Abortion: An abortion is the termination of a pregnancy. There are two commonly held views on the question of when a pregnancy begins. Some consider a pregnancy to begin at conception (that is, the fertilization of the egg by the sperm), while others consider it to begin with implantation (when the embryo implants in the lining of the uterus).

Because the statutes that would be enforced through the proposed regulation, in part, sought to protect "individuals and institutions from suffering discrimination the basis of conscience," the HHS further proposed that "the conscience of the individual or institution should be paramount in determining what constitutes abortion within the bounds of reason." Therefore, inasmuch as "both definitions of pregnancy are reasonable and used within the scientific and medical community," the Department proposed to define abortion as

"any of the various procedures—including the prescription and administration of any

(Continued)

CASES AND CONTROVERSIES (CONTINUED)

drug or the performance of any procedure or any other action—that results in the termination of the life of a human being in utero between conception and natural birth, whether before or after implantation."[54]

Questions for Analysis

1. Under the HHS proposal, would there be any way for a woman to prove she's not pregnant? If not, what are the implications?

2. There is no scientific evidence that hormonal methods of birth control—for example, birth control pills, implants, injectables, "morning-after pill"—can prevent a fertilized egg from implanting in the womb. Would the HHS proposal, nevertheless, have the effect of including them under the classification of "abortifacients"?

3. Under HHS's proposal, anyone working for a federal clinic, or a health center that receives federal funding, apparently could prevent a woman from accessing most prescription birth control on grounds of conscientious objection to abortion. Explain by appeal to moral principle(s) why you favor or oppose such legislation.

4. Do you agree with the following criticism of the HHS proposal?

   … HHS proposes that anyone can enforce his or her own definition of abortion "within the bounds of reason." And, it would seem the bounds are pretty far flung. Most dangerously, perhaps, this new rule establishes a legal precedent that may eventually be used as a basis for banning the most popular forms of birth control along with what is, in fact, abortion.[55]

REFERENCES

1. Paul D. Simmons, "Religious Liberty and Abortion Policy: Casey as Catch-22," in *The Ethics of Abortion*, Robert M. Baird and Stuart E. Rosenbaum, eds., Amherst, NY: Prometheus Books, 2001, p. 146.

2. Phillip E. Hammond, David W. Machacek, and Eric Michael Mazur, *Religion on Trial: How the Supreme Court Trends Threaten Freedom of Conscience in America*, Walnut Creek, California: AltraMira Press, 2004. Quoted in Mark C. Modak-Truran, "Religion on Trial," *Law and Politics Book Review*, August 2005, pp. 626–631. Retrieved June 3, 2008, from http://www.bsos.umd.edu/gvpt/lpbr/subpages/reviews/hammond-machacek-mazur805.htm.

3. Hammond, Machacek, and Mazur, p. 152.

4. Hammond, Machack, and Mazur, p. 111.

5. Anthony Lewis, *Freedom for the Thought That We Hate: A Biography of the First Amendment*, New York: Basic Books, 2008.

6. Ibid., p. 148.

7. Joan C. Callahan, "The Fetus and Fundamental Rights," in *The Ethics of Abortion*, 3rd ed., Robert M. Baird and Stuart E. Rosenbaum, eds., Amherst, NY: 2001, p. 296.

8. Ronald M. Dworkin, *An Argument About Abortion, Euthanasia & Individual Freedom*, New York: Knopf Doubleday Publishing, 1993, p. 26.

9. Hammond, Machacek. and Mazur, p. 115.

10. Simmons, p. 148.

11. Emily Bazelon, "Is There a Post-Abortion Syndrome," *New York Times Magazine*, January 21, 2007, pp. 42, 44.

12. Stephanie Simon, "Absolutists Turn Against Other Foes of Abortion," *The New York Times*, June 6, 2007, p. A22.

13. Susan Gorney, "Gambling with Abortion," *Harper's Magazine*, November 2004. Retrieved April 25, 2008, from http://www.catholiccincinnati.org/tct/CT%20Anniversary/week7.html.

14. David J. Merkowitz, "In Essentials, Unity; In Non-Essentials, Liberty; In All Things, Charity," *The Catholic Telegraph*, 2006. Retrieved May 12, 2008, from www.catholiccincinnati.org/tct/CT%20Anniversary/week7.html.

15. Alan Wolfe, "Political Science 358: American Culture War," Spring 2008. Retrieved May 2, 2008, from www.bc.edu/centers/boisi/meta-elements/pdf/PO_358_Spring_2008.pdf.

16. W. A. Criswell, "The *Roe v. Wade* decision runs counter to the moral sense of the American people," *Christianity Today*, February 16, 1973. Retrieved May 1, 2008, from http://www.christianitytoday.com/ct/2003/januaryweb-only/1-20-32.0.html.

17. Austin Cline, "Abortion Rights, Privacy, Sexual Autonomy: Christian Right is Wrong on Abortion," *About.com: Agnosticism/Atheism*, 2008. Retrieved May 1, 2008, from atheism.about.com/od /abortioncontraception/p/PrivacyAutonomy.htm.

18. Neela Banerjee, "The Abortion-Rights Side Invokes God, Too," *The New York Times*, April 3, 2006, p. A12. Retrieved May 12, 2008, from http://www .nytimes.com/2006/04/03/us/03breakfast.html? _r=1&oref=slogin.

19. Evangelical Lutheran Church in America, "Social Statement on Abortion," August 28–September 4, 1991. Retrieved May 3, 2008, from http://www .elca.org/socialstatements/abortion/.

20. Presbyterians Pro-Life, "A Voice for Renewal in the Presbyterian Church (USA)," Retrieved May 8, 2008, from www.ppl.org/voiceren.html.

21. The Archives of the Episcopal Church, "The Acts of Convention," September 1994. Retrieved May 14, 2008, from www.episcopalarchives.org/cgi-bin/ acts_new/acts_resolution-complete.pl?resolution= 1994-A054.

22. "Religion Taking A Left Turn," *CBS Evening News*, July 10, 2006. Retrieved July 15, 2008, from www .cbsnews.com/stories/2006/07/09/eveningnews/ main1786860.shtml.

23. David Novak, "Be Fruitful and Multiply: Issues Related to Birth in Judaism," in *Celebration and Renewal: Rites in Judaism*, Rela M. Geffen, ed., Philadelphia: The Jewish Publication Society, 1993, pp. 16–19. Retrieved May 8, 2008 from http:// www.peopleforlife.org/novak.html.

24. Garry Wills, "Battling Abortion Isn't a Holy War," *Los Angeles Times*, November 4, 2007, p. M7.

25. Pope John Paul II, "Evangelium Vitae (The Gospel of Life)," *L'Osservatore Romano*, Weekly Edition in English, April 5, 1995. Retrieved April 17, 2008, from http://www.ewtn.com/library/ENCYC/ JP2EVANG.HTM.

26. Mary Leonard, "Bush Woos Catholics On Abortion Nominee, Echoes Pope's 'Culture Of Life' Phrase." *Boston Globe*, October 9, 2000. Retrieved April 25, 2008, from http://graphics.boston.com/news/ politics/campaign2000/news/Bush_woos_Catholics_ on_abortion+.shtml.

27. William Saletan, "Three Decades After Roe, a War We Can All Support," *The New York Times*, January 22, 2006, p. A17. Retrieved April 22, 2008, from http://www.nytimes.com/2006/01/22/opinion/ 22saletan.html.

28. Nicholas Riccardi, "Forces of Abortion Shift to States," *Los Angeles Times*, November 23, 2007, p. 27.

29. See note 27 above.

30. Monica Casper and Lynn Morgan. "Constructing Fetal Citizens," *Anthropology Newsletter*, December 2004, pp 17–18. Retrieved April 25, 2008, from http://www.aaanet.org/press/an/infocus/repro- rights/Casper.htm.

31. Lynn Morgan, "Life Begins When They Steal Your Bicycle: Cross-Cultural Practices of Personhood at the Beginnings and Ends of Life," *The Journal of Law Medicine & Ethics*, March 1, 2006, pp. 8–15.

32. Monica Davey, "Grass-Roots Grand Juries Become latest Abortion Battlefield," *The New York Times*, June 7, 2008, p. A1.

33. See note 30 above.

34. Morgan, p. 8.

35. Office of Media Relations, United States Council of Catholic Bishops, "Catholic Bishops' Official Ap- plauds President Bush for Signing the Unborn Vic- tims of Violence Act—'Laci and Conner's Law,'" April 1, 2004. Retrieved May 23, 2008, from http:// www.usccb.org/comm/archives/2004/04-063. shtml.

36. Noam N. Levey, "Antiabortion Measure Falls Short in House," *Los Angeles Times*, December 7, 2006, p. A23.

37. Stephanie Simon, "Abortion Foes Work to Expand Informed-Consent Laws," *Los Angeles Times*, April 12, 2007, p. A9.

38. Neela Banerjee, "Church Groups Turn to Sono- gram To Turn Women From Abortions," *The New York Times,* September 24, 2008. Retrieved October 15, 2008 from http://query.nytimes.com/gst/ fullpage.html.

39. See note 38 above.

40. Cynthia Gorney, "Gambling with Abortion: Why Both Sides Think They Have Everything To Lose," *Harper's Magazine*, November 2004, pp. 33–46. Retrieved April 27, 2004, from http://www. harpers.org/archive/2004/11/0080278.

41. Shaila Dewan, "To Court Blacks, Foes of Abortion Make Racial Case," *The New York Times*, February 26, 2010. Retrieved March 1, 2010, from http:// www.nytimes.com/2010/02/27/us/27race.html.

42. Greg M. Shaw, "The Polls-Trends: Abortion," *Public Opinion Quarterly*, Fall 2003, pp. 407–429.

43. Stephanie Simon, "The New Abortion Warriors," *Los Angeles Times*, January 22, 2008, p. A1.

44. "Abortion and Birth Control," *PollingReport.Com*, May 7–13, 2009. Retrieved June 8, 2000 from www.pollingreport.com/abortion.htm.

45. Quoted in Gail Collins, "The Wages of Rages," *The New York Times*, February 20, 2010, p. A15.

46. Madonna Kolbenschlag, "Abortion and Moral Consensus: Beyond Solomon's Choice," *The Christian Century*, February 20, 1985, pp. 179–183.

47. Frances Kissling and Kate Michelman, "Abortion's Battle of Messages," *Los Angeles Times*, January 22, 2008, p. A19.

48. George J. Annas, "The Supreme Court and Abortion Rights," *The New England Journal of Medicine*, May 24, 2007, pp. 2201–2207.

49. Alta Charo, "The Partial Death of Abortion Rights," *The New England Journal of Medicine,* May 24, 2007, pp. 2125–2128.

50. NA, "Frequently Asked Questions: U.S. Supreme Court Upholds Federal Ban on Abortion Methods," ACLU. Retrieved April 25, 2009, from www.aclu. org/reproductiverights/abortionbans/29845res20070523.html.

51. "Provisions of South Dakota's 2005 'Informed-Consent' Law for Abortion." Retrieved April 25, 2009, from http://content.nejm.org/content/vol359/issue21/images/large/01t1.jpeg.

52. NA, "Both Sides Claim Victory in Ruling Over South Dakota's Abortion Law," *The New York Times*, August 21, 2009, p. A20.

53. Zita Lazzarini, "South Dakota's Abortion Script—Threatening the Physician-Patient Relationship, *The New England Journal of Medicine*, November 20, 2008, pp. 2189–2191.

54. Christina Page, "HHS Moves To Define Contraception as Abortion," *The Huffington Post*, July 15, 2008. Retrieved April 24, 2009, from http://www.huffingtonpost.com/cristina-page/hhs-moves-to-define-contr_b_112887.html.

55. See note 54 above.

Chapter 11

The Assisted Reproduction Debate I: Principled Considerations

On July 25, 1978, British and American media descended on a hospital in Oldham, England, to investigate the rumor that a healthy baby girl named Louise Joy had been delivered by cesarean section to John and Lesley Brown, an English working-class couple. The rumor was true and reproductive medicine would never be the same.

TEST-TUBE BABIES

As recounted by bioethicist Albert Jonsen:

> After nine years of trying to become pregnant, Mrs. Brown was told that her fallopian tubes had been damaged by an earlier ectopic pregnancy and that she would not be able to conceive. They were referred to [obstetrician Dr. Patrick] Steptoe, who had consulted with [physiologist R.G.] Edwards. Ova were retrieved from Mrs. Brown by laparoscopy, fertilized with Mr. Brown's sperm in vitro, and reimplanted in Mrs. Brown. Mrs. Brown was the first patient to carry her implanted embryo to term.[1]

Infertility, the condition for which Mrs. Brown sought treatment, refers to the inability to conceive after one year of unprotected intercourse, if under 35 years of age, or six months if over 35. Also considered within infertility is the inability to sustain a normal pregnancy. Some commentators believe that infertility is a disease, whereas others object to that characterization because they believe *disease* implies that an inability to become pregnant is a pathological condition requiring medical intervention.[2] Either way, statistics show that infertility affects millions of individuals and couples, 90 percent of whom are treated with medications or surgeries. For the remainder, like Mrs. Brown, there are alternative treatments to assist reproduction.

Considered pioneering in its time, the fertility treatment Mrs. Brown underwent, in vitro fertilization, or IVF, is today responsible for more than 50,000 babies born annually in the United States, according to the American Society for Reproductive Medicine (ASRM). Worldwide, three million babies have been born using IVF or other reproductive technologies.[3] Initially, IVF offered little more than a 5 percent chance of pregnancy; today the rate is nearly 25 percent. Not only has the success rate of IVF improved, so have people's feelings about it.

In *Pandora's Baby* (2003), a book about the first test-tube babies, science writer Robin Marantz Henig describes how the artificial process by which Louise Brown was conceived initially met with protests, suspicion, and even disgust. Religious conservatives decried it as "a violation of God's plan."[4] Creating a baby outside the body was even viewed as threatening the very fabric of civilization. The harshest critics predicted that baby Louise and babies like her would turn out to be freaks—genetic defectives or chromosomally damaged beasts. This hasn't happened. Today Louise Brown is a perfectly normal adult with a naturally conceived toddler of her own, and the procedure, though expensive and intricate, is done routinely and often is covered by medical insurance. Nevertheless, those initial fears contributed to a ban on federal financing for IVF, driving its development into the private sector, where it has grown into a self-regulated $3 billion dollar industry.[5]

Thirty years ago bioethicist Leon Kass said that the new reproductive technologies would raise some of the most important questions that individuals, couples, and society could ask themselves: "questions about the responsibility of power over future generations; questions about awe, respect, humility; questions about the kind of society we will have ...."[6] Kass was right. As we'll see in this chapter, assisted reproductive technology, or ART, does indeed test our understanding of "embodiment, gender, love, lineage, identity, parenthood, and sexuality."[7]

ASSISTED REPRODUCTIVE TECHNOLOGY

Although various definitions of ART have been used, the Centers of Disease Control and Prevention (CDC) adopted the following one in 1992:

ART includes all fertility treatments in which both eggs and sperm are handled. In general, ART procedures involve surgically removing eggs from a woman's ovaries, combining them with sperm in the laboratory, and returning them to the woman's body or donating them to another woman. They do NOT include treatments in which only sperm are handled (i.e., intrauterine—or artificial—insemination) or procedures in which a woman takes medicine only to stimulate egg production without the intention of having eggs retrieved.[8]

The IVF procedure described in the CDC's definition accounts for almost all ART procedures, which have produced about 200,000 babies since 1981.[9] As with Mrs. Brown, in IVF multiple unfertilized eggs, termed ova or oocytes, are surgically removed from the ovary and, in a complex and delicate procedure, are mixed with sperm outside the body in a petri or glass dish (*in vitro* is Latin for "in glass"). The fertilized eggs—3- to 6-day-old microscopically small, relatively undifferentiated masses of cells or blastocysts—cannot develop into full human beings unless implanted into a uterus. They contain no nervous system, no heart, and no specialized human tissues.

Most clinics today allow embryos to grow in lab culture for at least three days after the eggs and sperm are mixed. Some even allow development for five days before transfer in order to decipher better which embryos are more likely to survive. The remainder must be disposed of, usually by freezing for later use, using for experimentation, or simply discarding. There are at least 400,000 embryos frozen in US clinics alone, but there may be as many as a half-million.[10]

I.V.F. procedures may use a woman's own eggs (called nondonor eggs), as with Mrs. Brown; or eggs from another woman (called donor eggs), first done in Long Beach, California, in 1984, just six years after the birth of Louise Brown. The sperm may be the husband's or partner's, or that of a donor. One of the fastest growing infertility treatments today, donor eggs are currently used in

12 percent of all IVF attempts.[11] In some cases, the pre-implantation embryo, or pre-embryo, is donated by a couple who produced extras during their own ART treatment. In 2008, British scientists reported using IVF to create embryos consisting of DNA from a man and two women. They believe that the technique could help to eradicate a whole class of hereditary diseases, including some forms of epilepsy.

Surrogacy

IVF sometimes plays a part in surrogacy, an infertility treatment in which a woman agrees to become pregnant for the purpose of gestating and giving birth to a child for others to raise. Depending on the arrangement, the surrogate may be the child's genetic mother or not. She agrees, usually in a pre-conception adoption contract and sometimes for pay (termed a commercial surrogacy), to carry the child for the commissioning party (or parties) and to give it to that individual or those individuals at birth.

There are two main types of surrogacy: complete and partial. In a complete (gestational) surrogacy, the commissioning couple undergoes IVF and the resulting pre-embryo is transferred to the surrogate, making the biological parents the rearing couple, and the surrogate the birth or gestational mother. In a partial (traditional) surrogacy, the surrogate agrees to be artificially impregnated by the "husband's" sperm and is, therefore, both the baby's biological and birth (gestational) mother, as distinguished from the child's rearing mother, the wife. In a variation, a donor egg may be fertilized in vitro by the husband, then implanted in another woman who carries the child to birth. In this case, the surrogate is the birth mother, the egg donor and the husband are the biological mother and father, and the husband and wife are the rearing parents. In still rarer situations, the surrogate mother is impregnated with donor sperm or donor embryo, in which cases there will be a rearing couple, biological parents, and a surrogate (birth) mother. If the surrogate (birth) mother is married, her husband also can be considered a father of the child.[12]

The Organization of Parents Through Surrogacy estimates that, in the United States, carriers have been responsible for the births of nearly 10,000 babies since 1976. The number is hard to pin down, however, since some people make carrier arrangements privately, especially in states where compensated surrogacy arrangements are illegal, such as in Michigan, Utah, and New York.[13]

Ethical Debates

In 2001 the New York State's Task Force on Life and the Law issued its analysis of reproductive technologies and recommendations for public policy to govern its use.[14] Identified in its *Executive Summary* of ARTs were the following three groups of commentators in the cultural discourse about infertility and its treatment:

Group 1. Some commentators oppose all uses of ARTs. Among their concerns is the fear that children created through ARTs will be viewed as commodities; that ARTs disrespect life; or that the availability of ARTs reinforces the view of women as primarily mothers and coerces all infertile women into attempting to become parents.

Group 2. Some commentators, on the other hand, believe that ARTs offer important benefits to infertile individuals and help alleviate the suffering that often accompanies infertility. They also say that scientific research and decisions about the use of ARTs should be left to the individuals involved, with the state playing a limited regulatory role. They say that procreative liberty, privacy, and autonomy matter most. Additionally, they argue that if, constitutionally, women have the right to have and rear children and if ARTs are the only way they can practice this right, then ARTs should be available and women should have access to them.

Group 3. Straddling 1 and 2, Group 3 commentators believe that individuals have a right to use ARTs but that other interests outweigh that right in certain circumstances. These commentators express particular concern about the impact of ARTs on children and third-party participants such as egg donors and surrogates. Many also question whether substantial resources should be spent on ARTs when existing children lack homes and many basic health care needs remain unmet. Although they aren't opposed to all ARTs, Group 3 commentators lean more toward Group 1 than toward Group 2.

The general positions of these three opinion groups can be sorted out according to whether they are based on principle or are empirical. Principle-based arguments for or against ARTs can be considered deontological in nature. On one hand, they may claim that moral worth is as much an intrinsic feature of assisted reproductive choice as of reproductive choice in general; and, therefore, infertile individuals generally should have access to ARTs. On the other hand, principle-based arguments may find something that is inherently objectionable about ARTs to suggest that they be prohibited or controlled. Empirical arguments for or against ARTs can be considered utilitarian because, on one hand, they find the value of ARTs in their worthy goals, ends, benefits, or consequences; or, on the other hand, they can find ARTs circumstantially objectionable.

The remainder of this chapter will consider four prominent principle-based arguments for or against ARTs: rights, respect for life, unity of marriage, and gender liberation and self-determination. The next chapter will take up the empirical arguments.

RIGHTS

Perhaps the most powerful, principle-based arguments in the ART debate are those that appeal to rights. Thus, supporters of wide access to ART—Group 2 commentators—argue from the right of procreative liberty; whereas those inalterably opposed to ART—Group 1 commentators—argue from the fetal right to life.

Procreative Liberty

In a 1986 essay for the *Southern California Law Review*, constitutional lawyer and bioethicist John A. Robertson coined the term "procreative liberty" for the widely acknowledged right to either have or

not have children.[15] Unlike some other societies (e.g., China), where individuals and couples are expected to procreate or not to beyond a limit, the United States imposes no such legal duties on its citizens. Americans may or may not have children. In this sense, procreative liberty can be viewed as a negative personal right, meaning that an individual "violates no moral duty in making a procreative choice and other persons have a duty not to interfere with that choice."[16] It would seem, then, as Robertson wrote, that "freedom to procreate noncoitally should also be recognized, since it may be the only way for the person to reproduce." By the same token, he argued,

> the use of sperm, egg, embryo, or uterus donors may also be necessary for the person to have or rear biological descendants. While the possibility of harms unique to IVF procreation should be explored, a plausible argument to extend procreative liberty to transactions involving the extracorporeal embryo can be made.[17]

Robertson's principle of procreative liberty is still read as incorporating two related bioethical principles: respect for privacy and autonomy, as they apply to making choices among the full array of reproductive technologies.

Life

As we saw in the previous chapter, religious and social conservatives say that the unborn is a human being from fertilization and, therefore, there is no such thing as "a right to abortion." The same logic plays out in their opposition to ART. For any view that associates full ontological status with fertilization, pre-embryos are human beings; and, therefore, ART inevitably raises concerns of fetal right to life.

Generally of acute concern to Group 1 commentators is the disposition of the multiple human beings that presumably exist as pre-embryos before implantation even occurs in the IVF process. For example, according to the *Instruction on the Respect for Human Life and Its Origin and on the Dignity of*

Procreation, issued in 1987 by the Vatican's Congregation for the Doctrine of the Faith, "Human embryos obtained *in vitro* are human beings and subjects with rights: Their dignity and right to life must be respected from the first moment of their existence."[18] The Vatican also includes freezing in its condemnation, because:

> [t]he *freezing of embryos*, even when carried out in order to preserve the life of an embryo—cryopreservation—constitutes an offense against the respect due to human beings by exposing them to grave risks of death or harm to their physical integrity and depriving them, at least temporarily, of maternal shelter and gestation, thus placing them in a situation in which further offenses and manipulation are possible.[19]

Although a principled argument from the right to life has broad religious support, it also has nonreligious appeal as an application of the widely accepted moral principle of equality. Again, on the assumption that pre-embryos are human beings, it is argued that it's as wrong to intentionally permit their loss or destruction as it would be with regard to any other human being. This leads some commentators, for example Robert George and Christopher Tollefsen, to oppose the production of spare IVF embryos and to propose that all pre-implantation embryos be transferred to a womb.[20] A growing number of Catholic theologians—William May, Germain Grisez, and Geoffrey Surtees among them—also support the adoption of prenatally frozen embryos as life saving.

To religious and social conservatives, the bulk of Group 1 commentators, the rights to life and equality have enormous appeal and serve to check the argument from reproductive liberty, exactly as fetal life does with choice in the abortion debate. To others, however, it merely recalls the whole ontological debate raised by abortion, notably the difference between *human life* and *person*. Thus, in 1987 the Ethics Committee of the American Fertility Society (ECAFS) responded to the Vatican's Instruction by noting:

> It remains fundamentally inconsistent to assign the status of human individual to the human zygote or early pre-embryo when compelling biologic evidence demonstrates that individuation, even in a primitive biologic sense, is not yet established…. The Committee notes that although the Instruction preliminarily addresses biologic evidence on early human development, these data ultimately are put aside in favor of a predetermined position (revelation) that is not persuasive.[21]

Philosophically and politically, the reason that the revelation-based position isn't "persuasive," according to ECAFS, harkens to that Jefferson-like compromise made at the birth of bioethics (see Chapter 3). Thus, while a public policy may coincide with religious teaching, religious teaching cannot be the basis of public policy. As ECAFS stated elsewhere, it is the woman's right to privacy that the Constitution protects as fundamental, including the right to autonomy in procreative decisions. Consequently, in ECAF's view: "[P]articular reproductive technologies can be banned only if they present compelling risks … imminent and substantial … that can only be satisfactorily met by outright prohibition." Acknowledging that the *Instruction* did cite risks to unity and stability of the family, ECAFS noted that the Vatican directive provided no evidence for such assertions, preferring to stand on theology, not science. As for freezing pre-embryos, ECAFS said, in utilitarian fashion, that "cryopreservation preserves life and avoids, in many instances, the hazards to mother and offspring of multiple pregnancy."[22]

It has also been pointed out—by the Italian bioethicist Maurizio Mori, for one—that if pre-embryos are accepted as persons, then the destruction of pre-embryos may rise to the level of genocide performed by nature, given their numbers that perish naturally. Writing in 1999, Mori noted the implicit irony: "We should therefore immediately invest the resources to rescue all naturally aborted early embryos in order to show that we take equality seriously." Mori realized that no serious analyst, including theologians, would think that ensuring the survival of those pre-embryos unable to live autonomously was a good way to modify nature. Indeed, it was this strong intuitive reaction that convinced Mori "how difficult it is to hold the thesis according to which the embryo is a person starting at the moment of conception."[23] For Mori and like minds, it is the disputable status of the pre-embryo that undermines its alleged right to life as a reason for opposing ARTs.

RESPECT FOR HUMAN LIFE

Some opposition to ARTs is based on respect for human life, as opposed to the belief that the pre-embryo has a right to life akin to a full human being. As early as 1979, for example, Leon Kass distinguished between what occurs spontaneously in natural reproduction from what doesn't, and asserted that only what occurs naturally in reproduction may be deliberately mimicked. Accordingly, IVF sometimes is permissible, despite the inevitable destruction of pre-embryos, because a like loss occurs routinely in natural reproduction. With the 1978 British breakthrough in reproductive medicine still fresh, Kass wrote at the time:

> In vitro fertilization and embryo transfer to treat infertility, as in the case of Mr. and Mrs. Brown, is perfectly compatible with a respect and reverence for human life, including potential human life. Moreover, no disrespect is intended or practiced by the mere fact that several eggs are removed to increase the chance of success. Assuming nothing further is done with the unimplanted embryos, there is nothing disrespectful going on. The demise of the unimplanted embryos would be analogous to the loss of numerous embryos wasted in the normal *in vivo* attempts to generate a child.[24]

As for the remaining embryos, Kass said they must not be transferred for adoption into another infertile woman; used for investigative purposes; be actively killed; or perpetuated *in vitro* ultimately, perhaps, into viable full-term babies (i.e., ectogenesis). All these options, he claimed, disrespect life by treating pre-embryos as "things or mere stuff."

Kass can be considered one of Group 3's more conservative commentators. He has held this highly restricted view of ART since the inception of modern bioethics in the early 1970s, when he framed the technology as an assertion of human will over human nature. Kass said that ART could only lead to "self-degradation and dehumanization."[25,26] His fear, which theologian Paul Ramsey publicly shared, was that once permitted, the logic of science, knowing no boundary, would be used to justify future extensions to later stages. Evoking the chilling images of the 1932 novel by the English writer Aldous Huxley (1884–1963), Kass predicted that, ultimately, human beings would be produced in *Brave New World* laboratories.[27,28] As he put it in a 1985 essay on the subject: "Once the genies let the babies into the bottle, it may be impossible to get them out again."[29] Thus, Kass condemned all ART with the exception of IVF to treat infertility in a case like the Browns. As head of the President's Council on Bioethics from 2002 to 2005, Kass, predictably, led the effort to stop human embryonic stem cell and cloning research.

Others, however, saw things differently from the outset. Philosopher Samuel Gorovitz read in the history of medical treatment and research a robust, collective capacity to exercise judgment and control. Besides, he pointed out, "[T]he likelihood of the subsequent exercise of judgment and restraint may largely depend on the principles that are used to justify first steps." Thus, in a rebuttal to Kass and Ramsey, also in 1985, Gorovitz wrote:

> If early-term abortion were justified by the principle that parents enjoy absolute dominion over their issue, the adoption of that principle would already have constituted a sanctioning of infanticide, and there would be no basis for stopping the slide down the slippery slope.[30]

By the same token, if the use of ARTs were justified by the principle that prenatal life is of no moral importance or that individuals enjoy absolute procreative liberty, there would be no basis for restraint on later-stage research and the fears of Kass, Ramsey, and others would be warranted. But that, said Gorovitz, just wasn't the case. The question was which ARTs were permissible, which were not.

Like Gorovitz, today's defenders of ART are quick to point out that history and deployment of biological research, in fact, do not support Kass's grim depiction, but rather a love and compassion for both new and existing life. It is true, they concede, that the question "When does life begin?" is not a meaningful question to most biologists, who by-and-large view life as a continuum. But, they say, this can't be equated with a disregard for prenatal life that ART will only foster. On the contrary, they point to evidence that suggests scientists view even human embryos donated for research in a special light and don't use them for trivial or scientifically worthless research.[31–33]

To his critics, then, Kass posed a conceptual slippery slope thirty years ago that continues to confuse reproductive debates. They say that respect for life can be practiced within a more liberal context of reproductive choice and access to ART than permitted by Kass' prohibition of most ARTs. Specifically, critics ask: If nondonor IVF, or implanting the pre-embryo of a couple seeking a child of their own, is acceptable, as with the Browns, why not donor IVF? Why not transferring a pre-embryo for adoption into another infertile woman? What is there exactly about nondonor IVF that respects life, whereas donor IVF does not?

It is at this point that the discourse often turns on another principle, one that appeals to the presumed nature of marriage, sex, and reproduction.

UNITY OF MARRIAGE, SEX, AND REPRODUCTION

Most religions cast marriage as a sacred institution created by God. From a cultural viewpoint, on the other hand, marriage is a contractually committed partnership between two individuals that includes various agreements, including sexual love, cohabitation, shared resources, and mutual childrearing. Both characterizations—the one sacred, the other secular—have been treated as principles to argue,

both against and for, reproductive choice that includes ARTs.

Religious Views

All three Abrahamic religions observe that, in Genesis, God created woman because "it is not good for man to be alone" (Gen. 2:18). This, they teach, makes marriage, in part, for companionship, love, and intimacy. Genesis also records God's command to "be fertile and multiply; fill the earth" (Gen. 1:28). This, the three faiths also teach, gives marriage a procreation purpose. Although the procreative function sometimes is associated more with Christianity than Judaism, Daniel B. Sinclair points out that halakhah, or Jewish law, starts with "procreative obligation," in contrast with reproductive autonomy. Sinclair, who is an authority on Jewish law and bioethics, says:

> Undoubtedly, one of the most important lessons to be learned from the halakhah is that reproduction, however it is carried out, is a serious and sacred task requiring the utmost responsibility and commitment. It constitutes the fulfillment of a religious commandment, whether biblical or rabbinic, and as such, is not a matter of choice, but of obligation.[34]

From the Judeo-Christian tradition, then, comes the teaching that God created marriage for a dual purpose: to join a man and woman in a physical and spiritual union and to share in his act of creation.

For the religious orthodox, this dual purpose of marriage generally is taken to mean that marital sex must be open to conception. In other words, while sexual union serves to strengthen a genuine, conjugal partnership, it must always be open to the generation of offspring, which is viewed as a gift of God—a privilege, not a right.

Another important aspect of the traditional religious teaching concerns the exclusivity of the marital relationship, which in the view of religious and social conservatives is threatened, possibly even sundered, by the introduction of ART.

BIOETHICS ACROSS CULTURES

Sunni and Shi' a Views of Reproductive Technology

"Sunni" and "Shi' a," the majority and minority branches of Islam, have been much in the news for the past ten years because of the US-led war in Iraq. Rarely if ever mentioned, however, is how the new reproductive technologies to overcome fertility have spread from the technology-producing nations of the world and are changing the understanding of how families can be made and marriages saved in the twenty nations of the Muslim Middle East.

Anthropologist Marcia C. Inhorn of the University of Michigan points out that throughout the greater Muslim world religion profoundly affects the practice of IVF in ways uncommon in Euro-America. In her own research in Egypt and Lebanon, for example, Inhorn has discovered that infertile Muslim couples have been extremely concerned about making their test-tube babies in the Islamically correct fashion. For many infertile couples this means seeking the "official" Islamic opinion on the practice of IVF in the form of a *fatwa*, or "a non-binding but authoritative religious proclamation made by an esteemed religious scholar."

With regard to IVF specifically, *fatwas* were issued thirty years ago in both Egypt and Saudi Arabia, the first two countries to open IVF centers, along with Jordan. Indeed, Egypt issued the first *fatwa* on medically assisted reproduction in 1980, two years after the birth of Louise Joy Brown, but a full six years before the opening of Egypt's first IVF center. Inhorn says that this official religious opinion has proven to be truly authoritative and enduring in all its main points for the Sunni Muslim world. That's significant because Sunni Islam embraces nearly 90 percent of the world's 1.3 billion Muslims, with the strictest form of Sunni Islam emanating from Saudi Arabia. As currently practiced in Sunni-majority Muslim countries such as Egypt, IVF is allowed, as long as it entails the union of ova from the wife with the sperm of her husband and the transfer of the resulting embryo(s) back to the uterus

of the same wife. The use of a third-party donor is not allowed, whether the person is providing sperm, eggs, or embryos. Furthermore, all forms of surrogacy are strictly forbidden. For Shi'ite Muslims—found in Iran and parts of Iraq, Lebanon, Bahrain, Saudi Arabia, Afghanistan, Pakistan, and India—third-party donors are permissible, thanks to a *fatwa* issued in the late 1990s by Ayatollah Ali Hossein Khamenei, successor to Iran's Ayatollah Khomeini (1902–1989). The Khamenei *fatwa* effectively permits donor technologies to be utilized so long as both the donor and the infertile parents adhere to Muslim codes regarding parenting. As a result of these unprecedented Iranian religious rulings favoring third-party gamete donation and surrogacy, infertile Shi'ite Muslim couples in Iran, as well as in Shi'ite-majority Lebanon and elsewhere throughout the Middle East, are beginning to receive donor gametes, as well as donating their gametes to other infertile couples. "Paradoxically," Inhorn writes, "the most conservative, male Shi'ite religious leaders in Iran have been the ones to adopt the most 'adventurous' attitudes toward third-party gamete donation. In doing so, they have offered reproductive fatwas with real potential to transform infertile gender relations in ways heretofore unanticipated in the Muslim world."

(SOURCE: Marcia C. Inhorn, "Religion and Reproductive Technologies: IVF and Gamete Donation in the Muslim World," *Anthropology News*, February 2005. Retrieved May 1, 2009, from www.aaanet.org/press/an/0502Inhorn.htm.)

Question

Do you think that Americans generally know about these developments in reproductive health in the Muslim world? Are these views consistent with the image of Islam that the news media project in reporting on the fast-moving political events and crises in the Middle East? Do they show that religion matters in understanding the social and cultural implications of the new reproductive technologies, which have spread around the globe?

Representative, again, are the words of the *Congregation for the Doctrine of the Faith*, which, quoting from Pope Paul VI's 1968 encyclical *Humanae Vitae (On the Regulation of Birth)*, expresses the official Catholic Church's teaching:

The Church's teaching on marriage and human procreation affirms "inseparable connection, willed by God and unable to be broken by man on his own initiative, between two meanings of the conjugal act: the unitive meaning and the procreative meaning. Indeed, by its intimate structure, the conjugal act, while most closely uniting husband and wife, capacitates them for the generation of new lives, according to the laws inscribed in the very being of man and of woman."[35]

This interdependence of marriage, sexual union, and openness to cocreation form a unity that confers value and meaning on each element. Therefore, according to the Vatican, if any of these three elements is disrupted, such as by separating procreation from marital sex, then so is that unity and the value that it confers.[36] According to Catholic doctrine, then, procreation may not morally be separated from marital sex.

Sometimes called the *inseparability principle*, this doctrine means that (1) reproduction must be the product of marital sex, and (2) any reproductive substitute for marital intercourse is immoral. Therefore, as stated in the *Instruction*, any procreation achieved from its separation from marital sex is "deprived of its proper perfection" and is, therefore, "not in conformity with the dignity of the person."

The inseparability principle effectively prohibits the use of all ARTs, because they invariably separate intercourse and conception, and, thus, are considered to go against the dignity of both human creation and conjugal union. (In theory it would permit their use in the very few cases where they might help the natural process but not replace it.) For the same reason, Catholic teaching would prohibit any form of artificial insemination, including from husband, because the semen used is obtained not from intercourse but usually masturbation, which, according to traditional Catholic teaching, is "an intrinsically and seriously disordered act."[37]

In contrast to the official Catholic opposition to ART, there exists a broad ecumenical and scientific consensus supporting both artificial insemination and IVF by husband (AIH and IVH). Many Christians, including Catholics, Protestant, and Anglican denominations, say that as long as infertility treatment isn't used to replace sex within marriage it's permissible.[38] As early as 1972, even an ethical committee of Catholic doctors accepted IVF in principle, while insisting that

once fertilized a person exists.[39] Moreover, some Catholic theologians consider the Vatican's position a misapplication of the inseparability principle.[40] Father Richard McCormick, for one, was a member of the Ethics Committee of the American Fertility Society that, in its 1987 response to the Vatican's *Instruction*, agreed that "the one conceived must be the fruit of his parents' love," but then wondered: "Why must that love inevitably mean sexual intercourse?"[41] Writing as a Jewish bioethicist, Sinclair has expressed a similar sentiment:

> ... where a married couple is desperate to have their own child and looks to assisted reproduction as the means for achieving this end, the act of reproduction becomes imbued with the same ingredient of marital love as that which suffuses the act of marital intercourse, and AIH should, therefore, be permitted.[42]

These religious moderates can invoke the Bible on the matter of assisted reproduction as confidently as conservatives do on the matters of marriage and lineage. Although the Bible attributes both barrenness and fertility to the will of God, that didn't always mean an infertile couple had no alternative but passively to accept and endure. In fact, by custom, a wife could give her maid to her husband and claim the child as her own. Ishmael (Gen. 20:17–18), Daniel (Gen. 30:2), and other biblical figures (Gen 33:4) are all the fruit of such arranged coital partial surrogacies.

Unlike the Catholic Church, which regards ART an unnatural intrusion into human reproduction, neither Jewish nor Islamic law has a comparable institutional, principled opposition to ART used in a marital context, according to Sinclair. Viewing ART, in theory, as no more "unnatural" than artificial limbs, both Judaism and Islam, minimally, permit IVF that involves a married couple whose sperm and eggs are used. Representative of this minimally permissive tradition in Jewish teaching is the following general statement from Steinberg's *Encyclopedia of Jewish Medical Ethics*:

> Judaism does not accept the view that nature is supreme and that technology ought not to be allowed to intervene in natural

processes. On the contrary, man is a partner with God and his role is to improve the world in all its aspects.[43]

Going further, Steinberg states that in the context of medical therapy, there is, in fact, a halakhic, or legal, obligation to develop new technologies in order to conquer all manner of physical disability, especially in an area in which the physical issue also affects the relationship between man and wife. In this way, ART doesn't replace sexual intimacy but extends it.

Some prominent rabbis have made a related point in challenging the Jewish prohibitionist characterization of IVF as strange or unnatural, as well as its hostility to the welfare of the offspring, whom it places outside the traditional family structure. Rabbi Avigdor Nebenzahl, for example, points to the human cost of denying IVF to a couple desperate to conceive their own child using the wife's eggs and womb. Such a course of action could lead to divorce, worries Nebenzahl, former chief rabbi of the Old City of Jerusalem.[44]

For its part, Islamic law permits artificial insemination, as long as it's the husband's semen and the marriage is intact. (See Bioethics Across Cultures, p. 214.) Although Islamic law prohibits the use of frozen semen used after a divorce or the husband's death, it allows freezing spare embryos so long as they are only used in subsequent cycles for the same couple, and the couple is still married.[10] Furthermore, although "the fate of the unused eggs has not yet been [officially] decided upon," obstetrician/gynecologist Dr. Hossam Fadel believes that eventually, under Islamic law, "it will be permissible to use them for medical research with the consent of the couple and within the appropriate guidelines."[45]

Secular Views

The principle-based argument from the unity of marriage, sex, and reproduction need not be religiously guided. For example, Kass made a similar argument, devoid of the theology, within his early, expressed reservations about ART. Thus, again in 1979, Kass wrote:

> Our separate embodiment prevents us as lovers from attaining that complete fusion of souls that we as lovers seek; but the complementarity of gender provides a bodily means for transcending separateness through the children born of sexual union. As the navel is our bodily mark of lineage, pointing back to our ancestors, so our genitals are the bodily mark of linkage, pointing ultimately forward to our descendants. Can these aspects of our being be fulfilled through the rationalized techniques of laboratory sexuality and fertilization? Does not the scientist-partner produce a triangle that somehow subverts the meaning of "two"? Even in the best of cases, do we not pay in coin of our humanity for electing to generate sexlessly? …[46]

Kass went on to condemn surrogacy for divorcing the act of conception from the act of intercourse and, thereby, denying the meaning of "the bond among sexuality, love, and procreation."[47] In the mid-1990s, Daniel Callahan similarly took aim at "anonymous sperm donations," which he said downgraded fatherhood and violated "a basic moral principle," that a man should be held responsible for the child he fathers.[48]

Kass and Callahan still attach great significance to ordinary coitus as the source of children. Although they have a lot of company in that conservative view, an equally well-represented progressive opposition wonders why this feature must define the unity of marriage and sex. Political scientist James Q. Wilson (The *Moral Sense*, 1993), for one, concedes that "marriage is about the union of a man and a woman for the purposes of having exclusive sex and procreating children" and that such an arrangement "has been the function of marriage in every culture as far as we have any cultural records."[49] Still, Wilson endorses ART. As he explained in 1999:

> If the child is born of a woman who is part of a two-parent family and both parents work hard to raise it properly, and if the child's life is not harmed by the fact that it was adopted, conceived artificially or in a petri dish, or even conceived with an egg or sperm from another person, we poor

mortals have done all that man and God might expect of us.[50]

Philosopher Bonnie Steinbock also has granted that siring children without rearing them can be irresponsible, but not in the context of sperm donation. As she wrote in a mid-1990s response to Callahan:

> … impregnating and abandoning a woman and one's biological child is not analogous to sperm donation. The sperm donor has not abandoned his child; he has provided some genetic material so that another man can be a rearing father, as real a father as possible. Why should we think that this is irresponsible? Even if we accept a prima facie obligation to take care of one's biological offspring, this responsibility can be transferred.[51]

But what about anonymous donations? Opinions again vary. In the past, donors were thought to confuse the issue by bringing a third party into the family, as Callahan suggested fifteen years ago. The trend today, however, is toward providing non-identifying information about the donor to the parents, who can then decide when the child should have it. Some even think it's a good idea for child and donor to meet at some point or even participate in the rearing.

GENDER LIBERATION AND SELF-DETERMINATION

Privacy, autonomy, reproductive rights, all coalesce in the largely feminist argument that associates ARTs with the principle of female liberation and self-determination, specifically the woman's right to decide for herself the circumstances under which she becomes a mother. The basic feminist contention is that, like men, women have (or should have) a right to use their bodies as they autonomously choose, reproductively speaking. Thus, if, (1) constitutionally, women have the right to have and rear children and if (2) ART is the only way they can practice that

right, then (3) as a principle of procreative equality, women should have access to ARTs. Some feminists argue, further, that a woman's right to control her reproductive function also extends to a choice to bear but not to rear a child, that is, to surrogacy.

Early on, however, the new reproductive technology troubled even feminists generally supportive of it. Among their concerns were questions about valid informed consent from both the subjects of the scientific studies that led to the development of IVF and, subsequently, from prospective mothers who might not be apprised of alternative social roles for women besides motherhood. But for so-called radical feminism, concerns went far beyond assurance of valid consent. To feminists like Mary O'Brien (*The Politics of Reproduction*, 1981) and Gena Corea (*The Mother Machine*, 1985), for example, ART represented not a victory for procreative freedom and autonomous choice but a defeat for gender liberation and self-determination. ARTs, they said, were yet another way that, historically, men had attempted to dominate women, this time by marginalizing their role in the birth process and controlling their reproductive functions. These feminists found surrogate motherhood especially obnoxious for turning women into breeding stock.

Today, feminists such as Janice Raymond, Andrea Dworkin, and Corea condemn reproductive technologies with all the vigor of the Vatican, ironically, one of the most patriarchal of institutions. What both the Church and radical feminism philosophically share in their opposition to implantation of contraceptives, IVF, and surrogacy is a hardy suspicion, if not condemnation of, the rationality of the Enlightenment. For the Vatican, the tradition of Enlightenment rationality has led to the autonomous self that recognizes no authority but itself.[52] For radical feminists, Enlightenment rationality represents the perpetuation of systematic abuses against women by men and the patriarchal structure of culture that men have created. Less radical, more mainstream feminists, on the other hand, typically measure the benefits of ARTs against the political effect on women as a whole, as did their counterparts in the 1980s, such as Ruth Hubbard and Marge Berer.[53–57]

BIOETHICS ACROSS CULTURES

ARTs and Women in India

In 2007 the Sama—Resource Group for Women and Health (RGWH), a New Delhi-based voluntary organization—released a study that showed ARTs have a negative impact on the lives of Indian women by further subjugating them in society and increasing pressure toward motherhood. Presented as boons to women, these procedures are, in fact, physically painful and emotionally stressful, the study found. What's more, the treatment, development, and proliferation of these technologies depend on India's social imperative to have a biologically related child. Women without children are blamed for their status, and ridiculed, abused and isolated socially, and often face desertion. Adoption is not seen as an option. The research also revealed an entire industry that cashes in on women's vulnerability and the social pressure to have a biological child at any cost. Thus, information provided on diagnosis, the process of "treatment," success rates, and side effects are distorted to portray these technologies positively. Media coverage of ARTs as medical breakthroughs—downplaying the associated risks and uncertainties—also adds to this picture, presenting a skewed reality. In an effort to offset the distorted and even glamorous depiction of ARTs, as well as their further commercialization, the Sama study recommended monitoring and supervising ART clinics, as well as formulating guidelines that "take cognizance of the unequal gender relationships, and ensure that the rights of women using these technologies are not compromised in any manner."

(SOURCE: Aarti Dahr, "Assisted Reproductive Technologies Counter-Productive to Women: Study," *The Hindu*, April 9, 2007. Retrieved April 28, 2009, from www.hindu.com/2007/04/09/stories/2007040901771300.htm.)

Question

Is there anything objectionable about glamorizing the reproductive industry or exploiting social mores in an attempt to market ARTs? Perform a Web search to see if US companies employ comparable tactics.

Despite still-divided opinion among feminists regarding rules governing the use of ARTs, there seems to be a substantial consensus about the values that should define ARTs. In 1990 professor of law Lori Andrews offered a statement akin to a bill of women's rights regarding ARTs:

- Infertility should be put into a larger social context to include not only physical barriers to fertility but also social ones to cover women whose children don't survive infancy.

- Women should have control of their bodies, including their gametes and conceptuses. Surrogates, for example, should be free to refuse any medical consultations or treatments and retain full decision-making control during pregnancy.

- Women should not be exploited, such as by being pressured into making arrangements for social or economic reasons.

- No prior screening for motherhood should be required.

- Women should be permitted to self-perform AI, which is part of the larger goal of non-medicalized childbirth.[58]

As ART continues to challenge our traditional understandings of motherhood, parenthood, and family, concerns have arisen about their social consequences. As we'll see in the next chapter, each side of the cultural discourse on ARTs feels that a strict communitarian analysis favors its perspective, as much as each is convinced that principles do.

CASES AND CONTROVERSIES

Dahl v. Angle: Who Owns Frozen Embryos?

In 2000, Drs. Darrell Angle and Laura Dahl—he an orthodontist, she a pediatrician—married and gave birth to a son. Four years later they decided to conceive again, this time by IVF treatment at the Oregon Health & Science University (OHSU). When the treatment failed, six spare embryos were frozen for indefinite preservation, and both parties signed an agreement naming Dahl as the default decision maker concerning the fate of the embryos, should the couple separate.

Soon afterward, the couple divorced and Dahl indicated that she wished to destroy the embryos because she "did not want anyone else to raise her child." She also feared that the child might one day contact his or her sibling, Dahl's naturally conceived son. Angle, on the other hand, urged the court to reconsider, and said he could not stand to let the small human lives he had fathered be destroyed. He suggested they be donated to another couple. "There's no pain greater than having participated in the demise of your own child," he told the court in vain. The embryos were to be destroyed, as Dahl desired.

Dr. Angle subsequently appealed the decision on grounds of "unfair distribution of property." He argued that his desire to preserve the embryos was more compelling than his wife's desire to avoid the birth of another child, biologically hers. Therefore, he claimed, the agreement they had signed should be considered null and ownership of the embryos should be assigned to him.

On October 8, 2008, the Oregon Court of Appeals denied Angle's appeal to keep the six frozen embryos alive, ordering them to be destroyed by thawing, as ordered by Dr. Dahl. The court unanimously agreed that Angle had no right to "impose a genetic parental relationship" on his ex-wife. While it avoided calling the embryos "property," the court did say that authority over the embryos constituted a matter of private property and the embryos' fate fell under the issue of "property rights."[59]

Questions for Analysis

1. What are the moral implications of considering frozen embryos "property"?

2. In *Dahl v. Angle* the court based its decision on several related state appellate court rulings, including Tennessee's *Davis v. Davis* (1992), which ruled that the interest of Junior Davis in not procreating outweighed the interests of his wife, Mary Sue Davis, in donating their embryos to another couple. Do you agree with the *Davis* ruling?

3. What status do you think the various ethical theories would give to frozen embryos—religious natural law, secular natural law, Kant's ethics, and utilitarianism, including preference utilitarianism?

4. Do you agree with the *Dahl* decision?

CASES AND CONTROVERSIES

What to Do with Frozen Embryos?

In 2005, after six heartbreaking years of trying to get pregnant, Gina Rathan and her husband, Cheddi, finally conceived a daughter through IVF. About a year later, when they conceived a second child naturally, the Rathans decided their family was complete. But their venture into the world of reproductive medicine was by no means over. In 2008, they received a bill from the infertility clinic for $750 for preservation of three frozen embryos left over from their IVF treatment. What to do?

"I don't see them as not being life yet," said Gina Rathan, 42, a pharmaceutical-sales representative. "I thought, 'How can I discard them when I have a beautiful child from that IVF cycle?'"[60]

The Rathans aren't alone in their dilemma. Many other former infertility patients also must wrestle with the fate of the cryopreserved several hundred thousand embryos in the United States. Couples with leftover frozen embryos—about half the people who undergo IVF procedures—have three choices: discard the embryos, donate them to research, or make them available to another couple for pregnancy. The default option is

(Continued)

CASES AND CONTROVERSIES (CONTINUED)

option is to leave the embryos in a vat of minus-310-degree liquid nitrogen, paying for the storage and deferring the decision. Thus, the Rathans' bill. Now, however, embryo-protection legislation could winnow the options of the Rathans and others like them.

Several states are considering proposals that would change the legal status of frozen embryos and possibly limit future infertility treatments. Georgia and West Virginia, for example, are considering legislation that would give "personhood" status to frozen embryos, and New Jersey legislators have moved to allow unused embryos to become "wards of the state." A bill in Indiana would make destruction of an abandoned human embryo a misdemeanor. In November 2008, Colorado voters soundly defeated an amendment to the state's constitution that would have effectively granted frozen embryos rights by defining a person to include "any human being from the moment of fertilization." A similar proposal on the federal level, HR 157, the Sanctity of Human Life Act, from Rep. Paul Broun (R-Ga), would define life as beginning with fertilization and, thus, grant stored embryos "all the legal and constitutional attributes and privileges of personhood."

Questions for Analysis

1. In your opinion, what is the icy clump of cells smaller than a grain of sand stored in a fertility clinic? What does your faith tradition teach?

2. Would you support the proposed legislation?

3. What would you do with stored embryos were they yours? Explain by reference to some moral principle(s).

4. According to the American Society for Reproductive Medicine's guidelines, a clinic can consider embryos abandoned and dispose of them if five years have passed without contact with the couple and if significant efforts have been made to reach the couple. Do you agree with this guideline?

5. Who do you think should determine the fate of frozen embryos?

CASES AND CONTROVERSIES

Love, Sex, and Marriage

In laying out the Catholic Church's teaching on surrogate motherhood, Joseph M. Incandela, Professor of Religious Studies at St. Mary's College, writes:

Is sex crucial for generating children? Or is it the case that as long as children come about from love, then parents are exercising proper stewardship over their offspring? The Church would answer "no" to this, for it holds that good intentions by themselves do not necessarily produce good actions. The Catholic tradition refuses to see human beings as moral mercenaries who purchase goodness by end results. But ... if the answer to that question is "yes" then love can be sexual love; love can be the willingness of a couple to go through the stress, expense, and physical hardship of an in vitro or GIFT procedure; or love can be found in a surrogacy arrangement in which a couple entrusts their hopes and dreams to another, who herself may well be responding to their plight out of an equally generous love.[61]

Questions for Analysis

1. Is it more the case that sex or love is crucial for generating children? Explain how your answer helps shape your view of ARTs.

2. Re-read "Early Induction in Ontario" (Bioethics Across Cultures, Chapter 9). Do you think that conservative Catholics would liken the moral rationale for this procedure to being "moral mercenaries who purchase goodness by end results"? How do you think Father Prieur might respond to this charge?

3. Some people compare surrogacy to adoption such that if adoption is morally acceptable, even praiseworthy, so is surrogacy. In what ways are adoption and surrogacy alike; in what ways are they different? Do you find the comparison morally compelling or not?

REFERENCES

1. Albert Jonsen, *The Birth of Bioethics*, New York: Oxford University Press, 1998, p. 305.
2. Department of Health, New York State, "Executive Summary of Assisted Reproductive Technologies: Analysis and Recommendations for Public Policy," *Executive Summary of the Task Force on Life and the Law*, October 2001. Retrieved April 25, 2008, from http://www.health.state.ny.us/nysdoh/taskfce/execsum.htm.
3. Peggy Ornstein, "In Vitro We Trust," *The New York Times Magazine*, July 20, 2008, p. 11.
4. See note 3 above.
5. See note 3 above.
6. Leon Kass, "The Meaning of Life—in the Laboratory," in *The Ethics of Reproductive Technology*, Kenneth D. Alpern, ed., New York: Oxford University Press, 1992, p. 107.
7. Ibid., p. 99.
8. Department of Health and Human Services, Centers for Disease Control and Prevention, "Assisted Reproductive Technology: Home," December 12, 2007. Retrieved April 22, 2008, from http://www.cdc.gov/ART/index.htm.
9. Tiffany Savickas and Kevin Myron, "PENN Study Emphasizes Need for National Guidelines for Assisted Reproductive Technology Programs," *Penn Medicine*, January 18, 2005. Retrieved May 27, 2010, from http://www.uphs.upenn.edu/news/News_Releases/jan05/ARTPguidelines_print.htm.
10. William Saletan, "Better Than Sex: The Growing Practice of Embryo Eugenics," *Slate*, September 16, 2006. Retrieved April 28, 2008, from http://www.slate.com/id/2149772/.
11. Peggy Ornstein, "Your Gamete, Myself," *The New York Times Magazine*, July 15, 2007, p. 36.
12. Hossam E. Fadel, "The Islamic Viewpoint on New Assisted Reproductive Technologies," *Fordham Urban Law Review*, November 1, 2002. Retrieved April 28, 2008, from http://www.encyclopedia.com/doc/1G1-97823700.html.
13. Baby Center Medical Advisory Board, "Gestational Carriers (Surrogacy)," *Baby Center*, September 2006. Retrieved April 25, 2008, from http://www.babycenter.com/0_gestational-carriers-surrogacy_4099.bc.
14. Department of Health, New York State, "Executive Summary of the Task Force on Life and the Law: Assisted Reproductive Technologies: Analysis and Recommendations for Public Policy," 1998, revised 2001. Retrieved June 9, 2009, from www.health.state.ny.us/nysdoh/taskfce/execsum.htm.
15. John A. Robertson, "Embryos, Families and Procreative Liberty: The Legal Structures of the New Reproduction," Southern California Law Review, July 1986, pp. 942–1041.
16. John A. Robertson, "Noncoital Reproduction and Procreative Liberty," in *The Ethics of Reproductive Technology* Kenneth D. Alpern, ed., New York: Oxford University Press, 1992, pp. 249–258.
17. Ibid., p. 250.
18. Vatican, Congregation for the Doctrine of Faith, "Instruction on Respect for Human Life in Its Origin and on the Dignity of Procreation," in *The Ethics of Reproductive Technology*, Kenneth D. Alpern, ed., New York: Oxford University Press, 1992, p. 87.
19. Ibid, p. 88.
20. Robert P. George and Christopher Tollefsen, *Embryo: A Defense of Human Life*, New York: Doubleday, 2008.
21. American Fertility Society Ethics Committee, "Ethical Considerations of the New Reproductive Technologies in the Light of Instruction on the Respect for Human Life in Its Origin and on the Dignity of Procreation, Supplement 1," *Fertility and Sterility*, February 1, 1988.
22. See note 21 above.
23. Maurizio Mori, "The Morality of Assisted Reproduction and Genetic Manipulation," *Cadernos de Saude Publica*, January 1999. Retrieved April 28, 2008, from www.scielo.br/scielo.php?script=sci_arttext&pid=S0102-.
24. Leon Kass, "The Meaning of Life—in the Laboratory," p. 103.
25. Leon Kass, "Babies by Means of In Vitro Fertilization: Unethical Experiments on the Unborn?" *The New England Journal of Medicine*, November 18, 1971, pp. 1174–1179.
26. Leon Kass, "The New Biology: What Price Relieving Man's Estate?" *Science*, November 1971, pp. 779–788.
27. Paul Ramsey, "Shall We 'Reproduce'?" *JAMA*, June 12, 1972, p. 1484.
28. Paul Ramsey, *Manufacturing Our Offspring: Weighing the Risks, The Hastings Center Report*, October 1978, pp. 7–9.
29. Kass, "The Meaning of Life—in the Laboratory," p. 108.

30. Samuel Gorovitz, "Progeny, Progress, and Primrose Paths," in *The Ethics of Reproductive Technology*, Kenneth D. Alpern, ed., New York: Oxford University Press, 1992, p. 119.

31. Anne McLaren, "A Scientist's View of the Ethics of Human Embryonic Stem Cell Research," *Cell Stem Cell*, June 7, 2007, pp. 23–26.

32. Gina Kolata, "Researcher Who Helped Start Stem Cell War May Now End It," *New York Times*, November 22, 2007, p. A1.

33. Martin Fackler, "Risk Taking Is in His Genes," *New York Times*, December 11, 2007, p. D1.

34. Daniel B. Sinclair, "Artificial Insemination Using the Husband's Sperm ("AIH"): Jewish and Catholic Positions," *Fordham Urban Law Journal*, November 1, 2002. Retrieved May 3, 2008, from http://goliath.ecnext.com/coms2/summary_0199-2476463_ITM.

35. Vatican, Congregation for the Doctrine of Faith, p. 91.

36. Kenneth Alpern, ed., "The Ethics of Reproductive Technology," New York: Oxford University Press, Inc., 2002, p. 41.

37. Pope Paul VI, *Persona Humana—Declaration on Certain Questions Concerning Sexual Ethics*, Sacred Congregation for the Doctrine of the Faith, December 29, 1975.

38. Joseph G. Schenker, "Assisted Reproductive Practice: Religious Perspectives," *Reproductive BioMedicine Online*, March 2005, pp. 310–319.

39. Guild of Catholic Doctors Ethical Committee, "In Vitro Fertilization," *Catholic Medical Quarterly*, May 1972, pp. 237–243.

40. Thomas A. Shannon and Lisa S. Cahill, *Religion and Artificial Reproduction*, New York: The Crossroad Publishing Company, 1988.

41. Richard A. McCormick, *The Critical Calling: Reflections on Moral Dilemmas Since Vatican II*, Washington: Georgetown University Press, 2006, p. 348.

42. See note 34 above.

43. Quoted in Sinclair.

44. See note 43 above.

45. See note 12 above.

46. See note 6 above.

47. See note 29 above.

48. Robert M. Veatch, "Can the Moral Commons Survive Autonomy? (includes commentaries) (In Search of the Good Society: The Work of Daniel Callahan)," *The Hastings Center*, November 1, 1996, p. 41.

49. "James Q. Wilson: The Power of His Written Word," *Los Angeles Times*, June 3, 2007, p. M11.

50. Leon Kass and James Q. Wilson, "The Ethics of Human Cloning," *The American Enterprise*, March 1999, p. 67.

51. Veatch, p. 46.

52. Richard John Neuhaus, *Catholic Matters: Confusion, Controversy, and the Splendor of Truth*, New York: Basic Books, 2006.

53. Rita Arditta et al., *Test-Tube Women*, Boston: Pandora Press, 1984.

54. Gena Corea et al., *Man-Made Women*, Bloomington, IN: Indiana University Press, 1987.

55. Boston Women's Health Book Collective, *Our Bodies, Ourselves: A New Edition for New Era*, New York: Touchstone, 2005.

56. Marge Berer, "Breeding Conspiracies: Feminism and the New Reproductive Technologies," *Trouble and Strife*, Summer 1986, pp. 29–35.

57. Peter Singer and Deane Wells, *The Reproductive Revolution*, New York: Oxford University Press, 1984.

58. Lori B. Andrews, "Feminist Perspectives on Reproductive Technologies," from *A Forum on Reproductive Laws for the 1990s*, circa 1990. Retrieved April 18, 2008, from http://www.barnard.columbia.edu/bcrw/archive/sexualhealth.htm.

59. Kathleen Gilbert, "Oregon Court Orders Frozen Embryos Destroyed, Considered 'Property Rights' Issue," *LifeSiteNews.com*, October 10, 2008. Retrieved April 29, 2009, from http://www.lifesitenews.com/ldn/2008/oct/08101008.html.

60. Shari Roan, "Infertility Patients Caught in the Legal, Moral, and Scientific Debate," *Los Angeles Times*, October 6, 2008. Retrieved April 29, 2009, from http://seattletimes.nwsource.com/html/nation-world/2008257408_embryos12.html.

61. Joseph M. Incandela, "The Catholic Church and Surrogate Motherhood," *The American Surrogacy Center*, May 1998. Retrieved May 1, 2009, from http://www.surrogacy.com/religion/catholic.html.

Chapter 12

The Assisted Reproduction Debate II: Empirical Considerations

The empirical arguments about assisted reproduction generally relate to their near and long-term impact on how we view reproduction, lineage, and the meaning of family. Another concern involves the well-being of offspring. Driving opinions in all these areas are strong feelings about the commerce of reproduction.

THE COMMERCE OF REPRODUCTION

More than 5,000 babies are born annually from donor eggs alone, according to the CDC. Actual egg donation, however, is thought to be much higher because the success rate is fairly low.[1] Given the current average cost of well over $50,000 for producing a baby through ART, the baby business is big business.

Already three billion dollars a year is spent on the commerce of conception, according to Harvard Family Professor Debora Spar. Although the American Society for Reproductive Medicine (ASRM) considers compensation to egg donors for expenses of $5,000 or more to require justification, and sums exceeding $10,000 inappropriate, ads in the student newspapers of prestigious colleges offer to pay young women with the right physical and mental assets as much as $25,000 for their eggs. A 2007 survey found the national average compensation for high-quality sperm was $4,217.[2]

Statistics like these are fodder to Group 1 critics of ART (see Chapter 11), who view reproduction as a sphere of intimately personal decision into which economic motives should not intrude. They claim that when the "stuff of life" is bought and sold like any other object of commerce governed by laws of supply and demand, then children become commodities bred by technology for certain traits.[3]

Few commentators would dispute that using embryos strictly for commerce disrespects human life. But plenty are quick to point out that not every ART arrangement is commercial. Many women generously and compassionately give their eggs, and men their sperm, with no more expectation of compensation than a blood or organ donor. But even where money is exchanged, should that matter? Group 2 commentators (see Chapter 11), in particular, observe that money is routinely exchanged for a variety of services without those services being "commodified," in law and medicine most notably. Moreover, as libertarian economist Donald J. Bordeaux points out, individuals and couples frequently family plan and consider economic costs in making family decisions, and yet we don't say that this cheapens and objectifies reproduction. Isn't a commercial ART arrangement an extension of family planning and economic assessment?[4]

Even if a commercial ART arrangement isn't of itself objectionable, opponents insist that there's always the possibility that it may impair the judgment of the donor about physical and psychological risks of egg extraction, a procedure that is both time consuming and uncomfortable and whose physical and psychological effects on the donor haven't been thoroughly studied. Does egg extraction jeopardize a donor's fertility? What are the possible psychological effects on a donor should she later find that she's unable to conceive? Where the donor is driven by money, say skeptics like the Hastings Center's Josephine Johnson, these questions might never be raised, thereby putting informed consent in doubt. "We hear about egg donors being paid enormous amounts of money," says Johnson. "How much is that person actually giving informed consent about the medical procedure and really listening and thinking as it's being described and its risks are explained?" Johnson feels that the real issue in whether the money can cloud the donor's judgment.

Must extending technological frameworks to personal relationships necessarily cheapen or destroy them? No, say their defenders, not any more than economic frameworks do. They point to online dating, which has been around now for about fifteen years and has grown into a half-billion dollar industry with twenty-one million subscribers, according to *Business Week*.[5] A Harris survey reports that matchmaking was responsible for 2% of the marriages in America in 2007—that's nearly

120 weddings a day.[6] This leads ART defenders to ask: Is using the Internet to bring adults together inherently unsavory? Is online matchmaking somehow degrading in a way that meeting someone at a church social, health club, or museum is not? Does making a member of a dating service submit to a personality inventory sully love and romance, degrade the participants, and pollute any subsequent relationship?

QUESTIONS OF LINEAGE

Whatever one thinks of ART and its commercialization, there's no doubt that it has staggering social implications. As Wendy McElroy says:

> A single infant can have more than two parents, all of whom might die of old age before he or she begins to teethe. If recent experiments on mice are an indication, a woman could abort a female fetus and, using its ovaries and eggs, later give birth to her own grandchild. Instead of having children during their peak career years, women could wait until retirement to raise a family. Women could reset their biological clocks at will.[7]

Opportunities for biological parenthood for single couples, same-sex couples, infertile individuals, and even the deceased thrill many people. But others fear that ART inevitably threatens clarity of lineage by introducing third parties into the transmission of life. They cite cases like the following:

- In the early 1990s a Virginia fertility doctor was found to have fathered as many as seventy-five children by inseminating patients with his own sperm.[8]

- In 1999 a white woman gave birth to one black and one white boy after an IVF mix-up at a New York clinic. The woman returned the black child to his biological parents when they sued for custody. Six years earlier, in Holland, another white woman gave birth to dark-skinned twins. DNA tests showed the

BIOETHICS ACROSS CULTURES

Wombs for Rent in India

In France, Australia, Spain, and China, commercial surrogacy is banned; in Italy almost every form of assisted reproduction is illegal; and in the US laws are highly ambivalent on the use of reproductive technology. Add to this murky world picture the cost—as much as $80,000 for a US surrogacy—and it's little wonder that couples from rich countries in the West are paying local women in developing countries for the use of their bodies.

In India, where tens of thousands a year die as a result of pregnancy and childbirth, surrogacy is estimated to be nearly a half-billion-dollar-a-year business. The reasons for the surrogacy boom in India are many, but most foreigners like the low costs, roughly $12,000, including the cost of foreign stay and travel. Other factors that make surrogacy in India attractive are high-quality health care and the availability of English-speaking physicians. Choosing surrogacy through a third-party clinic in India also gives couples a "guarantee" that the surrogate is taking every precaution with the pregnancy. Only women between the ages of 18 and 45 who already have children act as surrogates. They are housed in dormitories, carefully monitored, and given constant medical attention, including counseling. To avoid possible conflicts, surrogates usually must sign contracts agreeing to give up the baby after the birth. Parents must provide medical expenses and need only be present at the time of in vitro fertilization and at the time of the birth. Most babies leave their surrogate mothers within one to two days after birth.

While images of poor, pregnant Indian women lying in rows or lined up for exams may strike some as "outsourcing pushed to a nightmarish extreme," to its defenders, these reproductive practices are just another example of the many legal and economic factors that have led Western businesses to send some of their operations to countries such as India in recent years. They say that if some Indian women choose to rent their wombs, isn't it their body? Former health minister S.K. Nana calls the arrangement a "win-win."

"It's a completely capitalistic enterprise. There is nothing unethical about it. If you launched it somewhere like West Bengal or Assam [both poverty-stricken states] you'd have a lot of takers."

One Indian woman earning up to $5000 for surrogacy services, or about ten years of her normal income, agrees. "From the money I earn as a surrogate mother, I can buy a house," says Nandani Patel, via a translator. "It's not possible for my husband to earn more as he's not educated and only earns $50 a month." From another woman comes a more noble reason for her surrogacy: "Beyond the money," she says, "there is the reward of bringing happiness to a childless couple in the United States."

(SOURCE: Yoo Jin Jung, "Outsourcing Pregnancy? *The Illinois Business Law Journal*, February 6, 2008. Retrieved from http://iblsjournal.typepad.com/illinois_business_law_soc/2008/02/outsourcing-pre.html; Judith Warner, "Outsourced Wombs," *The New York Times*, January 3, 2008. Retrieved May 2, 2009, from http://warner.blogs.nytimes.com/2008/01/03/outsourced-wombs; Henry Chu, Wombs for Rent, Cheap, *Los Angeles Times*, April 16, 2009. Retrieved May 2, 2009, from http://www.truthout.org/article/wombs-rent-cheap.)

Question

What are the moral issues involved in outsourcing surrogacy? Is it just another capitalistic practice? Compare and contrast the views of preference utilitarianism and feminism on commercial surrogacy in countries like India.

---

hospital had mistakenly mixed sperm from her husband with that of a black man. In this case the woman kept the twins, as did a white couple in England after a similar mix-up at an IVF clinic in 2002.

- In 2006 a grandmother in California carried out a pregnancy for her own daughter. That feat, in fact, was accomplished fifteen years earlier by Arlette Schweitzer, a 42-year-old school librarian in South Dakota, who in 1991 became the first woman in the United States to give birth to her own grandchildren when she bore the twins of her daughter (who was born without a uterus) after IVF. Schweitzer used the eggs of her daughter and sperm of her daughter's husband.

- Also in 2006, Carmela Bousada, a 67-year-old Spanish woman, became the world's oldest new mother when she gave birth to twins. The woman, who became pregnant after deceiving California fertility specialists about her age (she said she was 55), receiving IVF treatment and giving birth for the first time, was a year older than a Romanian woman who had a baby girl in 2005 at the age of sixty-six. The woman had been pregnant with twins, but one was stillborn.[9,10]

■ In 2009 an Ohio woman agreed to carry to term and turn over to his biological parents a baby boy, after learning that the fertility clinic had transferred the wrong embryo to her womb. In Michigan a gestational carrier got a court order to retrieve the twins she bore after learning that the contracting mother was being treated for mental illness.

Critics of ARTs say that by introducing confusion of lineage, practices like IVF, embryo transfer and adoption, and especially surrogate pregnancy threaten the integrity and welfare of the offspring, family, and society just as incest and adultery do. Beyond this, they charge that ART threatens other matters of lineage and marriage, including duties of parents and children, rules governing blood relations and inheritance, and the child's putative right to know the identity of his or her mother and father. Then there are the problems suggested by a Pennsylvania case in which a child was granted three legal parents.[11]

"If more children are granted three legal parents," asks Elizabeth Marquardt of the Institute for American Values and author of *My Daddy's Name Is Donor* (2007), "what is our rationale for denying these families the rights and protections of marriage?" Indeed, if we allow three legal parents, why not even more? Marquardt is among those commentators with a warning for America: "[G]et ready for the group-marriage debate." (See end-of-chapter case *Jacob v. Shultz-Jacob*.)

Religious Considerations

Certainly for those with conservative religious beliefs, ART can pose problems related to clarity of lineage. There is, for example, in orthodox Judaism a minority prohibitionist view of any departure from natural procreation as fundamentally objectionable because it turns the act of marital love into a "mechanical act" bereft of human qualities, thereby causing lineage confusion and harming the traditional family structure. Egg donation and surrogacy can also flout Jewish law that associates Jewish identity with birth to a Jewish mother.

Issues of lineage and marriage also trouble traditional Islamic law, specifically with respect to donor IVF. The Qur'an states: "Then has He established relationships of lineage and marriage...."[12] The use of donor sperm, eggs, or embryos results in the biological father or mother being different from the "married couple." This confusion of lineage is similar to adultery in Islamic law. Also, unclear lineage can ultimately result in incest, the strictest guidelines notwithstanding.

At the same time, though, the Bible is, itself, ambiguous on the most controversial ART of all: surrogacy. For example, when Sarah can't bear him an heir, she tells her husband Abraham: "Consort with my maid; perhaps I shall be built up through her." In other words, following custom, Abraham is to produce an heir with another woman, in this case the Egyptian maidservant Hagar, and he and Sarah shall adopt the child as their own. True, the Sarah/Hagar relationship didn't succeed. In a rage, adoptive mother Sarah drove off biological mother Hagar and her child, Ishmael. Still, an angel of God who promised that Ishmael would father a nation rescued the outcasts.

What to make of this biblical tale? Such arrangements of partial surrogacy evidently weren't unusual or considered adulterous in biblical times. Nor were they viewed as inevitably effecting confusions of lineage. Granted, they sometimes didn't pan out. Strong maternal instincts, pride, jealousy, all rear up to doom the Sarah/Hagar/Ishmael relationship. In this, theirs can be read as a cautionary tale of the problematic nature of such arrangements. Still, by one interpretation, "From the Torah's perspective, which is to say, from God's, there is no guilty party in the story of Sarah and Hagar."[13]

For defenders of ART, then, including many religious liberals, the Bible can be read as holding a rather modern, nuanced view of surrogates: as women looking after the baby for the parents, rather than giving up the baby. It can be interpreted as implying the need for such arrangements not only for infertility brought by age, but infertility in the presence of medical conditions such as hysterectomy after cancer, repeated miscarriage, or any health condition that would make carrying a child dangerous. Indeed, say their defenders, ARTs make fertility possible without what makes adultery immoral: sexual intercourse.

Legal Considerations

Modern law further strengthens the case for ART. Although it generally shows comparable concern for the biological mother and father, contemporary law also makes a place for fresh understandings of parenthood and relational complexities introduced by the new ART.

New York, as one example, requires informed consent for all gamete retrieval and requires gamete banks to limit the number of times gametes from a particular donor can be used to establish pregnancy. Also, non identifying medical and genetic information about the donor must be kept and made available to the child when she or he reaches the age of majority or earlier, with consent of the child's parents. Donors may also consent to releasing identifying information about themselves to any resulting children. Before selecting gametes or embryos, recipients are told whether the donor has agreed to be identified to any resulting children.

Beyond this, like many states, New York addresses the complexities of assisted reproductive parenthood. When a married woman undergoes any artificial insemination by donor (AID) procedure, for example, her husband is considered the legal father of any resulting child, provided he has so consented and the procedure was performed by a licensed physician. Men who donate semen and women who donate eggs to gamete banks relinquish their parental rights and responsibilities at the time of donation, not to be overridden by future circumstances, including the marital status of the woman who ultimately uses the semen.

As for gestational surrogacy arrangements, rights and responsibilities reflect both the genetic and gestational contributions of motherhood. Thus, if both genetic and birth mother agree, the genetic mother is recognized as the child's sole legal mother. If both assert parental rights, each has standing as a biological parent to seek custody and other rights, as would be the case in disputes between, say, divorcing parents. And, as in such cases, the best interests of the child are used to determine a resolution. Thus, one biological mother is ordinarily awarded custody, the other maternal rights. Where problems do arise, it's often because of laws regarding gay unions or marriage.[14] But even there, courts have ruled basically as they do in divorce cases, for example awarding joint custody of children when a couple separates.[15–17]

Perhaps marriage and family law is broad-shouldered enough to bear the relational complexities brought by ARTs. But the fact remains, say critics, surrogacy is largely unregulated. Indeed, it is fertility doctors who mainly control third-party reproduction arrangements, and when postnatal disputes arise outcomes vary according to state. California law, for example, upholds the validity of surrogacy contracts whereas Michigan views surrogacy as contrary to public policy and surrogacy agreements unenforceable. Practically, this means that Californians who hire surrogates are far more likely to keep the babies if disputes arise than their Michigan counterparts.[18] To critics, the lax regulatory atmosphere and unsettled law governing the new reproductive technologies suggest that the child's best interests are best served within the traditional family, not in the nontraditional ones that ARTs make possible.

THE MEANING OF FAMILY AND THE WELL-BEING OF OFFSPRING

When it was reported in December 2006 that Mary Cheney, the openly lesbian daughter of Vice President Dick Cheney, announced that she and her longtime partner Heather Poe were expecting a baby, conservative leaders across the country voiced dismay. Janice Crouse of Concerned Women for America, which promotes biblical values and family traditions, described the pregnancy as "unconscionable."

"It's very disappointing that a celebrity couple like this would deliberately bring into the world a child that will never have a father," Crouse said. "The best thing we can do for a child is to provide a father and a mother."[19]

Another conservative Christian analyst, Carrie Gordon Earll of Focus on the Family, expressed empathy for the Cheney family and depicted the pregnancy as unwise. "Just because you can conceive a child outside a one-woman, one-man marriage doesn't mean it's a good idea," she was quoted as saying. "Love can't replace a mother and a father."[20]

Such reactions that greeted the Cheney announcement reflect the views of a broad spectrum of Americans whose objection to ARTs is that they threaten our traditional understanding of family. For many people today, "family" means what sociologists term the "nuclear family": married female and male parents with children. (Recent research, however, reported in the 2010 book Counted Out: Same-Sex Relations and Americans' Definitions of Family, suggests that the majority of Americans now say their definition of family includes same-sex couples with children, as well as married gay and lesbian couples, and unmarried cohabiting couples with children.) Traditionally, a heterosexual married couple has been the preferred nuclear environment for raising children. This belief and value have helped shape the widespread understanding of acceptable childbearing and rearing.

Consistent with this depiction, popular morality, as well as law, traditionally have viewed as "natural" and "ideal" that children know and grow up with their biological parents; otherwise they're thought to be at risk. From this assumption it is then argued that, because ART makes alternative—that is, "unnatural" and less than "ideal"—families possible, ART is objectionable. Among those alternative families would be ones headed by single individuals or same-sex couples. In some way or other—perhaps by social isolation or by creating gender identity,

self-identity, or sexual orientation problems—these alternative family arrangements are thought to put children at risk.[21,22]

In the case of the older parent served by ART, critics also worry about the best interests of the child. One major question is whether parents will be able to cope with toddlers at retirement age. "[E]ven when they have those kids and die," says bioethicist Arthur Caplan of well-known older fathers such as Strom Thurmond (1902–2003), Tony Randall (1920–2004), Larry King, or Clint Eastwood, "they've always had to have partners young enough to bear children. There's always been a parent there." And, lest we forget, they didn't have to bear the child. Making Kass's point is the aforementioned Carmela Bousada, who nearly died during her pregnancy when her kidneys threatened to fail, and the twin boys she delivered prematurely by cesarean section had to be placed in incubators. As for the possibility that she may leave her sons prematurely parentless, Bousada said she is looking for a younger man to marry and be their father.[23]

Defenders of ARTs answer these charges with empirical data of their own. In 2000, according to the US Census Bureau, 34% of lesbian couples and 22% of gay male couples were raising at least one child under 18 in their home.[24] Extensive data have been collected on the estimated 6 to 14 million children being raised by at least one gay or lesbian parent, usually as a result of a heterosexual relationship. After reviewing these data, the American Psychological Association has found no basis for asserting that there would be a higher rate of psychological or social problems among children born in those settings.[25] Similarly, the Ethics Committee of ASRM declared in 2006:

> There is no persuasive evidence that children raised by single parents or by gays and lesbians are harmed or disadvantaged by that fact alone. [Therefore, fertility] programs should treat all requests for assisted reproduction equally without regard to martial status or sexual orientation.[26]

Most definitively, a nearly 25-year study, reported in 2010, concluded that children raised

BIOETHICS ACROSS CULTURES

Dead Men To Father Children in Israel and England

In 2007 an Israeli court said a woman could be inseminated with the sperm from a known, dead man. Four
years earlier, when Staff Sgt. Keivan Cohen was killed
in the Gaza Strip, his parents had his sperm extracted
and frozen, then fought a legal battle for the right to
use it to inseminate a woman he never met. They chose
a 35-year-old unmarried economist. The Cohens argued that their son had expressed a wish to become a
father. "I'm terribly sad that I don't have my boy; it's a
terrible loss," Cohen's mother said. "But I'm also happy
that I will have a grandchild to hold, and that I succeeded in carrying out my son's will."

Two years later, in February 2009, a 42-year-old
widow in England received permission to conceive a
child using sperm from her dead husband. Doctors retrieved sperm from the man, who was in his late thir-
ties, hours after he died unexpectedly during routine
surgery in June 2007. Although she didn't have written
consent from her dead husband, the widow said it was
her dead husband's wish to have a sibling for the couple's existing daughter. As it's illegal to use sperm
without written consent in the United Kingdom, the
widow needed permission to export the sperm to the

United States where she would undergo fertility treatments. A judge granted permission on the basis that
the couple had consulted a gynecologist for fertility
advice a week before the husband died.

(SOURCE: "Dead Man May Yet Be a Father," *Los Angeles Times*, January
30, 2007, p. A-8. Retrieved May 2, 2009, from articles.latimes.com/2007/
jan/30/world/fg-donor30; Ben Leach, "Widow Wins Right To Have Child
by Dead Husband," *The Telegraph*, February 1, 2009. Retrieved May 2,
2009, from www.telegraph.co.uk/health/healthnews/4421988/Widow-
wins-right-to-have-child-by-dead-husband.html.)

Question

Do these two cases differ in any morally significant
way? What moral issues are involved in postmortem
sperm donation? Is it moral to use a husband's cryopreserved sperm after his death without his explicit
approval? Imagine a situation of a mother and father,
devastated by the sudden death of their adolescent
son, who request that his sperm be removed and frozen. Their intent is to purchase an egg, fertilize it with
his sperm, and hire a surrogate to carry and bear the
child, whom they will then adopt. Do you think this
should be permitted under the organ donation law,
which gives next of kin the right to donate a dead
person's body parts and decide on the recipient?

in lesbian households were psychologically well-
adjusted and had fewer behavioral problems than
their peers.[27]

As for the comparative physical well-being of
children born following artificial conception, there
is some evidence of an increased risk of some congenital birth defects and gastrointestinal tract abnormalities. Although the risk is still low, infants
conceived through ART, for instance, have almost
double the risk of cleft lip than infants conceived
naturally.[28] Also, although the technology often is
used to bypass male infertility problems caused by
chromosomal abnormalities, the child can still inherit
the underlying genetic problems, along with subtle
genetic changes that might occur while the embryo
is developing in the lab, possibly setting the offspring
up for childhood cancer. The biggest risk, though,
remains multiple births. About 45% of ART pregnancies result in twins and roughly 7% in triplets or

more. Carrying more than one baby dramatically
increases risks to both mother and child.[29]

On the other hand, the social development of
ART children seems quite normal. Research shows
that children born of ART not only function well
but also may have better relationships with their
parents than children conceived naturally.[30–31] One
study, in The Netherlands, found children conceived
by IVF in two-parent families to be the object of
more maternal involvement and pleasure than were
children of similar parents whose offspring had been
conceived without IVF.[32] Susan Golombok of the
Center for Family Research at Cambridge University in England reports comparable findings.[33]

Beyond this, defenders of ARTs point out
that the law, in fact, already has expanded its traditional limits for human reproduction within the
nuclear family. Recognizing that persons other
than heterosexual married couples—singles, gays,

and lesbians—have interest in having and rearing offspring, all states now allow such individuals to be foster parents. All but one allow them to adopt. Why, then, ART proponents ask, should fertility treatment not be extended to unmarried persons, including homosexuals? Isn't that illegal discrimination based on sexual orientation?

By the same token, many same-sex couples have interest in having children within marriage, that is, in approximating the ideal of the nuclear family. Feminist Andrews, for example, argues that alternative family structures—such as lesbian single-parent households— should be valued and protected as much as the traditional biologically related family is, because they provide "many of the same emotional, physical, and financial benefits...."[34] Therefore, says Andrews, the nontraditional family should have the same legitimate choices that traditional families have, including access to ART.[35]

As of June 2009, forty-three states had laws prohibiting same-sex marriages—twenty-nine of those with constitutional amendments specifically defining marriage as between a man and a woman. However, many of those prohibitions are being challenged in court. Gay and lesbian activists also hope to challenge the 1996 federal "Defense of Marriage Act" that defines marriage as between a man and a woman.

CONCLUSIONS

As New York's Task Force on Life and the Law made plain in its analysis of reproductive technologies: ART is here to stay. The question then becomes: What values, criteria, and rules will govern its use, including access to ART and its administration?

Although these matters are far from settled, a recent study sponsored by the Center for Bioethics at the University of Pennsylvania School of Medicine sheds important light on the values that currently govern access to ART.[37] The study began in 2001 when a six-member expert panel—including infertility specialists, bioethicists, an obstetrician/gynecologist, and a clinical psychologist from an ART clinic—developed a survey and refined it into a final questionnaire that asked about a variety of

Beyond matters related to our understanding of the family and to the welfare of children, there's another aspect of this debate, one that to some commentators in Groups 2 and 3 (see Chapter 11) smacks of a deep corruption: holding the infertile population to tests and standards that don't apply to the fertile population. In the words of Professor of Law Emily Jackson of the London School of Economics:

> ... we do not burden fertile people with the requirement that they demonstrate that they are capable of producing psychologically well-balanced [or even healthy] individuals prior to conception. And even when we know that a person's alcoholism, record of domestic violence or history of abuse poses a statistically significant risk to the well-being of their offspring, we are not entitled to prevent them from having children. If protecting the civil liberties of the fertile population prohibits us from policing conception among those who may actually pose a serious risk of causing psychological harm to their offspring, it seems incongruous that a possibly groundless fear of psychological harm to children born through assisted conception should be used to challenge the continued provision of services to would-be parents.[36]

ethically and socially challenging cases. A total of 210 out of 369 ART program directors responded to the anonymous self-administered, mailed questionnaire. Among the findings, four stood out.

1. Written policies on access to services are present at less than half of the ART clinics.

2. Universal agreement does not exist on any issue.

3. "... the majority of the ART programs believe that they have the right and responsibility to screen candidates before providing them with assisted reproductive technologies to conceive a child ... the key value being that they ensure a prospective child's safety and welfare and not risk the welfare of the prospective mother."

4. There is a significant variation across programs in their reported likelihood of turning away candidates, with some clinics more permissive in terms of access to services than others, while some are more restrictive.

Regarding 4—the lack of uniformity in screening candidates for ART—the researchers found that 79% of clinics treated single women, 27% treated patients with a history of schizophrenia, 10% treated patients who abuse alcohol, 7% treated human immunodeficiency virus–positive women, and 2% said they would treat patients previously convicted of child abuse. When program directors were addressed with a hypothetical situation in which the prospective "mom" in a couple was addicted to marijuana, 33% of the respondents said they would accept the couple for ART services, whereas 47% of programs would have denied the couple access. The researchers also found that a couple on welfare is as likely to be granted access as they are to be denied.

Clearly, the data demonstrate considerable variability in policy among clinics on most access-to-services questions, with a troublesome inconsistency in the candidate-screening practices of different ART programs in the United States. In the opinion of bioethicist Caplan, one of the study's authors: "The frequency of these variations highlight the need for a formal policy and common guidelines for candidate screening utilized by all ART facilities." The results also underscore the importance of ongoing discussion of the ethical and legal issues related to access and the need to develop consistent methods to deal with complex cases. Georgetown University law professor Naomi Cahn, author of *Test Tube Families* (2008), believes that this can be done without sacrificing reproductive privacy, through carefully crafted government regulation that the reproductive industry currently lacks. Still, even with improved and uniform methods leading to national or professional guidelines for screening program candidates (as in the United Kingdom), there still lurks a most complex moral problem.

At the advent of bioethics in the early 1970s, theologian Paul Ramsey spoke for many who worried that the science of artificial reproduction would come between husband and wife, thereby sullying the marital relationship. This hasn't occurred, at least not widely. But Ramsey also warned that assisted reproduction would lead to wider genetic manipulation, including human cloning, as parents increasingly attempted to influence the traits of their offspring and were encouraged to do so. This, in fact, is occurring. What does it mean when medicine "undertakes either to produce a child without curing infertility as a condition or to produce simply the desired sort of child"? For Ramsey it meant that medicine has lost its way "into an entirely different human activity—manufacture (which most want to satisfy desire)." Whether Ramsey was right is at the heart of the trait selection debates to be considered in the next two chapters.[38]

CASES AND CONTROVERSIES

In re Baby M: First Surrogacy Case

On February 6, 1985, William Stern and Mary Beth Whitehead entered into a surrogacy contract which provided that through artificial insemination using Mr. Stern's sperm, Mrs. Whitehead would become pregnant, carry the child to term, bear it, deliver it to the Sterns, and afterward do whatever was necessary to terminate her maternal rights so that Mrs. Stern could thereafter adopt the child. Mrs. Whitehead's husband, Richard, was also a party to the contract. Mrs. Stern was not, although she was to be given sole custody of the child in the event of her husband William's death. In return for her surrogacy, Mrs. Whitehead was to be paid $10,000 after the child's birth and on delivery to Mr. Stern.

After several artificial inseminations over a period of months, Mrs. Whitehead became pregnant. The pregnancy was uneventful, and on March 27, 1986, Baby M was born, named "Sara Elizabeth Whitehead" by Mrs. Whitehead in order to keep the surrogacy arrangement private.

According to court records, Mrs. Whitehead realized, almost from the moment of birth, that she could not part with the child. She had felt a bond with her even during pregnancy. Some indication of the attachment was conveyed to the Sterns at the hospital

(Continued)

CASES AND CONTROVERSIES (CONTINUED)

when they told Mrs. Whitehead what they were going to name the baby. Whitehead apparently broke into tears and indicated that she did not know if she could give up the child. She talked about how the baby looked like her other daughter, and made it clear that she was experiencing great difficulty with the decision. Despite her conflicted feelings, Whitehead turned the child over to the Sterns on March 30 at the White-heads' home, as agreed upon.

The Sterns were thrilled with their new child. They had planned extensively for its arrival, far beyond the practical furnishing of a room for her. It was a time of joyful celebration—not just for them but for their friends as well. The Sterns looked forward to raising their daughter, whom they named Melissa. While aware by then that Mrs. Whitehead was undergoing an emotional crisis, they did not yet realize its depth or implications.

Later in the evening of March 30, Mrs. Whitehead became disturbed and disconsolate, and the next day she went to the Sterns' home and told them how much she was suffering. Fearing that Mrs. Whitehead might commit suicide, the Sterns agreed to Mrs. Whitehead's request to have the baby in her possession for one week, after which she would surrender the child to them. It was not until four months later, after a series of attempts to regain possession of the child, that Melissa was returned to the Sterns, having been forcibly removed from the home where she was then living with Mr. and Mrs. Whitehead, a home in Florida owned by Whitehead's parents.

In the ensuing legal battle over possession of the child, a trial court awarded "Baby M" to the Sterns, with limited visitation rights to Mrs. Whitehead. On appeal, Mrs. Whitehead contended that the surrogacy contract was invalid because, she said, it conflicted with public policy, since it guaranteed that the child would not have the nurturing of both natural parents—presumably the state's goal for families. She further argued that the contract deprived her, Baby M's natural mother, of her constitutional right to the companionship of her child, and that it conflicted with statutes concerning termination of parental rights and adoption. With the contract thus voided, Mrs. White-head claimed primary custody with visitation rights to Mr. Stern, both on a "best interests of the child" basis, as well as on the policy basis of discouraging surrogacy contracts. She maintained that even if custody would ordinarily go to Mr. Stern, here it should be awarded to her in order to deter future surrogacy arrangements.

On February 3, 1988, the Supreme Court of New Jersey invalidated surrogacy contracts as against public policy, but affirmed the trial court's "best interest of the child" analysis. The Supreme Court remanded the case to family court. On remand, the lower court awarded William Stern custody and Mary Beth Whitehead visitation rights.[39]

When she turned eighteen in March 2004, Melissa Stern initiated the process of allowing Elizabeth Stern to adopt her, which involved terminating Whitehead's parental rights. As of March 2007, Melissa was a junior at George Washington University majoring in religious studies and hoping to become a minister with, per-haps, her own children some day. On the twentieth anniversary of her groundbreaking case, she told a lo-cal magazine, referring to the Sterns, "I love my family very much and am very happy to be with them. I'm very happy I ended up with them. I love them, they're my best friends in the whole world, and that's all I have to say about it."[40]

Questions for Analysis

1. Should the Sterns—a biochemist and a pediatrician—have been allowed to leverage their relative affluence to have Mary Beth Whitehead, a high school dropout married to a sanitation worker, become pregnant and give away a baby that was genetically half hers?

2. In voiding the surrogacy arrangement, the New Jersey Supreme Court said, in effect, that biology trumps a contract. Do you agree with this ruling?

3. Due largely to the Baby M case, gestational car-riers, who have no genetic relationship with the children they bear for other couples, have since replaced paid surrogates in New Jersey; and they may not be paid any more than medical and legal expenses. Do you think this is wise social policy?

4. *Baby M* involved traditional surrogacy, i.e., a surrogate mother whose egg was used. In 2009 New Jersey expanded the *Baby M* decision to gestational surrogate mothers by ruling that a gestational surrogate who gave birth to twin girls was their legal mother, even though she was not genetically related to them. Do you agree that there is no significant difference between tradi-tional and gestational surrogacy?

5. Evaluate the practice of surrogate motherhood from the perspectives of natural law, utilitarian-ism, and Kant's ethics.

6. Evaluate this case in the context of the critique of autonomy presented in Chapter 6 under "Sug-gested Off-Setting Principles."

CASES AND CONTROVERSIES

Jacob v. Shultz-Jacob: Three Adults with Parental Rights

During the time they lived together in York County, Pennsylvania, from about 1996 to 2003, Jodilynn Jacob and Jennifer Shultz, two lesbian women, had a commitment ceremony in Pittsburgh and formed a civil union in Vermont. Jennifer took the last name Shultz-Jacob. Jodilynn subsequently became the birth mother of two children, conceived through donor insemination. The sperm donor was Carl Frampton, a long-time friend of Jennifer, who remained actively involved in the lives of his offspring and the birth mother.

In February 2006, several months after the women had decided to end their partnership, birth-mother Jodilynn relocated with the children to Dauphin County, PA, and soon thereafter, Jennifer filed a lawsuit in York County Court, naming Jodilynn and Carl as defendants, seeking legal and physical custody of the children. The court made a temporary award of primary custody to Jodilynn while the case was pending, with partial custody, or visitation rights, for Jennifer and Carl, the children's biological father.

In April, 2006, while the custody case was pending in York County Court, Jodilynn filed a complaint in Dauphin County Court, seeking child support payments from Jennifer. The court awarded her payments of $983 per month, on the theory that Jennifer was in fact the children's parent and, therefore, should be legally obligated to contribute to their support. For her part, Jennifer appealed this ruling, arguing that because Carl was now essentially a third legal parent of the two children, he should be required to pay part of the child support. The York County judge was open to the concept of the three adults sharing a legal relationship to the children, but the Dauphin County judge rejected Jennifer's request. On April 30, 2007, however, a Pennsylvania Superior Court panel ruled for Jennifer, and Carl was added as a party to the case with child support obligations.[41]

Questions for Analysis

1. Do you agree with the Superior Court's ruling that a child can have, simultaneously, three adults who are financially obligated to the child's support and are also entitled to visitation?

2. Supporters of this decision say that if two parents are good for children, three are better.[42] Do you agree?

3. What is the possible harm, if any, if other US courts follow Pennsylvania's decision?

4. If more children are granted three legal parents, is there any rationale for denying these families the rights and protections of marriage?

5. Are the aforementioned "Suggested Off-Setting Principles"(Chater 6) relevant to this case?

CASES AND CONTROVERSIES

Wanted: A Few Good Sperm for Choice Mothers

Many women today are considering or have chosen single motherhood. According to Single Mothers by Choice, a 25-year-old support group,

> A single mother by choice is a woman who decided to have or adopt a child, knowing she would be her child's sole parent, at least at the outset. Typically, we are career women in our thirties and forties. The ticking of our biological clocks has made us face the fact that we could no longer wait for marriage before starting our families. Some of us went to a doctor for donor insemination or adopted in the United States or abroad. Others accidentally became pregnant and discovered we were thrilled.[43]

The number of single mothers by choice is expanding, Jennifer Egan reported in a 2006 *New York Times* piece, although no one knows by how much because "choice mothers," as they're sometimes called, aren't separate statistically from, say, unwed teenage mothers.[44]

According to Egan, in her profile of single women, "Sperm donors, like online daters, answer myriad questions about heroes, hobbies and favorite things,"

(Continued)

CASES AND CONTROVERSIES (CONTINUED)

searching for just the right donor sperm to conceive a child. One woman Egan interviewed, a 39-year-old executive named Karyn, reported being smitten with one donor's profile. "'You can tell he comes from a warm family, some very educated,'" Karyn told Egan. The donor had worked as a chef and had "proven fertility," meaning that at least one woman conceived using his sperm. He was also free from sexually transmitted diseases (STDs) and testable genetic disorders. Karyn especially liked that he was an "identity-release donor" (also called an "open donor" or a "yes donor"), which meant he was willing to be contacted by any offspring who reaches the age of eighteen.

When Karyn called the sperm bank the next morning to inquire further about the donor, a worker told her: "I have to be honest. He's very popular, and I only have eight units in store right now. I'm not sure how much longer he might be in the program."

Like an impulsive shopper, Karyn said, " 'I'll take the eight units.'" The price of $3,100 included six months of storage. The sperm bank that Karyn used was one of the few that had photos, and she knew right away that "he was the one." She carried a wallet-size copy of the donor's photo between her MetroCard and her work ID: "a fair, sharp-featured young man in a crisp white shirt, his arms crossed."

Karyn's first insemination try didn't work, but she wasn't discouraged. There was still one last chance for her to become pregnant before her fortieth birthday.

"In a perfect world, I'll get pregnant this cycle," she told Egan, and vowed that she and baby would "live happily ever after."

Questions for Analysis

1. Another woman profiled in the article assessed two sperm donors as follows: "'Thick hair, which is also nice because if I happen to get a son, I don't like bald guys.... [this one is] six feet but he only weighs 150. Which is good. If I have a girl, she wants to be skinny, and if she can eat what she wants, that's perfect.'" Does this kind of social engineering concern you?

2. Discuss the implications of creating a kind of reproduction and parenthood in which men are almost unnecessary.

3. It seems that, while many women like the ones Egan profiled have given up on romance or marriage, they have not given up on motherhood. What does your faith tradition teach about these new ways of becoming a mother and starting a family?

4. Can you imagine yourself ever DNA shopping, or contributing sperm or eggs to those who are?

5. Evaluate the practice of conception through donor insemination from the perspectives of principlism, virtue, care (including feminism), and narratives. (See Chapters 4 & 7.)

REFERENCES

1. Roni Caryn Rabin, "As Demand for Donor Eggs Soars, High Prices Stir Ethical Concerns," *The New York Times,* Mary 15, 2007, p. D6.

2. Sharon N. Covington and William E. Gibbon, "What Is Happening to the Price of Eggs?" *Fertility and Sterility,* May 2007, pp. 1001–1004.

3. Department of Health, New York State, "Executive Summary of Assisted Reproductive Technologies: Analysis and Recommendations for Public Policy," *Executive Summary of the Task Force on Life and the Law,* October 2001. Retrieved April 25, 2008, from http://www.health.state.ny.us/nysdoh/taskfce/execsum.htm.

4. Donald J. Boudreaux, "A Modest Proposal to Deregulate Infant Adoptions," *The Cato Journal,* Spring/Summer 1995. Retrieved April 25, 2008, from http://www.cato.org/pubs/journal/cj15n1-7.html.

5. "C'mon, Baby, Light My Brain Cells," *Business Week,* October 13, 2005. Retrieved May 2, 2008, from http://www.businessweek.com/technology/content/oct2005/tc20051013_964490.htm?campaign_id=rss_tech.

6. John Tierney, "Hitting It Off, Thanks to Algorithms of Love," *The New York Times,* January 29, 2008, p. D1.

7. Wendy McElroy, "Feminists Against Women: The New Reproductive Technologies," *Wendy McElroy.com,* May 30, 2008. Retrieved, May 26, 2010, from http://www.wendymcelroy.com/e107_plugins/content/content.php?content.111.

8. "Amy Harmon, "Are you My Sperm Donor? Few Clinics Will Say," *The New York Times*, January 20, 2006, p. A1. Retrieved May 1, 2008, from http://www.zetetics.com/mac/reason.htm.

9. "Spanish Woman, 67, Becomes a Mother with Birth of Twins," *Los Angeles Times*, December 31, 2006, p. A4.

10. Kay S. Hymowitz, "The Daddy Dilemma" *Los Angeles Times*, April 16, 2007, p. A15.

11. Elizabeth Marquardt, "When 3 Really Is a Crowd," *The New York Times*, July 16, 2007, p. A17.

12. Hossam E. Fadel, "The Islamic Viewpoint on New Assisted Reproductive Technologies," *Fordham Urban Law Journal*, November 1, 2002. Retrieved April 28, 2008, from http://www.encyclopedia.com/doc/1G1-97823700.html.

13. Shana Roskies, "Chayei Sarah," *Ritualwell.org: Ceremonies for Jewish Living*. Retrieved May 2, 2008, from http://www.ritualwell.org/lifecycles/pregnancyinfertility/infertility/Hayyei%20Sarah.xm.

14. Department of Health, New York, Executive Summary of the Task Force on Life and the Law, "Executive Summary of Assisted Reproductive Technologies: Analysis and Recommendations for Public Policy," October 2001. Retrieved May 15, 2008, from http://www.health.state.ny.us/.

15. Adam Liptak, "Ruling Lets Women Share Rights in Fight Over Custody," *The New York Times*, November 29, 2006, p. A20.

16. Adam Liptak, "Judge Dissolves Civil Union in Custody Fight," *The New York Times*, June 19, 2007, p. A14.

17. NA, "Birth Mother Ordered to Surrender Daughter," *The New York Times*, December 30, 2009, p. A18.

18. Stephanie Saul, "Building a Baby, With Few Ground Rules," *The New York Times*, December 13, 2009, p. A1.

19. David Crary, "Groups Mixed on Mary Cheney's Pregnancy," *Washiongtonpost.com*, December 6, 2006. Retrieved April 27, 2008, from www.washingtonpost.com/wp-dyn/.content/article/2006/12/06/AR2006120600221.html.

20. Johanna Neuman, "A Pregnant Pause in Right Wing," *Los Angeles Times*, December 7, 2006, p. Al5.

21. William R. Avison, "Single Motherhood and Mental Health: Implications for Primary Prevention," *Canadian Medical Association Journal*, March 1997, pp. 661–663.

22. J. Cairney, M. Boyle, D. R. Offord, and Y. Racine, "Stress, Social Support and Depression in Single and Married Mothers," *Social Psychiatry and Psychiatric Epidemiology*, September 2003, pp. 442–449.

23. Bob Pool, "Fooling Nature, and the Fertility Doctor," *Los Angeles Times*, January 30, 2007, p. A12.

24. John Bowe, "Gay Donor or Gay Dad?" *The New York Times*, November 19, 2006. Retrieved April 29, 2008, from http://www.nytimes.com/2006/11/19/magazine/19fathering.html.

25. American Psychological Association, Public Policy Office, "Briefing Sheet: Same Sex Families & Relationships," Washington, 2006. Retrieved May 1, 2008, from www.apa.org/ppo/issues/lgbfamilybrf604.html.

26. The Ethics Committee of the American Society for Reproductive Medicine, Fertility and Sterility, "Access to Fertility Treatment by Gays, Lesbians, and Unmarried Persons," November 2006, p. 1333. Retrieved May 2, 2008, from www.asrm.org/Media/Ethics/fertility_gaylesunmarried.pdf.

27. Nanette Gartrell, "U.S. National Longitudinal Lesbian Family Study: Psychological Adjustment of 17-Year-Old Adolescents," *Pediatrics*, June 7, 2010, p. 2009.

28. Jennita Reefhuis, et al., "Assisted Reproductive Technology and Major Structural Birth Defects in the United States," *Human Reproduction*, November 16, 2008. Retrieved November 18, 2008, from http://humrep.oxfordjournals.org/cgi/reprint/den387v3.

29. Valerie Ulene, "Babies, the Easy Way?" *Los Angeles Times*, August 11, 2008, p. F3.

30. Susan Golombok, "New Families, Old Values: Considering the Welfare of the Child," *Human Reproduction*, September 1998, pp. 2342–2347.

31. Susan Golombok, *Parenting: What Really Counts?*, New York: Psychology Press, 2000.

32. Leon Kass and James Q. Wilson, "The Ethics of Human Cloning," *The American Enterprise*, 1999, p. 67.

33. Peggy Ornstein, "Your Gamete, Myself," *New York Times Magazine*, July 15, 2007, p. 58.

34. Lori Andrews, "Surrogate Motherhood: The Challenge for Feminists," in *The Ethics of Reproductive Technology*, Kenneth D. Alpern, ed., New York: Oxford University Press, 1992, p. 206.

35. Ann Warren, "IVF and Women's Interests: An Analysis of Feminist Concerns," *Bioethics* 2, January 1988, pp. 37–57.

36. Emily Jackson, "Reproductive Technologies: What About Me? The Child of A.R.T.," *Pro+Choice Forum*. Retrieved April 30, 2008, from www.prochoiceforum.org.uk/revpast5.asp.

37. Andrea D. Gurmankin, Arthur L. Caplan, and Andrea M. Braverman, "Screening Practices and Belief of Assisted Reproductive Technology Programs," *Fertility and Sterility*, January 2005, pp. 61–67.

38. Paul Ramsey, "Shall We 'Reproduce'? II. Rejoinders and Future Forecast," *JAMA*, June 12, 1972, p. 1481.

39. "First Surrogacy Case—In re Baby M," *The Medical and Public Health Law Site*, February 3, 2008. Retrieved April 20, 2009, from http://biotech.law.lsu.edu/cases/cloning/baby_m.htm.

40. Jennifer Weiss, "Now It's Melissa's Time," *New Jersey Monthly Magazine*, March, 2007. Retrieved April 29, 2009, from http://www.reproductivelawyer.com/news/babym.asp.

41. Arthur S. Leonard, "Pennsylvania Court Finds Three Adults Can Have Parental Rights," *Leonard Link*, May 1, 2007. Retrieved May 1, 2009, from http://newyorklawschool.typepad.com/leonardlink/2007/05/pennsylvania_co.html.

42. Elizabeth Marquardt, "When 3 Really Is a Crowd," *The New York Times*, July 16, 2007. Retrieved May 1, 2009, from www.nytimes.com/2007/07/16/opinion/16marquardt.html.

43. Single Mothers by Choice, 2009. Retrieved May 2, 2009, from http://www.singlemothersbychoice.com.

44. Jennifer Egan, "Wanted: A Few Good Sperm," *New York Times Magazine*, March 19, 2006. Retrieved May 1, 2009, from http://www.nytimes.com/2006/03/19/magazine/319dad.html.

Chapter 13

The Prenatal Testing Debate I: Embryo Screening

P renatal testing is testing that provides information about the health or condition of the embryo or fetus. Nowadays, many pregnant women are using prenatal tests to screen out diseases and disabilities such as neural tube defects, Down Syndrome, chromosome abnormalities, and genetic diseases. Although prenatal testing can be performed before the fertilized egg is embedded in the uterus, that has only been possible since 1990. Before then tests could only be done weeks into a pregnancy, sometimes with results that weren't really conclusive until after the birth.

THE BOY IN THE PLASTIC BUBBLE

It wasn't until he was 12 years old that Carol Ann Vetter touched the hand of her son David for the first time.[1] Afflicted with a rare hereditary disease, severe combined immunodeficiency (SCID), that made him defenseless against any germs, David had lived inside a sterile isolator "bubble" since his birth on September 21, 1971. In October of 1983, doctors infused David with two ounces of his sister's bone marrow, hoping that would help him make his own antibodies and free him from the bubble. Unbeknownst to them, the bone marrow contained traces of a dormant virus, which produced hundreds of cancerous tumors in the boy. David left his bubble on February 7, 1984, and died fifteen days later.

When David Vetter died, he was known to the world as "the boy in the plastic bubble." As depicted on the PBS program *American Experience* (April 10, 2006), his life was "a tragic tale ... of unendingly committed caregivers and resourceful scientists on the cutting edge of medical research." The program duly noted that David's ordeal also raised some of the most difficult ethical questions of our age. "Did doctors, in a rush to save a child, condemn the boy to a life not worth living? Did they, in the end, effectively decide how to kill him?"

Within ten years of David's death, treatments for some forms of SCID improved, such as bone marrow transplant drugs. Also in the early 1990s, children like David were among the first beneficiaries of an exciting new branch of medicine: gene therapy. By snipping and splicing DNA, scientists were able to replace defective genes in the white blood cells of SCID patients with normal genes. Unfortunately, the treatment wasn't a cure. As white bloods cells live only a few months, the patients had to come back for repeated treatments. There was also the possibility they would develop leukemia. All of this led opponents to urge scientists to wait until stem cells, the source of all the body's tissues, could be identified and used to cure all blood cells in children. Some skeptics of genetic engineering went even further. Lawyer Jeremy Rifkin, for example, said that genetic scientists were playing God and that any tampering with nature, no matter how well intentioned, set a dangerous precedent.[2] Nevertheless, on September 14, 1990, SCID's victim Ashanthi DeSilva, a 4-year-old from suburban Cleveland, became the first person ever to receive human-gene therapy. Ashanti is not completely cured and still takes treatments, but, as one commentator observes, "that she's alive today—let alone healthy and active—is due to her gene therapy, and also helps prove a crucial point: genes can be inserted into humans to cure genetic disease."[3]

Granted, people like Ashanthi DeSilva were lucky to be born at the advent of gene therapy. But, perhaps, they were also lucky to have missed—just missed—the advent of another technology, called pre-implantation genetic diagnosis (PGD). Prior to the use of PGD, or embryo screening, prenatal diagnosis was limited to testing a fetus through amniocentesis and chorionic villus sampling (CVS). One tests the amniotic fluid, the other placenta tissue; both are done weeks into a pregnancy. PGD, on the other hand, provides a couple with more conclusive information about the genetic health of the embryo *before* it is implanted in the uterus. That means informed decisions about the path a pregnancy should take, including deselecting embryos with genetic mutations that cause catastrophic afflictions like that of Ashanthi DeSilva.

PGD was first used in 1990 to screen against genetic mutation for cystic fibrosis. Today not only can the procedure select against hundreds of different genetic conditions, including SCID, it can also be used to create compatible donors, generate stem lines, and even select the sex of the child. Given the nature of its uses, PGD is very much part of today's debates in reproductive ethics. This chapter and the next are about this centerpiece in the dazzling reproductive revolution and the moral controversies that swirl about its applications.

MEDICAL USES OF PRE-IMPLANTATION GENETIC DIAGNOSIS

PGD was first developed for patients at risk of having children with serious genetic disorders, which often discouraged them from having their own biological children. These couples, according to two fertility experts, are often faced with attempting a type of "Russian Roulette" to have children, "many times having to confront the difficult decision to terminate an affected pregnancy." Illustrative of their predicament is the following hypothetical:

> Consider a woman known to be carrying an X-linked disease with a 50% risk of an affected male in each pregnancy. In addition, her daughters have a 50% risk of being carriers, but are unlikely to be clinically affected. She may not wish to become pregnant if she has to make decisions about an affected child in a viable pregnancy. However, she would become pregnant if she knew she had conceived a daughter, and with preimplantation diagnosis this possibility becomes a reality. PGD thus eliminates the need for possible pregnancy termination after prenatal diagnosis of a genetically affected fetus.[4]

A PGD test consists of the removal of a cell to test for abnormalities when the fertilized egg has reached the 6-to-8-cell stage, usually the third day. If normal, the cell is then implanted with its remaining cells. The technically complex and expensive procedure consists of the following steps:

1. The woman is given drugs to produce "super-ovulation." She normally produces many eggs, which are collected.

2. As for a standard IVF procedure, the eggs are placed in a dish and are fertilized by donated sperm (usually from the woman's partner).

3. About three days after IVF, when each successful embryo has divided to about the 8-cell level, one or two cells are removed and subjected to a molecular analysis. If a genetic defect is found, the embryo from which it was taken is destroyed.

4. Typically, three of the embryos that are free of abnormalities are implanted in the woman's womb. The others are destroyed.

5. Sometimes none of the embryos develops into a fetus, and the procedure is repeated. Often, one or even two embryos, rarely three, do live and develop into fetuses, which are later born as single births or twins, rarely triplets.

None of this causes the pre-embryo any apparent harm and, for the most part, the process has resulted in the birth of healthy children.[5]

PGD carries up to a 3 percent chance of failing to detect a mutation, or a mistake in a cell's DNA.[6] Those odds recently improved when British scientists announced a significant refinement of PGD. Rather than searching for an altered gene linked to a genetic disease, such as cystic fibrosis or Huntington's disease, the new technique—called pre-implantation genetic haplotyping (PGH)—looks for DNA "fingerprints," or markers, near the gene. Because the defective gene can be different for different families, the markers, by contrast, can be applied to many families, thereby offering more couples a more reliable test.

The advantage of a PGD (or PGH) screen is not only that couples of high genetic risk don't have to gamble on a birth; neither must they wait for days for the results of an alternative test. Literally overnight, a PGD result is known, whereas in an amniocentesis the blood needs to be tested over a week or more. This is significant because the pre-embryos need to be placed in the womb on the fifth day, or only 48 hours after reaching the required size of 6 to 8 cells.

Although PGD was originally intended for having healthy children, it has also become useful for creating compatible donors, generating stem cells, and selecting sex.

Having Healthy Children

PGD was initially used to target a handful of fatal childhood diseases such as Tay-Sachs. Today PGD technology can be used to decipher embryonic cells for over two hundred diseases, including spina bifida and spinal muscular atrophy, the leading killer of babies under two.[7] According to a 2006 survey conducted by the Genetics and Public Policy Center (GPPC), nearly three-quarters of American PGD clinics typically provide embryo screening to detect and discard embryos with abnormalities involving a missing or extra chromosome, which can result in miscarriage or severe and usually fatal birth defects.[8] Sometimes screening only for the sex chromosomes is medically relevant. Males, for example, are more likely than females to develop autism. Sex preselection may also be useful to avoid other types of sex-linked genetic disorders, such as Duchenne's muscular dystrophy and hemophilia. PGD is also being used, increasingly, to target dispositions to diseases that may never strike or, if so, not until adulthood. Colon cancer, for example, ordinarily doesn't develop until age 45 to 55 and is curable with early detection. The prenatal procedure is also being applied to less serious conditions such as arthritis.

Creating Compatible Donors

For prospective parents with detectable genetic disorders, PGD is a procedure that allows them to have healthy children. But for others, it's a way to treat an already-existing ill child.

"If you're screening embryos for the benefit of future kids," asks William Saletan of the online news magazine *Slate*, "why not do it for kids already here?" Saletan, who writes a column called *Human Nature* and has written extensively on the current trend toward embryo eugenics, explains:

> Some embryos are particularly suited to donate cord blood to a sick elder sibling; nearly one-fourth of American PGD clinics have sorted embryos for this purpose. Originally, this was done for diseases such as Fanconi's anemia, in which the

embryo could be checked both for its own sake—to avoid the bad gene—and for the blood match. Today, however, it's also being done for leukemias that have no clear genetic cause. In the GPPC survey, 6% of clinics that perform PGD admit they've used it to identify which embryos are useful donors, even when the test offers the embryos no benefit.[9]

The Nash family of Colorado were the first to go through this process of creating a "savior sibling." Their child Molly was born in 1994 with Fanconi's anemia, a rare genetic disease that causes many problems, the most serious of which is inadequate bone marrow production. Molly's poor bone marrow production meant that she would develop leukemia and die, possibly within a few years. The Nashes, who wanted a second child anyway, used IVF and PGD procedures to make sure that their second child would be disease free and a compatible donor to their sister. A month after Adam was born in 2000, Molly was treated with radiation and chemotherapy to completely destroy her bone marrow. She was then given a transfusion of Adam's umbilical cord blood. Her chances of survival increased from 42 percent with cord blood transplant from an unrelated marrow donor to 85 percent with a transplant from a matched sibling. There was no danger at all to Adam.[10]

Generating Embryonic Stem Cells

Human embryonic stem cells (ESCs, or hESCs) can develop into any type of cell in the human body, and thus have vast research and medical potential. Usually, ESCs are grown from a mass of cells harvested from the embryo in a procedure that destroys it. But PGD offers an alternative. The single cell used in PGD for genetic diagnosis, in theory, could be used to create stem cells for therapeutic use. Molecular biologist and enthusiast of the procedure, Robert Lanza of Advanced Cell Technology, a California biotech company, explains why:

> Normally the cell is taken in the IVF clinic and used immediately for testing. What

we're saying is, let it grow overnight, there is still time to do the test and implant the embryo, and then use the rest of the biopsy for stem cell generation. It doesn't change the outcome of the test, it doesn't present any other risk to the embryo, and it ensures that there is a cell line out there that matches the child and his or her siblings.[11]

Of course, because only a small percentage of embryos used in IVF clinics actually undergo PGD, IVF with PGD would have limited use for stem cell generation. "Other than that," however, according to Zev Rosenwaks, director of New York's Center for Reproductive Medicine and Infertility, "the procedure seems like a perfectly reasonable proposition for cases when PGD is already being performed."[12]

THE ETHICAL DEBATE

As a technology, PGD clearly is one of the fruits of a science "devoted to the relief of man's estate," to recall Francis Bacon's pithy phrase (see Chapter 1). And yet, there's general agreement that as a reproductive practice PGD needs close ethical, legal, and social scrutiny. At the center of that scrutiny are two sorts of objections that arise most forcefully in the cultural discourse about this remarkable technology.[13] The first relates to creating and discarding pre-embryos; the second to selecting traits.

Embryo Creation and Destruction

To parents like the Nashes, PGD is a lifesaving procedure. Instead of watching their child waste away and die, they can have the possibility of a cure. Also, if the transplant doesn't work, they will have another, healthy child to love.

But not everyone applauds the use of IVF and PGD to create a child to treat a sibling. Vigorous cultural opposition comes from religious and social conservatives who, variously, view the disposal of unacceptable embryos as murder, object to the creation of what they call "designer babies," and openly warn that IVF and PGD are the first steps down a slippery slope to manufacturing babies for spare parts. Some cultural liberals share some of these concerns, but the most vocal opposition comes from religious and social conservatives who consider the three-day old early embryo, or blastocyst, "a human being just like you and me; and it deserves the same respect that our laws give to us all," in the words of Senator Sam Brownback (R-Kan.).[14] Like Brownback, who is a convert to Roman Catholicism, those who consider the unborn a person from conception object to the destruction of pre-embryos and, therefore, oppose most uses of PGD.

In 1987 the Congregation for the Doctrine of the Faith published the most detailed religious teaching on this area in *Donum Vitae (Gift of Life)*. As noted in the previous chapter, the basic Vatican instruction with respect to all ARTs is "assist, do not replace, natural sexual intercourse." Thus:

> [A]ny means that attempts to assist the act of sexual intercourse to achieve its natural end of procreation while keeping intact the exchange of love is morally acceptable. Any means that replaces, bypasses, or substitutes for sexual intercourse in order to produce a child is morally unacceptable.[15]

Also worth noting is the wholesale importation of the biblical narrative into the contemporary conversation. As formulated by biblicist Cyril Tennant:

> Man has a dignity and an important role as a controller and steward of the rest of creation. At the same time, he is to recognize his limitations and to be humble, both because of his position in relationship to God, and also because he is essentially flawed and imperfect as a result of the fall. Taking these doctrines together, his task in controlling creation and caring for it is to seek to restore it to its pristine pre-fall perfection, not to arrogate the place of God by seeking to improve on it. This has particular importance for genetic

technologies: the production of "designer babies" or "superhumans" is equally wrong.[16]

In contrast, those who endorse delayed personhood don't consider the destruction of pre-implantation embryos inherently objectionable, although they often oppose its nonmedical use, as for social sex selection. To its enthusiasts, not to exploit available biotechnology is caving in to an antiquated view of human nature out of step with modern science, namely: that children are a gift of a God who best knows what's best for us. Canadian geneticist Robert Haynes puts it this way:

> For three thousand years at least, a majority of people have considered that human beings were special, were magic. It's the Judeo-Christian view of man. What the ability to manipulate genes should indicate to people is the very deep extent to which we are biological machines. The traditional view is built on the foundation that life is sacred.... Well, not anymore. It's no longer possible to live by the idea that there is something special, unique, even sacred about living organisms.[17]

Trait Selection

In addition to the creation and discarding of embryos, a second set of objections to PGD as a reproductive practice relates to the selection itself.

Principled Considerations It is frequently argued, religiously, that trait selection is against God's will for human reproduction and life's meaning and purpose. Because children, regardless of traits, are a gift from God, by intervening in the divinely directed course of reproduction, as by trait selection, we are playing God and, therefore, denying God's wisdom of what is best for us.[18]

The secular counterpart of this principled objection is that trait selection is simply unnatural. Both Leon Kass and the President's Bioethics Council he once chaired have argued, deontologically, that trait selection bypasses the established

BIOETHICS ACROSS CULTURES

Eugenics Around the World

Genetic counselors typically insist that they are not trying to "improve" the population, as in eugenics, but rather allowing parents informed reproductive choice. But research conducted in the mid-1990s by the American sociologist and ethicist Dorothy Wertz and her colleague, John Fletcher, pointed up a gap between this professional ideal and the actual practice of genetic counseling.

Wertz found that only geneticists in English-speaking countries and Northern Europe (ENE) can make any claim to non-directiveness and abandonment of eugenic thinking. In Eastern and Southern Europe, the Middle East, Asia, and Latin America (designated as Rest Of the World, or ROW), geneticists not only hold eugenic ideas, but also see no problem in directing their clients in accordance with those ideas. Here are a few examples from Wertz's survey:

- In response to the clearly eugenic suggestion that "An important goal of genetic counseling is to reduce the number of deleterious genes in the population," 13 percent of geneticists in the United Kingdom agreed. In Eastern and Southern Europe an average of 50 percent did, and in China and India nearly 100 percent did.

- An average of 20 percent of ENE geneticists felt that, given the availability of prenatal testing, it is not fair to society knowingly to have a child with a serious genetic disorder. (The survey also revealed huge discrepancies between geneticists about what counts as "serious.") In ROW, majorities of geneticists supported this view, rising to nearly 100 percent in some countries.

- Substantial minorities of both ENE and ROW geneticists would advise voluntary sterilization for institutionalized women with mental handicap of varying severity.

- Approximately 15 percent of ENE and majorities of ROW geneticists admitted that they would provide biased prenatal counseling (emphasizing negative aspects of a condition without actually suggesting termination) for a variety of child- and adult-onset genetic diseases. For conditions judged more serious, nearly 30 percent of US genetics professionals would provide negatively slanted counseling. Conversely, where the condition is viewed as less serious, they would give more positive counseling. Wertz says that giving clients biased information is worse than being directive, because it does not offer the client an opportunity to disagree with the counselor. None of the geneticists said that they thought that giving biased information was dishonest.

Wertz's discovery that genetic counselors underestimated the degree to which they contravened their professional norms in practice has led her to conclude, "[E]ugenics is alive and well."

(SOURCE: David King, "The Persistence of Eugenics," GenEthics, Issue 22. Retrieved May 5, 2009, from www.hgalert.org/topics/geneticDiscrimination/eugenics.htm)

Question

What are the moral issues involved in genetic counseling? What bioethical principles does it raise? Do you agree with Wertz's assessment of giving biased information? Do you think that scientific and cultural conditions today could lead to a new generation of active eugenics?

natural means of human reproduction and, on that ground, is wrong, regardless of intention. By this account, "human reproduction is a 'gift,' of nature if not from God. Any form of selection or manipulation turns the child into a 'manufacture' and thus impairs human flourishing."[19-21]

In Kass's words:

Sexual reproduction—by which I mean the generation of new life from (exactly) two complementary elements, one female, one male, (usually) through coitus—is established (if that is the right term) not by human decision, culture, or tradition, but by nature: it is the natural way of all mammalian reproduction. By nature, each child has two complementary biological progenitors. Each child thus stems from and unites exactly two lineages. In natural generation, moreover, the precise genetic constitution of the resulting offspring is

BIOETHICS ACROSS CULTURES

Biotechnology in China

In 1986, Deng Xiaoping (1904–1997), the leader of the People's Republic of China, took steps to put science in his socialist state on an equal footing with the West. One of Deng's target areas was American-dominated biotechnology.

Under Deng's strategy, China began to ramp up biotech research and development, with impressive, if at times freakish, results. Working in a military medical research institute, Chinese biomedical scientists grew dog bladder tissue on the back of a mouse in 2001. The following year a team of researchers at the Beijing Genomics Institute managed to produce in just three months a rough draft of the genome of one strain of rice. Beyond this, Chinese scientists boasted of having cloned human embryos in 1999, using rabbit eggs and human DNA, ostensibly to be used for isolating stem cells and possibly harvesting spare organs and tissues. (The United States didn't accomplish this feat until 2001, using only human materials.) Meanwhile, the Chinese Ministry of Health approved plans for the country's first state-run stem cell bank. Although smaller than stem cell banks in the United States, it promised to be the largest such bank in Asia.

Overseeing these developments in biotechnology is a still authoritarian Chinese government, with complete power to chart a social course that, in its view, makes cultural sense. A policy enacted in 1998, for example, requires scientists to get government permission before using China's "human genetic resources"—a category that includes organs, tissues, blood samples, and any genetic materials, products, or even information. The goal is to ensure that these human "resources" are "rationally utilized." For the same reason the government announced plans to develop a new "genetic information card" that would convey certain genetic information about the cardholder. By 2009, bar codes representing the full biological characteristics of a person had been issued in a handful of Chinese cities, with more to come.

(SOURCE: The Editors of *The New Atlantis*, "Chinese Bioethics?," *The New Atlantis*, Spring 2003, pp. 138–140. Retrieved May 4, 2009 from http://www.thenewatlantis.com/publications/chinese-bioethics; Jiang Yuxia, "Gene ID Cards Issued To Help Chinese Street Children Find Parents," *China View*, January 3, 2008. Retrieved May 4, 2009, from news.xinhuanet.com/english/2008-01/03/content_7360752.htm)

Question

Does the Chinese focus on the good of society rather than the good of the individual set bioethics in China fundamentally at odds with Western bioethics? Given the global nature of modern science, what are some of the international ramifications of Chinese biotech research? Do you think DNA-based biometric identification cards are a good social policy?

determined by a combination of nature and chance, not by human design: each human child shares the common natural human species genotype, each child is genetically (equally) kin to both parents, yet each child is also genetically unique.[22]

Testament to its force, this argument has appeal to many cultural liberals.

Still, the arguments from the will of God or from nature have critics. One is Dr. Mark Hughes of Wayne State University, who helped develop PGD. Dr. Hughes says he is often asked: "Aren't we playing God?" In answer, Hughes says he asks:

But isn't having a flu shot, or a heart bypass, or an appendectomy, or cancer treatment, playing God too? Medicine, by its very nature, interrupts nature. It tries to block the normal course of things so that a child with meningitis doesn't so often die from it. Darwin would predict that these are the "weak" and nature should take its toll. Medicine makes drugs, makes surgical advances, designs imaging techniques to see problems before they occur. In medicine, we generally treat the patient and his/her family … we don't treat all of civilization.[23]

Stanford Professor of Law Hank Greely, who specializes in the biosciences, expresses a similar viewpoint:

> Almost everything man has done, at least since the invention of agriculture, can be viewed either as against God's will or as unnatural. A principled line between permissible human actions and impermissible ones is hard to draw.[24]

Empirical Considerations   A common empirical, as opposed to principled, objection to the increased use and application of genetic screening concerns the ambiguity of its result. The more gene-hunters find disease-linked DNA mutations, the greater the number of people who will have to deal with agonizingly uncertain outcomes.

As noted earlier, even if allowed to mature to a live birth, a genetically defective fertilized egg will not always generate a disorder or disease in the individual. It all depends on the penetrance of various genetic variations, called alleles. The allele that causes Huntington's, for example, has a 100 percent penetrance, which means the presence of the allele guarantees that the disease will develop. But that isn't nearly always the case. The risk of some diseases being tested, such as Gaucher disease, is less than 50 percent. In other words, half of all children with a diagnosis of Gaucher disease will never experience its symptoms, including pain, organ enlargement, and anemia. The rest can lead normal lives with treatment. Still, according to a study of this potentially serious but treatable metabolic disorder among Ashkenazi Jews, one-quarter of fetuses found to have Gaucher disease were aborted over an eight-year period.[25] Of further concern is the discarding of flawed embryos that *might* cause a disease or disorder, but not until well into adulthood,

when effective treatment or even cure might be available, as with colon cancer.[26] The tragic irony of such cases is that in our quest to preselect healthy children we may be deselecting them.

"This is just the tip of the iceberg," says Dr. William R. Wilcox, who treats Gaucher patients. "There will be a time when we have the ability to screen for thousands of diseases in one blood spot. What are you going to terminate for?"[27] Wilcox is horrified by the prospect of genetically testing for diseases that are imminently treatable.

But to the tests' defenders, not to offer screens would be unfairly denying couples genetic information about their offspring. "It's an opportunity to gain information which some people might want," says one genetic counselor. "It's their decision about what they want to do with that information."[28]

Giving tests for treatable disease or ones with ambiguous results isn't the only empirical concern of test critics. Their larger fear is that genetic screening of prospective children will move us toward a eugenic world in which children are valued more for their genotype than for their inherent characteristics, eventually ushering in a world of "designer" children in which genetic engineering of offspring becomes routine.[29]

In this vein, Harvard philosopher Michael J. Sandel worries that the tendency toward genetic tinkering threatens human dignity and ultimately will leave us with nothing to affirm but our own will. In Sandel's view, there's simply something wrong with parents selecting the kind of child they will have, including its sex.[30]

With that observation, we are poised to consider, in the next chapter, the morally controversial practice of prenatal testing for nonmedical sex selection.

CASES AND CONTROVERSIES

The Genetic Information Nondiscrimination Act

Consider three Americans: U, S, and A. U has an increased genetic risk for colon cancer, S has a family history of colon cancer, and A has a colonoscopic finding of several large, benign polyps. Most colorectal polyps never become cancer, but virtually all colorectal cancers begin as benign growths. Under the Genetic Information Nondiscrimination Act (GINA) of 2008, health insurance companies may not refuse to cover and may not raise premiums for U and S, although genetic information or family history puts them at higher risk for colon cancer. The basic idea is to spread the cost of insuring U and S over a larger insurance pool, which inevitably raises the costs for those whose risks are low or unknown. The sharing of this risk is thought appropriate, because U and S bear no personal responsibility for their genes. Their bad luck, in short, could have befallen any of us. Such is not the case with A, however. Under GINA, insurers could refuse to sell A an individual policy or could increase his or her premiums. What's more, if A is enrolled in an employer-sponsored group health plan, insurers could raise the rates for everyone in the group.

Questions for Analysis

1. Underlying GINA is an egalitarian impulse: to protect people with an elevated risk of illness through no fault of their own, as a consequence of their genes, for example, or their family history. Explain by reference to ethical principle why you think the GINA policy is fair or unfair.

2. Are people like A any more responsible for their increased risk than people whose genes predispose them to illness?

3. How have advances in genetic testing left A worse off than he or she otherwise would be?

4. In theory, the application of GINA rests on our current knowledge of the genetic basis of disease. How has this led to the arbitrary distinctions that GINA has created between U and S, on the one hand, and A, on the other?

CASES AND CONTROVERSIES

The Genetic Matchmaker

Tay-Sachs is an incurable, single gene disorder that kills children. Named after British ophthalmologist Warren Tay (1843–1927) and American neurologist Bernard Sachs (1858–1944), Tay-Sachs frequently occurs among Ashkenazi Jews. The rate of the disease among that group, who are from Central and Eastern European descent, is about 1 in every 3,000 births—nearly 100 times higher than other ethnic groups. Because Tay-Sachs is inherited in an autosomal recessive fashion, both parents must be carriers of the defective gene to have an afflicted child. If both parents are carriers, they have a one in four chance for each pregnancy of having a child with Tay-Sachs.

In 1983, after losing four of his own children to Tay-Sachs disease, Rabbi Josef Ekstein, an ultra-Orthodox Jew in Brooklyn, founded Dor Yeshorim (Hebrew for "Generation of the Righteous") with the express purpose of using knowledge of human genetics to prevent future suffering and death from Tay-Sachs. Dor Yeshorim representatives visit Orthodox high schools and draw blood samples from students, who are then issued a number. The samples are screened for genetic disease and the results stored in Dor Yeshorim's offices. When young Orthodox men

and women reach a marriageable age, and receive a recommendation from a *shadchan*, or matchmaker, about a potential mate, they or their parents call Dor Yeshorim, which retrieves the assigned numbers for each member of the potential couple and checks to see if they are carriers of genetic disease. If they are, they are told that a union is not advisable.

Since its founding nearly forty years ago, Dor Yeshorim in the United States, Europe, Canada, and Israel have tested more than 135,000 people. No children with Tay-Sachs disease have been born to Ashkenazi Jews who have participated in Dor Yeshorim's screening program. Soon after its founding, the organization added testing for a range of other conditions that are not always fatal, including conditions that are late-onset or that range in the severity of their expression—such as cystic fibrosis and Gaucher's disease. Dor Yeshorim representatives say the organization will continue to add any and all genetic tests available to its menu of screening options.

What looks like an unqualified success story in harnessing the knowledge of human genetics to rid us of dread diseases has, in fact, invited controversy. "This is what happens when you have people with no scientific orientation who want to do good," says Rabbi Moshe David Tendler, a professor of medical ethics at Yeshiva

(Continued)

CASES AND CONTROVERSIES (CONTINUED)

University. "The question arises, when do you stop? There are close to 90 genes you wouldn't want to have. Will this lead to people showing each other computer print outs of their genetic conditions? We'll never get married." Rabbi Tendler, a microbiologist and teacher of Talmudic laws, has been especially critical of Dor Yeshorim's devotion to nondisclosure of each individual's carrier status. By keeping the test results secret and only giving approval or disapproval of a match, the testing program avoids counseling every carrier of a genetic disease. But "[w]hen a match is proposed and nothing happens," Rabbi Tendler points out, "people naturally ask, why didn't this happen? They submitted to Dor Yeshorim and then decided not to get married. This reveals immediately to their entire Jewish community that there are two people who are blemished."

In fact, recent research about gene-carrier status and community stigma suggests that stigmatization of carriers for purposes of marriage has occurred within the Orthodox Jewish communities. According to Brooklyn oncologist Mark Levin of Genetic Testing, "Anxiety appears to be increased in identified carriers.... Among high school students, nearly half of carriers felt 'worried or depressed.'"[31]

Questions for Analysis

1. What moral issues does genetic screening raise?

2. Does Dor Yeshorim's premarital screening program hew more to the belief in the obligation of one generation to the next or to the eugenic imperative to eliminate the unfit?

3. As a program of genetic screening like Dor Yeshorim's expands to nonfatal and late-onset genetic conditions, do the ethical boundaries become more ambiguous?

4. Could genetic findings that target a group, such as Jewish people, as a market for commercial genetic tests create a perception of group members as tainted?

5. More from Rabbi Tendler: "My grandparents were born in America. The American ethical and moral values are very important to me.... The idea that Dor Yeshorim has genetic information and refuses to share it with the person who it belongs to is unfair, irrational, and almost anti-American. If you submit blood, you should be able to have the results."[32] What "American ethical and moral values" do you think Rabbi Tendler has in mind? Does Dor Yeshorim have a moral obligation to share blood results with the individuals who submitted the blood? If you knew that you were a carrier of a genetic disease, would you have an obligation to tell the person you intended to marry?

CASES AND CONTROVERSIES

Growing a Baby with a Disorder

Instead of seeking to eliminate a disorder that affects one out of a thousand Americans, including themselves, Candace McCullough and Sharon Duchesneau, a lesbian and deaf couple from Maryland, deliberately solicited a deaf sperm donor. Through an IVF procedure, Sharon gave birth to a baby boy who, months later, was determined to be mostly deaf. The new mother, a former intern in the bioethics department of the National Institutes of Health, was quoted as saying in a 2002 *Washington Post Magazine* profile: "A hearing baby [would have been] a blessing. A deaf baby [is] a special blessing."[33]

But not everyone shared that opinion. "I think all of us recognize that deaf children can have

perfectly wonderful lives," said bioethicist Alta Charo, adding:

> The question is whether the parents have violated the sacred duty of parenthood, which is to maximize to some reasonable degree the advantages available to their children. I'm loath to say it, but I think it's a shame to set limits on a child's potential.[34]

Nancy Rarus agrees with Charo. A staff member at the National Association of the Deaf, Rarus feels that her deafness has limited her choices. "I can't understand why anybody would want to bring a disabled child into the world," she says, speaking for herself, not the organization.[35]

But, like Duchesneau and McCullough, many people in the deaf culture do not share the popular view—institutionalized in the Americans with Disabilities Act of 1992—that deafness is a disability to be repaired. For them, it's a cultural identity to be proud and accepting of. Duchesneau and McCullough share this fundamental view. According to the *Post* profile,

> [T]hey see deafness as an identity, not a medical affliction that needs to be fixed. Their effort—to have a baby who belongs to what they see as their minority group—is a natural outcome of the pride and self-acceptance the Deaf movement has brought to so many.[36]

So framed—as a profound expression of one's beliefs, values, and self-identity as a member of an oppressed minority—a couple's reproductive choice to have a deaf child is, then, basically no different from the choice, say, of a proud, self-accepting African-American couple to have a child of their same color. In both cases, admittedly, the parents are imposing certain difficulties on the children, notably prejudice and discrimination. But, by the same token, both believe that they can be better parents to their children for sharing a particular trait—blackness or deafness.

Unimpressed with such a characterization, Dr. Robert J. Stillman of the Shady Grove Fertility Center in Rockville, Maryland, is among the majority of fertility specialists who deny requests to use the latest reproductive technology for having children with a defective gene, such as those associated with deafness or dwarfism. "In general," says Stillman, "one of the prime dictates of parenting is to make a better world for our children. Dwarfism and deafness are not the norm." Dr. Yury Verlinsky of Chicago's Reproductive Genetics Institute agrees. "If we make a diagnostic tool," he says, "the purpose is to avoid disease."[37]

Questions for Analysis

1. Is deafness a disability to be repaired or a cultural identity to be proud of?

2. What are the moral issues involved in deliberately having a baby with what is widely viewed, medically and culturally, as a disorder?

3. Do you think Duchesneau, McCullough, and their doctors are properly or improperly using PGD?

4. Evaluate a request for having children with a defective gene from the perspective of principlism. How would alternatives to principlism—care, existentialism, feminism, narratives—frame the issue?

REFERENCES

1. Liza Munday, "A World of Their Own," *Washington Post*, March 31, 2002, p. W22.
2. See note 1 above.
3. Darshak M. Shanghavi, "Wanting Babies Like Themselves, Some Parents Choose Genetic Defects," *The New York Times*, December 5, 2006, p. D1.
4. "PGD," *Male Infertility Clinic*. Retrieved June 12, 2009, from www.drmalpani.com/book/chapter26 .html.
5. Nicholas Wade, "Journal Clarifies Report on a Stem Cell Finding," *The New York Times*, November 23, 2006. Retrieved May 2, 2008, from www .advancedcell.com/recent-news-item/ journal-clarifies-stem-cell-report.
6. Amy Harmon, "Selection of Embryos Is on the Rise for Couples," *The New York Times*, September 3, 2006. Retrieved May 22, 2008, from http://www .iht.com/articles/2006/09/03/news/embryo.php.

7. Shanghavi, p. D5.
8. Susannah Baruch, David Kaufman, and Kathy L. Hudson, "Genetic Testing of Embryos: Practices and Perspectives of U.S. IVF Clinics," *Fertility and Sterility*, September 20, 2006. Retrieved May 8, 2008, from www.fertstert.org/article/PIIS0015028 206038933.2006.
9. William Saletan, "Better Than Sex: The Growing Practice of Embryo Eugenics," *Slate*, September 16, 2006. Retrieved June 2, 2008, from http://www .slate.com/id/2149772/.
10. B. A. Robinson, "Pre-Implantation Genetic Diagnosis (PGD) & Haplotyping (PGH)," *Religious Tolerance*, September 20, 2007. Retrieved August 20, 2008, from http://www.religioustolerance.org/ abo_pgd3.htm.
11. Kate Baggott, "Ethical Stem Cells?," *Technology Review*, August 24, 2006. Retrieved June 2, 2008, from http:// www.technologyreview.com/Biotech/17356/.

12. See note 11 above.
13. John A. Robertson, "Extending Preimplantation Genetical Diagnosis: The Ethical Debate," *Human Reproduction*, March 2003, pp. 465–471.
14. Michael J. Sandel, "Embryo Ethics," *The Boston Globe*, April 8, 2007. Retrieved August 21. 2008, from www.boston.com/news/globe/ideas/articles/2007/04/08/embryo_ethics/.
15. Fr. Tom Knoblach, "A Brief Ethical Primer on Artificial Reproductive Technologies in the Catholic Tradition," *Dioceses of St. Cloud*, April 2005. Retrieved from www.stcdio.org/OMF/RespectLife/ART.html.
16. Cyril Tennant, "Creation and Man: A Christian View," *International Seminar on Human Genetic and Reproductive Technologies: Comparing Religious and Secular Perspectives*, Cairo, Feb. 6–9, 2006. Retrieved June 12, 2008, from http://www.islamset.com/ioms/cairo2006/abstracts/cyril_tennant.html.
17. Andrew Kimbrell, *The Human Body Shop: The Engineering and Marketing of Life*. San Francisco: Harper San Francisco, 1993, pp. 233–234.
18. Theresa Moss, "Boy or Girl: You Choose," *Virtue Magazine*, November, 28, 2006. Retrieved June 12, 2008, from www.virtuemag.org/articles/boy-or-girl-you-choose.
19. See note 18 above.
20. Leon Kass, *Life, Liberty and the Defense of Dignity: The Challenge for Bioethics*. San Francisco: Encounter Books, 2002.
21. The President's Council on Bioethics, "Human Cloning and Human Reproduction: An Ethical Inquiry," July 2002. Retrieved June 12, 2008, from www.bioethics.gov/reports/cloningreport/research.html.
22. Leon Kass, "Brave New Biology," *Mercator NET*, March 31, 2006. Retrieved June 18, 2008, from http://www.mercatornet.com/articles/brave_new_biology/.
23. MSNBC News Chat, "A New Way of Making Babies," *Live Talk*, June 26, 2003. http://www.msnbc.com/modules/newsweek/talk/062603_hughes.htm.
24. Hank Greely, "Seeking More Goodly Creatures," *Cerebrum: the Dana Forum on Brain Science*, Fall 2004. Retrieved June 2, 2008, from www.law.stanford.edu/publications/stanford_lawyer/issues/74/SeekingMoreGoodlyCreatures.html.
25. Shachar Zuckerman, et al, "Carrier Screening for Gaucher Disease: Lessons for Low-Penetrance, Treatable Diseases," *JAMA*, September 19, 2007, pp. 1281–1290.
26. Ontario Consultants on Religious Tolerance, "Preimplantation Genetic Diagnosis (PGD) & Haplotyping (PGH): Current Status; Objections; Advantages," *ReligiousTolerance.org*, September 20, 2007, Retrieved May 30, 2008, from http://www.religioustolerance.org/abo_pgd2.htm.
27. Karen Kaplan, "Genetic Tests Offer Knowledge, Not Wisdom," *Los Angeles Times*, September 19, 2007, p. A19.
28. See note 27 above.
29. See note 13 above.
30. Michael J. Sandel, *The Case Against Perfection: Ethics in the Age of Genetic Engineering*, Cambridge, MA: Belknap Press, 2007.
31. Christin Rosen, Eugenics—Sacred and Profane, *The New Atlantis*, Summer 2003, pp. 78–89. Retrieved June 15, 2009, from http://www.thenewatlantis.com/publications/eugenics-sacred-and-profane.
32. See note 31 above.
33. Liza Mundy, "A World of Their Own," *The Washington Post*, March 31, 2002, p. W22.
34. See note 33 above.
35. See note 33 above.
36. See note 33 above.
37. See note 7 above.

Chapter 14

The Prenatal Testing
Debate II: Sex Selection

Although prenatal testing for sex selection is sometimes medically advisable, since the early 2000s PGD for nonmedical or social sex selection has risen with the overall increase in the use of the procedure.

There are two principal ways of guaranteeing the sex of a child after conception, one within the uterus, the other outside it. In the first, termed prenatal diagnosis, a sonogram or amniocentesis is used to determine the sex of the unborn. If the sex is undesired, an abortion can be performed. In the second, PGD is used to selectively implant an embryo of the desired sex. Today PGD technology offers virtually a 100 percent success rate for obtaining the desired sex in a baby without manipulating or engineering genes.

Banned in most countries, nontherapeutic PGD use for sex selection is legal in the United States, and unregulated. Although many US fertility clinics will do sex selection only in the case of inheritable genetic diseases, some offer it to couples who prefer one or the other. According to the GPPC survey (see Chapter 13), 42 percent of clinics permit the use of PGD for "nonmedical sex selection." That figure jumps to 80 percent if PGD is performed for other medical reasons.[1]

In 1998 the journal *Human Reproduction* reported an alternative preconception sex selection procedure called MicroSort. Developed at the Genetics and IVF Institute in Fairfax, Virginia, MicroSort involves sorting sperm and then inseminating the woman with sperm stacked to create a boy or a girl. The Institute charges about $2,300 a try and offers the service exclusively for family balancing.[2] Originally created by the Department of Agriculture to select sex in livestock, sperm sorting is less controversial than PGD because it's done at the time of conception and doesn't necessarily create excess embryos. But it's also less accurate. So far, 91 percent of couples who wanted girls got them. The success rate for boys is lower, at 76 percent. Some people combine the two procedures, using sorted sperm to fertilize the eggs in the petri dish in the hope that, when tested, most of the embryos will be of the desired sex.[3]

As a mix of technological, economic, cultural, and ideological developments revive the ethical debate about sex selection that has lain relatively dormant since the mid-1990s, controversy heats up, with six topics generally getting the most attention. Two involve (1) the proper use of technology and (2) the particular technology used: preconception MicroSort versus postconception PGD. The other four topics concern the social impact of widespread use of the new technology, especially as it relates to: (3) misogyny, sexism, and gender stereotypes; (4) sex ratios in local populations; (5) commodification of reproduction; and (6) consumer eugenics.[4]

PROPER USE OF TECHNOLOGY

The attack on social sex selection typically begins with the charge of abuse of reproductive technology. Specifically, some fertility specialists balk at the idea of family balancing, the most common reason for nonmedical sex selection. "What are you balancing?" asks critic Dr. Mark Sauer of Columbia University. "It discredits the value of an individual life." As for the few patients who request the procedure, Sauer says: "I look them straight in the face and say, 'We're not going to do that.'" Northwestern's Dr. Ralph Kazer concurs with Sauer, alluding to *Gattaca*, the futuristic film about a society that places people according to their DNA: "*Gattaca* was a wonderful movie. That's not what I want to do for a living."[5]

Dr. Yury Verlinsky of Chicago's Reproductive Genetics Institute disagrees. After embryo screenings, some patients ask the PGD expert about the sex of the embryos, and in his view it's their right to. "I tell them it's normal," Verlinsky says, "and I tell them it's male or female ... It's their embryo. I can't tell them which one to transfer." But the parents can, thereby, select the sex of the child.[6]

The January 26, 2004, issue of *Newsweek* contained a series of articles about pre-implantation social sex selection that featured a number of couples who had used PGD to select the sex of their babies. When asked by Virtue Magazine whether, with the aid of the new reproductive technology, she'd made herself God in choosing the sex of her child, one mother recently insisted that neither she nor the doctors were playing God. "You know," said Sharla Miller, who was interested in balancing her family,

> it's just like every other procedure the medical field can do for you. When our oldest son had spina bifida, they fixed that. Were they playing God? No, they were making it so he could walk and so he could function properly.[7]

In a recent US survey of 999 people who sought genetic counseling, a majority—anywhere from 56 to 75 percent—said they supported prenatal genetic tests for the elimination of life altering and threatening medical conditions, including mental retardation, blindness, deafness, cancer, heart disease, dwarfism, and shortened lifespan from death by five years of age. Far fewer respondents, albeit 10 percent, said they would want genetic testing for athletic ability, while another 10 percent voted for improved height. Nearly 13 percent backed the approach to select for superior intelligence, according to the survey conducted by researchers at the New York University School of Medicine.[8]

PRE- VS. POSTCONCEPTION TECHNOLOGY

Although not always for the same reasons, Christian religions agree that social or nontherapeutic sex selection is wrong regardless of the means, Micro-Sort's postconception or PGD's preconception. The Catholic Church, for instance, deems all treatments "illicit" that are used to create life without sexual intercourse between a husband and wife, because embryos created by ARTs are not the "fruit of a conjugal union."[9] The Anglican Church also opposes the nonmedical use of sperm sorting and embryo selection, not because it's inherently evil, but because it has not yet been widely used and tested, "and there is as yet unquantified and unknown potential harm to the child." Another of the Anglican Church's objections is that PGD destroys embryos, which it believes should be treated with respect. It does permit their destruction, however, "for important reasons of significant risk of serious genetic conditions, or for treating infertility." Consistent with this condition, in 2003 the United Kingdom's head of the Human Fertilization and Embryology Authority recommended that parents not be allowed to select the sex of their babies except on compelling medical grounds.[10]

The orthodox Jewish views on nonmedical sex preselection tend to be more nuanced than the Christian.[11] As Joseph Schenker of Hebrew University points out:

> The requirement for a man to procreate by having a minimum of two children—a boy and a girl—is obligatory according to Jewish law…. According to both schools [of Hebrew thought in the Talmud], Beit Shamai and Beit Hillel, in order to fulfill the obligation of procreation at least one son is required. Therefore the application of sex preselection for nonmedical indications may be of practical importance using the method of sperm separation or sex selection of pre-embryo by PGD.

Schenker also notes that Islam permits sex selection on an individual basis through available medical means according to the wishes of a married couple.[12]

Where the major religions generally do not distinguish between sperm sorting and PGD for sex selection, ASRM does. Basically, ASRM supports preconception interventions, while discouraging the use of elective postconception selection. In other words, sperm sorting, as with MicroSort technology, is okay because it is noninvasive and doesn't involve discarding embryos of the "wrong sex." But out of concern and respect for the embryo, ASRM currently discourages the use of PGD exclusively for sex selection.[13] Some doctors, however, have publicly objected to ASRM's

distinctions. Norbert Gleicher of the Center for Human Reproduction, for example, doesn't believe it's ethical to offer a patient a technique, that is, sperm sorting, that has a significant error rate compared to an alternative, PGD.[14]

SEXISM

Aside from the preceding matters, which deal with the nature and use of PGD technology, there are several topics that address the social impact of its widespread use, specifically in sex selection. One of those topics is sexism.

Marcy Darnovsky, associate director of the Center for Genetics and Society in Oakland, California, points out that throughout the 1980s and early 1990s sex selection troubled virtually all feminists and others in the United States who addressed the issue. Some, like Helen Bequaert Holmes, associated any deliberate trait selection with eugenics.[15] Others viewed sex selection as symptomatic of a sexist society that discriminated against individuals on the basis of gender. Mary Anne Warren even wondered whether the practice should be called "gendercide."[16] Even feminists of that era who were unbothered by sex selection offered but tepid support.[17]

At the same time, feminists feared that any effort to limit sex-selective abortions, especially in the United States, would threaten women's reproductive rights. So, they were reluctant to condemn the practice of sex selection outright. Warren, for example, despite her misgivings, argued that choosing the sex of one's child was sexist only if its intent or consequence was discrimination against women. More recently, feminist Mary Briody Mahowald has expressed a similar view, while voicing concerns that pressures on women to enhance traits of offspring may create new discrimination against them.[18]

This feminist ambivalence toward the practice reflects medicine's own uncertainty about the connection, if any, between social sex selection and sexist attitudes. Currently, for example, ASRM doesn't consider it sexist or devaluing to a child for individuals or families to select a sex other than the one they already have, given the different experiences involved in raising boys and girls.[19] But earlier, in 1999, ASRM objected to sex selection because it could lead to gender stereotyping and overall gender discrimination. Even on a small and sporadic scale, its ethics committee asserted at the time, individuals or families using PGD to make a gender selection such a choice:

> remain vulnerable to the judgment that no matter what their basis, they identify gender as a reason to value one person over another, and they support socially constructed stereotypes of what gender means. In doing so, they not only reinforce possibilities of unfair discrimination, but they may trivialize human reproduction by making it depend on the selection of nonessential features of offspring.[20]

The American College of Obstetricians and Gynecologists (ACOG) still holds that view, sanctioning only therapeutic sex selection. It insists that even if sincere about family balance, the very act of choosing a baby's sex "may be interpreted as condoning sexist values."[21]

For her part, Darnovsky worries about the negative worldwide impact, especially in South Asia, should sex selection become an established business in the United States. Quoting *Fortune* magazine, she writes:

> "It is hard to overstate the outrage and indignation that MicroSort prompts in people who spend their lives trying to improve women's lot overseas."[22]

SEX RATIOS IN LOCAL POPULATIONS

In fact, much of the worry about sex selection derives from what has happened in China and India, where preferences for boys has led to widespread aborting of female fetuses[23] and skewed sex ratios favoring males. Mindful of these developments, the United Nations officially opposes sex

selection for nonmedical reasons, while Canada, Australia and Britain, among other nations, have outlawed the practice entirely.[24]

But proponents say that China and India are not the United States, where sex selection is not done for social but personal reasons, such as family planning. As a result, say fertility specialists, there's no danger of skewing sex ratio.

Dr. James Grifo, who directs New York University's Fertility Center and generally opposes using embryo testing just for sex selection, selectively honors patient requests for information about the sex of the embryo. If, for example, a patient is already having an embryo screen for medical reasons, has a child, and wants one of the opposite sex, Grifo informs her. "It's the patient's information, their desire," he says. "What are we to decide, to play God?" As for unbalancing sex ratios and local populations, Grifo says:

> I've got news for you, it's not going to change the gender balance in the world. We get a handful of requests per year, and we're doing it. It's always been a controversy but I don't think it's a big problem. We should preserve the autonomy of patients to make these very personal decisions.[25]

Dr. Jeffrey Steinberg's Fertility Institutes, which permits first-child sex selection, agrees that the choices shake out to 50-50: "Reproductive choice, as far as I'm concerned, is a very personal issue," Steinberg says. "If it's not going to hurt anyone, we go ahead and give them what they want."[26] Of the more than 2,000 babies he's helped conceive, Steinberg says he gets about equal requests for boys and girls.[27]

Sociologist Barbara Katz Rothman agrees that a strong shift in the sex ratio isn't likely in the United States. What concerns the City College of New York sociologist, however, are the more subtle modifications affecting birth. When American parents choose the sex of their children, Rothman points out, the first child is more likely to be a boy, and sometimes that first is the only child. "We know a good deal about the effects of birth

BIOETHICS ACROSS CULTURES

Chinese Bias for Baby Boys

A study released on April 10, 2009 in the *British Medical Journal* showed that a bias in favor of male offspring has left China with 32 million more boys under the age of 20 than girls, creating "an imminent generation of excess men." For the next twenty years China can do nothing to avoid having increasingly more men than women of reproductive age.

Analyzing data from the 2005 national census survey, researchers found births of boys in China exceeded births of girls by more than 1.1 million. There were 120 boys born for every 100 girls. This disparity was perhaps unsurprising in light of China's one-child policy and the urge of couples to have sons.

The trend toward more male than female children intensified steadily after 1986, as ultrasound tests and abortion became more available. "Sex-selective abortion accounts for almost all the excess males," the *BMJ* paper said. The researchers reported that the gap was widest among children ages 1 to 4, a sign that the greatest imbalances among the adult population lie ahead. They also found more distortion in provinces that allow rural couples a second child if the first is a girl, or in cases of hardship. Those couples were

determined to ensure they had at least one son, according to the study. Among children born second, there were 143 boys for 100 girls.

A bias for boys has led to the widespread practice of aborting female fetuses in other nations, such as in South Korea (SK), where for years the government tended to tolerate the illegal practice, seeing a high birthrate as an impediment to economic growth. The policy worked. SK's fertility rate, which stood at 4.5 children per woman in the 1970s, fell to 1.19 by 2008, one of the lowest in the world. SK is currently having its first serious discussion of the ethics of abortion.

(SOURCE: Sharon LaFraniere, "Chinese Bias for Baby Boys Creates a Gap of 32 Million," *The New York Times*, April 9, 2009, p. A5; Choe Sang-Hun, "A Korean Doctors' Group Wants To Halt Abortion," *The New York Times*, January 10, 2010, p. 10.)

Question

What are some of the social consequences of large numbers of excess males? Is China and SK's experience with sex selection applicable to the United States? Is abortion for sex selection or population control moral?

---

order," Rothman reminds us. First-born children tend to be rule-following achievers, for example, whereas the youngest are inclined to be creative and rebellious. Adding gender to birth order troubles Rothman.

> Think of a community in which most boys are big brothers or only children, and most girls are little sisters. Picture, say, a kindergarten room with that distribution of children—with the boys stronger and more ambitious, given gender stereotypes reinforced by birth order; the girls more spoiled and demanding, flouting the rules, and doing things their own way. Where would such a community be? Because of the cost, it's a class thing. Think rich neighborhoods, elite private schools. Now think long term: What might be the consequences for our society if there are more

only-children and first-born sons and more later-born daughters among the elite, the people most likely to run the government, the business, the world?[28]

Rothman's concerns may not be borne out, but it could be decades before we know for sure the large-scale social changes of sex selection. By then the changes will have altered society. "We won't have the research to see the big picture until we're living in it," Rothman warns.[29]

COMMODIFICATION OF REPRODUCTION

Many of today's upscale magazines and even large circulation newspapers carry ads for IVF clinics, egg donors, surrogate mothers, and a variety of

BIOETHICS ACROSS CULTURES

Clinics' Pitch to Indian Émigrés

The immigrant experience usually involves a conflict between old customs and new choices. But, in a strange twist, for Indians in the United States and Canada, new freedoms may be helping perpetuate an age-old preference for boys.

In an effort to capture one of North America's fastest growing ethnic groups, companies are pitching products and procedures to Indian émigrés to preselect the sex of a child. "Desire a Son?" asked a recent ad in *India Abroad*, a weekly newspaper for Indian expatriates in the United States and Canada. "Pregnant?" asked another. "Wanna know the gender of your baby right now?" Such ads would be illegal in India, as would ads that claim to increase the odds of having a male child. Abortion has long been controversial in India, and the country has struggled to discourage women from exploiting medical technology to assure themselves sons. But the traditional bias against female children runs deep and accounts for a widening gender gap. A 1989 study of sex selection in New York City found that "all the foreign-born couples in the study—mostly from Asia and the Middle East—preferred boys."

In India, the number of girls per 1,000 boys has dropped to 927 from 962 between 1981 and 2001. The preference for males in India and in many other cultures is driven by economics. Boys have more job opportunities than girls and are expected to support parents in their old age. They also inherit property. Girls, by contrast, are seen as economic burdens, whose marriage comes with a costly dowry. But while India tries to stamp out the tradition, the open medical marketplace in the United States could prolong it, something which distresses many Indian-Americans. "As immigrants, we really had a chance of starting with a clean, fresh slate," said Shamita Das Dasgupta, a founder of Manavi, a New Jersey group that provides counseling for abused South Asian women.

"But we also know that's not possible because we bring our own baggage with us." Dr. Das Dasgupta adds:

> So it makes me scared when something like this happens with impunity, where people are saying, "We are offering a service the community will practice anyway." These practitioners are taking advantage of a practice that is totally misogynous, and unless the good-thinking people of our community stand up and let their voices be heard, such practices will continue happening.

It isn't just Indian immigrants who have carried over their preference for sons to this country. Demographers see a significant statistical deviation among other Asian-American families, such as Koreans and Chinese, favoring male children and, thus, sex selection techniques, such as PGD or sperm sorting.

(SOURCE: Susan Sachs, "Clinics' Pitch to Indian Émigrés," August 15, 2001. Retrieved May 7, 2009, from www.nytimes.com/2001/08/15/nyregion/clinics-pitch-to-indian-emigres-it-s-a-boy.html; Sam Roberts, "U.S. Births Hint At Bias for Boys In Some Asians," *The New York Times*, June 15, 2009, p. A1.)

Question

Several fertility specialists decided to advertise in Indian newspapers after seeing an increase in the number of Indian clients coming for gender selection. One was Dr. Masood Khatamee, who conducted the 1989 New York study. Khatamee is a professor in the obstetrics and gynecology department at the New York University School of Medicine and executive director of the Fertility Research Foundation. "I have not really put any ads anywhere before except in *New Yorker* magazine," Dr. Khatamee points out. "I don't know now if I did the right thing or the wrong thing." What would you say to Dr. Khatamee?

---

sex-selection techniques. Little wonder. Market research suggests that about a quarter of Americans would like to be able to select the sex of their child. Analysts say that the market for sperm sorting in the United States alone amounts to between $200 and $400 million, if it is "aggressively marketed."[30] In her recent book on the subject, Liza Mundy of the *Washington Post* even cast profit motive as the main driving force in the new ART.[31]

Perhaps the leading player in the burgeoning reproductive industry, Genetics & IVF Institute (GIVF) bills itself as " the world's largest, fully integrated, specialized provider of infertility and genetics services." With a website worthy of its boast, GIVF lures prospective client/patients with pictures of attractive, young women; adorable babies; and flashing pitches for services like "free infertility consults," "special pricing for two donor eggs cycles," and "new pricing for multicycle contracts."[32]

As sex selection increasingly takes on the trappings of the marketplace, many fear that the traditional importance of generating a child will shrivel in importance. They say that sex selection commercializes reproduction, commodifies children, and harms the parent/child relationship. The Catholic Bishops' Conference has even branded sperm sorting "one step in an act of manufacture of a child."[33] The Catholic Linacre Centre for Healthcare Ethics in Britain has also warned of the commodification of children conceived through gametic manipulation:

> [H]e or she is *produced* by a process very similar to the manufacture of an object: a process only explicable in terms of the parent or parents' desire to "make" a child. The danger is that the parents will be more inclined to think of their child as an object of possession if the child comes into being by means of an act with the symbolic content of *production*. The impact of this symbolic content can, indeed, be seen in the widespread abuse of the "products" of non-sexual conception: these embryos are mass-produced, screened, discarded, used in experiments, etc. There is therefore nothing abstract about concern to protect the symbolism of natural procreation; such concern is amply justified by the way many children (though not, of course, all children) are treated after non-sexual conception.[34]

Religious-based reservations notwithstanding, what effect sex selection has on those involved has yet to be determined. Researchers at Houston's Baylor College of Medicine currently are doing a long-term study of its social and health effects on children and families. In the meantime, we're left to cautiously extrapolate from studies of families with donor children.

In the most extensive longitudinal study to date, Susan Golombok, the director of the Center for Family Research at Cambridge University, has compared families with donor children, as well as those who used conventional IVF and those who conceived naturally. In 2006, when researchers last checked in, the donor-conceived children, who were then 12 years old, were unusually well-adjusted. What's more, their parents, and those who used conventional IVF, appeared more involved with their kids' lives than those who had conceived naturally.[35]

But even if sex selection is shown to do no serious long-term harm to children or families, that, of itself, is not likely to placate opponents who insist that it still insults the unconditional love a parent should have for a child. Philosopher Michael Sandel, for example, a member of the President's Council on Bioethics, doesn't worry about safety, coercion, or exploitation with respect to sex selection. Instead, in *The Case Against Perfection* (2007) he bases his opposition on two criteria. First, some kinds of enhancement violate the norms embedded in human practices. Second, parents are supposed to cultivate children through unconditional as well as conditional love. In his opinion, selecting a baby's sex and other traits fails both tests and betrays the parent-child relationship.

CONSUMER EUGENICS

San Antonio's Abraham Center of Life recently opened the world's first human embryo bank. A cause of celebration to some, for others the Center represents a step toward still another disturbing social impact: "designer babies."

Besides being able to select egg or sperm donors, "adopt" leftover embryos, or have embryos created for them, prospective parents can now choose from pre-embryos made at the Center in advance for unspecified recipients. The new service has been described as "the first time anyone has started turning out embryos as off-the-shelf products."[36]

Some bioethicists view this development not only as yet another sign of a troubling trend to treat pre-embryos like any other commodity—"like ordering a computer from Dell," as one puts it.[37] Some go even further, such as Robert P. George, a member of the President's Council of Bioethics, who says:

> This is just more evidence that we haven't been able to restrain this move towards treating human life like a commodity. This buying and selling of eggs and sperm and now embryos based on IQ points and PhDs and other traits really moves us in the direction of eugenics.[38]

The basic idea behind eugenics is to "enhance" children before they are born, to improve them beyond their expected abilities or, perhaps, beyond humanity's normal range. The day is soon coming when couples can select embryos based not only on sex, but height, weight, eye color, and even IQ. Rothman, George, and many others fear that gender selection could lead to a "slippery slope" of customizing offspring in more ways than just their gender, such as for high intelligence, beauty, coordination, perfect pitch, or whatever else parents desire. Critics worry about the unintended consequences of such practices.

For example, if parents made similar choices, then genetic diversity could be reduced. Also, genetic combinations that might enhance a desired goal could also result in disease or disability, either for those whose genes were altered or for their progeny. Perhaps the most troubling of the unforeseen effects is the abuse of trait selection. What's to guarantee that it will always be used benignly? It could turn malignant, should government start specifying traits. Philosopher/economist Francis Fukuyama is among those who oppose sex selection, fearful that it inevitably will lead to engineering of other offspring traits and ultimately to "designer" children.[39]

James Q. Wilson shares the general concern about the unintended consequences of sex selection. "We do not want families planning to have a movie star, basketball player, or high-energy physicist as an offspring," the political scientist says. But, at the same time, Wilson is unclear as to how to draw those limits. If we can't solve that puzzle, he would favor sharply limiting the sources of the embryo that can be implanted in a woman. "Perhaps the best solution," Wilson suggests, "is a kind of screened lottery akin to what doctors performing in vitro fertilization now do with donated sperm. One can match his race or ethnicity and even select a sex, but beyond that he takes his chances."[40]

Another significant category of objections to trait selection relates to equality, fairness, and justice. It's feared, for example, that trait selection would be based on affordability, thereby depriving a huge population of equal access and opportunity. This has potential consequences for the integrity of the so-called game of life. Not only would the unenhanced be "playing" at a disadvantage, the efforts and accomplishments of the enhanced would be suspect and diminished. Just think of Barry Bonds, Roger Clemens, Alex Rodriguez, and Mark McGwire and the controversies their alleged drug enhancements stirred up.

Although it's helpful to identify concerns such as unintended consequences, equality, and fairness, John A. Robertson is among those who feel it's premature to decide what uses, if ever feasible, would or should be permitted. "Such tests," he says, "are too far off in the future to make informed judgments about them now. Until they are closer to practical reality, they should not be an important factor in determining the acceptability of more feasible uses."[41]

Dr. Hughes agrees, when he emphasizes the "huge difference between identifying a gene mutation and identifying gene combinations that could lead to enhancements." By way of illustration, Hughes says:

> A disease like sickle cell anemia is caused by one typographical error in three billion letters of the human genome. If you have two copies of the typo, you have sickle cell, one typo and you are a healthy carrier of it. But, say you were going to try to abuse PGD and use it to select "for" something ... a trait like intelligence. Well, that is pretty silly. Intelligence is almost certainly determined by many genes, not just one like sickle cell anemia.[42]

As for the fears about unintended consequences, Stanford law professor Hank Greely wonders if prenatal genetic enhancement is "meaningfully different from other, accepted forms of enhancement" before and after birth—such as eating well, taking prenatal vitamins, and encouraging children to grow into "responsible, loving, and moral adults." Of prenatal care, Greely writes:

> One can argue that it is more permanent, but other enhancing interventions may have permanent effects, too. Prenatal care can have permanent consequences; teaching a foreign language to a child may have consequences that can neither be reversed nor duplicated by teaching her as an adult. And, if gene therapy ever becomes possible, at least some genetic effects might be reversed by replacing alleles. One can also argue that prenatal genetic enhancement will have longer-lasting effects because it will be passed down from generation to generation. But humans long ago carefully constructed a mechanism to pass down advantages from generation to generation; we call it a family. Some families have few advantages to pass on; others pass on, with greater or lesser success, personalities, education, money, and even high political office.
>
> Prenatal genetic enhancement is different from other forms of enhancement, but then each form of enhancement is different from all the others. Before we decide whether and how to regulate prenatal genetic enhancement, we need to decide not just how it differs from other forms of enhancement, traditional and new, but how, and if, those differences are important enough to justify regulation.[43]

CONCLUSIONS

As the wisdom and morality of prenatal social sex selection continue to exercise us, rapid advances in the human genome project and genetic engineering only threaten to confound things. Consider that the day is near when sex can be determined by targeting the genes for particular early modification, as opposed to selecting embryos of a particular sex for implantation, as with PGD. Regardless of whether one considers the pre-embryo a person, genetic engineering raises a question of making decisions for not-yet-existent children without their consent. In fact, genetic enhancement, generally, has been criticized as fundamentally coercive from the future child's perspective, because decisions are being made about the traits of these not-yet-existent children without seeking their consent.[44] This objection looms large when the issue is essentially a sex change operation without informed consent. Some commentators view this as a violation of autonomy.

Philosopher Matthew Liao, who has a special interest in the ethics of the new biosciences, writes:

> ....even though a person does not yet exist (the embryo is not yet a person), genetic engineering affects an identifiable individual. In particular, the embryo would have developed to become a person of a particular sex except for one's act, which has caused this embryo to become a person of a different sex. As an adult, this person could complain that he or she could have been different had the modification not taken place. The fact that the harm to the embryo takes place only at a future date does not change the fact that an act of harm—in this case, a violation of autonomy—has been committed against an identifiable individual....[45]

By contrast, selected embryos in PGD that are brought to existence cannot complain about being harmed embryos, because, were different embryos selected, they wouldn't have existed. "The issues of consent and autonomy do not arise," says Liao, "because such selection is the same as when a child is conceived in the normal way where the issues of consent and autonomy also do not arise." The embryo in genetic engineering, however, can complain about being harmed, "as it could have existed in a different state, except for the modification done to it." For Liao, then, PGD is preferable to genetic engineering for sex selection. By this account, those who believe that embryos are persons and who want to select the sex of their offspring seem left with only one ethical option: the more unreliable method of sperm sorting.

A final point: Genetic testing is changing medicine not only for the unborn, but for the born as well. And, like prenatal testing, adult testing raises many concerns.

Since April 2003, when scientists announced they had sequenced the human genome—the full collection of genes that produces a human being—genomic information has grown exponentially.[46] New knowledge about how our genes affect our health is transforming the way diseases are understood, diagnosed, treated, and even predicted. Today, thanks to a comprehensive catalog of human genetic variation, first published in April 2005, gene tests are available for more than 1,500 conditions, with most of the growth in the area of common diseases. And now, as genetic screening gets cheaper and faster, researchers are hunting down the biological origins of more-complex disorders that involve multiple genes—diabetes, Alzheimer's, heart disease, cancer, heart disease, cystic fibrosis and blood disorders, even depression. "We are on the leading edge of a genuine revolution," says noted physician-geneticist Francis Collins, former director of the National Human Genome Research Institute.[47] If the scientists are right, genetic tests for

some of these diseases could be available in a matter of months. Indeed, in March 2010, it was reported that, for the first time, researchers had decoded the entire genome of patients to find the exact genetic cause of their diseases.[48] Then, just two months later, researchers raised the science and technology of genetic engineering to a new level by creating an artificial life form in the laboratory (see case "Synthia" that follows).

Although genetic testing promises valuable risk assessment information, it also raises many thorny issues. The most basic question, perhaps, is whether to get a genetic test for a disease for which there is currently no cure. There is also the fear that insurance companies could increase premiums for those who test positive. Then there's the issue of whether a given test accurately predicts and diagnoses a particular disease as promised. Most important is the question of what to do with the test information, specifically a positive test that determines risk but not inevitability of disease. Should one take pre-emptive measures? Might insurance companies limit coverage to someone who had learned that he was at risk, yet showed no signs of having a disease?[49] Would positive tests be interpreted as a "pre-existing" condition that would preclude getting health insurance in the first place? Would they become part of the job application and lead to discrimination? Hard questions such as these loom ahead as our scientific culture moves deeper into the revolution in genetic testing and engineering.

CASES AND CONTROVERSIES

Genetic Risks: To Disclose or Not To Disclose?

As genetic testing becomes more sophisticated and widespread, the catalog of genetic risks it can detect will expand. Increasingly, physicians may find themselves in an ethical dilemma such as the following:

> Mrs. B has a family history of breast cancer and has become worried about getting can-

cer herself. Her family physician, Dr. T, refers her for genetic testing. Her results show that she has the BRCA1 mutation, [which is associated with a risk of developing breast or ovarian cancer].

Mrs. B attends post-test genetic counseling and clearly understands the implications of the results for herself and her daughter (aged 29), who is also Dr. T's patient. Dr. T receives a copy of the test results and strongly recommends that Mrs. B inform her daughter of her own risk, but Mrs. B declines to do so immediately. Dr. T offers to inform the daughter on Mrs. B's behalf, but Mrs. B declines the offer. The daughter is getting married in 6 months, and Mrs. B does not want to worry her. She says that she may tell her daughter herself after the wedding. The daughter finds a pamphlet about a familial breast cancer program in her mother's study. During a visit with Dr. T, the daughter asks if she should be concerned.[50]

Questions for Analysis

1. State the nature of Dr. T's dilemma in terms of conflicting duties.

2. What are the principal benefits and harms of nonconsensual disclosure?

3. What should Dr. T do?

4. Do you think that before testing, physicians should inform patients that, under specific circumstances, they will disclose relevant genetic information to family members if the patient refuses to do so? Discuss the pros and cons.

5. In order to find out if they have a high genetic risk for breast or ovarian cancers, women like Mrs. B have to get a test sold by its patent holder, Myriad Genetics, at a cost of more than $3,000. But in a far-reaching decision, a federal judge in New York recently struck down patents to two human genes linked to hereditary breast and ovarian cancers, BRCA1 and BRCA2. In his 2010 decision, United States District Court Judge Robert W. Sweet found that the company's patents were invalid because the genes are "found in nature," and products of nature can't be patented. In effect, the judge agreed with the plaintiffs' argument that "[h]uman genes, even when removed from the body, are still products of nature" and, therefore, each human being's cells shouldn't be private property. For its part, Myriad argued that the work of isolating the DNA from the body transforms it and makes it patentable. Explain why you agree or disagree with this decision, which, if upheld, could throw into doubt the patents covering thousands of human genes and reshape the law of intellectual property.[51,52]

CASES AND CONTROVERSIES

Made-to-Order Babies

The Fertility Institutes, headed by Dr. Jeffrey Steinberg, is the world's largest and most successful PGD sex selection program. It boasts:

> Unlike many programs offering sex selection only to very limited couples with known genetic disorders in the family, we make sex selection available to all patients seeking to balance their families or assure themselves that a pregnancy will result in ONLY the gender outcome they desire (www.fertility-docs.com).

The Institutes' cost of sex selection with 99.9 percent guarantee of chosen gender, including IVF fee, is about $20,000. Although designing other traits wasn't available in 2004 when Dr. Steinberg was profiled on the CBS news program *60 Minutes*, the fertility specialist said he was already fielding requests for eye color and advised couples to call back in five or ten years, when he might be able to accommodate

not only their preferences in eye color, height, and personality, but also in the capacity of their offspring to achieve "self-transcendence."[53] (Indeed, according to one prominent geneticist, the VMAT2 gene is the "God gene" associated with spirituality.)[54] Sure enough, by 2009 the Los Angeles fertility clinic was offering a new service that would allow couples to choose their baby's physical traits, including eye and hair color.

But not everyone welcomes this development. Dr. Mark Hughes, a pioneer of PGD, calls the whole idea "absurd."

> We receive calls from some asking whether we would use PGD for sex selection. We won't. Most groups won't. We became doctors and scientists in order to diagnose, treat and eventually cure human disease. The last time I checked, your gender was not a disease. If there is no pathology then we shouldn't be involved. Besides, we are too busy helping couples avoid disastrous diseases.[55]

(Continued)

CASES AND CONTROVERSIES (CONTINUED)

Reproductive biologist Barry Zirkin of Johns Hopkins agrees. "This [sperm sorting]," he says, "is not curing a disease and it's not curing a societal problem. There is no reason for haste and every reason to be cautious."[56] John Lantos of Kansas City's Center for Practical Bioethics calls trait selection a plain "outrage to my sense of justice that people would rather waste resources on something like this rather than things that really matter."[57]

None of this criticism deters Dr. Steinberg, who says he's just moving ahead with science. "Genetic health is the wave of the future," he confidently professes. "It's already happening and it's not going to go away. It's going to expand. So if they [his critics] have major problems with it, they need to sit down and really examine their own consciences because there's nothing that's going to stop it."[58]

Questions for Analysis

1. Some critics, including Lantos, say that trait selection is "frivolous, but not necessarily unethical." Do you agree, or do you think it's unethical?

2. How would principlism frame the issue of trait selection?

3. What concerns might an application of Callahan's ecological and vital institution principles raise about trait selection? (See Chapter 6.)

4. What objections to trait selection might religious and social conservatives raise? What reasons for concern might social liberals express?

5. As sex selection most often prevents the birth of female children, does it devalue women as a group?

CASES AND CONTROVERSIES

Slouching Toward Gattaca?

In the 1997 science fiction film *Gattaca*, PGD is used in a future society to ensure that children carry only the "best" hereditary traits of their parents. Indeed, would-be parents who don't use the reproductive technology to ensure ideal offspring are viewed as antisocial, and their progeny are scornfully labeled "in-valids" and consigned to low-level, menial jobs. The "valids," on the other hand, whose genetic traits have been carefully screened and can be easily genotyped, qualify for professional employment and the best opportunities. Given this genetic discrimination, Vincent Freeman, an in-valid with a congenital heart condition and one of the last "natural" babies to be born, has no chance of fulfilling his lifelong desire of being selected for a manned space mission to Saturn. So, in order to improve his chances, Freeman assumes the identity of perfect specimen Jerome Morrow, and subsequently learns to deceive DNA and urine sample testing to conceal his real identity. Things turn dark for Freeman, however, when a colleague suspects his real identity and the police begin to investigate.

Questions for Analysis

1. Do you think that society inevitably would discriminate against those it perceives as having an undesirable trait that can be prevented or eliminated?

2. It's been argued that the mere decision of preventing the birth of a child with a given trait such as sex, hair color, or height is a form of discrimination. Do you agree?

3. It's also been argued that ensuring the most advantaged birth possible is really no different from giving children every advantage possible after they're born. Is it?

4. In *Gattaca* two kinds of eugenics, in effect, are practiced: negative and positive. Negative eugenics discourages reproduction by persons having genetic defects or inheritable, "undesirable" traits, whereas positive eugenics encourages reproducing by persons with "desirable" traits. Is there a moral distinction to be made between negative and positive eugenics such that one is morally permissible but the other is not?

5. Evaluate the use of PGD in *Gattaca* from the perspectives of religious natural law, utilitarianism, and Kant's categorical imperative.

6. Gattaca is supposed to be a society in the "near future." Is there any evidence to believe that we are becoming Gattaca-like?

CASES AND CONTROVERSIES

The Creation of "Synthia"

In May 2010 the American scientist J. Craig Venter introduced the first artificially created genome, nicknamed "Synthia."[59] Venter, one of the first scientists to sequence the human genome, explained that "Synthia" is "the first self-replicating species we've had on the planet whose parent is a computer." In other words, Synthia isn't a clone or a genetically modified organism, but "a new, entirely artificial life form created in a laboratory," by constructing a bacterium's "genetic software" and transplanting it into a naturally occurring microbe with its DNA stripped out.[60] Venter said that the breakthrough would benefit humanity by creating bacteria to perform specific functions, such as producing fossil fuels or medicines.[61] Some scientists hailed Venter's creation as an advance in synthetic biology; others downplayed it. Julian Savulescu described Venter's announcement as "creaking open the most profound door in humanity's history, potentially peeking into its destiny." The Oxford University ethicist added that Venter "is not merely copying life artificially or modifying it by genetic engineering. He is going towards the role of God: Creating artificial life that could never have existed." Savulescu warned darkly of "unparalleled" risks. "This could be used in the future to make the most powerful bioweapons imaginable," he said.[62] For his part, President Obama asked the Presidential Commission for the Study of Bioethical Issues to study the implications of the development.

Questions for Analysis

1. Were you a member of the president's bioethics commission, what implications of the new science and technology of "synthetic life" might trouble you?

2. Do you think that the creation of life from non-life, i.e., fully synthetic cells, challenges religious notions about the creation of life and the concept of a soul?

3. Venter believes that creating synthetic bacteria is important scientifically and philosophically. As he says, "It's certainly changed my views of the definitions of life and how life works."[63] But others aren't as sanguine. John Brehany, for one, the executive director and ethicist at the Catholic Medical Association, says: "We must be very prudent in how quickly and extensively we try to apply this technology." Although "[w]e are empowered and entitled by God to exercise responsible stewardship over creation," Brehany cautions against hubris. "It would be unfortunate if this invention contributed to the false impression that human beings have replaced God or can play God," he points out. "Only if we understand our proper place in the order of creation can we avoid destructive abuses of this powerful invention."[64] Is Venter's achievement consistent or inconsistent with your

REFERENCES

1. Phoebe S. Berman, "Genetic Testing of Embryos: Practices and Perspectives," *Fertility and Sterility*, September 2006. Retrieved May 1, 2008, from www.dnapolicy.org/resources/PGDSurveyReportFertilityandSterilitySeptember2006withcoverpages.

2. E. F. Fugger, S. H. Black, K. Keyvanfar, and J. D. Schulman, "Births of Normal Daughters after MicroSort Sperm Separation and Intrauterine Insemination, In-vitro Fertilization, or Intracytoplasmic Sperm Injection," *Human Reproduction*, September, 1998, pp. 2367–2370.

3. Denise Grady, "Girl or Boy? As Fertility Technology Advances, So Does an Ethical Debate," *The New York Times*, February 6, 2007. Retrieved May 2, 2008, from www.nytimes.com/.../health/06seco.html?n=Top%2FReference%2FTimes%20Topics%2FPeople%2FG%2Fgrady%2C%20Denise.

4. Marcy Darnovsky, "A New Chapter in the Sex Selection Debate," *Gene Watch*, January–February 2004. Retrieved July 8, 2008, from http://www.gene-watch.org/genewatch/articles/17-1darnovsky.html.

5. Claudia Kalb, "Brave New Babies," *Newsweek*, January 26, 2004. Retrieved May 12, 2008, from http://www.newsweek.com/id/52878?tid=relatedcl.

6. See note 5 above.

7. Theresa Moss, "Boy of Girl: You Choose," *Virtue Magazine*, November 28, 2006. Retrieved June 12, 2008, from www.virtuemag.org/articles/boy-or-girl-you-choose.

8. Angeline Duran Piotrowski, "Myth 22: People Who Use Genetic Testing Want Designer Babies," *Mommy Myth Busters*, January 26, 2009. Retrieved June 20, 2009, from http://mommymythbuster.wordpress.com/2009/01/26/myth-22-people-who-use-genetic-testing-want-designer-babies/.

9. The Pontifical Academy for Life, Tenth General Assembly, Final Communiqué on "The Dignity of Human Procreation and Reproductive Technologies. Anthropological and Ethical Aspects," February 2004. Retrieved May 22, 2008, from www.ewtn.com/library/CURIA/PALHUPRO.HTM.

10. Michael Cook, "UK Authority Rules Out Sex Selection," *Bioedge*, January 7, 2003. Retrieved June 7, 2008, from http://www.australasianbioethics.org/Newsletters/100-2003-11-14.html.

11. Sherman Silber, et al, "Religious Perspectives of Ethical Issues in ART: Infertility, IVF and Judaism" *Middle East Fertility Society Journal*, September 2005, pp. 200–204.

12. Joseph G. Schenker, "Gender Selection: Cultural and Religious Perspectives," *Journal of Assisted Reproduction and Genetics*, September 2002, pp. 400–410.

13. See note 3 above.

14. Beth Whitehouse, "Pick a Gender and Start a Controversy," *Newsday*, July 14, 2004. Retrieved June 12, 2008, from cosmos.phy.tufts.edu/mhonarc/nonsexist-parenting/msg00110.

15. Helen Bequaert Holmes, "Sex Preselection: Eugenics for Everyone?" in *Biomedical Ethics Reviews, 1985*, James M. Humber and Robert F. Almeder, eds., Clifton, NJ: Humana Press, 1986, pp. 39–72.

16. Mary Ann Warren, *Gendercide: The Implications of Sex Selection*. Lanham, MD: Rowman & Littlefield Publishers, 1985.

17. See note 4 above.

18. Mary Briody Mahowald, *Genes, Women, Equality*. New York: Oxford University Press, 2000, p. 12.

19. Ethics Committee of the American Society of Reproductive Medicine, "Preconception Gender Selection for Nonmedical Reasons, *Fertility and Sterility*, May 2001, pp. 861–864.

20. See note 19 above.

21. American College of Obstetrician and Gynecologists, "ACOG Committee Opinion No. 360: Sex Selection," *Obstetrics & Gynecology*, April 1, 2007, pp. 475–478.

22. Marcy Darnovsky, "Sex Selection Moves to Consumer Culture," *Genetic Crossroads*, August 20, 2003. Retrieved June 2, 2008, from http://www.geneticsandsociety.org/article.php?list=type&type=139.

23. Erik Eckholm "Desire for Sons Drives Use of Prenatal Scans in China," *The New York Times*, June 21, 2002, p. A3.

24. Therese Hasketh, Li Lu, and Zhu Wei Xing. "The Effects of China's One-Child Family Policy after 25 Years," *The New England Journal of Medicine*, September 15, 2005. pp. 1171–1176.

25. See note 3 above.

26. See note 3 above.

27. Lisa Napoli, "I'll Have a Girl, Please," *Marketplace*, September 12, 2006. Retrieved June 21, 2008, from http://marketplace.publicradio.org/shows/2006/09/12/AM200609121.html.

28. Barbara Katz Rothman, "The Consequences of Sex Selection," *The Chronicle Review*, February 24, 2006, p. B16. Retrieved July 2, 2008, from http://chronicle.com/weekly/v52/i25/25b01601.htm.

29. See note 28 above.

30. *Australasian Bioethics Information Center*, Michael Cook, ed., August 22, 2003. Retrieved June 8, 2008, from http://www.australasianbioethics.org/Newsletters/089-2003-08-22.html.

31. Liza Mundy, *Everything Conceivable: How Assisted Reproduction Is Changing Men, Women and the World*. New York: Knopf, 2007.

32. Genetics and IVF Institute. Retrieved June 18, 2008, from http://www.givf.com.

33. Albert Mohler, "The Ethics of Sex Selection: A View from Britain," *crosswalk.com*. Retrieved June 8, 2008, from http://www.crosswalk.com/1231725/.

34. Helen Watt, "The Diane Blood Case," *Linacre Centre for Healthcare Ethics*, 1997. Retrieved July 1, 2008, from http://www.linacre.org/dblood.html.

35. Peggy Ornstein, "Your Gamete, Myself," *The New York Times Magazine*, July 15, 2007, p. 58.

36. Rob Stein, "'Embryo Bank' Stirs Ethics Fears," *Washington Post*, January 6, 2007, p. A1.

37. See note 36 above.

38. See note 36 above.

39. Francis Fukuyama, *Our Posthuman Future: Consequences of the Biotechnology Revolution*, New York: Farrar, Strauss and Giroux, 2002.

40. Leon Kass and James Q. Wilson, "The Ethics of Human Cloning," *The American Enterprise*, 1998, p. 67.

41. John A. Robertson, "Extending Preimplantation Genetic Diagnosis: The Ethical Debate," *Human Reproduction*, March 2003, pp. 465.

42. MSNBC News Chat, "A New Way of Making Babies," *Live Talk*, June 26, 2003. http://www.msnbc.com/modules/newsweek/talk/062603_hughes.htm.

43. Hank Greely *Cerebrum: the Dana Forum on Brain Science*, Fall 2004. Retrieved August 8, 2008, from www.dana.org.

44. Leon Kass, *Life, Liberty and the Defense of Dignity: The Challenge for Bioethics.* San Francisco: Encounter Books, 2002.

45. S. Matthew Liao, "The Ethics of Using Genetic Engineering for Sex Selection," *Journal of Medical Ethics*, February 2005, pp. 117. Retrieved July 28, 2008, from http://www.pubmedcentral.nih.gov/tocrender.fcgi?iid=139644.

46. Kathy L. Hudson, M.K. Holohand, and Francis S. Collings, "Keeping Pace with the Times—The Genetic Information Nondiscrimination Act of 2008," *The New England Journal of Medicine*, June 19, 2008, pp. 2661–2663.

47. Claudia Kalb, "Peering into the Future: Genetic Testing," *Newsweek*, December 11, 2006. Retrieved June 8, 2008, from www.upstreambio.com/downloads/Peering_Into_Future.

48. James R. Lupski et al, "Whole-Genome Sequencing in a Patient with Charcot–Marie–Tooth Neuropathy," *The New England Journal of Medicine*, March 10, 2010. Retrieved March 11, 2010, from http://content.nejm.org/cgi/content/full/NEJMoa0908094?query=TOC.

49. Robert Pear, "Growth of Genetic Tests Concerns Federal Panel," *The New York Times*, January 18, 2008, p. 12.

50. Mireille Lacroix et al, "Should Physicians Warn Patients' Relatives of Genetic Risks?" *CMAJ*, February 26, 2008. Retrieved June 15, 2009, from http://www.cmaj.ca/cgi/content/full/178/5/593.

51. John Schwartz and Andrew Pollack, "Judge Invalidates Human Gene Patent," *The New York Times*, March 29, 2010. Retrieved April 1, 2010, from http://www.nytimes.com/2010/03/30/business/30gene.html?scp=1&sq=myriad&st=cse.

52. Smriti Rao, "Court Strikes Down Patents on Two Human Genes; Biotech Industry Trembles,"

Discover, March 30, 2010. Retrieved April 1, 2010, from blogs.discovermagazine.com/.../court-strikes-down-patents-on-two-human-genes-biotech-industry-trembles/.

53. *60 Minutes*, "Babies by Design," April 14, 2004.

54. Dean H. Hamer, *The God Gene: How Faith Is Hard-Wired into Our Genes*, New York: Anchor Books, 2005.

55. MSNBC News Chat, "A New Way of Making Babies," *Live Talk*, June 26, 2003. http://www.msnbc.com/modules/newsweek/talk/062603_hughes.htm.

56. See note 47 above.

57. See note 47 above.

58. Laura Bauer, "Custom-made Babies? It's a Possibility," *The San Diego Union-Tribune*, March 8, 2009. Retrieved June 18, 2009, from www3.signonsandiego.com/stories/2009/mar/08/1n8designer002232-custom-made-babies-its-possibili/?uniontrib.

59. Daniel G. Gibson et al., "Creation of a Bacterial Cell Controlled by a Chemically Synthesized Genome," *Science Express*, May 20, 2010. Retrieved May 24, 2010, from http://www.sciencemag.org/cgi/content/abstract/science.1190719.

60. NA, "Venter: Artificial Life Cell Will Benefit Humanity," *BBC Newsnight*, May 20, 2010. Retrieved May 22, 2010, from http://news.bbc.co.uk/2/hi/programmes/newsnight/8696148.stm.

61. Ridhar Adhikari, "Synthetic vs. Real Life: Is There a Place for Both?," *Science*, May 21, 2010. Retrieved May 23, 2010, from http://www.technewsworld.com/story/Synthetic-vs-Real-Life-Is-There-a-Place-for-Both-70049.html.

62. Marielena Montesino de Stuart, "The Modern Prometheus Redux: The Creation of 'Synthia,'" *Spero News*, May 22, 2010. Retrieved September 12, 2010, from http://www.speroforum.com/a/33389/site/site/privacy.asp.

63. Susan Watts, "Assessing the Impact of Venter's 'Synthetic Life,'" *BBC News*, May 20, 2010. Retrieved May 22, 2010, from http://www.bbc.co.uk/blogs/newsnight/susanwatts/2010/05/assessing_the_impact_of_venter.html.

64. See note 61 above.

Chapter 15

The Stem Cell
Debate I: Background
and Terminology

In the 1960s, biologists discovered that certain stem cells in our adult bodies retain an almost embryo-like power to spawn other cells. Stem cells in bone marrow, for example, continue to breed blood cells, and skin stem cells breed skin. The source of these particular-tissue forming stem cells is the zygote formed at conception. Twenty years later, in 1981, scientists first successfully removed mouse stem cells and stored them in a lab. This procedure was repeated with human cells in 1998 by Dr. James Thomson at the University of Wisconsin, building upon the research of such scientists as Leroy Stevens, who years earlier had shown that damaged or altered stem cells could stimulate certain cancers, including leukemia, breast cancer, and some brain cancers.[1] Then, in the late 1990s, enormous hope followed the news that scientists succeeded in using stem cells in mice to cure paralysis, diabetes, and brain disease.[2]

The great promise of stem cells comes from their unique potential to develop into any cell type in the body. This gives them extraordinary replacement value, allowing them to function as a sort of repair system for the body. According to the National Institutes of Health (NIH), stem cells

> can theoretically divide without limit to replenish other cells as long as
> the person or animal is still alive. When a stem cell divides, each new
> cell has the potential to either remain a stem cell or become another
> type of cell with a more specialized function, such as a muscle cell, a red
> blood cell, or a brain cell.[3]

By coaxing them to become whatever cells are needed, scientists believe that stem cells will provide new therapies and treatments for an array of diseases and medical conditions, such as macular degeneration, as well as for spinal cord injuries, burns, and even male infertility.

Despite its potential to revolutionize our understanding of human biology, stem cell research is morally controversial and culturally divisive. Indeed, according to *Science* magazine, stem cell research has triggered "one of the most contentious public debates in the history of biomedical science."[4] The next chapter deals with the profound moral and religious disagreements at the heart of the cultural discourse surrounding stem cell research. In preparation for that discussion, this chapter provides background and basic terminology, including a review of how stem cells are obtained.

LOOSENING THE STEM CELL BINDS

At his first prime-time presidential address, August 9, 2001, George W. Bush became the first president to provide federal funds for stem cell research. Although they are present in us from conception to death, most scientists today believe that stem cells derived from early embryos offer the most promise because they have the potential to develop in all of the tissues in the body. Most scientists also believe, as Bush noted in his speech, that

> rapid progress in this research will come only with federal funds [because they] help attract the best and the brightest scientists [,] ensure new discoveries are widely shared at the largest number of research facilities and the research is directed toward the greatest public good....[5]

Nevertheless, the Bush endorsement of stem cell research came with one big stipulation: Federal funds could only be used for research on the roughly twenty existing stem lines, or masses of stem cells with the same genetic code, that private research had isolated from embryos. This condition, while not banning stem cell work, did mean that no research money could go to scientists who either created or used fresh lines of ESCs after August 9, 2001.

Five years later, stem cell research occasioned another "first" for President Bush. On July 19, 2006, the president cast his first veto by rejecting legislation of a Republican-controlled Congress that would have overturned the earlier research restrictions by expanding federally supported ESC research. With a backdrop of infants born through IVF using PGD procedure—sometimes called "snowflake babies" or "adopted embryos"—Bush said the proposed Stem Cell Research Enhancement Act violated his principles on the sanctity of human life by encouraging the destruction of embryos left over from fertilization procedures. Perhaps in an attempt to head-off the objection that such embryos would be destroyed anyway, the president confessed:

> I felt like crossing this line would be a mistake, and once crossed we would find it almost impossible to turn back. Crossing the line would needlessly encourage a conflict between science and ethics that can only do damage to both, and to our nation as a whole.[6]

About a year later, in June 2007, Bush again vetoed the Stem Cell Research Enhancement Act, this time sent by a Democrat-controlled Congress. "Destroying human life in the hopes of saving human life is not ethical," Bush said on that occasion.[7]

By defying Congress twice in less than a year, the president had placed himself squarely on the side of leaders of the Christian Right and many social conservatives. At the same time, he set himself against a majority of voters, many members of his own political party, and the scientific community, who feared American scientists were losing ground to their counterparts in less restrictive countries. Clearly, by blocking an expansion of stem cell research, the president had reinserted himself into a moral, scientific, and political debate in a quickly moving field roiling at the confluence of technology and autonomy, on one hand, and deep-seated, religiously based cultural taboos, on the other.

It was, thus, that both sides enthusiastically received the news, on November 2, 2007, that two teams of scientists—one from Wisconsin, the other from Japan—had turned human skin cells into what appeared to be ESCs without having to make or destroy an embryo. As widely depicted, "the discovery, if it holds up, should provide an unlimited supply of stem cells without the ethically controversial embryo destruction and the restrictions on federal financing that have impeded work on human embryonic cells."[8] Still, as we'll presently see, though the new technology did dodge significant ethical problems, it also created some new ones, thereby ensuring that the stem cell debate was not likely over. Indeed, at its 2008 convention, the Republican Party adopted a decidedly conservative, pro-life platform that advocated "a ban on all embryonic stem cell research, public or private."

With the election of Democrat Barack Obama, a new era for stem cell research began, and with it more controversy. Within days of his inauguration in 2009, the new president announced that he would lift restrictions on federal financing for ESC research. Immediately thereafter, the US Food and Drug Administration's approved the first-ever study of a treatment based on human embryonic stem cells, using discarded embryos from in vitro fertilization procedures. In response, the Georgia legislature swiftly moved to limit ESC research in that state, and anti-abortion groups nationwide promised similar efforts in other states. In April 2009, the NIH proposed guidelines to allow research with federal financing, but only on stem cells derived from surplus embryos at fertility clinics. To the dismay of some scientists, no research funding would be available for stem cell lines created solely for research purposes. Along with the new guidelines came rigorous eligibility standards revolving around informed consent that included giving donors the ability to change their minds until their embryos were actually used. All these regulations became part of the Stem Cell Research Enhancement Act of 2009.[9] Just when the matter appeared settled, in August 2010 a federal judge blocked NIH funding of ESC research, ruling that the support violated a federal law–the Dickey-Wicker Amendment–barring the use of taxpayer money for experiments that destroy human embryos. In response, Sen. Arlen Specter (D-Pa.) introduced a bill that would update

guidelines on federal funding for embryonic stem cell research and circumvent the ruling.

While it may be dizzying to follow the political tit-for-tat in the ongoing stem cell wars, it's flatly impossible to understand what's at issue or have an informed opinion without some scientific background. A good place to start is with some basic terminology.

EMBRYONIC AND NON-EMBRYONIC STEM CELLS

The many different types of human stem cells fall into one of two broad categories: embryonic or non-embryonic. Human embryonic stem cells, or ESCs (or hESCs), are those that exist only in days-old human embryos, called blastocysts; or, earlier, in blastomeres, which are the cells generated after the fertilized egg's first few divisions. Non-embryonic, or "adult stem cells," exist in different fetal and adult tissues, such as aborted or miscarried fetuses; pregnancy matter such as umbilical cord, placenta, or amniotic fluid; menstrual blood; and adult tissue and organs.

According to Do No Harm, a group that calls itself "The Coalition of Americans For Ethical Research," non-embryonic source stem cells have produced treatments for at least seventy-two ailments, including spinal cord injuries, rheumatoid arthritis, and sickle cell anemia.[10] Blood-forming stem cells from bone marrow or from umbilical cord or placenta blood, for example, are used in transplantation procedures, particularly to treat leukemia and compromised immune systems, as from chemotherapy.[11] They're also used in treating some other cancers. Still, the consensus of scientific opinion is that the most promising stem cells for cell therapy treatment and for understanding the mechanisms of disease are to be derived not from non-embryonic sources but from human embryos, that is, ESCs.[12]

ESCs are highly adaptable cells that have been termed *pluripotent* for their remarkable potential to become any one of the body's more than two hundred types of cells.[13] "Indeed," says the Manhattan Institute's Peter Huber, who frequently writes on drug development and technology, "these ultrayoung cells are so extraordinarily versatile that they—and they alone—are capable of breeding something even younger than life."[14]

By contrast, *multipotent* adult stem cells can renew themselves and multiply to yield a limited number of different cell types of their tissue or organ. Studies suggest that some adult stem cells, skin for example, may have plasticity, a feature that allows them to yield cell types other than from the specific tissue or organ from which they originate. Such flexibility also has been demonstrated in placenta, cord blood, and bone marrow stem cells.[15–18] In an especially provocative study, scientists in Australia have demonstrated that nasal stem cells from patients aged 2 to 80 could develop into cells of heart, liver, kidney, muscle, brain, and nerve; they've also produced "patient specific stem cells" from over forty patients for study.[19] In 2007, research scientists in the United States managed to isolate stem cells from the testes of mice,[20] and some scientists have even proposed that adult stem cells can be coaxed backward into ESCs. In any event, perhaps within five years, according to Huber:

> a mother in the early stage of pregnancy will routinely direct her obstetrician to extract and stash away some embryonic cells for the future benefit of her unborn child. When the child gets to be 40 and has early Parkinson's or some other degenerative disease, another doctor will pluck those cells out of the freezer and cultivate a perfect cure. And if instead the child is fated to suffer nothing but the degenerative disease of old age, why then, he or she will have the option of curing that affliction, too. Restarting the biochemical clock for the body as a whole when you're 80 will be as straightforward as restarting it for any one specific tissue or organ when you're 40.[21]

DIFFERENTIATION

Hours after fertilization, the single cell that we all begin as divides to form blastomeres. Within five days, about 150 cells have formed the blastocyst,

at the core of which are ESCs. As long as these cells remain stem cells, they can divide indefinitely. But once they start to differentiate, they cannot. Differentiation is the process during which the unspecialized cell becomes specialized, or turns into the body's various types of mature cells, such as bone, heart, or brain cells.

Since 2001 scientists have been learning how to grow ESCs in the lab and how to make them differentiate into the sort that might be useful in therapy, such as liver and heart cells. This procedure is enormously complicated and has yielded mixed results. Producing heart cells, for example, is easier than producing pancreas cells. It's also not known how the lab-grown mature cells will function properly when introduced into a patient's body. Their very strength, or versatility and growth capacity, make ESCs unstable and hard to control, as evidenced by a story out of China of a man who was treated with ESCs for Parkinson's disease, only to die of a brain tumor apparently caused by the cells.[22]

LINES

Before stem cells can begin to differentiate or specialize, scientists extract them from the blastocyst (or, less frequently at present, from blastomeres), store them to prevent differentiation, and allow them to keep dividing. The result is a mass of stem cells with the same DNA (deoxyribonucleic acid), or genetic code, called a line. Once established, a line can be grown in the lab indefinitely, and cells can be frozen for storage and used by many researchers for their experiments. As long as the line continues to reproduce, many researchers can draw from this supply for their experiments indefinitely.[2] Some scientists think that the development of new drugs and helping the body self-repair are potentially the most exciting prospect for stem cell lines.[23] As for the problem of tissue rejection, scientists may someday be able to modify ESCs in the laboratory by using gene therapy or other techniques to overcome this potential obstacle.

OBTAINING STEM CELLS

Until the 2007 milestone, when scientists coaxed mature human skin cells to behave like embryonic ones, there were two main ways to obtain ESCs, both from embryos: (1) from IVF embryos prior to implantation or (2) from embryos specifically created for research. Now a third can be added: reprogrammed skin cells, termed induced pluripotent stem, or iPS, cells.

Pre-Implantation or Spare Embryos

The estimated twenty ESC lines in existence in 2001 when President Bush limited federal funding have by now become genetically degraded and, thus, ill-suited for research.[24] There is, however, a replacement source frozen in the nation's 450 fertility banks. According to a 2003 RAND corporation study, there were about 400,000 pre-implantation embryos, or blastocysts, stored in cryopreservation that were created during IVF procedures and donated with informed patient consent. Most of these spare embryos are slated for fertility treatment, according to RAND, who put the number designated for research at 2.8%. But a more recent study puts that figure much higher, inasmuch as nearly 60% of fertility patients say they are willing to donate their stored embryos for stem cell research.[25]

If, then, research could proceed on just a fraction of the stored embryos, say one-quarter, that would give scientists 100,000 embryos (compared to 11,200 previously estimated by RAND), resulting in 2,000 to 3,000 viable stem cell lines (instead of 224–336).[26] That number could be higher if, as is likely, the number of stored embryos is today closer to a half-million.

Created Embryos

The second primary way to obtain stem cells involves embryos created specifically for research purposes, either by (1) parthenogenesis or (2) somatic cell nuclear transfer (SCNT). Both methods provide a genetic match with the donor, but SCNT provides a match for anyone's use. (In 2006, researchers reported cultivating a colony of ESCs from apparently dead embryos, but their research values have yet to be determined.)[27]

Parthenogenesis Parthenogenesis, or stimulation of unfertilized eggs, is often called "virgin birth," because the eggs are made to develop without sperm. The stem cells derived from these products of stimulated unfertilized eggs are a potential source of transplants because they closely match the immune system of the recipient. In theory, then, a woman who wants a transplant to treat a condition such as a spinal cord injury or diabetes could provide eggs to a lab, which in turn could create tissues that her body wouldn't reject. Because parthenogenetic embryos, both of whose sets of chromosomes carry a female imprint, are not viable, there are fewer moral obstacles to deriving their stem cells than by using SCNT, which employs cloning technology.[28]

Somatic Cell Nuclear Transfer SCNT is a technique that involves extracting the nucleus, where the genetic material is held, from an unfertilized donor egg and replacing it with the nucleus extracted from a specialized or adult cell such as a skin cell. Given the proper signals, this single cell will begin to divide as if newly fertilized, resulting in a new entity that has the genetic constitution virtually identical to the donor somatic cell.[29] (In 2001, Advanced Cell Technology [ACT] became the first company to successfully test this procedure to the six-cell stage.)

SCNT, then, basically consists of three steps: (1) removing the nucleus of a donor's egg; (2) replacing the egg's nucleus with a second donor's somatic, or nonreproductive, body cell, such as hair, skin, or blood; and (3) "fertilizing," by applying an electric discharge to fuse the cells together to begin the process of differentiation, or dividing. After a few days the product can either be (A) implanted into a uterus and let develop into a baby; or (B) have its stem cells extracted for research purposes. "A" is called reproductive cloning and is widely, if not universally, opposed. "B," which has elicited considerable scientific interest, is termed nuclear transplantation or, more popularly, therapeutic or research cloning.[30,31]

BIOETHICS ACROSS CULTURES

Japanese Create Fatherless Mouse with Three Mothers

In April 2004 Japanese scientists demonstrated that the creation of a baby mouse did not require a paternal role. The mouse, named Kaguya, was the product of two female mice. Since all genetic material was derived from a female, Kaguya was promoted as a "virgin birth." Technically speaking, however, she wasn't parthenogenic, or the product of a virgin birth, since she didn't originate from a single source of genetic material; two females contributed to her birth. In creating Kaguya, scientists combined one normal mouse egg and a genetically manipulated mouse egg to form the "parthenogenic" embryo, which they then implanted into a surrogate female mouse.

Although this process is not reproducible (as of yet) in humans, researchers are nevertheless uncovering the keys for controlling early human development and producing artificial gametes. It typically takes about ten years for a scientific breakthrough in animal models to be applied to humans. But since its dawn in 1978, with the first baby born through IVF, reproductive technology has progressed at a breathtaking speed, which suggests that the application of the Japanese achievement to the human system isn't far off.

At the same time, commentators point out that creating an embryo from two eggs would be a crazy way for us to reproduce.

(SOURCE: Nancy L. Jones, "Three Mothers Make a Baby: Is that Sex? Yes, Or Maybe?," The Center for Bioethics & Human Dignity, June 9, 2004. Retrieved May 21, 2009, from http://www.cbhd.org/resources/reproductive/jones_2004-06-08.htm)

Question

In the opinion of Nancy L. Jones, Professor Public Health Sciences at Wake Forest University School of Medicine: "If Kaguya's mode of creation were to be extrapolated to humans, the very basis of our society would be shattered—opening nearly endless possibilities for overcoming the normal reproductive barriers for mammals that requires both male and female genetic contributions." Discuss some of the "shattering" social implications of such an event. In 2004 the President's Council on Bioethics published a report entitled *Reproduction and Responsibility: The Regulation of New Biotechnologies*. Among its recommendations are prohibitions against "attempts to conceive a child by any means other than the union of egg and sperm." On what moral grounds would you support or oppose this recommendation?

Reprogrammed Stem Cells

Rarely in science does anyone who starts a controversial field also end it. But that's how James Thomson characterizes his involvement in the stem cell controversy. It was Thomson's lab at the University of Wisconsin—together with one in Japan—that first captured stem cells from spare embryos in 1998, destroying the embryos in the process and triggering the "stem cell wars."[32] The same teams seemed to end the cultural conflict in 2007 when they induced stem cells from skin cells, without ever using a human embryo.[33,34]

The new technique, called induced pluripotent stem (iPS) cells, consists of adding just four genes to ordinary adult skin cells. The genes somehow reprogram the skin cells to become stem cells that genetically match the donors and, therefore, wouldn't be rejected by their immune systems. The genetically

matched cells would also enable scientists to study complex diseases such as Alzheimer's in the laboratory.[35]

The iPS technique obviates the donation of women's eggs and, significantly, avoids controversial cloning. Indeed, so confident is Thomson that his discovery will end the stem cell debates that he was quoted as predicting: "A decade from now [it] will be just a funny historical footnote."[36] His optimism was rewarded in 2008 when researchers from Harvard and Columbia Universities used iPS technique to take adult skin cells from two elderly sisters (aged 82 and 89) with a genetic form of Lou Gehrig's disease and reprogrammed them into cells resembling ESCs. In creating the disease-specific, individualized human cells, scientists proved that embryonic-like stem cells specific to both a person and disease can be manufactured using adult human cells. Shortly afterward,

BIOETHICS ACROSS CULTURES

ESC Research in Iran

After slowly developing scientifically for several hundred years, Iran is now starting to invest in science and taking a leadership role in the Middle East. Major developments are occurring in that country in ESC research with the full support of the government.

At present, Iran permits stem cell research and therapeutic applications in the "pre-ensoulment stages" of fetal development. As bioethicists Mansooreh Saniei and Raymond De Vries note:

> Islam is unique among world religions in that the embryological development of humans has been extensively discussed and described in the divine scripture, the Qur'an, and commented on in detail by Prophet Mohammad and the Imams, exemplary teachers who are descendants of the Prophet. Ensoulment is generally believed by Muslim scholars to take place at 120 days after conception (although a minority belief indicates ensoulment takes place 40 days after conception).... Based on theological and ethical considerations derived from the Qur'an passages that describe the embryonic journey to personhood developmentally, and the rulings that

treat ensoulment and personhood as occurring over time almost synonymously, it is correct to suggest that Shi'ite and a majority of Sunni jurists will have little problem in endorsing ethically regulated research on stem cells that promises potential therapeutic value.

Although Iran currently has no comprehensive legal framework for research on human embryos, it has issued guidelines, one of which prohibits generating human embryos for research purposes. However, under the guidelines embryos left over from assisted reproduction treatments may be used for research purpose.

(SOURCE: Mansooreh Saniei and Raymond De Vries, "Embryonic Stem Cell Research in Iran: Status and Ethics," *Indian Journal of Medical Ethics*, October-December 2008. Retrieved May 22, 2009, from http://www.issuesinmedicalethics.org/164ie181.html)

Question

What, if anything, is ethically different about generating embryos exclusively for research and doing research on spare embryos? Do you agree with the Iranian (and American) distinction, or is the nature of the embryo generation morally irrelevant to you?

---

researchers announced that they had expanded their library of disease stem cells to include, among others, Parkinson's, juvenile diabetes, Down Syndrome, and two forms of multiple sclerosis. Then, in 2009, Chinese researchers took a giant step closer to creating medically useful stem cell lines when they reprogrammed cells to create live offspring with normal organs and body tissue in mice.

CLONING

Cloning involves the manipulation of a cell so that an identical copy of the donor can be produced from it. In simple terms, cloning is the production of multiple and identical copies. The copies could be cells, plants, and even whole animals. Currently, cloning is widely used by farmers for the

vegetative reproduction of plants and by gardeners whenever they take a cutting. Various animals have been cloned, including frogs, mice, sheep, and cows, but not chickens or poultry. The most famous clone was Dolly (1997-2003), a sheep cloned by Ian Wilmut of Roslin Institute in Scotland from an udder cell of a six-year-old sheep. In 2007, researchers at the Oregon National Primate Research Center reported cloning of monkey embryos, extracting stem cells from the clones, and stimulating their development into brain neurons and heart cells. In 2008, a South Korean company began offering clone pet dogs at a cost of $150,000. In the same year, scientists in Japan reported successfully cloning a mouse from a body that had been frozen for sixteen years.[37]

To date, nontherapeutic cloning—SCNT for humans, or human cloning—has not been documented and is widely opposed. Research or therapeutic cloning, on the other hand, has elicited considerable scientific interest. Although most human embryos made for research are made through SCNT, the procedure has not escaped the moral controversy that bedevils stem cell research, generally. As the new reprogramming technique, iPS, bypasses the need for embryos to obtain stem cells, it avoids cloning and, thus, has been widely viewed by people outside science as quelling the moral debates that trouble the field. But most scientists hold a more guarded view and, in fact, stress the need to continue funding for traditional (i.e., SCNT) ESC research. This means that the moral and political debates about stem cell research that we now turn to are likely to remain among the most fiercely contested battlegrounds in reproductive ethics.

CASES AND CONTROVERSIES

The *Pernkopf Anatomy*

It's commonplace to assume that the fine anatomy illustrations used in medical training have come from willing donors who have selflessly left to science the gift of their bodies for the education of future generations. Evidently, this isn't always the case. In 1996 a body of evidence suggested that a well-known medical atlas favorably compared with the work of Vesalius (1514–1564) was a product of Nazi evil genius.

The *Pernkopf Anatomy*, an authoritative multivolume text, was produced during the Third Reich by Eduard Pernkopf (1888–1955) and his four associates, all members of the Nazi party. Although the identities of the cadavers used by Pernkopf and his associates to produce the exquisitely detailed illustrations have not been conclusively determined, there's the distinct possibility that Pernkopf used the murdered bodies of men, women, and children from the Holocaust for his atlas of anatomy.

Pernkopf, who was a successful anatomist, was also a fervent believer in National Socialism and joined the Nazi party in 1933. Soon after Hitler invaded Austria in 1938, Pernkopf was chosen as Dean of the Vienna Medical School, where his first assignment included purging the medical school faculty of all Jews and "undesirables." As a result, most of the faculty was lost, including three Nobel Laureates. In his first official speech to his selected faculty members, Pernkopf expressed his beliefs as follows:

> To assume the medical care—with all your professional skill—of the body of the people which has been entrusted to you, not only in the positive sense of furthering the propagation of the fit, but also in the negative sense of eliminating the unfit and defective. The methods by which racial hygiene proceeds are well known to you: control of marriage, propagation of the genetically fit whose genetic, biologic constitution promises healthy descendants: discouragement of breeding by individuals who do not belong together properly, whose races clash: finally, the exclusion of the genetically inferior from future generations by sterilization and other means.[38]

As of 1997, the University of Vienna provided all libraries carrying the *Pernkopf Atlas* with an insert titled "Information for Users of *Pernkopf Atlas*." The insert provided the political background of Pernkopf along with this statement:

> Currently, it cannot be excluded that certain preparations used for the illustrations in this atlas were obtained from (political) victims of the National Socialist regime. Furthermore, it is unclear whether cadavers were at that time supplied to the Institute of Anatomy at the University of Vienna not only from the Vienna district court but also from concentration camps. Pending the results of the investigation, it is therefore within the individual user's ethical responsibility to decide whether and in which way he wishes to use this book.[39]

In 1998 a commission at the University of Vienna issued a final report of its investigation of the Institute of Anatomy. It could neither prove nor disprove the suspicions surrounding the *Pernkopf Anatomy*.

(Continued)

CASES AND CONTROVERSIES (CONTINUED)

Questions for Analysis

1. Should we study and learn from illustrations that may have been made of the corpses of those killed for that purpose?

2. Is it ethical to let *Pernkopf's* excellent illustrations, so useful to medicine, go to waste?

3. Ethical responsibility seems to pull in two directions with respect to the use of *Pernkopf*. Can the same be said of using human embryos in experiments and research; or of using viral vaccines, such as Varivax and Maruvax II, that were generated from aborted fetuses?

4. In 1998, the White House asked the National Bioethics Advisory Commission to give an opinion on the disposition of human embryos. It concluded:

[I]n the light of public testimony, expert advice, and published writings, we have found substantial agreement among individuals with diverse perspectives that although the human embryo and fetus deserve respect as forms of human life, the scientific and clinical benefits of stem cell research should not be foregone.

The commission recommended that the federal government sponsor and fund such research, "but only if it is conducted in an ethically responsible manner." (For the full text, see http://bioethics.gov/pubs.html). Do you agree with the commission's conclusion and recommendation? What principle would you use for determining whether research on human embryos is conducted in "an ethically responsible manner"? Would the principle, whatever it was, be equally applicable to Pernkopf's likely use of Holocaust victims?

CASES AND CONTROVERSIES

Irreconcilable Differences

President Obama's policy will not end the stem cell debate, any more than his predecessor's did. As Christian bioethicist David Fletcher says:

Perhaps the most crucial and fundamental debate will be between those with a traditionally, biblically based view of the sacredness and inviolability of human life and those who ... find no intrinsic value in embryonic human life in comparison with the values that can be promoted by its destruction.[40]

Fletcher cites Peter Singer as representative of the latter group for dismissing the standard Judeo-Christian belief that "human beings have a special place in the world, that there is a world of moral difference between a human being and any other creature."

Admittedly, according to Singer, human embryos are potential children, but the Australian philosopher doesn't believe that that confers any special status on them. Only, Singer claims, if someone has a good reason for bringing the embryo into existence—such as a childless couple trying to conceive using the embryo—does the embryo have value and should be given a chance at developing. Therefore, Singer concludes, it makes sense to use embryos freely for research, and all the more so because sentient animals would be used less.

Predictably, Singer's argument seems "odd" to Fletcher, even if, as Fletcher puts it, "we wish to call the embryo only a potential person and not a person from the moment of conception." Fletcher explains as follows:

If something has the potential to develop into and become a thing of great value, it would normally be valued even before the time that it comes to realize this potential. For example, if we had a bulb of a rare and valuable species of tulip, the value of the flower it will become would cause us to value the bulb now, perhaps every bit as highly as an adult specimen. It is inconceivable that we could value the tulip but disregard the tulip bulb, or that we could value the living child or adult, but fail to value it in its earlier stages of development into that state.

Questions for Analysis

1. Do you think that Fletcher satisfactorily answers Singer?

2. What moral theory is Fletcher employing to confer special status on a fetus?

3. The pro-life community is divided on the ethics of stem cell research, and even more sharply on the ethical acceptability of allowing funding only for research on already established stem cell lines, not the creation of new ones by the further destruction of embryos. As Fletcher says:

> Some would argue that the use even of existing lines would be to profit from and thus to condone the destruction of embryonic human lives, and might draw an analogy to the use of the *Pernkopf Anatomy*. Others, while uneasy about the source of the stem cell lines, share with most people the desire that important research be done to benefit the sick.[41]

Explain by appeal to moral principle(s) which side you favor.

4. Singer wrote (in the *Manchester Guardian*, August 21, 1999):

> Other things being equal, there is less reason for objecting to the use of an early human embryo, a being that has no brain, no consciousness and no preferences of any kind, than there is for objecting to research on rats, who are sentient beings capable of preferring not to be in situations that are painful or frightening to them.[42]

What moral principle underlies this opinion? Do you agree with Singer or do you disagree based upon a competing principle?

CASES AND CONTROVERSIES

The Missyplicity Project

The Missyplicity Project is the first serious attempt to clone a pet dog. It takes its name from Missy, a mongrel rescued from a dog pound and adored by her wealthy California owner. Indeed, so beloved was Missy that in 1998 she was flown under the supervision of BioArts International, a biotech startup, to Texas A&M University to have her DNA preserved forever. Missy had been spayed, so she couldn't have puppies. Not that her devoted owner wanted Missy's offspring; she wanted an exact replica. And so began the Missyplicity Project.

When word of BioArts's feat spread, the fledgling company was inundated with requests to clone other loved animals, leading to the founding of another company—Genetic Savings and Clone—which allowed other wealthy owners to bank their pets' DNA. But cloning Missy was no mean task, and when she died in 2002, at the ripe old canine age of fifteen, she faded from the news.

Then, in 2005, as if returning from the dead, Missy, or rather her clone Mira, turned up in South Korea, along with two other puppies, Chingu and Sarang. There had been two other puppies, but they died soon after birth. The three Missy clones were introduced to the world via a video, posted on YouTube in the summer of 2008. The voices of skeptics were silenced when tests conducted by the Veterinary Genetics Laboratory at the University of California concluded that the three dogs were, indeed, clones. The YouTube piece also made mention of a dog-cloning "auction" named Best Friends Again, organized in the manner of an eBay sale, open to all. Bids were invited over a five-day period with the top bidders getting to clone their pet. The bidding raised about $750,000, with the five highest bidders in the BioArts auction remaining anonymous. A spot was reserved for a sixth dog, free: Trackr.

Trackr, an Alsatian, had recently retired from a police search-and-rescue team in Halifax, Nova Scotia, when news of the 2001 World Trade Center attacks broke. Knowing Trackr's unique qualities, and that there was a shortage of search-and-rescue dogs in New York, his owner drove for fourteen hours, and arrived early on September 12. This remarkable dog, now 15,

(Continued)

CASES AND CONTROVERSIES (CONTINUED)

was responsible for finding the last survivor from the rubble, Genelle Guzman McMillan, a 30-year-old employee of the Port Authority who worked on the 64th floor of the North Tower.

"'What you've got to understand is that Trackr is my best friend and lifelong companion,'" says his owner, James Symington, a former Canadian police officer. "'He's changed my life in ways I can't explain. To know that his legacy was going to go on is the greatest gift I've ever received. If Trackr's double has even 70 per cent of him, then I'll put him to work for the search-and-rescue team—and I'll be dusting off my gloves, too.'"[43]

Trackr died in April 2009. In June, Symington received five clone puppies from the South Korean lab that had performed the Missyplicity project.

Questions for Analysis

1. What moral issues, if any, does commercial cloning of companion animals raise?

2. Given the current pet overpopulation problem, which costs millions of animals their lives and millions in public tax dollars each year, what social value, if any, does the cloning of pets have? Does

it matter, morally, that it may not have any social value?

3. Cloning is an imperfect science and potentially dangerous for the animals involved, including the clone, which carries a high risk for substantial health complications. Also, surrogate mothers who bear the cloned embryos until delivery may have to endure surgical procedures due to complications from pregnancy. Do you think that nonmaleficence toward animals can override a human's desire for a companion pet; or is it the case that animals can't and don't have rights?

4. Cloning can only replicate the pet's genetics, which influence but do not determine its physical attributes or personality. In fact, a pet's personality, which is what their owners generally desire to preserve, is the trait least likely to be replicated by cloning. What's more, the cloned companion animal may not even physically resemble the original pet.[44] In the light of these facts, is a commercial cloning company exploiting the emotional attachment of owners to their pets through deception, or isn't it?

5. Would you clone a pet?

REFERENCES

1. Kaspar Mossman, "Stem Cells Cause Cancer," *Scientific American Mind*, April 2006. Retrieved July 8, 2008, from http://www.sciammind.com/issue.cfm?issuedate=Apr-06.

2. Raja Mishra, "What Can Stem Cells Really Do?" *Boston Globe*, August 21, 2001. Retrieved April 30, 2008, from http://www.mult-sclerosis.org/news/Aug2001/WhatCanStemCellsReallyDo.html.

3. National Institutes of Health (NIH), "Stem Cell Information," December 20, 2006. Retrieved June 9, 2008, from http://stemcells.nih.gov/info/faqs.asp.

4. Anne Drapkin Lyerly and Ruth R. Faden, "Embryonic Stem Cells: Willingness to Donate Frozen Embryos for Stem Cell Research," *Science*, July 6, 2007, pp. 46–47.

5. President George W. Bush, "President Discusses Stem Cell Research," *The White House* August 9, 2001. Retrieved July 2, 2008, from http://www.whitehouse.gov/news/releases/2001/08/20010809-2.html.

6. Sheryl Gay Stolberg, "First Bush Veto Maintains Limits on Stem Cell Use," *The New York Times*, July 20, 2006, p. A1.

7. Sheryl Gay Stolberg, "Bush Vetoes Bill Removing Stem Cell Limits, Saying 'All Human Life is Sacred,'" *New York Times*, June 21, 2007, p. A21.

8. Andrew Pollack, "After Stem-Cell Breakthrough, the Real Work Begins," *The New York Times*, November 27, 2007, p. D1.

9. Editorial, "Stem Cell Compromise," *The New York Times*, April 23, 2009, p. A24.

10. "Do No Harm: The Coalition of Americans for Research Ethics." Retrieved July 1, 2008, from www.stemcellresearch.org/.

11. Paolo De Coppi et al, "Isolation of Amniotic Stem Cell Lines with Potential for Therapy," *Nature Biotechnology*, January 7, 2007, pp. 100–106.

12. Europa Bio, the European Association of Bio-Industries, "Human Stem Cell Research: A Novel Technology that Will Benefit Patients: Information

and Position Paper," November 19, 2003. Retrieved June 12, 2008, from http://www.europabio.org/articles/article_254_EN.doc.

13. See note 2 above.

14. Peter Huber, "Fountain of Youth," *Forbes.com*. July 4, 2005. Retrieved June 11, 2008, from http://www.forbes.com/forbes/2005/0704/098.html.

15. T. Miki et al, "Stem Cell Characteristics of Amniotic Epithelial Cells," *Stem Cells*, November 2005, pp. 1549–1559.

16. C. P. McGuckin et al, "Production of Stem Cells with Embryonic Characteristics from Human Umbilical Cord Blood," *Cell Proliferation*, August 2005, pp. 245–255.

17. B. J. Crain, S. D. Tran, and E. Mezey, "Transplanted Human Bone Marrow Cells Generate New Brain Cells," *Journal of Neurological Science*, June 2005, pp. 121–123.

18. W. Murrell et al, "Multipotent Stem Cells from Adult Olfactory Mucosa," *Developmental Dynamics*, June 2005, pp. 496–515.

19. Shahin Rafii et al, "Generation of Functional Multipotent Adult Stem Cells from GPR125+ Germline Progenitors," *Nature*, September 20, 2007, p. 346.

20. Dr. Ray Bolin "Stem Cells and the Controversy Over Therapeutic Cloning," *Probe*, 2005. Retrieved September 14, 2010, from http://www.probe.org/site/c.fdKEIMNsEoG/b.4218221/k.48BC/Stem_Cells_and_the_Controversy_Over_Therapeutic_Cloning.htm.

21. See note 14 above.

22. See note 20 above.

23. See note 12 above.

24. Ricardo Alonso-Zaldivar and Karen Kaplan, "Loosening of Stem Cell Limits Backed," *Los Angeles Times*, March 20, 2007, p. A12.

25. NA, "Fertility Patients Favor Donating Unused Embryos for Research," *Forbes*, June 20, 2007. Retrieved June 2, 2008, from http://www.forbes.com/forbeslife/health/feeds/hscout/2007/06/20/hscout60576.html.

26. See note 24 above.

27. Rick Weiss, "Researchers Report Growing Stem Cells from Dead Embryos," *Washington Post*, September 23, 2006, p. A3.

28. Constance Holden, "Stem Cell Research: Primate Parthenotes Yield Stem Cells," *Science*, February 1, 2002, pp. 779–780.

29. See note 12 above.

30. Stanford School of Medicine, *The Dean's Newsletter*, March 7, 2005. Retrieved June 10, 2008, from http://deansnewsletter.stanford.edu/archive/03_07_05.html.

31. Bert Vogelstein, Bruce Alberts, and Kenneth Shine, "Please Don't Call It Cloning!" *Science*, February 15, 2002, p. 1237.

32. James A. Thomson et al, "Embryonic Stem Cell Lines Derived from Human Blastocysts," *Science*, November 6, 1998, pp. 1145–1147. Retrieved June 8, 2008, from http://www.sciencemag.org/cgi/content/full/282/5391/1145.

33. James A. Thomson et al, "Induced Pluripotent Stem Cell Lines Derived from Human Somatic Cells, *Science*, December 21, 2007, pp. 1917–1920. Retrieved June 18, 2008, from http://www.sciencemag.org/sciencexpress/recent.dtl.

34. Shinya Yamanaka et al, "Induction of Pluripotent Stem Cells from Adult Human Fibroblasts by Defined Factors," *Cell* November 20, 2007, pp. 1–12. Retrieved June 8, 2008, from http://cellnews-blog.blogspot.com/2007/11/yamanaka-turns-human-fibroblasts-to-esc.html.

35. Takashi Tada, "Genetic Modification-free Reprogramming to Induced Pluripotent Cells: Fantasy or Reality?" *Cell Stem Cell*, August 2, 2008, p. 121.

36. Gina Kolata, "Researcher Who Helped Start Stem Cell War May Now End It," *The New York Times*, November 22, 2007, p. A22.

37. Sayaka Wakayama et al, "Production of Healthy Cloned Mice from Bodies Frozen at 20 °C for 16 Years," *PNAS*, November 3, 2008.

38. Quoted in Vanessa Ruiz, "The Pernkopf Anatomy Atlas: Tainted Beauty," *Street Anatomy*, April 1, 2007. Retrieved May 20, 2009, from http://streetanatomy.com/blog/2007/04/01/the-pernkopf-anatomy-atlas-tainted-beauty/.

39. See note 38 above.

40. David B. Fletcher, "The Stem Cell Controversy," *Center for Applied Christian Ethics*, 2005. Retrieved May 22, 2009, from http://www.wheaton.edu/CACE/HotTopics/StemCellResearch.htm.

41. See note 40 above.

42. Quoted in Fletcher.

43. Tom de Castella, "Pet Cloning: Best Friends Reunited," *The Daily Telegraph*, January 21, 2009. Retrieved May 21, 2009, from www.telegraph.co.uk/family/4296547/Pet-cloning-Best-friends-reunited.html.

44. "Cloning of Pets: The HSUS Statement," *The Humane Society of the United States*, 2009. Retrieved May 22, 2009, from www.hsus.org/pets/issues_affecting_our_pets/hsus_statement_on_the_cloning_of_pets.html.

Chapter 16

The Stem Cell Debate II: The Ethics of the Science

In sorting out the ethics of stem cell research, it helps to distinguish three different ethical categories as they relate to: (1) the individuals who do the research, (2) the research itself, and (3) the social impact of the research. In the context of ESC, reproductive biologist Anne McLaren (1927–2007), whose pioneering work led to IVF in humans, termed these three categories personal ethics, research ethics, and social ethics.[1] These distinctions are not black and white, but rather they grade into one another, and often an ethical issue may relate to more than one category.

PERSONAL ETHICS

In 2005 the scientific community was rocked by the news that two South Korean studies demonstrating the cloning of human embryos had been fabricated. Dr. Hwang Woo Suk admitted that he and his team had not created cloned human embryos by means of SCNT, as they'd claimed in 2004. The embryos, in fact, originated from the eggs of female members of the lab team. Dr. Hwang was fired and charged with fraud and embezzlement.

Within and outside Korea, the Hwang case stands as a powerful example of a failure of personal ethics, which McLaren wrote shortly before her death:

> relates to personal morality, avoiding cheating, dishonesty, irresponsibility, but also failure to observe good practice [such as] failure to follow the rigorous requirements of Good Manufacturing Practice (GMP) but also failure to get informed consent, or giving inadequate information to patients, too little or sometimes too much.[2]

Hwang's personal failure brought shame not only to himself and his team but also to South Korean science and the worldwide scientific community. Other lapses in professional conduct, though less egregious, are more common.

For example, given its spectacular health and financial potential, stem cell research is likely more susceptible to exaggerated claims and false hope than to fake research. Although most scientists are uncertain about the potential of nonembryonic or adult stem cells, that hasn't stopped some people from betting on their curative powers. Reportedly, "[t]here are companies that offer to extract and store stem cells from adult blood, from fat removed by liposuction, from children's baby teeth after they fall out, and even menstrual fluid."[3] Many thousands of people have taken the bait. About a half-million families in the United States alone are estimated to have their children's stem cells—typically cord blood—stored in private tissue banks for their own use. Their thinking is that should their newborns become sick and need a bone marrow transplant, his or her own stem cells would be available to provide a perfect match, whereas there is only about a 25% chance that a sibling will match.[4]

The widespread marketing of cord cryopreservation has caught the attention of the American Academy of Pediatrics, which issued a report in 2007 to guide physicians in responding to parents' questions about it. Noted in the report were recommendations about

> appropriate ethical and operational standards, including informed consent policies, financial disclosures, and conflict-of-interest policies for physicians, institutions, and organizations that operate or have a relationship with cord blood–banking programs.[5]

The report specifically warned of (1) the low likelihood of cord blood's use for childhood diseases, (2) the safety of a child using his or her own cord blood in some cases of pediatric cancer, (3) the vulnerability of parents to the emotional effects of marketing for cord blood banking, and (4) physician financial conflicts.

RESEARCH ETHICS

According to McLaren, research ethics refers to "the actual research itself: what material is being used, what is its source, what are researchers doing with it."[6] Predictably, much of research ethics is about the destruction of the early embryo. But also of concern is the moral difference, if any, between spare embryos—those left over from fertility treatment—and embryos deliberately created for research. Additionally, alternatives to destruction of embryos raise their own ethical questions.

Destruction of the Early Embryo

The concerns about the moral status of the early human embryo that we encountered earlier—in our coverage of abortion, ARTs, PGD, and trait selection—also dominate ethical discussions about various types of embryo research. Thus, while the consensus view is that a new, unique genetic constitution is formed at fertilization, when human life begins and when the unborn attains personhood remains unsettled and controversial. Any answer largely determines the fate of embryo research. In the words of Princeton's Robert George, a member of the President's Council on Bioethics:

> If human embryos are not human beings, then (1) the promise of advances in scientific knowledge, (2) the prospect of developing useful therapies, and (3) the general principle of liberty of scientific inquiry would make an overwhelming case for funding research involving embryo destruction. If, however, human embryos are human beings, then the case for a ban on funding destructive embryo research—and, indeed, a ban on the research itself—would be powerful. To dislodge it, advocates of the research would have to show either that the deliberate killing of some human beings to benefit others can be justified by some sort of utilitarian calculus; or they would have to demonstrate that human beings do not have a right to life throughout their existence, but acquire such a right only at some point in their development.[7]

As with other reproductive issues, the most contentious opposition to ESC research comes from religious and social conservatives, who invariably equate the human embryo from its earliest stages as a single-cell organism with a neonate or a fully grown adult human being. In the words of Richard M. Doerflinger, of the United States Conference of Catholic Bishops: "[T]he human individual, called into existence by God and made in the divine image and likeness ... must always be treated as an end in himself or herself, not merely as a means to other ends...."[8] From this premise follows the official Catholic prohibition of all forms of ESC research, a view shared by many evangelical Protestants and (Eastern) Orthodox Christians.[9] Evangelicals and fundamentalist Christians often cite the Bible (e.g., Psalm 139:13–16; Jeremiah 1:4–5) as the basis of their opposition to ESC research. Accordingly, from (1) the biblical teaching that human existence begins at conception and (2) ESC research requires the destruction of a living human being, they conclude:

> No amount of promised "benefit" to society or to medical knowledge can justify the killing of a human for spare parts. The end does not justify the means. It is never ethical—in fact, it is morally reprehensible—to mark people for death in order to conduct utilitarian experiments on their body parts.[1]

Embryonic research, in short, is, like abortion. Indeed, Doerflinger equates them, when he writes:

> These stem cells are taken from embryos while they are still living. In effect, the harvesting of cells is itself the abortion—i.e., it is the act that directly destroys a live embryo—and the method of destruction, using microsurgery to extract the embryo's inner cells from the outer trophoblast, is determined entirely by the needs of the stem cell researcher.[11]

A secular version of this argument is offered, again as in the trait selection debate, by Leon Kass. Thus, the special status of humans in the Book of Genesis should be heeded not because of the biblical authority, but because the message reflects a cosmological, or self-evident, truth. Kass is representative of those opponents of cloning for embryo research who say they are not defending Judeo-Christian beliefs but "human dignity."[1]

George, on the other hand, and Christopher Tollefsen stake their case on science. As noted in Chapter 8, the morally conservative law professor and the philosopher, both traditional Catholics, argue that personhood begins at conception with the possession of a developmental program. Therefore, in their view, even research that poses the slightest threat to the embryo must be banned, along with the production of research embryos. As for existing spares, they should be transferred to a womb.[13]

Non-ESC research, by contrast, is not murder, religious and social conservatives say, because it does not require the loss of life. This makes experiments on adult stem cells, including the new reprogramming method iPS, a "legitimate field of study, well within the will of God."[14] This leads conservatives to distinguish between ethical non-ESC research, on the one hand, and unethical ESC research, on the other.

Mindful of this ethical/unethical distinction, when he was House Republican leader, Tom DeLay (R-Tex.) supported legislation to encourage research on stem cells drawn from cord blood, but adamantly opposed all legislation supporting ESC research. On one occasion, in 2004, while opposing a bill that would have allowed discarded embryos to be used as sources of stem cells, the born-again Christian cast himself in the spirit of the three main Abrahamic religions and declared: "An embryo is a person, a distinct internally directed, self-integrating human organism. We were all at one time embryos ourselves. So was Abraham. So was Mohammed. So was Jesus of Nazareth." The Catholic bishops of the United States concurred, issuing a statement opposing such research as "immoral, illegal and unnecessary."[1]

DeLay's comments notwithstanding, there is no monolithic religious view on ESC. Some liberal Catholic theologians, for example, permit ESC research in the 14-day period between "conception" and "individuation." Representative of this religious progressive viewpoint, Margaret Farley of

Yale Divinity School has written that the human embryo is not considered

> in its earliest stages (prior to the development of the primitive streak or to implantation) to constitute an individualized human entity with the settled inherent potential to become a human person. The moral status of the embryo is, therefore (in this view), not that of a person; and its use for certain kinds of research can be justified. (Since it is, however, a form of human life, some respect is due it—for example, it should not be bought and sold.)[1]

Farley opposes reproductive cloning and earmarking stem cells for therapeutic treatment. Other than that, a liberal Catholic view like hers permits research on spare embryos.

The National Committee on Eugenics of the United Church of Christ (UCC) also takes a generally permissive position on ESC research. The UCC doesn't "object categorically to human pre-embryo [i.e., an embryo in the first 14 days after fertilization] research, provided the research is well justified in terms of its objectives, that the research protocols show proper respect for the pre-embryos, and that they are not implanted."[17]

For its part, Judaism generally extends the period of ESC research even longer, up to 40 days, which is for many Jews the morally significant point in the embryo's development. It is true that not all Jewish scholars agree with this mainstream view. Eric Cohen, for instance, with the Ethics and Public Policy Center in Washington, doesn't think 40 days is a significant moment. Cohen, like Kass a former member of the President's Council on Bioethics (2001–2007), places the beginning of life at conception.[18]

Still, the widespread Jewish view on ESC research parallels its progressive view on IVF and PGD. As noted by physician Sherman Silber, as the soul has not entered the body prior to the fortieth day, "[e]mbryo research to promote life is, therefore, acceptable." Apart from its theology, the great value that Judaism places on medicine and healing lends further support to ESC research.

"[N]ot only is therapeutic cloning acceptable," Silber says, "but it is an obligation to do any research which can enhance and promote life-saving treatment such as stem cell and cellular replacement therapy."[19]

For their part, conservative Muslims say it is immoral, even infanticide, to destroy embryos at any stage in order to harvest stem cells. More liberal Muslims, however, who believe that the embryo does not have a soul until later stages in its development are open to allowing ESC research.[20] "The key issue," according to Muslim theologian Omar Sultan Haque, "is that just because an embryo is a member of our species does not mean that it has the same moral status as a child with diabetes." Of the tens of thousands of frozen embryos created by IVF clinics and slated to be discarded, Haque says:

> [D]estroying them with regulations and under the equally, if not greater, moral needs of the living—suffering children, for example, whose moral status no one would debate—is consistent with respecting the moral status of an embryo....[21]

Haque, who teaches at Harvard Medical School, is especially critical of what he terms "irresponsible deontology" that ignores the "necessity of tradeoffs amongst competing moral demands."

Hassan Hathout, gynecologist and author (*Reading the Muslim Mind*, 1995), is another prominent Muslim who says that in Islam stem cell research on pre-implantation embryos may be justified as the lesser of two evils, if the aim is to save actual patients suffering serious illness. The Muslim view also permits therapeutic transgenic engineering, or gene manipulation involving the introduction of the genes of one species to another for the purpose of combating illness and alleviating suffering. Outside this necessity, genetic engineering is impermissible in Islam, as is reproductive cloning. Therapeutic cloning used for purely research purposes, on the other hand, may be permissible during the very early stages, before body systems are formed including the nervous system.[22]

This division of religious opinion on the destruction of the early embryo in ESC research was

---

Bioethics Across Cultures

Embryonic Stem Cell Research Worldwide

Policies surrounding ESC research vary across the world. Here is a snapshot of them as of 2005, from LeRoy Walters, professor at the Kennedy Institute of Ethics at Georgetown University.

The most conservative policy prohibits human embryo research, not even permitting experimentation with existing ESC lines. In Europe, countries such as Italy, Ireland, and Norway follow this policy. In some other European countries, such as France and Germany, a slightly more liberal policy is in place that allows research with existing ESC lines but prohibits research on new lines derived through the destruction of embryos. This was the position of the United States prior to 2009. After that, and continuing toward more liberal policies, the United States joined Spain, Russia, Iran, Canada, and Australia, which all permit the derivation of new ESC lines but only through the use of

unused embryos from infertility clinics. The most liberal policy permits SCNT to produce new ESC lines, as in a growing number of countries, including Belgium, India, Israel, South Korea, and the United Kingdom.

(Source: Susan Morrissey, "Human Embryonic Stem Cell Debate," *Chemical & Engineering News*, October 26, 2004. Retrieved May 23, 2009, from http://pubs.acs.org/cen/news/8243/8243earlygov2.html.)

Question

Do you approve or disapprove of the trend toward liberalizing ESC research policies worldwide? Does the position of other countries influence your view of what US policy should be? Do you support the United Nations ban on all forms of cloning?

(Adopted by the General Assembly on March 8, 2005, with 84 votes for [including the United States], 34 against, and 37 abstentions.)

---

palpably in evidence at a March 2007 forum titled "Religious Perspectives on Stem-Cell Research," sponsored by the Harvard Stem Cell Institute, in conjunction with Harvard Divinity School and the Boston Theological Institute. In the end, the panel, with representatives of the three Abrahamic faiths, couldn't agree on the moral status of the embryo and thus reached divergent views about the permissibility of stem cell research. At the same time, they all welcomed medical advances and agreed that an embryo was nascent human life that deserved respect. "I think we've got a true moral dilemma that our tradition and our scripture do not fully address," panelist Llewellyn Smith concluded. The UCC theologian urged continuing dialogue, saying, "We are a long way from a clear answer ... and a long way from successful implementation of these therapies."[23]

Spare versus Created Embryos

Generally sharing the ground of theological agreement at the Harvard conference—respect for the fetus and desirability of scientific advances—are

biologists who study the process of fertilization. As McLaren said of her colleagues:

> "When does life begin?" is not a meaningful question to most biologists, as life is a continuum. Nonetheless, scientists that I have talked to who actually use donated human embryos in their research do view them in a rather special light because they are human, and would not want to use them for trivial or scientifically worthless research.[24]

Presumably, then, these same scientists, including James Thomson, would use donated human embryos for research intended to reduce human suffering, as opposed to letting them languish in IVF clinics, perhaps ultimately to be discarded.[25]

In fact, this position is the policy of an increasing number of countries that permit embryo research on donated or spare embryos, including ESC lines derived from them. It is argued, that, although research on spare embryos means using them as a means to other people's ends, they are not *merely* being so used. In other words, the embryos are not being disrespected. On the contrary, as McLaren pointed out:

> Any eight-celled embryo seen down a microscope is beautiful, but if it is a human embryo, one views it with added respect, and it seems unethical to have to discard it when it could contribute to scientific knowledge and the reduction of human suffering. Indeed, if there is no welcoming uterus, that new unique genetic constitution could still survive in a pluripotent human ES cell line.[26]

This is basically the position of Gene Outka, a self-professed Augustinian Christian who employs a principle first formulated by theologian Paul Ramsey. As conceived by Ramsey, the "nothing is lost principle" provides a way to resolve parity-conflicts, where one physical life collides directly and immediately with another physical life, and we cannot save both. Ramsey's nothing-is-lost principle permits the intentional killing of innocent life under two conditions: (A) when the innocent will die in any case; and (B) when other innocent life will be saved.[2] While seriously doubting that Ramsey would do so, Outka, nonetheless, has extended the theologian's principle to the contemporary ESC debate as follows:

> ... [I]t is correct to view embryos in reproductive clinics who are bound either to be discarded or frozen in perpetuity as innocent lives who will die in any case, and those third parties with Alzheimer's, Parkinson's, et al., as other innocent life who will be saved by virtue of research on such embryos.... [I]t is the absence of prospects of *these* innocents [i.e., the embryos] that partly extends the first exempting condition. It is the enhancement of prospects to *other* innocent life that partly extends the second exempting condition. (*Less* will be lost, or at least, *someone* may benefit.)[2]

This characterization, generally shared by scientists, religious, and cultural liberals, and a growing list of countries, governs ESC research, then, according

to the following moral distinction. On one hand, research on spare embryos (i.e., ones conceived to enhance fertility but that will never be implanted) is permissible; on the other hand, the creation of embryos in order to disaggregate them is impermissible.

But is this popular distinction morally significant? Ironically, both extreme conservative and extreme liberal thought are united in insisting that there is no relevant moral difference between spare embryos and ones deliberately created for research.[2]

On the extreme conservative side are opponents such as Doerflinger of the US Catholic bishops, who insist that using the parts of something that will die is not the moral equivalent of using parts of something already dead. Moreover, according to Doerflinger, policing a policy that allows research on spare embryos would be impossible. What, for example, would prevent a fertility clinic from producing a few more embryos from a couple, ostensibly as part of their fertility treatment but, in fact, to ensure a supply of research subjects?[30] By this conservative measure, then, President Bush's moral distinction between federal and private ESC research support was fatuous, if not hypocritical; and his allowance of research on existing lines, that is, those created prior to August 9, 2001, but not after that date, gave inscrutable moral weight to a date.

By the same token, extreme liberals say that if the use of spare embryos is moral, then so is the deliberate creation of embryos for research. As John A. Robertson points out, once it's decided, in utilitarian fashion, that the end justifies the means, as in the case of using spare embryos to relieve human suffering, then the same utilitarian logic argues for creating research embryos as justifiable means to attain the identical end.[31] By this yardstick, the Bush policy, again, made no sense morally because it only permitted, in the interest of the public good, (private) research on spare embryos, while condemning their creation for the same end.

Both extremes in the cultural discourse, then—as represented by Doerflinger and Robertson—seem to agree that either ESC is morally permissible or it isn't, regardless of how the embryos are derived. The predominant middle or moderate position, represented by Outka and taken by Bush and subsequently by President Obama, claims that the derivation of the embryos matters: Embryos left over from fertility treatment may be used in research, but under no circumstances, private or public, may embryos be created exclusively for that purpose.

Alternatives to Embryo Destruction

In the process of extracting the cells to produce a stem cell line, the days-old blastocyst is, of course, destroyed. This, as we've seen, is a substantial moral, theological, and political sticking point for anyone who considers the blastocyst a person. Three possibilities for perhaps meeting this objection are parthenogenesis, the blastosphere method, and conversion of adult stem cells into ESCs, as with the iPS technique. Unfortunately, none has succeeded in bridging the gap in the discourse between supporters of ESC research and its hard-line critics.

Parthenogenesis Although the parthenogenic embryo contains a complete complement of human DNA, it cannot complete gestation. It can, however, produce stem cells that are genetically matched to the egg donor.

The Hwang team, unwittingly, may have pulled off the world's first human case of parthenogenesis when they were falsely claiming to have produced a human clone. If they did, suggests Nicholas Wade of *The New York Times*, it may go down as one of science's greatest ironies; for what was actually accomplished—perfectly matched replacement cells—was, perhaps, more significant than what was faked.[32] In any event, parthenogenesis strikes some as an ethically acceptable way to create stem cells. As Dartmouth ethicist Ronald M. Green says:

> People will see that these are activated eggs.... They do not of themselves ever develop into a human being. This is not anything biologically or morally like a human embryo, and it's a very good way of trying to provide human embryonic stem cells that does not involve the destruction of an embryo.[33]

But Catholic priest Tad Pacholcyzk, of the National Catholic Bioethics Center in Philadelphia, isn't convinced.

> My view is that if these [stimulated eggs] grow as organized embryos for the first few days and then arrest, they may just be very short-lived human beings. One is very possibly dealing with a defective human being. And at a minimum, the benefit of the doubt should be given here, and these embryos should not be created for the purposes of destroying them.[34]

Biochemist Nancy L. Jones of LaSalle University, a private Catholic institution, agrees that the parthenogenic embryo presents the same moral problems raised by embryos created deliberately for research. As she explains:

> If ... a parthenogenic embryo (known as a "teratoma" or tumor) occurred naturally, we would not contest its destruction. Applying the "principle of double effect," we would assent to the surgical removal of such an entity because there is no available treatment to heal it and since removing it will save the mother's life. However, to specifically create an embryo fated for early death is ethically troublesome.[35]

The Blastomere Method In August 2005, Dr. Robert Lanza, of the biotech firm Advanced Cell Technology (ACT), created a stir when he showed that it is theoretically possible to grow ESC lines and still preserve the blastocyst, at least in the case of mouse embryos. Using the PGD technique on mice, Lanza

> extracted single cells out of sixteen mouse blastocysts, then grew two of those cells into new embryonic stem cell lines. The embryos from which the cells were removed were then implanted back into the wombs of mice where they developed into healthy pups, about as successfully as a control group of normal mouse pups.[36]

Then, in January 2008, the Lanza team reported that they had duplicated the method using human embryos: creating several colonies of human embryonic stem cells without harming the embryos from which they were derived.

In theory, then, a single cell, a blastomere, could be removed from an eight-cell human embryo and coaxed to multiply into a colony of stem cells in a dish. The remaining seven cells could then be implanted in a womb to complete gestation. The loss of a single cell—or even two—at that early stage is not known to cause developmental problems in children born by this procedure.[37,38] Fertility doctors perform such "single-cell biopsies" thousands of times every year to test the genetic health of embryos conceived by IVF, with little or no apparent effect on the remaining seven cells' ability to form a normal baby.

Even if proved scientifically sound, Lanza's method, which like parthenogenesis avoids embryo destruction, doesn't placate religious and social conservatives. For example, Monsignor Elio Sgreccia, who heads the Vatican's Pontifical Academy for Life, claims that Lanza's method of producing stem cells remains an in vitro form of reproduction, which the Catholic Church prohibits. He also says that the research is "manipulation" and that it "doesn't solve the ethical problems" regarding ESC research.[39] Catholic bishops spokesperson Doerflinger has also accused Lanza of deceiving the public about details of his work. "We're against manipulating, harming, assaulting embryos for their cells even if it doesn't always kill them," Doerflinger says of the official Catholic view.[40] Even biologist McLaren admitted that, even if the blastomere approach could be repeated with human cells, it might not circumvent the central ethical problem. "At that [8-cell] stage," she explained,

> each cell of a human embryo could be totipotent, in that it could give rise to an entire individual, so using it instead for making an ES cell line would be equivalent to using an embryo for the same purpose and just as impermissible.[41]

Morality and theology aside, the blastomere method has been criticized scientifically on several grounds. For one thing, scientists can derive many more stem cell lines through traditional methods. Also, the blastomere approach wouldn't allow researchers to study "disease specific" ESCs for disorders such as Alzheimer's and diabetes. Beyond this is the appearance of scientific research being subordinated to religious and political concerns. For example, when he resigned from ACT's ethics board in 2000, bioethicist Glenn McGee, an ESC research supporter, called the for-profit firm's research a "pitiful attempt to look morally acceptable, rather than do valuable science."[42]

iPS Less than six months after scientists in the United States and Japan said in June 2007 that they had succeeded in changing mouse skin cells into what appear to be embryonic stem cells, the Kyoto and Wisconsin teams announced that they had adapted the technique to human cells. In so doing, they raised the possibility that a patient's skin cells could be used to generate a new heart, liver, or kidney cells that might be transplantable and would not be rejected by the patient's immune system. Lead scientists Yamanaka and Thomson cautioned, however, that key hurdles remained before the new reprogramming technique was ready for clinical use. The most serious was that the viruses used to turn on the genes could cause cancer, while one of the genes itself tended to cause tumors. But then, in March of 2009, news came from Canada that that obstacle apparently had been overcome. Stem cell researchers there said they had devised a way to reprogram mouse and, for the first time, human fibroblasts without the use of harmful viruses. (Fibroblasts are fiber-producing connective tissues.) This astonishing feat effectively enables scientists to make patient-specific stem cells for disease modeling, drug screening, and perhaps someday cell replacement therapy. The Toronto breakthrough also seems to bear out researcher Lanza's earlier characterization of cutting-edge research in iPS as "the biological equivalent of the Wright brothers' first airplane."[43]

Morally, because it does not involve the destruction of embryos, the iPS method of converting ASCs into ESCs, would, like parthenogenesis and the blastomere methods, skirt the problem of embryo destruction. And, because it doesn't involve eggs or embryos, iPS avoids many of the ethical issues raised by therapeutic cloning. This is why religious and social conservatives universally applauded the revolutionary technique.[44]

But while opponents of ESC research were calling the reprogrammed cell innovation a vindication of their ethics and the end of immoral ESC research, involved scientists gave reasons for pause. They pointed out, for one thing, that it wasn't yet known whether reprogrammed cells would prove as functional as ESCs, whose research was much more advanced and had shown great promise. So, why abandon a line of research that hadn't failed? Indeed, they emphasized that research on both types of cells were closely related and crosschecked each other. The breakthrough with mature cells, for example, was made possible largely by ESC research, underscored by Thomson's key role in both. In fact, Thomson himself was quick to note:

> This is not the end of embryonic research.... It will take a couple of years to sort out whether this [reprogramming] might differ from embryonic stem cells in some unexpected way. It would be a shame to drop embryonic research.[45]

Also giving pause was the nagging moral question posed by those possibly half-million embryos stored in fertility clinics. Was it better to use them, with donor consent, for research; or, as will otherwise most probably happen, destroy them? The iPS breakthrough did nothing to resolve this matter. Nor has progress in reprogramming silenced the cloning debate. It is true, for example, that the Chinese achievement of reprogramming mature skin cells of mice to an embryonic-like state, then using the resulting cells to create live mouse offspring, may lead to the development of medically useful stem cells for treating human disease without resorting to controversial laboratory techniques. But it also may make it easier to create human clones and babies with specific genetic traits.

Doubtless, genetically programming human skin cells to behave like ESCs opens a new chapter in using stem cells to fight disease. But, again, it probably won't end the stem cell debate. In fact, there's the potential for increased polarization. Traditional opponents of ESC research now insist that human embryos aren't necessary, and therefore—given the availability of a less controversial method—it is ethically unjustifiable to pursue research using embryos. Supporters, on the other hand, insist that it would be extremely foolish, unscientific, and wasteful to place all bets on a single approach; therefore, it is unethical to abandon ESC research. For them the prudent course is to pursue parallel science, at least until the new alternative is fully tested.

SOCIAL ETHICS

In a 2006 poll of Americans nationwide, the Genetics and Public Policy Center (GPPC), a nonpartisan research institution, found that 67% of Americans approved of ESC research. This level of support was largely consistent regardless of sex, race, age, political affiliation, and religion. The only exceptions were fundamentalist and evangelical Christians, and yet even 50% of them also supported the research.[46] In another poll, this one conducted in 2007 by Opinion Research Corporation, 60% of adult Americans thought the government should either place no restrictions on government funding of stem cell research or ease the current restrictions to allow more stem cell research, while 30% favored keeping the current restrictions, and 16% no federal funding at all.[47]

If such surveys accurately reflect moral opinion, a clear majority of Americans find stem cell research unobjectionable. But, as the expression goes, the devil is in the details. In this regard, the work of Matthew Nisbet is worth noting.

In 2004 Nisbet, a communications professor at American University, reported on his effort to get a reliable quantitative sense of trends in public opinion about stem cell and cloning research.[48] Based on a "meta-analysis" of hundreds of questions from numerous opinion surveys, Nisbet concluded that ESC research and, specifically, therapeutic cloning remained unresolved, and that the issue may mark a new era of divisive and deadlocked "biopolitics." At the core of the conflict are two fears. The first is the feared disruption that ESC research will have on our traditional understanding of human nature, procreation, and personal relationships. The second deals with perceived threats to social justice.

Disruption of Traditional Understanding

Polls show that Americans overwhelmingly have strong reservations about anything that smacks of cloning. They strongly oppose reproductive cloning, and only about a third of them favor legislation permitting therapeutic, or research, cloning. If stem cell research must move forward, then, the American public prefers that scientists make use of either extra embryos left over from in vitro clinics or adult cells.

At first glance, the public reservations about research/therapeutic cloning may be perplexing because SCNT skirts the moral thicket posed by reproductive cloning. But SCNT still must deal with the question of the humanity of the embryo, which is central to the entire ESC debate. And even if the problems raised earlier by George in this respect can be sidestepped—by not considering the early embryo a human being—there still lurks, palpably in the public mind, the fear that research cloning could lead to the production of babies, or reproductive cloning. Indeed, it seems impossible for the public mind to distinguish research from reproductive cloning, as they pertain to our traditional understanding of human nature, procreation, and personal relationships. This is why a grasp of human cloning is vital for understanding today's political dialogue about research (or therapeutic) cloning.

Human Cloning   At present the United States and many other countries ban reproductive cloning partly because of reasons of health and safety. Additionally, there are potential legal and psychological problems to consider with reproductive cloning. Critics including George and Kass worry about the impact on our most basic and personal relationships. Consider that a child cloned from its mother would be its mother's genetic twin; its grandfather would be its genetic father; and its siblings would be its

genetic children.[49] Then there's the disturbing prospect of animal-human hybrids, or chimeras, which threaten to blur the distinction between human and animal. How is society to consider a sentient ape? Would such a creature, *should it*, be accorded individual rights?[50] George sums up the view of the many, on both sides of the cultural divide, who oppose reproductive cloning, including himself:

> [They] insist that it is a dehumanizing procedure that will lead our culture down the road—or further down the road—to the commodification of human life. They argue that it constitutes treating children as products of manufacture—"made" rather than "begotten"—compromising their individuality and raising a knot of serious problems pertaining to kinship, identity, and self-image. They warn that it will exacerbate the difficulty children already have when parents become obsessive in their expectations for their children and seek to live vicariously through them.[51]

The fear of nontraditional procreation and its effects on marriage and family take another turn when one contemplates the possibility of reversing the cloning process. Consider that in cloning, stem cells are derived from eggs. But what about reversing the process—deriving eggs from stem cells? Unfertilized eggs, in fact, have been derived from the embryonic cells of mice and pigs, although not from humans. Whether these oocytes can then be fertilized and support embryonic development isn't known. But suppose that eggs were derived from stem cells and then introduced into clinical practice. Then, presumably, both oocytes and sperm could be produced from ESC lines of either sex. In that event, critics of nontraditional procreation point out, same-sex marriages could produce their genetically own babies, without the need for reproductive cloning.[52]

On the other side, those tolerant of reproductive cloning point to the control that people would have over the qualities and genetic characteristics of their offspring. So framed, reproductive cloning extends hope to some who otherwise couldn't have

---

Bioethics Across Cultures

Human-Animal Hybrid in Britain

On April 1, 2009, British scientists at Newcastle University confirmed that they had created human-animal hybrid embryos for the first time, in an effort to develop new stem cell treatments for disorders such as Parkinson's disease, stroke, and diabetes. The scientists merged human genetic material with cow egg cells that had most of their own genetic material removed. The resulting hybrid embryos were genetically 99.9 percent human and 0.1 percent cow. They lived for three days. Ultimately, the researchers would like such embryos to live for up to six days so that they can take embryonic stem cells from them and grow the cells into mature tissue, thereby avoiding the use of human eggs or normal human embryos. Over the objections of those opposing stem cell research and abortion, the government proposed to legitimate the procedure by allowing scientists to use human-animal hybrid sources of stem cells. Scientists developing treatments for incurable diseases would be allowed to grow the hybrid embryos for no longer than two weeks, and implanting them into a human womb would not be permitted. The proposal, submitted in May, marked a turnaround for the government, which just the year before had proposed a complete prohibition on hybrid embryos. Still prohibited under the new proposal would be the creation of so-called true hybrids, which involves fertilizing a human egg with animal sperm or vice versa.

(Sources: Steve Connor, "Cows and Human Cells Used in Embryo," *Independent.ie*, April 2, 2008. Retrieved May 22, 2009, from www.independent.ie/world-news/europe/cow-and-human-cells-used-in-embryo-1334808.html.)

Question

The Catholic Church immediately described human-animal hybrid research as "monstrous," on the grounds that it meddles with the basic essence of what constitutes human identity. Do you agree or do you support such research as a morally acceptable way to obtain stem cells?

---

children; and, to those who have lost a child, it offers the comfort of a genetic copy of the child. Beyond this, to its advocates reproductive cloning is a simple matter of reproductive liberty.

Research cloning, to repeat, doesn't mean human cloning, nor does it necessarily lead to it. But the public clearly fears it will, thus inviting political manipulation. This is why, outside scientific circles, discussions of therapeutic cloning can quickly veer off the path of rational analysis into the quicksand of "baby cloning."

Parthenogenesis and iPS   The other two methods of obtaining stem cells, parthenogenesis and iPS, also raise concerns about nontraditional procreation. For example, if researchers can overcome some genetic deficiencies incurred via parthenogenesis, in theory they could provide a way for a single female or a female couple to procreate. This would further undermine traditional procreation, according to critics, besides raising questions about the morality of sacrificing such embryos to scientific experimentation.[53]

While reprogramming skin cells, iPS, avoids destroying embryos, it nevertheless raises its own controversial issues of human fertility. If, for example, the induced stem cells can be transformed into sperm and egg cells—as has been done in mice—that would alter how we think about human fertility. In theory, for instance, the new method would allow people to reproduce after death as long as they banked a tissue sample. A person wouldn't even have to be alive, then, to create sperm or eggs. Such a possibility likely would offend those who object to any form of reproductive manipulation, either in principle or out of concern for unintended perverse effects.

Against these concerns to our traditional understanding, defenders of ESC research are quick to point out that the security of traditional assumptions about marriage, procreation, and family vanished a long time ago, with IVF. In a larger sense, they say, the changes that IVF have brought and its widespread approval should remind us that things change, including people and their traditions. Our cultural view of marriage, procreation, and families is an inherited way of thinking that isn't fixed in cement but subject to modification as changing conditions and new experience warrant.

Still, there is the matter of how we would think of the products of nontraditional procreation. As we saw in the preceding chapter, genetic screening is becoming easier all the time. Once accustomed through, say, parthenogenesis to viewing some embryos as "lesser humans" or "nonhumans," would it also be easier to regard the genetically flawed embryo the same way? Would that, in turn, dispose us to abort, donate to research, or even create for research, embryos known to carry genetic flaws— all with moral impunity? Such speculations bring Nancy L. Jones, out of prudence, to assess the "longer-term dangers" of parthenogenic human embryo research.[54] She writes:

> I am persuaded that there is a deeper concern intrinsic to the creation of embryos for destructive research. This deeper concern pertains to humankind's accountability for our genetic offspring and the very processes and "building blocks" of reproduction. Experimenting on parthenogenic human embryos will likely have far-reaching consequences for our ability to control the initial steps of procreation— potentially including those of nontraditional procreation, e.g., by enabling the creation of embryos who do not require paternal imprinting to develop normally. I am persuaded that our offspring has even far greater significance—borne out in the fact that they are created in the image of God—than that typically ascribed to them. Even the intrinsic design and function of sperm and eggs may be instructive to the parthenogenic issue. One question that is not often asked is whether our "seed" should be used for non-reproductive purposes, or, rather, reserved

only for the realm of procreation of human beings created in the image of God. As scientists seek to manipulate and artificially stimulate human eggs in the parthenogenic process, they should perhaps focus on *what they are doing*—and the implications of such— rather than on just *what they are creating*.[55]

Threats to Social Justice

Beyond matters related to our cultural understanding of human nature, procreation, and family, stem cell research raises several concerns of social justice. One is the question of priorities. How can spending billions of dollars on stem cell research be justified when, for example, more people die worldwide of pneumonia and diarrhea than anything else?[56]

Another issue concerns accessibility to stem cells. If, for instance, cord blood banking is a good idea, is it fair that only people who can afford it will be able to have a chance at a life-saving therapy for their children? This question may diminish as unrelated cord blood banks expand. But it won't disappear, because the banks presumably will be integrated into the present limited access, "fee for service" system.[57]

Then there's the matter of compensation. Any research project that involves making embryos by fertilization, SCNT, or parthenogenesis requires unfertilized eggs. But donated oocytes are in short supply. In Britain, the government compensates women who donate eggs for stem cell research. In the United States, paying donors for eggs donated for clinical use is permitted, as in infertility treatment, but not for research. Is such a policy fair or discriminatory? If donors are to be compensated, will paying donors for eggs commodify oocytes and exploit women, possibly subjecting them to long-term health risks?

Beyond this is the question of monopolies and profit. Before we move much deeper into stem cell research, we need to answer two questions. (1) Is it permissible that scientific advances be monopolized by a handful of companies; and (2) is it permissible for gain or profit to be the prime objective of such activities?

CONCLUSIONS

For the vast majority of religious and social conservatives, ESC research probably represents a threat to the divine spark that they believe exalts human beings. They think that, by destroying embryos left over from fertilization procedures, ESC research destroys life made in the image of God. Also, in the case of cloning, it enables humans to remake themselves in their own image. For those who espouse traditional morality and social mores, then, ESC research likely represents not simply humans "playing god," but, in fact, becoming God, the equivalent of Adam's original sin of prideful disobedience.

If modern post-Enlightenment history is any indication, the theological and spiritual objections that religious and social conservatives raise will not likely stop the advance of ESC research, any more than they have halted advances in birth control or IVF. Still, the inexorable tide of science will not drown out voices of concern. Like "the Pill" or the "test-tube baby," ESC research inevitably will raise questions about human nature, procreation, family, personal relations, and individual rights that will continue to challenge our most cherished and profound beliefs. For religious and social conservatism, alternatives to traditional understanding are to be resisted as a road that leads to the dehumanized rationality of *Brave New World*. For religious and social liberalism, those alternatives should be met with a dedicated pursuit of knowledge and an exercise of our willful rationality. These opposed perspectives harken back to ancient debates, while at the same time occupying the center of discussions about the new embryology and its associated technologies.

CASES AND CONTROVERSIES

Cloning and Cultural Conflict

To its supporters, ESC research represents merely another technology that extends human choice and with it the boundaries of human existence. As such, it is not an expression of human willfulness against God or nature, but in the words of Patrick Stephens, "the willful product of [our] own rationality, the manifestation of [our] conceptual mind." Stephens is in charge of current affairs at the Objectivist Center of the Atlas Society, a research and advocacy organization devoted to spreading the thought of American novelist and philosopher Ayn Rand (1905–1982). Of special importance to Rand were the Enlightenment values of reason, individualism, freedom, and achievement. Continuing in this tradition, Stephens is among those who extol the expansion of human choices and limits when he writes of human cloning:

> … it is the extension of choice and the pursuit of knowledge that offer man the opportunity to expand the boundaries of his existence. In the end, man's spirit, that within him which searches for truth and morality, that part of his mind that aspires and dreams —his soul—is ultimately the product of his

own design. Man's spirit is, fundamentally, not a gift or an accident, but the product of a lifetime's achievement. His soul is the willful product of his own rationality, the manifestation of his conceptual mind. It is not the shallow shudder of humility that ennobles a man's soul, but the enraptured embrace of knowledge, opportunity, and choice.[58]

No one could disagree more with this view than Leon Kass, who recoils at the prospect of humans taking an increasingly active role in their own being. Thus, with respect to cloning, Kass has written:

> We are repelled by the prospect of cloning human beings not because of the strangeness or novelty of the undertaking, but because we intuit and feel, immediately and without argument, the violation of things that we rightfully hold dear. Repugnance, here as elsewhere, revolts against the excesses of human willfulness, warning us not to transgress what is unspeakably profound. Indeed, in this age in which everything is held to be permissible so long as it is freely done, in which our given human nature no longer

commands respect, in which our bodies are regarded as mere instruments of our autonomous rational wills, repugnance may be the only voice left that speaks up to defend the central core of our humanity. Shallow are the souls that have forgotten how to shudder.[59,60]

Questions for Analysis

1. Discuss Stephens's statement with reference to the language of the Enlightenment.

2. Show how, although it never mentions God or religion, Kass's argument nevertheless has a religious sentiment to it. With which secular moral theory would you associate it: natural law, utilitarianism, or Kant's ethics?

3. To which aspects of principlism do Stephens and Kass seem to give priority?

4. Describe the views of human nature that underlie these opposed positions on cloning.

5. Do you think that the disagreement between Stephens and Kass goes beyond cloning? Does it capture the polarities of the so-called culture war (see Introduction)?

6. With whom are you more inclined to agree, Stephens or Kass?

CASES AND CONTROVERSIES

NIH ESC Guidelines

President Obama's 2009 Executive Order removing limitations of NIH funding for ESC research required the Secretary of HHS to provide funding guidelines. In April of that year, HHS published the following draft for the public consultation process that ultimately would direct the NIH regarding the types of embryonic stem cell research that are within its mandate to support. Under the proposed guidelines, the NIH could only support ESC research that meets the following criteria:

1. the ESCs were derived from human embryos that were created for reproductive purposes, but were no longer needed for this purpose;
2. the ESCs were obtained consensually, without coercion or remuneration; and
3. the ESCs were donated for research purposes, and for which the proper documentation can be assured.

NIH would be prohibited from funding ESC research if:

1. the research involved introducing human ESCs or iPS cells into non-human primate blastocysts;
2. the research includes the possibility that human ESCs or iPS cells may contribute to the germ line (sperm or egg) of a non-human animal; or if

3. the ESCs were derived from other sources, such as somatic cell nuclear transfer, parthenogenesis, and/or IVF embryos created for research purposes.[61]

Questions for Analysis

1. Show how the HHS guidelines tried to balance scientific interests and the anti-ESC sentiment. Do you think it succeeded?

2. In a press release following publication of these guidelines, the President of the Family Research Council stated: "The research that President Obama supports is not sound science and will destroy human life." Do you agree?

3. These guidelines would also restrict funding for scientists pursuing research involving ESCs derived from nonreproductive IVF, or SCNT. Unsurprisingly, these limitations provoked objections from stem cell biologists who argue that these technologies are important therapeutic avenues for the development of disease-specific human ESCs. Assuming they are correct, would you drop or keep the funding restriction? Answer by appeal to moral principle(s).

4. Many people, including some members of the President's Council on Bioethics, are concerned that an embryo cloned for research purposes—

(Continued)

CASES AND CONTROVERSIES (CONTINUED)

from a sick person, for example—could be implanted and gestated. In response, bioethicist Bonnie Steinbock has written:

... why would anyone want to do that? If the intention is simply reproduction, IVF embryos are a lot easier to come by. And if the intention is to get an embryo of a particular genome for

reproductive purposes, why would an embryo cloned from a sick patient be desirable? Concerns about cloning for reproductive purposes need not preclude cloning for research or eventual therapeutic purposes.[62]

Do you agree with Steinbock that reproductive cloning need not rule out therapeutic cloning?

CASES AND CONTROVERSIES

Frozen Embryos: The Personal Decision Behind the Public Controversy

"Ingrid Jansson peers through a vapor of liquid nitrogen at frozen embryos conceived for her in a petri dish four years ago. It's the first time she's eyed the surplus from the in vitro fertilization procedure that brought her son Dylan, now 3, into the world." That's how *USA Today* recently began a story about people like Jansson, who must decide what to do with excess embryos after their families are complete.[63]

"'It's surreal,' says Jansson, 39, as an embryologist fishes out the thin straw containing eight embryos stored at a fertility clinic where she was treated and now works as a nurse. 'I don't think about them much, because I have two (children) at home that keep me busy.'"

Only Jansson and other gamete providers are legally entitled to decide what to do with their excess eggs: discard them, offer them to other couples, donate them to research, or pay to keep them frozen indefinitely. At a major institution, New York's Weill-Cornell Medical School, 54% of the clinic's patients who have finished their families ask to have their embryos destroyed, 43% donate them to basic science unrelated to stem cells, and 3% offer them to other infertile couples. It's estimated that about 150 babies were born that way between 1998 and 2006.

What is already a difficult decision can quickly become more complex when husband and wife disagree, as with the Janssons. Ingrid, who is not religious,

wants to donate her embryos for research. She says giving them to an infertile couple is "not an option," because it "would be like giving away my own child, my own DNA." Her husband Gardner is Catholic, and he objects. He says stem cell research, which dismantles embryos, is "destroying human life" and opposes it for his "son's siblings." The irony of their situation isn't lost on the Janssons. They never imagined they'd have spares after all they did to get pregnant. Now they disagree on what to do with the extras.

Questions for Analysis

1. What should be done with excess embryos?

2. Do you think that a decision about what to do with spare embryos should be a private decision or do you think that the government should legislate regulations?

3. If the government should legislate regulations, what moral principles ought it follow? Does principlism provide clear guidance for social policy in this area? Broadly speaking, what policy would a strict adherence to principlism suggest?

4. What offsetting principles, if any, do you think should balance principlism in crafting social policy?

5. What does your faith tradition teach about the morality of each choice facing people like the Janssons? What would you do with spare embryos, were they yours?

REFERENCES

1. Anne McLaren, "A Scientist's View of the Ethics of Human Embryonic Stem Cell Research," Cell Stem Cell, June 7, 2007, pp. 23–26.

2. Ibid., p. 24.

3. Andrew Pollack, "Questioning the Allure of Putting Cells in the Bank," The New York Times, January 29, 2008, p. D1.

4. Melissa Healy, "Stem Cell Hope, Hype," Los Angeles Times, March 5, 2007, p. Fl.

5. Mitchell Cairo et al., "Cord Banking for Potential Transplantation," Pediatrics, January 2007, pp. 165–170.

6. See note 2 above.

7. Robert P. George, "The Ethics of Embryonic Stem Cell Research and Human Cloning," Family Research Council, May 23, 2007. Retrieved July 9, 2008, from http://www.frc.org/get.cfm?i=PD02D5.

8. Richard M. Doerflinger, "The Ethics of Funding Embryonic Stem Cell Research: A Catholic Viewpoint," Kennedy Institute of Ethics Journal, June 1999, pp. 137–150.

9. Gene Outka, "The Ethics of Stem Cell Research," Kennedy Institute of Ethics Journal, December 2002, pp. 176–213. Retrieved July 2, 2008, from http://www.bioethics.gov/background/outkapaper.html.

10. NA, "What Should a Christian's View Be on Stem Cell Research?" Got Questions Ministries, 2009. Retrieved June 18, 2009, from http://www.gotquestions.org/Christian-stem-cell-research.html.

11. Doerflinger, p. 139.

12. John Tierney, "Are Scientists Playing God? It Depends on Your Religion," The New York Times, November 23, 2007, p. D1.

13. Robert P. George and Christopher Tollefsen, Embryo: A Defense of Human Life, DoubledayNew York, 2008.

14. See note 9 above.

15. Stephen Pollard, "The EU and Stem Cell Research," The Spectator, August 4, 2007. Retrieved July 22, 2008, from http://www.spectator.co.uk/the-magazine/features/68717/why-europe-may-soon-split-along-religious-lines.thtml.

16. Quoted by Outka.

17. NA, "The Moral Status of the Embryo," Harvard Magazine, May–June, 2007. Retrieved May 5, 2008, from http://harvardmagazine.com/2007/05/the-moral-status-of-the.html.

18. See note 17 above.

19. Sherman Silber, M.D., "Religious Perspectives of Ethical Issues in ART: 4. Infertility, IVF and Judaism," Middle East Fertility Society Journal. September 3, 2005, pp. 200–204.

20. Christi Dabu, "Stem-Cell Science Stirs Debate in Muslim World, Too," The Christian Science Monitor, June 22, 2005. Retrieved July 8, 2008, from www.csmonitor.com/2005/0622/p15s02-wogi.html.

21. See note 17 above.

22. Dr. Hassan Hathout, "Human Genetic and Reproductive Technologies: Comparing Religious and Secular Perspectives—An Islamic Perspective," International Seminar on Human Genetic and Reproductive Technologies: Comparing Religious and Secular Perspectives, Cairo, February 6–9, 2006. Retrieved August 9, 2008, from http://www.islamset.com/ioms/cairo2006/abstracts/hassan_hathout.html.

23. See note 17 above.

24. McLaren, p. 25.

25. Gina Kolata, "Researcher Who Helped Start Stem Cell War May Now End It," The New York Times, November 22, 2007, p. A22.

26. See note 24 above.

27. Paul Ramsey, War and the Christian Conscience: How Shall Modern War Be Conducted Justly? Duke University PressDurham, NC, 1961, pp. 171–191.

28. See note 9 above.

29. See note 9 above.

30. See note 8 above.

31. John A. Robertson, "Ethics and Policy in Embryonic Stem Cell Research," Kennedy Institute of Ethics Journal, June 1999, pp. 109–136.

32. Nicholas Wade, "Within Discredited Stem Cell Research, a True Scientific First," The New York Times, August 3, 2007, p. A16.

33. Associated Press, "Embryonic Stem Cells Created Using Unfertilized Eggs," Los Angeles Times, June 29, 2007, p. A31.

34. See note 33 above.

35. Nancy L. Jones, "The Stem Cell Debate: Are Parthenogenic Human Embryos a Solution?" The Center for Bioethics, June 2, 2003. Retrieved July 7, 2008, from http://www.cbhd.org/resources/stem-cells/jones_2003-06-02.htm.

36. Mark Henderson, "Stem Cell Breakthrough Opens Way To 'Spare Part' Tissue Banks," TimesOnLine,

October 17, 2005. Retrieved June 30, 2008, from www.timesonline.co.uk.

37. Carina Dennis and Erika Check, "'Ethical' Routes To Stem Cells Highlight Political Divide," Nature, October 20, 2005, p. 1076.

38. Helen Pearson, "Early Embryos Can Yield Stem Cells … and Survive," Nature, August 24, 2006, p. 858.

39. Maria Sanminiatelli, "Vatican Critical of Stem Cell Creation," Washingtonpost.com, August 26, 2006. Retrieved June 13, 2008, from http://www. washingtonpost.com/wp-dyn/content/article/ 2006/08/26/AR2006082600535.htmle8/26.

40. Claudia Kalb and Debra Rosenberg, "Embryonic War—Scientists and Ethicists Put the Latest Stem-Cell 'Breakthrough' Under the Microscope," Newsweek, September 4, 2006. Retrieved May 6, 2008, from kasusa.squarespace.com/national/2006/ 8/28/embryonic-war-newsweek.html.

41. See note 24 above.

42. See note 40 above.

43. Alan Boyle, "Skin Cells Made to Mimic Stem Cells," MSNBC, November 20, 2007. Retrieved June 20, 2008, from www.msnbc.msn.com/id/ 21886974/.

44. See note 25 above.

45. Michelle Turcotte, "Breakthrough Should Not End Embryonic Research," The Daily Cardinal, November 26, 2007. Retrieved May 6, 2008, from http://www.dailycardinal.com/article/1289.

46. Sam Berger, "The Silent Stem Cell Majority," Center for American Progress, February 22, 2006. Retrieved June 7, 2008, from www.americanprogress.org/issues/2006/02/b1433729.html.

47. USA Today/Gallup Poll, April 13–15, 2007. Retrieved June 4, 2008, from http://www.pollingreport.com/science.htm.

48. Matthew C. Nisbet, "Trends: Public Opinion About Stem Cell Research and Human Cloning," Public Opinion, Spring 2004, pp. 131–154.

49. Patrick Stephens, "Cloning: Toward a New Conception of Humanity," The Objectivist Center, April 1, 2001. Retrieved June 4, 2008, from http:// www.objectivistcenter.org/cth–228Cloning_Toward_New_Conception_Humanity.aspx.

50. See note 49 above.

51. See note 7 above.

52. See note 1 above.

53. See note 35 above.

54. See note 35 above.

55. See note 35 above.

56. See note 17 above.

57. "Cord Blood Banking," Keep Kids Healthy.com. Retrieved July 8, 2008, from http://www.keepkidshealthy.com/pregnancy/cord_blood_banking.html.

58. See note 49 above.

59. Leon R. Kass, "The Wisdom of Repugnance," New Republic, June 2, 1997, pp. 17–26. Retrieved June 11, 2008, from http://www.people.umass.edu/jak-locks/Phil164/kass.doc.

60. Leon R. Kass, "Cloning of Human Beings," testimony presented to the National Bioethics Advisory Commission, March 14, 1997. Retrieved June 11, 2008, from www.all.org/abac/clon-sec.htm.out.

61. Ryan Ward, "NIH Releases Draft of Embryonic Stem Cell Guidelines- Overly Restrictive, Overly Permissive, or Just Right?" Connecting for Kids, April 23, 2009. Retrieved May 22, 2009, from http://sickkidsus.org/2009/04/nih-releases-draft-of-embryonic-stem-cell-guidelines-overly-restrictive-overly-permissive-or-just-right/.

62. NA, "Bioethics Forum: Federal Funding of Embryonic Stem Cell Research," The Hastings Center Report, May–June 2009. Retrieved June 20, 2009, from http://www.thehastingscenter.org/Bioethics-forum/Post.aspx?id=3298.

63. Andrea Stone, "Each Stored Embryo Is a Stem Cell Debate," USA Today, January 30, 2007. Retrieved May 21, 2009, from www.usatoday.com/educate/ college/healthscience/articles/20070204.htm.

PART IV

Issues at the End of Life

INTRODUCTION: JACK'S BACK

On June 1, 2007, Dr. Jack Kevorkian, the 79-year-old retired Michigan pathologist dubbed "Dr. Death" for admitting he assisted at least 130 deaths from 1990 to 1999, left prison after eight years, still convinced that people have a right to die and the law should recognize it. Greeting Kevorkian along the road to the prison were a handful of supporters holding signs like "Jack, Glad You're Back" and "Jack, We're Glad You're Out of the Box."

Throughout the 1990s Kevorkian had challenged authorities to make his actions legal. He repeatedly and publicly expressed the view that the individual owns his or her life and, therefore, has the moral right to decide when and how to end it, despite laws to the contrary. "You think I'm going to obey the law? You're crazy," he said in 1998, shortly before being accused and then convicted of the deliberate killing of a man suffering from Lou Gehrig's disease who had sought his assistance to die. The sentence—10 to 25 years for second-degree murder—was reduced because of good behavior and bad health.

As a condition of his release, the medicide advocate promised never to participate in another planned death. But Ruth Holmes, Kevorkian's legal assistant, insisted that her client's views on the subject were unchanged. "This should be a matter that is handled as a fundamental human right that is between the patient, the doctor, his family and his God," Holmes said of Kevorkian's beliefs. Kevorkian agreed.

In an interview shortly after regaining his freedom, Kevorkian told a Detroit television station that physician-assisted suicide, or PAS, had to be legalized. "I'll work to have it legalized. But I won't break any laws doing it," he said.[1] (Michigan has had a law banning assisted death since 1998 when, one month after Kevorkian's conviction, voters overwhelmingly rejected an assisted-suicide referendum.) But not everyone was taking Kevorkian at his word. Right to Life Michigan, a group opposed to planned death, publicly expressed its distrust of Kevorkian's pledge. So did Michigan Catholic Conference, vowing to mobilize public opposition, as it did in 1998. A Conference spokesperson called assisted suicide "an affront to the dignity of the human person, a crime against life, and an attack on humanity."[2]

The controversy that still dogs Kevorkian is symptomatic of yet another category of dilemmas—besides those in reproductive technology—posed by the wonders of modern medicine, where dazzling gains in extending life come at a steep price. Thanks to modern medicine's awesome capabilities to intervene in and redirect the natural course of disease, we can anticipate longer life. But we also dread how we may die: tethered to machinery tended by strangers orchestrating our death.

In the last quarter of the last century, US courts heard many cases that bear on how much influence any of us can exercise over the circumstances of our death, including *Quinlan* (1976), *Perlmutter* (1980), and *Cruzan* (1990). Today, largely because of those rulings, competent or formerly competent patients through their surrogates have a well-established right to refuse any medical treatment, even if that means allowing a disease to progress on its natural, fatal course—indeed, even if it means the death of a viable fetus (*In re Fetus Brown*, Illinois Appellate Court, 1997). Still unresolved, however, is whether a competent adult who so wishes should ever be assisted to die.

Given its centrality in end-of-life issues, voluntary death is the common interest of several chapters of Part IV. Chapter 19 shows how PAS is a recent turn in the long and complex history of voluntary death, while Chapters 20 and 21 join the debates about its morality and legalization. Chapter 22 takes up the troubling prospect of rationing health care at the end of life. Language clarification being important in these matters, we begin, in Chapters 17 and 18, with some key conceptual concerns, including the meanings of "death," "suicide," and "euthanasia."

The theme of PART IV is that end-of-life issues ultimately owe their controversy to many of the same irreconcilable divisions that drive the cultural discourse about issues at the beginning of life: opposed views about the definition of human life and personhood, the purpose for existence, the reach of personal liberty, and the nature of the ideal society.

REFERENCES

1. "Kevorkian Released from Prison After 8 Years," *MSNBC News Services*, June 1, 2007. Retrieved March 25, 2008 from http://www.msnbc.msn.com/id/18974940/.
2. "'Dr. Death' Kevorkian Released from Jail; Helped Suicides," *Monsters and Critics.com*, June 1, 2007. Retrieved April 1, 2008 from http://news.monsters andcritics.com/usa/news/article_1312240.php/Dr_Death_Kevorkian_released_from_jail_helped_suicides__Roundup_.

Chapter 17

Definition and Criteria of Death

There has been a rapid rise in the number of kidneys, livers, and other body parts surgeons are harvesting through a controversial approach to organ donation. The procedure involves removing organs from a patient minutes after the heart stops beating and doctors declare the patient dead. Federal officials, transplant teams, and organ banks promote the practice as an efficient way to expand the donor pool, as well as to give dying patients and families the gift of giving life. The Joint Commission on Accreditation of Healthcare Organizations even requires that hospitals have such a procedure in place in order to be accredited. But some doctors and bioethicists object to the practice, saying it raises "the disturbing specter of transplant surgeons preying on dying patients for their organs, possibly pressuring doctors and families to discontinue treatment, adversely affecting donors' care in their final days and even hastening their deaths."[1]

The controversial protocol in question is termed "donation after cardiac death," or DCD, and in at least one instance its aggressive use has led to criminal charges against a transplant surgeon in the death of an organ donor.

DCD AND THE DEATH OF RUBEN NAVARRO

DCD typically involves a patient with severe brain damage who, as a result, requires life-sustaining treatment such as a ventilator. With appropriate patient consent that includes "do not resuscitate," or DNR orders, the patient is disconnected from life support and the heart slows. Once it stops, brain function ceases. As soon as death is declared, a transplant team waiting nearby can start removing organs, ordinarily within thirty minutes to ensure their viability. Most donor protocols call for a five-minute delay before the patient is declared dead after heart stoppage. However, doctors at some hospitals wait three minutes, others two. In Denver, surgeons at Children's Hospital wait 75 seconds before starting to remove hearts from infants, to maximize the chances that the organs will be usable.[2]

DCD donors usually are medicated to make sure they don't suffer as life support is withdrawn, and they're often given blood thinners to help preserve the organs. But some say those measures may hasten death. In 2007, a San Francisco transplant surgeon was criminally charged with excessively prescribing drugs to a patient in order to hasten his death and harvest organs sooner.

The patient, Ruben Navarro (1981–2006), a physically and mentally disabled man, had been revived and placed on life support after being found in cardiac and respiratory arrest at a nearby long-term care facility on January 29, 2006. Because his brain had been irreparably damaged from lack of oxygen, there was no expectation of recovery. So, Navarro's family agreed to donate his organs; and late on February 3, four days after he was discovered, Navarro was taken to the operating room and had his life support removed. But his heart continued to beat, despite the administration of many times the normal doses of drugs. After waiting the requisite thirty minutes, staff returned Navarro, 25, to intensive care where he died the next morning, about eight hours later. In the interim, his organs had deteriorated and were not suitable for transplant.[3]

Dr. Hootan Roozrokh, a 33-year-old surgeon, faced felony charges for his role in the transplant. Although unprecedented, the strong sanction was warranted, in the opinion of some within and outside the medical profession. Typical of their view was the opinion of one bioethicist who said that if the physician's intention was "to kill the person, have the person die sooner, but the person didn't actually die, that's attempted murder."[4]

Even before the incident, some hospitals had questioned the ethics of removing life support from a patient for the purpose of retrieving organs. To them it smacked of hastening death. After all, the narcotic morphine and the sedative Valium or Ativan can depress breathing and cause death in patients like Navarro. And when the patient's circulatory and respiratory functions start to fail, and physicians choose not to reverse and restore them, they are bringing death sooner than later, albeit by omission. To its many defenders, however, DCD is absolutely crucial to improving the life prospects of the nearly 100,000 on the nation's organ waiting list; the estimated one new patient in the US who is added to that number every thirteen minutes; and

the eighteen who die each day waiting for organs.[5] Add to this the approximately 50% of infants who die while awaiting a donor organ and the many who die with parents wanting to donate their infants' organs but cannot.[6]

For those locked in debate over the propriety of DCD, the core ethical issue is about permissible letting die, on the one hand, and impermissible killing or deliberately hastening death, on the other. But, perhaps, something more fundamental underlies the discourse, namely, the difference between dying and being dead. How, in fact, do we know when death has occurred?

According to some analysts, Ruben Navarro couldn't possibly have been the victim of something akin to attempted murder, because he wasn't alive to begin with; he was actually dead when the "life support" was removed. "Life support," they'd submit, is a misnomer in such cases. What's really being supported are organs. PVS (persistent vegetative state) patients including Navarro, Schiavo, and the thousands of others in US hospitals are, properly speaking, on "organismic support," not "life support" in any meaningful sense of the word "life."

Some commentators would say the same of patients in a minimally conscious state (MCS). MCS, as distinguished from PVS, is a condition where the patient exhibits inconsistent and erratic responsiveness often enough that it can be distinguished from the unconscious reflexive responses that characterize PVS or deep coma. But the outlook for both is basically the same. As one neurologist puts it:

> The facts show that PVS is the result of a brain that is badly, and chronically, injured, and meaningful clinical recovery from PVS is possible only in the hopes and dreams of patients' loved ones and supporters. The prognosis may not be much different with MCS. These latter ill-fated patients are bedbound, need full nursing care, are double incontinent, drift away during attempted conversation, and are unable to participate in rigorous rehabilitation programs as a result of their inability

to perform complex tasks and retain information in their stored memory.[7]

Even if most physicians would not consider PVS or MCS patients dead, doctors themselves do disagree on the exact point when a patient can be declared dead, suggesting that the question of when life ends is as debatable as when it begins. In the Navarro case, a jury avoided commenting on Navarro's status and acquitted Dr. Roozrokh of trying to speed his death.

Currently there are four main conceptual approaches to defining and determining death: heart-lung, whole brain, higher brain, and brain-stem. All of these formulations assume that life requires the integrated functioning of an organism. When that's lost, so is life. But exactly when that occurs is debatable. As we'll see in this chapter, each formulation gives an answer with implications for morally appropriate treatment for patients like Ruben Navarro or Terri Schiavo, but even for MCS patients and those suffering from incurable disorders such as Lou Gehrig's disease.

TRADITIONAL HEART-LUNG DEFINITION

Imagine a terrible auto accident. A husband and wife occupy one of the cars. Authorities on the scene pronounce the man dead and rush the unconscious woman to a hospital, where she spends the next seventeen days in a coma due to severe brain damage. On the morning of the eighteenth day she dies. Or did she? Some time afterward a relative contesting the couple's estate claims that the two died simultaneously. Did they?

In an identical case about a half-century ago, the Supreme Court of Arkansas ruled that, since the unconscious woman was breathing, she was alive.[8] In making its decision the court relied on a time-honored understanding of death as "the cessation of life; the ceasing to exist; defined by physicians as a total stoppage of the circulation of blood and a cessation of the animal and vital function

consequent thereon, such as respiration, pulsation, etc."[9] This traditional definition of death is variously termed *heart-lung*, *cardiopulmonary*, *cardiorespiratory*, or *clinical death*. By whatever name, according to this time-honored understanding, death occurs when circulation and respiration permanently cease. Down through the years different ways have been used to determine this, placing a stethoscope to the chest and listening for a heartbeat being a familiar one. Another, prior to the development of modern critical care, was simply observing that the patient was cold, blue, and stiff.[10]

Using heart-lung functioning as the criterion of death served well enough until challenged in the 1960s by two major medical developments addressed in Chapter 3: (1) breakthroughs in biotechnology; and (2) advances in transplant surgery.

Recall that the first advances in biotechnology, such as mechanical respirators and electronic pacemakers, made it possible to sustain breathing and heartbeat indefinitely in patients with head trauma, stroke, or other neurological injuries. This meant that, according to the traditional formulation of death, individuals who had lost all brain functions were technically still alive because they had respiration and circulation, albeit artificially maintained. Yet to many, notably relatives of the permanently comatose and those who cared for them, such persons were effectively dead.

The second medical development, advances in transplant surgery, brought the need for hearts and other organs from newly dead bodies. Artificially supported patients were, potentially, a rich source of organs, as they could provide blood-circulating organs right up to the time of removal. The problem was that these individuals could not be considered dead by the traditional criteria because, technically, they had heart-lung function. It was only irreversible heart stoppage that triggered the widely accepted "dead donor rule," which simply states that patients must be declared dead before the removal of any vital organs for transplantation. Fearing criminal or civil liability for removing organs before heart stoppage—part of the larger concern of medical researchers and biomedical institutions over legal liability[11]—physicians pressed for a reconsideration of the traditional heart-lung formulation of death.

WHOLE-BRAIN DEATH DEFINITION

To deal with the challenges of biotechnology and transplantation, an ad hoc committee of the Harvard Medical School was formed in the 1960s. In 1968 the committee, headed by Dr. Henry Beecher (1904–1976), proposed a new formulation of death. Based on brain function, the new definition would make some patients with devastating neurological injury suitable for organ transplantation under the dead donor rule.[12]

In the traditional view, if and only if heart-lung function was permanently lost might a patient be declared dead. Now, the committee proposed the permanent loss of all functions of the whole brain as enough for declaring death. Thus, patients could be declared dead when the *entire* brain irreversibly ceased functioning. Such a nonfunctioning brain was interpreted as exhibiting:

1. unreceptivity and unresponsively to applied stimuli and inner need;

2. lack of movement and breathing for at least one hour while being observed continuously by physicians; and

3. lack of reflex action, such as blinking or eye movement.

For a confirmatory test of this approach, the Beecher committee recommended the use of an electroencephalograph (EEG), where a flat electroencephalogram would confirm a permanently nonfunctioning brain.

A 1981 presidential commission report titled *Defining Death* reinforced this alternative formulation of death by proposing what became the Uniform Determination of Death Act. With the UDDA, the nation had a second legal standard of death: irreversible cessation of all functions of the entire brain, both cerebellum and brainstem. The new definition was termed *whole brain death* or, more popularly, *brain death*.

Currently, both approaches to death—heart-lung and whole brain—are used throughout the United States. An individual, including one artificially supported, can be declared dead who has sustained irreversible loss of either (1) circulatory and respiratory functions or (2) all functions of the entire brain, including the brainstem, the lowest part of the brain that controls vital functions such as heartbeat and breathing. Note that PVS patients such as Terri Schiavo are not considered "brain dead" since it is not their *entire* brain that has irreversibly ceased functioning, only their *higher* brain, or that part ordinarily considered to be uniquely characteristic of humans. Assuming he had a working brainstem, the same applies to Navarro, who, per DCD protocol, staff was monitoring for cardiac arrest while having his life support withdrawn.

Transplantation units and health care facilities nationwide welcomed the new whole-brain definition, and for good reason. As transplant and cancer surgeon Pauline W. Chen succinctly puts it:

> Whether you are transplanting a liver or a heart or a kidney or a pancreas, the better the donor is, the better your patient's outcome will be. And the very best of those donors is one who, when under the knife, is as close to alive as possible....[13]

The new, whole-brain definition also found support among Catholics, Protestants, and the pro-life lobby, who generally viewed it as less offensive than euthanasia.[14] Some scholars attribute the silence of Catholic opposition largely to a view Pius XII had expressed years earlier. In his 1957 allocution *Prolongation of Life,* the pope stated that while death was the complete and final separation of the soul from the body, "it remains for the doctor and especially the anaesthesiologist, to give a clear and precise definition of 'death' and the 'moment of death' of a patient who passes away in a state of consciousness."[15] Two leading Catholic theologians of the day rescued the pope's evaluation from seeming arbitrary and, thus, undermining the traditional religious view of life's sacredness from conception to death. Germain Grisez and Joseph Boyle argued as follows: (1) An organism is an integrated system, and (2) death is the irreversible loss of integrated organic function; therefore, (3) as the organ that maintains the "dynamic equilibriums" of the system, death occurs when the functioning of the entire brain is completely and irreversibly lost.[16]

In recent years, the religious and pro-life support that initially greeted the whole-brain definition of death has ebbed. So has enthusiasm for the work of the Beecher committee in general. Despite sharp divisions of opinion, there does seem to be a consensus of opinion on at least one point: Science can determine that the heart and lungs or the brain have permanently ceased to function, but medical facts alone cannot determine if a patient in such a condition is to be determined dead. That is a value judgment shaped by philosophical, ethical, religious, legal, and public policy considerations.[17] As an upshot, defining death has become controversial, fueled by the notoriety of cases like Navarro, where patients may appear to be killed for their organs or have their lives ended by organ removal.

CHALLENGES TO THE WHOLE-BRAIN FORMULATION

Currently there are three major challenges to the whole-brain formulation of death. They are, according to its preferred formulation of death: (1) traditional heart-lung, (2) higher-brain, or (3) brainstem.

Return to the Heart-Lung Formulation

From the outset, one assumption of the whole-brain definition was that when irreparable brain damage is more or less total to the whole brain, both cerebral cortex and brainstem, individuals cannot possibly return to spontaneous, respirator-free body activity. This accounts for the Beecher committee's use of the term "brain-death," that is, death according to a neurological or cortical as opposed to a cardiopulmonary criterion.

But some traditionalists continue to question the committee's reliance on spontaneous respiration, a brainstem function, claiming that artificially sustained

life is life nonetheless. Others consider the loss of the central nervous system, even of brain function, as irrelevant to the task of defining death. Breathing and blood flow, they point out, are not subsystems that, like the growth of hair or nails, function locally and display biochemical activity for themselves. They are, rather, activities whose functions extend throughout the total system and ensure the preservation of other parts. This would make circulation and respiration at least as important as brain activity—perhaps more important—because brain activity depends on them. Still other commentators claim that a distinct line between life and death cannot be drawn.

Although some traditionalists have used such criticisms of whole brain to revitalize the heart-lung definition, the traditional cardiopulmonary formulation is rarely used today in the United States as the exclusive criterion of death. Notable exceptions are found among some orthodox Jews and fundamentalist Christians who view heart-lung as the only criterion fully respectful of God-created human life and consistent with biblical teaching.

Adopt a Higher-Brain Formulation

Considerations of brain state certainly expanded the definition of death and the number of qualifying patients. Still, the whole-brain death formulation doesn't go far enough to suit scientists and philosophers who don't see why *all* functions of the *entire* brain have to be permanently lost before a declaration of death. Why not merely the permanent loss of *higher* functions, such as consciousness, thought, and feeling? Using this neo-cortical standard, a physician could declare a patient dead with brain functions that have no role in sponsoring consciousness, such as brainstem reflexes.

If adopted, a higher-brain criterion could make the irreversible loss of functioning in the cerebral cortex the primary physiological standard for defining death, as it is the cerebral cortex wherein lies the capacity for conscious life, a commonly accepted hallmark of personhood. Significantly, this higher-brain standard can be met prior to whole-brain death, which, again, must include death of the brainstem, or that part of the brain that allows spontaneous breathing and heartbeat but not consciousness. A patient in a permanent coma, then, or one who, like Schiavo or Navarro, is "awake but unaware" would meet the higher-brain but not the whole-brain standard of death. The higher-brain formulation, therefore, would give a basis for declaring dead tens of thousands of patients currently maintained in the United States. Included also would be those scant few patients with badly damaged brains who, though ostensibly conscious, show some preserved cognition, as revealed by magnetic resonance imaging (MRI).[18] Neither the whole-brain nor heart-lung definitions would permit declarations of death in any of these cases.

Consider the famous case of Sunny von Bulow (1932–2008), whose husband, Claus, was convicted of trying to kill her with an overdose of insulin in 1982, before being acquitted in 1985. The incident was the basis of the 1990 movie *Reversal of Fortune*. For twenty-eight years, until her death in 2008, Sunny von Bulow was maintained in an irreversible coma with such brain damage that, according to experts, she would never regain consciousness. Still, she could breathe on her own, her eyes occasionally opened, and she showed sleep-wake sequences. So, was she alive or dead all that time? By two interpretations—heart-lung and whole-brain—she was alive. By another—higher-brain—she was dead, and had been since 1980.

Adopt a Brainstem Formulation

The third challenge today to whole-brain death accepts the validity of declaring death on neurological grounds but contends that a permanently nonfunctioning brainstem—ordinarily determined by simple, low-tech, bedside tests such as checking the pupils—is always adequate for determining death. Proponents are led to this view by the fact that consciousness as well as heart and lung function depend on a functioning brainstem. This makes the brainstem-dead, regardless of cardiac prognosis, because they are irreversibly unconscious and apneic.[19,20]

Its supporters claim that a brainstem formulation offers advantages over both the higher-brain and whole-brain definitions. First, spontaneously breathing vegetative patients like Schiavo would be considered alive, thus avoiding the cultural problems of the higher-brain formulation by which such patients would be declared dead. Also considered alive would be patients in a "locked in state," that is, patients who look unconscious but are conscious, as opposed to PVS patients, who look conscious but are unconscious. Locked-in syndrome is caused by damage to the brain's lower but not upper portions, whereas PVS results from damage to the upper but not lower parts of the brain. Second, the brainstem formulation avoids common objections to whole-brain death that some patients declared "brain dead" in fact retain neuronal life above the level of the brainstem.[21]

Heart-lung, higher-brain, and brainstem formulations directly challenge whole-brain death. But like whole-brain, heart-lung and brainstem formulations are *biological* concepts, whereas higher-brain is *psychosocial*. It is the higher-brain, or neocortical, formulation, then, that uniquely calls into question whole-brain's fundamental conception of death itself, and with it the status of patients like Terri Schiavo and Ruben Navarro. (See chart below.) With that distinction there emerges an excruciating question. As more and more of us engage the long twilight struggle with aging and profound and irreversible cognitive impairment, individuals, families, and society must decide: Is death better understood as a biological concept or as a psychosocial concept?

Biological Death		Psychosocial Death
(Navarro and Schiavo alive)		(Navarro and Schiavo dead)
Heart-lung	X	
Whole-brain	X	
Higher-brain		X
Brainstem	X	

THE BIOLOGICAL VS. PSYCHOSOCIAL DEBATE: ORGANISMS VS. PERSONS

According to the heart-lung, whole-brain, or brainstem definitions, individuals are dead when they have permanently lost what is essential to them as an organism—respiration and circulation, all brain activity, or simply brainstem function, respectively. By any of these formulations, then, death is strictly an organismic or a biological concept.[22] The higher-brain definition, in contrast, associates death with the irreversible loss of what is essential to an individual as a person—for example, consciousness or cognition—not just as a biological organism. This makes death a psychological and social concept.

Is the death of a human being rightly understood only biologically, as the permanent loss of functioning of an organism as a whole? Or may it also and perhaps better be understood psychologically and socially, as, for example, the permanent loss of consciousness or the capacity for consciousness? When we say that someone is dead, precisely what are we referring to—merely a biological organism that has permanently ceased to function; or something more, perhaps an entity that has permanently lost capacities uniquely human?

These abstract philosophical questions, like their counterparts about the beginning of life (see Chapter 8), have their own serious clinical and moral implications. They raise questions about the status—alive or dead—and appropriate treatment of those thousands of PVS patients being maintained artificially at an annual cost of billions of dollars.[23] But the numbers and costs of PVS patients are small compared with the hundreds of thousands who likely will suffer from catastrophic cognitive impairment, as the number of the elderly demented rises significantly over the next quarter century.[24] What are we to say of those who are alive but not living—of the loved one who, stricken with a disease such as Alzheimer's, slowly leaves us all alone, with no memories or recognition of us?

Death of the Organism: A Biological Perspective

Consistent with the Beecher committee's new, whole-brain formulation of death, the 1981 President's Commission said that the status of PVS patients should not alter our understanding of death as the permanent cessation of the functioning of the organism as a whole. The commission pointed out, first, that the loss of all brain functions permanently

disrupts the integrated functioning of heart, lungs, and brain. There can be no spontaneous breathing, the heart will soon stop, and the organism as a whole will die. So, although the commission recognized whole-brain death, it didn't depart from the traditional biological or organismic understanding of death.[25]

The commission also said that the many thousands of PVS patients were alive because, even though they were permanently unaware, they still exhibited integrated functioning of brain, heart, and lungs. In its view, these organs "assume special significance ... because their interrelationship is very close and the irreversible cessation of any one very quickly stops the other two and consequently halts the integrated functioning of the organism as a whole." So long as there was integrated functioning of the circulatory, respiratory, and central nervous system, then, the "organism as a whole" was to be considered alive.

Finally, the President's Commission emphasized that these cases of "partial brain impairment"—such as, Schiavo, Navarro, von Bulow—were different in kind, not just degree, from cases of "complete and irreversible loss of brain function." It emphatically stated:

> The President's Commission ... regards the cessation of the vital functions of the entire brain—and not merely portions thereof, such as those responsible for the cognitive functioning—as the only proper neurological basis for declaring death. This conclusion accords with the overwhelming consensus of medical and legal experts and the Public.

Today that consensus may not be as "overwhelming" as it was thirty years ago; but it still stands, supported by the traditional understanding of death as the permanent cessation of the functioning of the organism as a whole. For heart-lung, whole-brain, and brainstem theorists, then, PVS patients are still alive given that they exhibit integrated functioning of most important organic subsystems, such as temperature regulation, spontaneous heartbeat, and normal blood pressure.

BIOETHICS ACROSS CULTURES

Japan's Organ Transplantation Law

Rather than defining "human death," Japanese law allows people to choose between traditional death and brain death. Thus, people who want to donate their organs after brain death has occurred record that intention on a donor card or label beforehand. When their brain death is diagnosed, they are considered dead, providing their family does not object. Those objecting to brain death and transplantation so indicate by not carrying donor cards. They are considered to be alive until the heart stops beating, the lack of brain functions notwithstanding. Japan's Organ Transplantation Law, then, has three pillars, namely, pluralism on human death; the donor's prior declaration principle; and family consent. From philosopher Masahiro Morioka comes the following summary of how the law is applied:

> First, a patient is "clinically" diagnosed as brain dead in a hospital. It should be noted that a "clinical" brain death diagnosis is to be distinguished from a "legal" brain death diagnosis. The clinical diagnosis is a tentative one. When a patient goes into a deep coma, for example, physicians try to reach a clinical determination of whether brain death has occurred. The determination does not require an apnea test (that is, a test to see whether breathing has stopped) since the test might be detrimental to the patient's body.
>
> If the patient does not have a donor card, or has declared against transplantation, then he or she is considered "alive" until the heart stops beating. Physicians are not allowed to reach a legal diagnosis of brain death (including an apnea test) on the patient.
>
> If the patient has a donor card, and the patient has agreed to brain death and organ

donation (and designated the names of transplantable organs on the donor card), then a transplantation coordinator comes and asks the family members if they also agree to legal diagnosis of brain death and organ removal for transplantation. If they agree, physicians start to make a legal diagnosis of brain death following the Japanese criteria for brain death, which include an apnea test. The transplantation team comes in. Organ procurement begins.

To the Western mind, the weight given "family consent" probably seems strange, as it is the patient who is dying. But for many ordinary Japanese, "the dying person and the family share the dying process and the death itself, and that even after the diagnosis of brain death the family continues to share the dying process with the patient." Morioka calls this phenomenon "brain death as a feature of human relationships," and bioethicist Yoshihiko Komatsu has called it "resonating death." By whatever name, this "human relationship-oriented analysis of brain death" has become very popular in Japanese bioethics, and supports the view that the family has some right to say something about the legal brain death diagnosis and the removal of organs.

(SOURCE: Masahiro Morioka, "Reconsidering Brain Death: A Lesson from Japan's Fifteen Years of Experience," *Hastings Center Report*, Fall 2001, pp. 41–46. Retrieved May 25, 2009, from http://www.lifestudies.org/reconsidering.html.)

Question

Why would a significant proportion of Japanese people who reject the idea of brain death also reject the notion that the essence of humans lies in self-consciousness and rationality? Do you approve or disapprove of Japan's Organ Transplantation Law?

Whether there's a moral obligation to maintain that life, however, is disputable.

Recall from the Introduction that religious and social conservatives insisted on maintaining Terri Schiavo, arguing that removing her feeding peg was tantamount to murder. Religious and social liberals, on the other hand, largely defended the withdrawal of hydration and nutrition as not killing

Schiavo—as, for example, by a lethal injection—but allowing her to die by removing unwanted and extraordinary means to preserve her life. Apparently, then, despite their differences, both positions assumed that Terri Schiavo was biologically alive. By the same token, those divided over the propriety of DCD must at least agree that a patient like Navarro is biologically alive; for DCD involves the orchestrated withdrawal of life support and monitoring of the onset of cardiac arrest.

To higher-brain proponents, however, these debates miss the point. Schiavo was neither killed nor allowed to die, they say. Schiavo was already dead because she had long since permanently ceased to function as a person. And Dr. Roozrokh did nothing wrong, unless perhaps violate some law against corpse desecration.

Death of the Person: A Psychosocial Perspective

As previously noted, a growing number of theorists object to the whole-brain standard, not because it goes too far in defining death, as some traditionalists claim, but because it doesn't go far enough. Higher-brain enthusiasts say that whatever makes us uniquely human, such as consciousness and cognition, is what matters in determining human death. Without awareness, without being able to think, reason, or remember, patients including Schiavo, von Bulow, or Navarro can't ever function as persons. Therefore, they're dead.

By this account, then, the whole-brain standard of death may adequately capture the death of non-human animals, but not a *human* death. Human beings are dead, say higher-brain theorists, when they are no longer persons. And that means when there is irreversible loss of *higher* brain functions. Without higher-brain functions, there can be no integration of the mind and body and, thus, no basis for asserting that *human* life is present.

Worth recalling here is Chapter 8's discussion of personhood, specifically the observation that most philosophers today tend to associate personhood with not just a single trait but a cluster of them. Similarly, not all higher-brain theorists are agreed on what it is that is essential to us as persons—what, philosophically speaking, is necessary for a human being to be a person. This is why they sometimes employ the purposely ambiguous term *higher-brain function*. It's "a way to make clear that the key philosophical issue is which of the many brain functions are really important," as bioethicist Robert Veatch explains.[26]

Noteworthy, too, is how this interest in significant brain functions for personhood turns the discourse about the proper understanding of death from the procedural to the philosophical/religious. Specifically, the question is less, as with Schiavo, "What does the patient want and who is entitled to say?"; or with Navarro: "What is proper organ transplant protocol and was it violated, perhaps criminally?" With the higher-brain view, the question is more: *What exactly is it that has lost life or ceased to be when we say that someone like Schiavo and Navarro, or you or me, are dead?*[27] Given the controversial nature of that issue, the higher-brain school, while attracting a considerable following, also has drawn its share of detractors, who are critical of its psychosocial, person-based perspective of death.

Problems with the Person-Based View Philosopher David DeGrazia of George Washington University is representative of critics of this neocortical concept of human death. DeGrazia has identified what he calls some "irresolvable tensions" with the person-based view.[28]

First of all, says DeGrazia, human beings undoubtedly are organisms as well as persons, which means that biological death still applies to humans. What, then, are we to make of permanently unconscious patients? Are they dead as persons but alive as organisms? Doesn't the person-based, higher-brain view imply two deaths for a single human being: one of the person and another of the organism? "This is somewhat odd," DeGrazia writes, "since we are accustomed to believing that there is just one death associated with every human being."

Another conceptual problem relates to the meaning of *personhood*. Because philosophers are not agreed on what constitutes personhood, any higher-brain standard that relies on a concept of it will prove controversial. More troublesome, the unsettled nature of personhood has grave, practical implications, as evident in DeGrazia's most serious objection to the higher-brain standard: the "slippery slope" upon which he sees the person perspective teetering.

DeGrazia fears that defining death as loss of personhood invites an expansion of those humans to be counted as dead, because personhood is generally thought to require more than consciousness or the capacity for consciousness. Whatever the character(s) of a person, presumably conscious individuals who lacked it (or them) are to be considered dead. Among these patients certainly would be ones like Schiavo and Navarro, but also, perhaps, such disabled individuals as Parkinson's and Alzheimer's patients; the mentally ill and retarded; and the frail elderly and the medically futile ill.

The Person-Based Reply For their part, person-based, higher-brain theorists say their critics again miss the point. When we permanently lose consciousness, they argue, we lose the possibility of any meaningful life, including *any* meaningful proposed candidate of personhood. We have no self-awareness, for example, or sense of personal identity—no sense of a self that persists from one moment to the next. We can't think, evaluate, or choose. We have no social existence. We can't speak, think, feel, work, or play. We can't befriend or love. In other words, we're alive, but don't have a life in any morally relevant sense. As philosopher James Rachels (1941–2003) wrote a quarter century ago:

> There is a deep difference between *having a life* and *being alive*. Being alive, in the biological sense, is relatively unimportant. One's *life*, by contrast, is immensely important; it is the sum of one's aspirations, decisions, activities, projects and human relationships. The point of the rule against killing is the protection of lives and the interest that some beings, including ourselves, have in virtue of the fact that we are subjects of lives…. In deciding questions of life and death, the crucial question is: Is a life, in the biographical sense, being destroyed or otherwise affected? If no the rule against killing offers no objection.[29]

Higher-brain theorists respond further that it is only from a biological or organismic perspective that an individual appears to die twice. There is, in fact, only one death, regardless of whatever biological

or minor brain functions might be present. Terri Schiavo didn't die twice, she died once—not in 2005, but in 1990 when she incurred catastrophic brain damage. Sunny von Bulow did not die twice; she died in 1980, not 2008. And Ruben Navarro died once, on January 29 not February 4, 2006, when his brain was irreversibly damaged. To talk about "two deaths," then, is to beg the question, which is simply whether the higher-brain standard is preferable to the whole-brain standard. And given that an uncovered whole-brain standard always reveals higher-brain functions, such as self-awareness or rationality, then why not define death by reference to the higher-brain standard?

As for potential abuses, Veatch, for one, thinks that it is the whole-brain formulation of death that stands on the slippery slope, not the higher-brain. After all, he says, for no good reason whole-brain effectively draws "a sharp line between the top of the spinal cord and the base of the brain (i.e., the bottom of the brain stem)," thereby discounting the significance of any spinal reflexes. But if spinal reflexes can be ignored in determining death, then why can't some brainstem reflexes as well? Why can't the wincing and the tearing of PVS patients like Schiavo? The typical reply is that brainstem reflexes are more integrative of bodily function; and, so long as the central nervous system can retain the capacity for integration, a person is alive. But Veatch doubts that brainstem reflexes are more integrative of bodily function than spinal reflexes. "Whatever principle could be used to exclude the spinal reflexes," he writes, "surely can exclude some brainstem reflexes as well."

By contrast, Veatch insists that defenders of the higher-brain formulation, like himself, in fact are avoiding the slipperiness by relying on

> classical Judeo-Christian notions that the human is essentially the integration of the mind and body and that the existence of one without the other is not sufficient to constitute a living human being. Such a principle as the higher-brain provides a bright line that would clearly distinguish the total and irreversible loss of

consciousness from serious but not total mental impairments.[30]

In effect, then, Veatch is saying that the higher-brain definition is more consistent with, say, the Catholic Church's traditional view of death as the complete and final separation of the soul from the body than is the whole-brain definition endorsed by Pius XII. Thus, the conclusion that aforementioned theologians Grisez and Boyle should have drawn is: As the organ that maintains the "dynamic equilibriums" of the system, death occurs when the functioning of the *higher* (not whole) brain is completely and irreversibly lost.

Other defenders of the higher-brain, person-based position have taken a less technical, more pragmatic approach to the whole-brain/higher-brain debate. Philosopher Martin Benjamin of Michigan State simply asks which conception of the human individual makes more sense. He believes there are powerful practical reasons for understanding human beings as persons, not merely as biological organisms. For one thing, such a view jibes with what really matters to us about human life and death: opportunities for acting and enjoying. Death makes all of this experience impossible; that's why it's a great loss.

Benjamin is also troubled by the fact that the whole-brain formulation effectively leaves patients who are in need of new hearts and livers waiting for the organs of PVS patients until the latter meet the UDDA. But by then the organs may no longer be suitable for transplantation. The same issue arises with the estimated 1,000 to 2,000 babies born annually in the United States with anencephaly, the total or near total absence of the cerebral hemisphere.[31] Anencephalic infants who aren't stillborn generally don't live longer than a few weeks. In some cases their kidneys and hearts, though undeveloped, could be transplanted to other infants who might die without them. For the transplants to have a reasonable chance of success, however, they need to be taken from these infants before they meet the criteria of whole-brain death. But even if the parents of the anencephalic infant agree to the transplant, the law does not permit this sort of organ donation. Beyond the matter of transplants,

higher-brain theorists like Benjamin hope that a shift from mainly a biological to a psychosociological conception of death may help settle an array of bioethical issues, including abortion, embryo and stem cell research, euthanasia, and assisted suicide.[32]

Veatch's reassurances not withstanding, it's worth noting that any attempt to separate the notion of personhood from biological life unsettles any belief that biographical life does not, of itself, determine personhood. The most obvious example is the Thomistic tradition, whose moral influence, as noted in Chapter 1, extends well beyond Roman Catholicism. According to Thomistic theology, biographical life is, itself, grounded in something else, namely, "the ultimate capacities of being a human being created in God's image." In other words, even after the irreversible loss of biography, part of what it means to be a person remains, namely, "being a human being, with a soul and created in God's image."[33] This remains a widely popular view in the cultural discourse on death and dying.

Still, liberal religious views exist today, even among some evangelicals, that comfortably separate the notion of personhood from biological life. Here's a representative example, from Professor of Philosophy Robert Wennberg of Christian Westmont College:

> Those operating within a Christian belief system may be attracted to the conclusion that death is the total and irreversible loss of the capacity to participate in God's creative and redemptive purposes for human life. For it is reasonable for Christians to believe that it is precisely this capacity, which endows human life with its special significance. More specifically, it is the capacity to shape an eternal destiny by means of decision-making and soul-making, and not mere organic functioning. Indeed it is reasonable to suppose that human organic life has no value in its own right but receives its significance from the fact that it can make possible and sustain personal consciousness, and thereby make possible the capacity to participate in God's

creative and redemptive purposes. However, when the human biological organism can no longer fulfill that function, its significance has been lost.... When an individual becomes permanently unconscious, the *person* has passed out of existence, even if biological life continues. There cannot be a person where there is neither the capacity for having mental states nor even the potentiality for having that capacity (as with infants). For persons are beings who have the capacity (potentially or actually) to think, will, affirm moral and spiritual ideals, love and hate, desire, hope, plan and so forth. Where no such capacities exist at all due to permanent loss of consciousness, there we no longer have an individual who commands the special respect due a person, because we no longer have a person.[34]

BIOETHICS ACROSS CULTURES

A Cross-Cultural Perspective on Brain Death

Many critics hold that the concept of human death should be one and universal and, therefore, the Japanese law on transplantations (see previous box) is seriously flawed. On one hand, according to the law, people without any brain functions are "dead" if they carry a donor card and the family does not object to the legal brain death diagnosis. On the other hand, they are "alive" either if they're not carrying a donor card or if the family objects to brain death. Critics insist that this variability is inconsistent and irrational, and sometimes call it the problem of a "bifurcated legal standard."

This criticism continues in the modernist assumption that science and technology can rid the world of its ills, improve the estate of its inhabitants, and lead to an increasingly better future. Specifically, it is held that science can provide objective grounds for resolving cross-cultural differences on such bioethical issues as brain death and organ transplants. The idea, traceable to the Enlightenment, is that with enough precise scientific understanding of a phenomenon—the exact moment of human death, for example—cultural differences over morality can be overcome and a universal moral code established, such as one dealing with the concept of human death and transplantations.

Is the modernist assumption correct? Can science not just inform ethical decision-making across cultures but arbitrate cross-cultural ethical disputes? To answer in the affirmative ignores a distinction David Hume first made in the eighteenth century and ever since has distinguished science from ethics. Simply put: "Is" doesn't mean "ought." This is shorthand for saying that science tells us about the world, whereas ethics tells us about how to live in the world. Precisely because how things are, or exist in the world, doesn't determine what we ought to do, individuals and cultures will differ morally, sometimes dramatically so.

Does this mean, then, that ethics is purely a matter of personal or cultural choice, as postmodern ethicists claim? Is a universal ethics impossible? Is ethics no more and no less than the creation of a particular culture? If the postmodernists are right in their relativistic ethics, then we seem left to accept cultural differences without any means of resolving cross-cultural disputes.

Richard Evanoff, who teaches environmental ethics at Aoyama Gakuin University in Tokyo, offers what he terms a "constructivist" alternative to the modern and postmodern oppositions.

In the constructivist view there are a variety of levels at which decisions can be made ... [and] a moral claim can be considered justified only if everyone who is affected by a particular decision has the opportunity to participate in the process by which that decision is made ... Accordingly, decisions which have consequences only for the individual should be made by the individual alone. When decisions made by an individual have consequences for others, however, then those others should also be consulted. If a decision affects larger groups or society as a whole, then all of those affected should be allowed to engage in the decision-making process. Indeed, if decisions have consequences which cross national boundaries, then cross-cultural dialogue is no longer an option but a necessity. It should be noted that this position is opposed to the view that decisions should be made by "experts," whether in government, science, or even bioethics. Rather, the role of politics, science, and ethics is to inform and illuminate the choices which the relevant moral agents themselves must make.

In the light of these considerations, Evanoff suggests that, because decisions related to brain death and organ transplants generally have no consequences for others, each culture be permitted to develop its own ethical stance on such issues. In fact, he tends to go further:

I would ... suggest that most bioethical decisions related to brain death, euthanasia, and similar issues can be plausibly made by individuals, their families, and doctors alone, in the absence of government control. The only role the state can legitimately play in such cases is to guarantee that any agreement

reached among the relevant moral agents has been arrived at in a fair and inclusive manner.

(SOURCE: Richard Evanoff, "A Cross-Cultural Perspective on the Relationship Between Science and Bioethics," *Eubios Journal of Asian and International Bioethics*, January 2001, pp. 11–13. Retrieved May 22, 2009, from http://eubios.info/EJAIB111.htm.)

Question

What would be an example of a decision that affects "larger groups or society as a whole"; one that has "consequences which cross national boundaries"? Explain why you think that a constructivist approach is or is not a plausible alternative to modernism and postmodernism. Do you agree with Evanoff that decisions about brain death and euthanasia be left largely to individuals, families, and their physicians?

LINGERING QUESTIONS ABOUT BRAIN DEATH

Besides inviting a spirited response from higher-brain theorists, the current whole-brain formulation of death continues to be criticized for conceptually confusing a definition of death with a permission to die. Some even say that the whole-brain formulation has been more harmful than helpful. Adding to the critical mix are those who say that any biologically based formulation fails to understand that death is not an event but a process.

Definition or Permission?

The *Report of the Harvard Committee to Examine the Definition of Brain Death*, the official sub-title of the Harvard Committee's 1968 report, implies that the committee was proposing an alternative *definition* of death. In the eyes of its supporters and many of its detractors, it did precisely that. For them the only issue involves the relative breadth of that definition. But amidst the critics is another school of thought, one that views the report as offering not a necessary new definition of death but criteria for permitting death to occur unopposed.

The concern of the Harvard Committee, it should be remembered, was plainly physiological, specifically with (1) the irreversible loss of reflex activity mediated through the brain or spinal cord, with (2) electrical activity in the cerebral neocortex, and/or with (3) cerebral blood flow. On the basis of medical facts—such as reflex activity and cerebral blood flow—the committee advocated whole-brain *criteria* for determining death. Because of its emphasis on organic integration as defining life, whole-brain enthusiasts read in the criteria a new definition of death, "brain death." On the other hand, committee reference to "consciousness," "personality," or "mental activity" permitted others to read a higher-brain *definition* in the criteria. By conflating criteria and definition, did the committee introduce conceptual confusion?[35]

The problem is medical facts alone can't yield a definition of death, as the whole-brain/higher-brain dispute suggests. Each side, for example, generally agrees on the medical facts in a PVS case such as Schiavo, von Bulow, or Navarro; but they dispute the interpretation of those facts. For *psychosocial* reasons, higher-brain theorists believe that the medical facts determine that these patients are dead. For *biological* reasons whole-brain theorists believe that they are still alive. These opposed viewpoints leave little doubt that a *definition* of death is fundamentally a philosophical, religious, and legal issue, not a medical one.

Now, if the medical facts in these cases invite interpretation, who is to say that the interpretation must necessarily favor one or the other, whole-brain or higher-brain orientations? Perhaps the facts are best interpreted strictly as *criteria* that do not *define* death but *permit* it to take place. If so, then what the Beecher committee proposed, albeit inadvertently, was not a set of conditions for *determining* death but for *allowing* it to occur. By this account, the committee, and later the President's Commission, weren't addressing the question of whether patients with irreversible loss of the entire brain were dead but rather how such patients should be dealt with. They were really saying—or should be viewed as saying—not that such patients are dead, but that they might be allowed to die, by turning off a respirator, for example.

The difference between definition and permission in these matters is morally important, for once patients are declared dead—as in "brain dead"—then they are no longer persons with certain moral and legal rights. They're corpses. And as corpses they can be treated, in the words of philosopher Hans Jonas, however "law or custom or the deceased's will or next of kin permit and sundry interests urge doing with a corpse." Once assured we're dealing with a corpse, Jonas asked as early as the mid-l960s, what's to stop us from maintaining the body in an artificially animated state as a source for life-fresh organs—as a "plant for manufacturing hormones or other biochemical compounds ... a self-replenishing blood bank?"[36]

Jonas happens to believe that a patient with irreversible loss of the entire brain is nonetheless a patient—"'an organism as a whole minus the brain,' maintained in some partial state of life so long as the respirator and other artifices are at work." So for him the question is not "Is the patient dead?" but "How should the patient be dealt with?" This latter moral question is basically asking: "Are we justified, let alone obligated, in artificially supporting the life of a brainless body?" No, say Jonas and others like him, whereas whole-brain and higher-brain enthusiasts treat the question as moot, because in their views the patient is already dead.

Help or Harm?

Although Hans Jonas rejected the Harvard criteria as a definition of death, he at least viewed the criteria as establishing needed ground rules for the modern, high-tech era for withdrawing life support. Others have been less charitable.

As early as the 1970s and 1980s, some critics were calling the Harvard criteria unnecessary and harmful. One of them, physician/bioethicist Norman Fost, revisited the issue in the late 1990s. His conclusion: Events over the last three decades prove that the new definition has failed its main original social purposes of (1) ending medically worthless treatment and (2) improving organ supply. Fost says:

> Overtreatment—the continuation of life-sustaining treatment on patients who have no reasonable prospects for meaningful survival and often no clear interest in or desire for such treatment—seems far more widespread today than in 1968, when the redefinition was proposed as the solution to that problem ... [and] organ supply lags further and further behind demand.[37]

Supporting Fost's second point: Currently, of the approximately 100,000 people on waiting lists for organ transplantations, less than a third will receive the needed organ. Nationwide, about seventeen people die each day waiting for a transplant.[38] Compounding things, according to Fost, the statutes have made it very difficult to develop sensible, coherent policies and practices on withholding and withdrawing life support from a wide range of patients as well as to have a more rational policy of organ procurement involving a much broader population of patients than those who are "brain dead."

Event or Process?

Any biologically based definition of death views death as an event in which the biological organism permanently ceases to function. It is further assumed that a single criterion—heart-lung, whole-brain, brainstem—demarcates the moment of death.

But some bioethicists believe that it may be impossible to pinpoint a single criterion of human death because death (or dying) in our high-tech medical environment is less an event than a process that defies demarcation by a single point. At various points along the way, capacities—respiratory, hormonal, cardiac—are compromised and must be supported. Does it make sense, then, to say that the organism died at some specific point in this process? Isn't it more reasonable to say that "the organism was fully alive before the chain of events began, is fully dead by the end of the chain of events, and is neither during the process"?[39]

Still, important questions demand specificity about when the organism actually died. When can life support be withdrawn, organs be harvested, or the body be cremated? For example, in 2003 the Michigan State Court of Appeals upheld a 2001 ruling allowing a divorce for a woman comatose since a 1994 auto accident. The woman had filed for divorce several times but had not followed through. Friends said that the woman, who had a $1.5 million dollar estate, planned to file again but was prevented from doing so by the accident. After she was hospitalized, her brother and legal guardian pressed the case. In the court's eyes, obviously, the woman was alive, that is, she hadn't reached that point that marks the moment of death. Absent this assumption, how would the court possibly decide such a case?

CONCLUSIONS

The lack of consensus about death has led some theorists to back a public policy that would implicitly acknowledge multiple, valid definitions of death. From these, patients or their legal surrogates could choose according to their own values and philosophies. Orthodox Jewish groups, for example, have lobbied a few states for a conscientious objection exception to the whole-brain definition of death to allow their belief that death only occurs when heartbeat and respiration cease.[40] New Jersey, in fact, operates under a whole-brain formulation of death, but permits patients for religious reasons to choose heart-lung criteria. Some say that offering a menu of options—heart-lung, whole-brain, higher-brain—would maximize personal freedom, square with the nature and ideals of a democratic and pluralistic society, and expedite organ transplants by decriminalizing cases that today are considered killing, as with PVS patients and anencephalic newborns. Japan's Organ Transplantation Law of 1997, as an example, permits people to choose which of two conceptualizations of death, traditional or brain, will be legally recognized at their death. "Japan's transplantation law shares this 'pluralism on human death' with New Jersey's brain death law," writes

Japanese philosopher Masahiro Morioka, "but while New Jersey considers brain death the default definition of death, Japan takes traditional death as the default."[41]

Others see only confusion and controversy in such a "cafeteria" plan. They doubt that the general public would grasp, let alone embrace, the validity of multiple meanings of death. Unacceptable to the many who view death as a profoundly spiritual event would be the implicit secular notion of reducing its definition to "just another" choice. Then there are the practical matters raised by conscientious choice, including insurance coverage and impact on heath care professionals who may consider the option selected inappropriate.

Such concerns have brought some commentators to submit that, perhaps, legal and social issues are best viewed as separate and distinct points in the process of dying that allow, even require, different answers. Accordingly, they propose "decoupling," or separating, such matters from a determination of death. For example, life support might be withdrawn when higher-brain function is permanently lost, whereas organs might be removed when the entire brain ceases to function. Neither decision, however, applies a single criterion of death justified by some definition of death. Circumstance rules: the best use of resources, for example, in the case of withdrawing life support; the greatest number or organs appropriately harvestable, in the case of organ removal. Although this utilitarian bias avoids the problems of multiple definitions, it may raise another as potentially divisive: voiding the "dead-donor rule." In any event, decoupling theorists strongly oppose the conscientious choice

model, generally preferring the current whole-brain formulation as a default position to their own.

Defining and establishing criteria of death clearly remain problematic, inevitably inviting different approaches and defenses. Ultimately, it may be enough to follow the suggestion of death as "the permanent and irreversible cessation of the relevant aspects of life, where different accounts select different aspects as relevant."[42]

CASES AND CONTROVERSIES

Terry Wallis: The Man Who Woke Up After Nineteen Years

On July 13th, 1984, Terry Wallis and two friends were involved in an ugly crash when the truck they were driving in through Arkansas's Ozark Mountains lost control and plunged over the face of a cliff, before falling to a dried-up river bed thirty feet below. Terry was 20 years old, with a wife, Sandi, and a six-week-old daughter. The crash delivered a massive blow to his head, and by the time rescuers were able to pull him from the gorge, he had already slipped into a coma. Three months later he emerged from the coma and was diagnosed as a vegetative quadriplegic.

According to the Official Terry Wallis website, Terry's condition confused his family.

> At times, for instance, he appeared alert; he could grunt and fidget as if irritated with his confinement in bed. His eyes sometimes tracked people who entered his room and he often appeared to understand what was going on around him. If his food was liquefied and spooned into his mouth, he could eat well enough. There were glimpses, in other words, that Terry was still "in there." The family bolstered their hopes.[43]

But doctors, allegedly non-neurologists, cautioned the Wallises that these reactions were pure illusion.[44] Even though he appeared to be there "every now and then," they said that Terry was "utterly incapable of cognition," and beyond rehabilitation. He was placed in a nursing home to receive full-time care.

Angilee Wallis, Terry's mother, took the loss of her son particularly hard. Indeed, she never accepted the doctors' diagnosis of Terry's condition and persisted in believing that her son could hear and understand her.

The Wallises even began to include Terry in family activities. According to the website:

> A quick flip through the Wallis family photo album will tell you how unusual this decision was. There's Terry in every single Christmas picture, year after year. He's propped up in the corner with a Santa Claus cap on his head, staring straight into the lens with his wide-eyed, gape-mouthed vacant expression while family and friends throw their arms around him and laugh and joke and share eggnog. There he is, too, sitting at the head of every Thanksgiving table, even though he couldn't eat the turkey; Terry's food had to be pureed in a blender before he could swallow it. There are photos of Terry fishing down by the lake—his father, Jerry, would take him down to lip of the water, prop him up in an old folding chair, and wrap his paralyzed fingers around the shaft of a rod and reel ....[45]

But through it all, Terry remained as silent as the family photos he appeared in.

Meanwhile, Sandi, buckling under the strain, took off with baby Amber, leaving behind a note: "I still care about Terry but I've got to go on with my life. I have to find someone who will give Amber a good home. If you want I'll file for a divorce but all I want is to not have any trouble ...."

Nineteen years passed, with the Wallises acclimating to life with and without Terry. And then, on June 11, 2003, almost to the day he'd been declared officially "brain-dead," Terry Wallis "woke up." His first two words were "Mom" and "Pam," the name of his longtime nurse. After that, Terry's vocabulary began to expand, and at present he continues learning to speak, count, and interact. On the details of his devastating accident, he remains silent.

His family calls it a miracle. Some neurologists say his brain has rewired itself by growing new connections from those that were severed in the accident. They say that scans of his brain—the first ever taken from a recovering comatose patient—show that it has developed "new pathways and completely novel anatomical structures to re-establish functional connections, compensating for the brain pathways lost in the accident."[46,47] Other neurologists are less sanguine. What the scans reveal, they say, are "just more neuronal tracts formed over many years in an already awake and aware—and not comatose—patient."[48] Still others consider the findings valuable and interesting enough to warrant further studies.

Questions for Analysis

1. Neurologists make a major distinction between "recovery" (meaning that the diagnosis is correct and there truly is exceptional improvement) and "discovery" (in which the diagnosis is incorrect and changes with more methodical examination). Which do you think applies in the Wallis case?

2. Pro-life activists used the experience of Terry Wallis in their effort to maintain Terri Schiavo's feeding tube. Do the neurological conditions of Wallis and Schiavo bear any resemblance to each other?

3. Is the case of Terry Wallis evidence of meaningful clinical improvement in a PVS patient; or evidence that PVS is sometimes, perhaps often, misdiagnosed?

4. Discuss the appropriate treatment for Terry Wallis according to the four conceptual approaches to defining and determining death.

5. What lessons would you draw from the Wallis case?

CASES AND CONTROVERSIES

Baby Theresa

Cephalic disorders are defects resulting from abnormal development of, or damage to, the brain and spinal cord. Anencephaly is one of the worst cephalic disorders, leaving the infant missing major parts of the brain and the top of the skull. Although anencephalic infants have no cerebrum or cerebellum, they do have a brainstem, a tiny stump of a brain that makes possible autonomic functions such as breathing and heartbeat. Anencephaly afflicts roughly 1,000 to 2,000 babies born in the United States annually. Most anencephalic infants are stillborn or die within a few hours or days after birth. Many cases of anencephaly are detected during pregnancy and aborted.[49]

In 1992 a Florida couple sued a local hospital to have their anencephalic newborn declared dead so that her organs could help sick infants survive. When the Pearsons made the unusual request to volunteer their baby Theresa's organs, physicians welcomed the offer, because the need for infant organs well exceeded the supply, and still does. But the hospital balked, citing the "dead-donor rule," which operates in Florida and throughout the United States to prohibit the removal or organs before the donor is dead. Because little Theresa had a brainstem, the hospital insisted that she was still alive. A Florida circuit court agreed, as did the Florida Supreme Court on appeal. "We find no basis to expand the common law to equate anencephaly with death," Justice Gerald Kogan wrote in the high court's ruling, issued November 12, 1992. "Although some babies might be saved by organs from anencephalics, there is not enough proof that such donations save lives," the judge wrote.[50] The decision thus left in place the traditional definition of death, based on heart and lung activity.

Nine days after she was born, Theresa's breathing stopped and her organs deteriorated for lack of oxygen, rendering them useless for transplantation.

Questions for Analysis

1. What are the moral issues involved in this case?

2. Was the parents' request morally right or wrong?

3. Evaluate this case in the context of the four conceptual approaches for defining and determining death.

4. Is it possible that secular ethical theories—natural law, utilitarianism, and Kant's ethics—could provide a moral justification for the Pearsons' request?

5. What good and harm did the court's decision do? Do you agree with it?

CASES AND CONTROVERSIES

In the Conservatorship of Wendland

A rollover auto accident in September 1993 put Robert Wendland in a coma for seventeen months. After he came out of his coma, it was determined that he was profoundly and permanently disabled, physically and mentally. Robert was paralyzed on his right side and could not talk or meaningfully communicate with assistive devices. He could not perform any activities of daily living, and couldn't swallow. He was fed and hydrated by means of surgically implanted tubes. He wasn't in a permanent vegetative state, but one termed a persistent indeterminate state by medical experts, who couldn't agree on his state of awareness. Robert never talked, but could follow simple commands with coaching. His wife and children never thought he recognized them, but he was able to catch a ball and put pegs in a board. On one point there was no disagreement: Robert Wendland lacked the mental capacity to make decisions about his life and future, and his physicians said he would never get any better.

About two years after the accident, Robert's wife, Rose, decided to stop the administration of food and fluid to him after Robert had repeatedly pulled this tube out of his body. Based on previous conversations with him about such matters and his values pertaining to living and dying, Rose and her children were convinced that Robert would not want to live under these circumstances and would refuse to be kept alive by medical treatment. When Robert's estranged mother, Florence, challenged Rose's decision, litigation ensued, and lasted over the next six years. A trial judge appointed Rose to be Robert's surrogate decision maker but wouldn't permit her to stop his tube feedings. After a court of appeal ruled in Rose's favor, Florence took the case to the next level, the California Supreme Court, to stop Rose from having Robert's artificial feeding stopped.

In 2001 California's high court ruled, 6-0, that Rose could not order life-giving food and water withheld from Robert, unless "clear and convincing evidence" proved that he wanted to die under those specific circumstances, and that he indicated that wish in a formal manner while "competent." At the same time, the court made it clear that the ruling only applied to conscious patients who were "not terminally ill, comatose, or in a persistent vegetative state," and only to persons who had not left "formal instructions" regarding their health care, or had not appointed a person to make health care decisions for them. Ironically, Robert Wendland didn't live for the decision. He died three weeks earlier, of pneumonia. His wife refused aggressive treatment and insisted upon all palliative measures so he could die in peace.

Questions for Analysis

1. Do you think the court made the morally right decision?

2. Do you agree with the court's exception from the reach of its ruling conscious, terminally ill, incompetent persons, and permanently unconscious persons?

3. In order to satisfy the *Wendland* standards, someone would have to provide "clear and convincing evidence," that is, "evidence so clear as to leave no substantial doubt [and] sufficiently strong to command the unhesitating assent of every reasonable mind...." To Rose's appeals attorney, Lawrence J. Nelson, this standard sounds like the highest evidentiary standard used in law, "beyond a reasonable doubt," as opposed to the lesser test common in civil matters, "more likely than not."[51] Which standard should operate in cases like these, the higher or lower?

4. Do adults have a moral obligation to make sure that medical decisions will be made for them, in the event of their incompetency?

5. Discuss this case in the context of the biological versus psychosocial debate, the definition or permission debate, and the help or harm debate.

6. How should medical decisions be made for people such as Robert Wendland, who have not formally delegated a surrogate and specified their wishes and values?

REFERENCES

1. Rob Stein, "New Trend in Organ Donation Raises Questions: As Alternative Approach Becomes More Frequent, Doctors Worry That It Puts Donors at Risk," *The Washington Post*, March 18, 2007, p. A3.

2. Mark M. Boucek et al, "Pediatric Heart Transplantation after Declaration of Cardiocirculatory Death," *The New England Journal of Medicine*, August 14, 2008, pp. 709–714. Retrieved August 22, 2008, from http://content.nejm.org/cgi/content/full/359/7/709.

3. Charles Ornstein and Tracy Weber, "Doctor Charged in Death of Donor," *Los Angeles Times*, July 31, 2007, p. A1.

4. Stein, p. A17.

5. Upstate New York Transplant Services, "Frequently Asked Questions," June 2010. Retrieved June 6, 2010, from http://www.unyts.org/?select=faq.

6. Joseph Brownstein, "When Does an Infant's Life End?" *ABC News*, August 14, 2008. Retrieved August 22, 2008, from http://abcnews.go.com/Health/Story?id=5575170&page=2.

7. Eelco F. M. Wijdicks, "Minimally Conscious State vs Persistent Vegetative State: The Case of Terry (Wallis) vs the Case of Terri (Schiavo)," *Mayo Clinic Proceedings*, September 2006, pp. 1155–1158. Retrieved May 22, 2009, from http://www.mayo clinicproceedings.com/content/81/9/1155.full.

8. *Smith v. Smith*, 229 Arkansas 579, 317 S.W., 2d 275, 1958.

9. *Black's Law Dictionary*, rev. 4th ed. 1968, p. 488.

10. Robert M. Troug and Franklin G. Miller, "The Dead Donor Rule and Organ Transplantation," *The New England Journal of Medicine*, August 14, 2008, pp. 674–675.

11. Tina M. L. Stevens, *Bioethics in America: Origins and Cultural Politics*, Baltimore: Johns Hopkins Press, 2003.

12. See note 10 above.

13. Pauline W. Chen, "Dead Enough? The Paradox of Brain Death," *The Virginia Quarterly Review*, Fall 2005, pp. 130–137.

14. Peter Singer, *Rethinking Life and Death: The Collapse of Our Traditional Ethics*, New York: St. Martin's Press, 1996, pp. 29–30.

15. Pope Pius XII, "An Address to an International Congress of Anesthesiologists," November 24, 1957. Retrieved June 20, 2009, from www.lifeissues.net/writers/doc/doc_31resuscitation.html.

16. See note 14 above.

17. Robert M. Veatch, "The Conscience Clause," in *The Definition of Death: Contemporary Controversies*, Stuart Youngner, Robert M. Arnold, and Renie Schapiro, eds., Baltimore: Johns Hopkins University Press, 1999, p. 140.

18. Martin M. Monti et al, "Willful Modulation of Brain Activity in Disorders of Consciousness," *The New England Journal of Medicine*, February 18, 2010, pp. 579–583.

19. Fred Plum, "Clinical Standards and Technological Confirmatory Tests in Diagnosing Brain Death," in *The Definition of Death*, pp. 34–69.

20. Chris Pallis, "On the Brainstem Criterion of Death," in *The Definition of Death: Contemporary Controversies*, Stuart Youngner, Robert M. Arnold, and Renie Schapiro, eds., Baltimore: Johns Hopkins University Press, 1999, pp 93–100.

21. Ibid., p. 95.

22. David DeGrazia, "Biology, Consciousness, and the Definition of Death," *Report from the Institute of Philosophy & Public Policy*. Retrieved March 2, 2005, from http://www.puaf.umd.edu/IPPP/winter98-biology_consciousness.htm.

23. Maura Dolan, "Out of a Coma, Into a Twilight," *Los Angeles Times*, January 2, 2001, p. A1.

24. Adelina Comas-Herrera et al, "Cognitive Impairment in Older People: Its Implications for Future Demand for Services and Costs," *Mental Health Research Review*, May, 2003. Retrieved June 7, 2010, from www.pssru.ac.uk/pdf/dp1728_2.pdf.

25. "Defining Death," *U.S. President's Commission for the Study of Ethical Problems in Medicine and Biomedical and Behavioral Research*, Washington Government Printing Office, 1981, Ch 1.

26. Robert M. Veatch, "The Impending Collapse of the Whole-Brain Definition of Death," in Tom Beauchamp and Robert M. Veatch, *Ethical Issues in Death and Dying*, 2nd ed., Upper Saddle River, N.J.: Prentice Hall, 1996, p. 40.

27. Martin Benjamin, "Pragmatism and the Determination of Death," in Thomas A. Maples and David DeGrazia, *Biomedical Ethics*, 5th ed. New York: McGraw-Hill, 2001, pp. 316–324.

28. See note 22 above.

29. James Rachels, *The End of Life*, New York: Oxford University Press, 1986, p. 26

30. Veatch, p. 42.

31. Steve and Patricia Karg, "Anencephaly Fact Sheet," *Anencephaly Net*, May 31, 2009. Retrieved June 7, 2010, from http://www.anencephaly.net/.

32. Benjamin, p. 324.

33. Moreland and Rae, p. 325.

34. Robert Wennberg, *Terminal Choices: Euthanasia, Suicide and the Right To Die*, Grand Rapids: Eerdmans, 1989, pp. 159–160. Quoted in Moreland and Rae, pp. 333–334, italics added.

35. Martin S. Pernick, "Brain Death in a Cultural Context," in *The Definition of Death: Contemporary Controversies*, Stuart Youngner et al, eds., Baltimore: Johns Hopkins Press, 1999, pp. 3–33.

36. Hans Jonas, "Against the Stream Comments on the Definition and Redefinition of Death," in Tom Beauchamp and Robert M. Veatch, eds., *Ethical Issues in Death and Dying*, 2nd ed., Upper Saddle River, N.J.: Prentice Hall, 1966, pp. 23–37.

37. Norman Fost, "The Unimportance of Death," in *The Definition of Death: Contemporary Controversies*, Stuart Youngner et al, eds., Baltimore: Johns Hopkins Press, 1999, pp. 161–177.

38. NA, "Racial and Religious Considerations," *Donor Alliance*, January 2010. Retrieved June 8, 2010, from http://www.donoralliance.org/info-page-16.

39. Baruch A. Brody, "How Much of the Brain Must Be Dead?" in *The Definition of Death: Contemporary Controversies*, Stuart Youngner et al, eds., Baltimore: Johns Hopkins Press, 1999, p. 79.

40. Tom Tracy, "Euthanasia and the Supreme Court's Competing Conceptions of Religious Liberty," *Issues in Law & Medicine*, Summer 1994. Retrieved August 30, 2008, from findarticles.com/p/articles/mi_m6875/is_n1_10/ai_n25022496/pg_2.

41. Masahiro Morioka, "Reconsidering Brain Death: A Lesson from Japan's Fifteen Years of Experience," *Hastings Center Report*, 2001, pp. 41–46. Retrieved September 1, 2008, from http://www.lifestudies.org/reconsidering.html.

42. John Martin Fischer, ed., *The Meaning of Death*, Stanford: Stanford University Press, 1993, p. 8.

43. NA, The Terry Wallis Fund. Retrieved May 20, 2009, from http://www.theterrywallisfund.org/history.html.

44. NA, "Brain Plasticity," *Planet Thrive*, May 2, 2009. Retrieved May 20, 2009, from planetthrive.com/cgi-bin/members/pub9990223062281.cgi?categoryid=0&action=viewad&itemid=9990314442222.

45. See note 7 above.

46. See note 44 above.

47. Emily Singer, "Why Did Terry Wallis Wake Up After 19 Years in Bed?" *Technology Review*, July 5, 2006. Retrieved May 25, 2009, from http://www.technologyreview.com/read_article.aspx?id=17103&ch=biotech.

48. See note 47 above.

49. Stanley J. Swierzewski, III "Cephalic Disorders," *Neurology Channel*, March 12, 2008. Retrieved May 26, 2009, from http://www.neurologychannel.com/cephalicdisorders/index.shtml.

50. NA, "Florida Court Rejects New Death Definition," *The New York Times*, November 15, 1992, p. 26. Retrieved May 26, 2009, from www.nytimes.com/1992/11/15/us/florida-court-rejects-new-death-definition.html.

51. Lawrence J. Nelson, "Persistent Indeterminate State: Reflections on the Wendland Case," *Issues in Ethics*, Winter 2003. Retrieved May 25, 2009, from www.scu.edu/ethics/publications/iie/v14n1/wendland.html.

Chapter 18

Conceptual Issues in Suicide and Euthanasia

U nlike many patients on respirators, the Italian poet and writer Piergiorgio Welby (1945–2006) was conscious and communicative right up until his death on the night of December 20, 2006. And his blogosphere left no doubt what he wanted: help to die.

THE ASSISTED DEATH OF PIERGIORGIO WELBY

Weeks earlier, the 60-year-old Welby, a long-time advocate of euthanasia and forty-year victim of muscular dystrophy, had appealed directly to Italy's president for legal permission for a doctor to sedate him and remove him from a respirator, to which he'd been attached for nine years. Welby said that he wasn't seeking to commit suicide but to end unwanted medical treatment. Nonetheless, the result would be certain death. While Italian law allows refusal of medical treatment, it prohibits assisted death, even with consent. The Catholic Church, a vital force in Italy, also opposes medical treatment that artificially prolongs life, while it also opposes assisted death. So, as far as Catholic Italy was concerned, any doctor who detached Welby's respirator risked prosecution.

When a judge formally ruled against Welby's request days before his death, Welby could have appealed the court's decision. Instead, he chose to perform an act of civil disobedience that would kill him. Fully lucid but losing his capacity to speak and eat, Welby enlisted the services of anesthesiologist Mario Riccio. About 11 p.m. on the night of December 21, Dr. Riccio injected Welby with sedatives; and then, at an unspecified time before his death, Riccio stopped the respirator. By 11:30 p.m. Welby was dead. The cause of death: cardiorespiratory failure, according to Riccio.

Hours after Welby's death was announced, conservative lawmakers demanded Riccio's arrest. A leader of the Christian Democratic Party, a small group with strong ties to the Vatican, said the death could not go unpunished, "if only because it was committed in such a violent, scandalous and exploitative way."[1] In response, a serene Dr. Riccio said: "The case of Piergiorgio Welby is not a case of euthanasia. It's a case of refusing treatment," something that "happens every day," quietly and privately.

Asked his opinion, Dr. Myles N. Sheehan, a Jesuit priest and physician at the Loyola University Medical Center in Chicago, tended to agree. The expert on the ethics of euthanasia said: "If it is done privately, there would be a way to accommodate [the] desire to discontinue life support as a burdensome therapy…. But if it is done publicly, it's a big mess, because of the direct link to euthanasia."[2] Indeed, what gave the case a particular political twist was that Welby had long been a spokesperson for euthanasia, as a key member of Italy's Radical Party's effort to have it legalized. To supporters and detractors alike, his very public death was viewed as part of his political campaign for greater rights for the terminally and incurably ill to end their lives.

Was Piergiorgio Welby's death euthanasia, as conservative lawmakers and the Vatican charged? Or was it a case of an artificial prolonging of life, as Dr. Riccio and supporters claimed? Did Riccio merely assist Welby to discontinue burdensome treatment that, as a patient, he had a right to refuse, under Italian law and Church teaching? Or in ending Welby's artificial life support did Riccio, in fact, violate both?

These difficult moral questions can't be answered without conceptual clarification of at least three terms that recur in end-of-life cases: "euthanasia," "killing," and "allowing to die." But before examining these terms, the present chapter engages a related matter: suicide.

Traditionally, a death caused by placing oneself in circumstances one knew to be life ending was considered an act of suicide. But, as we're about to see, some modern philosophers have employed carefully selected cases of voluntary deaths to challenge this traditional, broad interpretation, and, thereby, narrow the scope of acts that count as suicides. As their analyses bear directly on voluntary death decisions at the end of life, they warrant consideration in discussions of physician-assisted suicide (PAS).

SUICIDE: THE PROBLEM OF DEFINITION

Emile Durkheim (1858–1917), the French social scientist and founder of sociology, applied the term

suicide to all self-administered acts, positive or negative, that result directly or indirectly in one's death. Durkheim's view has inspired broad definitions of suicide associated with foreknowledge. Accordingly, so long as an individual knew that an act would bring about his death, that act is properly termed suicide.[3]

But should suicide be defined so broadly? Is every act of voluntary death with foreknowledge really suicide, that is, the intentional termination of one's own life? Several kinds of examples have been proposed recently—self-sacrificial and coerced deaths among them—that challenge the breadth of the foreknowledge criterion and, with it, the conventional interpretation of "intentional" as "foreknowing."

Self-Sacrificial Deaths

In 1910 the explorer Captain Lawrence Oates (1880–1912) set out with Robert Scott's Antarctic Expedition and was one of the party of five to reach the South Pole on January 17, 1912. On their return trek, it is believed that the confluence of two events determined the grim fate of both Oates and the party: The explorers became dangerously delayed by weather, and Oates became severely lamed by frostbite. Convinced that his crippled state would pose further delays, Oates walked out into a blizzard, deliberately sacrificing his life to save his comrades. (The other two of Scott's remaining companions—Petty Officer Evans had succumbed prior to Oates—may also, in effect, have taken their own lives. In her recent, gripping account of the doomed party, author/ scientist Susan Solomon speculates that Dr. Wilson and Lieutenant Bowers sealed their fates by loyally remaining behind to tend a dying Scott, himself a victim of frostbite.)[4]

Was the self-sacrificial act of the gallant Captain Oates suicide? No, some would say, because presumably Oates didn't want to die but to save his comrades. Although he knew the blizzard would claim him—he had foreknowledge—his intention was not to end his own life but to save the lives of others. And, besides, it wasn't Oates who claimed his life, it was the blizzard.

Not everyone, however, finds this analysis persuasive. Philosopher Tom Beauchamp, for one, believes that Oates's heroic sacrifice was "plausibly a suicide because of the active steps that he took to bring about his death."[5] In short, Oates put himself in harm's way. Still, Beauchamp does think that some voluntary deaths are not suicides, such as those "coerced" or "forced."

Coerced Deaths

Consider the case of a captured soldier who, given a choice by the enemy of being executed by them or by himself, chooses to commit suicide. Clearly he intended to take his life. But he didn't *freely* intend to; coercion to death underlay his self-killing. The same can be said of Socrates, who was forced to drink the poison hemlock. Analysts like Beauchamp call such deaths "coerced self-killings," not suicides.[6] They make the same distinction of voluntary deaths of persons suffering from fatal diseases who refuse treatment and, consequently, hasten their deaths. Were their conditions treatable, on the other hand, and the individuals intended to die by refusing ordinary treatment, then the resulting deaths would be suicides rather than coerced deaths.

Clearly the degree of personal autonomy, or freedom, a person has plays a significant role in Beauchamp's concept of suicide. But so does one's role in effecting the death-causing circumstances, as his analysis of the Oates case shows. In Beauchamp's view, then, "an act or omission is a suicide if a person intentionally brings about his or her death, unless death is (a) coerced or (b) is caused by conditions that are not specifically arranged by the agent for the purpose of bringing about the death."[7]

Representative of an opposed viewpoint, philosopher Manuel Velasquez offers the following counter instance to Beauchamp's view. Imagine a man takes his own life when threatened with exposure of a dark secret he harbors. "Is this coerced death not a suicide?" Velasquez asks. It is, Beauchamp agrees, but only if the threat is *not* death. If the threat is death, and the threat is credible and such that the threatened party cannot resist it, Beauchamp insists that the death is not a suicide. Velasquez disagrees. Velasquez also challenges Beauchamp's characterization of Captain Oates's death as suicide. Oates did not intentionally walk out into the blizzard to die but to save the lives of his companions; therefore Velasquez does not consider the death a suicide.

Velasquez is thus led to the following definition of suicide, which contains the two main elements of the traditional legal definition: intention and causation.

> Suicide is the act of bringing about a person's death, provided that: (1) death is brought about by that person's own acts or omission, and (2) those acts or omissions are (a) intentionally carried out (b) for the purpose of bringing about death by those concretely particular means that actually brought death about.[8]

By this account, Oates's death would not be a suicide because, (b), his primary intention was not to end his life but to save the lives of his party.

On the other hand, Velasquez does share the general view of philosophers that Socrates' death was not a suicide, but not because of diminished autonomy, as Beauchamp says, but because his death is more properly assigned to his executioners.[9] By the same logic, presumably, some of the traditional Christian martyrs did not commit suicide when they cooperated in their own deaths rather than renounce their religious beliefs. Nor did "certain holy women," as Augustine called some virgins who took their own lives at the time of persecution, rather than lose their chastity. In this vein, the *Declaration of Euthanasia* (1980) of Pope John Paul II asserts:

> ... one must clearly distinguish suicide from that sacrifice of one's life whereby for a higher cause, such as God's glory, the salvation of souls or the service of one's brethren, a person offers his or her own life or puts it in danger (cf. Jn. 15:14: *"Greater love has no man, than this, that a man lay down his life for his friends"*).

Elsewhere in the same document the pope condemns euthanasia but supports the right to refuse extreme measures to preserve life. Thus, patients who die as a result of fatal diseases for which they refuse futile treatment are not suicides, according to the church's official teaching. Velasquez and Beauchamp would agree, but for different reasons. For Beauchamp and some other philosophers, such patients lacked full autonomy; for thinkers like Velasquez, the Catholic Church, the AMA, and some other organized bodies, the disease and not the patient caused the death.

The modern problem of defining suicide can be viewed as an extension of the absorbing, centuries-old dialogue in western civilization about the propriety of self-killing. For over two thousand years some of the West's greatest minds, both religious and secular, have debated the permissibility of suicide. As we'll see in the next chapter, their views, which have indelibly shaped the modern mind and contemporary discourse, have run the gamut from outright condemnation of suicide as "self-murder" to unapologetic defense of it as a sometimes-honorable act.

EUTHANASIA

Compassion is the ordinary motivation for assisting in the suicide of a terminally ill patient. Convinced that a patient's death is preferable to his present existence, someone—usually a physician—helps a patient to die by providing the means, such as lethal drugs and instruction for their use. The same desire for compassionate relief of pain and suffering of a terminally ill patient typically motivates today's act of euthanasia (from the Greek *eu*, good, and *thanatos*, death). Indeed, if euthanasia is viewed informally as "help with a good death," then PAS is a form of euthanasia. The difference, which some consider morally significant, is that unlike PAS, in which the patient self-administers the physician-provided lethal means, in euthanasia the physician—or at least someone other than the patient—administers the lethal means for what is

believed to be the patient's own good. So, in PAS the patient takes his own life; in euthanasia someone else takes the patient's life.

Among the patients for whom euthanasia is sometimes considered are: premature neonates with potentially fatal medical complications; severe trauma victims in severe pain and almost certain to die; the gravely ill aged; and those dying in the last stages of incurable disease. It was the 1998 *60 Minutes* broadcast of the euthanasia of Thomas Youk that ended the assisted death work of Dr. Jack Kevorkian. With individuals like Youk, the term euthanasia carries the meaning of "mercy killing," for the purpose of ending extreme suffering. That popular label suggests the importance of distinguishing between two interpretations of euthanasia, one narrow, and the other broad.

DEFINITION: NARROW AND BROAD INTERPRETATIONS

Some philosophers define euthanasia narrowly as intentional killing, which can take the form of an act, termed active or positive euthanasia; or a failure to act, termed passive or negative euthanasia.

In active euthanasia (AE), someone—ordinarily a physician—intentionally causes the patient's death by performing an action, such as administering a lethal injection. In passive euthanasia (PE) someone—again ordinarily the physician—causes the patient's death by not taking usual and customary action, such as not providing antibiotics to help a terminally ill patient survive pneumonia. AE brings on death through intervention; PE brings on death through nonintervention. In AE an action is taken that causes the death; in PE an action is not taken that would have prolonged the life. Central to both is intention.

According to the narrow interpretation, unless the death is intentionally caused by what was or was not done, there is no euthanasia. For example, suppose a doctor determines that commencing a treatment will be of no help to a dying patient or to one incurably ill such as Welby; or once started the treatment will be ineffective. The physician, together with the patient and the family, decide to withhold or withdraw the treatment, knowing that death will quickly follow. It does. Now, ordinarily, according to the narrow interpretation of the term, what occurred is not euthanasia but "allowing to die." As bioethicist J. Gay-Williams says, after defining euthanasia with specific reference to intentionally taking the life:

> The failure to continue treatment after it has been realized that the patient has little chance of benefiting from it has been characterized by some as "passive euthanasia." This phrase is misleading and mistaken. In such cases, the person involved is not killed ... nor is the death of the person intended by the withholding of additional treatment.... The aim may be to spare the person additional and unjustifiable pain, to save him from the indignities of hopeless manipulations, and to avoid increasing the financial and emotional burden on his family. When I buy a pencil it is so that I can use it to write, not to contribute to an increase in the gross national product. This may be the unintended consequence of my action, but it is not the aim of my action. So it is with failing to continue the treatment of a dying person. I intend his death no more than I intend to reduce the GNP by not using medical supplies. His is an unintended dying, and so-called "passive euthanasia" is not euthanasia at all.[10]

According to this narrow interpretation, euthanasia, active or passive, (as well as PAS), is always to be condemned as outright killing. By contrast, allowing to die, when properly carried out, is a sound medical practice supported by law and professional ethics. In Dr. Ricci's view, he allowed Piergiorgio Welby to die; he didn't kill him by euthanasia.

Other philosophers, however, prefer to interpret euthanasia more broadly, as including both acts of killing and allowing to die. They say that if euthanasia is always wrong, then so is allowing to die because it is a form of euthanasia. Alternatively, if allowing to die is not always wrong, then neither is euthanasia necessarily wrong.

In this broad interpretation, euthanasia is not always an act of killing, because it includes allowing to die. Thus, AE encompasses acts of painlessly and deliberately ending the lives of people suffering from terminal or possibly incurable conditions like Welby's. PE includes acts of deliberately allowing such patients to die by withholding or withdrawing treatment. So, whereas the narrow interpretation always prohibits euthanasia and sometimes permits allowing to die, the broad interpretation, discarding "allowing to die" as an irrelevant artifice, can permit either form of euthanasia. According to the broad interpretation, Dr. Ricci performed an act of PE on Welby. Italian authorities and church officials agreed. And because for them any form of euthanasia is impermissible, they condemned Ricci's action and sought to prosecute him.

Much of today's public debate about assisted death trades on one or the other understandings of euthanasia. So, it's important to give the broad/narrow distinction some thought. Specifically, is the distinction between "killing" and "allowing to die" a phantom, as the broad interpretation says? Or is it, as the narrow interpretation claims, a meaningful, morally significant distinction?

KILLING VS. ALLOWING TO DIE

In rejecting challenges to the constitutionality of laws prohibiting physician-assisted suicide, the US Supreme Court, instructively, has invoked the "killing" versus "allowing to die" distinction. Consider *Vacco v. Quill* (1997).

Vacco involved three gravely ill patients whom New York law prohibited from dying with the assistance of their physicians, one a hospice physician, Dr. Timothy Quill. According to several philosophers writing as friends of the court (*amici curiae* in Latin) in support of the patients, who had since died: "Whether a doctor turns off a respirator in accordance with the patient's request or prescribes pills that a patient may take when he is ready to kill

BIOETHICS ACROSS CULTURES

Suicide Tourists

When Craig Ewert, an American university professor living in Great Britain, faced the prospect that he would vegetate the rest of his life, he sought sanctuary in Switzerland. Ewert, 59, suffered from severe nerve system damage that, within a very short period of time, had left him paralyzed. Once in Switzerland, he followed up on arrangements he'd made earlier at the euthanasia clinic Dignitas (Latin for "dignity"), which helps those with terminal illnesses and severe physical and mental illnesses to die assisted by doctors and nurses.

Founded in 1998 by Swiss lawyer Ludwig Minelli, Dignitas operates under Swiss law, which, since 1940, has permitted assisted suicide provided it is done for altruistic reasons, never for self-interest. Dignitas ensures compliance by following this procedure:

> [T]he person who wishes to die meets several Dignitas personnel, in addition to an independent doctor, for a private consultation. The independent doctor assesses the evidence provided by the patient and is met on two separate occasions, with a time gap between each of the consultations. Legally admissible proof that the person wishes to die is also created, i.e., a signed affidavit, countersigned by independent witnesses. In cases where a person is physically unable to sign a document, a short video film of the person is made in which they are asked to confirm their identity, that they wish to die, and that their decision is made of their own free will, without any form of coercion. Such evidence of informed consent is entirely private and is not intended to ever be made public. The evidence is created and stored purely for use in any possible future legal dispute regarding the person who wishes to die, e.g., allegations that someone was forced to commit suicide. Finally, a few minutes before the lethal overdose is provided, the person is once again reminded that taking the overdose will surely kill them. Additionally, they are asked several times whether they want to proceed, or take some time to consider the matter further. This gives the person the opportunity to stop the process. However, if at this point the person states that they are determined to proceed, a lethal overdose is provided and ingested.

Craig Ewert set up a special timer, which he himself constructed, that switched off his respirator automatically after he took a high dosage of a sleeping drug. He died on December 26, 2006, in his hospital bed with his wife, Mary, by his side. The event was filmed for broadcast on British television. It subsequently aired in the United States, on March 2, 2010, as a documentary titled *The Suicide Tourist,* presented by the PBS program *Frontline.* When Ewert's death was broadcast in England, it was condemned by TV watchdog MediaWatch-UK, which feared that the subject of PAS might "influence... the public or other sufferers into making a similar action."

Dignitas made international news in July 2009 with the announcement that one of Britain's most distinguished orchestra conductors, Sir Edward Downes, had joined his wife in drinking a clinic-provided lethal cocktail of barbiturates. Sir Edward, 85, was not terminally ill, but he was blind and increasingly deaf; his wife, Lady Joan, 74, was in the final stages of terminal cancer. According to the couple's children who

himself, the doctor acts with the same intention: to help the patient die."[11,12] In other words, according to this view, the accepted practice of knowingly administering powerful, death-hastening pain relievers to dying patients is morally no different from "killing." Earlier the Second Circuit of the US Court of Appeals had ruled it discriminatory to allow a person on life support to end her life by removing such treatment, while those who are not connected to life support would be denied similar access to death. In other words, the law violated the equal protection clause of the Fourteenth Amendment. *Vacco* reversed that decision and accepted the traditional distinction between killing and allowing to die in its reversal.

Today the legalization of PAS deeply divides the medical profession and the broader society. Despite that, there is professional and social consensus that killing and allowing to die are morally different.

accompanied them to the Swiss clinic, their parents decided to end their own lives after fifty-four years together, rather than continue to battle serious health problems. "They wanted to be next to each other when they died," their son said, adding: "It is a very civilized way to end your life, and I don't understand why the legal position in this country doesn't allow it." Attempting suicide is not a criminal offense in Britain, but assisting others to kill themselves is.

As of 2009, none of the family members and friends who have accompanied 117 Britons to the Zurich clinic has been charged with an offense. Nevertheless, just a few weeks after the Downes deaths, Britain's House of Lords unanimously declared that UK laws on assisted suicide interfere with the right to respect a private life under the European Convention on Human Rights, and ordered the director of public prosecutions to promulgate a policy stating in which circumstances he would prosecute in assisted dying cases. Earlier, Debbie Purdy, 46, a British woman suffering from multiple sclerosis, had asked the House of Lords to order prosecutors to say whether they would charge her husband if he took her to Dignitas. Author Terry Pratchett, who has Alzheimer's disease, even urged the creation of special panels for hearing appeals of seriously ill people to die legally. Roiling things further was the arrest of Ray Gosling, a veteran BBC broadcaster, after he confessed in a television program that, in the early 1980s, he had smothered to death an ex-lover who had AIDS.

The new guidance came on February 25, 2010, just a week after the Gosling bombshell. It basically distinguishes between malicious intent and compassionate support. For example, a case where the person who assisted a suicide stood to gain financially from the death would be prosecutable. Among the factors

against prosecuting would be evidence that the suspect had sought to dissuade their loved one from suicide, and that the terminally ill person had "reached a voluntary, clear, settled and informed decision to commit suicide."

(SOURCES: NA, "Dignitas (Euthanasia Group)," *Wikipedia*, May 20, 2009. Retrieved May 26, 2009, from http://en.wikipedia.org/wiki/Dignitas_ (euthanasia_group); Lajla Mlinarić Blake, trans., "Decided To Die in Hospital in Front of Camera," *Limun.HR*, December 12, 2008. Retrieved May 26, 2009, from http://limun.hr/en/main.aspx?id=384707; John F. Burns, "With Help, Conductor and Wife Ended Lives, *The New York Times*, July 14, 2009. Retrieved July 28, 2009, from http://www.nytimes.com/2009/07/15/world/europe/15britain.html?_r=1; James Lumley and Lindsay Fortado, "U.K. Assisted Suicide Rules to be Clarified after Lords' Ruling," Bloomber.com. Retrieved July 31, 2009, from http://www.bloomberg.com/apps/news?pid=20601102&sid=aT_lip0LZfA0; "Professor Craig Ewert's Final Moments To Be Broadcast on TV," *Times Online*, December 10, 2008. Retrieved March 8, 2010, from http://www.timesonline.co.uk/tol/life_and_style/health/article5315633.ece.)

Question

Alois Geiger, a Dignitas physician, says suicide "is a human right." Were Ewert, the Downeses, and the 840 like them who used the services of Dignitas as of March 2008, exercising a "human right," or weren't they? Geiger blames the monotheistic religions, particularly Christianity, for the prohibition against suicide. But, he asks, "What if there is no God?" He argues that suicide should be an option for those who do not believe. What do you think? How do you feel about the guidelines issued by Britain's director of public prosecutions? Do you share MediaWatch's anxiety about the Ewert death film, or do you find social value in its broadcast?

(SOURCE: Hilary White, "'Suicide Is a Human Right': Dignitas Suicide Doctor," *LifeSiteNews.Com*, October 27, 2008, http://www.lifesitenews.com/ldn/2008/oct/08102704.html.)

Many clinicians, for example, intuitively sense an important difference between turning off a ventilator, as Dr. Ricci did with Piergiorgio Welby, and giving a lethal injection, as Dr. Kevorkian did with Thomas Youk. "If their intuitions are confused or mistaken, however," worries Daniel P. Sulmasy, an attorney/philosopher, "physicians and other health care professionals will have one less reason for refraining from the practices of euthanasia and assisted suicide."[13]

Organized religious and professional bodies share Sulmasy's concern. Accordingly, in its earliest and subsequently reaffirmed statement on euthanasia of December 4, 1973, the House of Delegates of the AMA adopted the following position:

The intentional termination of the life of one human being by another—mercy killing—is contrary to that for which the medical profession stands and is contrary to the policy of the American Medical Association. The cessation of the employment of extraordinary means to prolong the life of the body when there is irrefutable evidence that biological death is imminent is the decision of the patient and/or his immediate family. The advice and judgment of the physician should be freely available to the patient and/or his immediate family.

The shared position of the Roman Catholic Church has been expressed more fully as follows:

Whatever its motives and means, direct euthanasia consists in putting an end to the lives of handicapped, sick, or dying persons. It is morally unacceptable. Thus an act or omission which, of itself or by intention, causes death in order to eliminate suffering constitutes a murder gravely contrary to the dignity of the human person and to the respect due to the living God, his Creator. The error of judgment into which one can fall in good faith does not change the nature of this murderous act, which must always be forbidden and excluded. Discontinuing medical procedures that are burdensome, dangerous, extraordinary, or disproportionate to the expected outcome can be legitimated; it is the refusal of "over-zealous" treatment. Here one does not will to cause death; one's inability to impede it is merely accepted. The decisions should be made by the patient if he is competent and able or, if not, by those legally entitled to act for the patient, whose reasonable will and legitimate interests must always be respected. Even if death is thought imminent, the ordinary care owed to a sick person cannot be legitimately interrupted.[14]

The positions of the church and the AMA are consistent with both law and cultural tradition, which prohibit only *killing*, or definite actions deliberately committed or omitted to end the patient's life. The paradigm case of patient killing is the physician who mercifully administers a lethal injection into a consenting, terminally ill adult to end the patient's life, as with Youk; or, alternatively, the physician who intentionally causes the patient's death by withholding or withdrawing a treatment that would have saved the patient's life, as with Welby.

In contrast to these deliberately death-causing acts of commission and omission are ones not intended to cause death, although death inevitably occurs sooner because something was done or not done. For example, when the symptoms of a dying patient cannot be eliminated by other appropriate and acceptable means, drugs sometimes are used to make the patient unaware of the symptoms, a practice termed terminal or total sedation. Administering increasing dosages of regular analgesic and sedative drugs that can suppress consciousness and hasten death is legal and considered a valuable therapeutic adjunct so long as the declared intention is to ease pain and suffering. This has been the official position of the Catholic Church since Pope Pius XII (1876–1958) approved it as a last resort in 1957: "If no other means exist, and if, in the given circumstance, this does not prevent the carrying out of other religious and moral duties."[15] Again, the excerpt quoted above from the *Catechism of the Catholic Church on Life*, concludes with the statement:

The use of painkiller to alleviate the sufferings of the dying, even at the risk of shortening their days, can be moral in conformity with human dignity if death is not willed as either an end or a means, but only foreseen and tolerated as inevitable. Palliative care is a special form of disinterested charity. As such it should be encouraged.

Notice that the same question that arises in defining suicide may be asked of the AMA and church's official positions: "Can an outcome (death) be foreseen and foreknown without being intended?" Yes, say the Catholic Church and AMA, among other bodies. Injecting a drug with the explicit intention of causing death is euthanasia and not permissible. But injecting exactly the same drug with the intention of relieving pain and even suppressing consciousness is *not* euthanasia and is permissible, even though it is foreseen and foreknown that, as a direct result of that act, life will be shortened.

The conventional emphasis on intention or aiming at death as the legal and moral determinant in end-of-life treatments applies equally to acts of omission. In theory, then, any end-of-life treatment that is omitted with the intention of causing the patient's death is passive euthanasia, and is not permissible. For example, had the physician in the earlier example deliberately withheld antibiotics to end the patient's life, that would be killing—murder, in fact, in all US jurisdictions and almost all other countries. The same would apply to an instance of disconnecting a terminally ill patient from a breathing machine, as with Welby; or making no effort to revive one in cardiac arrest, if the intention was to cause the patient's death. Some of its critics say that DCD (donation after cardiac death) is on the slippery slope of at least passive euthanasia; and, depending on intention, possibly active euthanasia when drugs are administered. Thus the charges against Dr. Hootan Roozrokh (see Ch. 17).

The moral significance of intention was behind Pope John Paul II's stunning pronouncement of March 20, 2004, that PVS patients should not be denied food and water.[16] To do so, he said, would amount to "euthanasia by omission," a viewpoint that contradicted existing policy followed by American Catholic hospitals. Although considered an "allocution"—an opinion rather than an encyclical—the pope's remark sent shock waves through the Catholic medical community, owing to the potential complications related to do-not-resuscitate orders and medical requests to end treatment. A year later, in 2005, Pope Benedict XVI adopted the position of his predecessor in the case of Terri Schiavo (see Introduction). Then, in 2009, the US Conference of Catholic Bishops issued a directive for Catholic health care ordering that anyone who needs a feeding tube to stay alive must have one surgically implanted and maintained indefinitely, irrespective of the patient's religious faith or expressed wishes. Inasmuch as 30 percent of Americans receive health care or reside in Catholic institutions—hospitals, nursing homes, assisted living centers, etc.—the new directive could affect thousands of patients who are not actively dying,

from those in permanent comas or vegetative states to those with advanced dementia or loss of ability to eat along with other sentient activity.

In contrast to those emphasizing the manner under which a death is caused, supporters of the broad interpretation insist that what matters are the conditions of a death.[17] This makes the allowing to die/passive euthanasia distinction a false one, an artifice for avoiding the full weight of moral intuition and analysis that support helping consenting adult patients with a merciful death. Rather than responding honestly to the dictates of logic and morality by modifying their condemnation of euthanasia, supporters of the narrow view, charge its critics, are engaging in a verbal sleight of hand. They are calling "allowing to die" what really are instances of "passive euthanasia." This allows them to have their cake and eat it, too—cause death but not intend it. They can kill but not be killers, according to critics.

A Distinction with or without a Difference?

Is the official distinction between euthanasia and allowing to die morally meaningful? Friends of the broad interpretation obviously don't think so. But proponents of the narrow view do.

Yes (Narrow Interpretation)   The defense of the passive euthanasia/allowing to die distinction rests on various grounds. First, say its defenders, the distinction coheres with ordinary language usage, which distinguishes between harms that are actively caused and ones that are permitted. More importantly, it identifies the cause and pinpoints responsibility. Thus, in euthanasia the physician directly causes the death; in allowing to die, the disease does. Not distinguishing between euthanasia and allowing to die would blur this important moral and legal distinction.

Additionally, its defenders say the distinction recognizes and honors the subtle but very real medical discrimination honored since the birth of medicine in the West. Tradition teaches that there is no greater harm than to kill a patient deliberately. But it also acknowledges that deliberately to leave a patient in treatable pain is also a great harm. What is the physician to do, then, when she can't both save a life *and* pain? Supporters say it is exactly the distinction between (passive) euthanasia and allowing to die that captures this kind of clinical dilemma, by distinguishing between permissible cases of allowing to die and impermissible cases of killing. Furthermore, it's this discrimination that enables physicians to meet their historical duty. On one hand, they are expected to avoid the harm of interfering with natural death by overtreatment. On the other hand, they are expected to avoid the great harm of deliberately killing the patient. Without such clear distinction, physicians would be in a moral muddle.

To its defenders, then, the euthanasia/allowing-to-die distinction may be conceptually awkward, but it creates a needed firewall or "psychological barrier" between acts of omission and commission.[18] To remove the distinction—to treat allowing to die as a form of euthanasia—would make killing acceptable and, perhaps, active euthanasia inevitable.

No (Broad Interpretation)   Philosophers Michael Tooley[19] and James Rachels gave the position that euthanasia/allowing to die is a false distinction its most forceful expression more than a quarter century ago. In the latter's widely anthologized 1975 article that first appeared in *The New England Journal of Medicine*, Rachels argued that the traditional killing/allowing-to-die distinction was fraught with inconsistencies and contradictions.

Consider, Rachels suggested, that if the difference between euthanasia and allowing to die is relevant anywhere, then it should be relevant everywhere. Thus, if someone saw a child drowning in a bath, wouldn't it be just as wrong to watch him drown as to push his head underwater? If emphatically yes, then why isn't it wrong to allow a suffering patient dying, say, of throat cancer to die? Suppose further that such a patient is certain to die in a few days even if his present treatment is continued, but he doesn't wish to go on. So, with his family's support, he asks his physician to put an end to his pain. Now, according to the conventional doctrine—seemingly the narrow view of euthanasia—the doctor may withhold treatment because the dying patient is in terrible pain and it would be wrong to

prolong his suffering needlessly. "But now notice this," Rachels wrote over thirty years ago:

> If one simply withholds treatment it may take the patient longer to die, and so he may suffer more than he would if more direct action were taken and a lethal injection given. This fact provides strong reason for thinking that, once the initial decision not to prolong his agony has been made, active euthanasia is actually preferable to passive euthanasia [i.e., "allowing to die"], rather than the reverse. To say otherwise is to endorse the option that leads to more suffering rather than less, and is contrary to the humanitarian impulse that prompts the decision not to prolong his life in the first place.[20]

In other words, whether active or passive, the outcome is the same: the death of the patient on humanitarian grounds. And that—the conditions under which the patient died—is what matters, Rachels argued, not the manner in which the death was caused.

While permissive of euthanasia, Philippa Foot is one of those philosophers who think the distinction between euthanasia and allowing to die *is* relevant. In a 1977 reply to Rachels' example of the drowning boy, Foot pointed out that while both killing and allowing him to drown are iniquitous acts, they are so for different reasons, and that makes all the difference in euthanasia. Killing the child violates justice, Foot said; no one has the right to push the child's head underwater. To leave him to drown, on the other hand, violates charity or benevolence by denying the child what is good for him. In Rachels' example justice and charity happen to coincide. But this isn't always the case, as Foot illustrated as follows:

> Suppose, for example, that a retreating army has to leave behind a wounded or exhausted soldier in the wastes of an arid or snowbound land where the only prospect is death by starvation or at the hands of an enemy notoriously cruel. It has often been the practice to accord a merciful

bullet to men in such desperate straits [an act of charity]. But suppose that one of them demands that he should be left alive? It seems clear [by the requirements of justice] that his comrades have no right to kill him though it is a quite different question [with regard to charity] as to whether they should give him a life-prolonging drug.[21]

Foot's point was that although the right to life can sometimes require positive service of others, it does not in this case. In other words, justice dictates that the soldier has a right to be left alone. But considerations of charity relieve the retreating army of any obligation to give him the means to prolong his life. In other words, it matters whether they opt to kill the soldier (which Foot believes would be wrong) or whether they allow him to die (which Foot believes could be acceptable). This distinction, she said, really matters in euthanasia.

For his part, Rachels would agree that killing the soldier would be wrong, because the soldier doesn't want to be killed. But what of *voluntary* cases of euthanasia as opposed to voluntary cases of allowing to die? In such situations, the foreseen outcome, death, is the same. For Rachels this means that it is irrelevant whether the death is aimed at (euthanasia) or merely foreseen. Merely foreseeing the death as certain is enough to characterize a doctor's ceasing treatment as intentional termination of life, according to Rachels. Again, the AMA, as well as all major religions and US jurisdictions, disagree, insisting that so long as the physician does not discontinue treatment to end the life she did not intentionally terminate it. But Rachels has argued further that any decision to withhold extraordinary means is based precisely on the same grounds as a decision to end the patient's life: a determination of whether the patient's life should be prolonged.[22]

VOLUNTARY AND NONVOLUNTARY DECISIONS

We could easily imagine, as a counterpart to Foot's suffering soldier, a terminally or incurably ill patient who "for her own good" would be better off dead, but wants to live. On the other hand, it's just as easy, as in Rachels' example, to pose a terminally ill patient or, like Welby, one who is incurably ill and wants to die, because he no longer regards his life as worth living. Then there are patients whose wishes are unknown—for example, formerly competent patients now in deep comas—Quinlan, Cruzan, Wendland, Schiavo—or never-competent patients, such as the severely mentally retarded. So, in addition to the challenges of defining euthanasia and distinguishing between killing and allowing to die, another conceptual issue in euthanasia discourse involves patient wishes. Patient decisions about life and death ordinarily are characterized as voluntary and nonvoluntary.

Voluntary Decisions

Voluntary decisions about death refer to cases of competent adult patients requesting or giving informed consent to a particular course of medical treatment or nontreatment. Included are cases in which patients: (1) take their own lives either directly or by refusing life-sustaining treatment; (2) request that physicians either perform a procedure that will end their lives or discontinue a procedure that would save their lives; or (3) designate others, for example spouses, to act on their behalf should their medical condition leave them unable to speak for themselves. The designation could take the form of an advance medical directive, such as a *Durable Power of Attorney for Health Care* (see Chapter 5). The instructions can be quite general, such as "Use your own best judgment" or "Do what you think is best." In that case the designee is charged with doing what she believes is in the patient's best interests. On the other hand, the directions might be more specific: "No resuscitation if there's cardiac arrest," for example, or "Comfort care measures only." Alternatively, a patient could instruct, "Keep me alive as long as possible," and, to this end, complete a *Right to Life* directive. Whatever the patient's wishes, one thing is certain: For a death decision to be voluntary, the patient's consent must be explicit.

BIOETHICS ACROSS CULTURES

"Compassionate Murder" in Canada

Robert Latimer, a Canadian farmer with a wife and five children, admitted to the police that he killed his daughter Tracy on October 24, 1993. Tracy was a 40-pound quadriplegic, a 12-year-old who functioned at the level of a three-month-old as the result of a severe form of cerebral palsy. She had been repeatedly operated on and at the time of her death was due for more surgery. Tracy couldn't walk, talk, or feed herself, though she responded to affection and occasionally smiled. She was in constant, excruciating pain that, inexplicably, nothing stronger than Tylenol could treat. Latimer said he loved his daughter and could not bear to watch her suffer any further. So "he placed her in the cab of his Chevy pickup, ran a hose from the exhaust to the cab, climbed into the box of the truck, sat on a tire and watched her die." On November 4, 1993, Latimer was charged with first-degree murder, and a year later convicted of second-degree murder.

Following his first conviction, the Supreme Court of Canada ordered a new trial when it was learned that the police, acting on orders from the government, had possibly tainted the case by questioning potential jurors about their views on religion, abortion, and mercy killing. Latimer stood trial again in October 1997 and a month later was again convicted of second-degree murder, with a recommendation for parole after a year, even though the minimum sentence for second-degree murder was twenty-five years with no chance of parole for ten years. Within weeks, however, the judge granted Latimer a constitutional exemption

from the minimum sentence for second-degree murder because, he said, the minimum sentence would constitute "cruel and unusual punishment." He explained that the law "recognizes that the moral culpability or the moral blameworthiness of murder can vary from one convicted offender to another." The judge called Tracy Latimer's murder a "rare act of homicide that was committed for caring and altruistic reasons. That is why for want of a better term this is called compassionate homicide." On appeal, the decision was reversed, and Latimer was ordered to serve a life sentence. Latimer then took his case to the Supreme Court arguing, first, that he had no choice but to kill Tracy; and, second, that a life sentence was cruel and unusual punishment. He lost.

In 2008 Robert Latimer won day-parole. He was eligible for full-parole on December 8, 2010.

(SOURCE: NA, "Compassionate Murder: The Law and Robert Latimer," *CBS News Online*, March 17, 2008. Retrieved May 28, 2009, from http://www.cbc.ca/news/background/latimer/.)

Question

Do you think that compassion and common sense dictated a reduced sentence and the granting of parole to Robert Latimer? Numerous disability rights groups, as well as the Catholic Church and the Evangelical Fellowship of Canada, argued that killing a disabled child like Tracy was no different from killing a non-disabled child and should carry the same penalty. Do you agree?

Nonvoluntary Decisions

Nonvoluntary decisions about death refer to cases in which the person who is to die does not make the decision, perhaps because of age or medical condition. Of special note, given its frequency, are the many nonvoluntary cases that arise because formerly competent patients never formally deputized someone to act on their behalf and expressed unambiguously what they wished done and not done, as apparently with Quinlan, Cruzan, Wendland, and Schiavo.

Inevitably such cases raise two important questions, as we saw in the cultural clash over Terri

Schiavo (see Introduction): What's best for the patient and what would the patient want if she could choose? The first is a medical matter, the second a moral and legal one. The Quinlans and Cruzans (see Chapter 3) were persuaded that discontinuing treatments was both in the medical and moral interests of their daughters. But families aren't always unified in their understanding of a loved one's wishes or best interests, as with Michael Schiavo and his in-laws, the Schindlers; or Rose and Florence Wendland (see case presentation, Chapter 17). Nor are physicians and families always on the same page. Generally, what competent adult patients wish or likely would wish takes moral and legal priority over their best medical interests where the two conflict. Still, the issue is far from settled.

Even when a patient is competent, it is not always easy to determine exactly what she wishes. Mixed messages, fear or denial of death, a false sense of protecting others, reluctance to talk about imminent death, and other factors on the part of patient, physician, or family can block a clear, unambiguous expression of patient wishes. As an upshot, a physician might administer an overdose of painkilling drugs in order to end a patient's suffering without letting the patient know beforehand that death will result. Because pain and suffering can always impede communication, hospice physician Quill urges colleagues to distinguish between the very common "transient yearning for death as an escape from suffering" and the extremely rare "requests for a physician assisted suicide death." In other words, "I wish I were dead" doesn't always mean, "Doctor, I want to die. Will you help me?"[23] Given the uncertainty of patient wishes, sometimes physicians are called on to use their best judgments. A 1998 study found that in one case out of six of the rare euthanasia or assisted suicide in the United States, it is the family or physician who requests it, without the patient's knowledge or request, even though the patient is conscious.[24]

When the voluntary-nonvoluntary distinction is paired with them, the narrow and the broad interpretations of the meaning of euthanasia each yields four kinds of death decisions. For the narrow interpretation there are:

1. Voluntary euthanasia: impermissible
2. Nonvoluntary euthanasia: impermissible
3. Voluntary allowing to die: permissible
4. Nonvoluntary allowing to die: permissible

For the broad interpretation:

1. Voluntary active euthanasia: permissible
2. Nonvoluntary active euthanasia: permissible
3. Voluntary passive euthanasia: permissible
4. Nonvoluntary passive: permissible.[25]

Thus, for the broad interpreters, a deliberate action to shorten a patient's life may be right if it's in keeping with the patient's wishes. For narrow interpreters, such an act is always wrong regardless of what the patient wishes. Of overriding moral consideration to the broad interpreters is patient autonomy, whereas to the narrow interpreters it is the nature of the act: killing. Interestingly, in the Welby case both sides—Dr. Ricci and his critics— took the narrow view. The difference is that what Ricci called permissible voluntary allowing to die (by discontinuing burdensome treatment), Italian lawmakers and the Catholic Church called impermissible euthanasia. Anyone taking the broad interpretation would call it a permissible act of voluntary passive euthanasia.

CONCLUSIONS

Besides voluntary and nonvoluntary decisions, a third kind of decision is at least theoretically possible. An *in*voluntary decision would be a decision to die contrary to the expressed wishes of the patient. Were a patient's life ended or shortened contrary to his wishes, that would be an involuntary decision. Overriding expressed patient wishes has been a moral threshold that neither philosopher nor physician has dared to cross, even theoretically. And for good reason. Whose life is it, anyway?—the

patient's. An act of overriding patient wishes to live would be murder.

It was the moral premise that individuals are entitled to determine the circumstances of their deaths that propelled the whole "right to die" movement of the 1970s. Giving patients and surrogates power to decide treatment turned existing standards, rules, practices, customs, and laws that interfered with free choice into potential instruments of involuntary decisions—that is, choices imposed on patients contrary to their expressed wishes. The exception is suicide. With few exceptions—the states of Oregon, Washington, and Montana—physicians in the United States may not assist patients in suicide.

Why this is so, and why a gathering number of people think it's time to change, traces back to a centuries old debate about the morality of suicide, which the next chapter discusses.

CASES AND CONTROVERSIES

Pope John Paul II: Life-Sustaining Treatments and Vegetative State

On March 20, 2004, speaking to participants in an international congress on the "vegetative" state, Pope John Paul II issued what was described as "the first clear and explicit papal statement on the obligation to provide food and water for patients in a 'persistent vegetative state.'"[26] Here's a portion of the pope's remarks:

> The sick person in a vegetative state, awaiting recovery or a natural end, still has the right to basic health care (nutrition, hydration, cleanliness, warmth, etc.), and to the prevention of complications related to his confinement to bed. He also has the right to appropriate rehabilitative care and to be monitored for clinical signs of eventual recovery.
>
> I should like particularly to underline how the administration of water and food, even when provided by artificial means, always represents a natural means of preserving life, not a medical act. Its use, furthermore, should be considered, in principle, ordinary and proportionate, and as such morally obligatory, insofar as and until it is seen to have attained its proper finality, which in the present case consists in providing nourishment to the patient and alleviation of his suffering.
>
> The obligation to provide the "normal care due to the sick in such cases"... includes, in fact, the use of nutrition and hydration.... The evaluation of probabilities, founded on waning hopes for recovery when the vegetative state is prolonged beyond a year, cannot ethically justify the cessation or interruption of minimal care for the patient, including nutrition and hydration. Death by starvation or dehydration is, in fact, the only possible outcome as a result of their

> withdrawal. In this sense it ends up becoming, if done knowingly and willingly, true and proper euthanasia by omission.
>
> In this regard, I recall what I wrote in the *Encyclical Evangelium Vitae*, making it clear that "by euthanasia in the true and proper sense must be understood an action or omission which by its very nature and intention brings about death, with the purpose of eliminating all pain"; such an act is always "a serious violation of the law of God, since it is the deliberate and morally unacceptable killing of a human person."

Questions for Analysis

1. Analyze the pope's statement with respect to natural law, with particular reference to his implied interpretation of how the doctrine of double effect applies to artificial hydration and nutrition (a.h.n.).

2. Do you agree that a.h.n. is always a "natural means of preserving life, not a medical act"? Does the obligation to provide "normal care to the sick" include a.h.n. to PVS patients?

3. In the opening paragraph, the pope outlines what he believes are the rights of treatment of PVS patients, but says nothing of the right of choice. In your opinion, do formerly competent patients who expressed the wish not to be maintained in a vegetative state have a right to have their wishes respected, or not?

4. Some right-to-die groups favor policies of withdrawing feeding tubes not because of special burdens involved in administration but because "'a denial of nutrition may in the long run become the only effective way to make certain that a large number of biologically tenacious patients actually die.'"[27] Do you think this is an adequate reply to the papal position?

5. Is the withdrawal of food and water from PVS patients euthanasia?

6. Religious liberals, probably many Catholics among them, generally maintain that the traditional teaching of the Church, in fact, allows the removal of a.h.n. from PVS patients. They reason that PVS involves a lethal pathology (inability to chew and swallow) and that circumvention of the pathology through a.h.n. imposes a grave burden (at least upon the family and perhaps society), or that such therapy is ineffective insofar as the purpose of life is concerned. Therefore, they say, removal of artificial hydration and nutrition does not violate religious natural law. Do you agree with their interpretation? Does the dispute between religious conservatives and religious liberals suggest anything about natural law theory?

CASES AND CONTROVERSIES

The Boston Declaration on Assisted Dying

The following Declaration was made at the 13th International Conference of the World Federation of Right to Die Societies held in Boston, Massachusetts, from September 1 to 3, 2000. After a brief statement of support for assistance in dying in response to "voluntary, rational, and persistent" requests, the delegates drew attention to other options, offered by palliative care.

> On this occasion, we wish to draw public attention to the practice of "terminal sedation" or "slow euthanasia" which is performed extensively today throughout the world in hospitals, nursing homes, and hospices and in private homes. This is carried out under the doctrine known as "double effect" by which a physician may lawfully administer increasing dosages of regular analgesic and sedative drugs that can hasten someone's death as long as the declared intention is to ease pain and suffering. Of course, the key word is "intention." Compassionate physicians, without publicly declaring the true intention of their actions, often speed up the dying process in this way. Many thousands of terminally ill patients are so helped globally every year.
>
> We feel that the only real difference between "terminal sedation" and a rapidly effective lethal dose is one of time, a slow death, over a few days, with life-shortening palliative drugs versus a more dignified and peaceful death, because it is not prolonged, and is determined by the patient. We urge other medical professionals, worldwide, to be more open about this form of physician-assisted dying.[28]

Questions for Analysis

1. Michael Irwin, a British physician who signed the Declaration and prominent member of a voluntary euthanasia group in the United Kingdom, says that terminal sedation amounts to euthanasia "because the comatose patient often dies from the combination of two intentional acts by a doctor—the induction of unconsciousness, and the withholding of food and water."[29] Is there no significant moral difference between euthanasia and terminal sedation?

2. Many Dutch doctors propose terminal sedation as an alternative to euthanasia. In The Netherlands terminal sedation usually involves more than just rendering a patient unconscious. It also entails withholding all food and fluids until the patient dies. Is terminal sedation, as practiced in The Netherlands, a way of letting patients die "naturally," or is it a form of slow euthanasia?[30]

3. Apply the ethical principles of autonomy, beneficence, informed consent, and the doctrine of double effect to the use of terminal or palliative sedation.

CASES AND CONTROVERSIES

Barney Clark's Key

In 1982, 62-year-old Barney Clark, a retired dentist from Seattle, became the first human to receive a permanent mechanical heart. Clark was dying of untreatable heart disease, but otherwise was of sound body and mind. He was described as having a strong will to live, with a thorough understanding of his disease, including the option of an artificial heart. Unlike a transplant, for which he was considered too old, Clark realized that the mechanical heart, while preserving his life, would drastically limit his mobility. For as long as he lived, he'd be tethered to a bulky compressor by two six-foot hoses. Given the novelty of the experience, it was impossible to predict Clark's quality of life. Recognizing the potential to make Clark's life overly burdensome, his doctor, Willem Kolff, gave Clark a key that could be used to turn off the compressor sustaining the artificial heart's action. Defending his decision, Kolff argued:

> [If Barney Clark] suffers and feels it isn't worth it any more, he has a key that he can apply.... I think it is entirely legitimate that this man whose life has been extended should have the right to cut it off if he doesn't want it, if life ceases to be enjoyable.[31]

Clark never used the key. Fifteen weeks after the historic operation, he died.

Questions for Analysis

1. Had Clark used the key, which of the following statements do you think would have been the most accurate description of his action and the cause of his death?
   A. forgoing extraordinary means of life-sustaining treatment
   B. withdrawing from an experiment
   C. letting nature take its course
   D. natural death
   E. euthanasia
   F. suicide[32]

2. If Clark had refused the heart and, as a result, died, would that have been suicide? If not, how would that have differed from, say, Clark's having intentionally shot himself?[33]

3. What if Clark had taken the mechanical heart in the belief that accompanying risks likely would hasten his death. Would that have been a kind of suicide?[34]

REFERENCES

1. Ian Fisher, "Italian Poet Dies With Help from a Doctor," *The New York Times*, December 22, 2006. Retrieved April 10, 2008, from http://www.nytimes.com/2006/12/22/world/europe/22italy.html.

2. Ian Fisher, "A Poet Crusades for the Right to Die His Way," *The New York Times*, December 20, 2006. p. A2.

3. Manuel Velasquez, "Defining Suicide," in Tom L. Beauchamp and Robert M. Veatch, *Ethical Issues in Death and Dying*, 2nd ed., Upper Saddle River, N.J.: Prentice Hall, 1996, pp. 106–111.

4. Susan Solomon, *The Coldest March*, New Haven, Conn.: Yale University Press, 2001.

5. Tom L. Beauchamp, "The Problem of Defining Suicide," in Beauchamp and Veatch, p. 116.

6. Ibid., p. 114.

7. Ibid., p. 115.

8. Velasquez, p. 109.

9. Ibid., p. 110.

10. J. Gay-Williams, "The Wrongfulness of Euthanasia," in Jeffrey Olen, Julie C. Van Camp, and Vincent Barry, *Applying Ethics: A Text with Readings*, 8th ed., Belmont, CA: Wadsworth/Thomson Learning, 2005, p. 180.

11. John Rawls et al, "Assisted Suicide: The Philosophers' Brief," *The New York Review of Books*, March 27, 1997. Retrieved February 4, 2005, from http://www.nybooks.com/articles/1237.

12. Ronald Dworkin, "Assisted Suicide: What the Court Really Said," *The New York Review of Books*, September 25, 1997. Retrieved February 4, 2005, from http://www.nybooks.com/archives/.

13. Daniel Sulmasy, "Killing and Allowing to Die: Another Look," *Journal of Law, Medicine, and Ethics*, Spring 1998, p. 57.

14. "Euthanasia," in *Excerpts from the Catechism of the Catholic Church on Life, Abortion, and Euthanasia*,

Staten Island: Priests for Life. Retrieved February 1, 2005, from http://www.priestsforlife.org/magisterium/catechismonabortion.htm#euthanasia.

15. Pope Pius XII, "Address to a Symposium of the Italian Society of Anesthesiology," February 24, 1957, *Catholic Mind*, May/June, 1957, p. 277.

16. Pope John Paul II, "Life Sustaining Treatments and Vegetative State: Scientific Advance and Ethical Dilemmas," March 20, 2004. Retrieved June 10, 2005, from http://www.lifeissues.net/writers/doc/doc_33vegetativestate.html.

17. Jeffrey Olen, Julie Van Camp, and Vincent Barry., *Applying Ethics: A Text with Readings*, 8th ed., Belmont, CA: Wadsworth/Thomson Learning, 2005, p. 172.

18. Philippa Foot, "Euthanasia," in Olen, Van Camp, and Barry, pp. 187–201.

19. Michael Tooley, "An Irrelevant Consideration: Killing Versus Letting Die," in *Killing and Letting Die*, 2nd edition, Bonnie Steinbock and Alastair Norcross, eds., New York: Fordham University Press, 1994, pp. 103–111.

20. James Rachels, "Active and Passive Euthanasia," in Olen, Van Camp, and Barry, p. 184.

21. Foot, p. 195.

22. James Rachels, "More Impertinent Distinctions and a Defense of Active Euthanasia," in *Killing and Letting Die*, pp. 139–154.

23. Timothy E. Quill, "Doctor I Want to Die, Will You Help Me?" *JAMA*, August 18, 1993, pp. 870–875.

24. Linda Emanuel et al, "The Practice of Euthanasia and Physician-Assisted Suicide in the United States," *JAMA*, August 12, 1998, pp. 507–513.

25. Olen, Van Camp, and Barry, p. 173.

26. Richard Doerflinger, "Pope John Paul II Affirms Obligation to Feed Patients in the "Vegetative" State," Free Republic, April 26, 2004. Retrieved May 28, 2009, from http://www.freerepublic.com/focus/fr/1124925/posts.

27. See note 26 above.

28. "The Boston Declaration on Assisted Dying," 13th *International Conference of the World Federation of Right To Die Societies*, Boston, September 1-3 2000. Retrieved May 25, 2009, from http://www.worldrtd.net/node/541.

29. Gillian Craig, "Terminal Sedation," *Catholic Medical Quarterly*, February 2002. Retrieved May 22, 2009, from www.catholicdoctors.org.uk/CMQ/Feb_2002/terminal_sedation.htm.

30. NA, "Dutch Continue To Rationalize and Expand Induced Death Practices," *International Task Force.org*, 2004. Retrieved May 22, 2009, from http://www.internationaltaskforce.org/iua31.htm.

31. Megan-Jane Johnstone, *Bioethics: A Nursing Perspective*, 4th ed., Chatswood, NSW: Elsevier Australia, 2004, pp. 280–282.

32. See note 31 above.

33. See note 31 above.

34. See note 31 above.

Chapter 19

Suicide in the West: A Brief History

On May 16, 2009, Isadore E. Millstone drove to the Daniel Boone Bridge, which carries Interstate 64 over the Missouri River and to the western suburbs of St. Louis, and jumped. He was 102 and, according to reports, simply "tired."[1]

THE SUICIDE OF ISADORE MILLSTONE

At a memorial ceremony for Millstone, the former chancellor of Washington University described him as "a hero of St. Louis," while leaders of the Jewish community recalled his generosity. "You can't drive in any direction," said the president of the Missouri Museum of History, "without being touched by Mr. Millstone."

Specializing in construction, Isadore Millstone founded Millstone Construction in 1927. The company built the old Busch Stadium and one of the nation's early double-decker highways, US 40, as well as banks, schools, and a synagogue. It also made Millstone millions. But to all outward appearances, money and material things meant little to the self-made millionaire. At the time of his death, Millstone lived in a single-story home and drove a Chevy Impala. What he did care about, though, was St. Louis and its people.

At Millstone Construction, the younger Mr. Millstone became known for his support of civil rights. He pressured unions to admit African Americans, and he started vocational schools for black men to become skilled tradesmen eligible for jobs as bricklayers, plumbers, and welders. While earning a fortune, he also earned a reputation for philanthropy, "donating millions of dollars to hundreds of charitable causes." When word of his death spread, relatives received calls, letters, and e-mails from common people such as postal workers, bartenders, and dry cleaners, all touched by his acts of kindness.

"I don't think any of us thought his life would end this way," said Tom Green, a lawyer and a friend for more than fifty years. A year earlier, Mr. Millstone had fallen and injured his shoulder. He took pain medication and complained about having a difficult time sleeping. "We'd tease him: 'Isadore, you're 102 years old,'" Mr. Green said.

Bob Millstone, who shared an office with his grandfather, described him as "a man who had known a lot of loss" and was simply "tired." "He lost his friends," his grandson said, "and he lost his friends' children." Millstone outlived his first wife by sixty-eight years, and his second died in 2007. His only two children, a daughter and a son, died at ages forty-four and sixty-eight, respectively.

Although Jewish law generally condemns suicide, no one condemned Millstone. Notably absent, in fact, were the strident arguments typically exchanged after such events. Mike Staenberg, the chairman of the Jewish Community Center, preferred to focus on Mr. Millstone's love for swimming, which he pursued well into his nineties. "This was a man who gave so much," Mr. Staenberg said. "And he got tired. He had been quite a swimmer. I guess he decided it was time to make one last dive into the water."

Isadore Millstone is one of thousands who take their lives every year in the United States. According to the National Institute of Mental Health (NIMH), slightly more than 30,000 Americans die by their own hand annually, a number that hasn't varied much in nearly a half century.[2] Each suicide is estimated to affect six other people intimately.[3] If, as statistics show, there is a suicide in the United States every eighteen minutes, then there are six new survivors every eighteen minutes as well. That meant, in the five years leading to 2004, 4 million people, or one for every sixty-two Americans was affected by the 738,000 suicides.[4]

Of course, numbers reveal nothing about why people take their lives. Mental disorders, drug and alcohol abuse, the loss of a job or partner—whatever the usual suspects, a suicide almost always is attributed to an "unconscious cry for help" rather than to a carefully calculated choice of death over life. But is it that simple? In fact, people throughout time have taken their lives to escape pain, suffering, illness, and, apparently like Millstone, the infirmities of old age. They've also done so out of despair or shame; to get revenge; to maintain dignity; or to preserve a cherished belief.[5]

Once we acknowledge nonmedicalized reasons for suicide, then the question arises: Can suicide ever be right? Ever moral? Can there be an honorable form of suicide—a so-called noble suicide? Some philosophers have thought so. They claim that suicide can be a rational, justifiable act. Can it? Could Isadore Millstone have acted *from* deliberation and not merely *with* deliberation? Did Craig Ewert and David and Joan Downes act rationally? (See Bioethics Across Cultures, "Suicide Tourists," Chapter 18.)

Or, on the other hand, does self-killing, including physician-aided, always deserve the condemnation it generally gets from religion? (In contrast to Christianity, Judaism, and Islam's denunciation of it, Confucianism and Buddhism are open to conditional suicide, for intolerable illness, as an example). Was Baruch Spinoza (1632–1677) right when he categorically denied any natural impulse for self-destruction? Is suicide, as the Dutch philosopher claimed, always the result of physical or psychological compulsion and never a rational act?[6] At the end, did Millstone, Ewert, and the Downeses act irrationally?

In the eighteenth century, at the height of the Enlightenment, David Hume made what is regarded as the first unapologetic defense of the moral permissibility of suicide on grounds of individual autonomy and social benefit. In making his case that suicide did not violate duty to "god, our neighbor, or ourselves," Hume was directly challenging each leg of a tripod that for more than a thousand years had supported the medieval Church's categorical condemnation of suicide and euthanasia on grounds of theology, social interest, and self-preservation. But the medieval Church was not original in its attacks on self-killing. Centuries earlier Plato and Aristotle had advanced the same arguments.

It is with the classical Greek perspective that we begin the enduring dialogue that has cast suicide, variously, as offensive, rational, sinful, beneficial, irresponsible, and socially useful. The palpable Western ambivalence about voluntary death persists in today's moral analyses of PAS.

BIOETHICS ACROSS CULTURES

Al-Qaida and Suicide Terrorism

Al-Qaida ("vanguard of the strong") is a fundamentalist Islamic group whose main objectives are to end foreign influence in Muslim countries and create a new Islamic caliphate, or Muslim rule. Its members generally believe that a Christian-Jewish alliance is conspiring to destroy Muslims and that the killing of bystanders and civilians is Islamically justified in *jihad*, or a religious duty. According to Islamic jurist and scholar Khaled Abou El Fadl, however, classical jurists viewed attack by stealth that indiscriminately killed the innocent as evil, and even had a name for the crime, *hiraba*. The crime of *hiraba*, or "waging war against society," was considered so serious that perpetrators were considered "enemies of humankind" and nowhere given sanctuary. Nevertheless, one of al-Qaida's devastating tactics is the suicide attack.

Conventional wisdom holds that al-Qaida members are mostly poor, uneducated, irrational, religious fanatics. But the work of Marc Sageman, an independent researcher on terrorism, challenges this stereotype. After 9/11, Sageman began collecting biographical material on about 400 al-Qaida terrorists to test the validity of popular conceptions about them. Sageman's research was published as *Understanding Terror Networks* (2004) and *Leaderless Jihad* (2007), both by the University of Pennsylvania. Here's what Sageman discovered:

- the vast majority of terrorists in the sample came from solid middle class backgrounds, and its leadership came from the upper class;
- only 13 percent of terrorists went to madrassahs, or Muslim schools;
- the vast majority came from families with very moderate religious beliefs or a completely secular outlook;
- 84 percent were radicalized in the West, not in their countries of origin;
- most had come to the West to study, and at the time they had no intention of ever becoming terrorists;

- 8 percent consisted of Christian converts to Islam, who could not have been brainwashed into violence by their culture;
- about two-thirds had attended college, in contrast to the less than 10 percent of their original communities who did so;
- many had studied engineering and most knew little about religion;
- three-fourths were married and two-thirds had children, often many children;
- about 60 percent of them had professional or semi-professional occupations;
- none had mental disorders; and
- all were recruited by al-Qaida through friendship and kinship rather than dedicated recruiters.

(Source Michael Bond, "The Making of a Suicide Bomber," *New Scientist*, May 15, 2004, pp. 34–37. Retrieved June 5, 2009, from http://indianmuslims.in/defying-the-myths-the-rational-educated-secular-prosperous-suicide-bomber/; Marc Sageman, Foreign Policy Research Institute, 2009. Retrieved June 5, 2009, from http://www.fpri.org/about/people/sageman.html.)

Question

All of us to a degree will give up our identity for group membership and solidarity. In other words, to keep our position in the preferred group, we're fully capable of suppressing our own beliefs and values, even to the point of overlooking the crimes and immorality of the group. It has been suggested, then, that suicide terrorists are merely extreme examples of a general class of behavior in which all of us engage. Do you think a person is capable of rational suicide for the goals of a group? What would a rational suicidal terrorist have to believe? Is it possible to explain the acts of 9/11, in which the perpetrators deliberately sacrificed themselves, in terms of rational choice?

(Source: Ronald Wintrobe, "Can Suicide Bombers Be Rational?" November 5, 2001. Retrieved June 5, 2009, from http://cas.uchicago.edu/workshops/cpolit/papers/suicide.pdf.)

SUICIDE AS AN OFFENSE TO GOD, NEIGHBOR, SELF: PLATO AND ARISTOTLE

In the dialogue *Phaedo*, Plato's great monument to death, Socrates speaks of a doctrine from "mystics" "who say that we men are put in a sort of lock-up, from which one must not release oneself or run away … ." Of this teaching Socrates professes no understanding, but agreement. "I believe," he affirms, "that this much is true: that we men are in the care of the gods, one of their possessions," concluding: "So … it is not unreasonable to say that we must not put an end to ourselves until God sends some necessary circumstance like the one which we are facing now [that is, his own death sentence]."[7]

Plato, to be sure, tolerated exceptions to the prohibition of suicide—notably, extreme misfortune and hardship, personal disgrace, and capital punishment self-administered. He also permitted voluntary euthanasia of the disabled and incurable, as well as for eugenic reasons, infanticide of defective newborns, and the products of certain incestuous unions (see *The Republic*, bk. iv, ch. xvi). But, in general, Plato considered voluntary death an offense against the divine, to be punished by disgraceful burials in solitary and unmarked graves. And such would be the funerary fate of suicides for centuries to come.

That it was legally prohibited figured prominently in Aristotle's condemnation of suicide. It was, in his view, a socially irresponsible act that weakened the state by depriving it of the services of a citizen. As he says in *Nicomachean Ethics*, "a certain loss of civil rights attaches to the man who destroys himself, on the ground that he is treating the state unjustly."[8] Also, according to Aristotle, the act of suicide went against the instinct of self-preservation and, therefore, was further to be condemned as an unnatural act.

SUICIDE AS A RATIONAL ACT: THE STOICS

Many cultures, including ancient Greece and Rome, have permitted and respected so-called rational suicide, that is, ending one's life for good reasons, as opposed to emotional or psychological ones. Not surprisingly, what constituted "good reasons" varied from culture to culture and sometimes even within cultures. For example, to the warrior Vikings, only those who died violently—in battle or by their own hand—were thought worthy of paradise, or Valhalla. For the elderly infirm among the ancient Scythians, suicide presented a most honorable alternative to overburdening their nomadic tribe.[9] And it was the promise of immediate heavenly reward that motivated many voluntary deaths among the early Christians.

To Plato, but not Aristotle, crippling grief or unrelenting disease was reason enough for both voluntary death and euthanasia. On this point, Plato differed from Pythagoras (569–475 BCE) and his followers, who, respecting the sanctity of life and viewing a hard death as punishment for past sins, discouraged suicide.[10] Plato also tolerated suicide for patriotism or personal honor; and the Greeks generally, as well as the Romans, believed that people should meet death with equanimity and comfort. As a rule, then, the ancients did permit suicide in the face of intolerable and irremediable life circumstances.

Within a century of Socrates' death in 399 BCE, many philosophers framed suicide as sometimes most reasonable and desirable. For example, to the Stoics, philosophers who flourished for centuries in Greece and Rome, suicide was a rational choice when life no longer seemed to accord with nature. This gave primacy, though not an unlimited freedom, to the individual rather than the community. Most Stoics believed that suicide was justified only when the individual could no longer live according to reason. They interpreted this state as a divine message to depart from life. Thus, when it was no longer possible to live the life nature intended—what today we might call poor "quality of life"—voluntary death was appropriate. And when was that? Only the individual could determine when life had so deteriorated as to warrant self-killing. As the Stoic philosopher Epictetus (55–135 CE) averred, "If the room is smoky, if only moderately, I will stay," but "if there is too much smoke I will go. Remember this, keep a firm hold on it, the door is always open."[11] And in a sentiment befitting many contemporary deaths, including those dispatched by Jack Kevorkian, the Roman philosopher Seneca (4 BCE–65 CE) wrote to his friend Lucilius:

> Living is not the good, but living well. The wise man therefore lives as long as he should, not as long as he can … He will always think of life in terms of quality not quantity…. Dying early or late is of no relevance, dying well or ill is …. Even if it is true [that while there is life, there is hope], life is not to be bought at all costs.[12]

True to his code, the Stoic Seneca took his own life rather than endure the blood lust of Nero (37–68), who three years later did the same rather than be flogged to death by order of the Roman senate.

SUICIDE AS SINFUL: AUGUSTINE AND AQUINAS

If the Roman Stoic could find honor and dignity in suicide, the early Christian could find in it a ticket to paradise. Indeed, the increasing popularity of suicide among early Christians as a way to heaven—and even to sainthood, as with suicidal virgins—evidently threatened the stability of the Church enough that Augustine urged his fellow bishops to join him in condemning suicide as a violation of the sixth commandment. "It is significant that in Holy Scripture no passage can be found enjoining or permitting suicide either in order to hasten our entry into immortality or to void or avoid temporal evils," he wrote in *The City of God*. And then, as if to dispel any doubt, he added: "God's command, 'Thou shalt not kill,' is to be taken as forbidding self-destruction."[13] Still, the medieval Church's *official* condemnation of suicide would not come until over a hundred years after Augustine's death when, at the Council of Braga in 562, suicide was pronounced a crime against God who, as creator of the universe and everything in it, was proclaimed the sole determinant of death and life.

In years following, the gravity of the offense showed in the harsh punishments instituted for suicide, such as the denial of burial rites or excommunication. Then, in the thirteenth century, Aquinas, drawing on the three classical arguments, categorically condemned suicide as a sin against self, society, and God. Thus, from *Summa Theologica*:

> It is altogether unlawful to kill oneself, for three reasons. First, because everything naturally loves itself, the result being that everything naturally keeps itself in being, and resists corruption as far as it can. Wherefore suicide is contrary to the inclination of nature and to charity, whereby every man should love himself. Hence suicide is always a mortal sin, as being contrary to the natural law and to charity. Secondly, because every part, as such, belongs to the world. Now every man is part of the community, and so, as such, he belongs to the community. Hence by killing himself he injures the community, as the Philosopher [Aristotle] declares (*Ethic* vii). Thirdly, because life is God's gift to man and is subject to His power, Who kills and makes to live. Hence whoever takes his own life sins against God, even as he who kills another's slave sins against the slave master and as he who usurps himself judgment of a matter not entrusted to him. For it belongs to God alone to pronounce sentence of death and life according to Deut. xxxii. 39, *I will kill and I will make to live.*[14]

The medieval Church's condemnation of suicide also extended to active euthanasia but not to passive, or allowing to die, which was tolerated as nonsuicide.

It was thus, says suicide scholar A. Alvarez of the evolution of feeling about suicide from classical to medieval times, that "an act which during the first flowering of Western civilization had been tolerated, later admired, and later still sought as the supreme mark of zealotry, became finally the object of intense moral revulsion."[15]

SUICIDE AS BENEFICIAL TO SELF AND OTHERS: HUME

In his 1577 description of Elizabethan England, chronicler William Harrison (1534–1593) tartly observed: "Such as kill themselves are buried in the field with a stake driven through their bodies."[16] Suicides, it seems, fared only a tad better than witches and thieves, who, imprudently failing to kill themselves, were variously hanged, burned, or beheaded. But about the same time that Harrison penned his chilling words, the church-sponsored

Elizabethan view of suicide as an unmitigated evil was about to be challenged—by a good French Catholic, no less.

In *A Custom of the Isle of Cea*, an essay presenting opposed arguments on suicide, Michel de Montaigne (1533–1592) insisted, "God gives us sufficient dispensation when he puts us in a situation where life becomes worse than death." Referring to the extension of the commandment "Thou shalt not kill" to suicide, Montaigne added: "I don't break the law made for crooks, when I take away my own property—thus I am not obliged to conform to the law made for murderers when I deprive myself of my own life." In Montaigne's view, pain and "the fear of a worse death" were "excusable incitements" for suicide. In the essay's most memorable aphorisms, Montaigne wrote: "For a desperate disease a desperate cure" and "The wise man lives as long as he ought, not as long as he can."[17] Other voices of the time echoed the sentiment, if not the eloquence, of the famous essayist that suicide was an individual choice.

- In 1516 the English humanist Sir Thomas More (1478–1535) defended euthanasia in his *Utopia*. Idealizing the functions of hospitals, More supported hastening the death of consenting patients with incurable illnesses, when sanctioned by a priest.[18] His pro-euthanasia stand apparently posing no obstacle to sainthood, More was canonized Saint Thomas More in the Roman Catholic Church by Pope Pius XI (1857–1939) in 1935.

- Francis Bacon, the creator of scientific induction we met in Chapter 1, conceived the role of physicians as "not only to restore the health, but to mitigate pain and dolors; and not only when such mitigation may conduce to recovery, but when it may serve to make a fair and easy passage" (*New Atlantis*, 1627).

- Other writers employed more theological arguments to challenge the religious prohibition on suicide, notably John Donne (1572–1631) in *Biathanatos* (1647). In that first defense of suicide in English, the metaphysical poet and cleric claimed that, whereas suicide often was

morally wrong, it could be acceptable if performed with the intention of glorifying God, not serving self-interest. Yes, Donne conceded, prohibitions of suicide had their place, but so did exceptions that proved the rule. In fact, he argued that Jesus took his own life and offered scriptural verse in defense of that controversial view, such as "No one takes life from me, I give it" (John 10:18).

- On the continent, the eighteenth century French *philosophes*—Baron d'Holbach (1723–1789), Voltaire, Baron de Montesquieu (1689–1755), Rousseau—all took a permissive view toward suicide, characteristic of Enlightenment thought generally. Rousseau's uncommon reservation involved obligations to others such as family. The sole exception among the principal French intellectuals of the day was Diderot (1713–1784), who, in the famous *Encyclopedie* (1765), based his opposition to suicide on the three classic arguments.[19]

Of the all the dissident voices, however, David Hume, the towering figure of the Scottish Enlightenment (1740–1790) who was raised as a Presbyterian, is considered to have made the first substantive attempt to defend the permissibility of suicide for reasons of both self- and social-interest. His *On Suicide* (1777) still stands as a full-throated rebuttal against the two thousand year condemnation of suicide as sin against God, neighbor, and self.

On Suicide

Perhaps the most compelling statement in any language of the Enlightenment's position on the subject,[20] *On Suicide* basically urged the potential suicide to decide after assessing the multiple interests and values involved. If, on balance, it was determined that either the individual or society benefited more from taking one's life than not, then the action was permissible, perhaps even praiseworthy.

In making his case, Hume used counter instances to the traditional disapproval of suicide. He submitted, for example, that if God was the creator of the universe, then in all things, great and small, his will was present—even in acts of self-killing. Therefore, suicide could not be a violation of divine will but could be a rational and reasonable act that occurred within the context of a divinely ordered universe. Notice how in the following passage Hume turned the classical metaphor of the suicide being like a soldier deserting his post without orders into a devastating boomerang:

> But you are placed by providence, like a centinel in a particular station, and when you desert it without being recalled, you are equally guilty of rebellion against your almighty sovereign and have incurred his displeasure. —I ask, why do you conclude that providence has placed me in this station? For my part I find that I owe my birth to a long chain of causes, of which many depended upon voluntary actions of men. But Providence guided all these causes, and nothing happens in the universe without its consent and Co-operation. If so, then neither does my death, however voluntary, happen without its consent; and whenever pain or sorrow so far overcome my patience, as to make me tired of life, I may conclude that I am recalled from my station in the clearest and most express terms.[21]

If, as an expression of liberty, suicide did not necessarily offend divine will, by the same token, Hume argued, it did not always threaten public order. It might even at times promote it, he suggested, as it would were one to become a burden to society or family. In such cases, he wrote, "my resignation of life must not only be innocent but laudable."[22] Beyond this, Hume argued that suicide could also be consistent with duty to self when "age, sickness, misfortune" rendered life intolerable, "worse even than annihilation."

But not all Enlightenment thinkers were as permissive of suicide. Locke, for one, condemned disowning one's right to life as preposterous as giving away one's inalienable and irrevocable right to liberty.[23] In Chapter 2 of his *Two Treatises of Government*, he invoked the traditional theological anti-suicide argument such that, being "servants of one sovereign Master, ... every one ... is bound to preserve himself, and not to quit his station willfully." Even more effusive in his opposition than Locke, Kant offered four arguments, three philosophical and one religious, for casting self-killing as always a violation of moral responsibility.

SUICIDE AS VIOLATING MORAL RESPONSIBILITY: KANT

Kant claimed that suicide was always wrong because it (1) involved a contradiction of free will, (2) degraded human nature, (3) was inconsistent with autonomy, and (4) violated the law of God. (Although 3 and 4 might be considered versions of 1 and 2, they'll be considered separately here.)

The Argument from Free Will

Kant believed that we could treat our bodies as we pleased so long as our motives were self-preservation. Consider an amputation: Part of the body is intentionally sacrificed for the preservation of the body as a whole. In contrast, because in taking one's life one obviously does not preserve one's person, suicide always involves the intention to destroy oneself. It robs oneself of one's person, thereby making it for Kant

> contrary to the highest duty we have towards ourselves, for it annuls the condition of all other duties; it goes beyond the limits of the use of free will, for this use is possible only through the existence of the Subject.

In terms of Kant's ultimate rule of morality, the categorical imperative (see Chapter 2), the maxim permitting suicide would be self-contradictory, since it would permit the power of will to destroy itself.

The Argument from Human Nature

Kant granted many circumstances when life ought to be sacrificed, chief among them whenever life conflicts with duty. Thus, "If I cannot preserve my life except by violating duties toward myself, I am bound to sacrifice my life rather than violate these duties." But suicide never qualified as a justifiable sacrifice of life, he argued, because life was the condition of everything else. Conscious that life was a trust reposed in us, we should recoil at the thought of breaking this trust by turning our lives against ourselves. An act of suicide, then, didn't merely devalue life; it degraded human worth and human nature. In his *Lectures on Ethics*, Kant wrote:

> Suicide is not abominable and inadmissible because life should be highly prized; were it so, we could each have our own opinion of how highly we should prize it, and the rule of prudence would often indicate suicide as the best means. But the rule of morality does not admit of it under any condition because it degrades human nature below the level of animal nature and destroys it. Yet there is much in the world far more important than life. To observe morality is far more important. It is better to sacrifice one's life than one's morality. To live is not a necessity; but to live honorably while life lasts is a necessity. We can at all times go on living and doing our duty towards ourselves without having to do violence to ourselves. But he who is prepared to take his own life is no longer worthy to live at all. The pragmatic ground of impulse to live is happiness. Can I then take my own life because I cannot live happily? No! It is not necessary that whilst I live I should live happily; but it is necessary that so long as I live I should live honorably. Misery gives no right to any man to take his own life, for then we should all be entitled to take our lives for lack of pleasure. All our duties towards ourselves would then be directed towards pleasure; but the fulfillment of those duties may demand that we should even sacrifice our life.[24]

Here, suicide is depicted as violating the categorical imperative because it is not treating humanity (i.e., one's own person) as an end in itself but simply as a means to pleasure or the avoidance of pain.

Alternatively, in Chapter 2 of his *Principles of Morals*, Kant famously depicted a suicide permit as failing the test of universalizability:

> A man reduced to despair by a series of misfortunes feels wearied of life, but is still so far in possession of his reason that he can ask himself whether it would not be contrary to his duty to himself to take his own life. Now he inquires whether the maxim of his action could become a universal law of nature his maxim is: From self-love I adopt it as a principle to shorten my life when its longer duration is likely to bring more evil than satisfaction. It is asked then simply whether this principle founded on self-love can become a universal law of nature. Now we see at once that a system of nature of which it should be a law to destroy life by means of the very feeling whose special nature it is to impel to the improvement of life would contradict itself, and therefore could not exist as a system of nature; hence that maxim cannot possibly exist as a universal law of nature, and consequently would be wholly inconsistent with the supreme principle of all duty.[25]

The Argument from Autonomy

According to Kant, and contrary to the Stoics and Hume, autonomy, properly understood, disallowed suicide. Kant did not share the Stoic, Humean, and humanistic view that a self-killing might be the justifiable act of a rational choice to die according to one's values and principles. On the contrary, he held that autonomy, rightly understood, argued against using one's freedom self-destructively. To do so would be to destroy the very existence that was necessary for freedom. In other words, a maxim that would allow a person to use freedom to end his/her life would fail the categorical imperative by being self-contradictory, because it would allow something external to limit that freedom.

Alternatively, suicide violated Kant's principle of humanity, which forbade intentionally using a person as a means to an end rather than as an end in himself. Thus, similarly to his argument from free will, Kant wrote:

> He who contemplates suicide should ask himself whether his action can be consistent with the idea of humanity *as an end in itself.* If he destroys himself to escape from painful circumstances, he uses a person merely as *a means* to maintain a tolerable condition up to the end of life. But a man is not a thing, that is to say, something which can be used merely as means, but must in all his actions be always considered as an end in himself. I cannot, therefore, dispose in any way of a man in my own person so as to mutilate him, to damage or kill him.[26]

The Argument from Divine Will

Finally, Kant, who was brought up as a Lutheran, believed that suicide opposed God's purpose and design, and, therefore, was always wrong. In reviving the classic appeal to divine will, Kant even borrowed the soldier and chattel metaphor of Plato, where, again, the suicide was classically framed as a deserter of his post and, therefore, deserving God's wrath.

Despite the obvious religious nature of this argument, it's worth noting that for Kant suicide was not wrong because God forbade it, but rather because it degraded and destroyed human nature. In reducing one's inner worth to a sub-animal level, suicide was an abomination that properly warranted the divine condemnation it got. Kant's argument from divine will, then, could be read as a religious version of the argument from human nature. For Kant—as well as for Georg W. F. Hegel (1770–1831), a professed Lutheran—the imperatives of reason validated the traditional religious condemnation of suicide and euthanasia.

The recurrence of the theological argument in the battle between traditional prohibition and enlightened permissiveness recalls the tension between faith and reason in the Age of Enlightenment that profoundly shaped views of the nature and purpose of morality. Recall that for Aquinas, Augustine, and their descendants in faith, morality was all about obeying the will of God. This view led them to an unqualified disapproval of suicide and euthanasia. For philosophers such as Hume and Kant, in contrast, morality was about following reason, and reason did not entail a single moral judgment about suicide. As it happened, reason led Hume to permissiveness, Kant to prohibition. The larger point, though, is that as reason, itself, gained cachet in moral discourse, the theological bulwark against suicide weakened. As a net result, suicide seemed less sinful and more rational, a trend that quickened with the maturation of scientific medicine in the nineteenth century.

SUICIDE AS A SOCIAL UTILITY: BENTHAM AND MILL

Medical ethicist Andrew Papanikitas points out, "It is generally regarded that the medical profession overtook the theological monopoly on death in the nineteenth century." Specifically, the ascent of scientific medicine made it possible to pinpoint incurable or terminal patients and, thus, candidates for euthanasia, in the modern usage of the term. As a result, says Papanikitas, "Until the end of the nineteenth century euthanasia was regarded as a peaceful death, and the art of its accomplishment."[27]

Utilitarianism, with its emphasis on liberty and challenge to state intrusion into demonstrably private affairs, gave the toleration of suicide and euthanasia added impetus. Nineteenth century utilitarians asked: *What business is it of government if the individual wishes to end his or her life rather than suffer an agonizing death? On what moral grounds can state interference that extends pain and suffering at the end of life be justified when the alternative, hastening death, promises an end to individual suffering? Whose interests are mainly at issue—the individual's or the society's?* With such questions, utilitarians launched a still echoing liberty-interest case for permissive euthanasia legislation.

But the impact of scientific medicine and utilitarianism reverberated well beyond philosophical circles. Throughout the nineteenth century, the medical profession increasingly addressed the subject of euthanasia. For example, "Medical Euthanasia," a famous lecture delivered by a physician, stressed the importance of treating patients, not just their diseases. Its author, Dr. Carl F. H. Marx, reminded his colleagues that a physician "is not expected to have a remedy for death, but for the skillful alleviation of suffering," before adding pregnantly, "and he should know how to apply it when all hope has departed."[28]

However, the first popular advocate of active euthanasia in the nineteenth century was not a physician or philosopher but a schoolmaster and essayist. In the first paper (1870) to appear in the United States and England dealing with the concept of "medical" euthanasia, Samuel Williams wrote:

> In all cases it should be the duty of the medical attendant, whenever so desired by the patient, to administer chloroform, or any other such anaesthetics as may by and by supersede chloroform, so as to destroy consciousness at once, and put the sufferer at once to a quick and painless death;

BIOETHICS ACROSS CULTURES

Field of Tears in South Korea

Even though it was harvest time, the tenant farmers of Jangsu left their paddy fields and assembled in the community hall to pay their last respects to a man who stabbed himself in the heart the week before in Cancun, Mexico, in protest against the World Trade Organization's efforts to open agricultural trade. Next to a four-foot-high photograph of the dead man, a banner reaffirmed his campaign: "Lee Kyung-hae [1947–2003] is our hero"; "Stop WTO agriculture negotiations which are killing millions of Korean farmers." Even the prime minister of South Korea sent condolences.

The WTO is an organization that deals with the rules of trade between nations. Farmers like Lee blamed the WTO for worsening their lives by systematic bias toward rich countries and multinational corporations. They said they were dying of burdensome debt and declining income. Unable to see a way out, some Korean farmers even spoke of committing suicide, others of running off in the middle of the night. And they saw no let-up, as their government sacrificed domestic agricultural protection to open markets overseas for the finance and manufacturing sectors. With 80% working as small-scale tenant farmers, they knew they could never compete head-on with rice produced by the huge agri-businesses of the United States, or apples grown in Chinese farms that could tap into unlimited cheap labor. The young were deserting the fields in droves, and in the past twenty years, Jangsu had lost half its population.

Such was the whirlwind of conditions that led to the events at the Mexican seaside resort of Cancun, on September 10, 2003, as ministers from 146 nations launched a five-day WTO conference aimed at breaking a two-year deadlock in trade liberalization talks. Prior to that, few outside the small farming town of Jangsu had ever heard of the 56-year-old farmers' leader, who was in the frontline with about 150 other Koreans trying to breach the barriers separating the protesters from the site of the WTO negotiations.

Climbing to the top of the fence, Lee turned to his compatriots and said: "Don't worry about me, just struggle your hardest." Then, on the sidelines of a protest of several thousand people, Lee stabbed himself in the chest with a knife. It pierced four centimeters into the left atrium of his heart. Below the security fence where he stabbed himself, Italian activists splattered themselves with red paint and shouted the slogan that Lee had made his own: "The WTO kills farmers." Outside the hospital where he died, sympathizers held candlelit vigils.

When he died after several hours, some protesters proclaimed Lee a martyr. During international solidarity rallies over the weekend, Cancun echoed with thousands of voices, chanting: "We are all Lee, we are all Lee." One official said: "Lee knew the Korean countryside is slowly dying, that farmers are living lonely, miserable lives. He wanted to tell the world. That is why he sacrificed himself and that is why we call him a hero." A farm association leader added, "His death is not a personal accident but reflects the desperate fighting of 3.5 million Korean farmers."

(Sources: NA, "South Korean Activist Kill Himself, Others Injured in Cancun Protest," *Agence France Presse*, September 11, 2003. http://www.commondreams.org/headlines03/0911-06.htm; Jonathan Watts, "Field of Tears," *Manchester Guardian*, September 16, 2003. Retrieved May 25, 2009, from http://www.globalexchange.org/campaigns/wto/1068.html.)

Question

How would you characterize Lee's suicide—as sinful, rational, beneficial, irresponsible, socially useful? How would you assign moral responsibility for it?

precautions being adopted to prevent any possible abuse of such duty; and means being taken to establish beyond any possibility of doubt or question, that the remedy was applied at the express wish of the patient.[29]

Williams' view circulated widely, although the medical profession largely ignored it. Under the influence of utilitarianism and social Darwinism—the belief that society's strongest and fittest should survive, while the weakest and unfit be allowed to die—the argument made the incurably sick dispensable.

Feeding into the nascent tendency to marginalize the socially "undesirable" were related ideas emerging with the new science of eugenics. Among

the most controversial proposals was sterilization of the disabled, the mentally ill, and those with hereditary disorders. The "social burden" depiction of such individuals reached a grisly climax in the twentieth century with the mass involuntary deaths that occurred in Nazi Germany. Among them were thousands of disabled people, as disability advocate Hugh Gallagher (1932–2004) horrifyingly showed in *By Trust Betrayed* (1995). And should the practice leave physicians of that day squeamish, they could always draw strength from a 1920 German publication titled *Consent to the Extermination of Life Unworthy To Be Lived*. The little book provided a rationale for ending lives thought unworthy to preserve.[30]

CONCLUSIONS

The ethics of suicide and euthanasia clearly have occupied philosophers and theologians for centuries. Central to the colloquy are broad principles about duties to self and to society, as well as fundamental beliefs about the value of human life, its nature, purpose, and origins. The principals engaged in the debate have been likened to a "Who's Who?" of Western intellectual history, "ranging from Plato and Aristotle in ancient Greece to Augustine and Thomas Aquinas in the Middle Ages, to Locke, Hume, and Kant in more modern times."[31]

This mix of religious and secular belief, modified by cultural conditions and demands, has shaped law, morality, and feeling about suicide. What once was a crime that brought punishment—loss of family inheritance for suicides or punishment for attempted suicide—today is decriminalized. But assistance in suicide generally remains a crime and resides at the heart of the intense cultural discourse about how much control we can exercise over how we die.

CASES AND CONTROVERSIES

The "Rational" Suicide of Carolyn Heilbrun

Writing under the pen name Amanda Cross, Carolyn G. Heilbrun (1926–2003) was the author of fourteen Kate Fansler mysteries, with the recurring theme of feminism and academic politics. But Heilbrun concealed her career as a mystery novelist to protect her career as a literature professor at Columbia University, where she was the first woman to receive tenure.

Although she wasn't ill, Heilbrun's suicide in her New York apartment on October 9, 2003, didn't come as a total surprise. Her writing foreshadowed it,

especially her 1997 book, *The Last Gift of Time*, in which she described life after age 70 as "dangerous, lest we live past both the right point and our chance to die." Two concerns that Heilbrun mentioned were her "inevitable decline" and becoming a burden on others, according to Barron H. Lerner, Columbia professor of medicine who knew her. Heilbrun's motto, he said, was "Quit while you're ahead." In the July 2003 issue of the *Women's Review of Books*, Heilbrun allowed that she feared "living with certainty that there was no further work demanding to be done." She had consented to life, she stated, "only on the terms of borrowed time." Lerner said that

> Heilbrun was suffering from none of the conditions commonly associated with suicide when she evidently took an overdose of pills and put a plastic bag over her head. She was neither terminally ill, in severe pain nor, apparently, depressed.

According to her son, Heilbrun felt that her life had been completed. The note she left behind supported that view: "The journey is over. Love to all," it read.[32]

Questions for Analysis

1. Was Carolyn Heilbrun's suicide "rational"?
2. Daniel P. Sulmasy, philosopher and ethicist at New York Medical College and St. Vincent's, a Catholic hospital in New York, says: "Anyone who is not mentally ill and chooses the irrationality of committing suicide has done something morally wrong." Many Christian denominations agree. Do you think that Heilbrun did something morally wrong or was her self-killing the fullest expression of her autonomy?
3. Would it be dangerous for society to condone the so-called rational suicide?
4. Do you think that permissive assisted death laws would obviate the need for healthy people like Heilbrun to preemptively end their lives?

CASES AND CONTROVERSIES

Final Exit Network

According to an undercover Georgia state investigator, when he told a right-to-die group he was suffering from cancer and wanted to kill himself, group officials were willing to provide the means: a helium tank and a plastic "exit mask." The investigator said group officials planned to have him asphyxiate himself with the mask while holding down his arms. Within minutes he would die, and the "exit guides" would remove evidence from the scene. After an investigation, four members of Final Exit Network were arrested in February 2009 on charges of racketeering and assisted suicide, including the group's medical director, Dr. Lawrence D. Egbert.

Founded in 2004, Final Exit Network is a nonprofit organization and a member of the World Federation of Right to Die Societies. It owes its name to a suicide manual it promotes, *Final Exit,* by Derek Humphry, who is chairperson of the Network's advisory board. The charges against its members specifically related to the suicide of John Celmer, a member of the Network and a case in its Exit Guide Program. The undercover investigation began after relatives of the Georgia man told the police they believed that the Network took part in Celmer's death. Celmer's mother said her son had long suffered from mouth and throat cancer, but Georgia investigators said he had overcome the disease by the time he killed himself and was instead embarrassed about a facial disfigurement. Celmer's wife, Susan, issued a statement of gratitude to the law enforcement officials who "pursued this matter vigorously."[33]

After the arrests of its volunteers, the Network posted this press release on its website:

> Final Exit Network does not 'assist' suicide in any way, nor do we encourage individuals to hasten their deaths ... . Members who avail themselves of the Exit Guide Program must be capable of performing every required function without assistance of any type. At any time during the process a member can change his or her mind. Final Exit Network has thousands of members. The Network's revenues come exclusively from memberships and donations. Contrary to the widely published news reports the Network never charges for its Exit Guide services. The $50 fee so widely reported is the annual fee members pay to support the mission.[34]

"Assisted suicide is Jack Kevorkian putting a needle in someone with a deadly substance," said Jerry Dincin, who became the network president after the

(Continued)

CASES AND CONTROVERSIES (CONTINUED)

arrests. "We provide information that we think is protected under the First Amendment." He added, "Final Exit Network is a leader in the fight for the last human right."[35]

Convicting Final Exit Network could well hinge on how involved the group was beyond providing information about suicide. "The idea that they don't push a switch or administer a shot doesn't protect them from liability," says Russell Korobkin, a law professor at UCLA. "But I think it will be problematic to prosecute them for providing information, which is entitled to First Amendment protections. It seems that [Final Exit Network] is being very careful to stay on the right side of the line on this."[36]

Dincin agrees, but the issue for him isn't about getting away with murder. "We realize the risk we take when we're willing to walk that fine line between what a jurisdiction might call assisted suicide and what we might call compassionate presence," he says. "But whose life is it anyway? I know that my life is mine. It doesn't belong to the Georgia Bureau of Investigation or any religious entity or any person. It belongs to me, and I have the right in extreme circumstances to take it."

Questions for Analysis

1. Evaluate this assertion: "If we are going to intervene in the natural act of dying and allow people to live even though disease is rampant in their body, we can't make someone's decision to die the one exception to our meddling."

2. It is sometimes claimed that so long as assisted suicide remains illegal, individuals will turn to nonphysicians to help them end their lives. Do you think this is a good reason to legalize PAS?

3. Is it possible to support what Final Exit Network does but not how it does it? Explain by appeal to moral principle(s).

4. Evaluate Dincin's analysis of the right to die:

   You could liken it to women's suffrage in 1910 … . Women had to fight for that and be arrested for that, but now they have that right, and I don't mind fighting for this right in the same way. When a terminally ill person's quality of life is so miserable that they think life is not worth living, I think it is their right to decide whether they want to take their own life.

5. If you had to judge, would you find Final Exit Network volunteers as their sympathizers view them as "compassionate, caring, loving angels of mercy"; or as their critics view them as murderers?

CASES AND CONTROVERSIES

The Suicide of Garrett Hardin

In the fall of 2003, renowned microbiologist Garrett Hardin, author of two groundbreaking essays in environmental ethics—"The Tragedy of the Commons" (1968) and "Lifeboat Ethics: The Case Against Helping the Poor" (1974)—died with his wife in a double suicide in Santa Barbara, California. He was 88, she 81. Both were in poor health—he suffered from heart trouble and the effects of childhood polio, she from a form of Lou Gehrig's disease. Both were long-time members of the Hemlock Society, an organization committed to providing "information about options for dignified death and legalized physician aid in dying." (With a membership of about 25,000, the Hemlock Society, which Derek Humphry founded in 1980, merged with End-of-Life Choices in 2003.)[37]

To those who knew the Hardins, their suicides, though stunning, were not out of character. The couple's firm, humanistic belief was that each of us controls our own fate. Indeed, it was the collective failure to recognize that humankind is the master of its own destiny, and then follow the logical and ethical path rather than the sentimental one, that led to so much human misery, according to Garrett Hardin.

"They did what they wanted to do," is how one of the couple's four children summed up the deaths of her parents. She added that they "felt very strongly that they wanted to choose their own time to die."[38] A close friend and colleague said, "Garrett and Jane … faced death as unflinchingly as they had embraced life. Their last act together was not desperate or cowardly, but brave and calculated."[39]

Evidence for these impressions tracks back to 1996 and an interview with the British magazine *Skeptic*. Conducted at a time when Dr. Kevorkian's notoriety had landed him on the investigative TV newsmagazine *60 Minutes*, the interview turned to the subject of assisted suicide:

SKEPTIC: What about assisted suicide, now best known because of Dr. Kevorkian's legal battles?

HARDIN: Look, I'm 81. I may be wanting that one of these days. Because of polio, I'm dependent on my arms. I can't walk. If I lose my arms, should I get in a wheelchair and have to have somebody push me around all the time? At that point, I'm going to be looking for Dr. Kevorkian. I don't want to sit in a wheelchair for the rest of my life.

SKEPTIC: But your mind is still sharp and you have contributions to make.

HARDIN: Ah, thank you for those kind words. I know how unsharp my mind is becoming. And though I appreciate the tact of other people, looking at my fellow oldsters, I know damned well we're going downhill. So, by association I say, "probably, me too."[40]

Questions for Analysis

1. Comment on the Hardins' suicides in the context of the perspectives presented in this chapter.

2. Were the Hardin suicides morally different from Heilbrun's?

3. On what moral grounds would you either approve or disapprove of the Hardin suicides?

4. What does your faith tradition teach about suicide in general, and suicides such as the Hardins' in particular. Do you or do you not wholly agree with this teaching?

REFERENCES

1. Dirk Johnson, "A Suicide at 102 Unites a City in Thanks for a Man's Life," *The New York Times*, June 16, 2009, p. A11.

2. Jeffrey A. Bridge et al, "Suicide Trends Among Youths Aged 10 to 19 Years in the United States: 1996–2005," *JAMA*, September 3, 2008, pp. 1025–1026.

3. "Suicide Facts and Statistics," *The National Institute of Mental Health*. Retrieved June 24, 2008, from http://www.nimh.gov/suicideprevention/suifact.cfm.

4. Steven Reinberg, "Suicide Rates Rise Among Baby Boomers," *The Washington Post*, October 21, 2008. Retrieved June 20, 2009, from www.washingtonpost.com/wp-dyn/content/article/2008/10/21/AR2008102100665.html.

5. Michael Bannigan, *The Pulse of Wisdom*, Belmont, CA: Wadsworth Publishing, 1995, p. 340.

6. Jacques Choron, *Suicide*, New York: Charles Scribern's Sons, 1972, p. 116.

7. Plato, *Phaedo*, Benjamin Jowett, trans., in *The Harvard Classics*, New York: P.F. Collier & Company, 1909, pp. 121–122.

8. Aristotle, *Nicomachean Ethics*, R. D. Ross, trans. Retrieved June 1, 2005, from http://www.ethics.sandiego.edu/theories/Aristotle/.

9. A. Alvarez, The *Savage God: A Study of Suicide*, New York: Bantam Books, 1971, pp. 52–53.

10. Ron P. Hamel, *Choosing Death: Active Euthanasia, Religion, and the Public Debate*, Harrisburg, PA: Trinity Press International, 1991.

11. Choron, p. 118.

12. Seneca, "Letter to Lucilius, No. 70," in *The Stoic Philosophy of Seneca*, Moses Hadas, trans., Garden City, NJ: Doubleday, 1987, p. 202.

13. St. Augustine, *City of God*, Gerald G. Walsh et al, trans., Bk. I, Ch. 20, New York: Image Books, 1958, p. 55.

14. Thomas Aquinas. *Summa Theologica*, Father of the English Dominican Province, trans., Benziger 1947 Edition. Second Part of the Second Part, Q. 64, Art. 5. Retrieved May 1, 2005, from http://www.ccel.org/a/aquinas/summa/home.html.

15. Alvarez, p. 71.

16. William Harrison, "A Description of Elizabethan England," *Hollinshed's Chronicles*, in *The Harvard Classics*, vol. 35, Charles W. Eliot, ed., New York: P. F. Collier & Son, 1910, p. 366.

17. Michele de Montaigne, "A Custom of the Isle of Cea," in *The Essays of Montaigne*, E. J. Trechmann,

trans. London: Oxford University Press, vol I, bk. II, 1927, pp. 336–351.

18. Thomas More, *Utopia*, in *The Harvard Classics*, vol. 36, New York: P. F. Collier & Son, 1910, p. 208.

19. Choron, p. 125.

20. Ibid., p. 127.

21. David Hume, "On Suicide," in *Of the Standard of Taste and Other Essays*, John Lenz, ed., Indianapolis: Bobbs-Merrill Educational Publishing, 1965, p. 157.

22. Hume, 159.

23. G.B. Ferngren, "The Ethics of Suicide in the Renaissance and Reformation," in *Suicide and Euthanasia*, B. A. Brody, ed., Dordrecht, Germany: Kluwer Academic Publishers, 1989, pp. 173–175.

24. Immanuel Kant, *Lectures on Ethics*, Louis Infield, trans., New York: Harper & Row Publishers/Harper Torchbooks, 1963, pp. 151–152.

25. Immanuel Kant, *Fundamental Principles of the Metaphysic of Morals*, T. K. Åbbott, trans., in *The Harvard Classics*, vol. 32, New York: P.F. Collier & Son, 1910, p. 332.

26. Ibid., p. 340.

27. Andrew Papanikitas, "Is It Historically Possible for a Consensus to Be Reached on the Subject of Euthanasia, Voluntary or Otherwise?" *Catholic Medical Quarterly*, February 2000. Retrieved March 15, 2005, from http://www.catholicdocors.org.uk/CMQ/FEB_2000/consensus_on_euthanasia.htm.

28. Derek Humphry, *The Right to Die*, New York: Harper and Row, 1986, p. 10.

29. Quoted in Papanikitas.

30. "When Death is Sought: Assisted Suicide in the Medical Context," Ch. 5, *The New York Task Force on Life & the Law*, October 2001. Retrieved February 7, 2005, from http://www.health.state.ny.us/nysdoh/provider/death.htm.

31. Ibid, pp. 77–78.

32. Barron H. Lerner, "A Calculate Departure," *Washington Post*, March 2, 2004. Retrieved May 22, 2009, from www.biopsychiatry.com/misc/suicide.html.

33. Paige Bowers, "Final Exit: Compassion or Assisted Suicide?" *TIME*, March 2, 2009. Retrieved May 25, 2009, from http://www.time.com/time/nation/article/0,8599,1882418,00.html.

34. Press Release, *Final Exit Network*, February 26, 2009. Retrieved May 26, 2009, from http://www.finalexitnetwork.org/.

35. Robbie Brown, "Arrests Draw New Attention to Assisted Suicide," *The New York Times*, March 10, 2009. Retrieved May 29, 2009, from http://topics.nytimes.com/top/reference/timestopics/subjects/e/euthanasia/assisted_suicide/index.html.

36. See 33 above.

37. Dianne Coleman, Steve Drake, and Paul Longmore, "The Real Hemlock Society," *Broad Reach Training & Resources*. Retrieved June 20, 2008, from www.normemma.com/arhemloc.htm.

38. Scott Steepleton "Pioneering Professor, Wife Die in Apparent Double Suicide," *Santa Barbara News-Press*, September 18, 2003. Retrieved June 25, 2008, from http://www.garretthardinsociety.org/tributes/obit_sbnews_2003sep18.html.

39. Leon Kolankiewicz, "Tribute to Garret Hardin," The Garrett Hardin Society, October 2003. Retrieved June 23, 2008, from http://www.garretthardinsociety.org/tributes/tr_kolankiewicz_2003oct.html.

40. Frank Meile, "Living Within Limits and Limits on Living: Garrett Hardin and Ecology, Economy, and Ethics," *Skeptic*, Summer 1996, pp. 42–46. Retrieved July 1, 2008, from http://www.lrainc.com/swtaboo/stalkers/fm_hardn.html.

Chapter 20

The Assisted Death Debate I: Individual Morality

Fighting the ravages of Lou Gehrig's disease, fearing the prospect of choking on her own saliva, unwilling to linger for months in steady decline, Velma Howard (1919–1995), 76, of Belleville, Illinois, made a decision.

THE ASSISTED DEATH OF VELMA HOWARD

On a weekend in 1995, Velma and her husband, also 76, together with their two sons—one a Texas businessman, the other a Kansas judge—gathered at a convenient central point, a motel in Joplin, Missouri. There, after a day spent reminiscing, Velma willingly drank a mix of sleeping medicine and alcohol, then pulled a plastic bag over her head to end her life.

Although her death was swift and peaceful, it hardly escaped the notice of local authorities. Both husband and a son were charged with felonies, the one for providing the poison-laced orange juice Velma drank, the other for reading instructions on self-killing from the suicide manual, *Final Exit*. In other words, Velma's husband and son were charged with the crime of assisted death.

Assisted death is usually considered a form of euthanasia in which an individual expressing a wish to die prematurely is helped to accomplish that goal by another person, either by counseling and/or by providing a poison or other lethal instrument. As with Velma Howard's, the assisted death may be regarded as a homicide or suicide by local authorities, and the person giving assistance may be held responsible for the death.[1]

When asked by a reporter if the case wasn't really a moral issue, the prosecutor replied: "This case doesn't have anything to do with whether it's right or wrong to commit suicide. It just happens to be illegal in Missouri to help somebody to do so." A year later, with influential high courts elsewhere debating the constitutionality of assisted suicide, authorities dropped all charges.

The prosecutor's distinction between the moral and the legal notwithstanding, it is, in fact, the widely held assumption that assisted death is always immoral that drives its widespread prohibition. By the same token, it is the view that assisted voluntary death can be moral that argues against its prohibition. So, as a practical matter, despite the moral/legal distinction, how we answer the question of individual morality, "Ought I ever practice assisted suicide or have it practiced on me?" does influence our answer to the question of social policy: "Ought PAS [physician-assisted suicide] be legalized?" Little wonder, then, that the most vociferous opposition to its legalization come from those individuals, bodies, and institutions that consider PAS immoral; whereas support for its legalization comes overwhelmingly from those who think PAS can be moral under carefully defined circumstances. Both positions harken back to the age-old dialogue about the permissibility of suicide sketched in the previous chapter.

For moral guidance about PAS, many people turn to some principle or rule, either religious or secular. What honors their particular standard they consider right; what doesn't they consider wrong. Others, on the other hand, who view morality less about rules and principles than about virtue seek guidance in the character qualities of those engaging in PAS. Derek Humphry, for example, defended the Howards as being "solid citizens, unanimous in their decision, with no hint of impropriety." They were "decent people," said the author of *Final Exit*, "trying to handle a difficult situation."[2] But critics saw in the Howards something different: a perversion of compassion and love.

As we'll see in this chapter, these two traditional approaches to individual morality—principle and virtue—play leading, if morally ambiguous, roles in the discourse about assisted death.

PRINCIPLES

The Introduction made the point that moral principles, rules, or laws conceive of moral judgments and actions in terms of the question "What ought I do?" To that question each offers an answer. "Do what will maximize happiness," for example, or "Do what God wants you to do." Whatever the answer, it takes the form of a principle (rule or law) of conduct. Although the principles vary, the underlying assumption of all principle-based morality is that a "What ought I do?" question has an answer. This means that a question such as "Ought

I ever practice assisted death or have it practiced on me?" can be answered, once and for all, as yes or no, according to the principle.

But is it that easy? The last chapter's historical overview showed that different principles have led to opposed views about the morality of suicide and euthanasia. Thus, Bentham and Mill could justify both by appeal to social utility, whereas Kant condemned them as irresponsible acts, according to his categorical imperative. Now we're about to see that the *same* principle can lead to *opposed* conclusions. In fact, an application of, traditionally, the three most prominent moral principles—utility, respect, and divine command—turns up morally ambiguous answers about the propriety of assisted death. They seem to say not yes *or* no, but yes *and* no. This helps explain how opposed voices in today's social debate, both religious and secular, sometimes invoke the same principle to condemn or condone assisted death. It also helps explain the differences even among those who otherwise share a general worldview. Whereas they endorse a governing rule of morality within that perspective, say divine command or utility, they don't share the same interpretation of it.

By no means, however, does the variance in interpretation of principle turn up only in discussions of PAS. From the outset, with Schiavo, and throughout the vexing disputes about reproductive ethics, we have seen examples of parties, religious and secular, in accord on a moral rule but at odds on its application. The PAS controversy offers a golden opportunity to explicitly draw attention to this phenomenon and, thereby, deepen understanding of its controversial nature.

Utility/Happiness

As we saw in Chapter 2, according to classical utilitarians such as Bentham and Mill, following the "greatest happiness" or utility principle means doing what likely will yield the greatest net happiness of all alternatives. But in utilitarianism's pleasure/pain calculation, a question naturally arises as to whose interests are to be considered—the individual's or the society's? Is the yardstick of utility to be applied to personal or group net happiness?

In fact, as noted, classical utilitarianism allowed for either, depending on circumstances. Accordingly, a utility argument for PAS has been made on grounds of both self-interest and social interest. Much the same can be said of "preference satisfaction" utilitarianism.

Self-Interest Viewed as an isolated action taken to relieve pain and suffering, and affecting only a handful of people, the assisted deaths of individuals such as Velma Howard fall squarely in the tradition of act utilitarianism. They are among the many opportunities for people to live their lives as they see fit, based on their own values and beliefs, so long as they don't harm others. Hence, for Bentham and Mill a proper application of the utility principle permitted suicide and euthanasia as a demonstrably private affair. (Perhaps true to his position, Bentham is rumored to have requested euthanasia at the end of his life, although it's not known whether it was administered.)[3]

By the same token the principle of "preference satisfaction" would permit both PAS and voluntary active euthanasia (VAE). Thus, it could be argued that patients like Howard face a future whereby they will be able to satisfy very few preferences, indeed. Such patients, who inevitably lack opportunities for satisfying desires, plans, projects, mobility, and independent living, should be permitted a coherent and informed preference for assisted death. The preference satisfaction argument, or some version of it, was the most common one among all of Dr. Kevorkian's assisted deaths, beginning with the first, 54-year-old Janet Adkins (1936–1990), who, though still active and mentally coherent, preferred to die before losing her mind to Alzheimer's disease and being reduced to infant dependency.

Some theorists use the self-interest argument today to reason that having PAS available might, in fact, help patients choose life. The idea is that given the PAS option, patients are less likely to fear and, therefore, avoid aggressive medical treatments that, while risky and painful, could extend their lives.[4] Also, patients might be less anxious over their worsening condition and the prospect of uncontrolled pain and suffering.[5] Physician Timothy Quill echoed

this point in describing his assisted death of a leukemia patient he called "Diane." In his controversial 1991 admission that appeared in *The New England Journal of Medicine*, Quill wrote: "… it was … evident that the security of having enough barbiturates available to commit suicide when and if the time came would leave her secure enough to live fully and concentrate on the present."[6]

Another prominent American physician has expressed a similar view. In a 1977 article, also in *The New England Journal of Medicine*, Marcia Angell drew the following lesson from the self-inflicted death of her terminally ill father:

> If patients have access to drugs they can take when they choose, they will not feel they must commit suicide early, while they are still able to do it on their own. They would probably live longer and certainly more peacefully, and they might not even use the drugs.[7]

In the same year, a patient echoed Angell's sentiment:

> I'm so afraid of pain and being dependent, of not having my body parts work. I don't know if I could do it or would do it [commit suicide]. But I want the feeling of having a choice of ending what may be a horrible situation.[8]

Like this one, many patients today—and nonpatients, for that matter—assume that the availability of a quick and painless death is always in their best interests. But is it? Some think not and turn self-interest into an argument *against* assisted death.

Philosopher J. Gay-Williams, for one, worries that "[b]ecause death is final and irreversible, euthanasia contains within it the possibility that we will work against our own interest if we practice it or allow it to be practiced on us."[9] Although directing his remarks at VAE, defined as intentional killing, Gay-Williams's argument seems equally relevant to PAS.

Consider that mistaken diagnoses and prognoses are possible, because medicine doesn't have complete and perfect knowledge. We may think we're dying when we're not or believe we have a disease when we don't. Beyond this, we may have more life than reasonable medical judgment would expect. Indeed, according to federal officials, about 10% of patients live longer than the anticipated six-month life expectancy that in part defines "terminal" under Oregon's assisted suicide permit.[10] Moreover, according to a 1999 study, more than one-quarter of Oregon physicians willing to write a lethal prescription for a patient request they received were not confident they could determine when a patient had less than six months to live.[11]

But the argument from self-interest *against* assisted death goes well beyond considerations of diagnosis or prognosis. Assisted death, say some of its opponents, precludes the potential benefits of therapeutic experimental procedures, not to mention possible cure from spontaneous remission. Also, if knowing assisted death is available can bring comfort, might not the same knowledge incline one to give up too easily or because of concern for others? Then there's the matter of clinical depression that might be driving a suicide decision, or simple fear. In Germany recently, a 79-year-old retired X-ray technician was assisted to kill herself, although she was neither sick nor dying. She simply preferred death to moving into a nursing home. So, rather than face the prospect of institutionalization, the woman asked Roger Kusch, a prominent assisted death campaigner, for a way to satisfy her preference. He obliged with counsel about how to commit suicide, and she took it, swallowing a deadly cocktail of an antimalarial drug and a sedative.[12]

Beyond this, some opponents of PAS express the view that dying is potentially an opportunity for profound learning and spiritual development. For both psychologist M. Scott Peck (1936–2005) and psychiatrist Elisabeth Kubler-Ross (1926–2004), assisted death could prematurely end what they considered a divinely decreed, developmental process.[13,14] Dr. Ira Byock, past president of the American Academy of Hospice and Palliative Medicine, also suggests that dying can offer unique opportunities for individual learning, growth, and personal satisfaction.[15] According to such commentators, dying and death are part of the continuum of a person's life.

For their part, supporters of assisted death from self-interest willingly concede all these points. Yes, they say, sometimes, though rarely, a terminal diagnosis is mistaken and an experimental procedure is lost. And, yes, more needs be done of a psychiatric and psychological nature to rule out volition-limiting depression, although depression of itself doesn't make a decision irrational. (As Angell says, "Some of the vegetative symptoms of depression are similar to the symptoms of terminal illness.") But what weight any of these improbable factors carries in an end-of-life decision is, ultimately, the patient's call. And that is at the heart of the matter, according to PAS advocates. They say that if self-interest or preference satisfaction is to be the determinant, then we need to trust the individual to sort out these essentially personal and private matters. Illustrative, perhaps, is the goodbye letter to Kusch, in which the woman thanked him, saying that if her death helped his battle it would fulfill her goal to have "the freedom to die in dignity." For defenders of assisted death, then, the liberty argument is as fresh today as when Bentham made it more than a century-and-a-half ago.

Social Interest Of course, unlike suicide, assisted death is not a wholly private act. In both PAS and VAE, at least one person is facilitating the death of another—for instance, Kevorkian, Riccio (see Chapter 18), Quill, the Howards. This makes assisted deaths matters of public concern and social policy, which we'll address fully in the next chapter. Suffice it here to note that rule utilitarians, as opposed to act utilitarians, look beyond self-interest—beyond the pleasure/pain calculation for self—and consider the impact of one's acts on others, now and in the future. Thus: *What if everyone in a situation like the Howards helped their loved one to die? What if every physician in a similar situation acted as Quill or Riccio did? What would the social impact be of such conduct? Might it, as has been variously suggested, coarsen the value of life? Inevitably be abused? Concentrate too much power in the hands of physicians? Alter the nature of the medical profession for the worse?*[16–18] Or, on the other hand, perhaps these risks are worth taking. Angell, who is the former Editor-in-Chief of *The New England*

Journal of Medicine, says it's impossible to avoid the slippery slope in medicine, or anywhere else for that matter. Consider proxies to terminate life-sustaining treatment. They can be abused, but is that reason not to have them? "The question," Angell writes, "is not whether a perfect system can be devised, but whether abuses are likely to be sufficiently rare to be offset by the benefits to patients who otherwise would be condemned to face the end of their lives in protracted agony."[19] In her view, a rule can be fashioned in such a way that its social benefits outweigh its costs.

Respect for Persons

For many moralists it isn't utility or happiness that should govern morality but the respect for persons that Kant had in mind when he wrote that rational nature exists as an end in itself. In practice, this means that we are never to use each other merely as a means to our own selfish ends but always as ends in themselves. So, to the question "What ought I do?," one version of Kant's answer is: "Always treat others as ends in themselves, never merely as means to ends." This makes Kantian respect all about honoring autonomy, reciprocity, and dignity. Applying these three ideals to assisted suicide, however, turns up the same moral ambiguity as implementing utility does, Kant's own prohibition of suicide notwithstanding (see Chapter 19).

Autonomy   According to Kant, we should never allow anything to condition our freedom. But this is precisely what we do, he said, when we use our freedom against ourselves to take our own lives. For Kant, then, irreversibly relinquishing autonomy is simply not consistent with autonomy itself.

Curiously, the utilitarian Mill made a similar argument. Autonomy does not justify all voluntary acts, he wrote in his famous essay *On Liberty*, and gave slavery as an illustration. The slave

... by selling himself for a slave ... abdicates his liberty; he forgoes any further use of it beyond that single act. He therefore defeats, in his own case, the very purpose

which is the justification of allowing him to dispose of himself.... The principle of freedom cannot require that he should be free not to be free. It is not freedom to be allowed to alienate his freedom.

Some contemporary philosophers have extended this analysis of individual freedom and autonomy to euthanasia. They argue that, like slavery, "death irreversibly alienates autonomy and cannot be condoned by appeal to autonomy."[20]

But the reason we can't sell ourselves into slavery, a demurral goes, has less to do with the nature of autonomy than the sheer social costs of slavery. The same applies to authorizing another to end one's life. By this account, context and cost are the only terms for considering the morality of euthanasia. That, in turn, requires a sensible analysis of autonomy itself.[21] For assisted death advocates, being autonomous or self-determining means choosing for themselves. It means acting for their own reasons or based upon their own goals and aspirations. Given the great variability among individuals about the matter, then, it's most important that they themselves control how and when they die.[22] This is the view of a great many agnostics, atheists, humanists, secularists, and non-Christians. But it is also a view of many liberal Christians in North America, such as the United Church of Christ, as well as the Unitarian-Universalist, Methodist, Presbyterian, and Quaker movements.[23]

But what about the complex frame of mind of many patients with advance disease and the lack of personnel trained in the care of the dying? Such concerns lead neurologist and hospice expert Kathleen Foley, for one, to doubt that a suicide decision in these cases is ever the end product of a competent person making a rational, autonomous decision.[24] Some studies support her view.[25]

Even if a suicide decision can be competent, other critics of assisted death assail it as an abuse of individual freedom. "Freedom to kill," Pope Benedict XVI has said, "is not a true freedom but a tyranny that reduces the human being into slavery." And: "Scripture, in fact, clearly excludes every form of the kind of self-determination of human existence that is presupposed in the theory and practice of euthanasia."[26] By the pope's reckoning, self-determination is not the right to die but to refuse disproportionate treatment.

Beyond this, even if individual autonomy argues for assisted suicide, the good of the community, both medical and social, is also relevant. And the good of the community, according to commentators such as Callahan, is never merely the aggregate of self-directing individuals.[27]

Reciprocity Besides autonomy, Kantian respect for persons is commonly associated with the principle of reciprocity, whereby, in the fashion of the Golden Rule, we treat others as we would want to be treated. This prompts a pro-PAS argument: If involuntary euthanasia is objectionable because it goes against a person's will, then why, by the same token (of reciprocity), isn't it equally objectionable to go against the will of a person who wants to die?

Consider, too, another apparent double standard at the end of life. Most everyone would agree that the dying ought to be treated alike. Are they? Terminally ill patients are permitted to refuse life-*preserving* treatment, but they are not permitted life-*ending* treatment. And yet, in both cases the foreseen outcome is identical: death. Isn't that unequal and, therefore, unfair treatment?

No, it's not, say critics of assisted death. Simply because we may want to die doesn't mean we have the right to die. A killer who has acted with full knowledge of the consequences of his act is effectively saying: "Since I don't mind your killing me, it's okay for me to kill you." That doesn't make killing right. Also, PAS opponents point to the traditional distinction between suspending life-prolonging treatment and intentionally hastening death. The first is permitting nature to take its course or "allowing to die"; the latter is interfering with that natural process, or killing (see Chapter 18). For the many who make such distinctions, legitimating conditions under which one person can kill another is not only wrong, it represents still another way that life is cheapened and made expendable in the "culture of death."

Dignity Kantian respect for persons also means that we allow them to live with dignity, as they see fit. For one person that may include fighting for the last breath of life. For another, lying in a hospital bed, wasting away to something hardly recognizable as human, let alone one's former self, is the ultimate indignity.

"Death with dignity" makes perfect sense, assisted death opponents say, in the context of a "natural death." In other words, it is a gross indignity to thwart nature by artificially maintaining life instead of allowing someone to die. PAS and VAE, by contrast, are actually avoiding a natural death rather than facing it. Killing the patient is the real indignity.

But assisted death supporters call "killing" a loaded term. They point out that unlike the other two methods of hastening death—withdrawing life-sustaining treatment and euthanasia, both of which can be performed even if the patient is unaware of the decision—assisted suicide requires the patient's knowledge and participation. Where, then, is the indignity with PAS? Isn't the real indignity thwarting an informed choice for an assisted suicide?

As for those who say such a choice can never be voluntary, there are those requests made earlier in life in advance directives and then repeated when desperately ill. As one Oregon cancer specialist says: "I think there are people who are perfectly sane, who know what their future holds for them, and then don't want that. Those are the ones who want the death with dignity."[28] Supporting this view are studies showing that most patients who have chosen suicide under the Oregon permit have not been depressed and socially vulnerable, with untreated pain and without access to good hospice care. They have been individuals for whom being in control and not dependent are their most important values when dying.[29,30] But for religious conservatives, that is precisely the rub.

Convinced that God creates each one of us out of love and that life is a sacred trust, today's heirs to the medieval religious legacy insist that it is God, not we, who control our lives and our time on earth. "God alone has the power over life and death,"[31] may be the words of Pope John Paul II, but it's a sentiment that most religions share and expect others to engage. In the words of Walter Cardinal (then Bishop) Kasper, President of the Pontifical Council for the Promotion Christian Unity:

> [T]he Church respects the autonomy of human reason; she respects Its [sic] claim to truth. But she also asserts her own claim to truth and thus does not excuse philosophy from the duty of confronting the claim of God's word and the question about the meaning of life and the transcendence of the human spirit.[32]

Placed in the larger context of bioethics, the cardinal is prescribing a noteworthy relationship between the secular and religious. On the one hand, he is saying, the church respects reason as expressed in secular ethical theories such as utilitarianism and Kant's categorical imperative. On the other hand, he also maintains that secular moralists are duty-bound by intellectual honesty to confront the religious viewpoint, presumably as expressed in divine command, as it applies, for example, to questions of suffering and death. With that distinction a question arises: Just what is the proper relationship of secular and religious bioethics? This question has sparked passionate discourse in contemporary bioethics, at times acrimonious and polarizing, with serious economic, political, and policy implications.[33] The Conclusion of this book addresses this contentious topic.

Divine Command

As noted in Chapter 2, there are two interpretations of how humans come to a knowledge of God's will. The first is through special revelation, or Sacred Scriptures. The second is through general revelation, or religious natural law; that is, through the human intellect independently of divine revelation. Both figure prominently in religious analyses of assisted death and, in the view of religious conservatives, they should shape secular opinion as well.

Scriptural Teachings Of the seven suicides recorded in the Bible, none is expressly condemned. Nevertheless, as with abortion, religious conservatives, especially, insist that the authority of the Bible alone establishes the sanctity of life regardless of its condition or stage (Gen. 2:6-7; Job 1:21-23; Ex. 20:13). They say that the Bible's suicides must be read as narratives or stories (see Chapter 7) that, although not condemning suicide are, nonetheless, intended to teach godly living.

Consider the death of King Saul, who, mortally wounded after battle, threw himself on his own sword. (See 1 Samuel 31:1-6; 1 Chronicles 10:1-6.) Of this suicide two commentators write:

> Saul's suicide is not an isolated incident without moral comment. It is the tragic conclusion to a literary masterpiece soaked with moral comments. Tragedy implies that what is, ought not to be. Saul's hunger for control puts him on the battlefield alienated from God, family, and friends. Killing himself fits his frequent use of death to deal with his problems. To claim that Saul's story commends suicide is to misinterpret completely the purpose of tragic narrative. As understandable as his suicide is, it remains a tragic conclusion that should never have happened....[34]

Conservative Christians extend this interpretation of such Old Testament narratives to the New Testament, where they find their reading reinforced. Accordingly:

> The New Testament offers a way of life and a set of values which call for hope and contentment in life in spite of pain and suffering. It stresses the value of every individual and the role each can play in this world. It offers a way to live with suffering, knowing that the afterlife will have none. But it also teaches that God's sovereignty extends to people's bodies and their lives. Paul declares to his fellow Christians "You do not belong to yourself, for God bought you with a high price. So you must honor

God with your body." ... the earliest Christians regarded suicide as incompatible with this perspective.[35]

For believers, then, the Bible offers perspectives on suffering and death that are incompatible with suicide, assisted suicide, and euthanasia. It variously casts suffering as potentially redemptive, a divine mystery, an act of self-sacrifice, and a consequence of human evil that God asks us to resist. Thus, in 2005, responding to the suggestion of his chief adviser that "[t]here is a very strong compassionate case for voluntary euthanasia," Rowan Williams, Archbishop of Canterbury, said:

> Do I have a right to die? Religious believers answer for themselves that they do not. For a believer to say: "The time could come when I find myself in a situation that has no meaning, and I reserve the right to end my life in such a situation," would be to say that there is some aspect of human life where God cannot break through. It would be to say that when I as an individual can no longer give meaning to my life, it has no value, and human dignity is best served by ending it. That would be in the eyes of most traditional believers, Christian or otherwise, an admission that faith had failed. It would imply that life at a certain level of suffering or incapacity could no longer be lived in relation to God.[36]

In objection, it's said that the Bible's seven cases of suicide are simply not analogous to today's PAS-prompting medical situations. Also, as with all narratives, the Bible's are open to multiple interpretations. Some scholars have even found in the Bible a religious framework for defending PAS and VAE.

For example, St. Paul admonishes: "We know that so long as we are at home in the body we are exiles from the Lord. We would rather be exiled from the body and make our home with the Lord" (Cor 5:6-8. The Revised English Bible). Philosopher Robert Baird of Baylor University interprets Paul's vision as a caution against biological idolatry. "This suggests," he says, "that the body can be too much with us, that the body is not the ultimate value. Life alone, simple biological existence, is not the highest value." Baird concludes that if life isn't an absolute good always to be preserved, then death isn't an absolute evil always to be avoided.

It's important to note that Baird, a member of the Society of Christian Philosophers, is not absolutizing autonomy. He also acknowledges that any assisted death decision is a communal one; and, at times, being a responsible patient requires accepting the debilitation of old age or injury and passively undergoing death. Still, in his view:

> This Christian rejection of the absolute value of biological existence, in conjunction with the God-given freedom and responsibility to live productive lives and to provide comfort to the suffering, provides prima facie justification for active voluntary euthanasia in certain cases of intense suffering, in circumstances when conscious life is no longer a possibility, and in other situations of pointless existence.[37]

Religious Natural Law   As noted previously (see Chapter 2), underlying all natural law ethics are two critical assumptions: (1) there are tendencies or dispositions built into human nature and the mind; and, therefore, (2) the mind can discover them. Both of these assumptions figure in the traditional natural law argument against assisted death, euthanasia in particular. Thus, from the observation that every human being has a natural inclination to continue living, it is then asserted that reason alone tells us that euthanasia sets us against our own nature. Additionally, it is said, in Aristotelian fashion, that euthanasia does violence to our dignity as conscious beings who are not only naturally disposed toward survival but are aware of this disposition.

But critics are quick to hoist natural law proponents with their own theory. On the assumption that it is rationality that makes us fully human, natural law enjoins us to use reason, to act rationally. Why at the end of life, then, are we to suspend the use of the very faculty that is the essence of our humanity? If natural law suggests anything, say friends of PAS, it is that competent individuals be left free to decide such matters for themselves. This largely explains exceptions to the general prohibition of suicide in Aristotle, Plato, and the Stoics, all of whom trusted to reason.

The religious version of natural law attempts to overcome this objection and its exceptions by interpreting nature's law in terms of divine will. Recall that, placed in the context of revealed religion, natural law is not only the law of nature and reason but also a reflection of divine mind and plan (see Chapter 2). According to Aquinas, one of the discoverable, basic moral precepts of natural law involves self-preservation. Thus, because we have an innate disposition to preserve our lives and avoid what destroys it, our reason tells us that life is a basic good that we should not deliberately destroy. To do so, as with acts of assisted suicide, for example, is an offense against God, as well as reason and nature, according to Aquinas and today's religious orthodox.

Still, determining appropriate treatment for the dying often poses conflicts between goods we're naturally disposed toward. What to do, for example, when the goods and goals of saving life and saving suffering conflict? To reconcile the tension of conflicting dispositions, Aquinas proposed the "principle of double effect" (see Chapter 2).

Double Effect Recall from our discussion of abortion (Chapter 9) that the principle of double effect recognizes some actions have more than a single outcome; sometimes bad things must come with good things. Dousing a dying patient with pain-relieving opiates, for example, saves pain, a good effect; *and* inevitably hastens death, putatively a bad effect. What morally matters in such cases, according to Aquinas, is intention. If the physician's intention is to save pain and not end life, under the principle of double effect it would permissible to "allow" death to occur. But it would be wrong to provide a large amount of opiate for the purpose of killing the patient.

The same reasoning applies to a decision to discontinue "disproportionate," "extraordinary," or "heroic" life-prolonging measures. These are medicines, treatments, and procedures that don't offer any reasonable hope of benefit to the patient and that involve excessive pain, expense, or other significant burdens. What constitutes "disproportionate treatment" in a clinical setting and who decides aren't always easy to determine. Still, the consensus of moral opinion, both religious and secular, invests in these distinctions enough to base moral judgments upon them.[38,39]

But sorting out actions by intention is tricky, as we saw earlier with Dr. Hootan Roozrokh (Chapter 17). When a dying patient is sedated, can the physician really limit his intention to a single good—saving pain and suffering—while not intending to destroy the other good, life itself? When a physician knows that a massive dose of opiate will end life along with pain, doesn't he really intend both? The larger, philosophical significance of this question is that if double effect doesn't work, then the unsettled conflict between fundamental goods may end up undermining the widely applied natural law theory itself.[40]

There's another difficulty with double effect and, implicatively, natural law. If we're naturally inclined to live, we are also naturally inclined to live free of pain. Minimizing pain, in short, is a natural human disposition that the application of double effect to end-of-life cases implicitly acknowledges. But where death may be hastened to relieve suffering, albeit not intentionally, isn't relief of suffering being given a higher moral priority than the maintenance of life? Aren't we actually saying, "To maintain life under these circumstances would be injurious"?

Now, if life saving can be "injurious," life saving can also be "non-injurious." According to double effect and natural law, we are always morally obligated to support non-injurious life saving (that is, "proportionate" or "ordinary" treatment); but we're not morally obligated to support injurious life saving (that is, "disproportionate" or "extraordinary" treatment). Usually, according to both religious and secular natural law, we may deliberately take measures to avoid injurious prolongation of life for reasons of burden and consent. In practice this simply means that a patient may heroically endure, but is not thus obligated. He may opt out when he judges the burden to be too great. The

BIOETHICS ACROSS CULTURES

Englaro Case Tears Italy Apart

The death of Eluana Englaro in Italy on February 9, 2009, echoed around the world. After a car accident in 1992, Eluana, then 21, lived for seventeen years in a vegetative state in a Catholic nursing home. However, her father, Beppino Englaro, thought that she would be better off dead. After years of legal battles, he won. Italy's highest court, the Cassation, allowed him to withdraw food and water. Three days later his daughter died, but not before involving the Vatican, reigniting debate in Italy over euthanasia, and bringing Italy to a constitutional crisis.

Politicians and commentators said that senior Italian cardinals and the Vatican had forced Prime Minister Silvio Berlusconi's government to step in at the last minute, defying the court order to discontinue life support. "This is murder," Berlusconi declared. "I would be failing to rescue her. I'm not a Pontius Pilate," a reference to the Roman procurator who ordered the crucifixion of Jesus and appears in all four canonical Christian Gospels. Then, when Italy's President Giorgio Napolitano refused to carry out Berlusconi's decree, the Vatican weighed in, voicing its support for Berlusconi and pleading Napolitano to change his mind. But Napolitano remained steadfast. He said that as head of state he had the say in constitutional matters and that the government, through its decree on Eluana, was interfering with a ruling made by Italy's independent judiciary. But Roman Catholic Church officials, conservative politicians, and others who campaigned to keep Eluana alive, said the court order amounted to euthanasia, a procedure not

permitted under Italian law, whereas refusal of medical treatment is. But time was against Berlusconi, the Vatican, and their many backers. Eluana, who was now 38, died before the Italian parliament could act on the decree and possibly halt the process that the court order had set in motion.

After her death, charges and countercharges flew around Italy and greater Europe. Berlusconi and the Vatican's health minister, Cardinal Javier Lozano Barragán, termed the action "murder." Pro-life groups branded the father of the dead woman a murderer. Beppino Englaro retaliated by suing for damages against those who he alleged had defamed him. Meanwhile, some political analysts characterized Berlusconi's opposition to the courts and the head of state as attempts to further cement his power in the country. James Walston, an American teaching Italian politics at the American University of Rome, said that Berlusconi was trying to reduce the power of the courts and the residual powers of the president. "If he succeeds, it's a form of coup," Watson said. "He is basically changing the Italian constitution. And he is doing this with the support of the Vatican, which is a strong ally."

For its part, the Vatican remained firm. "May God forgive them," a senior Vatican official said, as the news that Eluana had died came through. But the former Archbishop of Milan, Cardinal Carlo Maria Martini, said terminally ill patients should have the right to refuse treatment. The cardinal, who has Parkinson's disease, said he opposed both killing the terminally ill and "unreasonably obstinate" treatments that keep

---

general obligation to preserve life, then, may be overridden if doing so results in disproportionate burden or, simply, is injurious. But if prolongation of life can be injurious or non-injurious, doesn't that imply that killing can be?

Consider the example of a cat writhing in pain after being mangled by a dog attack. In putting the cat out of its misery, philosopher Richard Brandt (1910–1977) once suggested that he had indeed killed the cat "but surely not *injured* it." Why? Because, said Brandt, we don't injure something by relieving its pain. "If someone is being tortured and roasted to death and I know he wishes nothing

more than a merciful termination of life, I have not injured him if I shoot him; I have done him a favor."[41] More generally, "I have not injured a person if I treat him in a way in which he would want me to treat him if he were fully rational, or in a way to which he would be indifferent."[42]

If Brandt was correct in his analysis, then the basic principle about killing needs to be phrased to take into account (1) whether the killing would be an injury and (2) the person's own wishes and directives. More important, the unqualified commandment "thou shalt not kill" (Ex. 20:13; Deut. 5:17) cannot be taken as a correct extension them alive. Senator Giulio Andreotti, who recently turned ninety and is as close to the Vatican as an Italian politician can be, simply said "the Calvary of Eluana" should never have been a political issue, alluding to the place in Jerusalem where the crucifixion of Jesus took place (Luke 23:33; Matt. 27:33). "We are dealing with a family which has been heavily tested by a tragedy, and no one can arrogate the right to decide it imperiously," the seven-time Christian Democrat prime minister said.

Meanwhile, comments coming from other European countries reflected a divided continent. Countries that permit assisted death—Belgium, The Netherlands, Luxembourg—were critical of Bersculoni's intervention, whereas the ultra-Catholic south, supported it. The harshest criticism of the Italian prime minister and the Vatican came from the left-leaning German daily *Die Tageszeitung*, which editorialized on February 10, 2009:

> The church can be happy to have such a willing advocate in Italy's government, one who does not hesitate to declare the Vatican's 'natural law'—the opposition to any form of assisted suicide—the sole standard. In this way the two men are letting the Englaro family feel the full weight of their authority. All of this has less to do with an ethical debate on euthanasia than with a church's pre-democratic claim to absolutism and its henchman, the state. This Roman alliance could not be more unholy.

(SOURCES: Richard Owen, "Tangled up in Politics," *The Tablet*, March 21, 2009. Retrieved March 24, 2009, from http://www.thetablet.co.uk/article/12668; DW Staff, "Right To Die Case Sparks Italian Constitutional Row, *Deutsche Welle*, February 2, 2009. Retrieved March 25, 2009, from http://www.dworld.de/dw/article/0,4010502,00.html; NA, "Englaro Family Sue for Defamation, "*Italy Magazine*, March 5, 2009. Retrieved March 26, 2009, from http://www.italymag.co.uk/italy/religion; NA, "Italy Faces Constitutional Crisis over Woman in Coma," *Algeria.com*, February 8, 2009. Retrieved March 30, 2009, from www.algeria.com/forums/world-dans-le-monde/24625-italy-faces-constitutional-crisis-over-coma-woman.html; Elisabetta Provoledo, "Italy Seeks To Clarify Right-To-Die Issue," *Boston.com*, February 11, 2009. Retrieved April 1, 2009, from www.boston.com/news/world/europe/articles/2009/02/11/italy_seeks_to_clarify_right_to_die_issues/; NA, "Italy: Coma Patient Eluana Englaro Dies After Berlusconi Row," *Cafebabel.com*, February 10, 2009. Retrieved May 28, 2009, from http://www.cafebabel.com/ita/article/28608/press-review-europe-death-italy-euthaniasia.html.)

Question

The case of Eluana Englaro deeply divided Italy and Europe generally over the influence of the Vatican. Undoubtedly, it will take time to heal the rift the case opened in a Roman Catholic country where the church holds much influence among politicians, who, themselves, split along religious rather than party lines on the issue. After Eluana's death, Giovanni Maria Vian, editor of the Vatican newspaper *L'Osservatore Romano*, wrote: "After weeks of anguish and polemics the time has come for a reflection that can unite believers and nonbelievers." What lessons would you draw from this case that "believers and nonbelievers" could agree upon? Are any of the lessons applicable to us here in America about political intervention in cases like these?

of natural law. It needs shaping by relevant considerations in assisted deaths, specifically considerations of autonomy and burden.

To the question of whether there's an obligation to sustain the life and suffering of a patient against his autonomous request for a termination of his existence, Brandt wrote, "Surely not." And he denied an obligation to refuse the patient death support. As he said, "What possible reason could be offered to justify the claim that [there is such an obligation] beyond theological ones about God's will and our being bound to stay alive at His pleasure?" But that, of course, is precisely the reason of

religious natural law that religious and many social conservatives publicly uphold.[43] Life is a gift of God, they say, and each individual is its steward. Thus, "only God can start a life, and only God should be allowed to end one. An individual who commits suicide is committing sin."[44]

VIRTUE

For virtue, or character, ethicists, the question "Ought I ever practice assisted death or allow it to be practiced on me?" can only be answered in reference to what it means to be a morally good person, and not—as principle-based ethicists hold—by appeal to some moral principle, such as utility, respect for persons, or divine command. Earlier, in Chapter 7, we saw that, following Aristotle, some contemporary virtue ethicists identify the good or virtuous person with particular character qualities, such as self-discipline, courage, compassion, flexibility, open-mindedness, even intuition. Above all, they identify the good person with Aristotle's notion of *phronesis*, or practical wisdom, which he viewed as a habit of mind that enables us to avoid the defects of excess and deficiency, and act in the mean.

Some modern virtue theorists associate *phronesis* with applying lessons learned to new situations in, perhaps, novel and creative ways. Thus, according to Joseph DesJardins, *phronesis* "requires us to fit our reasoning to the situation and to avoid forcing the situation into preconceived categories."[45] This makes the morally permissible action one that a person of *phronesis* or practical wisdom would perform in the circumstances. What makes the action permissible is not that a virtuous person would perform it, but certain other characteristics of the act, such as its being courageous or compassionate. What a virtuous person does, then, suggests the action is permissible, without establishing it as so. The question therefore becomes: Would a virtuous person—a person of *phronesis* or practical wisdom—ever assist death?

In one sense, no. If, as Aristotle held, the point of life is to attain *eudaimonia*—that is, to fulfill ourselves through the development of our character—then acts of suicide obviously make that impossible.[46] Certainly this is a significant consideration for virtue ethics, which is profoundly concerned with the effect of what we do on what we become. But virtue ethics is also about how what we do *reflects* what we are. So, it can be asked: *What does an assisted death decision say of one's moral character? What sort of people generally practice PAS/VAE or have it practiced on them? Do they tend to be virtuous—for example, temperate, persevering, honest, rational, and compassionate? Why do they choose to end their own lives or help others do so? Are their reasons selfish or unselfish? Well-considered or rationalizing? Have their lives, in general, exhibited characteristics we admire, or not?*

Some public figures have answered with generalizations they have formed based on extensive studies of so-called suicide personalities.[47] For example, Burke Balch, a lawyer who directs the Department of Medical Ethics for the National Right to Life Committee, flatly says that people attempting suicide are "deranged and in need of psychological help, and, therefore, in no position to make an accurate assessment of their circumstances."[48] This leads Balch and other Christians generally to urge compassionate counseling, as with hospice, together with medical and psychological care as an alternative to assisted death.

But is this assessment fair and accurate? Can an assisted death decision *ever* be rational, even courageous and compassionate? Certainly Dr. Timothy Quill thinks so.

Quill, who knew leukemia patient "Diane" for eight years, describes her as an "incredibly clear, at times brutally honest, thinker and communicator," with "a strong sense of independence and confidence." Although alternately fearful, angry, and sad upon learning she had an acute form of the blood disease, these emotions were not the main determinants of her decision. On the contrary, says Quill, "... she had a remarkable grasp of the options and implications"; and "it was extraordinarily important to Diane to maintain in control of herself and her own dignity during the time remaining to her. When this was no longer possible, she clearly wanted to die."[49]

If virtue ethics is only about becoming a good person and cultivating morally desirable character traits, then Diane seems to have failed, because she made *her own* further moral development impossible. But from another perspective, she succeeded. In Quill's opinion, Diane exhibited a high order of virtue. And if the virtuous life is also about teaching and inspiring and presenting ideals or models for others, then, on her physician's testimony, Diane's life and death serve as an exemplar. Indeed, fully persuaded that he and her family gave Diane the best possible care,

Dr. Quill retrospectively says of his patient's impact on him:

> Diane taught me about the range of help I can provide if I know people well and if I allow them to say what they really want. She taught me about life, death, and honesty. And about taking charge and facing tragedy squarely when it strikes. She taught me I can make small risks for people that I really know and care about.[50]

In a word, Diane made Dr. Quill a better physician, and Timothy Quill a better man.

Diane's professional impact on *Dr.* Quill reminds us that, beyond the general interest in moral character or integrity, some forms of virtue ethics address character strengths as they relate to particular social roles or professions. Given the physician's central role in assisted death, this aspect of virtue ethics bears some attention, especially because opposed constructions of "the good doctor" have divided physicians as well as the general public.

Roles and Professions

Taking their lead from the Hippocratic Oath's most important injunction—"do no harm"— many physicians and others would agree that the virtuous physician, the "good doctor," avoids assistance in death. The AMA goes further, saying that PAS threatens the integrity of the medical profession. In the language of virtue ethics, then, the AMA's assisted death prohibition partly defines professional excellence in end-of-life medical decisions. It is what the profession's governing body thinks is necessary both to be a good doctor and to sustain medicine as a social institution.

Not everyone, however, agrees with this interpretation of the Hippocratic Oath. Why they don't relates to an important philosophical point about virtues.

According to Alasdair MacIntyre, current standards of excellence never once-and-for-all define a socially based practice; they only *partially* do.[51] At any given moment, then, what medicine is depends on a way of understanding the practice of medicine that has developed over hundreds of years. As such, medicine's standards of excellence are subject to review, criticism, amendment, and change by its practitioners. Historically, for example, physicians were held to the Hippocratic prohibition of abortion: "I will not give a woman an abortive remedy." But today a physician who does an abortion can still be widely, though not universally, considered a good or virtuous doctor who does not threaten the survival of medicine as a social institution. With respect to abortion, then, the understanding of the practice of medicine has changed. That change has effectively expanded the conception of excellence in the practice of medicine to allow for abortion, vigorous and sometimes violent opposition notwithstanding.

On the other hand, the prohibition of assisted death, which appears in the same Hippocratic passage as the abortion prohibition, still largely stands: "I will neither give a deadly drug to anybody if asked for it, nor will I make a suggestion to this effect." Even more than abortion, many today feel that this traditional prohibition needs reinterpretation in the context of the complex, technology-driven end-of-life issues that arise in a modern clinical setting. Excellent medical practice, they suggest, should include assisted death, and a Dr. Quill should stand as a good or virtuous doctor. (Some also point out that Hippocrates' famous injunction upon physicians was actually about suicide in general, but not specifically PAS or VAE.)[52]

Is prolonging life the limit of a physician's responsibility to a patient? Or does it sometimes go beyond that to include helping patients die? What is to be regarded professional excellence in employing life-prolonging measures?

For religious and social conservatives and the AMA, the test is reasonable quality of life and level of function, defined by the patient's own life goals, supported by hospice-style terminal care. On the other side are cultural liberals and physicians who feel that when suffering cannot be relieved it would be an abrogation of medical power to abandon the patient, especially when through that same power the patient's life and suffering have been artificially extended. In the language of character ethics, according to the progressive view, not to assist the consenting patient's death can fall short of

BIOETHICS ACROSS CULTURES

The Groningen Protocol

On November 28, 2000, Holland became the first country in the world formally to legalize euthanasia. Under the law doctors are immune from prosecution provided they follow strict guidelines when performing a "mercy killing." The patient must be in intolerable pain, face "a future of unremitting and unbearable suffering," and make the request. Additionally, there must be no reasonable alternative solution to the patient's situation; their doctor must always consult another independent physician; and the euthanasia must be performed with due medical care.

Despite its circumspection, the controversial law hardly ended the 25-year-old debate in The Netherlands, pitting right-to-die campaigners and the medical profession against Holland's religious communities, whom the legitimization of a long-tolerated process outraged. It "will open the floodgates," critics warned, and give doctors "a license to kill." A Calvinist Party leader warned: "Only God can decide when life ends .... Already many old and lonely people are made to feel there is no point in living, now those suffering from dementia will be at increased risk of having others decide on whether they live or die." Five years later, religious sentiment seemed prophetic.

In 2005, Dutch pediatrician Eduard Verhagen admitted that he had given lethal injections to four babies born with spina bifida, a condition that prenatal surgery sometimes corrects. Verhagen said,

> All four babies had spina bifida—not the usual type, but severely affected children where this was not the only problem. They were in constant pain. In the last minutes or seconds you see the pain relax and they fall asleep ... at the end, after the injection, their fists unclench and there is relief for everyone in the room. Finally they get what they should have been given earlier.

Verhagen, who works at Groningen University Medical Centre, was one of a group of doctors who at the time were proposing a procedure that came to be called the Groningen Protocol to decide how much a child has to be suffering for lethal injection. The Groningen Protocol states that:

> diagnosis and prognosis must be certain; hopeless and unbearable suffering must be present; the diagnosis, prognosis and unbearable suffering must be confirmed by at least one independent doctor; both parents must give informed consent; the procedure must be performed in accordance with the accepted medical standard.

In an interview on National Public Radio, Verhagen said, "We felt that in these children the most humane course of action would be to allow the child to die, and even actively assist them in their death .... And in extreme cases, the best way to protect life is to sometimes assist a little bit in death."

Adopting the Groningen Protocol makes Holland the first country in the world to allow "baby euthanasia."

(SOURCES: Thaddeus M. Baklinski, Pediatric Neurosurgeons Criticize Dutch Practice of Euthanasia on Babies with Spina Bifida," *LifeSiteNews.com*, January 16, 2008. Retrieved May 23, 2009, from www.lifesitenews.com/ldn/2008/jan/08011610.html; NA, "Euthanasia Doctor Admits to Killing 4 Newborns with Lethal Injections," *LifeSiteNews.com*, April 27, 2005. Retrieved May 23, 2009, from http://www.lifesitenews.com/ldn/2005/apr/05042706.html; Isabel Conway, "Holland Is First Country To legalize Euthanasia," *The Independent*, November 29, 2000. Retrieved May 22, 2009, from http://www.independent.co.uk/news/world/europe/holland-is-first-country-to-legalise-euthanasia-622930.html; Matthew Campbell, "Holland To Allow 'Baby Euthanasia,' *Times Online*, March 5, 2006. Retrieved May 25, 2009, from www.timesonline.co.uk/tol/news/world/article737519.ece.)

Question

With which ethical principle(s) would you associate permissive assisted death policy in Holland? Prior to the Groningen Protocol, physicians and parents generally withdrew treatment and let the infant with untreatable disease and unbearable suffering die "naturally," an approach religious opinion generally tolerated and one practiced all over the world. From a moral point of view, is there any difference between this practice and administering, say, a lethal dose of morphine, given that the result is the same: death?

The Groningen Protocol has angered opponents of euthanasia who warn of a "slippery slope" leading to abuses by doctors and parents who will be making decisions for individuals incapable of expressing a will. Others welcome more openness about a practice that, according to doctors, goes on secretly anyway. What is your view of the likely effects of the Groningen Protocol?

professional excellence for failing the core bioethical principles: respect for persons (for not respecting autonomy), nonmaleficence (for extending pain or suffering), beneficence (for not conferring a benefit), and even justice (for not repairing the harm done by extending the life in the first place). To abandon such patients, in brief, can be a professional failure, whereas assisting their deaths, as with "Diane," can be professional excellence.[53]

But even granting Quill's compassion and respect for his young patient, is that enough to justify physician-death assistance? No, say Quill's critics, who view the physician's cooperation in Diane's death as a perversion of compassion, as did critics of Dr. Riccio in the death of Piergiorgio Welby (Chapter 18). Dr. Edmund Pellegrino, for one, writes: "The moral psychology of an act has a certain weight in assessing an agent's guilt, but not in changing the nature of the act itself."[54] Rather than improving the physician-patient relationship, and thus the practice of medicine, Pellegrino believes that Quill's misplaced compassion threatens both by presenting "opportunities for conscious or unconscious abuse of [physician] power." He warns that "[w]hen assisted suicide is legitimated, it places the patient at immense risk from the 'compassion' of others," adding: "Misdirected compassion in the face of human suffering can be as dangerous as indifference." For Pellegrino, a Georgetown University professor of medical ethics who has written widely on the importance of virtue in the practice of medicine, compassion requires the constraint of moral principle in the matter of assisted death.[55]

Perhaps so, but can't we say the same of principle? Uncoupled from virtue, isn't principle subject to abuse? It was Adolf Eichmann (1906–1962), after all, who deported millions of European Jews to death camps and later quoted Immanuel Kant at his trial (session 105). Is the highest ethical imperative of the physician to save life no matter what the cost in suffering? No, says physician Angell, "The highest ethical imperative of doctors should be to provide care in whatever way best serves patients' interest, in accord with each patient's wishes."[56] By the ethic of care, then, assisted death is for some physicians a natural extension of the physician's calling to heal. And if

healing is the highest medical imperative, then some doctors support PAS for that reason. Dr. Quill couldn't heal Diane's body, but he could heal her overwhelming sense of helplessness. The same applies to Dr. Riccio.

But to opponents of assisted death, the proper response to such patients is sympathy and empathy, period. Patients like Diane, they say, underscore not the need for assisted death but rather the profound inadequacy of pain control and general care for the chronically ill and dying. Cultural denial and avoidance of death support this social and professional failure, they say.[57,58]

On the other hand, Quill was empathetic. A former hospice physician, he was also an expert in pain relief. Indeed, according to philosopher Nancy Jecker, who is partial to the ethic of care (Chapter 7), the source of Quill's moral quandary was the laudable personal relationship he'd formed with Diane over the years. As a result, Diane wasn't merely a patient of Quill's; she was a particular person whose ends and good Quill ultimately held as his own. Were their relationship impersonal—were Diane "just another patient"—then Quill could have detached from her specific needs and invoked some abstract rule appropriate to his role as a doctor. He might have reasoned, for example, that doing PAS would undercut the trust in the medical profession, "while ignoring the actual basis of Diane's trust in him." Alternatively, he might have invoked the Hippocratic maxim "Do no harm," "while discounting what harm meant to Diane." Doing either, Jecker believes, would have been an evasion of Diane's moral claim on Quill owing to their laudable personal relationship.[59]

Jecker is saying that being a physician does not permit one to engage in PAS, but being a physician *in a personal relationship with a patient* may. Quill's experience, then, leads Jecker to conclude, "the love and care one harbors for a particular person may impel one to intervene and hasten death." Care and concern, in short, may make it impermissible to stand by and allow a protracted illness to run its painful course.

In Oregon two groups have organized with opposed positions on PAS. The one that opposes

PAS, the so-called pro-life group, calls itself Physicians for Compassionate Care. The one that favors PAS, the so-called pro-choice group, calls itself Compassion in Dying. That both draw their inspiration from the same virtue, compassion, is emblematic not only of deep divisions about the morality of assisted death but also of the difficulty of applying virtue theory to that issue. Our examination of principle-based theory turned up exactly the same challenge. Neither principle nor virtue, it seems, casts unambiguous light on the morality of assisted death. This inherent difficulty of implementing moral theory in individual, end-of-life situations defines the struggle to reach cultural consensus and form social policy about PAS, as we'll see in the next chapter.

CASES AND CONTROVERSIES

The Coup de Grace

In the pivotal scene of *The Coup de Grace*, the American author Ambrose Bierce (1842–1914?) captures the physical horror of war, when Captain Madwell encounters his friend, Sergeant Halcrow, lying mortally hurt after a Civil War battle. "The only visible wound," Bierce writes, is "a wide ragged opening in the abdomen" that is "defiled with earth and dead leaves." Protruding from the wound is a "loop of intestine." Madwell, an experienced warrior, has never seen a wound like it. But he does recognize the dark figures on a wooded hill fifty yards away as a herd of swine, feeding on the dead and wounded soldiers. The captain draws away his eyes and fixes them again upon what remains of his friend.

> The man who had suffered these monstrous mutilations was alive. At intervals he moved his limbs; he moaned at every breath. He stared blankly into the face of his friend and if touched screamed. In his giant agony he had torn up the ground on which he lay; his clenched hands were full of leaves and twigs and earth. Articulate speech was beyond his power; it was impossible to know if he were sensible to anything but pain. The expression of his face was an appeal; his eyes were full of prayer. For what?
>
> There was no misreading that look; the captain had too frequently seen it in eyes of those whose lips had still the power to formulate it by an entreaty for death. Consciously or unconsciously, this writhing fragment of humanity, this type and example of acute sensation, this handiwork of man and beast, this humble, unheroic Prometheus, was imploring everything, all, the whole non-ego, for the boon of oblivion. To the earth and the sky alike, to the trees, to the man, to what ever took form in sense or consciousness, this incarnate suffering addressed that silent plea.
>
> For what, indeed? For that which we accord to even the meanest creature without sense to demand it, denying it only to the wretched of our own race: for the blessed release, the rite of uttermost compassion, the coup de grâce.[60]

Out of cartridges, Madwell draws his sword from the scabbard and, with his left hand, tears the sergeant's shirt away from his chest and places the sword just over the heart. Then, with all his strength and weight, he thrusts downward.

Questions for Analysis

1. Is Madwell justified in putting his friend "out of his misery"?

2. If Madwell doesn't act as he does, what will he be responsible for?

3. How is a battlefield euthanasia like this one different from the more familiar cases of euthanasia today?

4. Is Foot's dying soldier illustration (Chapter 18) relevant to Bierce's depiction?

5. Which ethical theories and principles do you think are the most relevant to a case like this?

6. If a friend or relative of yours were clearly going to die and were in agonizing, unmitigated pain, without the possibility of any medical attention, what would you do if you were sure he or she wanted you to hasten death?

CASES AND CONTROVERSIES

Hurricane Katrina: Mercy Killing When Disaster Strikes

On September 1, 2006, two days after the costliest and one of the deadliest hurricanes passed east of New Orleans, conditions at local medical centers resembled battle zones. Power and sanitation were out. Basements flooded, knocking out generators. Without air conditioning, hospital temperatures soared to 100 degrees, affecting food supplies. The ability to get clean running water and dispose of waste products were also compromised. Such were the conditions that Dr. Anna Pou found herself working under at New Orleans' Memorial Medical Center, as she strived to provide care to patients.

Like other hospital personnel, Dr. Pou had to decide who the most critical patients were and who could be safely moved, because all of the patients could not be relocated at the same time. Who would go first? Who would have to wait or even be left behind? Swift but well-considered decisions had to be made. Unfortunately, not all of the patients at Memorial and some other area hospitals made it out alive. According to authorities, thirty-four fatalities were reported from Pou's Memorial Medical Center alone.

In the aftermath of Hurricane Katrina and amidst rumors of mercy killings at flooded hospitals, the State Attorney General's office opened an investigation, leading to the arrests of Pou and nurses Cheri Landry and Lori Budo, the following summer. The three were charged with being principals to second-degree murder in the deaths of four elderly patients, accused of administering lethal amounts of morphine and the sedative Versed to elderly patients who might have survived the hospital ordeal. Accusing the three women of "playing God," State Attorney General Charles Foti said that at least four hospital administrators knew of plans to give lethal injections to patients deemed too sick to survive, including a 92-year-old man. Through their attorneys, Pou and the nurses vigorously defended their actions and proclaimed their innocence.[61]

The sensational charges led to a spirited debate about the ethics of mercy killing and the responsibilities of doctors and nurses who are required to stay behind when an area has been evacuated ahead of an approaching storm. From right-to-die advocate Derek Humphry came this opinion:

> It seems to me that this New Orleans hospital medical team was placed in a terrible situation with the dying people in their care. Thus the most humane thing to do, rather than abandon them to die in appalling conditions caused by the hurricane, was to quietly hasten their inevitable ends with sedative drugs.[62]

The Military Ethicist David Perry cited a possible exception to the military prohibition of mercy killing: "'[I]t might be worse to let this person die of starvation or suffocation or drowning if the person didn't want that … than to do something more actively.'" Steven Miles, bioethicist at the University of Minnesota Medical School, suggested that the defendants were less likely trying to kill the patients than relieve their pain. But other ethicists and doctors weren't as understanding or forgiving. Noted University of Pennsylvania bioethicist Arthur Caplan, for one, said that either the personnel were trying to save themselves and didn't want to feel guilty about abandoning their patients; or, given the conditions, all possibility of maintaining the patients had to come to an end. Either way, said Caplan, their behavior was inexcusable under American law.[63]

On July 24, 2007, a grand jury declined to indict Dr. Anna Maria Pou. Prosecutors earlier had declined to charge the two nurses also blamed for the deaths. Two years later, however, a *New York Times Magazine* article prompted authorities to reevaluate the events surrounding the patient deaths. The article quoted two other doctors who admitted to hastening patient deaths.[64]

Questions for Analysis

1. Compare the post-Katrina events with those depicted in *The Coup de Grace*.

2. Explain why you think the grand jury did or did not reach the morally right decision.

3. Is a physician ever justified under conditions like those created by Hurricane Katrina in administering a quick and painless death to a patient; or is that always wrong, even if it means abandoning the patient to a slower and more painful death? Justify your view by moral principle(s).

4. What should we, as a society, expect of medical personnel like Dr. Pou in the face of a natural or human-made disaster?

5. Discuss this case in the context of the disagreement between James Rachels and Philippa Foot over the distinction between euthanasia and allowing to die, as discussed in Chapter 18.

CASES AND CONTROVERSIES

Does Responsible Care Include Assisted Dying?

In response to the growing legalization of assisted suicide, a contributor to Medscape's Physician Connect (MPC), a physician-only discussion board, asked: "Would you consider writing a lethal prescription for a terminally ill patient who wants to die, if such an action was legal in your state?" The resulting discussion showed that physicians are as divided about assisted suicide as the US public.

Some responses, like this one, echoed the position of the AMA: "Killing is not within the purview of a physician .... For those of us who take our responsibility honestly and seriously, euthanasia will never be acceptable." But some respondents pointed to the preeminence of individual autonomy in modern bioethics, such as this view from an emergency medicine physician: "Modern American medical ethics is very concerned about patient autonomy, the right of every patient to determine his or her own medical care, which, to be internally consistent, would include voluntary termination of life." From an oncologist came an even stronger endorsement of patient choice:

> Our job is to do what is in the best interest of our patients ... whether we agree with it or not. What if 'do no harm' means 'let me end my life' in a particular situation? One should have a right to die in a dignified, honorable manner and not after months of emaciation on a ventilator.

Then there were those responses that showed ambivalence, such as one from the internist who wrote:

> If we continue to let patients suffer when our pain control measures have reached their limit, aren't we causing harm? If we put a patient on a morphine drip and continuously increase the rate to maintain some degree of comfort, we can produce respiratory arrest. Isn't that euthanasia? Frankly, I don't know what I'd do if I lived in a state where euthanasia was legal.

Other physicians chose to frame the question in terms of pain control rather than assisted dying. A family medicine physician commented, "I dare suppose that most people who express a wish to die are primarily communicating a wish to end their suffering, but that death is neither the sole nor best treatment option." Others frankly admitted inadequate knowledge of pain management and problems caring for the terminally ill. One contributor said:

> I had an acquaintance who thought she would end her mother's suffering by administering a large dose of morphine. Fact was the patient was in pain, and when an adequate dose was supplied, she slept for 8 hours. No need for euthanasia, just adequate pain management.

Then there were those physician-respondents who thought that those desiring a quick, pain-free death needn't involve them at all. "Their lethal medication is right in their medicine cabinet or on the over-the-counter shelves at their pharmacy. Why should they involve their docs?" A psychiatrist commented, "I just don't want my name on the bottle or referral. I trust they will have the ingenuity to figure it out by themselves." But another psychiatrist objected to this view, commenting:

> We already are entrusted to hold their lives in our hands. How is this different? It is a contrived and artificial standard to expect patients to kill themselves—and hope they do it properly—so the physician will not need to sully his or her hands with a personally distasteful matter.

Amidst all the divergent opinion, on one point there can be no disagreement: If more states legalize PAS, it won't be only MPC physicians who will be asked, "Tell me, doctor, where do you stand on physician assisted death?"[65]

Questions for Analysis

1. Does the "good doctor" ever assist a patient to die?

2. Do you agree with the AMA and many physicians who say that PAS threatens the integrity of the medical profession?

3. Is it consistent with the Belmont principles for physicians to remain uninvolved in a patient's suicide?

4. Which of the stated positions to MPC's inquiry most closely resembles yours? On what moral principle(s) do you base your view?

5. What would you recommend to avoid inappropriate application of unrestricted right-to-die laws?

REFERENCES

1. NA, "Assisted Death," Medical Dictionary. Retrieved June 20, 2009, from http://medical-dictionary. thefreedictionary.com/assisted+death.

2. Derek Humphry and Mary Clement, *Freedom To Die: People, Politics, and the Right-to-Die*, New York: St. Martin's Press, 1998. Retrieved February 7, 2005, from http://www.assistedsuicide.org/ typical_example.html.

3. James Rachels, *The Elements of Moral Philosophy*, 4th ed., New York: McGraw-Hill, 2003, Ch. 4.

4. "Issues and Controversies: Assisted Suicide Update," *Facts on File News Services*, November 21, 1997. Retrieved February 1, 2005, from http://www.facts. com/icof/00057.htm.

5. Dan Brock, "Voluntary Active Euthanasia," *Hastings Center Report*, March–April, 1992, pp. 10–22.

6. Timothy E. Quill, "Death with Dignity: A Case of Individualized Decision Making," *New England Journal of Medicine*, March 7 1991, p. 692.

7. Marcia Angell, "The Supreme Court and Physician-Assisted Suicide—The Ultimate Right," *The New England Journal of Medicine*, January 2, 1997, p. 50.

8. Timothy Egan, "Suicide Comes Full-Circle, to Oregon," *The New York Times*, October 26, 1997, p. A1.

9. J. Gay-Williams, "The Wrongfulness of Euthanasia," in Jeffrey Olen, Julie C. Van Camp, and Vincent Barry, *Applying Ethics: A Text with Reading*, 8th ed., Belmont, CA: Wadsworth/Thomson Learning, 2005, p. 180.

10. Jane Cys, "HCFA Won't Punish Doctors for Long-living Hospice Patients," *American Medical News*, October 9, 2000. Retrieved February 3, 2005, from http://www.ama-assn.org/amednews/2000/10/ 09gvsb1009.htm.

11. Linda Ganzini et al, "Oregon's Physicians' Attitudes About and Experiences With End-of-Life Care Since Passage of the Oregon Death with Dignity Act," *Journal of the American Medical Association*, May 9, 2001, p. 2363.

12. Mark Landler, "Assisted Suicide of Healthy 79-Year-Old Renews German Death on Right to Die," *The New York Times*, July 3, 2008, p. A8.

13. Elisabeth Kubler-Ross, *On Death and Dying*, New York: Scribner Classic, 1997.

14. M. Scott Peck, *Denial of the Soul*, New York: Harmony Books, 1997, p. 152.

15. Ira Byock, *Dying Well: Peace and Possibilities at the End of Life*, New York: Riverhead Books, 1997.

16. "When Death is Sought: Assisted Suicide in the Medical Context," *The New York Task Force on Life & the Law*, October 2001. Retrieved February 7, 2005, from http://www.health.state.ny.us/nysdoh/ provider/death.htm.

17. Leon Kass, "I Will Give No Deadly Drug," in *The Case Against Assisted Suicide*, Kathleen Foley and Herbert Hendin, eds., Baltimore: Johns Hopkins Press, 2002, pp. 17–40.

18. Daniel Callahan, "When Self-Determination Runs Amok," in Ralph Baergen, *Ethics at the End of Life*, Belmont, CA: Wadsworth/Thomson Learning, 2001, p. 223.

19. Angell, p. 52.

20. Ezekiel Emanuel, "Euthanasia: Historical, Ethical and Empiric Perspectives," in Ralph Baergen, *Ethics at the End of Life*, Belmont, CA: Wadsworth/ Thomson Learning, 2001, p. 211.

21. John Lachs, "When Abstract Moralizing Runs Amok," in Ralph Baergen, *Ethics at the End of Life*, Belmont, CA: Wadsworth/Thomson Leaning, 2001, p. 231.

22. Brock, p. 10.

23. "Religion and Spirituality," *Death with Dignity National Center*, Portland, 2008. Retrieved September 6, 2008, from www.deathwithdignity. org/historyfacts/religion.asp.

24. Kathleen Foley, "Medical Issues Related to Physician Assisted Suicide," testimony before Judiciary Subcommittee on the Constitution, April 29, 1996. Retrieved February 1, 2005, from http://www.2. soros.org/death/testimony.htm.

25. James H. Brown et al, "Is It Normal for Terminally Ill Patients To Desire Death?" *American Journal of Psychiatry*, February 1996, pp. 210–211.

26. Eunice K. Y. Or, "Pope Benedict XVI Vows To Stand Firm Against Abortion and Euthanasia," *Christian Today*, May 9, 2005. Retrieved June 19, 2009, from www.christiantoday.com/article/pope. benedict.xvi.vows.to.stand.firm.against.abortion. euthanasia/2815.htm.

27. Callahan in Ralph Baergen, *Ethics at the End of Life*, Belmont, CA: Wadsworth/Thomson Learning, 2001, p. 223.

28. "Dying Wishes," *CBS Sunday Morning*, March 17, 2002. Retrieved March 1, 2005, from

http://www.cbsnews.com/stories/2002/03/15/
Sunday/main503851.shtml.

29. See 28 above.

30. Linda Ganzini, "Oregon's Physicians Perceptions of Patients Who Request Assisted Suicide and Their Families," *Journal of Palliative Medicine*, June 3, 2003, pp. 381–390.

31. Pope John Paul II, *The Gospel of Life*, New York: Random House, 1995, p. 121.

32. Bishop Walter Kasper, "Reflections on the Holy Father's Encyclical *Fides Et Ratio*," *L'Osservatore Roman Romano*, Weekly English Edition, April 28, 1999, p. 5. Retrieved June 20, 2009, from www.ewtn.com/library/theology/fides11.htm.

33. Terrence McEachern, "Book Review of Ford, Norman M., *The Prenatal Person: Ethics from Conception to Birth*" *Theoretical Medicine and Bioethics*, September 2006. Retrieved June 18, 2009, from http://www.springerlink.com/content/5m12605634l7761/.

34. Donald P. O'Mathuna & Darrel W. Amundsen, "Historical and Biblical References in Physician-Assisted Suicide Court Opinions," *Notre Dame Journal of Law, Ethics, and Public Policy* Volume 12, Issue No. 2 (1998) pp. 473–496. Retrieved July 20, 2008, from http://www.xenos.org/ministries/crossroads/donal/suicide.htm#Ref53.

35. See note 34 above.

36. "Anglican Church Leader Rowan Williams Says Euthanasia and Assisted Suicide Unacceptable," *LifeSiteNews.com*, January 20, 2005. Retrieved September 6, 2008, from http://www.euthanasia.com/rowan.html.

37. Robert M. Baird," "In Defense of Active Voluntary Euthanasia: A Religious Framework," *Christian Ethics Today*, February 1997. Retrieved July 19, 2008, from www.christianethicstoday.com/Issue/009/Is%20There%20a%20Right%20To%20Die%20by%20Robert%20M.%20Baird_009_24_.htm.

38. Pope John Paul II, "Life-sustaining Treatments and Vegetative State: Scientific Advances and Ethical Dilemmas," March 20, 2004. Retrieved February 13, 2005, from http://www.lifeissues.net/writers/doc/doc_33vegetativestate.html.

39. E. Fritz Schmerl, "The Right to Die Is Ethical," *Euthanasia: Opposing Viewpoints*, Neal Bernards, ed., San Diego: reenhaven Press, Inc., 1989, pp. 31.

40. Manuel Velasquez, *Philosophy: A Text with Readings*, 8th ed. Belmont, Ca.: Wadsworth/Thomson Learning, 2002, p. 521.

41. Richard B. Brandt, "A Moral Principle About Killing," in Jeffrey Olen, Julie Van Camp, and Vincent Barry, *Applying Ethics*, 8th. ed., 2005, p. 205.

42. Ibid., p. 206.

43. George J. Marlin, *The Politician's Guide to Assisted Suicide, Cloning, and Other Current Controversies*, San Francisco: Smith-Morley, 1998.

44. See note 23 above.

45. Joseph R. DesJardins, "Virtues and Business Ethics," in William H. Shaw and Vincent Barry, *Moral Issues n Business*, 9th ed. Belmont, Ca.: Wadsworth/Thomson, 2004, pp. 90, 98.

46. Gay-Williams, p. 181.

47. Brown et al, pp. 210–211.

48. Burke J. Balch and Randall K. O'Bannon, "Why We Shouldn't Legalize Assisting Suicide," *National Right to Life*. Retrieved February 3, 2005, from http://www.nrlc.org/euthanasia/asisuid3.html.

49. See note 6 above.

50. See note 6 above.

51. Alasdair MacIntyre, *After Virtue*, Notre Dame, Ind.: University of Notre Dame Press, 1981.

52. Ludwig Edelstein, *Ancient Medicine*, Owsei Temkin and C. Lilian Temkin, eds. Baltimore: The John Hopkins University Press, 1967, pp. 11–12.

53. Howard Brody, "The Physician's Role in Determining Futility," in Thomas A. Mappes and David DeGrazia, *Biomedical Ethics*, 5th ed., New York: McGraw Hill, 2001, pp. 344–350.

54. Edmund Pellegrino, "Compassion Needs Reason Too," in *Dying, Death, and Bereavement 02/03*, George E. Dickinson and Michael R. Leming, eds., Guilford, Conn.: McGraw-Hill/Dushkin, 2002, pp. 96–97.

55. Ibid., p. 97.

56. Angell, p. 51.

57. Kathleen Foley and Herbert Hendin, eds. *The Case Against Assisted Suicide*, Baltimore: Johns Hopkins Press, 2002.

58. Diane Meier et al, "Characteristics of Patients Requesting and Receiving Physician-Assisted Death," *Archives of Internal Medicine*, July 14, 2003, pp. 1573–1542.

59. Nancy Jecker, "Giving Death a Hand: When the Dying and the Doctor Stand in a Special Relationship," in Ralph Baergen, *Ethics at the End of Life*, Belmont, CA: Wadsworth/Thomson Learning, 2001, p. 171.

60. Ambrose Bierce, "The Coup de Grace," *American Literature*. Retrieved May 30, 2009, from http://www.americanliterature.com/Bierce/SS/TheCoupdeGrace.html.

61. NA, "New Orleans Doctor Cleared of Mercy Killing," *The Raw Story*, July 24, 2007. Retrieved May 28, 2009, from http://rawstory.com/news/afp/New_Orleans_doctor_cleared_of_mercy_ 07242007.html.

62. Angela Morrow, "Deaths of Patients in Hurricane Katrina Aftermath: Disaster Casualties, Mercy Killing or Murder?" *About.com*, September 18, 2006. Retrieved May 29, 2009, from http://dying.about.com/b/2006/09/18/follow-ups-on-deaths-ann-richards-memorial-daniel-smiths-second-autopsy.htm.

63. See note 62 above.

64. Sherri Fink, "Strained by Katrina, a Hospital Faced Deadly Choices," *The New York Times Magazine*, August 25, 2009. Retrieved October 1, 2009, from http://www.nytimes.com/2009/08/30/magazine/30doctors.html.

65. Nancy R. Terry, "Does Responsible Care Include Helping a Patient to Die?" *Medscape Today*, January 30, 2009. Retrieved May 29, 2009, from http://www.medscape.com/viewarticle/587294.

Chapter 21

The Assisted Death Debate II: Social Policy and Law

Physician-assisted suicide (PAS) and voluntary active euthanasia (VAE) pose the question: "Is it ever morally permissible for us as individuals to practice assisted death or have it practiced on us?" But assisted death isn't only a question of personal morality; it's also a question of social morality. As with reproductive issues, discussions about assisted death also address the limits of public and collective life, about what society will permit and prohibit. In the context of the culture-war concept (see Introduction), assisted death—as much as abortion, social sex selection, or stem cell research—is about who we are; it concerns how we as a society will order our lives and govern ourselves. And exactly like those reproductive matters, this makes the question of its legal permissibility, "Should PAS be legal?" part of the much larger question: "What is the ideal society?"

In November 2008 voters in the state of Washington were asked to decide whether the ideal society does or does not permit physician-assisted suicide.

THE FINAL CAMPAIGN OF BOOTH GARDNER

"This will be my last campaign," said Booth Gardner, former governor of Washington. "This will be the biggest fight of my career." While political, the campaign that the former governor of Washington was referring to was also intensely personal. Burdened by an unrelenting loss of basic functions since his Parkinson's disease diagnosis fourteen years earlier, Gardner was fighting for a right-to-die law in that state.

Washington's proposed Death with Dignity Act would let a doctor prescribe lethal drugs to patients given less than six months to live. At the time Oregon was the only state with such a law. Passed by voter initiative in 1994 and upheld by the US Supreme Court in 2006, Oregon's Death with Dignity Act permits a physician to prescribe lethal drugs for mentally competent, terminally ill Oregon residents eighteen or older who want to end their own lives—the law does not permit euthanasia—provided: the patient is expected to die of a terminal illness within six months, and diagnosis and prognosis are confirmed by a consulting physician. (See case presentation at end of chapter: "Oregon's Death with Dignity Act.")

Although the Washington permit probably wouldn't help him, because Parkinson's isn't terminal, Gardner strongly identified with the fight to permit assisted death. "There are people like me everywhere who are coping with pain," he said, "—they know that their next step is death. When death is inevitable, we shouldn't force people to endure agonizing suffering if we don't have to." The two term Democratic governor summed up the logic of his battle simply: "*My* life, *my* death, *my* control."[1]

Opposing the initiative, called I-1000, the Roman Catholic Church played a big part in defeating a like measure in 1991 by a margin of 8 percent, 54–46. Other conservative Christians joined with the church to form a powerful religious front against I-1000. But they weren't alone, by any means. Progressive perspectives, described as being "infused with feminism and with the politics of minority and disability rights," expressed "some of the most influential opposition arguments," as they have across the nation in opposition to death-with-dignity laws.[2]

Chairing the religious/secular coalition in Washington was Chris Carlson, who, like 71-year-old Gardner, is a Democratic activist and Parkinson's victim. In 2005, Carlson, 61, was diagnosed with cancer that responded well to experimental treatment. "That points to a major flaw in this initiative," Carlson said, referring to his experience. "Doctors can with some authority tell someone they have six months or less to live. I was supposed to be dead two years ago, but I'm still here." For Carlson and other opponents, passing the initiative would be tantamount to legalizing an "irrational and selfish act."

Gardner's son Doug, 45, agreed with that assessment. "We don't need Booth and Dr. Kevorkian pushing death on us," the born-again Christian said of his father's campaign. "Dad's lost. He's playing God, trying to usurp God's authority."[3] But proponents like Gardner didn't see it as "pushing death"

on anyone. In fact, they eschewed the term "assisted suicide" for "aid in dying," which, they felt, better captured what the terminally ill want: the option to avoid suffering.

Initiative supporters had until July 4, 2008, to turn in 225,000 valid signatures. They collected nearly 320,000, enough to put the controversial measure on the ballot in the fall. On November 4, I-1000 passed by a margin of 59% to 41%, making Washington the second state in the nation to allow doctors to hasten death. A month later, in the case of a 75-year-old man with terminal cancer, a Montana judge found: "It is the individual patients who should be entitled to make these critical decisions for themselves and their families, and not the government" (See case presentation at end of chapter: "*Baxter v. Montana*").

Whether or not a doctor should ever be allowed to prescribe a lethal dose of drugs to a dying patient is a question of collective, not individual decision-making. But like individual action, collective action can be moral or immoral. And, like individual action, whether it is one or the other depends on how well it is supported by moral principles.

Often the relevant principles are the same. For example, believing that individually *and* collectively we should be concerned with human happiness, one would understandably view utility as an important principle of social morality. Likewise, concern with fairness collectively as well as individually makes respect for persons just as important for social morality as for individual morality.

But individual morality isn't always the same as social morality. For example, in the I-1000 debate undoubtedly there were some who would hold themselves to a prohibitive moral standard that they would not want legislated, perhaps out of respect for individual liberty. Others, by contrast, might practice assisted suicide, or have it practiced on them, but still not favor permissive legislation, perhaps out of fear of potential abuse and social harm. Still others probably were uncertain of their own view and would tolerate either permission or prohibition, so long as everyone was treated equally. The point is that sometimes additional principles are needed to guide social policy. Whatever those principles, presumably we prefer them because they serve the social good by moving us closer to the ideal society.

Historically, when philosophers have inquired into the kind of society we should ideally be, they inevitably have answered: a just society. But whereas there is widespread agreement that the best society is the just one, there is lively disagreement about the best principles of social justice, with *individual rights, equal treatment, and general welfare* vying for priority. In the abstract, these principles, which are traceable to the political thought of the Enlightenment, are not controversial. But their interpretation can be. As we're about to see, opposed sides in the cultural discourse about the legalization of PAS endorse the same principles: retentionists, who want to retain prohibitions of assisted death; and abolitionists, who want to abolish them in favor of permissive legislation.

INDIVIDUAL RIGHTS

Recall from Chapter 2 that in ethics a right is generally considered a justified claim or entitlement to something against someone.[4] Basically, this means that if somebody has a right to something, then somebody else has a duty, either not to interfere or possibly to help. It is this language of rights that dominates the public debate about assisted death, where "the right to die" (or "pro-choice") is pitted against "the right to life" (or "pro-life").

Today when PAS advocates assert a right to die, they ordinarily mean two things: (1) Competent, terminally ill adults are entitled to be left alone in choosing to hasten their deaths; and (2) the right to die implies obligations of others. Accordingly, pro-choice supporters typically advance the right to die in both (1) a negative sense, meaning no one may interfere with the patient choice; and (2) a positive sense, meaning someone (e.g., a physician) must (i.e., is obligated to) assist the death. By this abolitionist standard, the just society is the one that permits such a right to die.

For its part, the "right to life" side draws strength from religious and social conservatives, especially Catholics and born-again Christians such as Doug Gardner, who are "set on defending the sanctity of life and the hegemony of God." According to a conservative reading of scriptural and religious natural law, as we saw in the preceding chapter, suicide is immoral. Therefore, to permit PAS would be tantamount to legislating immorality, something anathema to the just society.

But, as the Washington referendum on assisted death showed, the fight against death-with-dignity laws is by no means just religiously driven. It also includes a mix of secular liberals from the ranks of the disabled, the poor, the elderly, racial minorities, and feminists. For these non-religious retentionists, the just society is the one that bans assisted death, not because life is sacred, but because each life warrants equal concern, and PAS jeopardizes the well-being of the weak and vulnerable.

For their philosophical force, both sides—right-to-die abolitionists and right-to-life retentionists—invoke two categories of general rights: human rights and welfare rights.

Human or Moral Rights

Recall, again from Chapter 2, that the Enlightenment's three secular moral traditions—secular natural law, Kant's ethics, and utilitarianism—all made a case for human, or moral, rights without appeal to religion or religious authority. In contrast to a legal right, which law supports, a claim to a human right is supported merely by one's humanity, regardless of law. So, whereas a legal right emanates from law or a legal system, a human right derives merely from being a human being. For many abolitionists, determining the manner of one's own death is a human right that should be supported by law. Specifically, they argue that competent, terminally ill adults have both (1) a vital liberty interest in being free from outside interference in their own death decisions; and (2) a claim to appropriate services and opportunities to make and act on this critical choice, including the assistance of appropriate parties (i.e., physicians).

In response, retentionists raise what they believe are the objectionable implications of this view. For example, they ask why limit the right to die to the competent, terminally ill adult. After all, people act from an array of complex motives, some of which, at least, would seem to give them a justified claim to assisted death. Incurable, but not life-threatening, disease comes to mind, as do severely life-limiting disabilities. Couldn't these be as plausible for justifying PAS as physical pain or debilitation? Its implications, in short, lead retentionists to doubt there is a human right to die.[5]

Supporting this criticism are two important 1997 US Supreme Court decisions, both of which reversed lower court rulings that constitutionally protected the "right to die" of terminally ill and mentally competent patients. In *Washington v. Glucksberg* and *Vacco v. Quill,* the Supreme Court found that the right of assistance in committing suicide is not a fundamental liberty interest protected by the Constitution, and that states, in fact, may protect the sanctity of life by banning PAS/VAE. Recall, from Chapter 18, that in *Vacco* the court rejected the "Philosopher's Brief," which argued "the right to exercise some control over the time and manner of one's death" is part of the fundamental "right to make the most intimate and personal choices central to personal dignity and autonomy." Authored by six philosophers—Ronald Dworkin, Thomas Nagel, Robert Nozick, John Rawls, T.M. Scanlon, and Judith Jarvis Thomson—the brief concluded that an American citizen has the right, in principle, "to live and die in the light of his own religious and ethical beliefs, his own convictions about why his life is valuable and where its value lies."

While rejecting this analysis, *Vacco,* as well as *Glucksberg,* nonetheless allowed states to permit PAS, as human rights activists are quick to point out. And of themselves the high court's decisions don't prove that assistance in dying is not a human right, only that it is not a constitutionally protected one, and that only for now. Another court may rule otherwise. Besides, abolitionists argue, the right to assisted death, like any other human right, does not originate in law, although the law's protection is always welcome. Basic human rights—from speech to religion to political assembly—suffer and wither throughout the world. For all of that, they are no less human rights, as human rights derive from the assumption that all human beings, merely by virtue of their being human, have certain inviolable entitlements. Assisted death is one such entitlement; and, therefore, the society that interferes with this human right is unjust, according to abolitionists who favor the argument from human rights.

Retentionists concede that judicial opinion, in the end, is just that, *opinion.* Nevertheless, they believe that judicial opinion currently casts doubt over the charge that PAS prohibition is a social injustice. In fact, they note, in both decisions the court properly specified as a constitutionally guarded human entitlement the right to discontinue or never initiate heroic life-prolonging measures. *Glucksberg* and *Vacco* also reaffirmed another human right: the basic right of competent patients to refuse medical treatment, in general, and to receive adequate pain relief at the end of life, *even if so doing hastens death.* The human, or moral, right a patient has, then, is to risk his life, not to take it. The just society makes this distinction, and thereby strikes a proper balance between individual liberty and the sanctity of life, according to retentionists.

In response, abolitionists partial to human rights cite another case, *Compassion in Dying v. Washington* (1996), where the Ninth Circuit Court of Appeals found (8 to 3) "no ethical or constitutionally cognizable difference between a doctor's pulling the plug on a respirator and his prescribing drugs which will permit a terminally ill patient to end his own life." Thus, if a Terri Schiavo (see Introduction) has a right to withhold or withdraw life support, she has an equal right to have her life actively shortened, since the result is the same, death.

But do the identical outcomes imply identical constitutional concerns? Quoting various court rulings, constitutional law expert Yale Kamisar explains why he thinks not:

> The right to terminate life support grows out of the doctrine of informed consent, a

doctrine "firmly entrenched in American tort law." "The logical corollary," of that doctrine, of course is "the right to consent, that is to refuse treatment." The other tradition, which has "long existed alongside" the first one, is the anti-suicide tradition. This is evidenced by society's discouragement of suicide (indeed, by the state's power to prevent suicide, by force if necessary) and by the many laws criminalizing assisted suicide.[6]

According to retentionist Kamisar, then, the right to end life-support is a clinical extension of the fundamental right of informed consent, whereas intentionally hastening death is not. In fact, tradition opposes it.

Taking another tack, abolitionists who invoke human rights say the right to refuse treatment implies a right to assisted death because refusal of treatment is an outgrowth of a well-established right of privacy, specifically bodily determination. Since you have the right to determine what happens to your own body, you can refuse treatment. From there it's easy to infer that you have the right to choose to end your life and to have support in so doing. Thus, in the Montana case the court ruled: "The Montana constitutional rights of individual privacy and human dignity, taken together, encompass the right of a competent terminally (ill) patient to die with dignity."

Retentionists concede that, although the right to refuse treatment may derive from the right to bodily self-determination, it is not a "right to die." True, patients may exercise the right of self-determination at the risk of death or even in order to die. But retentionists say that the right of refusal of medical treatment is about protection from unwanted interference, not permission to decide whether to live or die. As Bonnie Steinbock points out, "There can be a reason for terminating life-prolonging treatment other than 'to bring about the patient's death.'"[7]

Regarding human rights, then, retentionists and abolitionists agree that, in theory, the just society is one that protects and does not interfere with a human right, whereas the society that fails this test is unjust. But they differ on the constitutional status of assisted suicide. Where at least some abolitionists see a constitutionally protected human right in assisted suicide, retentionists see only a constitutionally protected human right in the protection of life. These different constitutional readings set up diametrically opposed concepts of how the ideal society deals with PAS. For abolitionists who invoke human rights, the just society protects and doesn't interfere with the human right to die; and, therefore, the society that prohibits PAS is unjust. For retentionists who invoke human rights, the just society protects and doesn't interfere with the human right to life; and, therefore, the one that permits PAS is unjust.

It's worth noting that religious and social conservatives typically object to PAS not because it interferes with a human right to life, but because it violates the principle of the sanctity of life. In the words of Pope John Paul II:

> No one is permitted to ask for this act of killing, either for himself or herself or for another person entrusted to his or her care, nor can he or she consent to it, either explicitly or implicitly. Nor can any authority legitimately recommend or permit such an action. For it is a question of the violation of the divine law, an offense against the dignity of the human person, a crime against life, and an attack on humanity.[8]

Indeed, to abolitionists including Ronald Dworkin, it is such a religious-grounded argument that is the only basis for opposing legalization of assisted suicide. But Dworkin, a legal philosopher, believes religious arguments are specious, because they confuse the "good" with the "right"; that is, they conflate "values that only register within particular communities" with "values that can be known by all." The pope's statement will, thus, register only with those who share the papacy's values.[9] Therefore, Dworkin says, forcing that perspective on dissenters, by retaining assisted suicide prohibitions, leads to oppression and loss of personal freedom. This makes a ban on PAS unjust in a pluralistic society like ours, according to Dworkin.[10]

Welfare Rights

An alternative, more cautious rights argument holds that, even if assisted death isn't a human, or moral, right, it is nevertheless a welfare right, as much as medical care itself is. By this is meant that the special circumstances or situations of the competent, terminally ill patients support a right to PAS that the just society should recognize. Therefore, a society that doesn't is unjust—not because it's denying individuals something they are entitled to as human beings (i.e., a human right) but something they're entitled to as a *special* category of human beings (i.e., a welfare right).

Retentionists readily admit the cruelty of any patient's suffering needless pain. Inadequate pain treatment for the dying has even been termed "the most prevalent crime in medicine today."[11] But that merely argues for improved palliative care, retentionists argue, including relief from emotional and spiritual suffering as well as physical pain. If there's a welfare right, they say, it is to adequate care, not assisted death.

Many abolitionists also defend PAS as a welfare right in the context of political theory. They point out that our capacity to reflect about our deepest convictions and goals is the basis of democratic systems of government. Therefore, because no area of critical choice is more basic an expression of personal morality and self-definition than how we're going to die, the fully democratic society allows (at least carefully regulated) assisted death as part of its commitment to its members' dignity and autonomy.[12]

For their part, secular retentionists admit that people have a critical interest in living their lives according to their own beliefs about what is good. And if it were strictly a matter of suicide, as with, say, the Hardins (see case "The Suicide of Garrett Hardin," Chapter 19), self-determination might be pertinent as a negative right, or a sphere of liberty that should not be interfered with. But assisted suicide, by definition, is proposed as a *positive* right, that is, an entitlement to aid and assistance in the act of self-killing. Kevorkian's patients and the hundreds in Oregon were not just asking to die, nor were the voters for Washington's Death with Dignity Act. They were asking to have physician assistance to die. That makes assisted suicide "no longer a matter of only self-determination," as one retentionist says, "but of a mutual, social decision between two people, the one to be killed and the other to do the killing."[13]

In response, abolitionists point out that individuals generally seek medical assistance in dying because either they can't end their own lives or they fear failing in the attempt. They need help to do it. Even if they don't need help, that doesn't take medicine off the hook, according to abolitionists who view PAS as a welfare right. Because it has a protected monopoly on, perhaps, the most expedient means of death, drugs, the AMA and those who support prohibition of PAS can't both insist on controlling access to lethal drugs and say: "Let the patient do the deed himself."

Some abolitionists even make the argument that access to life-ending drugs would put an end to the controversy of physician involvement. Philosopher John Lachs of Vanderbilt University, for example, writes:

> This restriction of human autonomy is due to the social power of medicine; it is neither surprising nor morally wrong, therefore, to ask those responsible for this limitation to undo some of its most noxious effects. If the medical profession relinquishes its hold on drugs, people could make effective choices about their future without the assistance of physicians. Even limited access to deadly drugs, restricted to single doses for those who desire them and who are certified to be of sound mind and near the end of life, would keep physicians away from dealing with death.[14]

For abolitionists like Lachs, then, even if self-determination in the context of assisted death cannot be shown to be a human right, it certainly stands as a legitimate welfare right that the just, democratic society recognizes, specifically by relaxing drug laws and, thereby, enlarging personal freedom and limiting physician involvement.

For their part, retentionists generally grant the significance of self-determination but say that, given that PAS involves a request for public cooperation, autonomy must bow to a broader notion of the public good. Religious retentionists add that individual valuations of the quality of life should not trump the sanctity of life. By either measure—the secular "public good" or the sacred "sanctity of life"—self-determination in the context of assisted suicide is not a welfare right, and the society that thinks and acts otherwise is unjust, according to retentionists.

BIOETHICS ACROSS CULTURES

YouTube Plea from Australia

Propped up on pillows, barely audible, Angelique Flowers had something she wanted the world to hear. So, the 31-year-old Melbourne writer took to the Generation X medium, YouTube, where she detailed the medical history behind her request for a pain-free, peaceful death.

Having suffered debilitating Crohn's disease since the age of fifteen, Flowers was diagnosed with advanced, aggressive colon cancer shortly before her thirty-first birthday in May 2008. Fearing a slow, painful death from a total bowel obstruction, Flowers searched the Internet for information about euthanasia and a dose of the lethal drug Nembutal. The search dominated her dying days, and her frustration at Australia's legal situation led her to film a haunting plea to Australian Prime Minister Kevin Rudd for voluntary euthanasia to be legalized.

Speaking softly into the camera from her hospice bed, a weak and wan Flowers said:

> I don't believe in stoicism. I freely admit to not being a brave soul who grins and bears the pain and soldiers on …. I deeply admire people who rise above the adversity and their suffering. But I haven't grown from my illness or become a better person from its torments. All I want after 16 years of painful Crohn's disease and now cancer is to die a pain-free peaceful death. Because euthanasia was banned in Australia I am denied this right …. The law wouldn't let a dog suffer the agony I'm going through before an inevitable death. It would be put down. Yet under the law, my life is worth less than a dog's.

Flowers allowed how the stress of having to hide her activity from her family, friends, and medical staff had made her final days even more painful, and she related how she even contemplated violent ways to end her life, such as jumping off a building. "I have been robbed of both my living and my dying," she said, adding:

> At a time when I want to spend what good days and precious moments I have left having meaningful time with the people I love, I've had to cut myself off, writing questions and notes, making inquiries, doing research. If euthanasia was legal, I could have ended my days as I chose, finding peace before leaving this world, not panic and more pain.

Angelique Flowers died three months later, evidently still in pain, medicated with massive doses of morphine, her worst fears realized. Her older brother, Damian, 34, was with her when she died. In her last hour, he reported holding a bowl under his sister's chin as she vomited fecal matter.

(SOURCES: "Angelique's Dying Letter to Prime Minister Rudd," *YouTube*, September 12, 2008. Retrieved May 25, 2009, from www.youtube.com/watch?v=jdxd_EFDd4s; Sherrill Nixon, "'Robbed of My Living and Dying,'" *The Sydney Morning Herald*, September 13, 2008. Retrieved May 23, 2009, from http://www.smh.com.au/news/national/robbed-of-my-living-and-dying/2008/09/12/1220857835038.html.)

Question

What are some of the underlying issues of euthanasia raised by this video letter? Do you think that Angelique Flowers had a right to assisted death? Compare the deaths (or dyings) of Angelique Flowers and Craig Ewert (see Bioethics Across Cultures, "Suicide Tourists," Chapter 18). In your opinion, which was the more humane? Do you think that someone, perhaps her brother, would have been morally justified in deliberaely ending Angelique's life at her request, as Captain Madwell did with his friend, Sergeant Halcrow (see case presentation, *The Coup de Grace*, Chapter 20)?

EQUALITY

A society that doesn't treat all citizens equally isn't just—on that all agree. But what exactly does equal treatment require of the just society? About that there is as much disagreement as there is about the requirements of justice itself.

The notion of "equal treatment under the law" offers a useful entry point into the complex topic of equality as it applies to assisted suicide. As noted in Chapter 2, to some people, equality under the law is strictly a procedural matter; that is, equal treatment means treatment according to the same laws and legal procedures.[15] Thus, whatever the prevailing restrictive laws allow in end-of-life decision making—medical directives, withholding/with drawing life-prolonging measures, terminal sedation—so long as all like patients are permitted the full measure of these rights and privileges, they are being treated equally.

Equal treatment as strictly procedural often supports a retentionist view of PAS that goes something like this in the cultural discourse: "Laws prohibiting PAS and governing end-of-life care, in general, are fine as they are. Don't change a thing. Just make sure that everyone gets the full benefit of what's permitted and is disallowed what is not."

The abolitionist counter-argument pits justice as fairness against the retentionist's justice as procedural equality. Again, along the lines sketched in Chapter 2, the argument from fairness trades on the fact that not all laws are fair and just; indeed, they can mask and perpetuate deep social injustice. That's exactly the case, some abolitionists argue, with very ill patients desiring assisted death: They simply don't enjoy the same measure of freedom as their counterparts who don't desire assisted death. For philosophical support, abolitionists sometimes cite the social justice theory of John Rawls.

Rawlsian justice requires that every person has a right to the greatest basic freedom compatible with a like freedom for all. In other words, social justice demands equal freedom for everyone. If freedom can be increased without violating that requirement, it must be. Currently, according to abolitionists who invoke equality, pro-life patients and their physicians have more freedom of conscience, choice, and action than pro-choice patients and their physicians. That's not fair, they say. Only by abolishing assisted suicide prohibitions can the latter group have an equal measure of freedom as the former and enjoy real "equal treatment under the law," or true procedural equality.

But would permitting PAS truly enlarge patient and physician freedom while not interfering with others? Retentionists doubt it. Turning the abolitionist argument on its head, they warn of an unequal, or "disparate," impact on members of vulnerable groups, such as the elderly, the poor, the treatably depressed, the disabled, and even on women.[16]

Disparate Impact

Consider the disabled. Currently there are about 50 million disabled Americans being "maintained" at tremendous expense. More than half of Dr. Kevorkian's patients were disabled, not terminally ill. It's well-established that the disabled don't always get health care, personal assistance, housing, or other supports they require. Nevertheless, cost-conscious health care providers, insurers, and taxpayers are aware of the huge costs of maintaining the disabled and are seeking cost-saving alternatives, perhaps even PAS. Anticipating a growing threat to the disabled, Not Dead Yet (NDY), a vocal disability organization, formed in 1996 to oppose legalized suicide.

Although approximately two-thirds of people with disabilities support the right of assisted suicide, according to a 1995 Harris Poll, NDY members aren't among them. Their fear is that, were assisted death legalized, the disabled and the socially disadvantaged could be pressured into choosing death because of economic circumstances, low-quality health care, or limited availability to medical services. The dreaded expediency rationale is akin to the one Kevorkian gave when he told a Michigan court in 1990: "The voluntary self-elimination of individual mortally diseased or crippled lives, taken collectively, can only enhance the preservation of public health and welfare."[17] If coerced to choose death, then such individuals would lose, not gain, personal freedom.[18] The ideal state can't allow this to happen, say retentionists who fear that legalized assisted death will result in unequal, or disparate, treatment of vulnerable groups such as the seriously disabled.

The potential disparate impact of legalizing PAS naturally worries the religious-minded, given religion's traditional role of providing special care and protection to vulnerable populations. But some secularists share the religious concern, such as Robert P. Jones of the Center for American Values in Public Life. A fervent liberal, Jones disagrees with Dworkin that the only bases for opposing the legalization of PAS are religious or moralistic, and, therefore, prohibitions are oppressive and illicitly abridge freedom. By contrast, Jones argues (in *Liberalism's Troubled Search for Equality*, 2008) that legalized suicide would pose a threat to the lives of the disabled because of the profound social inequalities they and members of other vulnerable groups face. In the matter of PAS, then, Jones is arguing that PAS threatens one of the two great building blocks of liberal political theory since the Enlightenment: that all lives are to be equally protected. In opting for "egalitarian justice," or universal equality, Jones is pitting himself against those secular progressivists like Dworkin who embrace the other great Enlightenment principle: individual liberty, or simply "free choice." For Dworkin assisted suicide is a constitutional right; for Jones it shouldn't even be legalized, let alone be considered as constitutionally protected. Again, for Dworkin prohibitions of assisted suicide strike at freedom; for Jones, they safeguard equality.

Law professor Carl Coleman of Seton Hall University is another vocal retentionist with strong interests in protecting vulnerable populations, notably those that society does not guarantee access to adequate health care. Prominent within that category are patients covered by assisted death permits such as Oregon's. Coleman's analysis suggests that any society that erects a framework for individuals' reluctantly choosing an option that they don't really want would be presumptively unjust.[19]

For their part, abolitionists think that legislation can be crafted to preclude the feared injustice, as it has been with refusing disproportionate life-prolonging measures. For example, predictions to the contrary notwithstanding, in the twenty-odd years that most states have permitted withdrawing life-sustaining medical treatment, there is no evidence that that right has been abused. Nor has any coercion been reported in Oregon.

Furthermore, abolitionists ask, who's to say that members of at-risk groups can't make informed, voluntary death decisions? As bioethicist Ronald A. Lindsay points out: "If assisted suicide can be a rational, moral choice for competent persons, then the disparate impact argument (if accepted) erects a barrier to the exercise of this rational, moral choice by anyone, *including* members of disadvantaged groups."[20] In other words, the prohibition of PAS could just as easily result in unequal treatment for high-risk groups as its legalization could. Abolitionists as well as retentionists, in short, can argue unfair discrimination. Lindsay, who is director of research and legal affairs at the humanist Center for Inquiry in Washington, DC, is one of those who, like Dworkin and the other signatories to the "Philosopher's Brief," argue that assisted suicide is a fundamental constitutional right.[21]

Some of today's abolitionists go further, claiming that legalizing assisted suicide actually might prevent some patients from seeking to end their lives, because most suicide decisions nowadays are done in private, without any possible controls such as counseling or referrals to hospice.[22] Who can say whether these patients really wanted to die? Properly regulated PAS, as in Oregon, at least would remove any lingering doubt about a patient's suicide decision.

Still, retentionists worry about the capacity of our medical system to implement even a carefully fashioned law. They fear it may not be equipped to make assisted death available, while ensuring that it is restricted to competent persons experiencing unrelenting suffering who have made a voluntary, informed, and settled decision to die. The danger lies in the systemic inadequacies in end-of-life care. Cost considerations may drive assisted death decisions, leaving unresolved questions like: *Have all the options been spelled out to the patient? Does she fully understand them? Does she want to relieve the family of burdensome care giving? Is he making a formal request to die or simply expressing a fleeting desire to?*[23]

Providing fodder for the retentionist concern about hasty or ill-considered death decisions, a 1996 study reported in *The New England Journal of Medicine* cited widespread abuses of legalized assisted death in Holland, including the deaths of competent patients without their express consent.[24] Then, too, there are the patients of Dr. Kevorkian who weren't terminal and the five autopsies that turned up no existent pathologies. To retentionists this points to untreated depression as influencing patient choice. Indeed, the results of a recent survey in Oregon suggests that the Death with Dignity Act does not always prevent patients with depression, a treatable condition, from receiving a lethal prescription.[25]

Also of note, the vast majority of individuals Kevorkian assisted to die were women, suggestive to some retentionists that women with disabilities are special victims of external oppression, whom permitting suicide would only further victimize.[26] Indeed, feminist progressivists such as Princeton bioethicist and law professor Susan Wolf[27] worry about the "unacknowledged images that may give the practice [of assisted death] a certain gendered logic." As she explains:

If women are expected, above all, to care for others, for children, parents, husbands, ... aren't they particularly likely to view their own lives as without value when they become so sick or disabled that they are the ones who must be cared for? Might they be especially likely, at that point, to see themselves as burdens and, if assisted suicide were legal, to request that their deaths come right away? And might this tendency be compounded by a cultural lineage exalting female suicide, a tradition going back ... to Greek tragedy, where suicide is carried out almost exclusively by women?[28]

In her own rejection of self-determined dying in assisted death, another leading feminist, Sydney Callahan, writes:

Feminist ideals of inclusive justice, care-taking and the interconnectedness of all the living require that we struggle against approving assisted suicide and euthanasia. Let there be no more recruits for the armies of domination and death.[29]

Collectively, then, cultural insights and developments, at home and abroad, persuade retentionists that permitting assisted death will inevitably increase the risk borne by patients whose lives already are treated with less respect and dignity in a medical context, notably the disabled and women. They say that the just society ought never permit such disparate or unequal impact, let alone foster it with misguided social policy.

For their part, abolitionists point out that the United States isn't Holland, that Kevorkian acted without professional or legal oversight, and that so far Oregon's assisted deaths have been about equally divided between women and men. What's more, feminists such as Diane Raymond, while granting the importance of analyses such as Wolf's and Callahan's, reject the notion that PAS is incompatible with the philosophy or goals of feminism.[30] Feminist bioethicist Jennifer Parks, similarly, thinks that in a social world where women are too often viewed as more emotional than rational, their well-considered requests for assisted dying can be too easily trivialized and discounted.[31] All of this leads abolitionists to say that it's premature to cry "disparate impact" prior to permissive legislation. First legalize PAS, they suggest; if it's then found that a group of people, say the disabled or women, is choosing assisted suicide in significantly greater numbers than would be expected, revisit the procedures in place for assisted death.[32]

THE GENERAL WELFARE

Together with rights and equality, the just society is thought to be one that promotes the general welfare, or the common good. But exactly what is in the "public interest" and how the government can rightly promote it are not always easy to ascertain.

Consider that approximately 20 percent of voters in the 2004 presidential election said that "values" were important to them. Of these, an overwhelming majority voted for President Bush over Senator John Kerry. Abortion, stem cell research, assisted death, gay marriage, the general "coarseness" of the culture, such were the "value issues" that these voters felt the government should act to end, prevent, or ameliorate. Apparently, these voters felt that the incumbent, more than the challenger, was more likely to address these matters.

In feeling that the general welfare includes a wholesome moral environment (whatever that is), these voters probably weren't any different from most of the approximately 100 million other voters. What distinguished them as culturally conservative, however, was that most likely believed that a wholesome moral environment includes restrictions on certain private behaviors. In many reproductive and end-of-life issues, they evidently support state paternalism.

State Paternalism

State paternalism refers to actions of government bodies or agencies over particular kinds of activities or procedures. Usually such controls take the form of government-enacted laws and regulations purportedly for the good of individuals or the society, regardless of individual preference.

Sometimes the reason for the paternalistic intervention is obvious; the potential harm is clear and present. Without most licensing and technical specifications, for example, both patients and the medical profession itself could suffer. Other times, however, the harm is less clear, and so the liberty limitation of the paternalistic intervention is more controversial. Thus, while licensing and drug standards may protect the patient-consumer and the medical profession, they also limit the variety of medical viewpoints, therapies, and medications that both consumers and physicians can legally choose from. In such cases, it's more difficult to discern the harm that individuals are supposedly

being protected from. Many Americans, for example, feel that the largely prohibited access to cheaper Canadian drugs or to medical marijuana are cases of illegitimate state paternalism in the health care and market choices of individual Americans. So, too, is assisted suicide, according to abolitionists. They want to know: "What exactly is the harm that a competent terminally ill adult voluntarily requesting assisted death is being protected from? What harm is the society being protected from?" Or more pointedly: "What gives the state the right to impose a tax of pain and suffering at the end of life?"

Self-Regarding vs. Other Regarding Virtues and Vices Relevant to the proper reach of state interference (or, alternatively, the proper limits on self-determination) in personal decision is the distinction that utilitarian Mill (see Chapter 2) made between "self-regarding" and "other-regarding" virtues and vices.[33] For example, drinking to intoxication in the privacy of one's own home is, arguably, a self-regarding vice in that it might directly harm the individual but not anyone else. Drinking and driving, on the other hand, is an example of an "other-regarding" vice, because it threatens direct harm to others.

Now, there's no dispute about laws against drinking and driving, because the harm that the government is protecting us from is palpable. But imagine the resulting furor were the private act of drinking alcohol banned. Where, most people would ask, is the direct *public* harm? Which of our rights is being violated by the individual act of private intoxication? Why ought the government interfere with what appears to be, in Mill's terms, not an "other-regarding" but a "self-regarding" vice? So also with assisted suicide, say abolitionists, who claim that if an individual wants to die a quick, painless death rather than a lingering, painful one, it's no one's business but his own—precisely the argument the original utilitarians made some 250 years ago.

But even if assisted death is a "self-regarding" act, many retentionists deny that is a harmless one. On the contrary, they say that people like Velma Howard and her family (see Chapter 18); or

"Diane" (see Chapter 20) and Piergiorgio Welby (see Chapter 18), and their physicians, all need to be saved from the moral harm of assisted death, as much as do those who have or practice abortions. Therefore, the government that limits individual freedom to practice assisted suicide or have it practiced on oneself promotes the general welfare, and, therefore, is just.

Abolitionists respond in classic utilitarian terms, to the effect: The only freedom that will not maximize happiness is the freedom to harm others. As assisted suicide does not directly harm others, and individual patients, their families, and physicians are in a better position to know what is best for them in these matters than paternalistic governments are, prohibitions are unjustified.

But, even granting no direct harm to others, might assisted suicide cause *indirect* harm? Might it devalue life, for example, or invite abuses? Today's retentionists answer in the affirmative.

The Case *for* Indirect Harm   The great slippery slope fear that continues to haunt the right-to-die movement is that were PAS legitimated euthanasia would inevitably follow. And with time it would extend to the disabled, the clinically depressed, the chronically debilitated, racial minorities, women with disabilities, even to the elderly and deformed newborns.[34] Indeed, the current cost-conscious, market-driven medical environment does little to allay this fear of runaway abuse. As avid retentionist Wesley Smith chillingly warns:

> When people learn that the drugs used in assisted suicide cost only $40 but it could take $40,000 to treat a patient properly so that they don't want a "choice" of assisted suicide, the financial forces at work become clear.[35]

Smith, who heads the bioethics program at the Discovery Institute, an advocate group for conservative public policy, fears that legalizing voluntary assisted suicide will inevitably lead to nonvoluntary euthanasia. Once PAS is considered "medical treatment," it could be argued, under the Fourteenth Amendment, that it would be discriminatory to deny it to those too young or incapacitated to request it. (Oregon Medicaid already pays for assisted suicide for poor residents as a means of "comfort care.") What's stopping the suicide permission from being extended to the mentally incompetent? Why, under the "substitute judgment" doctrine, couldn't surrogates choose what the person would want if competent? Retentionists like Smith then depict a culture where infants, the mentally ill and retarded, the confused and senile elderly, all would be considered "entitled" to have someone else enforce their "right to die." Ultimately, in the sinister depiction of former Surgeon General C. Everett Koop, "Auschwitz could be in the offing."[36] Where, then, is the freedom to choose if you can be killed, even though you never expressed a wish to die?

Then there are those cases where, though present, autonomy is not equally available to a patient, such as to those of limited means or deeply depressed. Thus, recalling the equality debate, feminist Wolf hints grimly of a future time when "a doctor ... confronted with a desperately ill and despairing woman, ... would be more likely to think, under [permissive] laws ... that she would be better off dead."

> Whether the patient requested death and the doctor swiftly agreed, or whether the doctor softly suggested it and the patient, confronting a verdict of her own worthlessness, consented, the results would be the same.[37]

Adding heft to the retentionist doomsday scenario are bioethicists who express other concerns about legalizing assisted death, such as the harmful effect on the physician-patient relationship; the diversion of resources from comfort care; and the adverse impact on families, health care, and medical services, including hospice.[38–40] Why change current law, they ask, when proper pain management can alleviate a patient's desire for a hastened death; and life can be shortened through prudent terminal sedation and dehydration? These analysts worry that relaxing current prohibitions on assisted suicide will, in short, only serve to encourage a "culture of death."

BIOETHICS ACROSS CULTURES

World Legal Opinion on Assisted Death

Today most countries and American states prohibit assisting suicide. Where it is permitted, medical tradition opposes it. In the world's developing nations, debates about PAS are as rare as their populations are healthy. Still, a look at laws worldwide turns up a rather mixed and ambivalent body of opinion concerning assisted suicide.

Europe Europe is the only place outside Oregon, Washington, and (for now) Montana where assisted suicide is legal. Since 1941 Switzerland has permitted both physician and nonphysician-assisted suicide, uniquely today with no residency requirements. Holland officially sanctioned assisted death, as well as voluntary euthanasia, in 2002, although it had been permitted since 1984 and practiced in The Netherlands well before then. Since 1975, public opinion polls have shown that a large majority of the Dutch population across the religious spectrum believes that physicians should be permitted to carry out euthanasia. In 2002, Belgium became the world's second country to allow euthanasia, despite the considerable outrage of its influential Roman Catholic clergy. Sweden and Norway don't prohibit suicide but have prosecuted assisters as accessories to murder, albeit lightly.

Asia In Asia and the Pacific, aging populations, especially in the more developed countries, are pressing medicine to address quality of end-of-life issues, including suicide. Although assisting suicide is generally illegal, penalties for it tend to be lenient. In some instances a mix of ambiguous law and long-standing custom complicates the whole matter.

In Japan, for example, assisted suicide is illegal. At the same time, other rulings from earlier times seem to permit it by distinguishing PAS from assisted killing. Further complicating the Japanese picture are traditional taboos on suicide, dying, and death, and the fact that patients frequently are not told they are terminally ill.

The Israeli Terminally Ill Patients Law of 2005, while prohibiting active euthanasia and PAS, permits the physician to withhold "periodic medical treatment" such as dialysis or other drugs from an incurably ill patient at the patient's request, provided the patient is suffering severe pain. However, the law forbids the termination of "continuous medical treatment" (e.g., connection to a life-support machine) on the grounds that such an act would cause the patient to die and, therefore, be active euthanasia. In an innovative solution to the dilemma of a patient's requesting to be disconnected from life-support, the law permits ongoing support to be converted from continuous to cyclical treatment by use of a timer device called a Shabbat timer. According to attorney Simon M. Jackson: "The timer operates for 24 hours at a time and sets off a red light or alarm after 12 hours as a reminder to reset it. The patient or his representative could at any time request an extension, but if the dying person insists he does not want his life extended, the timer would turn off the respirator at the end of the cycle."

Still, what about those patients who might be delivered from agony and indignity were the assisted death that they desire permitted? The Dutch people, evidently, identify with such a plight more than with being a possible victim of abuse. So do abolitionists in the United States, who methodically attempt to muffle each retentionist alarm in making their own a case *against* indirect harm.

The Case *against* Indirect Harm Regarding the potential for abuse, abolitionists see exaggeration in recent reports of widespread abuses in Holland.[41] But it's mainly here at home, in Oregon, where they take their stand against charges of potential abuse. To them the experience of that pioneering northwestern state belies the specter of a horrific slippery slope.

Oregon's law clearly safeguards against coercion and requires the PAS process be stopped if any is detected. So far there's been no indication of jeopardy for members of the most vulnerable groups. For example, according to Oregon's Department of Human Services, between 1998 and 2003 rates of participation in PAS actually *decreased* with age and were highest among the better educated and those with deadly conditions, specifically terminal cancer and Lou Gehrig's disease. What's more, referrals to hospice *increased* to about 32 percent, which is almost double the national average and higher than any other state.

In 1994 delegates from the National People's Congress in the Republic of China proposed a law in support of euthanasia, and in 1995 thirty delegates again urged passage after the imprisonment of a man who assisted his terminally ill wife to commit suicide. Despite these efforts, euthanasia remains officially illegal in China. But given the challenges of providing quality care to burgeoning elderly populations there and throughout the Far East, the issue is unlikely to fade.

The only place in Asia where PAS was ever legal was in the sparsely populated Northern Territory of Australia, and there only for a nine-month period ending in March, 1997. Interest in permissive legislation, however, has spawned the lobby group Exit International, founded by Dr. Philip Nitschke, "Australia's Dr. Kevorkian."

Africa South Africa may soon have the most liberal euthanasia laws in the world, if the Law Commission's recommendations are accepted. Under the proposed "End of Life Decisions Act," South Africa doctors would be permitted to end the lives of terminally ill patients, at the patient's request, by providing or administering a lethal dosage of a drug. The Act would allow a medical practitioner under certain conditions to stop the treatment of a patient whose life functions are being maintained artificially, and permit a competent person to refuse life-sustaining treatment if he chooses to die. A physician would also be allowed to honor a patient's advance directive, if the patient has requested the cessation of treatment. Most significantly, the Act would sanction active voluntary euthanasia or physician-assisted suicide.

(SOURCES: "Assisted Suicide Laws Around the World," *ERGO*, November 22, 2004. Retrieved May 1, 2009, from http://www.assistedsuicide.org/suicide_laws.html; John Griffiths, Alex Bood, and Heleen Weyers, *Euthanasia and Law in the Netherlands*, Amsterdam: Amsterdam University Press, 1998; Simon M. Jackson, *Jewish Law in Our Times*, "The Israeli Terminally Ill Patients Law, 5766-2005 (Part II)." Retrieved March 25, 2010, from http://www.torahmitzion.org/eng/resources/showLaw.asp?id=801.)

Question

Religious critics of assisted death laws often attribute their liberalization to moral relativism. Representative is this statement by Frontline Fellowship, a Bible-based evangelical mission in Africa: "Confusion over human rights as they relate to judicial pronouncements arises from moral and intellectual relativism. If it is assumed that no absolute law exists, then it follows that an individual's rights must be equally relative.... When a nation moves away from the absolutes of God's law we can expect an immediate substitute to fill the void. Unfortunately, the 'human rights' idea has become the alternative to God's Law." Do you agree that the liberalization of assisted death laws is attributable mainly to moral relativism? What other factors might be in play? Do you think that the use of the "Shabbat timer" is a good way to balance the values of sanctity of life and individual autonomy?

(SOURCE: "Religious Freedom at Risk in South Africa," *Frontline Fellowship*. Retrieved May 22, 2009, from http://www.frontline.org.za/articles/religious_freedoms_at_risk.htm.)

Overall, one-third of Oregonians who die are enrolled in a hospice program and two-thirds have completed an advance directive before death, versus the national average of about 20 percent.[42,43] Far from being coerced by a flawed system, economic necessity, or rapacious HMOs (who, in fact, never get involved in a PAS decision in Oregon), patients opting for PAS in 2002, about equally divided between women and men, gave as their top reasons: losing autonomy (84%), decreasing ability to participate in activities they enjoyed (84%), and losing control of bodily functions (47%).[44] As for its impact on the physician-patient relationships, Oregon's suicide permission has been utilized so infrequently that it's currently impossible to calculate the law's effects on clinical practice.[45] But so far there's no evidence of a toxic effect. If anything, the encouraging figures on the utilization of medical directives and hospice suggest more honest and open physician-patient communication.

The abolitionist case for indirect harm then turns to alternatives to PAS, notably pain control and terminal sedation. They point out that, statistically, at least 5 percent of terminally ill people will still die suffering, even with the best pain care. But the other 95 percent also risk not getting good pain control because of stringent regulations of the Drug Enforcement Agency (DEA), which leave doctors fearing investigation and worse.[46] What's more, dying of starvation and dehydration while heavily sedated, though legal in all the states, is unpredictable. It can take up to two weeks, as with Terri Schiavo (see Introduction). The prescription used under Oregon's law, by contrast, usually renders the patient asleep within a few minutes and dead within a few hours. Beyond this, the wishes of the dying who prefer comfort care are fully respected, which tends to underscore Dr. Angell's observation that "good comfort care and the availability of physician-assisted suicide are no more mutually exclusive than good cardiologic care and the availability of heart transplantation."[47]

Finally, some abolitionists today would oppose collective action to protect the public morality strictly on utilitarian principle. They believe that in a free society the general welfare is never advanced at the cost of individual freedom that does no *direct* harm to anyone else.

Such are the profound disagreements about the nature and likelihood of indirect harm that leave retentionists and abolitionists predictably divided about the sheer possibility of writing or enforcing a suicide permit. Retentionists doubt that a meaningful law can be written or enforced that guarantees safeguards, because PAS occurs in the context of private and confidential doctor-patient relationship. Abolitionists say that it is precisely the sacredness of the physician-patient relationship that can and should serve as the foundation for a "safe law." Absent that, they believe that society will continue to abandon patients to their suffering, cruelly leaving them to devise ways and means to take their own lives, perhaps like Percy Bridgman (1882–1961), the Nobel laureate in physics who shot himself rather than die of metastatic cancer. His suicide note read: "It is not decent for Society to make a man do this to himself."[48]

CONCLUSIONS

After years of debate and legal wrangling, as a society we have reached some areas of social agreement on the care and treatment of the terminally ill. Today, for example, physicians honor the resuscitation wishes of patients. This means that should they suffer cardiac or respiratory arrest while hospitalized, the terminally ill or very old who so desire will not be revived. Patients also have the right to refuse life-sustaining treatment, including IVs, food, and water. Although undertreating end-of-life pain is still a serious lapse, pain relief is a top priority. The law, as well as a moral, religious, and professional consensus, recognizes a right to the most powerful analgesics, even if they shorten life.

Agreement eludes us, however, on the issue of assisted suicide. In the preceding chapter we saw how the same principle of individual morality can be used to support or oppose the morality of voluntary death. Now we see that powerful moral arguments from identical principles of social justice can support opposed propositions: "The just society permits assisted death" vs. "The just society does not permit assisted death." It is within this moral impasse that today's social debate about PAS takes place. It's also within a political stalemate that we must fashion social policy regarding assisted death. What to do?

We could do nothing. We could maintain the status quo, which seems to be a policy of toleration without legalization. Then again, we could respond aggressively.

On one hand, we could heed to the cultural conservatives, and some liberals, and ban assisted death on the federal level, including any initiatives such as Oregon's Death with Dignity Act. Any physicians who didn't comply could be prosecuted and, conceivably, sued for malpractice. On the other hand, we could follow more progressive tendencies and legitimate PAS. As in Oregon and Washington, strict rules could specify the conditions for permitting assisted death. Tests of mental competency; insurance of adequate comfort care; and, if we follow the lead of Dr. Quill, "a meaningful doctor-patient relationship" could be among the necessary criteria.[49]

Whichever option we choose, especially the liberty-limiting prohibition, a broad consensus of professional and public opinion acknowledges the moral importance of providing quality end-of-life care, including palliative, or comfort, care. From the patient's perspective, research shows that this includes five focal points: adequate pain and symptom management, avoiding inappropriate prolongation of dying, achieving a sense of control, relieving burden, and strengthening relationships with loved ones.[50,51]

Here isn't the place for discussing these patient interests and, possibly, rights. But it is appropriate to suggest some constituents of a genuine moral commitment, on the part of society and the medical profession, to meeting these elements of quality end-of-life care that bridge the cultural divide.[52] Required is a substantial investment of human and financial resources in research and development that address not only the physical needs of dying patients but also their psychological, spiritual, and emotional requirements, as well as those of their families. At a minimum, this calls for the removal of irrational barriers to effective pain management, such as cruelly restrictive regulation of narcotics. Also, patients and families need to be encouraged to issue directives, not just preferences. Most important, quality care at life's end must be based on need, not affordability. It must be seen as a universal right, not a privilege of wealth. And because none of this is possible without a cast of professionals who by inclination, training, and character can offer quality care to the dying and their families, reforms in medical education already underway must keep apace.[53]

Anything less than these social and professional developments would make the society that preaches life and prohibits assisted death heartless, and the one that preaches choice and permits assisted death dangerous—and both breathtakingly hypocritical. We may be understandably divided on whether the just society is the one that prohibits or permits assisted death. But on two points there can be no reasonable disagreement between retentionists and abolitionists: The just society ensures the highest quality end-of-life care, and by that measure we have a long way to go.

CASES AND CONTROVERSIES

Oregon's Death with Dignity Act

Under Oregon's Death with Dignity Act, which has been in effect since October 1997, a physician may, under certain circumstances, legally prescribe lethal drugs for mentally competent, terminally ill Oregon residents eighteen or older who want to end their own lives. Besides the age, residency, and mental competency requirements, the Oregon death permit contains the following provisions:

1. The patient must be expected to die of a terminal illness within six months.
2. The patient must make his or her requests at fifteen day intervals, one of which must be a written request supported by two witnesses.
3. Before writing the prescription the physician must wait at least fifteen days after the patient's initial request and at least forty-eight hours after the written request.
4. The physician must fully inform the patient about the diagnosis and prognosis, as well as feasible alternatives such as comfort care, hospice, or pain control.
5. Both the attending physician and consulting physician must certify that the patient is mentally competent, is acting voluntarily, and has made an informed choice.
6. If either physician believes that the patient's judgment might be impaired, the patient must be referred for counseling.

Although Oregon's criteria resemble Holland's, they differ significantly. Unlike in Oregon, the Dutch do not require "witness support," thereby granting a larger measure of patient freedom. In fact, in 1984 when the Dutch Medical Association compiled its requirements for doctors to follow in order for euthanasia to be acceptable, it stated that "the patient must experience his suffering as unacceptable for him."[54] Also notable: The "suffering," although unbearable and hopeless, need not be physical pain; and Dutch law has no life expectancy requirement. Finally, in The Netherlands euthanasia is permissible, but not in Oregon.

(Continued)

CASES AND CONTROVERSIES (CONTINUED)

Through 2008, 401 people, representing about one in 1,000 deaths, had used the Oregon law to take their lives, although 1 in 50 dying patients discussed the possibility with their doctors and 1 in 6 with their families.[55] Most were cancer patients. The top reasons given by patients for wanting to end their lives were: losing autonomy (84%), decreasing ability to participate in activities they enjoyed (84%), and losing control of bodily functions (47%).[56] There has not been widespread abuse, as feared, in part apparently because doctors and nurses have done a good job on end-of-life palliative, or comfort, care.

Bills modeled after Oregon's Death with Dignity Act were introduced in four states in 2003—Arizona, Hawaii, Wisconsin, and Vermont—and one stalled in committee, in California in 2005. In North Carolina two physician legislators introduced a bill calling for banning such legislation, while thirty-eight states already have done so. Seven states have either adopted case law or interpreted homicide statutes to criminalize PAS. Its legal status remains undetermined in Nevada,

Utah, Wyoming, and Hawaii. In November 2008, residents of the state of Washington voted 58% to 42% to allow physician-assisted suicide. The Washington Death with Dignity Act is modeled on the Oregon law. In December 2008, a Montana judge ruled that doctor-assisted suicide is legal (see case presentation *Baxter v. Montana* below).

Questions for Analysis

1. Do you approve of Oregon's Death with Dignity Act?

2. What is your greatest concern about a permit like this one?

3. Evaluate the morality of Oregon's law in terms of the principles of social justice discussed in this chapter.

4. In what way(s), if any, do you think the law could be improved?

5. Explain why you think PAS should or should not be prohibited by federal law?

CASES AND CONTROVERSIES

Dying and the War on Drugs

In 2006 Oregon's Death with Dignity Act was litigated in the US Supreme Court (*Gonzales v. Oregon*). The basis for the litigation was the US Attorney General's claim that Oregon's practice violated the Controlled Substances Act (CSA), because it lacked a "legitimate medical purpose." The attorney general (AG) depicted the actual "taking of drugs to commit suicide as drug abuse." The state of Oregon, a group of terminally ill patients, and a physician-pharmacist challenged the AG's interpretive rule. In a 6-3 decision upholding the Oregon law, the US Supreme Court found the AG's assertion of power to regulate medical issues was "both beyond his expertise and incongruous with the statute [CSA] purposes and design."

Although it was the first time that the Supreme Court directly passed judgment on legislation permitting states to actively assist dying, the decision was not widely viewed as a major victory for right-to-die advocates. Its immediate legal impact was to allow Oregon physicians to continue to prescribe drugs under

the Death with Dignity Act without fear of federal penalty. On the other hand, there's nothing to stop those who oppose PAS from continuing to try to use the CSA to impede the practice; or from pressing Congress to enact a nationwide assisted-suicide ban.

As a legal matter, *Gonzales v. Oregon* pitted the traditional power of the state to regulate medicine against the federal government's authority to regulate drugs. As a practical matter, the case was a key part of the government's $19 billion anti-drug campaign emphasizing drug abuse as a moral evil which needed to be eradicated and warranted punishment, as opposed to a medical/social scourge which called for education, containment treatment, and rehabilitation. Central to the administration's moralistic effort was the strict enforcement of all drug laws, meaning: no relaxation of any drug law for any purpose, including use as medicine. Thus, various efforts were made to discourage physicians from prescribing high levels of opiates for pain control; to defeat drug reform initiatives; and to roll back popular medical marijuana laws.

Ten years earlier, in 1996, California voted to legalize the sale of marijuana to people with a doctor's prescription, and since then hundreds of dispensaries sprung up throughout the state. But marijuana was still illegal under federal law, and DEA agents raided many of the dispensaries under both the Clinton and Bush administrations.

On March 17, 2009, Eric H. Holder, Jr., President Obama's new attorney general, outlined a shift in the enforcement of federal drug laws, saying the administration would effectively end the frequent raids on distributors of medical marijuana. In the future, Holder said, the Justice Department's enforcement policy would now be restricted to traffickers who falsely masqueraded as medical dispensaries and used medical marijuana laws as a shield. But, as the expression goes, the more things change the more they stay the same. In fact, providers of medical marijuana still face jail time, and the federal government still discourages research into the medicinal uses of smoked marijuana. That's probably one reason that there is no solid evidence that legalizing marijuana use provides benefits over current therapies.[57]

On January 18, 2010, his last day in office, Governor John Corzine of New Jersey signed a measure that made the state the fourteenth in the nation to legalize the use of marijuana to help with chronic diseases such as multiple sclerosis.

Questions for Analysis

1. What are some of the effects of the federal government blocking marijuana research?

2. Drugs often are used in indigenous and shamanistic religions as part of health practices. But Judaism, Christianity, and Islam disapprove of the use of most drugs. Representative of their view is this moral condemnation from the *Catechism of the Catholic Church*, derived from the Fifth Commandment's prohibition of killing:

   The use of drugs inflicts very grave damage on human health and life. Their use, except on strictly therapeutic grounds, is a grave offense. Clandestine production of and trafficking in drugs are scandalous practices. They constitute direct co-operation in evil, since they encourage people to practices gravely contrary to the moral law.[58]

   Do you agree with the church's position? Should religious beliefs influence social policy and laws?

3. For Dr. Richard Payne, a professor of medicine and divinity and director of the Institute for Care on the End of Life at Duke Divinity School, the ethics of providing desperate patients access to marijuana are clear. "It's not a great drug," he says, "but what's the harm?" Do you agree?[59]

CASES AND CONTROVERSIES

Baxter v. Montana

Experts agree that Montana offers excellent pain management and palliative care for the suffering terminally ill. But as of December 2008, it offered Robert Baxter something else: assisted suicide.

Baxter, a 75-year-old, retired truck driver terminally ill with leukemia, together with two other patients and four physicians, sought the right to assisted suicide and freedom from prosecution under the state's homicide laws. On December 5, 2008, Montana District judge Dorothy McCarter ruled that the state law banning assisted suicide violated not only the right to privacy guaranteed in the state constitution but also the constitutional clause that reads, "The dignity of the human being is inviolable." McCarter found a "fundamental right" for the terminally ill to "die with

dignity." She also found a concomitant physicians' right to be free from "liability under the State's homicide statutes" if they assist a patient in death with dignity. "If the patient were to have no assistance from his doctor," McCarter explained, "he may be forced to kill himself sooner ... in a manner that violates his dignity and peace of mind, such as by gunshot or by otherwise unpleasant method, causing undue suffering to the patient and his family." McCarter also said:

Respect for the dignity of each individual— a fundamental right protected by ... the Montana Constitution—demands that people have for themselves the moral right and moral responsibility to confront the most fundamental questions ... of life in general, answering to their own consciences and

(Continued)

CASES AND CONTROVERSIES (CONTINUED)

convictions.... [And, referencing Justice Anthony Kennedy's famous "mystery of life" passage from the 1992 abortion case *Planned Parenthood v. Casey*]: The most intimate and personal choices a person may make in a lifetime, choices central to personal dignity and autonomy are central to liberty protected by the Fourteenth Amendment. At the heart of liberty is the right to define one's own concept of existence, of meaning, of the universe, and of the mystery of human life. (*Baxter v. Montana*)

Baxter died before the opinion was issued. The case is being appealed to the Montana Supreme Court.

Questions for Analysis

1.   Is assisted suicide a "fundamental right"?

2.   Criticizing McCarter's ruling, pro-life activist Wesley Smith wrote:

     In essence, Judge McCarter ruled that the individual's right to act upon such

metaphysical beliefs trumps all but the most compelling state interests. But if that is so, how can assisted suicide possibly be limited to the terminally ill? Many people suffer more profoundly—and for longer—than people who are dying. Thus, once the right to end suffering through "death with dignity" is deemed "fundamental," how can people with debilitating chronic illnesses, the elderly who are profoundly tired of living, those in despair after becoming paralyzed, or indeed anyone in other than transitory existential agony be denied the same constitutional right as the terminally ill to end it all?[60]

Do you agree with Smith that the Montana decision effectively puts the nation on a slippery slope, one step closer to permitting assisted death for almost any reason?

3.   What moral principle or principles underpin McCarter's decision?

CASES AND CONTROVERSIES

The "Euthanasia Underground"

Drawing on his research with HIV/AIDS patients in California and Australia, Roger S. Magnusson calls it the "euthanasia underground" and "the underbelly of medicine and nursing." But, despite the significant number of doctors—from 4 to more than 10 percent—and nurses who admit in surveys to have written at least one "lethal prescription" or provided at least one lethal injection, relatively little is known about the circumstances in which doctors participate in PAS/VAE. Also undetermined are whether their assistance results in what is perceived to be a good death for the patient, and the long-term impact of involvement on health care providers themselves. Thus, the reason for Magnusson's extensive interviews with health professionals who secretly assist patients to die. Here are some of the professor of law's key findings:

■   Some of the doctors and nurses saw themselves at "the vanguard of a new ethic of caring: one that

encompassed assisted death as part of their professional role." Others showed stress and fatigue about trying to make sense of it anymore.

■   In many cases doctors and nurses miscalculated the dosages required to achieve death, resorting in panicked desperation to "suffocation, strangulation, and injections of air."

■   No guidelines or stable criteria exist for providing appropriate procedure.

■   Also absent is any sort of quality assurance mechanism that patients aren't acting out of depression or dementia, and that they've had adequate counseling for palliative care.[61]

Beyond this, Magnusson reports:

Covert PAS/AVE [i.e., VAE] has spawned a culture of deception. Deceit is all pervasive. It encompasses the methods used to procure euthanasia drugs, the planning of the death itself, and the disposal of the body and associated paperwork. Prior to death, doctors admitted to fabricating symptoms in order to create a plausible clinical basis for the prescription or administration of escalating dosages of drugs. In other cases, drugs were simply stolen, or hoarded and redistributed by health carers, patients, and even care organizations. Lying on death certificates, and on cremation certificates, was universal. The true nature of these underground practices, however, adds a worrying new dimension to the statistics. We need a new debate: one that takes account of underground PAS/ AVE, and is honest about the risks that prohibition, as well as legalization, pose for patients.[62]

Questions for Analysis

1. Illegalities aside, are the doctors and nurses who participate in the "euthanasia underground" doing anything that is morally wrong?

2. Evaluate the conduct of the underground physicians from the perspectives of principles and virtue.

3. Does the widespread occurrence of illicit euthanasia provide a good reason for legalizing PAS, or does it make you less supportive of its legalization?

4. Are there any comparisons to be drawn between Magnusson's findings and pre-*Roe* abortion (see Chapter 9)?

REFERENCES

1. Jane Gross, "Landscape Evolves for Assisted Suicide," *The New York Times*, November 11, 2008, p. D8.

2. See note 1 above.

3. Daniel Bergner, "Death in the Family," *The New York Times Magazine*, December 2, 2007, p. 40.

4. Manuel Velasquez, *Philosophy: Text with Readings*, 8th ed., Belmont, CA: Wadsworth/Thomson Learning, 2002, p. 638.

5. Yale Kamisar, "The Reasons So Many People Support Physician-Assisted Suicide and Why These Reasons Are Not Convincing," in Ralph Baergen, *Ethics at the End of Life*, Belmont, CA: Wadsworth/ Thomson Learning, 2001, p. 183.

6. Ibid., p. 180.

7. Bonnie Steinbock, "The Intentional Termination of Life," in Bonnie Steinbock and Alastair Norcross, eds., *Killing and Letting Die*, 2nd ed., New York: Fordham University Press, 1992, p. 123.

8. Pope John Paul II, "Declaration on Euthanasia," Sacred Congregation for the Doctrine of Faith, May 5, 1980. Retrieved June 20, 2009, from www. vatican.va/.../rc_con_cfaith_doc_19800505_ euthanasia_en.html.

9. Robert P. Jones, *Liberalism's Troubled Search for Equality*, quoted in Wesley J. Smith, "Liberalism's Troubled Search for Equality," March 5, 2008. Retrieved June 19, 2009, from www.discovery.org/ a/4503.

10. Ronald Dworkin et al, "The Philosopher's Brief," *The New York Review of Books* March 27, 1997. Retrieved June 19, 2009, from www.nybooks.com/ nyrev/WWWarchdisplay.cgi?

11. Ronald Melzak, "The Tragedy of Needless Pain," *Scientific American*, February 1990, p. 27.

12. John Lachs, "When Abstract Moralizing Runs Amok," in Ralph Baergen, *Ethics at the End of Life*, Belmont, CA: Wadsworth/Thomson Learning, 2001, p. 232.

13. Daniel Callahan, "When Self-Determination Runs Amok," in Ralph Baergen, *Ethics at the End of Life*, Belmont, CA: Wadsworth/Thomson Learning, p. 224.

14. Lachs, p. 230.

15. See note 12 above.

16. Jeffrey Olen, Julie C. Van Camp, and Vincent Barry, *Applying Ethics: A Text with Readings*, 8th ed., Belmont, Ca: Wadsworth/Thomson Learning, 2005, p. 18.

17. Steven J. Taylor, "Death With Dignity' For People Who Are Not Dying?" *Center on Human Policy*, Syracuse University, April 2000. Retrieved September 19, 2010, from http://thechp.syr.edu/ death_with_dignity.htm..

18. "When Death Is Sought: Assisted Suicide in the Medical Context," *The New York Task Force on Life & the Law*, October 2001. Retrieved February 1, 2005, from http://www.health.state.ny.us/nys-doh/provider/death.htm.

19. Carl Coleman and Tracy H. Miller, "Stemming the Tide: Assisted Suicide and the Constitution," *Journal of Law, Medicine & Ethics*, Winter 1995, p. 393.

20. Ronald A. Lindsay, "Should We Impose Quotas? Evaluating the 'Disparate Impact' Argument Against Legalizing Assisted Suicide," *Journal of Law, Medicine & Ethics*, Spring 2002, p. 7.

21. Ronald A. Lindsay, *Future Bioethics: Overcoming Taboos, Myths, and Dogmas*, Amherst, NY: Prometheus, 2008.

22. Stephen Jamison, *Final Acts of Love: Families, Friends and Assisted Dying*, Los Angeles: Jeremy P. Tarcher, 1996.

23. Coleman and Miller.

24. Marcia Angell, "Euthanasia in The Netherlands, Good News or Bad?" *The New England Journal of Medicine*, November 28, 1996, pp. 1676–1678.

25. Linda Ganzini et al, "Prevalence of depression and anxiety in patients requesting physicians' aid in dying: cross sectional survey," *BMJ*, October 8, 2008, p. 1682. Retrieved October 9, 2008, from http://www.bmj.com/cgi/content/full/337/oct07_2/a1682.

26. W. Carol Cleigh, "Attempted Suicide, Completed," *Ragged Edge Online*, Issue 2, 2001. Retrieved July 20, 2008, from http://www.ragged-edge-mag.com/0301/0301ft4.htm.

27. Susan Wolf, "Gender, Feminism, and Death: Physician-Assisted Suicide and Euthanasia," in *Feminism & Bioethics: Beyond Reproduction*, Susan M. Wolfe, ed., New York: Oxford University Press, 1996, pp. 282–317.

28. Bergner, p. 41.

29. Sydney Callahan, "A Feminist Case Against Self-Determined Dying in Assisted Suicide and Euthanasia," *Studies in Profile Feminism*, September 22, 1995, pp. 303–315.

30. Diane Christine Raymond, "'Fatal Practices': A Feminist Analysis of Physician-Assisted Suicide and Euthanasia," *Hypatia*, Spring 1999, pp. 1–25.

31. Jennifer Parks, "Why Gender Matters in the Euthanasia Debate," *Hastings Center Report* 30(1), pp. 30–36.

32. Lindsay, p. 14.

33. Olen, Van Camp, and Barry, pp. 19–20.

34. Ian Dowbiggin, *A Merciful End: The Euthanasia Movement in Modern America*, New York: Oxford University Press, 2003.

35. Wesley Smith, "Dying Cause," *National Review Online*, May 20, 2003. Retrieved February 3, 2005, from http://www.nationalreview.com/comment/comment-smith052003.asp.

36. C. Everett Koop, "The Right To Die," in Robert M. Baird and Stuart E. Rosenbaum, eds. *Euthanasia: The Moral Issues, (Contemporary Issues in Philosophy)*, Amherst, NY: Prometheus, p. 69.

37. Bergner, p. 42.

38. Peter Singer and M. Siegler, "Euthanasia— A Critique," *The New England Journal of Medicine*, June 28, 1990, pp. 1881–1883.

39. Arthur Caplan, "Will Assisted Suicide Kill Hospice?" in Bruce Jennings, ed., *Ethics in Hospice Care*, Binghampton, NY: Haworth Press, 1997.

40. James Bernat, "The Problem of Physician-assisted Suicide," *Seminars in Neurology*, 17, 1997, pp. 271–279.

41. See note 22 above.

42. S. W. Tolle, "Care of the Dying: Clinical and Financial Lessons from the Oregon Experience," *Annals of Internal Medicine*, 1998, vol. 128, pp. 567–568.

43. S. W. Tolle, A. G. Rosenfield, V. P. Tilden, and Y. Park, "Oregon's Low In-hospital Death Rates: What Determines Where People Die and Satisfaction with Decisions on Place of Death?" *Annals of Internal Medicine*, 1999, vol. 130, pp. 681–685.

44. "Assisted-suicide Number Continue To Rise in Oregon," *American Medical News*, March 24/32/2003. Retrieved February 3, 2005, from http://www.ama-assn.org/amednews/2003/03/24/prs0324.htm.

45. Linda Ganzini et al, "Oregon's Physicians' Attitudes about and Experiences with End-of-Life Care Since Passage of the Oregon Death with Dignity Act," *JAMA*, May 9, 2001. pp. 2263–2269.

46. Arthur Caplan and David Orentlicher, "The Pain Relief Promotion Act of 1999," *JAMA*, January 12, 2000, pp. 255–258.

47. Marcia Angell, "The Supreme Court and Physician-Assisted Suicide—The Ultimate Right," *The New England Journal of Medicine*, January 2, 1997, pp. 50–53.

48. Sherwin Nuland, *How We Die*, New York: Alfred A. Knopf, 1994, p. 152.

49. Timothy E. Quill, "Doctor, I Want to Die, Will You Help Me?" *Journal of the American Medical Association*, August 18, 1993, p. 873.

50. Peter Singer, Douglas K. Martin, and Merijoy Kelner, "Quality End-of-Life Care," *Journal of the American Medical Association*, January 13, 1999, pp. 163–168.

51. Institute of Medicine, "Accountability and Quality in End-of-life-care," in *Approaching Death: Improving Care at the End of Life*, Washington, D.C.: National Academy Press, 1997.

52. Last Acts, "Means to a Better End: A Report on Dying in America Today," 2002. Retrieved February 9, 2005, from http://www.americangeria trics.org/product/positionpapers/quality.shtml.

53. Rose Virani and Dalia Sofer, "Improving Quality End-of-Life Care," *American Journal of Nursing*, May 2003, pp. 52–60.

54. John Griffiths, Alex Bood, and Heleen Weyers, *Euthanasia and Law in the Netherlands*, Amsterdam: Amsterdam University Press, 1998.

55. Stuart Glascock, "A Personal Battle over Right To Die," *Los Angeles Times*, June 22, 2008, p. A13.

56. Andis Robeznieks, "Assisted-Suicide Numbers Continue To Rise in Oregon," *American Medical News*, March 24/31, 2003. Retrieved June 22, 2009, from www.ama-assn.org/amednews/2003/03/24/ prsc0324.htm.

57. Gardiner Harris, "Researchers Find Study of Medical Marijuana Discouraged," *The New York Times*, January 19, 2010, p. A18.

58. "Article 5, The Fifth Commandment, 2291," *The Catholic Doors Ministry*, Saskatoon, Canada. Retrieved March 20, 2009, from http://www.cath olicdoors.com/catechis/subject.htm.

59. See note 56 above.

60. Wesley Smith, "Euthanasia Comes to Montana," *Weekly Standard*, December 29, 2008. Retrieved May 28, 2009, from http://www.weeklystandard. com/Content/Public/Articles/000/000/015/ 930uapms.asp.

61. Roger S. Magnusson, *Angels of Death: Exploring the Euthanasia Underground*, New Haven: Yale University Press, 2002.

62. Roger S. Magnusson, "'Underground Euthanasia' and the Harm Minimization Debate," *The Journal of Law, Medicine & Ethics*, October 1, 2004. Retrieved June 20, 2009, from http://www.allbusiness.com/ legal/3587146-1.html.

Chapter 22

Rationing Health Care at The End of Life

"The U.S. health care system is in crisis."[1] That is how the Senate Finance Committee began its description of policy options for financing comprehensive health care reform, published on May 20, 2009. The report pointed out that the crisis is not limited to the estimated 46 million who lack health insurance, but extends to the insured who are worried about increasing costs.

Rising health care costs have a huge impact on federal and state health care programs. Forty-six percent of health care spending comes from Medicare, Medicaid, and other government-sponsored programs.[2] Medicare is the federally administered system of health insurance for persons aged sixty-five and over. Medicaid is a federally and state-funded health program for persons unable to afford medical treatment. Together they cover close to 100 million people. According to the 2009 Medicare Trustee Report, the Medicare Hospital Insurance Trust Fund runs out in 2017, two years earlier than in 2008's report. Spending for Medicare and Medicaid is projected to increase 114 percent in ten years, while GDP is expected to grow by just 64 percent over the same period. In 2008, health spending in the United States represented 16.6 percent of our GDP, a much higher share than any other industrialized country. That share is expected to rise to over 20 percent by 2018, an amount representing $4.4 trillion in annual spending.[3]

The cost growth of Medicare, which currently insures about 45 million Americans, has risen steadily and rapidly since its inception in 1965, although less so than for private health insurance.[4] Medicare is expensive because it serves the very disabled and the elderly. Most of its spending is for hospitalizations, about 33 cents out of every dollar spent on health care. In just twenty years from now, the percentage of the population sixty-five years old or older is expected to reach more than 20 percent. The fastest growing age group is the population aged eighty and over—the very group that tends to require expensive and intensive medical care.[5]

The projected demands from a growing elderly population on a health care system that is already taxed to the breaking point, together with continual advances and availability of expensive life-extending technology, have led to troubling questions about society's ability to meet future health care demands. But already controversial decisions to limit health resources are being made, sometimes in a most dramatic fashion.

THE DEATH OF BARBARA WAGNER

Barbara Wagner (1944–2008) of Oregon was a waitress, school bus driver, home health care aid, and great-grandmother. Wagner was also a smoker who developed lung cancer. Her condition forced her to wear an oxygen tube, paid for by the Oregon Health Plan (OHP), the state's Medicaid program, as were a wheelchair, chemotherapy, radiation, and a special bed. As her health worsened, Wagner pinned her hopes for survival on Tarceva, a new chemo drug her oncologist recommended that cost about $4,000 a month. Less than 10 percent of patients like Wagner, with advanced lung cancer, respond to the drug, with a chance to extend life from an average of four to six months. Given the treatment's costs and limited benefit, OHP would not approve it. In an unsigned letter, plan officials informed Wagner: "Treatment of advanced cancer that is meant to prolong life, or change the course of this disease, is not a covered benefit of the Oregon Health Plan."[6] The plan would pay for comfort care, pain and symptom management, and "physician aid in dying."

The decision shocked Wagner. "To say to someone, we'll pay for you to die, but not pay for you to live, it's cruel," she told a local newspaper. In a TV appearance Wagner expressed her determination to live. "I'm not ready, I'm not ready to die," she said. "I've got things I'd still like to do."

Portland physician William Toffler, an outspoken critic of PAS and founder of Physicians for Compassionate Care, called the letter's message disturbing. "People deserve relief of their suffering, not giving them an overdose," Toffler said, adding that the state has a financial incentive to offer death instead of life. Whereas cutting-edge chemotherapy drugs can cost thousands of dollars a month, drugs for assisted death cost less than $100.

Dr. Som Saha, who chairs the commission that sets OHP policy, called Toffler's an "unfortunate interpretation." Saha said that state health officials don't consider whether it is cheaper for someone in the health plan to die than live. He did admit, however, that they must consider the state's limited dollars when dealing with a case like Wagner's. "If we invest thousands and thousands of dollars in one person's days to weeks, we are taking away those dollars from someone," Saha said.

Others officials also attempted to defend the plan's decision. Dr. Walter Shafer, the state's medical director, pointed out: "We can't cover everything for everyone," and "We try to come up with policies that proved the most good for the most people." Plan administrator Dr. Jeanene Smith added, "We need evidence to say it is a good use of taxpayers' dollars."[7]

Wesley J. Smith, the prominent conservative bioethicist, said he was not surprised by events in Oregon. "We have been warning for years that this was a possibility in Oregon.... This isn't the first time this has happened. A few years ago a patient who needed a double organ transplant was denied the treatment but would have been eligible for state-financed assisted suicide.... [A]ssisted suicide is always covered. And now, Barbara Wagner was faced with that very scenario."[8]

Patients like Wagner can appeal a decision to deny coverage. She did twice and lost both times. However, her physicians contacted the drug's manufacturer, Genentech, who agreed to give her the medication free. Wagner died in October 2008, shortly after starting the new chemo regimen.

Coming as it did amidst the Obama administration's push for health care reform, the Wagner case provided a backdrop for conservatives like Betsy McCaughey, New York's former lieutenant governor, to insist that parts of the proposed legislation would deliberately drive the sick and elderly to early graves. Former Republican vice presidential candidate Sarah Palin saw "Obama's death panels" lurking, that is, government bureaucrats who would decide who got care and who didn't. And at a town hall meeting in his home state of Iowa, Republican Senator Chuck Grassley urged: "We should not have a government program that determines if you're going to pull the plug on grandma."

Meanwhile, abortion opponents were threatening to sink any health care reform without language barring the procedure. "Let's face it. I want to see health care," Representative Bart Stupak (D-MI) told ABC's *Good Morning America* on March 3, 2010. Nevertheless, the pro-life Catholic insisted, "we're not going to bypass the principles of belief that we feel strongly about." But sixty leaders of religious orders representing 59,000 Catholic nuns exposed the perdurable rift between conservative and liberal Catholic theology, when they sent a letter to federal lawmakers urging them to pass the Senate health care legislation. The nuns decried the "false" information circulating about abortion provisions and said the bill's "historic investments" for pregnant women were the "REAL pro-life stance." The nuns' letter, together with a matching view of Catholic hospitals, was a stunning departure from the position of the US Conference of Catholic Bishops, which denounced the proposed legislation.[9] For his part, Stupak dismissed the nuns, saying: "When I'm drafting right to life language, I don't call up nuns." Instead, Stupak said that he conferred with other groups, including "leading bishops, Focus on the Family, and The National Right to Life Committee."[10]

Amidst late-hour wrangling over the limits on insurance coverage of abortions, the president made clear his intention to "establish an adequate enforcement mechanism to ensure that federal funds are not used for abortion services," thereby continuing the longstanding prohibition on using taxpayer money for abortions known as the Hyde Amendment (see Chapter 10). Satisfied by the executive order, Stupak and other anti-abortion Democrats dropped their opposition and, just before midnight on Sunday, March 21, 2010, provided the critical votes needed to pass the historic but politically divisive legislation

that would affect about one-sixth of the nation's economy. (Shortly thereafter, under fire for the abortion deal, Stupak announced his retirement from the US Congress.)

Although reforming the current patchwork of public and private health insurance inevitably creates ideological division fueled by such hot-button issues as assisted death and abortion, on one point partisans agree. "Responsible health care reform must provide health care coverage for all Americans while at the same time reduce the rate of growth in health care spending," in the words of the Senate Finance Committee report. These goals must be achieved in a fiscally responsible manner with sustainable sources of funding. This is only possible, according to most experts, with some kind of health care prioritization, such as what Barbara Wagner confronted. As one commentator puts it: "No free society in the contemporary technologic era of medicine can provide everyone with every medical intervention and survive."[11] In brief, when it comes to health care reform, there are no free lunches.

HEALTH CARE RATIONING

Rationing refers to the controlled distribution of resources, particularly scarce goods or services. When the resources happen to be health care related—for example, organs, medicines, procedures, treatments, and therapies—health care is being rationed.

Like Barbara Wagner, patients typically experience health care rationing as a conflict between what their physicians consider the best treatment for them medically and ethically and the treatment the patient's insurance covers. The result is a delay or a denial of treatment. This makes health care rationing inevitably a conflict between medicine and money. At the same time, as health care policy consultant Heinz Redwood notes, while "the motivation of health care rationing is primarily financial, the intention is to be fair (i.e., 'equitable allocation')" in selecting patients and setting priorities.[12] This leads to the more precise definition of health care rationing as: "planning for the equitable allocation, apportionment, or distribution of available health resources." But establishing a criterion of fairness is very difficult.

In the 1960s, philosophers and bioethicists struggled to generate principles of equity to govern justice between racial and ethnic groups. Today some of them have taken on an analogous task: generating principles of equity to govern "justice between age groups."[13]

ARGUMENTS FOR AGE-BASED RATIONING

In 1995, the US Census Bureau noted that "not too far into the future," the growth of America's elderly population, which had recently moderated, would accelerate. In fact, so rapid would its growth be that by the middle of the present century, the Bureau said that "it might be completely inaccurate to think of ourselves as a Nation of the young: there could be more persons who are elderly (65 or over) than young (14 or younger)!" The Census Bureau forecast that by the year 2050 the elderly population would have doubled to 80 million. By that year, as many as 1 in 5 Americans could be elderly. Most of this growth, according to the Bureau, would probably occur between 2010 and 2030, when the "baby boom" generation entered its elderly years. During that period, the number of elderly would grow by an average of 2.8 percent annually. By comparison, annual growth will average 1.3 percent during the preceding 20 years and 0.7 percent during the following 20 years.[14]

As the ranks of the elderly swell, today's policy makers are scrambling to meet the challenges of increasing demands on the nation's health care resources. But even before the Census Bureau issued its sobering assessment, bioethicists and population planners were suggesting that health care should be rationed by age. In a 1983 speech to the Health Insurance Association of America, the economist Alan Greenspan frankly wondered "whether it is worth it" to spend nearly one-third of Medicare on just 5 to 6 percent of Medicare insurees who

die within the year. In 1984 Richard Lamm, then governor of Colorado, was widely quoted as stating that older persons "have a duty to die and get out of the way of younger generations."[15] Then, in 1987, bioethicist Daniel Callahan wrote a highly controversial book titled *Setting Limits,* criticizing the nation's health care system for devoting disproportionate health resources to the elderly. With that work, the idea of age-based rationing of health care emerged as a public issue.

The elderly, Callahan noted, generally require expensive treatments and high-tech intervention that often are ineffective and yield little benefit to society. The young, by contrast, typically require far less costly interventions, such as vaccinations, exercise programs, and basic health education. Callahan flatly urged the elderly population, whom he called "a new social threat," to step aside and sacrifice for the young.[16] In arguing that age-based rationing would be best for society, Callahan was making a largely utilitarian argument, based on the greatest good for the greatest number. Others made the same case, not from cost-effectiveness but from distributive justice, which, recall from Chapter 2, refers to the fair and proper distribution of public benefits and burdens among members of the community.

Some advocates of age-based rationing noted that the elderly received a disproportionately high share of the overall health care resources, and they said that was unjust. Others framed the question of justice more in terms of needs than equal treatment. Frances M. Kamm, for example, made the need for health care inversely proportional to age. The Harvard professor of philosophy and public policy defined needs in terms of how much adequate conscious life a person will have had before death, and then correlated conscious life with age. By this account, younger persons are usually "needier" than older ones, that is, the young "need" more years of life than the old, being worse off without them than the old would be.[17] Related arguments made the point that because the elderly had enjoyed the opportunity to live a long time, it was only fair for the old to give the young a similar opportunity. These views were indebted to the so-called fair innings argument, or FIA.

The Fair Innings Argument

Perhaps the main justification for age-based rationing was, and continues to be, the "fair innings argument."[18]

According to the FIA, everyone is entitled to some normal life span, say, 70 years. So, for health care resources to be distributed fairly, every person should receive enough health resources to give them the opportunity to live a normal life span. Those who live less are cheated, while those who live more have received a bonus. Alternatively, those who have been cheated have suffered an injustice by not getting their fair share, whereas those who have received a bonus suffer no such injustice, because they received more than their fair share. The FIA requires, then, that (1) everyone be given an equal opportunity to reach the appropriate threshold of a normal life span; and (2) having reached that threshold, they are not entitled to more. Philosopher John Harris, who is currently the Editor-Chief of *The Journal of Medical Ethics*, drew out the implications of the fair innings view as early as 1970, in an introduction to medical ethics, in which he wrote:

> I am inclined to believe that where two individuals both equally wish to go on living for as long as possible our duty to respect this wish is paramount .... Each person's desire to stay alive should be regarded as of the same importance and as deserving the same respect as that of anyone else, irrespective of the quality of their life or its expected duration. This would hold good in all cases in which we have to choose between lives, except one. And that is where one individual has had a fair innings and the other not. In this case, although there is nothing to choose between the two candidates from the points of view of their respective will to live and both would suffer the injustice of having their life cut short when it might continue, only one would suffer the further injustice of being deprived of a fair innings—a benefit the other has received .... The fair innings argument

points to the fact that the injustice done to someone who has not had a fair innings when they lose out to someone who has is significantly greater than in the reverse circumstances. It is for this reason that in the hopefully rare circumstances where we have to choose between candidates who differ only in this respect we should choose to give as many as possible the chance of a fair innings.[19]

The Prudential Lifespan Account

In 1985, and again in 1988, Normal Daniels, a Harvard professor of population ethics, advanced an argument for age-based rationing he called Prudential Lifespan Account, or PLA.[20,21] Daniels's PLA traded on John Rawls' social contractarian view of justice.[22] Although Rawls never directly addressed health policy, even by the late 1980s numerous writers were nonetheless grounding their views about how best to distribute medical resources in the Rawlsian theory of justice. Among them was Daniels, who specifically adopted the strategy Rawls used in *A Theory of Justice* (1972) in trying to identify and justify basic principles of justice.

Daniels imagined a group of prudent planners convening for the purpose of deciding on the ground rules for their society, in particular on the rules governing economic distribution. No one in the group knows anything about themselves personally or about what their individual situation will be once the rules are chosen. Behind what Rawls called this "veil of ignorance," the group must agree on the rules of governance. For Daniels, this meant, most significantly, that the participants didn't know how old they were or whether, in life's lottery, they would or would not reach a normal life span. Under these conditions, Daniels asked: What rules would prudent planners likely choose to govern their relationships, assuming that scarce and expensive life-extending resources could be made available to those who will have reached a normal life expectancy only by giving fewer services to those who have not? In other words, group members could have what they needed for living a longer than normal life span only if they agreed to forego access to what they needed when young to live a normal life span. What would they choose under these conditions?

In Daniels' view, the prudent planner would choose to ration by age, making life-extending resources more available to the young than to the very old. As he wrote recently in a reconsideration of his view: "More precisely, if we consider only information about life-years saved, and if rationing by age and rationing by lottery both yield the same life expectancy, it is not imprudent to prefer an increased chance of reaching that life expectancy through age rationing."[23]

ARGUMENTS AGAINST AGE-BASED RATIONING

Unsurprisingly, Callahan's *Setting Limits* inspired a wave of opposition, some of it challenging the cost-effectiveness assumptions behind his defense of age-based rationing. Critics argued that it wasn't so much a substantial aging population that was driving up health care costs but new medical technologies and their intensive application, as well as the structure and utilization of the health care systems, both public and private.[24] Moreover, even granting the need for health care rationing, Callahan's critics questioned whether age-based rationing would yield the expected results; and even if it did, they said there was no guarantee that the savings would redound to the young or make a significant dent in overall health care expenditure. Others wondered whether rationing was even required and, if it were, why other alternatives weren't preferable, such as transferring funds from other areas, notably defense spending (which for fiscal 2010 was $663.8 billion).

Economics aside, early critics of age-based rationing cited what they believed would be its enormous and intolerable moral and social costs, notably the abandonment of the elderly and the loss of their potential social contributions, as well as the loss of respect for persons and the value of all life. Robert Binstock, a professor of medicine and bioethics at Case Western Reserve University, was among those who also worried about the impact of age-based rationing on those it was supposed to treat more fairly: the young, who, as their years mounted inevitably would come to realize that they, too, would soon be considered too old for health care. Beyond this was the fear that once begun, age-based limiting would set a precedent for denial of health care access, to other "socially unproductive" groups, such as the disabled.[25]

Like its proponents, those who opposed age-based rationing also stood squarely on the ground of distributive justice, and still do. Equal treatment, they insisted, requires that individuals be treated equally in the absence of morally relevant reasons for treating them differently. And age, they argued, was no more relevant in allocating health care than race, sex, or religion was in distributing jobs. In hiring, what counted were qualifications; in health, what counted were patient needs. Illustrative of following a strict egalitarian approach to resource allocation, philosopher and lawyer Duff Waring of York University recently gave a spirited defense of random patient selection, under which Waring favors selection criteria that equalize opportunity, as opposed to best outcomes or fair innings. He argues that the best way to equalize opportunity is through a random selection by lottery, which he believes will affirm both a common humanity and the equal value of lives.[26]

Other philosophers have taken special aim at the FIA or "fair share of life" positions. Michael Rivlin, for one, says:

> Being fair does not … mean that we should discriminate against elderly patients on the grounds of fairness. This being the case … there are no grounds for using age as a basis for rationing health care on the basis of the FIA.[27]

Biomedical expert Alan Williams is another who believes that the FIA would mean greater discrimination against the elderly, outweighing any efficiency objectives.[28] Others object to the FIA's definition of "normal life span" as life expectancy at birth. Current gerontological theories, they say, suggest as a more suitable criterion for normal life span the idea that one's life is limited biologically, that is, to the aging process. As technology allows people to live longer, as a result of retarding the aging process, the FIA's notion of "the normal life span" loses its conceptual force. With that, as one commentator says, "the fair innings argument will no longer be able to justify denying people health-care resources because they have lived longer than the normal life span."[29]

As for the Prudential Lifespan Account, Daniels himself still believes it has relevancy to health care rationing. But he has given up on such arguments because of persistent disagreement about basic principles of justice. Even when there's agreement on other aspects of a just health care system, such as universal access to whatever services are provided, the lack of consensus after some thirty years of serious debate on distributive principles of health care has sent Daniels in another direction. Nowadays, he is most interested in finding an agreeable process for resolving disputes about rationing problems.[30]

THE HIGH COST OF END-OF-LIFE CARE

Although both the sides to the age-based rationing debate were, from the outset, in fundamental disagreement about cost effectiveness, social outcomes, and especially principles of distributive justice, both acknowledged the substantial investment of Medicare in end-of-life care, which has only increased since the 1980s. Of special note here is that today Medicare pays for the health care of 8 in 10 Americans who die each year. These costs are extremely high just before death, and our health- care system is set up to try everything because of many factors, including financial incentives for provider and patient preferences.[31] Of the $2.3 trillion allocated for health care in 2009, 10% to 12% was spent on end-of-life care. About 1 in 4 Medicare dollars—or approximately $120 billion in 2009—went to care during the last year of life. Thirty percent of that amount was spent in the last six months, while almost half was spent in the

last thirty days.[32] At an institution such as U.C.L.A., where patients may be seen by dozens of specialists and spend weeks in the hospital before dying, Medicare pays about $50,000 during a patient's last six months of life. That figure contrasts with $25,000 at the Mayo Clinic in Rochester, Minnesota, where doctors closely coordinate care, scrupulous to avoid expensive, unpromising treatments.[33]

While Medicare's $120 billion expenditure represents a sizable increase in absolute dollars compared to forty years ago, significantly it is not a greater proportion of the nation's GDP. To Professor of Public Policy Donald Taylor of Duke University, the persistence of this proportion suggests that "some care is futile and neither extends nor improves quality of life."[34] It is this observation that already in part drives the allocation of health care resources, as in the case of Barbara Wagner, and explicitly interjects the following proposition into the discussion of health reform and prioritization:

> [I]f our aim is to use costly resources more effectively, then we ought to deny treatment to all patients whose prognosis indicates a short life span, chronic illness, or little likelihood of improvement in the quality of life, rather than denying treatment simply on the basis of age.[35]

Were the United States to follow Taylor's proposition and, for example, press hospitals to behave more like Mayo and less like U.C.L.A., the country could save about $700 billion a year, by some estimates.[36] Indeed, under health care legislation pending in Congress in the spring of 2010, hospitals like Mayo would be rewarded for providing more cost-effective care, whereas high-cost centers like U.C.L.A. might be penalized by receiving lower government payments. Should the nation adopt such a policy? Should we, in effect, ration health care by medical futility? Would that be fair?

RATIONING BY MEDICAL FUTILITY

It's widely known that sometimes physicians use the notion of "medical futility" not to pursue treatment requested by patients or surrogates.

As distinguished from health care rationing, which involves an insurance provider or societal decision about the allocation of beneficial treatments among patients, futility is a medical decision about whether a treatment will benefit a patient. The two practices intersect when it is argued that a judgment of medical futility should influence a judgment to ration health care.

Although as old as Western medicine itself, the concept of futility also emerged in the 1980s, when "physicians started to assert that certain life-sustaining treatments should be withdrawn or withheld because they no longer met the legitimate goals of medicine and were thus 'futile.'"[37] Then, in 1990, several bioethicists drew the profession's attention to the quantitative and qualitative roots of medical futility that they thought offered a practical approach to its definition and application. Applying these traditions to contemporary medical practices, L. J. Schneiderman, Nancy Jecker, and Albert Jonsen proposed the following:

> [Quantitatively]: [W]hen physicians conclude (either through personal experience, experiences shared with colleagues, or consideration of published empiric data) that in the last 100 cases a medical treatment has been useless, they should regard that treatment as futile.... [Qualitatively]: If a treatment merely preserves permanent unconsciousness or cannot end dependence on intensive medical care, the treatment should be considered futile.[38]

In a 1996 update of their original article about medical futility, the authors took pains to point out that they were not endorsing "the use of futility by physicians as a cover for cost-containment strategies." "Such deception," they wrote, "makes a mockery of the physician's assertion of professional integrity." At the same time, however, they were quick to add:

> [I]f the medical profession retreats to the position that it has no internal professional values and merely provides whatever patients, families, or insurers are willing to

pay for, it can no longer claim to be a healing profession, that is, a group committed to helping and serving the sick. Instead, medicine becomes a commercial enterprise satisfying the desires of others.[39]

Perhaps so, but the problem is that disputes about medical futility inevitably pit physician professionalism against modern patient self-determination.

Physician Beneficence vs. Patient Autonomy

Physicians and patients or their surrogates don't always agree about what "futile" means and when a treatment or procedure is rightly termed "futile." For example, a physician might consider CPR or artificial feeding futile because the treatment itself is useless or the condition of the patient makes it so, whereas the patient or family might disagree. Cases such as *Quinlan*, *Perlmutter*, and *Cruzan* could be viewed as the opposite: physicians resisting the discontinuation of treatment that patient or family deems useless and dehumanizing. In conflicts over a judgment of medical futility, it is patient or surrogate resisting the physician's judgment to withhold or discontinue the treatment. Either way, the parties are in disagreement about what constitutes "futile treatment."

As in *Quinlan*, *Perlmutter*, and *Cruzan*, courts of final jurisdiction consistently have weighed in on the side of individual autonomy. This can be taken as a permission if not a "right to die" by refusing life-sustaining treatment. But does individual autonomy include a complementary "right to live" that supersedes a physician judgment to terminate treatment because of futility? Can patient autonomy override physician beneficence and compel treatment at the end of life that a physician believes is medically worthless? If the answer is yes, then patients are entitled to a certain level of health care regardless of their condition; the physician is obligated to provide it; and the case for rationing by futility loses much of its moral force. If, on the other hand, the answer is no, then patients have no such claim and the physician no such obligation, thereby greatly strengthening the case for rationing by futility.

Any serious discussion of rationing by futility, then, must first come to grips with the morality of a judgment of medical futility itself. In the competition between traditional physician beneficence and modern patient self-determination: *Can patient autonomy ever compel physicians to make futile interventions at the end of life? Can it make doctors give treatment they know provides no demonstrable medical benefits and, thus, violates the beneficence principle?*

ARGUMENTS FOR A JUDGMENT OF FUTILITY

In general, the case for making a judgment of medical futility (or, alternatively, for limiting patient autonomy) appeals to: (1) the nature and history of medicine, including its traditional values and professional standards; and to (2) social justice. Specifically, arguments from professionalism have been made to support 1, whereas arguments from responsible stewardship have been made to advance 2.

Professionalism

For 2,500 years patient autonomy in Western medicine has never been strictly subjective, but has always been limited by considerations of beneficence. The traditional norm of beneficence directs physicians to apply their insights and techniques only for patients' good; to provide treatment that they believe is beneficial, or at least not harmful to patients. As we saw in Chapter 4, noninjury or nonmaleficence can be derived from beneficence.

Hippocrates, for example, urged his colleagues "to follow that system of regimen which, according to (your) ability and judgment (you) consider for the benefit of (your) patients." This exhortation recognized the limitations of medicine. Thus, patients overwhelmed by disease were not to be treated, a point made by Plato, who was a contemporary of Hippocrates. In *The Republic* Plato has Socrates say: "[M]edicine was not meant for such people and they should not be treated though they might be richer than Midas."[40] Again, Socrates says

through Plato: "... where the body was diseased through and through, [the physician] would not try by nicely calculated evacuations and doses, to prolong a miserable existence ...The physically unsound (he) will leave to die."[41]

This classical tradition lives on. Today's AMA's Professional Code of Ethics, for example, tells physicians "not (to) provide or seek compensation for services that are known to be unreasonable and worthless." In this vein, the Society of Critical Care Medicine issued a "consensus report" in 1990 asserting that health care providers have the right to refuse requested "burdensome" therapy, including: "treatment for which they think 'loss of function' (is) ... disproportionate to 'benefit'—even though the patient thinks the 'benefit' of continued life is worth the 'loss of function.'"[42] Two years earlier, a specialist in CPR outcomes wrote in a leading medical journal that in some cases of extremely poor quality of life, for example severely demented patients, the health care team should be permitted to withhold CPR without informing patients or families.[43] Numerous scholarly professionals have lent their weight to this view that physicians should be free to disregard unreasonable family preferences for resuscitations.[44–46]

Ordinarily, respecting patient autonomy best respects beneficence. Physicians, therefore, are rightly charged with understanding patient values, feelings, and concerns. Still, the argument from professionalism denies that patient and family choices are sacrosanct. On the contrary, it asserts that physicians have a right to exercise their own autonomy to practice medicine responsibly. This means that when patient and family choices or demands are unreasonable, physicians are duty-bound to set them straight, to influence patient and family to make a rational choice. To do otherwise—to accede to treatment with no medical indication or scientific validity—violates beneficence. Furthermore, as Catholic bioethicist James Drane and physician John Coulehan point out, it insults patient and family autonomy by giving the false impression that a "sphere of decision making exists where (rationally) there is none ...."[47] In so deceiving patients and families, physicians fail their duty to practice medicine responsibly. They violate both their own autonomy and the patient's, according to Drane and Coulehan.

The argument from professionalism, then, views the patient's right to choose as limited and properly understood only by reference to the physician's right and duty to practice medicine responsibly. The AMA's Council on Ethical and Judicial Affairs frankly states: "Patients should not be given treatments simply because they demand them." This means that physicians ought not administer treatment whose harm outweighs any foreseeable medical benefit, despite patient wishes. To do so is a misrepresentation of professional knowledge and skills; in a word, medical fraud.[48]

Responsible Stewardship

According to the argument from responsible stewardship, providing treatment that fails to achieve the desired physiological effects wastes scarce resources—time, equipment, even transplantable organs—that could be used to achieve desired social ends. Topping the list of scarce resources nowadays is money.

Besides the thousands of PVS (persistent vegetative state) patients being maintained in the United States, traumatic brain injury leaves more than 75,000 people with long-term disabilities each year.[49] According to the US Government Accountability Office (GAO), as a nation we spent about $183 billion for long-term care for all ages in 2003. That's about 13 percent of all health care expenditures. Public programs, primarily Medicaid and Medicare, paid for about 69 percent of those expenditures. What the future costs of long-term care will be is uncertain, but it's a safe bet that they'll be considerably more than the already substantial costs.

To expand an earlier point, futility and cost are, in theory, separate issues, the former dealing with achieving medical goals, the latter with their price. In practice, however, at least since the early 1990s, cost and futility have been linked. That was when Dr. George Lundberg, then editor of *JAMA*, proclaimed futile care policies as one criterion of health care cost control, saying: "Certainly tens and probably scores of millions of dollars annually could be saved" and "major savings can be realized by eliminating futile care and limiting unneeded care of 'medicine at the margins.'"[50] Lundberg implicatively tied the issue of medical futility and "the fair, equitable, and appropriate distribution of medical resources in society." Given our current health care environment of both limited resources and access, he was saying: Unreasonable medical care is simply unfair and unacceptable.

Although many find the insinuation of rationing into the futility debate crass or irrelevant—tantamount to placing a price tag on human life—Peter A. Clark and Catherine M. Mikus aren't among them. One an ethicist, the other an attorney, Clark and Mikus point out that "medical resources in this country *are* limited and must be conserved." As a matter of justice, they say, "patients/surrogates cannot be given the absolute right to demand any medical treatment they choose .... if [they were], those treatments would be given at the expense of the poor, the powerless, and the marginalized...." This means that the physician has a special responsibility to avoid this injustice by practicing prudent stewardship of scarce medical resources in determining what constitutes reasonable medical treatment. For their part, patients and families "must agree to restrict their self-advocacy to what is fair and equitable for all."[51]

In tandem, the arguments from professionalism and stewardship make a powerful one-two punch for making judgments of medical futility and limiting patient autonomy, and for laying the philosophical ground for rationing by futility. Supporting this view is a recent finding of Dartmouth researchers that medical centers spending the most on end-of-life care seem to have no better results than hospitals spending much less.[52] Still, there exists strong cultural opposition to rationing by futility.

ARGUMENTS AGAINST A JUDGMENT OF FUTILITY

The proper role of physicians is to diagnose and treat, not to determine which lives are worth preserving, which not. It is upon this proposition that

---

BIOETHICS ACROSS CULTURES

QALY in the UK

For decades health care economists have used a unit called QALY (for quality-adjusted life-year) for comparing benefits that different forms of health care achieved. Countries do also, the United Kingdom among them.

The UK's National Health Service (NHS), working with an independent agency named National Institute for Clinical Excellence (NICE), has adopted the QALY "to compare different drugs and measure their clinical effectiveness." The basic idea behind the QALY is that the comparative costs and benefits of competing treatments for a condition can be calculated and then used as a basis for deciding which treatments are sufficiently cost-effective to be provided at public expense, and which are not.

NICE considers many factors when measuring a patient's quality of life, in terms of their health, including "the level of pain the person is in, their mobility, and their general mood." The QALY method helps measure these factors by using them as a basis for assigning a quality of life rating, which can range from "negative values below 0 (worst possible health) to 1 (the best possible health)." A QALY measurement gives an idea of how many extra months or years of life of "a reasonable quality" a person might gain as a result of treatment, which is particularly important when considering treatments for chronic conditions.

After establishing a QALY measurement, NICE then compares it with cost effectiveness—"that is, how much the drug or treatment costs per QALY."

This is the cost of using the drugs to provide a year of the best quality of life available—it could be one person receiving one QALY, but is more likely to be a number of people receiving a proportion of a QALY—for example, 20 people receiving 0.05 of a QALY. Cost effectiveness is expressed as "£ [pounds] per QALY." Each drug is considered on a case-by-case basis. Generally, however, if a treatment costs more than £20,000–30,000 [about $33,000–$50,000] per QALY, then it would not be considered cost effective.

Thus, in 2008 NICE gave a preliminary recommendation to the NHS not to offer the drug Sutent for advanced kidney cancer, because it exceeded $50,000 for extending life for a year, while offering only about six months extra life. British and US media immediately ran sensational stories about "penny-pinching bureaucrats sentencing sick people to death." Jack Rosser, 57, was one of these sick people.

"It's immoral," Rosser's wife said of the NICE refusal. "They are sentencing him to die." In its January 15, 2009, issue, the conservative monthly *The American Spectator* described Rosser as "one of NICE's many victims" and said that NICE "regularly hands down death sentence to gravely ill patients." Then, linking the British system of health care to Democratic proposals for health care reform, the article's author, health care consultant David Catron, asked whether we want a health care system in which "soulless bureaucrats arbitrarily put a dollar value on lives."

---

some within and many outside the medical profession take their stand against making judgments of medical futility or limiting patient autonomy. Specifically, they say that there is both (1) a lack of social agreement about what medical futility is and (2) uncertainty of diagnosis and prognosis. At the same time, (3) physicians are duty-bound by social contract to support patient/surrogate determination of medical futility.

No Consensus about the Definition of Futility

While endorsing medical futility, the AMA nevertheless concedes that "futility" "cannot be meaningfully

defined," because it involves a judgment about which there simply is no consensus. This reflects an understanding of medical futility as always a subjective judgment with aforementioned qualitative and quantitative aspects. Qualitatively, a judgment of futility is an opinion about what lives are worth preserving. Quantitatively, it's an opinion not only about likely outcome, but what degree of likelihood is worth pursuing. Clearly, physicians and patients (or families) sometimes will differ on these aspects of futility. They won't always give identical answers to the question, "How much of what kind of life is worth maintaining?" Indeed, physicians themselves disagree about quantitative and qualitative thresholds

Under a withering media blitz, NICE reviewed its recommendation about Sutent, and in March 2009 recommended the drug be provided because so few patients needed it and because of "special end-of-life considerations."

Despite the adverse publicity cases such as Rosser generate, the British overwhelmingly like their health care system. Asked in 2008 if they had confidence in their country's "health or medical systems," 73 percent of Britons said they did. This compared with 56 percent in the United States. There is also anecdotal support from people with experience with both systems, such as Cathy Arnst, who covers health and medicine policy for *Business Week*. Writes Arnst:

When my grandmother was a frail 96-year-old, she fell and broke a hip. Despite our family's better judgment, [US] doctors talked us into hip replacement surgery, from which she never fully recovered. She did not walk again, she quickly fell into dementia, and died with six months. I doubt very much she would have had that wasteful operation in a European nation. Then there was my mother, who died of an asthma attack at age 64. But first, the hospital was able to revive her enough to put her on a ventilator. Although she had a living will, and her family wanted the machinery disconnected, she lived in a deep coma for another five weeks, unresponsive, essentially a vegetable. I cannot imagine the financial cost, and I am all too aware of the emotional cost. Again, I do not think that would happen in a European nation. But take a look at England, home of "socialized medicine." My husband died of a brain tumor in London despite the uniformly excellent care he received, all free thanks to the National Health Service. In his final month cancer was found in his liver, but the doctors felt there was no point in putting him through any more painful treatments. We agreed and he died peacefully in hospice.

(SOURCE: Cathy Arnst, "How Would You Ration Health Care?" *Business Week*, June 30, 2009. Retrieved September 20, 2009, from online.wsj.com/article/SB123060332638041525.html; Peter Singer, "Why We Must Ration Health Care," *The New York Times Magazine*, July 19, 2009. Retrieved September 10, 2009, from http://www.nytimes.com/2009/07/19/magazine/19healthcare-t.html; National Institute for Health and Clinical Excellence, "Measuring Effectiveness and Cost Effectiveness: The QALY," *National Health Service*, 2009. Retrieved September 9, 2009, from http://www.nice.org.uk/newsroom/features/measuringeffectivenessandcosteffectivenesstheqaly.jsp; David Catron, "Obamacare Could Kill You," January 15, 2009. Retrieved September 5, 2009, from http://spectator.org/archives/2009/01/15/obamacare-could-kill-you.)

Question

Would you favor a role for QALYs if a reformed US health care system explicitly accepted rationing, or prioritizing, health care?

---

for futility.[53–55] This has led some critics to despair of defining "medical futility" to everyone's satisfaction.[56–59]

Socially and morally, there's little debate, if any, about suspending treatment in cases when a treatment is impossible, harmful, or ineffective. For example, no one seriously contends that a physician must honor a request to transplant a kidney into a patient who is imminently dying. On another point there is also strong professional agreement: "[A]utonomy does not require physician compliance with a patient request where clear and convincing evidence shows no benefit. Where the evidence is clear and convincing, autonomy is irrelevant."[60] In fact, the vast majority of patients who die in ICUs (intensive care units)—at least 90 percent, according to one study—do so following a decision to limit therapy based upon physician recommendation to withhold or withdraw life support.[61] But that would still leave about 10 percent of ICU patients/surrogates and an unspecified number outside ICUs who, despite recognizing that medical science is powerless to improve their quality of life, insist on living.

The relatively small yet morally significant number of physician–patient/surrogate conflicts show, according to defenders of strict patient autonomy, that society is uncertain of futility in hard cases. In practice this means no clear guidelines for resolving cases in which physicians recommend, "Stop treatment," and patients and families say, "Not yet."

Whose wishes to follow? Should society favor the patient/surrogate's autonomy or the physician's in those, admittedly, rare cases in which the two clash? Put into a larger context of social rules and policies, the question becomes: When there's a lack of social agreement, how ought society determine which of two competing policies to adopt?

One traditional way to resolve the conflict of competing social policies is to apply the utilitarian yardstick of the lesser harm. Thus, it could be asked: Which is the lesser societal offense, stifling the autonomy of the patient/surrogate or the physician? The one involves a choice of life, the other a choice of treatment. So framed, life trumps treatment. To bioethicists such as Robert Veatch and Carol Spicer, this makes preempting physician autonomy the lesser societal offense. As they write:

> If a patient or surrogate is demanding life-prolonging care that his or her clinician believes is futile and a violation of his or her integrity to provide, we have a head-on clash between a patient's or surrogate's choice for life and the provider's autonomy. A society that forces people to die against their will produces more offense than one that forces healthcare providers to provide services that violate their consciences. If society must offend, the lesser offense is preferred.[62]

To its proposers, the argument from lack of social consensus not only affirms patient autonomy in futility cases, it also responds to the argument from professionalism. It says regarding futile care: Patient/surrogate autonomy matters more than the physician's right and duty to practice beneficent medicine.

Uncertain Prognoses/ Mistaken Diagnoses

Discontinuation of treatment based on futility presupposes that the proposed treatment won't work. It won't achieve its intended outcome with respect to patient survival or quality of life. But some recent studies challenge this assumption. Specifically called into question has been the physician's ability to accurately predict short-term mortality even in gravely ill patients. Sometimes enough data can't be collected; other times applying the data to individual patients is

the problem. Then there's drawing the line between "futile" and "reasonable" care. What exactly constitutes a "futile" rate for a treatment: 0%? 10%?[63] Physicians disagree. The point is that if objectively determining medical futility is tricky, on what scientific basis can physicians make a unilateral, beneficent treatment decision on grounds of futility?

Beyond the difficulties inherent in diagnosis and prognosis, there are some troubling cases of patients misdiagnosed as vegetative. A famous one involved a Tennessee police officer who, though only slightly conscious for eight years, suddenly awakened one day in 1996 to talk, joke, and reminisce coherently with family for about eighteen hours. Similarly, in 2002 Terry Wallis suddenly spoke his first words after nineteen years of silence, the tragic aftermath of an auto accident that left him in a deep, extended coma. (See case presentation, Chapter 17). In 2006 a Belgian man who spent the previous twenty-three years incorrectly diagnosed as PVS regained consciousness and reported he could hear everything around him the entire time. More recently, in 2010, European researchers learned that a 29-year-old man who was mute and immobile in a vegetative state could, in fact, communicate in response to simple questions. Though often poignantly fleeting and exceptional, these spontaneous flashes of lucidity offer warnings about making hasty PVS diagnoses, especially in the early stages of an injury or medical episode. Some critics also argue that few futile treatments can confidently be said to have less than 1 in 100 chance of success.[64]

Social Contract

Patient autonomy enthusiasts also say that physicians shouldn't be permitted, unilaterally, to discontinue life-sustaining treatment, because of the implied contractual relationship between them and society. They point out that physicians accept upon licensure a "public trust" to use "their monopoly on medical knowledge to preserve lives when the appropriate decision makers want them preserved."[65]

Another take on the social contract argument is mindful of the substantial duties to patients, legal and moral, that physicians assume when licensed to practice medicine. Among the most basic: providing patients adequate care and not abandoning them. If in good conscience physicians feel it's unethical to treat patients who have poor quality of life, then they should transfer the patient to a colleague, exactly as they should were their ethics challenged by the patient's refusal of life-prolonging treatment. In this way they can honor both their conscience and the ethics of the profession.

CONCLUSIONS

Notwithstanding the cultural controversy that inevitably surrounds public cases of a judgment of medical futility, hospitals across the country are enacting polices, albeit quietly and sensitively, to enable physicians to override patient or family wishes on a case-by-case basis. Notably included in this development are institutions with historically religious affiliations that don't always accede to the faith-based feelings of their clientele. Sometimes, as with Terri Schiavo (see Introduction), Christian patients or their families cite religious justification for insisting on aggressive end-of-life medical care. For example, they may invoke the sanctity of life that is worth preserving at all cost, the hope for a miracle, the refusal to abandon the "God of faith," or the belief that suffering is redemptive. But for every reason given to extend treatment, an alternative religious interpretation points to the legitimacy of limiting treatment.[66] Many religiously affiliated hospitals are employing these counter-interpretations to justify instituting futile care policies.

Supporting this widespread institutional trend are two recent studies showing that a surprising number of frail elderly in nursing homes are suffering from futile care at the end of their lives. Reported in 2009, one of the studies found that, not only didn't dialysis support improve these patients' quality of life, it actually harmed it.[67] The other showed that many with advanced dementia would benefit more from hospice care than aggressive treatments, given their six months life expectancy.[68] Such studies argue for palliative, or comfort, care as an option to many more patients at the end of life. But, of course, end-of-life care is a divisive issue, so divisive that it intruded into the great national health care reform debate of 2009–2010. It was after one proposal included Medicare reimbursement for physician consultations about end-of-life options when critics branded the counseling "death panels" and a step toward euthanasia. While denying those claims, the Obama administration nonetheless dropped the Medicare benefit, which would have included palliative care. It's a supreme irony that the availability of such consultations, intended to give patients and their proxies an opportunity to learn the options and make choices, should be characterized as "death panels." In fact, *absent them*, physicians, bioethicists, attorneys, and committees increasingly will be empaneled to make the decision about when it's time to die.

The State of New York, on the other hand, passed a law in August 2010 requiring physicians of terminally ill patients to offer them or their representatives information about prognosis and options for end-of-life care, including comfort and hospice care as well as the possibilities for further life-sustaining treatment. The legislation took on special significance when, at about the same time, researchers reported that patients with terminal lung cancer who began receiving end-of-life comfort care immediately upon diagnosis not only felt better but lived longer.[69]

CASES AND CONTROVERSIES

The Case of Helga Wanglie

One of the most anthologized modern cases of medical futility occurred in 1991. It involved an 86-year-old PVS patient named Helga Wanglie.

After being treated for a broken hip she suffered after a fall in her Minneapolis home in December 1989, Wanglie was moved to a nursing home. The following month respiratory complications landed her back in the hospital where she was placed on a respirator before being transferred in May of 1990 to a long-term care facility specializing in treating respirator-dependent patients. While there Wanglie suffered a heart attack

(Continued)

CASES AND CONTROVERSIES (CONTINUED)

that left her with severe and permanent brain damage. By the end of May she was back in the hospital, maintained by a respirator and artificial food and liquid. She was ultimately diagnosed as PVS.

Helga Wanglie had left no instructions about how she wished to be treated under such conditions, which rendered her incapable of suffering but also of indicating preference. Given the extended care required to maintain her in PVS, medical staff were inclined to withdraw the ventilator, because it couldn't restore consciousness. But Mrs. Wanglie's husband and conservator, Oliver, 87, refused. He insisted that everything be done to keep his wife alive, over physician objections that so doing would go beyond the limits of "reasonable care."

With the family thwarting their medical judgment, hospital administrators and medical staff petitioned to appoint an independent conservator who might elect to have Mrs. Wanglie's ventilator removed. Physician Steven Miles, who served as the ethical consultant for the hospital, argued that a physician should not have to prove that medical care does not serve a patient's medical interest, whereas Oliver Wanglie insisted that all life-prolonging medical treatment be continued.

In a ruling issued July 1, 1991, the probate court rejected the hospital's position and turned over full guardianship to Oliver Wanglie. Three days later, on the Fourth of July, Helga Wanglie died of multi-system organ failure, leaving behind $750,000 in medical expenses. The family's health insurance covered most of the bills.

Questions for Analysis

1. Explain why, in your opinion, the court did or did not make the right decision.

2. Evaluate the court's decision from the perspectives of preference utilitarianism and Kant's ethics.

3. Evaluate the following statement on futile care, which comes from the board of the National Catholic Partnership on Disability:

   ... we note that the overall cost of providing ordinary or proportionate care to patients on life support often far exceeds the expense of life-sustaining measures themselves. However, to withhold or withdraw such measures because a patient's earlier death may obviate the need for such ordinary care and hence ease financial burdens on health care providers or the community at large would effectively constitute euthanasia. Alternatively, where life support itself proves exceptionally costly, patients, in their free and informed discretion, can selflessly forgo it to save the community expense; but no one can make this choice for another. Thus, without clear evidence of their patients' intent, health care providers can withhold or withdraw life-support because of expense only when the cost is so disproportionate to its hoped-for prolongation of life that it would be plainly unreasonable for patients to have chosen otherwise.[70]

CASES AND CONTROVERSIES

Gilgunn-Massachusetts General Hospital

Four years after *Wanglie*, in April 1995, a Massachusetts court decided whether doctors must provide medically futile treatment that patients have requested. The case involved Catherine Gilgunn, who in May of 1989 slipped and fell in her home, injuring a hip. It wasn't the first time the 71-year-old had so hurt herself. Three other times Gilgunn had been hospitalized to repair a broken hip, and she didn't want to return to the hospital. Complicating matters was Gilgunn's generally poor health. She'd recently undergone a

mastectomy for breast cancer, suffered a stroke, and was diagnosed with Parkinson's disease. She also suffered from diabetes and heart disease. Following her mother's wishes, Joan, Gilgunn's 30-year-old daughter, allowed her mother to delay hospitalization for several weeks.[71]

On June 7, 1989, with her mother's condition deteriorating, Joan finally took her to Massachusetts General Hospital (MGH). Nine days later and just before surgery, Catherine experienced a series of grand mal seizures that couldn't be controlled for about two weeks, leaving her in a coma with extensive brain damage. Joan, who was her mother's surrogate, informed physicians, with the approval of Mr. Gilgunn and the other five children, that Catherine always said she "wanted everything done" that was medically possible. Despite this, Catherine's attending physician wrote a DNR order on July 5th. The Hospital's Optimum Care Committee (OCC) supported the physician's decision. Its chairperson, Dr. Ned Cassem, took the view that "the family's wishes were irrelevant since CPR was not a genuine therapeutic option." Still, Gilgunn's physician revoked the DNR order two days later. However, the following month a new attending physician, Dr. William Dec, wrote the DNR order, once again with the backing of the OCC, which said that CPR would be "medically contraindicated, inhumane, and unethical." Catherine was subsequently weaned from the ventilator and died on August 10, 1989.

Joan Gilgunn subsequently sued Drs. Cassem and Dec and Massachusetts General, alleging neglect and infliction of emotional distress. On April 21, 1995, a jury ruled against her. In so doing, the court, apparently for the first time, ruled that a hospital and staff need not provide care they deemed futile, even if a patient or her surrogates request it.[72]

Questions for Analysis

1. What was the Gilgunn case about? The opposed lawyers differed in their replies. Joan Gilgunn's lawyers, led by Donald E. McNamee, said the case was about "how society treated its most vulnerable members, people like Mrs. Gilgunn who could not speak for themselves." In contrast, Frank E. Reardon, a lawyer for the hospital, countered that the case was about "the limits to patients' rights, and whether doctors and hospitals should be required to provide care that they believe is futile and only prolongs the process of dying." Make the case for each side and determine which is stronger.

2. During the trial the judge asked the jury whether Mrs. Gilgunn would have chosen to be resuscitated with CPR or to be kept on a ventilator if she had been able to express herself. The jury said that, yes, she would have. He also asked if the jury found such care futile. Again, the jury answered yes.[73] Do you agree with the jury that a judgment of medical futility should override patient autonomy?

3. John J. Paris, a Jesuit priest and an ethicist at Boston College who testified for the defense, expressed relief at the verdict. "If this had gone the other way," Father Paris said, "if they had in fact said that she had wanted CPR and that failure to provide it violated the standard of care, then you would have every doctor and every hospital believing that they have to provide every treatment a patient demands."[74] Do you think Father Paris gives a compelling reason for judgments of medical futility?

CASES AND CONTROVERSIES

The Death of Toddler Emilio Gonzales

Today some states have passed laws giving hospitals the right to make life or death decisions without patient consent and against family wishes. Indeed, across the nation hospital ethics committees are putting in place futile care or inappropriate care protocols.[75] In 1999, for example, then-Governor George W. Bush signed the law that gives Texas hospitals the authority to stop treatment if doctors say the treatment is "inappropriate." As of 2007 some dozen Texas hospitals had discontinued treatment against family wishes. One celebrated case involved a toddler named Emilio Gonzales (2005–2007), who had a rare genetic disorder—Leigh's disease—that was ravaging his central nervous system, leaving the child unable to see, speak, or eat.

In December 2006, Catarina Gonzales brought her son, Emilio, to Seton Children's Hospital with a collapsed lung. The next day, the 14-month-old was placed on life support in the facility's pediatric ICU. Without a ventilator, doctors said little Emilio would die within hours.

It wasn't long before staff at the Catholic hospital and the young mother clashed over Emilio's care. Doctors and hospital officials said that the treatment was painful to the child and useless against his illness and, therefore, should be stopped. Gonzales, on the other hand, insisted on keeping her son on the

(Continued)

CASES AND CONTROVERSIES (CONTINUED)

ventilator, allowing him to die "naturally, the way God intended." Both invoked Roman Catholic teachings to support their positions.

Meanwhile, the battle over the life of Emilio Gonzales was gaining national attention. Advocacy groups for the disabled and pro-life organizations campaigned for the child's right to life and even ordered the governor to order a "stay of execution" for Emilio. Joining them were some medical ethicists such as Lainie Ross, who argued that it was the family's call, not the physician's or hospital's. "Who am I to judge what's a good quality of life?" the University of Chicago pediatrician was quoted as saying. "If this were my kid, I'd have pulled the ventilator months ago, but this isn't my kid."

But other bioethicists saw it differently. Arthur Caplan, for example, expressed support for the Texas law giving the hospital the right to make life or death decisions, even if the family disagrees. "There are occasions when family members just don't get it right," he said. "No parent should have the right to cause suffering to a kid in a futile situation."[76]

On March 12, 2007, the hospital, in compliance with Texas law, told Catarina Gonzales that unless she could find an alternative treatment facility they would turn off her son's ventilator in ten days. Local Bishop Gregory Raymond supported the doctors' decision. "It is my responsibility as a shepherd to make sure we are respecting human life and that we are not in any way carelessly taking human life or not respecting the dignity of human life," the bishop said.[77]

Meanwhile, Gonzales said that she'd sought counsel from her priest, and she believed that God would take her son when it was time. Her conscience told her, she said, to keep fighting to keep Emilio alive until that time came. Supporting her were some organizations, such as the Robert Powell Center for Medical

Ethics, an arm of the National Right to Life Committee, that fights to protect people with disabilities. According to the Powell Center, Catholic teaching backed Gonzales's view, not the hospital's. Both sides drew comparisons with Terri Schiavo to support their opposed positions.

When the hospital's ultimatum to Gonzales appeared before Guy Herman, the Travis County probate judge ordered the doctors to continue treating Emilio while his mother looked for another facility that would take him. Weeks passed and before a final ruling could be issued, Emilio Gonzales, then 19 months old, died on May 19. A statement by family attorney said:

> God chose to take Emilio at this time.... He left on God's terms. He left on the terms that Catarina felt were best for her son, which is to die when his body could no longer live.... At least he did die when God took him and not because his tube was pulled.[78]

Questions for Analysis

1. With whom are you more inclined to agree: Lainie Ross or Arthur Caplan?

2. Do you agree with Bishop Raymond that the hospital was respecting human life?

3. Was the hospital justified in issuing the ultimatum?

4. Explain how religious natural law and the doctrine of double effect might support *and* oppose hospital futility policies.

5. Discuss futile care policies in the context of Callahan's ecological and vital institution principles (see Chapter 6).

REFERENCES

1. "Financing Comprehensive Health Care Reform: Proposed Health System Savings and Revenue Options," May 20, 2009. Retrieved September 10, 2009 from finance.senate.gov/.../complete%20text%20of%20financing%20policy%20options.

2. Sally C. Pipes, "Obama Will Ration Our Health Care," *The Wall Street Journal*, December 30, 2008. Retrieved September 1, 2009, from online.wsj.com/article/SB123060332638041525.html.

3. Centers for Medicare and Medicaid Services, NA, "Trustees Report 7 Trust Overview," *U.S. Department of Health & Human Services*, May 12, 2009. Retrieved September 2, 2009, from http://www.cms.hhs.gov/ReportsTrustFunds/.

4. Donald H. Taylor Jr., "A Bipartisan Way to Cut Medicare Costs," *The News Observer*, August 14, 2009. Retrieved September 1, 2009, from http://74.125.95.132/search?q=cache:Oxm38q5NNkQJ:

www.newsobserver.com/opinion/columns/story/1646448.html+Medicare+costs+at+end+of+life&cd=9&hl=en&ct=clnk&gl=us.

5. NA, "Hospital Bills Top Health Care Tabs," *The Washington Times*, September 22, 2006. Retrieved September 8, 2009, from http://www.washingtontimes.com/news/2006/sep/22/20060922-111548-6683r/.

6. Conn Carroll, "This Is What Government Health Care Looks Like," *The Heritage Foundation*, August 21, 2009. Retrieved September 3, 2009, from http://blog.heritage.org/2009/08/21/this-is-what-government-rationed-health-care-looks-like/.

7. Jeffrey Lord, "The Ultimate Cost Saver," *The American Spectator*, August 18, 2009. Retrieved September 1, 2009, from spectator.org/archives/2009/08/18/the-ultimate-cost-saver.

8. Tim Waggoner, "Oregon Offers to Pay to Kill, But Not to Treat Cancer Patient," *LifeSite News.com*, June 4, 2009. Retrieved September 2, 2009, from www.lifesitenews.com/ldn/2008/jun/08060402.html.

9. Helene Cooper, "Nuns' Backing of Bill Shows Rift Over Extent of Its Restrictions on Abortion," *The New York Times*, March 20, 2010, p. A11.

10. Amanda Terkel, "Stupak Dismisses Nuns' Letter: I Don't Listen to Them, I Listen to 'Leading Bishops' and Focus on the Family," *Think Progress*, March 17, 2010. Retrieved March 19, 2010, from thinkprogress.org/2010/03/17/stupak-nuns/.

11. Gregory W. Rutecki, "Rationing Medical Care to the Elderly Revisited: Futility as a Just Criterion," *Journal of Biblical Ethics in Medicine*, vol. 7. No. 3. 2003. From http://www.bmei.org/jbem/volume7/num3/rutecki_rationing_medical_care_to_the_elderly_revisited.php.

12. Heinz Redwood, "Does Ageism Affect Health Care Rationing?" *HealthandAge.com*, October 10, 2002. Retrieved September 1, 2009, from www.healthandage.com/Does-ageism-affect-health-care-rationing.

13. Robert H. Binstock, "Age-Based Rationing of Health Care," *Encyclopedia of Aging*, 2002. Retrieved September 25, 2009, from www.encyclopedia.com/doc/1G2-3402200019.html.

14. US Census Bureau, "Sixty-Five Plus in the United States," May 1995. Retrieved September 2, 2009, from http://www.census.gov/population/socdemo/statbriefs/agebrief.html.

15. Robert H. Binstock, "Scapegoating the Old," in John B. Williamson, Diane M. Watts-Roy,

Eric Kingson, eds., *The Generational Equity Debate*, New York: Columbia University Press, 1999, p. 165.

16. Daniel Callahan, *Setting Limits: Medical Goals in an Aging Society*, Washington: Georgetown University Press, 2003.

17. Frances M. Kamm, *Morality, Mortality. Volume I: Death and Whom To Save From It*, New York: Oxford University Press, 1993.

18. A. B Shaw, "Age as a Basis for Healthcare Rationing: Support for Ageist Policies," *Drugs & Aging*, December 1996, pp. 403–5

19. John Harris, "The Value of Life," in Helga Kuhse and Peter Singer, eds., *Bioethics: An Anthology*, 2nd ed., Wiley-Blackwell, 2006, pp. 435–436.

20. Norman Daniels, *Just Health Care*, London: Cambridge University Press, 1985.

21. Norman Daniels, *Am I My Parents' Keeper? An Essay on Justice Between the Young and the Old*, New York: Oxford University Press, 1990.

22. John C. Shevory, "Applying Rawls to Medical Cases: An Investigation into the Usages of Analytical Philosophy," *Journal of Health Politics, Policy and Law*, Winter 1986, pp. 749–764.

23. Norman Daniels, *Just Health: Meeting Health Needs Fairly*, New York: Cambridge University Press, 2007, p. 178.

24. See note 13 above.

25. See note 13 above.

26. Duff Waring, *Medical Benefit and the Human Lottery: An Egalitarian Approach*, Dordrecht, The Netherlands: Springfield, 2005.

27. Michael Rivlin, "Why the Fair Innings Argument Is Not Persuasive," *BMC Medical Ethics*, December 21, 2000. Retrieved September 1, 2009, from http://www.biomedcentral.com/1472-6939/1/1.

28. Alan Williams, "Intergenerational Equity: An Exploration of the 'Fair Innings' Argument," *Health Economics*, December 4, 1998, pp. 117–132.

29. Anthony Farrant, "The Fair Innings Argument and Increasing Life Spans," *Journal of Medical Ethics*, 2009. Retrieved September 2, 2009, from jme.bmj.com/cgi/content/abstract/35/1/53.

30. Norman Daniels, "Justice, Health and Health Care," in Rosamond Rhodes, M. Pabst Battin, and Anita Silvers, eds. *Medicine and Social Justice: Essays on the Distribution of Health Care*, Oxford University Press, 2002, pp. 14–15.

31. Jonathan Gruber, *Public Finance and Public Policy*, 3rd. ed., New York: Worth Publishers, 2009.

32. Cathy Arnst, "How Would You Ration Health Care?" *Business Week*, June 30, 2009. Retrieved September 2, 2009, from online.wsj.com/article/SB123060332638041525.html.

33. Reed Abelson, "Weighing the Medical Costs of End-of-Life Care," *The New York Times*, December 23, 2009, p. A20.

34. Donald H. Taylor Jr. "A Bipartisan Way to Cut Medicare Costs," *The New & Observer*, August 14, 2009. Retrieved March 18, 2009, from sanford.duke.edu/news/features/taylor_com081409.php.

35. See note 34 above.

36. See note 33 above.

37. Daniel Callahan, "Our Burden Upon Others: A Response to John Hardwig," in John Hardwig et al, *Is There a Duty To Die? and Other Essays in Bioethics*, New York: Routledge, 2000, p. 144.

38. L. J. Schneiderman, N. S. Jecker, Albert R. Jonsen, "Medical Futility: Its Meaning and Ethical Implications," *Annals of Internal Medicine*, June 15, 1990, pp. 949–954.

39. L. J. Schneiderman, Nancy S. Jecker, Albert R. Jonsen, "Medical Futility: Response to Critiques," *Annals of Internal Medicine*, October 15, 1996, p. 669.

40. Plato, *The Republic of Plato*, Francis Macdonald Cornford, trans., New York: Oxford University Press, 1945, Bk. III, p. 98.

41. Ibid., p. 97.

42. Tom Tomlinson and Howard Brody, "Futility and the Ethics of Resuscitation," *JAMA*, September 12, 1990, pp. 1276–1290.

43. David O'Steen and Burke J. Balch, "What's Wrong With Involuntary Euthanasia?," *Pregnant Pause*, September 6, 2000. Retrieved September 5, 2009, from http://www.pregnantpause.org/euth/whyin.htm.

44. D. J. Murphy, "Do-not-resuscitate Orders. Time for Reappraisal in Long-term-care Institutions," *JAMA*, November 11, 1988, pp. 2098–2101.

45. L. J. Schneiderman and N. S. Jecker. *Wrong Medicine: Doctors, Patients, and Futile Treatment*, Baltimore: Johns Hopkins University Press, 1995.

46. Howard Brody, "The Power to Determine Futility," in Howard Brody, *The Healer's Power*, New Haven, CT: Yale University Press, 1992.

47. James F. Drane and John L. Coulehan, "The Concept of Futility: Patients Do Not Have a Right to Demand Medically Useless Treatment," in Tom L. Beauchamp and Robert M. Veatch, *Ethical Issues in Death and Dying*, 2nd ed., Upper Saddle River, NJ: Prentice-Hall, 1996, p. 389.

48. Howard Brody, "The Physician's Role in Determining Futility," in Thomas A. Mappes and David DeGrazia, *Biomedical Ethics*, 5th ed., New York: McGraw Hill, 2001, p. 347.

49. Maura Dolan, "Out of a Coma, Into a Twilight," *Los Angeles Times*, January 2, 2001, p. 16.

50. George D. Lundberg, "American Health Care Systems Management Objectives, The Aura of Inevitability Becomes Incarnate," *JAMA*, May 19, 1993, pp. 2254–2555.

51. Peter A. Clark and Catherine M. Mikus, "Time for a Formalized Medical Futility Policy," *Health Progress*, July–August, 2000. Retrieved September 3, 2009 from http://www.chausa.orgPUBS/PUBSART?/ISSUE=HP0007&ARTICLE=F.

52. Abelson, p. A1.

53. J. R. Curtis, D. R. Park, M. R. Krone, and R. A. Pearlman, "The Use of the Medical Futility Rationale in Do-not-attempt-resuscitation Orders," *JAMA*. April 12, 1995, pp. 124–128.

54. S. Van McCrary, J. W. Swanson, S. J. Youngner, H. S. Perkins, and W. J. Winslade, "Physicians' Quantitative Assessments of Medical Futility," *Journal of Clinical Ethics*, Spring 1994, pp. 100–105.

55. S. J. Youngner, M. Allen, H. Montenegro, J. Hreha, and H. Lazarus, "Resolving Problems at the Intensive Care Unit/Oncology Unit Interface," *Perspectives in Biology and Medicine*, Summer 1988, pp. 299–308.

56. R. D. Truog, A. S. Brett, and J. Frade, "The Problem with Futility," *The New England Journal of Medicine*, March 19, 1992, pp. 1560–1564.

57. E. H. Morreim, "Profoundly Diminished Life. The Casualties of Coercion," *Hastings Center Report*, Nov.–Dec.1994, pp. 33–42.

58. S. J. Youngner, "Medical Futility and the Social Contract (Who Are the Real Doctors on Howard Brody's Island?)," *Seton Hall Law Review*, 1995; 25, pp. 1015–1026.

59. R. A. Gatter Jr. and J. C. Moskop, "From Futility To Triage," *The Journal of Medicine and Philosophy*, February1995, pp. 191–205.

60. T. J. Prendergast, "Futility and the Common Cold. How Requests for Antibiotics Can Illuminate Care at the End of Life," *Chest*, December 1996, p. 836.

61. T. J. Prendergast and J. M. Luce, "Increasing Incidences of Withholding and Withdrawal of Life Support from the Critically Ill," *Respiratory and Critical Care Medicine*, January 1997, pp. 15–20.

62. Robert M. Veatch and Carol Mason Spicer, "Futile Care: Physicians Should Not Be Allowed to Refuse

to Treat," in Tom Beauchamp and Robert M. Veatch, *Ethical Issues in Death and Dying*, 2nd ed., Upper Saddle River, N.J.: Prentice Hall, 1996, p. 396.

63. Ian Kerridge and Michael Lowe, "When Treatment Is Futile: Ethical Uncertainty and Clinical Practice," *Student BMJ*, March 1997. Retrieved February 7, 2005, from http://www.studenbmj.com/back_issues/0397/data/0397ed.2htm.

64. B. A. Brody and A. Halevy, "Is Futility a Futile Concept? *The Journal of Medicine and Philosophy*, April 1995; pp. 123–144.

65. See note 62 above.

66. Allan S. Brett and Paul Jersild, "'Inappropriate' Treatment Near the End of Life: Conflict Between Religious Convictions and Clinical Judgment," *Archives of Internal Medicine*, July 28, 2003, pp. 1645–1649.

67. Manjula Kurella Tamura, et al, "Functional Status of Elderly Adults Before and After Initiation of Dialysis," *The New England Journal of Medicine*, October 15, 2009, pp. 1539–1547.

68. Susan L. Mitchell, et al, "The Clinical Course of Advanced Dementia," *The New England Journal of Medicine*, October 15, 2009, pp. 1529–1538.

69. Jennifer S. Temel et al., "Early Palliative Care for Patients with Metastatic Non-Small Cell Lung Cancer," *The New England Journal of Medicine,* August 19, 2010, pp. 733-742.

70. Board of Directors, National Catholic Partnership on Disability, "NCPD Board Statement on 'Futile Care,'" August 22, 2008. Retrieved March 20, 2010, from http://www.ncpd.org/policy/church/ncpd/statements/futilecare.

71. Healthcare Ethics "Gilgunn-Massachusetts General Hospital," *Ascension Health.* Retrieved September 4, 2009, from http://www.ncpd.org/policy/church/ncpd/statementshttp://www.ascension-health.org/ethics/public/cases/cases_GL.asp/futilecare.

72. Gina Kolata, "Court Ruling Limits Rights of Patients," *The New York Times*, April 22, 1995. Retrieved September 10, 2009, from http://www.nytimes.com/1995/04/22/us/court-ruling-limits-rights-of-patients.html.

73. See note 72 above.

74. See note 72 above.

75. Lawrence J. Schneiderman and Alexander Morgan Capron, "How Can Hospital Futility Policies Contribute to Establishing Standards of Practice?" *Cambridge Quarterly of Healthcare Ethics*, October 2000, pp 524–531.

76. Elizabeth Cohen, "Fight Over Baby's Life Support Divides Ethicists." *CNN.com*, April 25, 2007. Retrieved April 22, 2008, from http://edition.cnn.com/2007/HEALTH/04/25/baby.emilio/index.html.

77. Eileen E. Flynn, "Emilio Gonzales and the Implications to Catholic Hospitals," *The Future Doc Wilson*, April 17, 2007. Retrieved May 2, 2009, from http://74.125.93.104/search?q=cache:GXbpXE6YKK8J:docwilson.blogspot.com/2007/04/emilio-gonzales-and-implication.

78. Gudrun Schultz, "Toddler Emilio Gonzales Dies Naturally from Terminal Illness," *Life Site* May 22, 2007. Retrieved June 28, 2008, from www.lifesite.net/ldn/2007/may/07052201.html.

Conclusion

Bioethics, Religion, and Liberal Democracy

I f the preceding chapters on issues at the beginning and end of life suggest anything about the current state of bioethics in the United States, it is that religion is a formidable presence in the public debate and formulation of social policy. This is not likely to change in the years ahead. Indeed, as biomedical research presses further into areas of life and death traditionally defined by religion, the moral and cultural conflicts we've noted are sure to keep simmering. With that, questions of institutional arrangements and constitutional order increasingly will intrude into the making of bioethical policy, forcing a balance between the sacred and the secular.[1] But how do we effect such a balance? Should religious interests influence national science policy? What place, if any, should religious beliefs, values, and language have in public debate? It seems fitting that a book about bioethics in a cultural context, one that purports to go beyond the issues, concludes with an examination of the relationship of religion, medical science, and public policy in a liberal democracy.

RELIGIOUS VS. SECULAR BIOETHICS

Religious ethics generally refers to ethics derived from supernatural revelation or guidance, as with the Abrahamic religions. Traditionally, Judaism, Christianity, and Islam have approached ethics as revealed truth from divine sources. They have treated ethics in the context of divine prescriptions for living such as the Ten Commandments. In practice, believers are expected to follow what their religion teaches them God wants them to do and to be. This makes (1) religious authority the primary source of moral truth; and (2) ethics a form of obedience, inseparable from theology.

   Secular ethics, by contrast, is not moral *theology* but moral *philosophy*, in which ethics is based solely on human faculties such as logic, reason, or intuition. Secular ethics is interested in what reasons there are to suppose certain actions are right or wrong, regardless of divine revelation.

The fundamental differences between sacred and secular ethics often lead to opposed and contradictory positions in bioethics. Consider the following practices, many of them the interests of earlier chapters:

> contraception; the use of abortifacients; prenatal diagnosis with the intent to abort defective babies; human embryo and human fetal research; abortion; human cloning; the formation of human chimeras (cross-breeding with other species); "brain birth" [i.e., formation of the neocortex]; "brain death"; purely experimental high-risk research with the mentally ill; euthanasia; physician-assisted suicide; living wills documenting consent to just about anything; and, withholding and withdrawing food and hydration as extraordinary means [of prolonging existence].[2]

According to most systems of secular ethics, writes bioethicist Dianne N. Irving, all of these practices could be ethical. For religious ethics, however, most, if not all, probably are unethical. "How is it," Irving asks, "that these two ethical systems lead to such opposite and contradictory conclusions?" Her answer: "It is because their conclusions flow necessarily from very different ethical principles, or premises."[3] Earlier, in Chapter 2, we saw how we have inherited both systems of doing ethics. These ethical traditions not only shape today's bioethical discourse, but they also influence understanding of political governance, and, therefore, they impact bioethical policy.

Consider, for example, that religious and many social conservatives embrace a *theological* vision. The defining conviction of this vision is belief in the core biblical teaching that we are *imago Dei*, made in the image of God (see Chapter 1), and that this "truth" should rule bioethical policy and decisions. Calling attention to this marriage of theology and Christian ethics, Francis Cardinal George, Archbishop of Chicago, has written:

> A Christian *bioethical* vision should ... be grounded in a Christian *anthropological* one, in the truths about the human person that

revelation—especially the risen Christ—discloses and reinforces. First among these is the dignity or value of each human person at every stage and condition .... [T]he revelation of our likeness to and the relationship with God, especially as revealed through the Incarnation and Christ's self-sacrifice, incontestably attests to this truth. The God in whose image each of us is created "knows" and "consecrates" us in the womb, and sent his only begotten Son, his Eternal Word, to "become flesh" and die for us on the Cross. In this light, acts that manipulate, marginalize, or kill human persons in any phase or condition are grave offenses that should be proscribed by civil law in a civilized society.[4]

By this account, the aforementioned procedures, practices, or treatments are immoral not only to conservative Catholics like Cardinal George, but to religious and social conservatives, generally. But beyond that, the prelate urges something that millions of Americans, given their own religious convictions, presumably would agree with: that a "Christian *bioethical* vision" be publicly supported by "civil law." In the cardinal's view, the society that does not implement this vision—that is, the one that permits even some of the aforementioned practices—cannot be a "civilized society," because it is not organized according to transcendent authority, or God's plan, which presumably prohibits such practices. Any talk of the "common good," therefore, must begin with the theological doctrine that the human being is an image of God, an *imago Dei*.

If Cardinal George's statement can be taken as a fairly accurate depiction of religious and social conservative sentiment about bioethics, then driving today's cultural discourse in bioethics is not only a deep division about the nature of ethics, but also about the nature of political governance. At issue is not just whether ethics is best understood as an aspect of religion and theology or as a rational study independent of them. Also up for review is the *political* question: *What is the proper relationship between religious and secular authority in the liberal democracy?* Not only are both of these questions mutually related, but they also profoundly relate to an understanding of today's moral conflicts. To ignore these questions—as for example, to fixate on specific issues, as important as abortion or stem cell research or assisted death is—is to miss the nature of the controversy, which is about how best to do ethics and to govern.

LIBERAL DEMOCACY

Although there is no universally accepted understanding of *liberal democracy*, two elements recur in all conceptualizations: the freedom of citizens and their basic political equality.[5] According to philosopher Robert Audi, this makes the liberal democracy individualist, because it doesn't subordinate the political structure to the interests of some ultimate party such as a monarchy or social class. Nor does it subordinate government to "the glory of God," "though religious ideals and other normative standards may inspire it and may figure quite properly in major aspects of its development."[6]

Underlying the individualist nature of a liberal democracy such as the United States are important preconditions, two of which, traceable to the Enlightenment, are significant culturally and bioethically. The first is a view of what humans are: rational beings capable of self-rule, that is, as determining and regulating their own social, economic, and political affairs. The other precondition relates to how we will order our lives and govern ourselves. Specifically, it calls for a division between theology and politics such that the state respects freedom of conscience and worship, while remaining neutral with regard to religion. This arrangement ensures freedom and protection of religious minorities. The liberal democracy, in brief, does not discriminate between particular religions or, for that matter, between religion and nonreligion. This is the contribution of the Enlightenment revolution in social and moral thought (see Chapter 2).

Clearly, these two preconditions played in the thinking of the framers of the Constitution. First, the framers obviously were committed to the view of human self-governance. But, second, and probably less understood, they were equally as committed to religious liberty. Their commitment to religion as a natural right kept the framers from allowing their own religious feelings to unduly influence the drafting of a political document of self-governance such as the Constitution. In Richard Rorty's words: "The Founding Fathers … asked people to think of themselves not so much as Pennsylvania Quakers or Catholic Marylanders but as citizens of a tolerant, pluralistic, federal republic."[7] Another philosopher, James F. Harris of William and Mary, the second college in the American colonies, tells us why:

> To jumpstart the process of framing a democratic constitution, the private religious beliefs of those doing the framing must be set aside. And this is exactly what the framers of the Constitution of the United States were able to do.[8]

None of this would have been possible, in Harris's view, if (1) Protestantism, as a result of the Protestant Reformation, had not recognized and adopted the Enlightenment view of a self-governing human nature; and (2) much of Protestant Christianity had not come to separate theology from politics and religion from everyday civic lives of individuals. "This is why," Harris says, "the distinction between the private, individual religious life and the public, civic secular life, which is crucial for Jefferson's separation of church and state, became possible."[9]

Now, these crucial suppositions—autonomous individualism and church state separation—don't mean that individual citizens of a liberal democracy and the groups they are members of can't have religious interests and values, or can't be motivated by religious beliefs and convictions. For religious reasons, many people don't practice or support the items on Irving's list, and their guaranteed liberty permits them to follow their consciences. Moreover, people of religious faith have the same right to express their opinions and participate in public affairs as their nonreligious counterparts, even to be conscientiously motivated to advocate policy on any of those items. In other words, a liberal democracy such as the United States protects the right of the religious to pursue a political vision, narrowly defined as the expression of a personal and private belief. But that changes at the point whereby the narrow personal religious interest turns to broad civic interest. It's one thing, for example, to hold that abortion or PAS is wrong and its practice violates the moral law of God; it's another to use that belief to justify the criminalization of abortion or PAS. At that point, whereby the personal and private turns social and public, the expectation of the liberal democracy kicks in. That expectation, simply put, calls for a translation of the religious belief or justification into a reason-based, as opposed to a faith-based, argument. Again, this is the practical meaning of Rorty's "happy, Jeffersonian, compromise" reached between the Enlightenment and religion, and upon which both the American nation and, two centuries later, modern bioethics were founded (see Chapter 3). Today, however, even as the author of that felicitous term admitted not long before his death in 2007, the "Jeffersonian Compromise" is being reconsidered.[10]

RETHINKING THE "JEFFERSONIAN COMPROMISE"

The "Jeffersonian Compromise" is, itself, part of today's culture strife and bioethical discourse, as legal and social conflict rage about where to draw the line between secular and sectarian. Driving these debates are aforementioned deep philosophical differences, including disagreements about "the sources of moral authority, about the nature of knowing and the limits of scientific rationality, about how best to live out one's sexuality, about purpose or accident in the universe."[11] As secular and religious viewpoints compete in the marketplace of ideas, many of today's conservative commentators are warming to the view that it is not always more neutral to favor the secular over the religious, as the traditional understanding of the "Jeffersonian Compromise" prescribes.[12] Basically,

they reason as follows: Beyond (1) the fact that all worldviews, secular as well as sectarian, rest on unprovable first principles, the "Jeffersonian Compromise" has led to (2) a double standard that favors the secular and to (3) the mistaken belief that the secular and the religious lack any common ground for dialogue.

Unprovable First Principles of All Worldviews

The case for reconsidering the "Jeffersonian Compromise" begins with the observation that *all* worldviews ultimately rest upon unprovable assumptions.[13] Take, for instance, empiricism's assumption that the world is a closed reality in which observation can detect cause and effect; or utilitarianism's assumption that happiness is the chief good. Those suppositions, it's asserted, are no more provable than the traditional religious assumption of the existence of a personal God who wants us to conduct our affairs in a particular way, both individually and collectively.

Again, like all religions, traditional Christianity appeals to foundational narratives that go against the notion of what's considered "public accessibility," such as the Genesis narrative. But, as theologian and bioethicist Courtney Campbell reminds us, secularism has its own "fictional portraits of human moral beginnings," for example the "state of nature," to "justify basic moral norms like liberty, equality, or distributive justice."[14] Why is the "state of nature" any more accessible to the theist than Genesis is to the atheist? Neither can be proved; both require a leap of faith. This "shared failing" of both systems comes as no surprise to physicist Paul Davies of Arizona State University, who calls "the very notion of a physical law" a theological construct in the first place. Davies writes:

> Isaac Newton first got the idea of absolute, universal, perfect, immutable laws from the Christian doctrine that God created the world and ordered it in a rational way. Christians envisage God as upholding the natural order from beyond the universe,

while physicists think of their law as inhabiting an abstract transcendent realm of perfect mathematical relationships.

And just as Christians claim that the world depends utterly on God for its existence, while the converse is not the case, so physicists declare a similar asymmetry: the universe is governed by eternal laws (or meta-laws), but the laws are completely impervious to what happens in the universe.[15]

Double Standard

Now, how exactly does the problematic nature of first principles, religious or secular, play out in bioethics? The short answer is: by providing unprovable basic assumptions about the universe that serve as foundations for doing bioethics. J. Budziszewski, professor of government and philosophy at the University of Texas, illustrates as follows:

> If I say that euthanasia should be illegal because murder violates the law of God, then obviously I suppose that there is a God, that He has a law, that this law ought to be obeyed, that it forbids murder, that euthanasia is murder, and that He commands the government to back Him up on such a point. If instead I say that euthanasia should not be illegal, then obviously I suppose either that there is no God, that even if there is a God He has no law, that even if He has a law it need not be obeyed, that even if it must be obeyed it does not forbid murder, that even if it does forbid murder euthanasia is not murder, or that even if euthanasia is murder He does not command the government to back Him up on such a point. If I seek relief from judgment in the doctrine that the state has neither the right nor the competence to decide such questions, then I deceive myself, for indecision is decision; to say that the state should not pass judgment on euthanasia is merely to suppose that euthanasia should be legal.

It is not enough to have no suppositions—at some point there must be a contrary supposition. That contrary supposition may be "secular," but it is still "religion" in that it is still about the meaning of the universe. The relevant distinction is not between a secular public life and a religious public life, but between a public life informed by a secular religiosity and a public life informed by the older religiosity that it opposes. A particular kind of morality and religion can be pushed out of the public realm, but morality and religion as such cannot be pushed out of the public realm.[16]

Budziszewski adds that what goes for deliberation also goes for deliberation about deliberation, that is, about the Constitution. Thus:

> It is no use to say that religion may be invoked in debate about particular laws but not in reference to the constitutional framework within which such debate is held. To banish the religions that call themselves religions is merely to free the religions that do not call themselves religions from the burden of competition—whether the utilitarian religion of Expedience, the yuppie religion of Autonomy, or the mammonist religion of Wealth.

And that, according to its critics, is precisely what the "Jeffersonian Compromise" has done: It has set up a double standard that victimizes religion.

More specifically, by framing religion strictly as a private matter, the "Compromise" has favored one perspective over another, such as by requiring people of religious faith to offer secular reasons for their judgments without imposing a symmetrical requirement on people having no religious faith. This strikes some as inherently unfair. After all, they say, if opponents of abortion or PAS cannot appeal to religious premises that secularists will reject, then how can its supporters use premises—for example, "the right to reproductive freedom" or "the right to assisted death"—that religious believers will reject?[17]

No Common Ground for Dialogue

Beyond this seemingly double standard thought to disadvantage people of religious faith, it has also been argued that the "Jeffersonian Compromise" assumes no commonality for meaningful dialogue between the religious and the secular. It is true, as David E. Guinn of DePaul University points out, and we saw repeatedly in our coverage of issues, "some of the faithful leap simply from grounding belief to conclusion, e.g., 'God said this, therefore cloning is wrong.'" But the same can be said of some people without religious faith, something we also saw. Recall how some ideological pro-choice activists say: "I'm a woman, therefore I have a right to decide about having an abortion." In contrast, says Guinn, who writes on American civil liberties:

> The better forms of religious argument not only assert a grounding belief, but also develop arguments to explain how that belief results in the judgment made in a particular situation. The nonbeliever does not need to accept the grounding belief in order to enter into the argument of the believer. The same rules of logic, coherence, and consistency apply to religious and nonreligious argument. Often, the person of faith will justify his argument by drawing upon illustrative examples and intermediary arguments that a person without faith can also use because the justifications are compatible with her own worldview and beliefs.[18]

Guinn believes, in other words, that religious and secular dialogue is possible within the shared standards of good argument. Illustrative, perhaps, is this point made by political scientist Robert B. Shelledy of Marquette University:

> [T]he Vatican has greater influence when its efforts resonate with secular justifications for particular policies. The Vatican's efforts in international debt relief, international religious freedom, and against the recent wars in Iraq demonstrate this finding.[19]

Furthermore, treating religion as strictly a private affair assumes that consensus must rest on a single justification for a policy. But, critics ask, is it necessary, let alone realistic, to expect people to alter their basic outlooks to reach a political policy judgment? Again, according to Guinn:

> Flexibility and compromise rest not at the level of fundamental belief but at the level of judgment about how those beliefs find expression in a particular situation. Therefore, the formation of public policy can result from a collection of overlapping but discrete public conversations addressed to particular audiences within the whole. The objective is consensus on a particular policy that may rest upon a pluralistically acceptable range of justifications.

Neo-liberalist Rorty said much the same: "The only test of a political proposal is its ability to gain assent from people who retain radically diverse ideas about the point and meaning of human life, about the path of private perfection."[20]

The preceding observations notwithstanding, the current reconsideration of the "Jeffersonian Compromise" does not necessarily favor the expression of institutional decision making in religious language, as, perhaps, religious fundamentalists might prefer. But, perhaps, its merit is the implication that the "separation" of church and state may not be as useful an idea in elucidating a liberal democracy's commitment to equality as the idea, say, of an "overlapping consensus" proposed by Guinn and others.

TOWARD AN OVERLAPPING CONSENSUS

Legal scholar and philosopher Martha C. Nussbaum has recently urged just such a construct: an "overlapping consensus" that acknowledges that (1) the state has a moral foundation and (2) this foundation may be religious for some people and nonreligious for others.[21] Such a construction seemingly would allow religious language in public bioethical debate,

BIOETHICS ACROSS CULTURES

Cross-Cultural International Bioethics

Darryl Macer is a professor at the Institute of Biological Sciences at the University of Tsukuba in Japan. Although a molecular biologist by training, Macer's area of specialization is bioethics, and he is director of the International Union of Biological Sciences (IUBS) Bioethics program. He is also founder-director of the Eubios Ethics Institute, a nonprofit group that aims to stimulate the international discussion of ethical issues, and how we may use technology in ways consistent with "good life" (*eu-bios*). Eubios aims at an integrated and cross-cultural approach to bioethics.

An ongoing concern of an organization such as Eubios involves an understanding and a clarification of the concept of "cross-cultural international bioethics." For example, how should cultural and religious beliefs be addressed within the rapidly growing field of bioethics? Cultural and spiritual traditions obviously vary, and sometimes even conflict. And yet, throughout the world it is these traditions that generally shape public policy, popular opinion, and private practice, even when not articulated explicitly. This leads Macer to recognize a common power in diverse cultural and spiritual traditions to motivate and guide. As he writes in *Bioethics Is Love of Life: An Alternative Textbook*:

> Despite the scientific world view that is prevalent among academics, most other people find religion to be a much more important source of guidance in life than science.... Any theory of bioethics that will be applied to peoples of the world must be acceptable to the common trends of major religious thought.

The chief implication of acknowledging the power of religions to motivate and guide is that one must address religious approaches and worldviews other than those dominant in Western society when addressing bioethical questions, particularly in a pluralistic society like the United States. As Macer says:

> In bioethics we should use not only the data of our own interpretations, but rather look for any other data that can aid us in understanding the real situation. Academics may often have abstract ideas, we need to come back to earth and look at reality. The data from surveys, and observations, reveals that there are fundamental similarities in

reasoning by individuals in different countries, despite diversity in social systems and even greater diversity in legal approaches to bioethics. I called this the universal bioethics approach.... [It includes an] understanding of local cultures, and ... the contribution of different peoples to bioethics.

Macer believes that we can't develop a complete bioethics without including this contribution, because that is what reveals the common ground. He writes:

> Harmony and naturality are desired by some people in all cultures, and in this century all peoples have abused power, not only in war.... We need to ask people in many countries what they think, we need to look at their religious and cultural history, and we have to see how they live. We cannot do this by television, we have to visit and live in different countries, we have to have some experience, ... above all, we have to be humble, and look towards the ideas of others, while also suggesting our own. In the words of the old prophet, "Listen, those of you that have ears to hear." This is cross-cultural international bioethics.

(SOURCES: "Darryl Macer," *United Nations University*, 2009. Retrieved June 5, 2009, from http://www.ias.unu.edu/sub_page.aspx?catID=78&d dlID=282; Darryl Macer, "The Future of International Bioethics," *Bioethical Web*, 1997. Retrieved June 5, 2009, from http://www.geocities.com/ athens/acropolis/9830/articulo8.htm; NA, "Can Religion Trump the Bioethics Debate?" *Emory University*. Retrieved June 5, 2009, from www. students.emory.edu/HYBRIDVIGOR/issue3/religion.htm.)

Question

Do you agree that any universal theory of bioethics must be acceptable to the common trends of major religious thought? What shared religious ground could you point to as building blocks of a bioethic theory that would be applicable to all peoples of the world? Macer believes that bioethics needs to incorporate, or at least acknowledge, the dominant threads of cultural, religious, and moral traditions in order to use technology in the service of "good life." By the same token, do you think that religious leaders and communities need to confront these difficult questions in open, frequent, and tolerant dialogue?

while continuing to restrict institutional decision making to religiously neutral or secular language. And, presumably, it would also hold all parties to the debate to the same standards of deliberation. Thus, if religious first principles are inadmissible, so are secular ones. If people of religious faith must offer secular reasons for judgments, then people of no religious faith are required to offer religious reasons. If the religious are expected to appreciate the value of logic and science, then secularists must openly consider faith and the nonrational concomitantly with the rational. In the words of Jürgen Habermas, a not-especially-religious philosopher:

> Whereas citizens of faith may make public contributions in their own religious language only subject to the proviso that these get translated, the secular citizens must open their minds to the possible truth content of those presentations and even enter into dialogues from which religious reasons that might well emerge in the transformed guise of generally accessible arguments.[22]

It's also important to bear in mind that, although religion offers answers to the profound questions of human nature and destiny embedded in bioethics, that does not mean such questions can only be answered theologically. On the contrary, as seen throughout this text, they can be answered without reliance upon sacred texts or theistic belief. At the same time, questions such as "What does it mean to be human?", "When does life begin and end?", "What is our place in creation?", or "What is the ideal society?" are inquiries into ultimate beliefs and values. As such they invite responses from everyone, faithful and nonfaithful alike. Those urging a reconsideration of the "Jeffersonian Compromise," then, are saying: "In order to answer these profound questions and to articulate the values held by the American people, it is necessary to engage people of faith without imposing secularizing barriers to their participation."

Finally, as for the widespread fear that any reconsideration of the "Jeffersonian Compromise" to involve the religious faithful in the formulation of public policy will violate church-state separation, it's important to keep in mind the great promise of the liberal democracy that Guinn reminds us of:

> To the extent that democracy and liberalism promise to respect each and every citizen, allowing them the full right to participate in the public forum, people of faith should not be excluded simply because they may disagree with the values of those controlling access to that forum. It is the task of democratic politics to find ways to accommodate the wide diversity within our pluralistic society.[23]

RELIGION IN PUBLIC BIOETHICS

Beyond considerations of internal logic and fair play that may recommend a rethinking of the "Jeffersonian Compromise," many commentators today think that there's tangible social value in including religious language in public bioethics. Dan Callahan is one who finds good reason for including the theological perspective in bioethics. He says that, although bioethics gained purchase when it shucked religion, "it also left behind insights and riches that cannot be supplied by an anti- or a-religious stance." To the Catholic-turned-atheist Callahan, this is a great loss; for, despite its classic separation of church and state, Callahan says that the United States is "a religious nation, in its history, its traditions, and among a majority of its people." Therefore, he believes that not factoring that reality fully into our public discourse about bioethics is to fail to take its work with sufficient seriousness.[24]

More specifically, in Callahan's view, theological ethics understands what secular ethics doesn't: the need to locate ethics within the larger framework of an interpretation of life and human destiny. Secular ethics, by contrast, operates according to an opposed premise: that there can be ethical systems and theories not dependent upon such a framework. This, according to Callahan, leaves secular ethics incomplete, resting on what reason alone can discover and develop, but which is itself only part of human nature. Religion, by contrast, offers an interpretation or revelation of reality that responds to the existential need for order, meaning, and coherence. It reminds us, he says, of the difficulty, if not impossibility, of talking about abortion or genetic manipulation or assisted death without engaging the ultimate questions about our nature, purpose, and destiny.[25] According to Callahan, the religious perspective is also able to take up "problems and puzzles" that purely secular, rational perspectives can't adequately deal with in any coherent, sensitive way. Religion can impart, for example, meaning to suffering, pain, disease, deformity, and death.

For his part, Lutheran theologian Martin E. Marty points out that religion is not necessarily hostile to the force of reason, indeed often welcoming it as a divine gift. At the same time, the religious voice on abortion, stem cell research, assisted death, or any other bioethical issue is grounded in many additional resources as well: intuition, memory, tradition, community, experience, hope, affection, generosity, altruism, sacrifice, kindness, devotion, service, compassion, love. As a result, says Marty, including religion in bioethical discourse "thickens the conversation" and "makes you listen, by addressing as it does 'the reasons of the heart that reason does not know.'"[26,27]

Other sympathetic commentators find additional reasons for the theological perspective in bioethics. For neurosurgeon D. Gareth Jones, religion places limits on scientific technique and directs biomedical technology "for human good rather than human degradation."[28] Although Jones is writing as a Christian theist, he says that religion's central concern with the meaning and sacredness of life makes religion a natural conduit for a much-needed ethic of care in medicine.

For her part, theologian Lisa Sowle Cahill finds great medical value in the wisdom of the Bible. In *imago Dei*, for example, she finds basic respect for others; in "love of neighbor" she sees an ethos of

compassionate service to the sick and suffering. Such narrative-borne insights, Cahill writes, "limit the role of market incentives in medicine and encourage caregivers to place 'autonomy' in the context of a network of support and genuine care." In this view, the "religious tradition captures the collective wisdom of the past and invites an affective, emotional, and very human type of moral discernment to which no abstract theory could do justice." It is in rediscovering our Judeo-Christian traditions, then, that we reconstitute our commitment to the dignity of the individual, according to this Catholic feminist.[29]

For commentators like Cahill, Marty, and Callahan, then, one of the great values of the theological perspective is that it has the effect of pushing the predominant questions of conventional bioethics— "What should we do?" and "Who should decide?"— to "fundamental issues that require a substantive account of the purpose of human life and destiny." "These," as Campbell notes, "are common questions of meaning that religious communities have devoted considerable attention to in their theologies, rituals, and practical ethics."[30]

At the same time, however, even if there is a strong case for including the religious perspective in public bioethics, religion is no less urged to translate its bioethical discourse into secular terms without attenuating or transforming its meaning. This is the challenge of being religious in a science-driven field in a pluralistic society. It's a challenge that requires religion be clear about its task in bioethics: Is religion's task to provide all biotechnological advances with ultimate meaning, which is religion's traditional undertaking? Or is the task of religion going to mean rational enlightenment, including Western scientific rationalism, equal rights, and pluralism? In other words, the issue isn't whether the moral and spiritual imperatives of religion aren't important for bioethics. They clearly are, for as Susan Neiman notes: "[R]eligion is … a way of trying to give shape and structure to the moral concepts that are embedded in our lives."[31] Rather, the challenge is how best to express the insights found in religious traditions. In the words of moral theologian and medical ethicist David Smith of Indiana University:

> We should look to fruitful ways publicly to express the insights found in religious traditions. This may or may not mean translation from one set of concepts into another; it may mean reinterpreting concepts with an eye to their contemporary relevance. The dialogue that results may enrich theology as well as the public conversation.[32]

Over a half century ago, the renowned Catholic theologian John Courtney Murray related pluralism to the vigorous engagement of people of different religious beliefs around the "common table" of discussion and debate.[33] Murray wrote in the late 1950s:

> By pluralism here I mean the coexistence within the one political community of

groups who hold divergent and incompatible views with regard to religious questions.... Pluralism therefore implies disagreement and dissension within a community. There is no small political problem here. If society is to be at all a rational process, some set of principles must motivate the general participation of all religious groups, despite their dissension, in the oneness of the community. On the other hand, these common principles must not hinder the maintenance by each group of its own different identity.[34]

Murray went on to argue that the "working out" of that political problem is itself "an exercise in civic virtue" and a theological imperative.[35] Murray's cool words are worth remembering in the heat of today's cultural discourse in bioethics.

CASES AND CONTROVERSIES

The Battle over Bioethics

Moral and religious perspectives traditionally have defined issues at the beginning and end of life. But increasingly today, legislation, court rulings, and government policies are confronting these matters, raising profound concerns about the morality of scientific biomedical research. The question then arises: How much influence should religious and moral interests affect national science policy and bioethics?[36] Alternatively: How much control, if any, should government exercise over the content of science?

On the right end of the continuum of positions are those culturally conservative individuals and groups that give government a central role in directing what science researches and develops. Representative is the position of the Traditional Values Coalition (TVC), a huge inter-denominational grassroots church lobby, speaking on behalf of over 43,000 Christian churches that subscribe to a code of morality based on the Old and New Testaments. In the fall of 2003, TVC circulated a list of National Institutes of Health grants that the coalition said involved research topics the government should not be funding, including AIDS initiatives. The

list contained the names of 157 researchers with NIH grants. TVC opposes studies on condom use and believes sex education programs are a waste of money. It also opposes abortion and stem cell research. However, it favors government support of programs advocating sexual abstinence.

Another outspoken voice on the right is Catholic Archbishop Charles Chaput of Denver, who recently accepted the Canterbury Medal, which is presented annually to honor those who have "most resolutely refused to render to Caesar that which is God's." In accepting the award, on May 7, 2009, the archbishop expressed concern about remarks President Obama made in his inauguration speech about restoring "science to its rightful place" during his administration. Chaput said that Obama and his supporters had "stressed his religious credentials many times," and that the president's faith is "one of the factors that made him attractive to voters last fall." Then he added:

> But from a believer's point of view, that makes the president's confusion about the "rightful place" of science—not just in his inaugural remarks, but in many of his words

(Continued)

CASES AND CONTROVERSIES (CONTINUED)

and actions since then—even more curious. The rightful place of science, like all human activity, is in the service of human dignity and under the judgment of God's justice. Science can never stand outside or above moral judgment.[37]

In contrast to these conservative views, on the left end of the positions continuum are liberal individuals and groups who are basically opposed to government shaping the content of scientific research according to religious and moral interest. For example, the Secular Coalition for America (SCA) is an advocacy group whose purpose is to "amplify the diverse and growing voice of the nontheistic community in the United States." SCA is committed to promoting reason and science as the most reliable methods for understanding the universe and improving the human condition. It encourages "the pursuit of knowledge, meaning, and responsible ethical codes without reference to supernatural forces," and it affirms a secular form of government that bases policy on "reason and science as the most reliable methods for understanding the universe and improving the human condition."[38]

Another group vitally concerned about government intrusion in scientific research is the Union of Concerned Scientists (UCS), which began as a collaboration of students and faculty at MIT in 1969 and is today an alliance of more than 250,000 scientists and concerned citizens. In 2004 UCS issued a report that more than sixty leading scientists signed, criticizing the Bush Administration's science policies. It read, in part:

> Political interference in federal government science is weakening our nation's ability to respond to the complex challenges we face. Because policy makers depend on impartial research to make informed decisions, we are mobilizing scientists and citizens alike to push for reforms that will enable our leaders to fully protect our health, safety, and environment.[39]

Somewhere in the middle—that is, somewhere between the most conservative and most liberal ends of the continuum representing the proper relationship of government and science—are numerous individuals and groups broadly united in trying to reconcile the interests of religion and morality with those of science. Here are some of those parties, as compiled by *ReligionLink*, an online service for journalists who write about religion:

- Brent Waters is director of the Center for Ethics and Values and assistant professor of Christian social ethics at Garrett-Evangelical Theological Seminary in Evanston, Ill. He is also an ordained minister in the United Church of Christ and co-editor of several books on religion and bioethics, including *God and the Embryo: Religious Voices on Stem Cells and Cloning* (Georgetown University Press, 2003). Waters says:

    Public policies should not be used as a means of implementing the teaching of a particular church.... Religious convictions, however, inform the moral vision of citizens and government officials, which are in turn incorporated into public policies. Consequently, overtly religious claims and values should inform public debate and deliberation on public policies in respect to science.

- Thomas Anthony Shannon is a professor of religion and social ethics in the department of humanities and arts at Worcester Polytechnic Institute in Worcester, Mass. He is co-author of *The New Genetic Medicine: Theological and Ethical Reflections* (2003). Shannon says religion should have a place at the table in any discussion about biomedical funding, but the challenge is for religious representatives to frame their positions in accessible and nondivisive language.

- David F. Kelly is a professor of theology and founding director of the Health Care Ethics Center at Duquesne University. He is author of *Contemporary Catholic Health Care Ethics* (2004). Kelly says the concerns of religion should be a part of any discussion on biomedical research and ethics, because religion "thickens the discussion" of what it means to be human. But he says it is wrong to decide questions of bioethics on the basis of theology alone—to use theology or religion as an "authority" on what we should or should not investigate.

- Dr. Albert Gunn is a professor of internal medicine and dean of admissions at the School of Public Health at the University of Texas Health Science Center at Houston. He has written several articles on bioethics and is a member of the Fellowship of Catholic Scholars. Gunn does not think of science as "freestanding" from religion, but says each side needs to encourage the other to deeper and more meaningful dialogue.[40]

Questions for Analysis

1. On what grounds would you justify scientific autonomy?

2. On what grounds would you restrict scientific autonomy?

3. Bioethicist David B. Resnik believes that "government involvement in scientific decision-making should usually occur through policies that control the process of science, rather than policies that control the content of science."[41] What is the difference between government controlling the process of science as opposed to controlling its content? Do you think it matters?

4. Bioethicist Arthur Caplan has been sharply critical of the President's Council on Bioethics and once initiated a petition to protest what he perceived as a lack of diversity of opinion. He says the challenge to religions is to transform their positions into secular language and not to object to science on the grounds that it is "wrong" because it conflicts with doctrine. Do you agree?

5. How much influence should religious and moral interests affect national science policy and bioethics?

6. Where would you locate yourself on the positions continuum in the ongoing "battle over bioethics"?

REFERENCES

1. Francis Fukuyama, *Our Post Human Future: Consequences of the Biotechnology Revolution*, New York: Macmillan, 2003.

2. Dianne Irving, "Which Medical Ethics for the 21st Century?" *Lifeissues.net: Clear Thinking about Crucial Issues*, March 14, 1999. Retrieved June 22, 2008, from http://www.lifeissues.net/writers/irv/irv_02ethics1.html.

3. See note 2 above.

4. Francis Cardinal George, "The Need for Bioethical Vision," in John F. Kilner, C. Christopher Hook & Diann B. Uustal, eds., *Cutting-Edge Bioethics: A Christian Exploration of Technologies and Trends*, Grand Rapids, MI: William B. Eerdmans Publishing Company, 2002, p. 97.

5. Robert Audi, *Religious Commitment and Secular Reason*, Cambridge: Cambridge University Press, 2000, p. 4.

6. Ibid, p. 6.

7. Richard Rorty, *Philosophy and Social Hope*, New York: Penguin Books, 1999, p. 88.

8. James Harris, "Religion and Liberal Democracy," *The Humanist*, May 1, 2006, Retrieved August 8, 2008, from www.thefreelibrary.com/Religion+and+liberal+democracy.-a0147057304.

9. See note 8 above.

10. Richard Rorty, "Religion in the Public Square: A Reconsideration," *Journal of Religious Ethics*, Spring 2003, pp. 141–149.

11. Peter Steinfels, "Religious Right May Be Fading, but Not the 'Culture Wars,'" *The New York Times*, February 16, 2008. Retrieved May 8, 2008, from www.nytimes.com/2008/02/16/us/16beliefs.html?scp=18&sq=immigration&st=nyt.

12. Michael McConnell, "Equal Treatment and Religious Discrimination," in Stephen V. Monsma and J. Christopher Soper, eds., *Equal Treatment of Religion in a Pluralistic Society*, William B. Eerdmans Publishing Company, p. 33.

13. Richard Rorty, "The Priority of Democracy to Philosophy" in Gene Outka and John P. Reeder Jr., eds., *Prospects for a Common Morality*, Princeton: Princeton University Press, 1993.

14. Courtney S. Campbell, "Religion and Moral Meaning in Bioethics," *Hastings Center Report*, July–August 1990, pp. 4–10. Retrieved August 2, 2008, from http://ccbs.ntu.edu.tw/FULLTEXT/JR-MDL/camp.htm.

15. Paul Davies, "Taking Science on Faith," *Los Angeles Times*, November 24, 2007, p. A31.

16. J. Budziszewski, "The Future of the End of Democracy (abortion law)," *First Things: A Monthly Journal of Religion and Public Life*, March 1, 1999, p. 15.

17. David Gordon, "A Man Possessed," *The Mises Review*. Retrieved May 10, 2008, from http://mises.org/misesreview_detail.aspx?control=160.

18. David E. Guinn, "A Necessary Player," *Second Opinion*, January 2002. Retrieved May 22, 2008, from http://papers.ssrn.com/sol3/papers.cfm?abstract_id=905127.

19. Robert B. Shelledy, "The Vatican's Role in Global Politics," *SAIS Review*, Summer–Fall 2004, p. 149.

20. Quoted in Guinn, p. 173.

21. Martha C. Nussbaum, *Liberty of Conscience: In Defense of America's Tradition of Religious Equality*, New York: Basic Books, 2008.

22. Jürgen Habermas, "Religion in the Public Square," trans. Jeremy Gaines, *European Journal of Philosophy*, April 2006, p. 9. Retrieved May 20, 2008, from http://www.law.nyu.edu/clppt/program2006/readings/Habermas.

23. See note 18 above.

24. Daniel Callahan, "Dialogue: Religion and Bioethics," *Lahey Clinic Medical Ethics*, Winter, 2000. Retrieved May 30, 2008, from www.lahey.org/NewsPubs/Publications/Ethics/JournalWinter2000/Journal_Winter2000_Dialogue.asp.

25. Albert Jonsen, *The Birth of Bioethics*, New York: Oxford University Press, 1998, p. 35.

26. Martin Marty, "Faith's Place at the Table: Why Religion Deserves to Be Integrated into Bioethics," *The Park Ridge Center Bulletin: Religion in Bioethics*, March/April 1999, p. 15. Retrieved June 12, 2008, from www.parkridgecenter.org/Page547.html.

27. Philip J. Boyle, "'Outing' Religion in Bioethics," *The Park Ridge Center Bulletin Religion in Bioethics*, March/April 1999, p. 2. Retrieved June 12, 2008, from www.parkridgecenter.org/Page547.html.

28. D. Gareth Jones, "Contemporary Medical Scandals: A Challenge to Ethical Codes and Ethical Principles," *Perspectives in Science and Christian Faith*, March 1990, pp. 2–14.

29. Lisa Sowle Cahill, "Finding Common Ground: Religion's Role in the Ethics Committee," *The Park Ridge Center Bulletin: Religion in Bioethics*, March/April 1999, p. 3. Retrieved June 12, 2008, from www.parkridgecenter.org/Page547.html.

30. See note 14 above.

31. Susan Neiman, *Moral Clarity: A Guide for Grown-Up Idealists*, New York: Harcourt, 2008. Quoted in Simon Blackburn, "Mind over What's the Matter," *The New York Times Book Review*, July 17, 2008, p. 15.

32. David H. Smith, "Religion and the Roots of the Bioethics Revival," in *Religion & Medical Ethics: Looking Back, Looking Forward*, Allen Verhey, ed., Grand Rapids, MI: William B. Eerdmans Publishing Company, 1996, p. 18.

33. Diana L. Eck, "Religious Pluralism: America in the Year 2000," *Yearbook of American and Canadian Churches*, National Council of Churches of Christ in the USA, 2000. Retrieved August 28, 2008, from http://www.electronicchurch.org/2000/2000_Essay.htm.

34. See note 33 above.

35. Tim Rutten, "The Catholic Choice," *Los Angeles Times*, August 27, 2008, p. A23.

36. Editor, "Religion, Politics and the Battle over Bioethics," *ReligionLink.com*, March 29, 2004. Retrieved June 2, 2009, from http://www.religionlink.com/tip_040329c.php.

37. NA, "Religious Convictions Crucial to US Public Debate, Archbishop Says," *Catholic News Service* May 15, 2009. Retrieved June 2, 2009, from http://www.catholicnews.com/data/stories/cns/0902253.htm.

38. NA, *Secular Coalition for America*, 2009. Retrieved June 2, 2009, from http://www.secular.org/about.html.

39. NA, "Scientific Integrity, Union of Concerned Scientists," February 18, 2004. Retrieved June 2, 2009, from http://www.ucsusa.org/scientific_integrity.

40. See note 36 above.

41. David B. Resnik, "Scientific Autonomy and Public Oversight," *Episteme: A Journal of Social Epistemology*, June 2008, pp. 220–238.

Index

Printed in the USA
CPSIA information can be obtained
at www.ICGtesting.com
JSHW050724110124
55227JS00003B/31